POLITICS
in the Age of Peel

POLITICS

in the Age of Peel

A study in the Technique of
Parliamentary Representation
1830 – 1850

SECOND EDITION
WITH A NEW INTRODUCTION

Norman Gash
Professor of History
University of St. Andrews

THE HARVESTER PRESS LIMITED
HUMANITIES PRESS INC

This edition first published in 1977 by
THE HARVESTER PRESS LIMITED
Publisher: John Spiers
2 Stanford Terrace, Hassocks, Sussex
and in the USA in 1977 by
Humanities Press Inc
Atlantic Highlands, NJ 07716

First published 1953 by
Longmans, Green and Co Ltd, London
and reprinted 1960 and 1964

Cataloging in Publication Data

British Library

Gash, Norman
    Politics in the age of Peel — 2nd ed.
    Bibl. — Index.
    ISBN 0-85527-139-6
    1. Title
    328.41'07'34   JN543
    Representative government and representation—
    Great Britian — History

Library of Congress

Gash, Norman
    Politics in the age of Peel.

    Bibliography: p.
    Includes index.
    1. Great Britain — Politics and government — 1830-1837.
    2. Great Britain — Politics and government — 1837-1901
    3. Elections — Great Britain. 1. Title.
    JN223.G3   1976   320.9'41'075   76-44360
    ISBN 0-391-00676-2

Printed in Great Britain by
Redwood Burn Limited, Trowbridge & Esher

ACKNOWLEDGEMENTS

My particular gratitude is due to the University Court of St Andrews whose travel grants materially eased the latter part of my researches; to Professor R. Pares who brought to my notice several sources I would otherwise have missed; to Dr George Pryde who read and criticized the section on the Scottish Reform Act; to my old friend Mr A. J. Taylor who elicited for me many of the details of F. R. Bonham's background, and through him, also to Mr J. H. H. Bonham; to Mr L. H. Hayter who put at my disposal copies of the Bonham letters in his possession; to the Editor of the *Reading Mercury* for the use of his office files at a time when copies were not available elsewhere; and to the staff of St. Andrews University Library for their unfailing help.

To two persons I cannot sufficiently express my debt. The first is Mr G. Kitson Clark of Trinity College, Cambridge, who read and criticized the typescript of this book and who, from the time he became aware of the work on which I was engaged, gave me most generous encouragement and advice. The other is my wife.

The United College,   NORMAN GASH
St. Andrews   *July 1952*

CONTENTS

INTRODUCTION

IT is an old saying that politics is the art of the possible. In the sphere of foreign policy, where the views and interests of other powers form the ordinary material of the diplomatist, the framework of limitations is obvious. In domestic policy it is less easily discerned but no less important. One of the most pervasive limiting factors, and one most difficult for the historian to reconstruct, is the ordinary working world of the politician: the medium, that is to say, in which the major political events take place as distinct from the events themselves. Yet the task of reconstruction must always be essayed. It is not possible to give a just account either of political events or of the careers of individual politicians without reference to the nature of the contemporary political world. As a fish is deprived of its lustre when taken from the water, so politics lose their colour and subtlety unless studied in their contemporary medium. It is essential for the historian to learn what were the political practices as opposed to the constitutional theories or legal machinery of the time; the restraints imposed by supporters as well as by opponents; the peculiar demands of indispensable political techniques; the unceasing conflict between ideal ends and imperfect means; and most important of all, perhaps, the implicit fundamental attitudes which condition everything but are often unconscious, or taken for granted, and therefore rarely discussed and recorded.

In the period immediately after the Reform Act of 1832 there is a particular need to reconsider British history in this light.[1] Because of its nearness to our own time, familiarity obscures the differences; and the differences are in any case often too subtle to catch the imagination. The political vocabulary then in common use (leaders, parties, whips, agents, associations, manifestoes, elections, voters, polls, constituencies), is largely identical with that of today. But to the early Victorians these terms did not always mean exactly what they mean to us, even though it is not always easy to define what they did mean. The difficulty is made greater by the fact that we have for the most part attributed, not perhaps too much

---

[1] For a stimulating essay on this subject see Mr Kitson Clark's paper on 'The Electorate and the Repeal of the Corn Laws' (*Trans. R. Hist. Soc.*, 5 ser., 1, 109 sqq.).

importance, but the wrong kind of importance to the Reform Act
of 1832. Landmarks are usually more conspicuous at a distance
than close at hand; turning-points rarely show any abrupt change.
The first Reform Act was both a landmark and a turning-point, but
it would be wrong to assume that the political scene in the succeeding generation differed essentially from that of the preceding one.
The word 'Reform' has, however, a certain ethical association.
There is a prejudice in favour of the view that the political
world after the Reform Act was morally purer. Perhaps it was,
but the change did not take place rapidly nor did it only begin in
1832. The fallacy is in using the Reform Act to symbolize certain
trends in politics that started long before and needed many subsequent years for completion. The result too often is a simplified
picture in which features regarded as 'good' are emphasized while
features regarded as 'bad' are ignored: the whole contrasting
agreeably with its companion piece of the unreformed era in which
the 'good' features are ignored and the 'bad' emphasized. How the
one grew out of the other; how the unreformed House of Commons
came to reform itself, are questions which by this process are not
readily answered.

In fact the pre-1832 period contained many new features which
it transmitted to the future; and the post-1832 period contained
many old features which it inherited from the past. Between the
two there is indeed a strong organic resemblance. This is not to
say that the Reform Act achieved nothing. Its ultimate effects
were considerable and there were some interesting, and rather
unexpected, immediate effects. But the continuity of political fibre
was tough enough to withstand the not very murderous instrument
of 2 Wm. IV., c. 45. As will be seen in subsequent chapters there
was scarcely a feature of the old unreformed system that could not
be found still in existence after 1832. Thus many small pocket
boroughs had been abolished by the Reform Act but over forty
in England and Wales alone, together with a dozen more that
regularly returned members of particular families, survived into
the third quarter of the nineteenth century.[2] Corrupt constituencies, open to the highest bidder, occupied a place in the reformed
structure of representation and two of them, Sudbury in 1844 and
St Albans in 1852, were disfranchised for gross and systematic
venality.[3] The ancient profession of borough-monger still survived

---

[2] Chh. 8 and 9, and Appendix D.   [3] Ch. 7.

here and there in congenial spots; and almost everywhere the tribe of solicitors and agents who grew fat on contested elections were promoting these operations for their financial rather than their political significance. There was no legal limit to the amount of money that could be spent on parliamentary elections and fortunes could be dissipated on a political career almost as easily as in the reign of George III.[4] Great peers still sent their nominees to the lower house. Landowners, merchants, clergy of all denominations, shopkeepers, employers, publicans, customers, and clients, habitually exercised their social and economic influence for political purposes.[5] Even the enfranchisement in 1832 of new industrial towns sometimes meant no more than the addition of landlords, such as the Ramsden family at Huddersfield, or industrialists, such as John Guest at Merthyr, to the existing 'electoral influences' listed by any competent parliamentary guide.[6] Nearly every constituency had some form of corruption peculiar to itself; and the borough electors as a class, whether old franchise holders or new £10 householders, customarily accepted, and often demanded, bribes.[7] As a last resort, physical force, sometimes of an extreme and unpleasant nature, was used to produce the required verdict on the hustings. Gang warfare between the hired bullies of rival political magnates, and electoral intimidation by radical mobs, were spectacles to which early Victorian England was hardened if not reconciled.[8]

Even at the other end of the political hierarchy old but not yet obviously anachronistic habits still clung. Though virtually all the prerogative powers of the monarch were now exercised in his name by the politicians, there was still no clear distinction in people's minds between the legal and the political conception of ministers as 'servants of the crown'. Wellington openly, Melbourne and Peel in the last analysis, considered loyalty to the crown as

---

[4] Though the legal limitation of the polling days to two, in place of the previous permissible maximum of fifteen days, did prevent the occasional protracted and enormously expensive county contests (such as the Yorkshire election of 1807) which were probably the most crippling feature of electioneering under the old system.

[5] Ch. 8.

[6] Practically the whole township of Huddersfield belonged to the Ramsden family of Byram Hall, Yorkshire. For that reason, when it was enfranchised in 1832, the constituency was extended to the parish. Without coming quite into the category of proprietary boroughs, Huddersfield in the eighteen-thirties was sufficiently under the control of the whig, Sir John Ramsden, to defy the efforts of radicals and tories to capture the seat (*Hansard*, 3rd ser., v, 901; x, 1154; Driver, *Life of Oastler*, 186, 255, 344, 358). For the Guest influence at Merthyr see below, Ch. 8.

[7] Ch. 5.   [8] Ch. 6.

the highest political duty of the statesman. The monarchs themselves were even less equivocal. William IV gave Peel the impossible task of forming a government in 1834 because his previous ministers had become unpalatable to him. The whigs, aided and abetted by their young sovereign, used the queen's name as a party cry in the general elections of 1837 and 1841; and only the partisan instincts of Victoria excluded the conservatives from office in 1839. Royal officials with seats in either house of parliament were expected to support the ministers of the day; and the court still intervened, where it could, in parliamentary elections on behalf of its recognized candidates. Not until 1845 did the crown indicate its wish to abandon this practice and then probably at the instigation of the German Albert rather than on the initiative of the Hanoverian Victoria.[9] Ministers themselves controlled as part of their normal functions an enormous mass of patronage which was still mostly distributed for political motives. When Peel died in 1850 political nomination was the standard means of recruitment for the civil service of the country.[10] The government chief whip was still known as the Patronage Secretary and held office in the Treasury. Constituencies containing naval dockyards were subjected to a special and sometimes decisive influence emanating from the political heads of the Admiralty. Chatham (which owed its existence as a parliamentary borough to the Reform Act) signalized itself by returning at every election from 1832 to 1852 the candidate recommended to it by the government of the day.[11]

This, of course, is not the whole picture but it is a necessary corrective to what too frequently passes as such. By the side of these old and familiar forms of political life, however, were new and remarkable developments. In the history of political party in this country the short reign of William IV is equalled in importance only perhaps by that of Charles II. The conservative party owes its name and origin to those who proclaimed themselves as conservators of the traditional institutions of the state against the reforming ministry of 1830–2.[12] The liberal party, though slower to emerge as a distinct concept, was primarily formed from an amalgam of old whiggery and new radicalism (together with certain eccentric strains of Canningite toryism and Peelite conservatism), which were welded together in the thirty years after

[9] Ch. 14.   [10] Ch. 13.   [11] Ch. 12.
[12] See the interesting note in Halévy, *History of the English People*, III, 68.

the Reform Act. On the technical side of party organization it was
the age of registration societies, constituency associations, the great
political Pall Mall clubs, and the central party agent.[13] The
registration clauses of the act, making legal enrolment of electors
a preliminary condition of voting, were designed to promote
economy and efficiency. They unexpectedly provided the greatest
single stimulus to the organization of the electorate for party
purposes that had so far been created by law. From it came the
spread of party associations in the constituencies, the rise of
the party agent watching chiefly over the electoral readiness of the
party in the country, and the immensely enhanced ability of the
parliamentary opposition to compete in political effectiveness with
the ministerial party. The general election of 1841 was the first in
which the government of the day, previously holding a majority in
the lower House, was defeated by a disciplined opposition organized
for electoral purposes. The development of these new aspects of
party organization, in addition to the traditional apparatus of
parliamentary leaders, whips, party meetings, and *ad hoc* election
committees, marks the real emergence of the party system in its
modern form.

But party organization did not function in a vacuum and it was
the extraordinary political and social tensions of the twenty years
following the accession of William IV that inspired the activity of
politicians and party managers. It was an age in which public
opinion exerted more direct and continuous pressure on the narrow
ring of parliamentary politicians than ever before. The close of
the French wars had opened the way to a flood of comment and
criticism; and the administrative reforms of the Liverpool ministry,
Catholic Emancipation, and the Reform Act itself, were only the
first-fruits of a power steadily growing in knowledge and effectiveness. The influence of the press was itself both a sign of public
interest in politics and a stimulant to it. Even before the Wellington
ministry went out of office in 1830 the existence of an eager and
critical public had enabled the principal newspapers to emancipate
themselves from the financial control of the politicians.[14] But
public opinion was a composite thing. There were many opinions
and though they overlapped, they did not always agree. There
were the violent opinions of the trade and political unions, the
chartists, the factory operatives, and the Short Time Committees

[13] Ch. 15.   [14] Aspinall, *Politics and the Press*, esp. Ch. XVI.

—the world of Oastler and Ashley. There were the opinions of the first generation of self-made and self-confident manufacturers, instinct with contempt for aristocratic government and all its ways, like Thornton in Mrs Gaskell's *North and South*; or the more persuasive, pseudo-scientific opinions of the small but influential group of Benthamites (the Fabians of the eighteen-thirties), who gave an unmistakable colour to nearly all government legislation of the time. There were the sharp and shallow opinions of ambitious shop-assistants and attorneys' clerks who attended mechanics' institutes and radical clubs; or the complacent though still liberal opinions of the more prosperous and settled middle classes who read the *Edinburgh Review*, the *Spectator*, or that great daily organ of opinion, *The Times*. It was an age, too, of powerful religious organizations: the Evangelicals, moderate on most things but capable of unregenerate stubbornness on their elected ground; the numerous body of English dissenters, often politically exalted by their sense of 'the exceptional possession of religious truth' and confirmed in self-righteousness by the bitter gulf of prejudice and history, described by George Eliot in *Felix Holt*, that lay between them and their socially more respectable Anglican neighbours. In Ireland there was Roman Catholicism and the agitation for the repeal of the Union; in Scotland Presbyterianism and the patronage controversy within the established Kirk that led to the Disruption of 1843.

Effective public opinion, moreover, was not the prerogative of the dissenters, of the new England of the industrial revolution, or of the urban middle classes in general. No estimate of political forces in the period after Waterloo is complete which fails to take note of the powerful agricultural opinion which was one of the prime factors in winning the elections for the reformers in 1831. The English county members almost to a man voted for the reform bill because the large English county electorates, formed by the old Lancastrian 40*s*. freeholders, believed that the time had come for the government to be reformed. But the parliamentary influence of the counties, particularly of the agricultural counties, did not expend itself with the Reform Act. Under the parliamentary leadership of Chandos in the thirties, Bentinck and Disraeli in 1846, it embarrassed each party in turn on the question of repealing the Malt Tax and split the conservative party in half on the repeal of the Corn Laws. If the farmers did not have their Cobden, Bright, and Fox, they had their Agricultural Protection Associations which as early as the thirties were giving concern to some old-fashioned tories who distrusted these demonstrations of initiative in areas conventionally controlled by the gentry. And in the crucial winter of 1845–6 the agricultural interest exerted enough pressure on parliament to ensure that even the prestige of a great statesman and the fidelity of the party officials could not save one of the most brilliant ministries of the century from destruction at the hands of its own supporters.[15]

The problem is how to draw in anything like accurate detail the physiognomy of politics in an age so complex. Yet there is in this labyrinth one focal point. All these influences were working in and upon the vast mass of static forces in the country—the great aristocracy, the country gentry, the Anglican Church, the universities, the legal profession, the established financial and commercial interests, the fighting services, the permanent civil service—that underpinned the traditional structure of the State. Here the dominating fact was that the old aristocratic society which had lost its supremacy in the country at large still retained its preponderant power in the narrowly based parliamentary constitution. Everything therefore depended on the disinterestedness with which this power was exercised, and this in the last resort depended on the six hundred and fifty members of the House of Commons. On them rested not only the careers of statesmen and the fate of legislative measures but the whole relation between public opinion and executive action, and the stability of government itself, in an age of social disorder at home and revolutionary example abroad. But to inquire into the conduct and thoughts of these men is necessarily to inquire also into the men themselves, the methods whereby they were returned to parliament, and the forces acting on them there. The chapters which follow constitute a study of this central problem: the technique of parliamentary representation. The chronological limits, generally though not consistently observed, are formed by the start of the reform crisis in 1830 and the death of Peel in 1850 which conveniently marks the end of that time of distress and passion which Dr Hammond with reason if not complete justice named 'the bleak age'. Many of the descriptions and generalizations hold good for the later period from 1850 to the

---

[15] For opinion in one agricultural county, see Ch. 11. Cf. also Kitson Clark, *ubi supra*, 124–5, and 'The Repeal of the Corn Laws and the Politics of the Forties' (*Econ. Hist. Rev.*, 2nd ser., IV, 1).

passing of the second Reform Act in 1867. But it was the first two
decades that were the proving time for the political system re-
modelled in 1832.

Since it is the 'reformed' system that is under examination, it
seemed a reasonable point of departure to consider what the framers
of that system thought they were doing and why they did it.[16]
For that, recourse has been had primarily to the reform debates in
parliament itself for there is no reason to doubt that in those
debates both ministers and opposition were expressing their
genuine convictions. Even if there were no other evidence, it can
hardly be supposed that in heated and exhausting debates on a
crucial measure, carried on intermittently for eighteen months, the
real opinions of men did not clearly emerge.[17] Next, since it was
an age in which the franchise was still a privilege, it is necessary to
ascertain who voted and where.[18] Only one man in seven had
the vote (in Ireland only one in twenty). The parliamentary
constituencies varied in size from two hundred to eighteen thousand
registered electors. The separate historical identities of England,
Scotland, and Ireland were perpetuated in different electoral
provisions for the three kingdoms. Even in drafting the reform
bill statistical uniformity had been deliberately rejected. In such
conditions the peculiarities of the legal system of representation
have a special political significance. For much of this Mr Seymour's
Electoral Reform in England and Wales 1832–1885 is already the standard authority. The emphasis in the present study is only on what is
germane to the subsequent political chapters or does not appear to
have received adequate attention even in Mr Seymour's generally
exhaustive study. For Scotland and Ireland, however, which lay
outside the scope both of Mr Seymour's book and of Professor
J. R. M. Butler's classic work *The Passing of the Great Reform Bill*,
the provisions of their respective reform bills, and the circumstances in which they were carried, are discussed in more detail.[19]

Once this framework has been set up, it is possible to consider
at greater length how the system worked in real life; what the
actual conditions were for both politicians and electors, the

[16] Ch. 1.
[17] Cf. Cockburn's remarks on the reform cabinet, September 1831: 'It is impossible
for the public declarations of any men to be more in unison with their private feelings
than theirs seem to be. Their confidential and unguarded language might have been
revealed to the world without any blot being found more than in their Parliamentary
statements.' (*Journal*, 1, 23.)
[18] Chh. 3 and 4.   [19] Ch. 2.

different types of constituency, and the peculiar influences at work within them. Since it is the nature and not the results of politics that is the object of inquiry, no chronological narrative is feasible. The method is necessarily analytical and the treatment topical. It may seem paradoxical that in order to arrive at a more integral view of the political scene, it should first be reduced to a collection of component elements. But though a narrative might display only too well the complexity of the subject, it is doubtful whether that complexity could be made comprehensible except by some such process of disarticulation. In turn this method entails the examination of actual samples of local conditions and is therefore immediately exposed to the criticism and correction of local historians. Such criticism must not only be risked but be invited. Only on an established basis of local history can national history of this kind be written. The chapter on Berkshire politics,[20] designed in part as a corrective to the topical method employed elsewhere, is also a personal contribution to this essential groundwork of knowledge.

Some gaps remain to be filled. There is still a lack of any general and authoritative study of the Irish political system in this period. The history of party organization is still to be written even though the outlines of the subject are becoming clearer. Fifty years ago M. Ostrogorski made a penetrating study of Victorian party machinery[21] but he only gave a backward glance to the age of Melbourne and Peel. Besides the special contribution to party history contained in his *Politics and the Press*, Professor Aspinall has sketched the parliamentary organization of parties in the early nineteenth century.[22] Mr Hill has explored the origins of conservative associations and operative societies in his *Toryism and the People 1832–46*. Limitations of space have excluded from the present work all but a marginal note on party finances and a chapter on some of the post-1830 developments, the Pall Mall clubs and the party agents, that have not yet received much comment.[23]

Only after the investigation of all these matters can the task be faced of establishing the relation between the course of political events and the medium in which they were formed. A discussion

---

[20] Ch. 11.   [21] *Democracy and the Organization of Political Parties*, 1.
[22] 'English Party Organization in the Early Nineteenth Century' (*E.H.R.*, XLI. 389 sqq.).
[23] Ch. 15, and Appendices C, J, and K.

of techniques is itself only a means to an end. It is misleading if it obscures the elements of tension, crisis, and change. It was in fact an age of exceptional tension in which a political world still heaving from the shock of Catholic Emancipation and Reform was being subjected to the disruptive social and economic pressures of post-Waterloo Britain. The age of Peel was also the railway age and the age of the chartists when an essentially aristocratic system of government was struggling with difficulty simultaneously to retain control over a parliament no longer amenable to executive influence, and to solve the urgent problems of an expanding industrial society.[24] In this unprecedented situation three features of the political system were outstanding: the oligarchic tradition of government, fundamentally administrative in outlook; the party system, moving slowly towards a programme as well as a philosophy of action; and the external forces of public opinion, often genuine, but also capable of being manipulated by men more adept and less scrupulous than the parliamentary leaders in the arts of mass propaganda. By the end of the century the party system was to emerge as the strongest of the three, having destroyed the aristocratic concept of 'the King's Government' on the one hand, and having made itself (at the cost of some concessions) the main channel of public opinion on the other. But in the age of Peel party was far from being in that dominant position, and between the three forces there existed a rough balance of power.

It was true of course that party took on a firmer outline after 1830. A remarkably continuous tradition of party in British parliamentary politics had existed since the seventeenth century and even before the Reform Act the party system had by no means been devoid of either principle or organization. The technical post-1830 developments, however, together with the issues thrown up by the reform crisis, immeasurably strengthened its control over politics. Nevertheless, it was working even after 1830 under the leadership of men who did not subscribe to a doctrine of party supremacy, still less of party infallibility, and in a society where local interests and opinions were still tenacious. The innumerable special influences that littered the electoral landscape did not always adjust themselves with nicety to party convenience. Even where voting was free, subordination to a centralized party

---

[24] For some discussion of this theme see my paper on 'Peel and the Party System' (*Trans. R. Hist. Soc.*, 5th ser., I, 47 sqq.).

organization would have seemed to many as servile as obedience to the whims of a borough magnate. Hence for all the imposing structure of organization and long political tradition, there were severe limitations on the national effectiveness of the two great parliamentary parties. This weakness (by modern standards) of party influence did not, however, result in a large floating vote. Too many other forms of control existed for the electorate to swing freely from one side to the other: the homogeneity of county society, proprietary boroughs, family boroughs, compromise agreements, bribery and intimidation, the social fixity of certain types of opinion, the influence of the executive, and the cement of political patronage. All these factors, moreover, were operating on a limited electorate (little more than 800,000 in this period) voting in public, which could be 'worked', in the language of the party managers, by methods inapplicable to the millions of the late-Victorian voters protected by secret ballot. At the general election of 1841, which turned out the whig ministry and installed that of Peel, less than half the constituencies were contested.[25] This was a stony and discouraging field for propaganda and significantly the two strongest expressions of political feeling in this period—the chartist agitation and the anti-Corn Law League—were extra-parliamentary movements.

Yet this did not absolve statesmen such as Peel from the responsibility of finding an answer to national movements of opinion or a solution to national problems. The aristocratic tradition did not conceive that a minister's duty was confined to the interests of his electoral supporters. Thus the dilemma was created. Government could not function without the co-operation of parliament; parliament could not function without the rigidity supplied by the party organizations. Yet the methods whereby members were returned to parliament offered no assurance that strong opinions and urgent problems in the country at large would be accurately reflected at Westminster. For men bred up to a genuine if limited sense of the national responsibility resting on ministers of the crown, the parliamentary parties could not be accepted as reliable interpreters of national duty.[26] Inevitably, therefore, such men took their stand not merely as leaders of great political parties but also as national statesmen, reserving their own right of judgement

[25] Ch. 10 and Appendix E.
[26] It is true that the repeal of the Corn Laws, like the reform bill itself, was passed by a parliamentary majority. But in neither case was it a party majority.

and appealing (if they appealed at all) to general non-party support. The dilemma would have been eased had the executive ministers possessed the means of influencing members of parliament that existed in the eighteenth century. It was to draw attention to this vital consideration that an attempt has been made in the last section of this book to describe and suggest the weakness of the surviving methods of direction from above.[27] Patronage, for example, continued and the justification of patronage was that it bound together on 'interested motives' an adequate number of people in support of 'the King's Government'. But patronage in this period was little more than a time-honoured and conventional function which, though contributing to executive influence, had been largely assimilated by the party organization. Its salient characteristic was that of a dying and ineffective system, from which most of the political value had been extracted. Direct executive control over elections, on the other hand, exemplified by Admiralty influence in the dockyard constituencies and by court influence in the two royal boroughs of Windsor and Brighton, affected only a negligible number of seats in the House of Commons. By comparison the unifying effect of the two great party political clubs, the Carlton and the Reform, and the evolution of the extra-parliamentary party agents, Parkes, Coppock, and Bonham, were far more significant factors. Yet party machinery, though as a rule the last element in a party to die, cannot be effective without the party rank-and-file. Whatever Peel's shortcomings as a leader, the official staff of whips and agents showed themselves completely loyal to him in 1846; yet that did not prevent the disruption of the party as a whole.

It is outside the scope of this book, however, to attempt the re-writing of the political history of the period. Its purpose is only to suggest some of the features in the contemporary political world which conditioned that history. For us in retrospect the age was one in which the strains and complexities of the slow movement from an aristocratic to a democratic system of government are thrown into sharp relief. To the statesmen of the time it was a tumultuous stream of old and new forces, tossing indistinguishably together, in which it was not easy to keep either balance or direction. Peel and Palmerston were the only really successful exponents of the parliamentary system as it existed between the

[27] Chh. 12–14.

first and second Reform Acts. Both were strong personalities; both conservative; both of national rather than party stature; both great House of Commons men. All these qualities were essential for success in a political structure which gave too little power to the executive, too much to the private member; too much to interest and too little to principle. Yet had their positions been reversed, it is doubtful whether Palmerston could have maintained himself. Though the elder of the two, he did not reach the summit of politics until he had succeeded not only to the position but to the work of Peel. By 1850 the major problems of the age had been met and solved, and the age of violence was giving way (in Professor Burn's phrase) to the 'age of equipoise'. Even Palmerston in the later and more peaceful era occasionally lost his footing. Peel did too, of course, and in a more memorable fashion. But Peel lived in the more turbulent if politically more fertile age and had profounder issues to confront. It is a paradoxical but illuminating commentary on the political techniques of the time that when he fell from parliamentary power in 1846 he was stronger and more popular in the country than he had ever been before

INTRODUCTION TO SECOND EDITION

Politics in the Age of Peel appeared in 1953. My interest in the subject began before the war and I resumed work on it after the gap of a decade in 1948. At that time the book was something of a pioneer effort. Since then, particularly in the years after 1960, there has been considerable activity in the field across which it tried to drive a few exploratory paths. Closer investigation has on the whole strengthened the view that electoral politics in the immediate post-reform era was a diverse and complicated process for which there are few simple explanations. In one sense this was only to be expected. Historical detail usually tends to emphasise the accidental and local at the expense of the characteristic and general. The moral is not that general statements should be avoided; rather the reverse. It is simply that one should be cautious of general statements that are more sweeping than the evidence on which they are based can justify. There are however particular reasons why early-Victorian politics are unusually difficult to analyse. Economic historians have pointed out that the haphazard, sporadic growth of early industrialism meant that the social and economic landscape of early nineteenth-century Britain is in many respects more complex than either the pre-industrial society which preceded it or the more specialised mass-industrial society which followed. In much the same way the piecemeal and limited movement towards a more equitable and more popular representative system and the growth of national parliamentary parties made the political landscape after 1832 more varied and contrasting than at either the beginning or the end of the century. There were immense differences in the size and character of constituencies as well as in the varieties of parliamentary franchise. Old electoral habits were tenacious but new practices and new forms of organisation were being evolved, sometimes with remarkable rapidity. National issues were growing in importance but they still had to compete with local issues and local methods of control; and the precise importance accorded to them in the provinces was not necessarily that attached to them in parliament or the national press. Issues, moreover, changed quite sharply from one election to another; M.P.s as well as electors transferred their allegiances; and both parties underwent severe internal strains.

Even with the refinements of electoral analysis that have been developed over the last thirty years, it is not easy to dissect this untidy political society. Dr. Nossiter's three-pronged formula of status, market and conscience — or in more familiar language, influence, bribery and opinion — is a useful approach to the problem of exploring electoral behaviour; but it can only be a starting-point. Techniques devised for a mass electorate casting their single votes into the security of the ballot-box are unconvincing when applied to general elections in which anything from a third to a half of the constituencies did not go to the poll; where electors, when they had the chance to use them, usually possessed two votes which they sometimes used to support candidates of opposing parties; for which pollbooks are not always available, and when they are, rarely provide all the information that is necessary to interpret them; and where, in the boroughs at least, the prospect of a close finish between rival candidates was likely even in the most respectable consituency to bring the marginal weapon of bribery into play. Occasionally, as in 1832 and 1841, one can discern the movement of a political current stronger than the aggregate of local forces; but even this is a matter of historical judgement rather than of scientific proof. On the whole the task of interpreting early-Victorian general elections is not one readily susceptible to collective treatment; it is best left to local historians, or rather, the historians of local constituences, judging each result in the light of their specialised knowledge of all the evidence. We are a long way from having enough of these regional studies; but a great deal has been done in the last twenty years.

As far as the boroughs are concerned (and the boroughs, still heavily and unfairly weighted in the electoral system, vastly outnumbered the county constituencies) some sentences written by Joseph Parkes in 1841 should be hung over the desk of any student of the electoral system between the first and second reform acts:

> Experience of 16 years active work in all classes of the Representation, and especially experience behind the Party scenes of the two last dissolutions, has convinced me — first; that the action of *political* principle & particular Cabinet policies on the English Borough Constituencies is much overrated: secondly; that the returns are much more influenced by particular *local* circumstances and the particular personal relations of *Candidates* than generally imagined: thirdly; that the returns are greatly influenced by the *sufficiency* & *purse weight* of *Candidates*: fourthly; that the Borough results in

England generally much baffle previous calculations of both parties. I have noted those calculations on 2 Dissolutions; & I have been struck by the *unexpected* gains and losses of *both* Parties. — I know Mr Holmes holds the same opinion.[1]

Parkes was the chief election agent of the Liberal Party. It is not unreasonable to think that he knew what he was talking about.

Even the counties emerge on examination as more complex entities than was at one time believed. Superficially, with large electorates, little bribery or violence, and a more homogeneous society, they might seem easier to explain; even if the situation is complicated by a high proportion of uncontested returns and peaceful electoral bargains. But a theory of 'influence' that does not take into account 'issues' is inadequate. In the agricultural constituencies it has become increasingly clear that the tenant farmers cannot simply be dismissed as a collection of deferential estate-packages which could be passed at will from one candidate to another. The deference of English rural society worked in two directions. Farmers and freeholders had been a growing political force ever since the Napoleonic War raised them to affluence and Waterloo threatened them with decline. Useful attention has been paid to the influence exercised by farmers' protection societies on Conservative M.P.s in the Corn Law crisis of 1845-46. But protectionist pressure was present much earlier, in most rural counties at the latest by the 1830s. It could be argued in fact that Peel's fate was decided not in 1846 by Bentinck and Disraeli but by farming votes and farming opinion in the general election of 1841. Even the agitation in agricultural constituencies over corn laws and malt tax in the previous decade was only a continuation of the post-war farmers' movement which produced Webb Hall's protectionist association and the unrest among the 'country party' in the House of Commons over Liverpool's economic policies in the early 1820s. One of the most useful contributions that could be made to the study of early nineteenth-century electoral history would be a detailed history of agricultural political opinion from 1815 to 1853. The bias of English historical writing towards urban, liberal and 'working-class' topics has left a serious imbalance here.

A greater interest has been shown, for obvious reasons, in party political history. Even so, the interest has been directed more towards the centre, where the evidence is fuller and more manageable, than to the provinces. There has been no sustained attempt, for example, to advance along the lines indicated by R.L. Hill in his book on *Toryism and the People 1832-46*, which came out nearly half a century ago. The disruption of the Conservative Party in 1846 and the looseness of the Liberal Party after 1841, together with certain other factors, did of course result in a decline of party feeling and party organisation in the middle of the century. This has led some historians whose real interest is in the post-1867 period to decry the significance of party in the 1830s. But few of these who have done serious work on post-1832 politics are likely to share that opinion. It is true that parties, in the new form they had assumed at the start of Victoria's reign, were feeling their way on such vital matters as internal discipline and agreed policy; that they had to contend with older traditions of political conduct; and that candidates, especially those with good local standing, made much of their independence when talking to their constituents. But of the importance of the party system in this period, and of the decisive shape it gave to parliamentary development, there can be little serious doubt. Here, as at other points, it is mainly the historians of individual constituencies and regions who have contributed most to this central aspect of early-Victorian political life.

Two further aspects of the subject may be mentioned. The first is the Reform Act of 1832 itself. The interesting feature here is that further investigation has not produced any essential change of interpretation; only a greater appreciation of the situation which shaped its character and consequences. We are more conscious of its defects, its tentativeness; of the inadequate experience of the cabinet, of their errors and miscalculations, their changes of mind and internal divisions; of the failure to realise many of their hopes, and the unexpected importance of some things which they regarded as matters of detail. The Reform Act was intended among other purposes to strengthen executive government: in the first two years after 1832 the reformed House of Commons made executive government almost impossible. Some thought it would extinguish party; it could now be argued that only the new party system made it work. Yet there is no cause for surprise in any of these things. Grey's cabinet were trying to do something never before attempted, with a minimum of preparation, with inadequate information and inadequate instruments. They found themselves as a result involved in a constitutional crisis which they never anticipated and which their opponents took rather more seriously than most who afterwards commented on their actions at a safe distance of time. It was not a simple situation and the act itself was far from simple, both in what it set out to do and (which is a different matter)what it actually accomplished. No neat formula to 'explain' the Reform Act is likely to be proved very satisfactory. Yet, looking at the situation before 1832 as well as in the years which followed, it is difficult not to conclude that the motives and intentions of Grey's ministry were in fact what they said they were; and that the bill itself was more important than its parts. Mr. Brock's detailed and authoritative study of the passing of the act, the first to appear since J.R.M. Butler's classic account half a century earlier, comes to substantially the same broad conclusions as the older book: namely, that Grey's achievement was one of great courage and statesmanship, simultaneously concessionary and conservative, designed not to prevent revolution (for that we shall never know) but, as Grey said in November 1830, to prevent the necessity for revolution. It was not a new conclusion. "The effect of the great Reform Bill," wrote Gladstone, "was not mainly numerical but moral". "It was not a good Bill," said Bright, "but it was a great Bill when it was passed". Subsequent examination has only confirmed the verdicts of these two great Victorian Liberals.

Finally, even the briefest survey should include a reference to Professor Aydelotte's work on the personnel of the 1841-47 House of Commons, the only nineteenth-century parliament which has been subjected to this form of statistical analysis. By tabulating data relating to individual M.P.s in a form capable of rapid manipulation, it has been possible for him to examine on a number of issues the relationship between the actual votes of M.P.s and certain personal and political attributes of those voting. This quantitative technique, as Professor Aydelotte has been at pains to emphasise, cannot be completely objective. The judgement of the historian is involved both in the selection of the initial data for analysis and in the interpretation of the results. Moreover, a system based on division lists can only record behaviour: it cannot analyse motive. To assess the motives of individual M.P.s would entail an examination of the conflicting pressures of party discipline, constituency influence and their own private convictions: a difficult task even with contemporary politicians, an impossible one when dealing with men who lived a century and a half ago. There are also subtler difficulties. An attempt, for example, to assess on this kind of statistical basis the extent to which parties consisted of men thinking alike on a number of public issues is complicated by the fact that parties were already in existence and that one of the objects of party organisation was to ensure that as far as possible it behaved as though its members thought alike, even when they did not. Nevertheless, Professor Aydelotte's careful and sensitive researches have told us much about the behaviour of politicians in the 1841 House of Commons. Negatively he has been able to disprove a number of loose generalisations; positively he has provided a firmer basis for observations arrived at by more empirical methods. Perhaps his most important contribution has been a weight of evidence to suggest that the most reliable key to an M.P.'s voting behaviour — other than his party affiliation — was not class, social background or economic interest but the kind of constituency he represented. That in itself is a sign how far the electoral system had developed since the eighteenth century.

Norman Gash

January 1976

BIBLIOGRAPHY TO SECOND EDITION

From the mass of books and articles which have appeared over the last twenty-two years, it is not possible to make more than a selection. But it is hoped that what follows will be of use to those who wish to pursue some of the topics with which *Politics in the Age of Peel* concerned itself.

(a) *Books*

Of the more general books H.J. Hanham's *Nineteenth Century Constitution* (1969) with its documents and commentary forms a valuable reference work. Another kind of introduction is provided by G. Kitson Clark's stimulating and suggestive *Making of Victorian England* (1962). The history of the 1830-41 period is covered by two specialised books. A. Llewellyn, *The Decade of Reform* (1972) is a straightforward history dealing with politics, social problems, foreign and imperial policy, and religion. Geoffrey B.A.M. Finlayson's *England in the Eighteen Thirties* (Foundations of Modern History series, 1969) has valuable discussions of the problems of reform and reform movements. N. Gash *Reaction and Reconstruction in English Politics 1832-52* (1965) deals with some of the major political problems, including the growth of political parties, which followed and to a large extent arose out of the Reform Act of 1832. The *Age of Peel*, (1968) by the same author, a small collection of documents with commentary for the years 1828-51, includes a number of political sections.

On the technical aspects of the electoral structure, Charles Seymour's classic work on *Electoral Reform in England and Wales* which first appeared in 1915 has been reprinted with an introduction by Michael Hurst (1970). J. Holladay Philbin's *Parliamentary Representation 1832 England and Wales* (New Haven, Connecticut 1965) is an invaluable reference work that deserves to be better known. It provides a detailed account of the electoral system at the time of the first Reform Bill, modelled on Oldfield's *Representative History*. W.B. Gwyn's *Democracy and the Cost of Politics in Britain* (1962) deals with the financing, legitimate and illegitimate, of parliamentary elections from 1832 to 1918. J.R. Vincent's *Poll Books: How Victorians Voted* (1967) is valuable but the material needs to be interpreted with care. For anyone carrying out research on the period two indispensable reference works have become more readily available as a result of reprinting: The first, covering the whole period from 1832 to 1910 is *McCalmont's Parliamentary Poll Book* ed. J.R. Vincent and M. Stenton (new edn. 1971). The second, with a long introduction by its editor Professor Hanham, is that invaluable handbook, *Dod's Electoral Facts from 1832 to 1853* (new edn. 1972).

On the reform act itself William H. Maehl Jr.'s *The Reform Bill of 1832* (New York, 1967) provides a useful compilation of extracts from historians ranging from Justin McCarthy to E.P. Thompson. A similar book designed specifically as an aid for university students is edited by J.B. Conacher, *The Emergence of British Democracy in the Nineteenth Century* (Major Issues in History, New York, 1971). About a third of its contents, mainly in the form of extracts from contemporary sources, is devoted to the first reform act. H.J. Hanham's *The Reformed Electoral System in Great Britain 1832-1914* (Historical Association pamphlet, 1968) is a good general introduction to a large subject.

John Cannon has an interesting discussion of the 1832 act in the closing chapters of his history of *Parliamentary Reform 1640-1832* (1973). What is likely to remain the definitive account is, however, Michael Brock's *The Great Reform Act* (1973) which takes account of the material which has become available since J.R.M. Butler's classic narrative and offers a thorough and intelligent survey of virtually every aspect of the passage and contents of the bill.

This might also be the place to mention two works which do not fit easily into a category of work done since the appearance of *Politics in the Age of Peel*. The first is A.S. Turberville's *The House of Lords in the Age of Reform 1784-1837* (1958), a posthumous work edited by Mr. R.J. White. Though the effective date of the book is 1945 rather than the year of actual publication, and it was in some respects old-fashioned even when it appeared, it is full of useful information and comment. The other is the late Professor Aspinall's *Three Early Nineteenth Century Diaries*. Indispensable for any study of the reform bill crisis, it not only includes copious extracts from the diaries of two Whigs (Littleton and Le Marchant) and one Tory (Ellenborough) but has a long, informative and authoritative introduction by the editor, whose knowledge of the political sources for this period was probably unrivalled. It appeared in 1952, by which date my own book was irretrievably committed in the hands of the printers, and any coincidence of view was unconscious, even if reassuring.

Though the history of the two main political parties still has to be tackled on any large scale, the gap is to some extent filled by Robert Blake's *The Conservative Party from Peel to Churchill* (1970), based on his Ford lectures for 1968, and by Donald

Southgate's *The Passing of the Whigs 1832-1886* (1962). The two fragments into which the Conservative Party was split in the 1840s have received rather closer attention. The Peelites have been dealt with in two complementary rather than competing works: *The Peelites 1846-1857* by W.D. Jones and A.B. Erickson (Ohio, 1972) which is particularly informative about the fate of the rank and file, and *The Peelites and the Party System 1846-52* by J.B. Conacher (1972) which concentrates on the leaders and the larger political issues. Their opponents form the subject of R. Stewart's *The Politics of Protection: Lord Derby and the Protectionist Party 1841-1852* (1971), an excellent study breaking new ground.

Chartism and the Anti-Corn Law League must be regarded as outside the present context, but a reference should be made to the growing interest in smaller pressure groups. *Popular Movements c. 1830-1850* ed. by J.T. Ward (Problems in Focus series, 1970) deals with various movements of agitation including parliamentary reform. *Pressure from Without in Early Victorian England* ed. Patricia Hollis (1974) is concerned with a slightly more esoteric group but has much that is indirectly of relevance for the general study of the structure of politics. A selection of papers of that indefatigable political wire-puller Francis Place is given in *London Radicalism 1830-1843* ed. D.J. Rowe (1970), including his retrospective narrative of the reform crisis. Space should also be found for a mention of a small book in a rare category — *A Victorian M.P. and his Constituents: The Correspondence of H.W. Tancred M.P.1841-1859* (Banbury Historical Society, 1969), which casts an interesting light on the relations between a backbench Liberal M.P. and the social organisations from which he drew support.

An even more valuable enlargement of the historical scene has come from the exploration of local and provincial politics. A useful background to rural society is provided by F.M.L. Thompson's *English Landed Society in the Nineteenth Century* (1963) and David Spring's *The English Landed Estate in the Nineteenth Century* (Baltimore, 1963). Donald Read's *The English Provinces 1760-1960* (1964) is a brave attempt at an unmanageable subject but has a section on the 1830-1860 period which is not without interest even though the interpretation of 'provinces' may be thought to be a trifle narrow. Alongside this may be placed the same author's *Press and People 1790-1850: Opinion in Three English Cities* (1961) which deals with the politics and the press in Leeds, Manchester and Sheffield. Patricia Hollis's *The Pauper Press, A Study in working class radicalism of the 1830s* (1970) is a detailed, scholarly study of popular journalism and working class politics in

London during the years 1830-36. Finally, there is a group of three regional political studies which illustrate in their different ways both the large contrasts between the different counties of England and the extent to which national issues and national organisations as well as purely local interests were beginning to be of importance in provincial Politics. As a collective introduction to the complexities of interpreting post reform politics at constituency level these could hardly be bettered. They are R.W. Davis, *Political Change and Continuity c. 1760-1885 A Buckinghamshire Study* (1972); R.J. Olney, *Lincolnshire Politics 1832-1885* (1973); and T.J. Nossiter, *Influence, Opinion and Political Idiom in Reformed England: Case Studies from the North-East 1832-1874* (1975).

(b) *Articles and Pamphlets*

From the mass of material that has appeared in article form a special place perhaps should be given to those by Professor D.C. Moore since they constitute the one sustained effort to establish a different interpretation of the Reform Act of 1832 from that generally accepted by British historians. It is not unfair to add, however, that to some of his critics Dr Moore's arguments seem to be based on an unduly rigid conceptual approach, using a rather narrow range of evidence: it is probably true to say that while his views have evoked interest they have not so far carried conviction to the majority of his fellow scholars. The argument can be followed in:-

'The Other Face of Reform', (*Victorian Studies*, V, 1961);

'Concession or Cure: The Sociological Premises of the First Reform Act', (*Hist. Journal*, IX, 1966);

'Social Structure, Political Structure, and Public Opinion in Mid-Victorian England', (*Ideas and Institutions of Victorian Britain, Essays in Honour of G. Kitson Clark*, ed. R. Robson, 1967); and (with E.P. Hennock) 'The First Reform Act A Discussion', (*Victorian Studies*, XIV, 1971)

A more permanent statement of his general views will be found in his recent book *The Politics of Deference* (Hassocks, Harvester Press, 1976). Other articles worth consulting are:-

W.O. Aydelotte: 'Voting Patterns in the British House of Commons in the 1840s', (*Comparative Studies in Society and History*, V, 1963)

'The Country Gentlemen and the Repeal of the Corn Laws', (*Eng. Hist. Rev.*, LXXXII 1967)

D.E.D Beales: 'Parliamentary Parties and the 'Independent' Member, 1810-1860', (*Ideas and Institutions of Victorian Britain*, ed. R. Robson, 1967)

G. Kitson Clark: 'The Electorate and the Repeal of the Corn Laws', (*Trans. R. Hist. Society*, 5 series, 1951)

David Close: 'The Formation of the two party alignment in the house of commons between 1832 and 1841', (*Eng. Hist. Rev.* LXXXIV, 1969)

W. Ferguson: 'The Reform Act (Scotland) of 1832: Intention and Effect' (*Scottish Hist. Rev.* XLV, 1966)

G.B.A.M. Finlayson: 'The Politics of Municipal Reform, 1835' (*Eng. Hist. Rev.* LXXXI, 1966)
    'Joseph Parkes of Birmingham 1796-1865: a Study in Philosophic Radicalism' (*Bulletin of the Inst. of Hist. Research*, XLVI, 1973)

W.E.L. Gilbert: 'Rye Reformed' (*Rye Museum Publications* n.d.)

Betty Kemp: 'The General Election of 1841' (*History*, XXXVII, 1952)

D. Large: 'The Decline of 'the Party of the Crown' and the Rise of Parties in the House of Lords, 1783-1837' (*Eng. Hist. Rev.*, LXXVIII, 1963)

Mary Lawson-Tancred: 'The Anti-League and the Corn Law Crisis of 1846' (*Hist. Journal*, III (2), 1960)

Norman McCord: 'Some Difficulties of Parliamentary Reform' (*Hist. Journal*, X, 1967)
    'Gateshead Politics in the Age of Reform' (*Northern History*, X, 1969)
    'Some Limitations of the Age of Reform' (*Britis' Government and Administration: Studies presented to S.B. Chrimes*, ed. H. Hearder and H.R. Loyn, 1974)

(with P.A. Wood) 'The Sunderland Election of 1845' (*Durham Univ. Journal*, LII new series, 1959)

J. Milton-Smith: 'Earl Grey's Cabinet and the Objects of Parliamentary Reform' (*Hist. Journal* XV, 1972)

David Spring: 'Lord Chandos and the Farmers 1818-1846' (*Huntingdon Library Quarterly*, XXXIII, 1970)

J.H. Whyte: 'Landlord Influence in Ireland 1760-1885' (*Eng. Hist. Rev.* LXXX, 1965)

D.G. Wright: 'A radical borough: parliamentary politics in Bradford 1832-41' (*Northern History* IV, 1969)

Part I

THE REPRESENTATIVE SYSTEM

Chapter One

THE PRINCIPLES OF THE REFORM ACT

WHEN whigs, tories, and radicals opened the grand national debate on the reform bill in 1831, it was an occasion for which it would have been necessary to go back to the Revolution of 1688 to find a parallel. Many constitutional changes had taken place since that time; but they had been for the most part gradual changes of administrative habit and convention rather than explicit and fundamental alterations in the legal conception of the constitution. Indeed, so long had the fabric of the constitution stood without formal change that it had acquired in the eyes of men like Eldon a kind of sacrosanctity; as though a prescriptive right against change could be gained by the mere passage of time. The crisis of 1831 was therefore all the more effective in revealing the attitudes of contemporary Englishmen to their most characteristic political institution. Nevertheless, as in 1689, it was a discussion not primarily of abstract principles, nor even of the application of principles to an actual situation, but of certain practical proposals from which principles might perhaps be deduced, though they were not in themselves essential to the work that was done. Had it been a question of abstract principles, the ground of difference between Grey's ministry and the opposition would have been narrow. It was because the controversy was over detail that room for a full-pitched battle was secured.

The parliamentary debate on the reform bill began in March 1831 and continued intermittently until the summer of 1832. Looking back now on that involved and protracted discussion, on the three successive English bills, the two Irish and the two Scottish bills, on the vehement argument in parliament, and the even more vehement participation of the public in that argument, it is clear that given the contemporary political assumptions accepted by both sides the tories were in the right. Almost every point that they made, every fear that they expressed, were good points and well founded fears, even though the whig majority rejected their validity and denied their justification. Sooner or later all the major prophecies of the opposition came true. In some cases it took a

3

century where they had anticipated a few decades; in others their predictions were vindicated within fifteen years where they themselves could scarcely have foreseen so sudden an onset of disaster. But taken as a whole the tory case against the reform bill was an accurate analysis of the real consequences of reform. That in itself, had it been accepted by their opponents, might have been sufficient to destroy the bill; since these consequences were so obnoxious, even in anticipation, to the majority of both parties in parliament, that it was imperative for the whigs to deny the accuracy of the opposition forecasts if they wished to retain the support of their own followers. For except on the specific measure before them there was a substantial amount of agreement between the parliamentary reformers and anti-reformers on political fundamentals; and conversely, therefore, agreement on what were political undesirabilities. Neither party was democratic; indeed, that adjective was still a term of abuse or condemnation among the ruling classes, and whigs as well as tories carefully dissociated themselves from its implications. Neither party was royalist in the sense of being a party pledged to the person of the monarch. Both were monarchical, in the sense of being a party anxious for the maintenance of the crown as an integral part of the constitution. Both were oligarchic and aristocratic; and though sensitive to public opinion both were opposed to demagogy. They were therefore in the position of two physicians, working according to the same science, but differing in their interpretation of a particular case. If the whigs had accepted the tory prognosis, they could scarcely have prescribed the remedy they did. Nevertheless, the tory prognosis was the correct one.

The case of the opposition was clear enough. Whether expressed confusedly by Wetherell, intemperately by Croker, or moderately by Peel, the common attitude can easily be distinguished among the intricate and laborious details of minor argument over schedule and franchise. In the first place the bill would inevitably destroy the existing balance of the constitution. Already the influence of the crown based on the control of patronage had been so diminished during the two preceding generations that it now scarcely counted in the scales. Under the new system the last major prerogative of the crown—the choice of ministers—would be confined within such narrow limits that in effect ministers would henceforth be imposed on the crown by the popular assembly.

He saw no prospect [Peel told the House] that the King would
hereafter be enabled to exercise an unpopular prerogative, however
necessary that prerogative might be to the permanent interests of
the country. . . . How could the King hereafter change a Ministry?
How could he make a partial change in the Administration in times
of public excitement with any prospect that the Ministers of his
choice, unpopular, perhaps, from the strict performance of necessary
duties, would be returned to Parliament?[1]

What was true of the position of the Crown applied also to the
House of Lords. The strengthening of the popular part of the
legislature meant a corresponding decline in the influence of the
non-elective house. Every diminution of aristocratic influence in
the representative system would widen the difference between the
two houses of parliament and deprive the constitution of the
checks and balances implicit in the character of the House of
Lords. So much emphasis was laid by the reform bill on the
popular aspect of the legislature that even while the fate of the
measure was still undetermined, the power of the House of Lords
seemed to be visibly shrinking. Who asked, observed Peel on
another occasion, what the House of Lords would do should the
reform bill pass the House of Commons. 'It seems taken for granted
that it must pass the House of Lords—that it would be vain to
oppose a measure that extends popular privileges, and is said to
be in conformity with the wishes of the majority of the people.'[2]
In such circumstances, with both Crown and House of Lords
weakened, if not actually paralysed, as independent working
features of the constitution, nothing would remain to challenge
the power of the elected branch of the legislature based on the
sovereignty of the people. The name and form of the monarchy
and peerage would be retained; but their significance would have
vanished and the whole balance of the constitution destroyed.
'When you have once established the overpowering influence of
the people over this House; when you have made this House the
express organ of the public voice; what other authority in the
State can—nay, more, what other authority in the State ought—
to control its will, or reject its decisions?'[3] And so, ultimately, on
the basis of the sovereign democratic legislature would be erected
the omnipotent and omnicompetent state.

---

[1] *Hansard*, 3rd ser., XI, 756–7.
[2] *Ibid.*, III, 906. [3] *Ibid.*, III, 905.

These were the most important, but not the only consequences of reform. It was Peel once more who pointed out that the bill would go far towards creating a division in the legislature between rural and industrial interests, divided geographically by a line of demarcation traceable across the face of England from the Wash to the mouth of the Severn. Of the fifty-six boroughs doomed by Schedule A,[4] five were north and fifty-one south of that line. On the other hand, the great majority of the new boroughs were situated north of the line, and (excluding London) only a mere half-dozen south of it. The stage was thus set for a struggle not of parties but of classes and economic interests. Alexander Baring, M.P. for Thetford, constituted himself the chief spokesman of those who feared that in a reformed parliament, the country interest would be swamped by the town interest. 'The field of coal', he told the house, 'would beat the field of barley; the population of the manufacturing districts was more condensed, and would act with more energy, backed by clubs and large assemblages of people, than the population of the agricultural districts. They would act with such force in the House that the more divided agriculturalists would be unable to withstand it, and the latter would be overwhelmed.' A few days later he renewed his warnings. 'In a Reformed Parliament, when the day of battle came, the country Squires would not be able to stand against the active, pushing, intelligent people who would be sent from the manufacturing districts.'[5]

Should indeed such an opposition of interests arise, there could hardly be any question which would prevail. Already before the Reform Act the Duke of Wellington had doubted the ability of the county representatives to maintain and protect the landed interests of the country without the assistance provided by the members sitting for the close boroughs. It was the latter, he thought, which were the 'true protectors of the landed interest'.[6] The act certainly increased the county representation of the kingdom; but the gain was, in the opinion of the opposition, far outweighed by the loss of the small boroughs, the weighting of the county franchise by tenants and leaseholders from urban areas, and the enfranchisement of the large industrial towns. It needed therefore no special perspicacity to foresee the coming onslaught on the Corn Laws.

[4] Second reform bill for England and Wales. Peel was speaking in committee, 27 July 1831 (*Hansard*, v, 410–11).   [5] *Ibid.*, v, 580, 614.   [6] *Ibid.*, vii, 1194.

Even in 1830 and 1831 innumerable petitions to the House of Commons had coupled the repeal of the Corn Laws with reform of the legislature, the ballot, and annual parliaments, in their list of political requirements. Across the narrow gap of fifteen years the tories could already look with apprehension to the time when the sacred cause of agricultural protection would go down before the influence of the inspired bagmen of Lancashire and the industrial north. Lord Wharncliffe was neither a reactionary nor an alarmist; but he told the peers in 1831 that 'he believed that when once this Bill was passed, the landed interest would find, when it was too late, that an opening was made for the total repeal of the Corn Laws'.[7] Behind this immediate threat there loomed even more menacing, if vaguer, vistas of destruction: the decline of property as the basis of society and of the constitution, and the surrender of the State to the confiscatory designs of the non-possessing classes. 'Take away', said Sadler, 'the influence thus possessed by the great masses of property. . . . The consequences are then certain . . . Prepare . . . for similar spoliations to those which have recently been witnessed in a neighbouring country, where property bereft of its political influence lost its rights, and only served to mark out its possessors to certain destruction.'[8] This was perhaps extravagant language; and yet in less than a lifetime an ex-minister of the Crown was to demand in public what ransom would property pay for the security it enjoyed.[9]

Against all this the reformers might argue that in point of fact the extension of the franchise under the reform bill was extremely moderate. At the most it would be a mere half-million of the educated and prosperous middle classes that would join the 'electoral nation'. But the brooding imagination of the opposition was impatient of these schoolroom arguments. Once admit the principle of breaking down the traditional structure of government in deference to popular demand, it then mattered little if on the first occasion a decent moderation confined the additions to the electorate within the half-million mark. It was the first step which marred all. Unlock the door and not only could it never be closed again but inexorably it would be shifted more and more open as the pressure from without increased. Exactly this metaphor was used by Peel himself. 'I was unwilling to open a door', he said

---

[7] *Ibid.*, III, 1003.   [8] *Ibid.*, III, 1536.
[9] Joseph Chamberlain at Birmingham, 1885.

in explanation of his opposition to reform, 'which I saw no prospect of being able to close.'[10] It was not necessary that the first generation of politicians bred by the new system should themselves be anxious to introduce fresh measures of democratization. It was enough that they had proclaimed the principle that government must follow the popular voice. On what was the reform bill based fundamentally except that it was desired by the people? But did the people always know what was right? And must statesmen look always to the passions and never to the interests of those that they governed? If so, the Reform Act could only be the first of a long series of changes, the end of which could not be foreseen. Even if those who wielded power immediately after the passing of the act were averse to further developments, they could not restrain the forces they had themselves unleashed. No doubt they would secure a temporary popularity from the mere passing of the measure and the enfranchisement of half a million voters. 'But these are vulgar arts of government; others will outbid you; not now but at no remote period; they will offer votes and power to a million of men, will quote your precedent for the concession, and will carry your principles to their legitimate and natural consequences.'[11] If room or pretext should in future be needed for criticizing the first Reform Act and substituting a second or a third, the whigs themselves had made ample provision for the contingency. The illogicalities of the reformed system were admitted on all sides; but the very men who applied rational criticism to the traditional structure had themselves produced a system crammed with anomalies, complexities, and absurdities, and displaying as illogical and arbitrary a set of arrangements as any that had preceded them. All the arguments used against the old system of representation could be advanced against the new. 'Your own arguments', as Peel rightly told the whigs, 'are conclusive against the stability and permanence of the arrangement you are about to make.'[12] It was less than twenty years later that Lord John Russell began to urge in a whig cabinet the need for a fresh instalment of parliamentary reform.

No doubt fear sharpened the imagination, and a natural desire to score in debate exaggerated the pessimism of the tory opposition. But it is clear that the debate over the reform bill of 1831 went to the roots of political philosophy; and that when stripped of

[10] *Hansard*, IV, 890.   [11] *Ibid.*, II, 1353.   [12] *Ibid.*, VII, 455.

ephemeral argument and selfish motive there remained at the core of the tory position a genuine body of principles ranged against the whole spirit of the Reform Act. Certainly the succeeding century was to vindicate in an impressive fashion the correctness of their prophecies. On this high historic and philosophical plane, therefore, the tory case against reform was irrefutable.

Politics, however, are rarely fought out in such a rarefied atmosphere. A party enjoying the freedom of opposition may be able to indulge in speculative refinements and look to the ultimate consequences of governmental actions. Politicians in office work within a much narrower and more practical context. If the tories were the better historians, philosophers, and prophets, the whigs were the better politicians. What counted for them was not the verdict of posterity but the force of contemporary society. The whigs could not afford, and perhaps had no right, to look too far ahead. 'Distant and eventual', had pronounced the greatest of all whigs, Sir Robert Walpole, 'must yield to present dangers.' Moreover in the long run the politician is the servant of the forces he directs. The deliberations of the cabinet committee on reform, and the Reform Act itself, were only symptoms of a much wider movement in the country. To ascribe solely to the decisions of a handful of ministers or to a single statute the immense political developments after 1832 is scarcely a tenable proposition. The whigs must bear responsibility for the Reform Act of 1832, but as instruments rather than as creators. The whole flank of the powerful intellectual position of the tories could be turned by one short question. What alternative was there to the whig proposals?

At the beginning of the parliamentary struggle Inglis had described the reform agitation as a 'state of diseased and feverish excitement' caused by the examples of France and Belgium, and denied that there was any general demand for reform in the country.[13] But support for that opinion gradually waned in the succeeding twelve months. It was significant that Peel in his first contribution to the long series of reform debates in 1831 and 1832 stated that he did not object to all reform, but merely to the particular bill brought forward by the whigs. Circumstances would have debarred him when last in office from bringing forward a motion for parliamentary reform. But out of office and as a private individual, he continued, 'I do not hesitate to avow, that

[13] *Ibid.*, II, 1094.

there might have been proposed certain alterations in our representative system, founded on safe principles, abjuring all confisca-
tion, and limited in their degree, to which I would have assented.'[14]
Indeed, when Wellington's tory government went out of office in
1830, all the ministers except the duke himself had told the king
that some reform of parliament would be necessary.[15] The
incoming whigs therefore did not so much create as merely
recognize the situation which confronted them when Grey first
formed his cabinet in November 1830. From the start this argument of necessity was consistently upheld. 'The perilous question
is that of Parliamentary Reform,' wrote the prime minister to Sir
Herbert Taylor, the king's secretary, in January 1831, 'and as I
approach it, the more I feel all its difficulty. With the universal
feeling that prevails on this subject, it is impossible to avoid doing
something; and not to do enough to satisfy public expectation (I
mean the satisfaction of the rational public) would be worse than
to do nothing.'[16] The whigs, then, took their stand on the fundamental principle of an irresistible demand in the country for
parliamentary reform; and on its logical corollary, the futility of
piecemeal or half-hearted legislation in answer to that demand.
The report which Grey himself received from his committee of
four took this argument as the criterion of their reform proposals.
'The plan of Reform proposed by His Majesty's Ministers', they
wrote, 'ought to be of such a scope and description as to satisfy all
reasonable demands, and remove at once, and for ever, all rational
grounds for complaint from the minds of the intelligent and independent portion of the community.'[17]

The question narrowed itself therefore not to the principle but
the degree of reform. Here the whig scheme, arbitrary and illogical
as it was, represented with rough accuracy the most that could be
pushed through parliament and the least that would satisfy the
country at large. That the tories regarded it as revolutionary and
the more extreme radicals as a betrayal was a reasonable indication
of its value as a national solution. But that sooner or later something in the way of parliamentary reform must take place was
apparent to most. With all its merits, the unreformed system had
by 1830 one gross demerit. It was not regarded as satisfactory by
the bulk of informed and influential opinion in the country. It was

[14] *Hansard*, II, 1344.   [15] *Corr. Wm. IV and Grey*, I, 186, 188.
[16] *Ibid.*, I, 52.   [17] *Ibid.*, I, Appendix A, 461.

this practical consideration that was the strength of the whig case. It was never better expressed than by Melbourne in the House of Lords on the occasion of the second reading of the reform bill in 1831. He acknowledged frankly that he had previously resisted reform.

> But [he added] all experience proves, when the wishes of the people are founded on reason and justice and when they are consistent with the fundamental principles of the constitution, that there must come a time when both the legislative and executive powers must yield to the popular voice or be annihilated. . . . When your lordships see, that on every occasion of public calamity and distress, from whatever cause arising, the people call for an alteration in the representation, and that the call is accompanied with a deep, rankling sense of injustice suffered, and of rights withheld, can your lordships suppose that an opinion so continually revived has not some deep-seated foundation, and can you be insensible to the danger of continuing a permanent cause for angry and discontented feelings to be revived and renewed at every period of public distress and public calamity?[18]

Indeed, reading this speech, suffused as it is with a kind of melancholy eloquence, one is reminded of the calm considered presentation of the case against reform put forward by Peel. Despite differences of background and temperament, Peel and Melbourne were together perhaps the truest diagnosticians of the reform crisis; the one opposing without hope, the other assisting without desire.

The defence of the whigs therefore is that they offered a practical remedy for a felt grievance.[19] What the tories said was true; but what the whigs did was necessary. They satisfied in a rough but substantial fashion the immediate demand in the country for

---

[18] *Hansard*, VII, 1179.

[19] An example of the persistence of the whig tradition is provided by the following passage, written in the second quarter of the twentieth century. The author, who was born in 1857 at a time when the great age of Pitt and Fox was still an after-glow in political memory, sat in parliament between 1885 and 1903 as one of the last of the genuine historic whigs, and lived to carry on into the age of Hitler the unbroken tradition of his vanished party. 'Though Whigs had talked of democracy and of "the Sovereign People" they were never democrats in the modern sense. They believed that Government was *a practical thing*, and did not exist to furnish a spectacle of uniformity nor to comply with logic, arithmetic or the theories of visionary politicians. They were for Liberty with a big L, for toleration and for justice, but they never confused inequalities with injustices and never desired to see administrations come and go by chance majorities or by the changing humours of millions of uninformed voters.' Sir Alfred Pease, *Elections and Recollections*, Preface, xiii.

parliamentary reform. 'They have done', said Macaulay in
vindication of his leaders, 'all that was necessary for the removing
of a great practical evil, and no more than was necessary.'[20]
Practical remedies, however, can only be applied to practical
abuses. What was it that the Reform Act, in the opinion of its
creators, was designed to do? In his speech introducing the first
reform bill, Lord John Russell went some way to answering that
question. The chief grievances of which the people complained,
he observed, were three in number. They were the nomination
of members of parliament by private individuals; the election of
members of parliament by close corporations; and the expense
of elections. The first grievance was to be met by the abolition of
all boroughs with electorates too small to preserve their independence and too isolated to be easily enlarged. The second was to be
met by the institution in all boroughs of a uniform £10 householder franchise. The third was to be met by a variety of measures:
the registration of voters, the reduction in the duration of elections,
the erection of separate polling stations in large constituencies; and
the splitting of large counties into divisions each returning their
own members.[21] Stated thus, the project of the ministers was
moderate to a degree; and indeed on Russell's own showing was
scarcely an adequate account of what the bill intended. In particular, it left almost out of account the question of the creation of
new constituencies.

Nevertheless it is clear that the emphasis of the first draft of the
reform bill was on the purification rather than on the enlargement
of the representative system. It is true that in Grey's opinion,
frequently expressed to the king, the essence of the bill lay in three
measures: the disfranchisement of the nomination boroughs, the
enfranchisement of the large towns, and the £10 householder
suffrage. But Grey, like most of the ministerial reformers, including the king himself, was also anxious for a reduction in the total
number of M.P.s. He wished to end a gross anomaly but he had no
desire to produce a rigid equality in borough representation.
Enfranchisement of new boroughs was doled out sparingly. As
originally proposed it was to be confined to towns with a population
of over 10,000, of which there were reckoned to be about thirty in
England.[22] The question of new constituencies thus took up only

[20] *Hansard*, ii, 1191.   [21] *Ibid.*, ii, 1060 sqq.
[22] *Corr. Wm. IV and Grey*, i, 68, 70, Appdx. A, 461 sqq.

a minor part in Russell's speech and from its place in the argument seemed almost to result from the *embarras de richesses* in the form of spare seats in the house made available by the abolition of borough seats in Schedules A and B. The initial plan of disfranchisement left 168 vacancies at the disposal of the ministry. But it was not proposed to fill them all up. Forty-two seats were to be allotted to the new boroughs (including eight to the new London boroughs) which by their population, wealth, and importance seemed to deserve representation. But this was to be balanced by additional seats for county members. 'As county members have unquestionably the most excellent class of constituents, they form of themselves a most valuable class of representation.' So Yorkshire, the only county with four members, was now to have six for its three ridings; twenty-six other counties were to be given two additional members; and the Isle of Wight was to be given one. Fifty-five seats, therefore, as compared with the forty-two new borough seats, were to be assigned to the counties. This of course was in England only. But nine additional members for Scotland, Ireland, and Wales, scarcely made a heavy inroad in the ministry's stock of empty seats and as originally calculated the House of Commons would have been reduced by sixty-two members under the first reform bill.[23] Even then, if to Russell's three explicit points is added a fourth, the question of new constituencies, it is obvious that no revolutionary expansion of the representative system was envisaged and that the counties were intended to receive as much if not more consideration than the towns.

Another statement of the basic objects of the reform bill was given by Palmerston two days later.[24] According to his analysis the existing system of representation suffered from five great blemishes. These were nomination by patrons, gross corruption among the lower classes of voters, inadequate representation of the larger manufacturing and commercial towns, the expense of elections, and finally the unequal and inequitable distribution of voting power between the middle and lower classes. The bill before the House, he claimed, would remedy all these defects. Apart from that the object of the government in framing the bill was threefold: firstly to give representation to the big manufacturing

[23] General Gascoyne's motion not to reduce the total representation of England and Wales, on which the first reform bill broke down, was in fact accepted later by the ministry.

[24] *Hansard*, II, 1318 sqq.

towns; secondly to add to the respectability of the electorate; and thirdly to increase the number of those enjoying the right of choosing their representatives in parliament. Both in his list of defects and in his analysis of objectives, therefore, Palmerston was more comprehensive than the first great spokesman on the ministerial side. Nevertheless he too followed Russell's example in stressing the importance of the additional county representatives. The great virtue of the bill, he concluded, was that it would provide a real national representation in the House of Commons, not only by reason of the enlarged representation of the industrial areas, but also—and even more importantly—by enlarging the representation of the county constituencies. 'For without meaning to disparage the manufacturing or commercial interests, he must say that he considered the soil to be the country itself.' There was thus ample agreement between the two speakers. Palmerston perhaps laid a shade more emphasis on the corruption of the electoral system and the importance of the new boroughs. On the question of elections, for example, he attributed much of the previous misgovernment and disregard of public opinion to the bribery and influence exercised at elections whereby 'parties came into parliament without constituents, or only with those whom they had purchased, and might sell again'; and he spoke with unwonted feeling of the existing mode of elections as 'the most offensive and disgusting that could be imagined'. But these were differences of stress rather than divergences of principle. In these two speeches, if anywhere, were contained the explicit declarations of the ministry on the purpose of the Reform Act. What they were is clear enough. It was to be seen later how justified were the hopes and calculations of the authors of the bill.

Apart from these specific observations on the part of two of the most prominent ministers in the House of Commons, a number of general points emerged in the course of the long discussions that dragged on for the next seventeen months. The most recurrent of these concerned the need to bring the middle classes within the orbit of the constitution. In explaining to the House why in 1822 he had championed the cause of reform which he had deprecated in 1819, Lord John Russell placed his whole case upon his awareness in the interval of the power and importance of this new social order. His motives, he said, were the great advance of the middle classes in wealth, intelligence, knowledge, and influence; the insufficient representation of that class in the House of Commons; and the obvious disinclination of parliament in its enacted measures to take that middle-class opinion into account.[25] This was said in public; but in private the whig leaders held the same view. Writing to a ministerial colleague in October 1831 Grey made a remarkable reference to 'the middle classes who form the real and efficient mass of public opinion, and without whom the power of the gentry is nothing'.[26] The middle classes deserved political recognition on their own merits. But the whig argument went deeper than this. From a profoundly conservative point of view, they asserted, it was expedient to enfranchise the middle classes because of the social and political considerations which such a measure would have. Not only did the exclusion of the middle classes from the constitution weaken the power of the government but it also strengthened popular discontent and disorder because the middle classes were inevitably forced thereby into an alliance with the lower classes. If on the other hand the middle classes, those 'vast masses of property and intelligence' as Macaulay termed them, were brought into an alliance with the old governing classes, the balance of the constitution would be restored. It was a significant proof of how widespread this feeling was in the minds of the reformers that an identical attitude was set out in the independent memorandum on Scottish reform submitted to Russell in November 1830 by Kennedy of Dunure.

The object of an extension of the Elective franchise in the Counties, Cities, and Burghs of Scotland [began the memorandum] must be to give satisfaction to the people of that country; and it is conceived that this may be done by extending the Elective Franchise to those classes, who possess property and knowledge. Much more is demanded by many, but it is hoped that it is not yet too late to make a change in the Franchise, the limit of which shall be the possession of property and intelligence; but any plan must be objectionable which, by keeping the Franchise very high and exclusive, fails to give satisfaction to the middle and respectable ranks of society, and drives them to a union founded on dissatisfaction, with the lower orders. It is of the utmost importance to associate the middle with the higher orders of society in the love and support of the institutions and government of the country.[27]

[25] *Hansard*, III, 309. [26] *Corr. Wm. IV and Grey*, I, 376 footnote.
[27] Cockburn, *Letters on Affairs of Scotland*, 258 sqq.

It was accordingly an essential purpose of the bill to reconcile to the constitution an influential part of the nation which until then had seemed to stand outside it; and, in so doing, to restore to the government that broad basis of national confidence which it had previously lacked and without which it could not efficiently exist. 'To property and good order', proclaimed Durham in the House of Lords, 'we attach numbers.' Once the bill was passed, he argued, the middle classes would be the friends and allies of the government. Then, if the poorer classes rose in discontent, they would find that their natural leaders had been taken from them and the forces of law and order immensely strengthened. Durham was careful to add that he had no reason to believe that the lower orders were disaffected. Nevertheless he had made his point and the history of chartism in the next two decades was to prove its accuracy.[28] In this light, therefore, the whigs appeared as the saviours of society, consolidating, pacifying, and uniting a much divided nation. It was a subtle and not entirely ungrounded argument.

It was at this point that the enfranchisement of the new boroughs assumed its real importance—one far greater than that indicated by Russell in his introductory speech of 1 March 1831. Indeed, at a later stage, he developed a more elaborate theory with regard to the fresh borough creations which followed logically from the main doctrine of the importance of the middle classes. There were, he said, three main principles on which the ministry had acted in the enfranchisement of new boroughs. They thought it desirable in the first place to give representation to important centres of trade and manufacture. They thought it desirable to bind a large class of people to the institutions of the country and to teach them to look to the House of Commons as the political tribunal where their grievances would be discussed and remedied. Lastly they believed that the House of Commons as the representative body of the nation would be improved by the addition of men qualified to take part in the discussions of all the new problems that might come before the legislature.[29] The £10 franchise and the new boroughs were thus the technical means of infusing fresh life into the narrow and unpopular governing system. The method itself involved the admission to the aristocratic *pays légal* not of the people but of the class most akin to the aristocracy in its wealth and

[28] *Hansard*, III, 1029.   [29] *Ibid.*, III, 309; XI, 44.

education, whose alliance was most to be valued, whose enmity was most to be feared. Even if that brought with it the risk of collision inside the ruling classes of the opposed interests of agriculture and industry, it was better that such a collision should take place within the parliamentary field, where its worst effects would be subdued by the responsibilities of office and the ties of party, than that it should take the form of a landowning parliament set against an unenfranchised industrial population of employers and employed. The essential point was to attach the middle classes to the aristocratic constitution. In all their references to 'the people' and to 'popular representation', the whigs clearly had this implication in mind. When Russell ended his introductory speech with a peroration stressing the need for a new political body which 'representing the people, springing from the people, and sympathising with the people, can fairly call on the people to support the future burthens of the country,'[30] he was using whig and not Lincolnian vocabulary. On the same evening Althorp made the assertion that the bill would give the 'people' of England an overpowering influence in the choice of representatives. This being greeted with ironic applause by Peel, he hastened to add that 'by the people he meant the great majority of the respectable middle classes of the country'.[31] Brougham in the House of Lords made an even sharper definition of the term. In speaking of the people's support, he informed the peers, he did not refer to the mob, or populace. 'But if there is the mob, there is the people also. I speak now of the middle classes . . . the most numerous and by far the most wealthy order in the community.'[32]

The last phrase in Brougham's explanation provides another approach to the problem. What the middle classes were in social terms, industrial and commercial property were in economic terms. It was wealth that gave the middle classes their status and it was wealth that the whigs wished to enfranchise. The object of the £10 householder vote, said Russell, was to give representation 'to the real property and to the real respectability' of the cities and towns. When all the changes contemplated by the reform bill had taken effect, the electorate would be fortified by 'about half a million of persons, and these all connected with the property of the country, having a valuable stake amongst us, and deeply interested in our institutions'.[33] The use of the possessive pronoun was

[30] *Ibid.*, II, 1089.   [31] *Ibid.*, II, 1143.   [32] *Ibid.*, VIII, 251.   [33] *Ibid.*, II, 1069, 1083.

revealing. In effect privileged wealth was being asked to admit unprivileged wealth to the close circle of the ruling class; and property was to be the certificate of probity and good behaviour. The principle commonly accepted in the eighteenth century, that the constitution was founded on property, was thus carried over into the Reform Act. 'There is no principle of our constitution,' said Lord Durham, 'there is no principle affecting the representative system, that has not property for its basis, and I am warranted in saying that the plan of the ministers is of this nature.'[34] The only difference was the realization by the whigs that a new type of property had arisen by the side of the traditional landed interest that was powerful enough to demand and deserve recognition. The qualifications of the new voters in both town and country therefore were made dependent on their relationship, whether direct or indirect, with property. The dispute was not on the principle of property qualification but on the details. With regard to the borough franchise it had at one point been decided to choose the £20 householder as the level of qualification. Only later realization that the result would be to transform many substantial towns into close boroughs induced the ministry to lower the standard. The £10 franchise was selected as a practical compromise between the desire to rest the franchise on an unassailable basis of property and the fear of creating narrow constituencies amenable to bribery and intimidation.

To state the case in the bare terms of economic dominance, however, would be to falsify the position. There were various intellectual and ethical arguments for requiring a minimum standard of wealth from the electorate which cannot be dismissed as mere pretexts. It was the social as much as the economic significance of property that counted. Hawkins, the whig member for Tavistock, put the matter concisely in the course of a speech which in print remains one of the ablest and most eloquent passages of the reform debates, though it was badly received by the House and criticized by the opposition as frigid and sarcastic. 'In a country', said Hawkins, 'where no public provision was made for the education of the people, it necessarily happened that a certain amount of income was the only general and practical criterion of a required degree of intelligence.'[35] Macaulay had earlier made the same point when he argued that in view of the distressed and

[34] *Hansard*, III, 1020.   [35] *Ibid.*, VII, 198.

ill-educated condition of the labouring classes, universal suffrage at that juncture was impractical and inadvisable, and indeed could only produce 'a destructive revolution'.[36] A more balanced statement of the ministerial position came from Jeffrey, the Scottish Lord-Advocate, who drew up the reform bill for Scotland and was thus an informed and authoritative spokesman. On the matter of property qualification, he said, it was generally agreed by all parties that the only reasons for requiring the electors to have property were firstly, that it was a kind of test or presumption that they had more intelligence and information than were usually to be found in persons of the very lowest condition; and secondly, it was a pledge of their interest in and consequent disposition to maintain that respect for property in general which all thinking men must feel to be at the bottom of civil institutions.[37] As a test of fitness and as a pledge of legality, therefore, the property qualification was indispensable. It was a blend of the Hanoverian sense of property with the Victorian instinct for education; and however incongruous the two arguments, they formed a powerful alliance in debate. Nobody in parliament advocated a franchise divorced from property or special responsibility. Even Hunt the radical, who constituted himself the champion of the under-privileged classes, contented himself with putting forward the claims of the tax-payers, the men liable to service in the militia, and all who fought in the army or navy, to have a share in the choice of representatives. His specific proposal was that householders paying an annual rent of £3 or more should be added to the electorate but he admitted that he was not in favour of universal suffrage.[38]

It was this conception of the electorate, or as it was more frequently styled in contemporary speech the constituency, that provided the real intellectual opposition to the ballot. If the constituency which literally created the House of Commons was itself to consist of a chosen body of electors, a special responsibility rested on them as spokesmen for the nation. In his first speech Russell spent some time in defending the decision of the government to omit the ballot from provisions of the bill. He argued that under any circumstances it would be impossible to eliminate all influence and that while the ballot would prevent an improper influence on the good voter, it would also prevent a beneficial influence being exerted on the bad voter. It was inadvisable that any class of

[36] *Ibid.*, II, 1192.   [37] *Ibid.*, III, 72.   [38] *Ibid.*, II, 1208 sqq.

persons should be left 'wholly irresponsible in the discharge of a great public duty'. No branch of the constitution was infallible, not even the electorate; and the public exercise of the voting function was a kind of constitutional check on the people to whom that function was entrusted.[39]

Of course other and less intellectual considerations affected the issue. To those radical purists who believed that the majority of the electorate were impelled by sinister forces, the ballot seemed to be the only immediately efficacious remedy. Conversely there was a strong desire on the part of the older governing classes to preserve public voting as the indispensable factor in maintaining their influence over the electors. But if the radicals identified themselves with the demand for the ballot, they had no copyright in electoral morality. The introduction of the ballot was seriously considered by the whigs when drawing up the reform bill and Althorp confessed in the House of Commons that he personally was in favour of it, although he did not think that its absence ruined the only chance of effectual reform.[40] After the elections of 1835 and 1837 more and more whigs were inclined to agree that the ballot, while not necessarily acceptable as a principle, might be a valuable barrier against the conservative revival. The tendency to ascribe electoral defeat to anything but the genuine will of the electorate was human; and even for some conservatives the ballot was not without its attractions. If radicals desired the ballot primarily to end land-owning intimidation in the counties, conservatives could hope that it would give them an advantage in the towns. 'It seemed to me', wrote Disraeli of his earlier career, 'that the borough constituency of Lord Grey was essentially, and purposely, a dissenting and low Whig constituency, consisting of the principal employers of labour —and that the ballot was the only instrument to extricate us from these difficulties.'[41] This eccentric strain in tory thought did not escape the cynical eye of Lord Palmerston. 'I should not be surprised', he wrote to Russell in 1835, 'to find some of these days Tories and Radicals combining to become Balloters, each hoping by such means to steal a march upon the others. For certainly the Radicals would lose power by ballot in many towns where they at present lord it over all.'[42]

Among both whigs and tories, however, there existed a strong

[39] *Hansard*, II, 1084–5.
[40] *Ibid.*, III, 1570–1.
[41] Monypenny, *Disraeli*, I, 222.
[42] Russell, *Early Corr.*, II, 73.

objection to the ballot, founded on something more principled than a mere apprehension of defeat and loss of influence. Here, as elsewhere, the conflict of opinion over a radical proposal revealed fundamental divergences. The radicals, instinctively and unconsciously perhaps, were moving towards universal suffrage as the only method of discovering the national popular will. When the electorate was equated with the adult population, each voter would represent merely himself and his personal interests, and it would be a legitimate precaution to guard him against the malign influence of others by ensuring the secrecy of his vote. The opponents of the ballot, on the other hand, based their view on the limited electorate, in which the vote was literally a franchise—a liberty and a privilege to be exercised by the elector with deliberation and foresight, and a proper sense of his own position. Where, in the whole United Kingdom, only one man in every seven had the vote, it was absurd to treat the electorate as the British people, the ultimate source of power. Just as the members of parliament represented their constituents, so did the electors represent the mass of unenfranchised population. Against men in such a responsible position, publicity was the necessary safeguard. Open voting was as imperative for the elector on the hustings as for the member in the lobbies of Westminster. The ballot meant the evasion of responsibility.

It would in my opinion be quite inefficacious as a remedy against bribery and intimidation [wrote Lord William Russell to John Russell in 1838] and would destroy the characters of Englishmen, certainly of the liberal party. What pitiful figures we should cut, sneaking up to the ballot box, looking with fear to the right and the left and dropping in our paper, the contents of which we are afraid or ashamed to acknowledge. Whilst the Tory comes forward like a man, and like an Englishman, and says openly and fearlessly who he votes for. I would rather never give a vote than give a concealed vote—the desire to conceal the votes is a bad sign of the times.[43]

This dislike of secrecy as a kind of stigma on the character of the individual whom it covered was not simply an ingenious argument. Nor was the feeling confined to the aristocratic classes, who conceivably had little to fear themselves from the publicity of their votes. W. E. Forster, for all his humble Quaker background and many radical impulses, shared in his youth the sentiments of

[43] *Ibid.*, II, 217.

William Russell. At a meeting at Bradford in 1848, held in connexion with the chartist movement, he told his audience that he hated secrecy and that he thought if they obtained universal suffrage they would not require the protection of the ballot.[44] There was room for a variety of opinions on the advantages of the ballot at the beginning of Victoria's reign; and the opponents of the device could be as sincere and disinterested as its advocates. Indeed to some people the passage of the Reform Act made the ballot appear not more but less indispensable. In a brief discussion on the ballot in the House of Commons during December 1830, some months before the introduction of the first reform bill, Hobhouse had argued that few of the English electors were men of property and that for such a class the ballot was their only defence. About seven years later, however, in February 1838, he noted that:

> at the House of Commons today Sir Robert Peel speaking on the question of the Ballot, made what I considered the true objection to that measure—namely, that it would take away that influence over the vote which preserves the representative system, in our country, from being of too democratic a character. To this opinion I incline. I think the Ballot before the Reform Bill, and without it, would have been a good measure; but I am not prepared to say the same of it after, and with the Reform Bill.[45]

However contradictory, both the main arguments against the ballot were logical deductions from a political theory which postulated property as the basis of the political constitution. If the electorate was regarded as a representative body, for whom publicity was a necessary aspect of their functions, the reason why they were singled out from the mass of the unenfranchised was their property qualification. If on the other hand it was considered that the necessity of maintaining influence over the electorate was the effective argument against the ballot, it was because of the underlying conviction that property must be secured in its predominant position in the constitution as against mere numbers. The fluctuations in the deliberations of the whigs when drafting the reform bill admirably illustrated the direct relationship between property and the ballot. When the drafting committee decided to include the ballot, they raised the borough franchise from £10 to £20.

[44] Wemyss Reid, *Life of Forster*, 124.
[45] Broughton, *Recollections*, v, 120, cf. also *ibid.*, vi, 224.

When the cabinet rejected the ballot, the lower £10 franchise was restored. Grey indeed told Sir Herbert Taylor that the ballot had not been proposed by the framers of the original report as good in itself but merely as a concession which would facilitate the raising of the elective franchise in the boroughs and the consequent diminution of popular influence. However, there was little enthusiasm for the £20 franchise, which appeared (without the ballot) in the first draft of reform submitted to the king. William himself offered no objection to a reduction of the borough qualification to £10, though he asserted that he would never consent to the ballot. The omission of the latter therefore was naturally followed by the reintroduction of the lower borough franchise.[46]

An extension of this fundamental principle is to be discerned in the attention paid to those organized and influential forms of property that had become socially distinct interests. In selecting the new boroughs for enfranchisement the criterion was not mere population; and only partially the size of the new electorate. The motive which operated as powerfully as any was the desire to secure representation for 'interests'. In a sense the whole commercial and manufacturing community was an interest which the ministry felt should be more equitably represented in parliament. But beyond that primary objective was the view that specific towns should be chosen for enfranchisement so that they could act as representatives for specific interests of various kinds. When the House of Commons went into committee on the first reform bill, Lord John Russell explained that on the question of enfranchisement the ministers did not look solely to population; they also took into account commercial capital and enterprise. Hence the population test was not a rigid rule. Indeed the ministers proposed 'as a counterbalance to the pure principle of population, to give representation to large towns possessed of manufacturing capital and skill'.[47] A few months later, when introducing the second reform bill in June 1831, Russell elaborated this simple proposition by arguing that under the new scheme the members for England and Wales would be composed of about 150 county and 280 borough representatives. The borough members fell into two categories: those representing great cities and towns, including all the big manufacturing interests, such as wool, cotton, coal, and

---

[46] *Corr. Wm. IV and Grey*, I, Appendix A; *ibid.*, 96, 111, 114. Cf. Halévy, *Hist. Eng. People*, III, 26–7. [47] *Hansard*, III, 1519.

the potteries; and the remainder who numbered about a hundred, drawn from boroughs with a population of from three to six thousand, not immediately representing any interest, but perhaps in consequence 'better qualified to speak and inform the House on great questions of general interest to the community'.[48] Even if this latter class did not represent the commercial interests, it is clear that they were designed to represent interests of a social or political type. At a later stage in committee Russell said that it was imperative to give representation to the populous industrial areas of the north but that the ministry had deliberately retained a class of small boroughs in order to ensure the representation of certain elements in the population that would otherwise be unrepresented. Here he was specifically referring to the forty boroughs of Schedule B (deprived of one member) and the additional thirty boroughs left intact although they did not possess a large constituency.[49] The argument, however, is still relevant. It was a fundamental point of the bill not to produce uniformity but to ensure that a mass of interests great and small, industrial and social, were adequately represented in the House of Commons. The great argument against the unreformed system was not its anomalous structure but the fact that it left unrepresented or insufficiently represented certain important interests and gave representation on a lavish scale not to interests but to individuals.

It resulted from this attitude that the new boroughs formed a practical selection rather than a category capable of statistical definition on a basis of population or electorate. Thus Frome was enfranchised, in spite of its relatively small population of 12,000, because it had a woollen industry and would represent the south-west of England as against the north. Whitby and Sunderland came in to reinforce the interests of the shipping industry. Walsall with a population of about 15,000 and some 800 £10 houses, justified its inclusion on the score of its iron and leather industries. The ministry consented to take Merthyr Tydfil out of its group of Welsh contributory boroughs and give it individual representation after powerful advocates in the House of Commons had dilated upon its four large ironworks, its thirty-three blast-furnaces, its population of 22,000, and its 4,000 houses. It is true that, along with a special interest, the ministry felt bound to insist on the presence of what Russell called the elements of a good constituency.

[48] *Hansard*, IV, 338.   [49] *Ibid.*, V, 421.

But it is also apparent that an electorate of six or seven hundred was regarded as sufficient if the other factors were there. Conversely one of the major arguments of the opposition in connexion with proposed new boroughs was that some of them did not represent any tangible interest. Those that incurred this condemnation were on the whole of two kinds. The first were the subdivisions of the overgrown and unwieldy metropolis. Thus, Peel, while admitting that he did not oppose a moderate measure of enfranchisement for such large, separate industrial towns as Birmingham, Manchester, and Leeds, criticized the creation of the new London boroughs. He argued that London was already sufficiently represented as an entity and that the further increase in the number of the London members was only justified on the principle of basing representation on population and wealth—a principle which the government had specifically rejected.[50] The second kind was composed of certain towns which formed an entity in the sense of having an identifiable area and character, and possessed a wealthy and numerous population, but seemed to the jaundiced eye of the opposition to represent no special interest other than the sum of the diverse interests of its electors. Such towns, to use the phrase applied by the Earl of Haddington to Brighton, were simply 'an example of an unmeaning mass of population'.[51] The phrase is illuminating for the concept of collective identity as opposed to numbers and aggregates of individuals. Cheltenham and Brighton, the two fashionable watering-places enfranchised by the act, were the chief objects of condemnation under this heading, and tory speakers vied with each other in finding insulting epithets to apply to these two new boroughs. Trevor spoke of the 'petty interests of the keepers of circulating libraries and vendors of oranges and lemonade at Cheltenham and Brighton'; and Baring, in defending the Cornish boroughs as representative of the mining and fishing industries, argued that it was of more consequence to leave some Cornish representation for those interests than to give members to Cheltenham and Brighton and 'such mushroom places as these which derived importance only from the migratory shoals which annually resorted to them'.[52]

Obviously what appeared to the ministry to be a judicious

[50] *Ibid.*, v, 666–9. [51] *Ibid.*, xII, 1259.
[52] *Ibid.*, v, 215; x, 1119, 1121.

selection of new boroughs might be regarded by the opposition as arbitrary and haphazard decisions. The way was thus left open for an endless succession of arguments conducted on a basis of comparison with selected and unselected towns. But the essential feature was the principle of selecting substantial interests and real communities for enfranchisement rather than attempting to build up a uniform structure on a numerical basis. The actual anomalies which the tories criticized at the time and which were to provide ground for rational objection thirty-five years later, were claimed by the whigs in 1831 as a decided merit in their scheme. In his reply during the opening debate on the first reform bill in March 1831 Russell acknowledged that the bill left anomalies in the representative system but firmly declared that this had been considered by the ministry and was a deliberate act on their part. 'Anomalies they found and anomalies, though not such glaring ones as now existed, they meant to leave. A regular distribution of an equal proportion of members to equal population might be a wise and great scheme, but the proposers of this measure had not thought fit to bring such a plan before Parliament.'[53]

There remains one final point to be considered. Behind the electoral structure as it was left by the Reform Act, with its retention of old practices and old anomalies, its guarded introduction of new forces, its essentially aristocratic and conservative nature, lay a factor not easily susceptible of translation into institutional terms—the power of public opinion. Of the consciousness within the House of Commons of its strength there can be little doubt, for both sides cited it as evidence for their opposed arguments. In particular the power of opinion as expressed through the medium of the press was generally acknowledged. Inglis, for example, when replying to Russell in the opening debate on the first reform bill, pointed out that in fact during recent years the House of Commons had grown steadily more independent. The influence of the crown and the peerage had waned; the House was corrupted neither by money, since no member took money for his vote; nor by place, since patronage had been rigidly circumscribed; nor by party, since the old party divisions and the control of party leaders had disappeared. On the other hand, by means of public agitation and petitions, above all by means of the press, public opinion had secured immense weight in the House. 'This', he said,

[53] *Hansard*, III, 307.

'is the real control, to which we all look more or less.'[54] At a subsequent period in the debate Sir James Scarlett, another tory, made a similar observation. 'At present', he remarked, 'no man can rise to deliver his sentiments in this House without exposing himself to the certainty of a comment upon those sentiments, by some public journal.'[55] The whigs claimed this force of public opinion as a virtue, and indeed as a necessary feature of the constitution. Only a government on which an enlightened and informed public opinion was constantly playing could be relied on to carry out its functions correctly. This did not mean mob-rule or ceaseless radical demands; but what the people wanted, said Russell, was a change in the character of the representation of the country on which they could henceforth rely to reform, retrench, and economize when necessary.[56] Hence one of the major whig arguments in favour of their bill was that it would result in a more constant and rapid action of public opinion on the legislature.

Both ministerialists and the opposition therefore were agreed on the strength of public opinion. The difference between them was that the tories believed that government had become so weak that it could not stand up to the weight of public opinion; the whigs believed that government had become so weak that it must have the reinforcement provided by public opinion. This latter aspect was most clearly put by Hawkins in the speech already referred to delivered in September 1831. With Inglis he agreed that the work of government had become increasingly difficult in recent years owing to the disappearance of various methods of influencing the House of Commons which had produced the majorities of the eighteenth century. He described the dilemma of the contemporary minister who, he said, was usually more liberal than his party—'slave, on the one hand, of that handful of dealers in parliamentary power whose zealous and faithful support he had no longer the adequate means of purchasing—hated, on the other hand, by the people, whose rights he would fain have granted, perhaps even at the sacrifice of his own interest, could such sacrifice have availed'. Nevertheless, the abolition of patronage had been the real cause of putting power into the hands of men prepared 'to try that newest and noblest of political experiments, a government by public opinion. And to this complexion must we come at last.' Matters had gone beyond the control of either tory or whig. 'The

[54] *Ibid.*, II, 1115 sqq.   [55] *Ibid.*, III, 788.   [56] *Ibid.*, III, 314.

narrow resting place, on which the old system yet stood, which the current of passing events had long been loosening, was pushed from its base by last winter's torrent.'[57]

This question of public opinion was fundamental to the whole issue of efficient government. Take for example the Duke of Wellington's argument that reform would make it impossible for the king's government to be carried on. That argument was only one of many to the professional tory politician. But to the duke it was the single window through which he gazed at the political scene. All measures were to be regarded from the point of view of executive government. 'A measure of Parliamentary Reform', he told the House of Lords, 'brought forward by government, ought to be a measure which should enable government to carry on the King's service in parliament according to the constitution as it was established at the revolution.' But the whig bill was not such a measure.[58] Yet it was precisely this point that the whigs turned into their strongest argument. 'The real question', said Russell, 'is whether without some large measure of reform, the business of the country can be carried on with the confidence and the support of the people.'[59] The whigs were in effect asking the tories not to surrender the powers of the aristocracy but to preserve those powers by opening their ranks and enlarging their basis. They denied that an aristocracy that was truly such— resident, public-spirited, of high private character and carrying out a national service—could lose its legitimate influence. But the constitution could not last much longer without 'an additional infusion of popular spirit, commensurate with the progress of knowledge and the increased intelligence of the age'.[60] It followed from this attitude that what the whigs expected to produce by the Reform Act was what in fact largely resulted. The strength and homogeneity of the aristocratic ruling classes, as witnessed in parliament, in the government, and in local administration, remained substantially intact after 1832; though to a greater extent than ever before public opinion, after its signal demonstration during the reform crisis, exercised ultimate control over the extent and direction of that rule. Ostensibly power lay in the same hands as before; but henceforth no politician on either side of the House could ignore with impunity the new responsibility which

[57] *Hansard*, VII, 210–12.
[58] *Ibid.*, III, 1069.
[59] *Ibid.*, II, 1087.
[60] *Ibid.*, II, 1089.

rested upon their chamber. He did not think, observed Hobhouse shrewdly in March 1831, that by the reform bill, or any other plan of reform, 'the complexion of the House, as to the members returned to it, would be much changed. The motives however that sent men into it would be totally different.'[61]

Not all reformers in 1831 nor all radicals after 1832 were satisfied that this increased dependence on public opinion would be powerful or durable enough. One of the constant objectives of political radicalism was to transform parliament from a debating club of the upper ruling classes to an assembly of delegates automatically recording the will of their constituents. Election pledges were in fact a radical device designed to secure that very end; and the mania, as Burdett described it, for demanding pledges which characterized the election of 1832, threw much light on an important aspect of radical philosophy. The particular problem was to ensure the same dependence on the electorate during parliament that the candidate was ready to profess during the election. 'Every elector should recollect that his representative is elected for the unreasonably long period of seven years and that he may therefore set his constituents at defiance for that period' was the warning of one radical pamphlet.[62] One obvious remedy for this undue liberty of the representative was to reduce the maximum duration of parliament. The radical demands for annual or triennial parliaments were thus attempts to enlarge the control of the constituents over their elected members. Such a reduction in the duration of parliaments and consequent multiplication of general elections had two aspects to recommend it. Firstly the electors were enabled to sit in frequent and periodic judgement upon the conduct of their representatives and pass sentence accordingly. Secondly, the continual burden of election expenses would rapidly impoverish and drive out of competition the candidates dependent on wealth for their return, and favour the popular candidates whose election costs were small and often defrayed by their partisans. This latter theory rested on the rather ingenuous assumption that an electorate relieved of all forms of corruption and intimidation would normally vote radical. It seemed plausible enough, however, in the hopeful days of 1831. But the movement for shorter parliaments never made a great amount of progress.

[61] *Ibid.*, II, 1294.
[62] National Political Union Pamphlet no. 15, written by Francis Place (Graham Wallas, *Life of Place*, 326–7).

The first report of the ministerial committee on reform did indeed recommend that the duration of parliament should be limited to five years; but there was little support even for this minor concession to radical thought. The king was against it and Grey, while acknowledging that his intention had been to reduce the length of parliament, considered it a comparatively unimportant point. The project was therefore quietly laid aside.[63] Events after 1832 helped to confirm this decision.

The picture drawn by radical pamphleteers of members setting their constituents at defiance for seven long years seemed a little over-coloured in the presence of the plain fact that four general elections under the Reform Act took place within the first ten years of its existence. It was true that the circumstances were peculiar and unlikely to be repeated. But if nothing was thereby detracted from the logic of the radical argument, propaganda on its behalf was made extremely difficult. In default of annual elections to reduce members of parliament to a proper state of dependence, the radicals advocated the enforcement of election pledges. 'Pledges are a makeshift for shorter parliaments', wrote Daniel Wakefield; and again, 'pledges, though by no means a perfect expedient, are the next best thing to shorter parliaments, for the electors I mean; and to Whigs and Tories the most hateful thing except annual parliaments'.[64] The traditional parliamentary politicians were not without some justification in their dislike of pledges; for the system involved a principle hostile to the traditional conception of parliament as a governmental machine. The radicals envisaged members of parliament in isolation, pledged and responsible to their electors alone. The whigs and tories, with a longer experience of parliamentary ways, looked first to the mustering of a strong party, accepting common principles and common discipline, which would be able to provide the steady majority of votes without which the administration of the country was impossible. If individual members allowed themselves to be pledged to any variety or combination of measures which their

[63] Halévy, *Hist. Eng. People*, III, 26, states that Grey flatly refused to consider reducing the duration of parliament. But it is difficult to see how this view can be maintained in the face of Grey's assertion to Taylor, 17 January 1831. 'It may be satisfactory to His Majesty to know, that I had intended to propose to reduce the term for which Parliaments are elected to five years; and though I think such a provision would have some advantages, it is a point to which I attach comparatively inferior importance.' (*Corr. Wm. IV and Grey*, I, 70).

[64] *Pledges Defended: a Letter to the Lambeth Electors* (1832).

constituents saw fit to impose on them, party discipline and party unity might become irrelevant. In the place of stable party votes working within recognized limits, there would be a shifting mass of groups without leadership or fixed basis, dissolving and reforming on each new issue. Complete dependence on an unorganized and uncontrolled electorate would produce an anarchy of individualism in the Commons, the destruction of party, and the end of stable government. If the danger was implied rather than imminent, the difference of principle was fundamental. Even the slight extent to which the pledges system penetrated party organization was not without embarrassment. Besides pledges, a similar and complementary device was contained in the demand that members of parliament should resign when requested to do so by their constituents. The ballot, shorter parliaments, pledges, and compulsory resignations all had one object: the transfer of initiative and decision from the floor of the Commons to the polling booth.

Some years later Sir Harry Verney, whose family could trace their parliamentary connexion back to the fifteenth century, testified on this exact point to the gulf between the aristocratic and radical views of the nature of the representative function. In a printed *Letter to one of his constituents*[65] he asserted that the more important need was not the ballot or the exact representation of each specific constituency but the discovery of men of talent to govern the country.

> The want [he wrote] which appears to me the most glaring in the present house of commons is that of superior men. There are plenty of men of business—men attentive to the necessities and interests of the classes and constituencies with which they are connected . . . Our object ought to be to draw out and place as our leaders in the public service men of superior ability, foresight and elevation of character.

It was a typical weakness of the radicals that they ignored this problem of government. They were intent on obtaining faithful delegates rather than able representatives, on securing control over their members rather than assisting a great party to capture the government. They looked to legislation to express the will of the people and regarded parliament primarily as a legislating

[65] London, 1848.

machine.[66] The task was to make the machine obey its masters. 'I had thought', wrote one radical pamphleteer, 'we had obtained a reform of parliament and that henceforth members were to be the instruments of the electors for the purpose of making laws.' Put against this Wellington's query, 'How is the king's government to be carried on?' and the antithesis between the two views, one executive and the other legislative, is complete. An element of both was, of course, necessary for lasting political success. Members had to be both the instruments of the electors for the expression of their will, and the instruments of the ministry for carrying on the government. In the party system lay the secret of the combination of functions.

The task of the whigs in 1831 was to effect an immediate reconciliation between the two apparently opposed viewpoints. Here, as on many other aspects, they produced a compromise solution, less attractive and less precise than the clear logical prescriptions of tory or radical, but perhaps of more practical value than either. While Wellington and others of his party were prophesying in parliament the decline of the executive power, the same foreboding was being expressed in private to his prime minister by William IV. Grey was willing enough to acknowledge the importance of the problem:

but in considering this matter [he wrote to Taylor] you must always take into view the present state of things. From the want of timely correction of many causes of just complaint, the Government has been driven to concessions to public feeling which may undoubtedly be found very inconvenient in future. But though it may appear somewhat paradoxical to say so, my conviction is, that this inconvenience will be less felt in a reformed House of Commons

[66] Cf. Lord John Russell in 1848. 'There have been in the course of the last thirty years very great changes in the mode of conducting the business of the House. When I first entered parliament it was not usual for Government to undertake generally all subjects of legislation . . . Two great changes have since taken place . . . The one, that since the passing of the Reform Bill it has been thought convenient, on every subject on which an alteration of the law is required, that the Government should undertake the responsibility of proposing it to parliament; and the other great change is that measures of all kinds are now discussed by a much greater number of members, and a far greater number of motions are made by individual members, than was formerly the case', and again, 'I must remind the . . . House that the supposed duty of the members of a Government to introduce a great number of measures to parliament, and to carry those measures through parliament in a session, is a duty which is new to the Government of this country . . . Let me call the attention of the House to the fact that the Ministers of the Crown are chiefly appointed to administer the affairs of the Empire.' (Walpole, *Life of Russell*, II, 93–5.)

than it is at present. The effect of a Reform will, I trust, be to restore confidence in that branch of the legislature. The want of that confidence at this moment is one great cause of its inability to resist popular clamour.[67]

The paradox was perhaps not very comforting to the king, but in those few sentences were contained the fundamentals of the whig attitude to reform, and its justification.

[67] *Corr. Wm. IV and Grey*, II, 32.

Chapter Two

SCOTLAND AND IRELAND

I⊤ is easy to forget in concentrating on the main struggle for reform of parliament in 1831–2 that the 'Reform Act of 1832' is a misnomer. We should properly speak of the Reform Acts of 1832, there being one for England and Wales, one for Scotland, and one for Ireland. In the parliament of 1830–1 the original reform bills for Scotland and Ireland were introduced soon after that for England and Wales, on 9 March and 24 March 1831 respectively, and an attempt was made to carry all three through the House concurrently. The defeat of the ministry on General Gascoyne's motion of 19 April, however, brought a dissolution of parliament and a general election. It was therefore necessary to begin again with the Scottish and Irish bills in the new parliament. The second Irish bill was introduced by Stanley on 30 June 1831, and the second Scottish bill on 4 July. The difficulty of dealing simultaneously with three controversial measures had nevertheless been impressed on the ministry by the events of the previous session,[1] and the real discussion on the Scottish and Irish bills was accordingly postponed until after the English bill had passed through committee and secured its third reading. It was thus not until 23 September 1831 that the Scottish bill was brought in for a second reading; and not until 27 September that it reached the committee stage. The neatness of the ministerial programme was again interrupted early in October by the rejection of the English bill in the House of Lords and the consequent prorogation of parliament. In the next session the Scottish and Irish bills once more gave precedence to the English bill. On 19 January they again appeared before the House of Commons; but it was not until May 1832 that they received a second reading.

Thus for over a year the two secondary reform bills were continually interrupted and frustrated by the vicissitudes undergone by the principal bill; and when at last there was a clear interval for discussion, the main battle of reform had been fought and won. Not unnaturally they received comparatively little attention both

[1] Althorp's statement in the House of Commons, 24 June 1831 (*Hansard*, IV, 350).

34

at the time and afterwards. In the earlier stages of the bills, when the English members had sufficient zest to join in the debates, there was a strong tendency for discussions to shift away from the details of the Scottish and Irish bills to the general principles of reform.[2] In the subsequent stages interest declined. This was particularly evident in the case of the Scottish bill. In the debate on the second reading in September 1831, for example, the discussion was confined almost entirely to Scottish members and though the party division was still apparent, it was clear that there was a general desire among all Scots M.P.s to secure greater representation for their country, and a general indifference to the issue among the non-Scots members of both parties. The same features were evident in the House of Lords where the debate on the Scottish bill was short and mild, and the remaining stages of its progress were rapidly traversed. The final passage of the Irish bill was not quite so peaceful. Inevitably the major contribution to debate came from the Irish members but the venom of religious controversy led to a vehement tory opposition which a quiet and moderate speech by Peel on the second reading failed to check; and even in the House of Lords a fierce note was sustained by the more Orange-minded peers. In point of fact, however, both bills were of immense significance. The English bill was made the test case and obviously affected the largest population and the greatest number of seats in the Commons. Yet within their narrower contexts the Scottish and Irish Reform Acts were far more revolutionary in their immediate effects than the moderate conservative measure for England and Wales.

A. THE SCOTTISH REFORM ACT

For Scotland the act was not so much reform as enfranchisement. 'It is giving us', wrote Cockburn, the whig Solicitor-General and himself part-author of the act, 'a political constitution for the first time.'[3] Recognition of this fact was implicit in the arguments of both whigs and tories. One of the most frequent points made by the opposition was the peace and prosperity enjoyed by Scotland

---

[2] E.g. debate on the Irish bill, 24 March 1831 (*Hansard*, III, 861 sqq.). Cf. Jeffrey to Cockburn, 4 March 1831: 'I have proposed to speak twice, but could never get in. I think I must tonight. But not a word has yet been said as to Scotland, nor do I think the House would bear three sentences on that insignificant subject. I must therefore go into the general question.' (Cockburn, *Life of Jeffrey*, I, 313.)

[3] Cockburn, *Journal*, I, 13.

in its state of political innocence and the extreme danger of thrusting upon it a political responsibility to which the country was unaccustomed and, some alleged, for which it was not fit. Lord Francis Leveson-Gower, member for Sutherlandshire, whose family was said to control all twenty-four votes in that county, went so far as to hint that the grant of reform to Scotland would bring back the troublous time of Fletcher of Saltoun with all its bitter animosities, its Highland clan feuds and Lowland sectarian strife, the return of priests to politics, and the oppression of the poor by the rich.[4] Even the Earl of Haddington, while admitting that in Scotland 'during the last three hundred or four hundred years except in some of the borough towns, nothing like a popular election had been known', urged the need for caution in introducing political changes that might break up the happy 'relations and dependencies of social life'.[5] The task of the ministry, therefore, in establishing a *prima facie* case for the need to create 'the elements of a good constituency' in Scotland was not very difficult.

The Union of 1707 had given to Scotland forty-five seats in the House of Commons. The machinery by which these seats were filled was controlled by a narrow oligarchy and invited all the exercise of corruption and influence which government could bring to bear. From 1707 to 1832 Scotland resembled one vast, rotten borough. 'The system of Scotland', declared Jeffrey, the Lord-Advocate, and his words were never seriously challenged, 'was not a representation of the Crown, nor of the peers, nor of the great landed proprietors; but, excluding all these, it was only the representation of a most insignificant oligarchy, not very high in rank or station, and of which the majority was not even connected with the great landed interests.'[6] The existing constituency for the thirty Scottish counties was less than 3,000 and excluding plural voters was reckoned at approximately 2,500. The burgh constituency, representing some sixty-six burghs, was under 1,500. The total Scottish electorate at the time of the Reform Act was thus under 5,000 and possibly less than 4,500; and this in a population of just over 2,300,000. The explanation of this excessively narrow electorate lay, of course, in the voting qualifications. In the burghs, which chose their representatives in groups by a method of indirect election, the franchise was in the hands of the self-elected town councils. Thirty-three electors returned the member for

Edinburgh, and the same number formed the constituency for Glasgow.

In the counties a peculiar development of Scottish law had gone far towards a divorce between the franchise and actual property by means of the 'superiority' system. Superiorities were a species of right derived from feudal law. They depended essentially on the power of the landowner to sell the property and fruits of the soil (*dominium utile* in Scots law, *anglice* beneficial interest) while retaining for himself the superiority over it (*dominium directum*), which gave him in law the right of voting at elections with respect to such property. In turn, however, the superiorities, now separated except in legal theory from property ownership, could be bought and sold as articles of merchandise and in fact consisted merely of pieces of parchment conveying to their possessors for the time being the right to vote. A brisk traffic was carried on in these superiorities, both at the hands of attorneys who found it a useful asset in their business, and also by members of the aristocracy who used them to create a system of private patronage. It resulted from this anomalous system that the Scottish county freeholders were frequently no more than the holders of parchment deeds and in all probability the system would have extended even further had not the practice existed on some large estates of forbidding in the entail the sale of superiorities. Even so the discrepancy between the nominal and actual character of the county electorate was striking. Jeffrey estimated that half of the 2,500 county voters merely owned superiorities and had no land of their own. In some constituencies the proportion of landless electors was far greater. In Argyllshire only 31 out of the 115 electors were landowners; in Bute only 1 out of 21; in Caithness 11 out of 47; in Dumbartonshire 19 out of 71; in Inverness-shire 38 out of 88.[7] But even apart from the character of these 'Paper' or 'Parchment Barons', as they were styled in Scotland, the roll of county freeholders in Scotland read like a list of pocket and rotten boroughs. The largest constituencies, Fife and Perthshire, had less than 240 voters; the smallest (Bute, Clackmannan, Cromarty, Kinross, Nairn, and Sutherland) had less than 30.

The effects of this system were to be seen in the character of the Scottish M.P.s in the eighteenth and early nineteenth centuries. Lacking any direct contact with the nation, and returned by a

---

[7] *Ibid.*, VII, 528 sqq. For the question of superiorities see also 1296–7 and II, 1079.

small and corrupt constituency, the Scots members had for long been notorious for their venality. With few exceptions they formed a steady court and ministerialist party, friends to whatever government was in power, provided their claims to place and profit were recognized. Scots M.P.s, it was alleged, had divided twenty-seven to five against Dunning's famous motion on the power of the Crown in 1780; and, even more remarkably, thirteen to five against the repeal of the Test and Corporation Acts in 1828.[8] As individuals they were for the most part nonentities; as a group their position as traffickers in patronage had made the expression 'a Scotch job' a notorious one south of the border. To a certain extent this was the inevitable consequence of the narrow franchise. In the counties, particularly, the reward to the individual voter was not as a rule in cash but in kind. Place, office, pension, and emolument, were the prizes sought by the Scottish elector; above all, commissions in the army and navy, and posts in India and other colonies. To purchase a superiority was in fact a recognized and reliable means whereby the respectable but indigent Scottish middle-class parent was able to provide for his younger sons. As a result any M.P. who could not obtain a tolerable share of ministerial patronage was unlikely to last long as a member for a Scottish county.[9] In these circumstances it was a remarkable tribute to the popular enthusiasm in Scotland for the reform bill that the 1831 general election produced a slight majority of Scots M.P.s in favour of the bill. It was generally estimated that eleven burgh and thirteen county members were in favour of reform; four burgh and seventeen county members against. Nevertheless the contrast with England, where the county members were almost solidly for the bill, was very striking.[10]

The object of the Scottish reform bill was to take down the whole of this electoral structure. 'No shred or rag', said Jeffrey, 'no jot or tittle of it was to be left.'[11] In this work of destruction the reformers were aided by the actual defects of the system they wished to destroy. The absence of any traditional system of local rights, the paucity of pocket boroughs, and the complete lack of any popular voice; all these features made it relatively easy to construct a new franchise. The original progenitors of the Scottish reform bill were Henry Cockburn and Thomas Francis

[8] *Hansard*, VII, 1054–6.   [9] See especially, *ibid.*, VII, 541–3, 563, 1048–9, 1107.
[10] Cockburn, *Journal*, I, 16–17; Omond, *Lord Advocates of Scotland*, II, 318.
[11] *Hansard*, VII, 536.

Kennedy of Dunure,[12] who had begun preliminary discussions on Scottish reform as early as September 1830. Cockburn, the abler and the better known of the two, was not in parliament, and was anxious that Kennedy should be the parliamentary leader. Sir James Graham who had greater interest and knowledge on Scottish affairs than any other of the leading whigs, and had already been turning his thoughts to the subject, was ready to concur with this choice and handed over the preparation of the bill to the two Scots with a recommendation that they should make taxation the basis of the new franchise. Not the least advantage that accrued from this early decision was that it forestalled any interference from Brougham in the control of Scottish reform.[13] But besides the need to avoid that contingency, which Cockburn felt certain would 'excite alarm in Scotland', it is clear that an independent movement for Scottish reform would have started even if the whig ministers had not included it in their general scheme of reform. As soon as the whigs were in office and announced the inclusion of Scotland in their reform plan, Kennedy was content to forward to Lord John Russell a memorandum on *Proposed Reform in Scotland* for the consideration of the ministers. This document, the fruit of his collaboration with Cockburn in the two preceding months, was the real basis of the Scottish reform bill. The general principles upon which it founded the cause of reform were entirely whiggish and conservative, but the paper also betrayed a slight fear that the ministry might not consent to a franchise sufficiently low to establish a respectable electorate. It probably represented, therefore, the least that Cockburn and Kennedy thought necessary and the most they thought the ministers would accept. The franchise was recommended as the first object of reform which, if properly dealt with, might by itself satisfy opinion in Scotland. It was suggested that the qualifications in the county should be land of the annual value of £10, other property of the value of £20; in the burghs occupation of houses or other premises of the annual value of £10. This, it was argued, was the minimum extension of the franchise that would meet the needs of reform in Scotland. In addition, 'further and great improvement' would be made if some redistribution of seats was carried out with the object of eliminating some of the smaller groups of burghs, uniting some of the

---

[12] M.P. for Ayr district, and later a whig lord of the Treasury.
[13] Cockburn, *Letters on Affairs of Scotland*, 239–44.

smaller counties so as to abolish the system of alternate elections, and granting representation to some of the larger towns.[14] The preliminary attitude of the Scottish reformers having thus been defined, the next step was to translate generalities into the language of the statute-book.

In December 1830 Cockburn, who in the meantime had been created Solicitor-General for Scotland, went down to London to confer with the ministers on the scheme of reform for Scotland. He remained there for a week, in close touch with the central whig committee of four, Russell, Graham, Durham, and Duncannon, who were drafting the English bill. The crucial point was the burgh franchise; and as soon as the £10 householder clause had been accepted, the remainder of the bill was a matter of detail. Cockburn, however, had no practical experience of popular election and, apart from his associate Kennedy, he was for security reasons allowed to consult only with Jeffrey, the Lord-Advocate. In the latter's hands the first draft was gradually enlarged and emended until in its final form it owed as much to Jeffrey as to its original parents. Cockburn, who was not a member of parliament, departed for Scotland at the end of a week and did not return south for further work on the bill until September 1831. Jeffrey remained for fourteen months on end at London, in 'ruinous attendance' on his political and parliamentary duties at the expense of his private legal practice. Though still in touch with Kennedy and Cockburn, he assumed more and more control of the details of the Scottish bill. In the end, therefore, the Lord-Advocate emerged not merely as the chief protagonist but as the principal architect of the Scottish Reform Act.[15] Nevertheless the activities of Cockburn in Scotland, sounding opinion and extracting information, and Kennedy's spade-work in London as the real if unofficial representative of the Scottish reformers at Westminster, formed the indispensable basis for the parliamentary performance.

As stated by Jeffrey in his speech introducing the bill on 9 March 1831, the intention of the ministry with regard to Scotland was threefold: to increase the representation of the towns, especially the larger towns; to establish a real system of representation based on a property qualification; and finally to remodel the system under which groups of burghs were combined to return one

---

[14] Cockburn, *Letters on Affairs of Scotland*, 258 sqq.
[15] Cockburn, *Journal*, I, 1–35; *Letters on Affairs of Scotland*, 238 sqq.

member in such a way as to eliminate or decrease the influence of the small burghs. As in the English bill, there were two salient aspects; the introduction of new types of franchise, and the redistribution of seats.

In the burghs direct voting was substituted for the machinery whereby the town councils each elected a delegate who had one vote in the election of members. The new franchise was the £10 household qualification[16] already proposed for England and Wales. In the spring of 1831 there was some question of raising the burgh franchise to £15 or £20; and even Jeffrey, at one point, much to Cockburn's anger, was prepared to concede the £15 franchise in order to facilitate the passage of the bill. 'My God! Only imagine Scotland having been degraded by a higher franchise than England or Ireland', wrote Cockburn to Kennedy on 22 April 1831, 'and this by the act of Jeffrey!' But Sir John Dalrymple, later Earl of Stair, and other Scots reformers fought the proposal and the government decided to retain the original qualification.[17] Fears that this would lead to a swamping of the urban electorate by a mass of inferior voters were clearly unfounded. It was reckoned that in the whole of Scotland there were 380,000 houses of which only 36,700 were of the annual value of £10 or more. Of these less than half were between £10 and £15 in value. In fact the voting qualification was drawn, if anything, too high, if the object was to produce individual constituencies that were sufficiently large to escape corruption and influence. Cockburn confessed to Kennedy that he had seen lists which showed that in some burghs the number of £10 householders was actually less than the voters under the unreformed system (i.e. the members of the town council).[18] In the larger and more prosperous towns the £10 franchise would produce a moderately sized electorate; in the smaller towns, in Jeffrey's opinion, rather 'a stinted one'. Thus Glasgow would probably produce some 5,000 voters; Edinburgh 4,000; the other towns singly or in groups about 1,000. Subsequent

[16] I.e. occupation as owner, tenant, or life renter of any house, shop, warehouse, or other building within the burgh limits, which separately or in connexion with any other house or building or land in the same burgh, occupied as owner or as tenant under the same landlord, was of the yearly value of £10. Residence and payment of assessed taxes formed a condition of voting. In addition, by a provision peculiar to Scotland, owners of £10 property within the burgh were entitled to vote, though not in occupation, provided they were resident elsewhere in the burgh or within the seven statutory miles.

[17] Cockburn, *Life of Jeffrey*, 1, 320; *Letters on Affairs of Scotland*, 315.

[18] *Letters on Affairs of Scotland*, 273.

experience confirmed this broad judgement. A parliamentary committee in 1834 reported that the average number of electors per representative in the Scottish cities and burghs was 1,362; though some, for example Dysart district with 507, Haddington district with 545, fell far below this standard.[19] The figures suggested by Jeffrey for the new Glasgow and Edinburgh constituencies were underestimates. In 1835 Glasgow had over 8,000 electors and Edinburgh just under that figure; both of these were two-member constituencies. Of the nineteen remaining urban constituencies nine were over and ten under the 1,000 mark.

In the counties the same principal was applied in framing the new franchise except that to qualify for the franchise it was necessary to be in actual ownership and not merely in occupancy of land, houses, feu duties, or other heritable subjects to the annual value of £10. In addition leaseholders of property worth £10 annually on a life lease or one not less than fifty-seven years, leaseholders of property worth £50 on a lease of not less than nineteen years, and *bona-fide* tenants of property worth £50, were also admitted to the franchise, together with the existing owners of 'parchment votes' (i.e. superiorities) for the remainder of their lives. The chief criticism levelled at the county qualification was that it would give a preponderant strength in those constituencies to the urban voter from the small towns outside the burgh system. It was Cockburn's opinion, on the other hand, that the bill as finally passed left too much power in the hands of the landlords. This aspect indeed was stressed by Lord John Russell in his comprehensive speech on the ministerial plan of reform delivered on 1 March 1831. In drawing attention to the defects of the old Scottish system in allowing the franchise to be divorced from ownership, he claimed that the bill would in effect restore electoral influence to the landed proprietors. In fact the new county franchise as settled by the act produced so restricted an electorate that the predominance of the landlord was made inevitable. Althorp, in repelling the claim for additional county representation in Scotland, pointed out that as it was, though some Scottish counties were superior in point of population to some English counties, in point of electorate the largest Scottish county constituency would scarcely equal the electorate of the smallest English counties. This was substantially true. It was reckoned in 1835

19 Parliamentary Papers (cited later as P.P.) 1834, IX, 269–70.

that Perthshire, the largest county constituency in Scotland, had an electorate of 3,700. In contrast the three smallest English counties (excluding the Isle of Wight, which returned one member separately) were Rutland with an electorate of 1,300, Huntingdon with 3,000, and Westmorland with 3,600.[20] The clear fact was that the smaller Scottish counties, under the new property qualification, could not possibly equal the larger, more prosperous, English counties where the normal propertied electorate was reinforced by the historic 40s. freeholder. The parliamentary committee of 1834 estimated that the average number of Scottish county electors per member was just over 1,000, or less than half the equivalent figure for the English counties. As an extreme example Bute had only 279 electors, and Caithness only 201.[21] There was thus the curious result that the average Scottish county constituency was smaller than the average Scottish burgh constituency; and that even after the Reform Act some of the Scottish counties had electorates that would have put them in peril of abolition under the famous Schedule A had they been English boroughs before 1831. In such circumstances complaints that the influence of landed property would not make itself duly felt in the county elections could not be taken very seriously.

In contrast therefore to the position south of the border, the small electorates in Scotland after 1832 were to be looked for among the counties rather than in the burghs. The smallest burgh constituency, Wigton district, was larger than no less than five county constituencies—Sutherland, Caithness, Orkney and Shetland, Bute, and Peebles. The anomaly, by English standards, was in large measure due to the Scottish practice of grouping individual towns together in burgh districts for purposes of collective representation. This system, which dated back to the Union of 1707, had secured the continued representation of places that, though royal burghs in status, were scarcely more than villages in fact. But it had the merit, in conjunction with the £10 householder franchise, of providing a reasonably large constituency for each burgh district. Logic and tradition therefore combined to retain it in the new act. Other than a certain reshuffling of the constituent elements of the various districts, only two major changes in this field were envisaged by the authors of the reform bill. The first was the detachment of certain large towns from their burgh districts to grant them independent representation. One of these, Glasgow, was given two members. Edinburgh, which alone of the Scottish towns had enjoyed individual representation between 1707 and 1832, was also given a second member. Moreover thirteen sizeable towns which, being burghs of barony, had hitherto been outside the scheme of burgh representation, were now brought within it, either as separate burgh constituencies (Paisley and Greenock) or as elements in the rearranged districts (Leith, Kilmarnock, and Peterhead among others). The second major alteration was the proposed disfranchisement of the Fife or Anstruther group of burghs on the grounds that they were little more than villages. Cockburn who wrote approvingly of the clause quashing 'the set of mean Fife burghs', was anxious to eliminate more of their type and considered that it was a serious defect of the act that this was not done. 'Clustering a number of unconnected towns together', he wrote, 'makes a bad constituency. Every member should be member for one known and visible place; but this is one of the many sacrifices we have been obliged to make of principles to management'.[22] The burgh district system which had been originally conceived in 1707 to reconcile the prescriptive claims of the Scottish royal burghs with the limited number of M.P.s allowed them under the Act of Union, had in the course of time accumulated a weight of vested interest behind it which even the reformers were obliged to treat with respect. In the end even the despised East Fife fishing villages (Anstruther Easter and Wester, Crail, Kilrenny, and Pittenweem) were brought back again to join St Andrews and Cupar in a new grouping of Fife burghs. As finally settled by the act, the burgh representation was divided between fourteen burgh districts, each with one member; five towns with one member each (Aberdeen, Paisley, Dundee, Greenock, and Perth); and two with two members each (Edinburgh and Glasgow). In all the total number of burgh M.P.s was twenty-three, an increase of eight on the pre-1832 figure.

As far as the counties were concerned, the structure of representation suffered little change. From 1707 to 1832 the Scottish counties had returned thirty M.P.s, comprising twenty-seven elected for each parliament by the same number of shires or stewartries, and three by three pairs of small shires. In the latter case each of the pair elected a member for alternate parliaments

[22] Cockburn, *Journal*, I, 12.

though constitutionally the member was representative for both. As settled by the Reform Act the number of county M.P.s remained the same. Twenty-seven shires returned one member each; the six remaining shires were combined into three groups (Elgin and Nairn, Ross and Cromarty, Clackmannan and Kinross), each group sharing one member. It had at one point been proposed to unite two other shires, Peebles and Selkirk, because of their inability to produce a sufficiently numerous constituency to justify individual representation. Jeffrey himself was always personally in favour of this solution.[23] The alternative was adopted in the committee stage of the bill of withdrawing the burghs of Peebles and Selkirk from the Linlithgow district of burghs and throwing them into their respective shires to make up the constituency. Even the opposition admitted that without these two towns the respective shires could scarcely muster 300 electors each. As it was, with the reinforcement provided by the county towns, Selkirkshire produced 430 electors in 1835 and Peebleshire 355. In similar fashion the burgh of Rothesay was withdrawn from its burgh district and thrown into the county of Bute. Looking at these changes solely from the point of view of the constituencies they produced, it might also be argued that there were two other points at least as open to criticism. Bute and Caithness, formerly an alternating pair of shires, were divided by the act into separate constituencies although in 1835 their electorates numbered only 310 and 246 respectively. While Sutherland, with an electorate in the same year of only 128, could not be justified by any principle set up by the reformers. To leave it as an independent constituency was to leave it, as it had notoriously been before the Reform Act, a nomination seat in the hands of the Leveson-Gower family.[24] There was, however, already considerable criticism from the opposition on the grounds that while Scottish burgh representation had been increased by half, the county representation remained at the point fixed in 1707. It would consequently have been very difficult in 1831 actually to reduce county representation. Geographical factors, on the other hand, put limitations on the extent to which the smaller shires could be combined in order to enlarge their

[23] Cockburn, *Life of Jeffrey*, I, 334.
[24] At the time of the Reform Act debates the electoral influence in Sutherlandshire was exercised by the Marquess of Stafford, whose wife was Countess of Sutherland in her own right. He was subsequently created 1st Duke of Sutherland in 1833. Francis Leveson-Gower, M.P. for Sutherland in the 1830 parliament, was the second son of the Marquess of Stafford.

constituencies. The alternate system of election which existed before 1832 allowed distant counties, such as Bute and Caithness, to be associated. The principle of joint election substituted by the act made geographical contiguity imperative. Indeed, to secure a more effectual geographical union of Clackmannan and Kinross, certain parts of Perthshire and Stirlingshire were annexed for parliamentary purposes to the first two counties. But this was obviously a practice that could not be carried very far without considerable protest. Yet there was no good reason why Sutherland and Caithness should not have been combined except that there would then have been a spare seat to be allotted elsewhere. In his memorandum of November 1830 Kennedy had in fact specifically recommended the union of Caithness with Sutherland, and Bute with Renfrewshire or Dumbartonshire.

In contrast therefore to the enfranchising clauses of the bill, where the reformers had a fairly clear field and where in consequence the effect of their work was most marked, the redistribution of seats was distinctly conservative. The existing pattern of burgh districts, and the existing pattern of county divisions, were made the basis of the new representative structure. The only fundamental change was the individual enfranchisement of some half-dozen larger Scottish towns. Even so, taking the Reform Act as a whole, its importance to the political life of Scotland was immense. In place of an electorate of 4,500 under the old system, the new electorate registered for the first reformed election totalled 65,000. It was with pardonable exaggeration that the Scottish reformers claimed that the act added not five but fifty members to the representation of their country.[25]

One issue of negative interest may be noticed. In September 1831 a petition was presented to the House of Commons from the universities of St Andrews and Edinburgh, praying for parliamentary representation to be given to the Scottish universities on the analogy of Oxford, Cambridge, and Trinity College, Dublin. No special interest was shown by the Commons in this suggestion although earlier Sir George Murray,[26] when presenting, in April 1831, a petition from the Presbytery of Dunblane for the enfranchisement of ministers of the Church of Scotland, confessed that he personally deprecated such a measure and would prefer, if the church

[25] This, of course, was said before the ministry allotted a further three seats to Scotland during the passage of the bill, making the total addition eight seats.
[26] M.P. for Perthshire.

was to be represented, that it should be through the appointment of higher church dignitaries to the House of Lords and the provision of Scottish university representation in the House of Commons.[27] The project was taken up over a year later by the Earl of Haddington in the committee stage of the bill in the House of Lords. He alleged that the degrees taken at the four Scottish universities between 1800 and 1830 amounted to nearly 7,000; and that though a large number of these were medical degrees, taken chiefly at St Andrews and Edinburgh, yet there remained nearly 3,000 Masters of Arts, mainly from Aberdeen and Glasgow. Even allowing for the fact that many of the medical graduates were not Scotsmen and had probably left the country, he argued that sufficient remained to form, together with the Masters of Arts, a good university constituency. He asked that one representative should be given to St Andrews and Glasgow, and another to Aberdeen and Edinburgh, to be elected by persons in office and graduates resident in Scotland. In fact Lord Haddington had already been privately urging the government to accept the principle of university representation for Scotland. As early as February 1831 he had submitted a proposal to Lord Grey which was reputed to have been favourably received. But most Scottish reformers regarded the scheme with dislike and Kennedy was asked to do his best to 'knock this foolish plan on the head'. Thus the idea had been considered and rejected by the authors of the bill long before Haddington made his proposal in the House of Lords.

> A few friends of the measure [wrote Cockburn] have been anxious to get at least one member for the four universities, but it won't do. It does in England and Ireland, because their universities have great and respectable constituencies. In Scotland a Master of Arts is no high honour. It implies no pecuniary or permanent connection with the college, and no importance is attached to it in the opinion of the country. According to the last accounts, there are not above 450 or 600 Masters of Arts in Scotland, above two-thirds of whom are ministers and schoolmasters; besides, I don't think that in itself politics do any good to any college.[28]

Brougham, who as Lord Chancellor introduced the Scottish bill in the House of Lords, opposed Haddington's motion on these

[27] *Hansard*, III, 1348–9.
[28] Cockburn, *Journal*, I, 11–12. It is not easy to reconcile these figures with those given by Lord Haddington.

grounds. He pointed out that the M.A. degree could be granted in Scottish universities without residence or examination, and that there was no true parallel with Oxford or Cambridge. If representation was to be given to Scottish universities, there should first be considered a new internal constitution for those universities. But at the moment all statutes of the universities which required conditions to the grant of degrees were a dead letter. The motion was therefore rejected.[29]

Despite the lack of enthusiasm for a special clerical or university vote,[30] a large number of Scottish M.P.s thought that their country was unfairly treated in the matter of representation. The original proposal of the ministry was to add five members to the existing total of Scottish members. But following the reintroduction of the Scottish bill in the parliament of 1831, a private deputation of Scots reformers requested Althorp to raise that figure to ten.[31] The outcome was the decision to increase the representation by eight members instead of the number first proposed. With that concession most reformers were satisfied although some professed still to believe that Scotland had received less than her needs merited. This, however, was hardly a tenable position in view of the size of the electorate under the new act. If population was to be made the criterion, the ministry had an easy, if somewhat unfair, rejoinder. It was pointed out in committee by Jeffrey, that as a mere matter of population Surrey and Middlesex together had 2,300,000 inhabitants, approximately the same as Scotland. Yet these two English counties, together with their boroughs, had only forty-three M.P.s as compared with Scotland's fifty-three.[32] There was only one point at which a rational case could have been made out for a further addition to the Scottish representation. That was in the case of the larger towns and cities. But it was precisely here that the opposition were most averse to an extension of the franchise and drew inspired pictures of the dire consequences of giving the vote to an inexperienced and turbulent crowd. 'He regretted the extension of the franchise', declared Sir William Rae, M.P. for Bute, 'because it was well known that Scotchmen seldom came together in a multitude, without causing bloodshed

[29] *Hansard*, xiv, 180 sqq.

[30] An amendment was actually moved on 6 June 1832 by Andrew Johnstone, M.P. for Fife district of burghs, to debar Scottish clergy from voting. This was opposed by the ministry and by several independent Scottish members and finally defeated (*Hansard*, xiii, 476).

[31] Omond, *Lord Advocates of Scotland*, ii, 320.

[32] *Hansard*, xiii, 332.

or at least riot. He besought hon. members to look at the Scotch character and they would find that what he said was true.'[33] This was merely one of a number of similar unflattering descriptions of the Scots national character made by their own countrymen in parliament. Even Cockburn, though he remarked at one stage on the impropriety of such reflections in the mouths of the Scottish M.P.s, virtually subscribed to the same view. 'The Scotch', he wrote, 'are bad mobbers. They are too serious at it; they never joke; and they throw stones. . . . An English mob exhausts itself upon itself, either in blows or fun; a Scotch mob acts because it hates its victim, and contains no corrective of its excesses in its own elements.'[34] Nevertheless, if the critics of the bill were caught between desire for more representation and fear of a larger electorate, there was always the comforting reflection that by individual means Scotland in reality enjoyed a wider representation in parliament than the letter of the constitution would suggest. In addition to the sixteen elected representative peers of Scotland in the House of Lords, it was estimated that about thirty of the remaining eighty Scottish peers were also peers of the United Kingdom and sat in the upper house by virtue of that qualification. As far as the House of Commons was concerned, it was pointed out in the course of the reform debates that, whereas it was highly exceptional for an Englishman to be returned for a Scottish constituency, there were many examples of Scotsmen sitting for English constituencies. Sir John Malcolm, M.P. for Launceston, observed that in the 1831 parliament no fewer than twenty-two Scots were members for English boroughs, himself being one of them;[35] and another migrant Scot Sir George Warrender, M.P. for Honiton, asserted that in the same parliament, the last under the unreformed system, actually more Scots sat for English constituencies than for Scottish, there being forty-five official Scottish representatives and an additional forty-seven Scots sitting for constituencies south of the border.[36] Admittedly it was also suggested that under the reformed system this supplementary representation would cease and that to maintain the existing Scottish element in the House of Commons more seats for Scotland would have to be provided. But it was not easy to see the logic of that conclusion even if its premises had been sound. Englishmen at least could feel

[33] *Ibid.*, III, 324. [34] Cockburn, *Journal*, I, 17.
[35] *Hansard*, V, 1359. [36] *Ibid.*, VII, 1303.

reasonably certain that the combination of Scots exclusiveness at home and Scots talent abroad would ensure at most times an adequate expression of the views and interests of the inhabitants of north Britain.

B. THE IRISH REFORM ACT

Introducing the second reading of the Irish bill in May 1832 Stanley, then Secretary for Ireland, asserted that of the three reform bills, it was the one most obnoxious to the tories and the one they considered most revolutionary.[37] His remarks were justified by the succeeding debate. Among the opposition Peel retained his good sense and moderation, criticizing specific details but agreeing that reform could not be given to England and Scotland and denied to Ireland. But from the benches behind him came violent and passionate protests. The reason for this is clear. Alone of the three reform bills, the Irish bill seemed to affect the actual unity and security of the United Kingdom. Virtually all the arguments of its opponents fell under two headings. On the political side they declared that the changes envisaged would strengthen the forces of Irish nationalism and so lead irrevocably to the repeal of the Union. On the religious side they declared that the changes would destroy the Protestant ascendancy and the Protestant Church in Ireland, and so remove the main basis of the Union. The history of Ireland in the next hundred years was to be a searching commentary on that text. O'Connell, on the other hand, considered that the bill was 'the first voluntary attempt for seven hundred years to combine the peoples of England and Ireland', and the first act of real justice to Ireland that had not been doled out, as Emancipation had been, in a mean and paltry spirit.[38] To the tories, therefore, the issue presented by the Irish reform bill was one of English ascendancy in Ireland; to the Irish party it was one of national revival. The technicalities of the bill tended to be lost in the greater background of the whole Anglo-Irish problem.

Yet viewed in a more restricted context, the Irish reform act is not without intrinsic interest. In particular it differed from the other two in this respect, that the existing structure of Irish representation was more rational and modernized, and therefore less in need of fundamental repair, than that of either England or Scotland. The Cromwellian experiments apart, no substantial

---

[37] *Hansard*, XIII, 120. [38] *Ibid.*, XIII, 159.

reshaping of the English system had taken place at all in modern times; the Scottish system dated back to the Union of 1707. But twice in the first thirty years of the nineteenth century there had been drastic statutory alterations in the Irish system. The changes that had taken place in 1800 and 1829 were not all, or even largely, to the liking of the Irish nationalists. But they had been the products of political forces still powerful in 1831 and as such could not be ignored or lightly rescinded by the whigs. Moreover one at least of those measures, the Act of Union of 1800, had been a reform act in effect if not in design. The paradox was presented, therefore, that the relatively uncontroversial Scottish bill was in fact the most revolutionary in its effects on the actual electoral system of its country; while the Irish bill, which aroused religious and national passions, possibly even deeper than the social and political passions engendered by the English bill, was less sweeping in the technical changes it involved than either of the other two bills.

In 1800, when the existing representation in the Irish parliament had to be trimmed down to proportions suitable for inclusion in the new parliament of the United Kingdom, a substantial measure of reform had taken place. Before the Union 300 Irish M.P.s sat in the parliament of Dublin. Under the terms of the Union Act only 100 Irish M.P.s were admitted to the parliament at Westminster. This loss of two-thirds of the representation was borne entirely by the Irish boroughs. The thirty-two counties continued to return their sixty-four knights of the shire; but no less than eighty-four boroughs were totally disfranchised. Of the remainder thirty-two were semi-disfranchised, returning one instead of the previous two members each. Dublin and Cork alone still elected two members each to complete the quota of a hundred members. In this drastic amputation the greater part of the Irish rotten and nomination boroughs were cut away. Of the importance of the Act of Union as a reforming and purifying measure there was general recognition in 1831; though the opposition as was natural turned the same set of facts into conflicting arguments. The whigs claimed that their bill was no more than a logical completion of the work of reform begun in 1800. The tories argued that since reform had already been carried through in Ireland there was no reason for any further tampering with its constitution. The main consequence, however, was that it was not necessary for the reformers of 1831 to make any but minor changes in the existing system of Irish representation. There were no rotten boroughs in Ireland in the sense of places enjoying representation that could not under any practical and acceptable franchise be provided with a respectable constituency; nor were there any important towns unrepresented whose influence and interests demanded a place within the parliamentary system. As finally passed, therefore, the act deprived no Irish borough or county of any of its members; nor added any new constituencies to the representative structure. The only changes in the representation were firstly the simple addition of one member each to the existing representation for the cities of Belfast, Limerick, and Waterford, the town of Galway, and the university of Dublin, making the total number of Irish members 105 in place of the 100 specified by the Act of Union; and secondly, the passing of the Irish Boundary Act redefining in a more rational way the geographical area of the parliamentary cities and boroughs.

But though a single clause of the bill was sufficient to effect all the changes in the distribution of seats which the ministry thought desirable, the question of the franchise was controversial in the extreme. The root of the problem here was the act of 1829. The grant of Catholic Emancipation in that year had been accompanied by two other precautionary measures designed as correctives to the effects of the principal act and as inducements to allow that act to go through. The first of these subsidiary measures was an act for the suppression of the Catholic Association as an illegal and dangerous body; the second was an act for the disfranchisement of the Irish 40s. freeholders and the raising of the property qualification for the Irish county voter to £10 per annum freehold. The result was the elimination of the great mass of Irish peasantry from the electoral system and the creation of Irish county constituencies almost as narrow as those that prevailed in Scotland before 1832. Estimates varied as to the number of Irish freeholders disfranchised in 1829. Sheil declared that the total was 200,000; Leader on another occasion said that the act had disfranchised 190,000 voters out of a total of 216,000, and that under the £10 qualification the new county electorate numbered only 19,000. O'Connell produced figures illustrating the effect of the measure on individual counties. In Galway 32,000 freeholders had been disfranchised; in Cavan 5,000; in Dublin county 10,000; and in Kerry nearly 4,000. In Antrim the electorate had been reduced from 7,000 to 700; in Tyrone from over 6,000 to under 400; in county Carlow to less than 200. Not surprisingly there were strong efforts on the part of the Irish nationalists to restore the pre-1829 franchise in the 1832 Reform Act. The ministry was not sympathetic. Stanley, who piloted the bill through the House of Commons, opposed a motion by O'Connell in this sense with the caustic observation that the great majority of the old 40s. freeholders were mountain and bogside squatters who had acquired their title to the land merely by long possession, and who in consequence formed a very low and venal class of voter. Russell, more tactfully, explained subsequently that the abolition of the 40s. franchise in 1829 had been an express condition of passing the Emancipation Act, and though he personally had not been in favour of that disfranchisement, he felt he could not now revoke it.[39] As it was the bill encountered some opposition on the grounds that it conflicted with the whole basis of the Emancipation Act. Lord Ellenborough, for example, in the upper house argued that a reform act for Ireland was *ipso facto* a breach of the earlier act since the latter had been passed on the clear understanding that it should be accompanied by a certain type of representative system in Ireland and it was only on the faith of this that Catholic disabilities had been removed.[40]

Nevertheless it was clear to the ministry that the Irish franchise could not be left in the condition it was in between 1829 and 1832. As Stanley logically observed, even if the tendency of the Irish bill was to destroy Protestant ascendancy in Ireland and give influence to the Roman Catholics, there could still be no going back on the decision of 1829 to admit members of that faith to a position of civil and political equality; and in that case reform could not be denied to Ireland, alone of the three kingdoms, on the grounds of a religious issue.[41] Reform of some sort, if the 'elements of a good constituency' were to be provided for the sister island, was certainly needed. If in the Irish counties the electorates were almost of Scottish proportions, the Irish boroughs could show even finer examples of constituencies in miniature. Of the thirty-three cities and boroughs, there were reckoned to be ten close and eight nomination boroughs at the time of the Reform Act. In the close boroughs, where the corporations usually formed the electorate, the constituencies numbered no more than thirteen

[39] *Hansard*, III, 198–9, 648; XIII, 570 sqq., 590.
[40] *Ibid.*, III, 1744.   [41] *Ibid.*, XIII, 120–1.

or fifteen voters. In the nomination boroughs the number of electors varied from 2 at Coleraine, 26 at Cashel, 94 at Clonmell, to 141 at Lisburn and 175 at Kinsale. The average constituency for these eight boroughs was eighty-one.[42] By ministerial standards, therefore, more than half the Irish boroughs needed enlargement.

The government was thus faced with the odd situation that whereas the representative structure in Ireland could be retained almost intact, important changes were necessary in the method of fashioning the electorate. The crux of the Irish bill was consequently the matter of the franchise. In the boroughs the main task was to break down the monopoly of corporations and borough patrons by the application of a uniform franchise low enough to bring a substantial proportion of the population into the electorate. Small electorates and not small populations were the defects of the old Irish system. Hence the introduction of the £10 householder qualification on the English model was the obvious remedy. In the ordinary boroughs the act vested the right of voting in the occupiers of houses, buildings, etc., of the annual value of £10, though in certain cities forming legal counties (counties of cities and counties of towns) the vote was also extended to £10 freeholders and £10 leaseholders. In addition resident freemen and freeholders and any others in legal possession of the franchise before the passing of the act were allowed to retain their right subject to certain conditions. The enfranchisement clauses, in so far as they affected the boroughs, were thus comparatively clear and logical. The real point at issue was whether the imposition of the £10 householder franchise would produce the respectable constituencies even after the geographical adjustments of the Boundary Act were taken into consideration.

It was precisely here that the Irish party brought forward their most severe criticisms of the bill. They asserted that even with the new franchise there would be some ten or eleven boroughs of less than 300 voters, inevitably perpetuating the old abuses of aristocratic influence and control. In some instances the alteration of

---

[42] The close boroughs were: Armagh, Bandon, Carlow, Dungannon, Ennis, Enniskillen, Portarlington, Sligo, Tralee, Belfast. Nomination boroughs: Athlone, Cashell, Clonmell, Coleraine, Dundalk, Kinsale, Lisburn, New Ross. It should be observed that the figures given here are merely as quoted and they conflict in some measure with other contemporary accounts, e.g. *Key to Both Houses of Parliament 1832*. But general confirmation of the figures is given by Stanley (*Hansard*, III, 861 sqq.; IX, 597 sqq.). They are to be found as a footnote to the report of Leader's speech in committee on the Irish bill, 13 June 1832 (*Ibid.*, XIII, 580–5).

boundaries, so far from purifying constituencies, would increase their dependence. Thus, it was alleged that Dungarvon and Youghal would become pocket boroughs of the Duke of Devonshire; and Bandon Bridge divided between the electoral influence of the Duke and Lord Bandon. In the committee stage of the final version of the bill, Dominick Browne, the member for co. Mayo, moved a motion on these grounds for the disfranchisement of the five smallest Irish boroughs—Portarlington, Mallow, New Ross, Enniskillen, and Bandon—and the redistribution of their seats among the counties and larger towns. The motion was defeated but Stanley significantly remarked that though in theory some Irish boroughs might deserve disfranchisement, the bill had been framed on the principle of no disfranchisement and he was loath to depart from that principle.[43] That the £10 household suffrage was in fact inadequate to secure constituencies of reasonable size was confirmed by subsequent statistics. Of the Irish boroughs in 1832 nine had registered electorates of over 1,000; ten had constituencies between 300 and 1,000; and no less than fifteen had constituencies of under 300. Of the last group, there were five boroughs—Tralee, Dungannon, Portarlington, New Ross, and Lisburn—with registered electorates of less than 200.[44] Though individual predictions of the effect of the Reform Act on specific Irish constituencies were often wide of the mark, there was complete justification for the general charge that the franchise had been fixed too high for a thorough purification of the borough constituencies to be made possible. Over half the Irish boroughs immediately after the Reform Act fell short of the standard minimum of 300 voters which the ministry itself had taken as a guide in dealing with the smaller English boroughs. It was an additional illustration, if that were needed, of the profoundly unequal effects obtained by applying an equal standard to all parts of the United Kingdom. As a result, Ireland, with an average constituency of 769 electors for each borough member, took third place in the class below Scotland and England.[45] But even that figure concealed the true position. The great majority of Irish boroughs were far below this average and only the presence of a

[43] *Ibid.*, XIII, 564 sqq.; XIV, 187 sqq.
[44] Mosse, *Parl. Guide* (1835). Owing to the inadequate information on the state of the registration in 1834 the compilers used the 1832 figures in drawing up their statistical table of voters in the Irish constituencies.
[45] P.P. 1834, IX, 269-70.

few great towns like Dublin (7,000 electors), Cork (over 4,000), Limerick (nearly 3,000), and Galway (over 2,000), reduced the balance against the small boroughs. Even after the Reform Act therefore influence and corruption flourished in the smaller Irish boroughs. 'These boroughs', wrote Morgan the second son of Daniel O'Connell, after experience of the reformed system, 'are vile places and I pity any man who has to do with them. That dirty little town of Youghal was more expensive to me than the county of Meath where we had to bring voters from twenty-four miles and further. As William Ford says, "In the towns it's the ready money down." '⁴⁶

In the counties the ministry was equally cautious in widening the franchise. The main limitation here was the precedent laid down only two years earlier by the Catholic Emancipation Act. As originally proposed in the first draft of the Irish bill, the existing £10 freeholders created in 1829 were to be joined by holders of property worth £50 per annum on a lease of not less than twenty-one years. The following session this was modified to £20 leaseholders for a term of twenty years. As was pointed out at the time, this was a lower franchise than was proposed for England. But it was anticipated that in view of the different economic conditions in Ireland it would not result in flooding the county constituencies with a mass of poor tenants. Nevertheless even this failed to satisfy the Irish party and when the bill was discussed in committee O'Connell severely criticized the limited county constituencies which the bill was likely to produce. He argued that the basic £10 freeholder electorate was in some counties extremely small, less than 300 in five Irish counties; less than 700 in another fifteen; leaving only twelve counties with a constituency of over 700. The other classes of electors proposed by the bill, he maintained, were too restricted to make any fundamental alteration to the general situation. He estimated that the addition under the bill would be only another 12,000, so that putting old and new electorate together the total constituency for the counties would be a mere 30,000. These figures were of course simply estimates and Stanley sensibly retorted that in fact the number of leaseholders who would be enfranchised by the act was wholly unknown. Nevertheless it is probable that the criticism had its effect on the ministry, for a week later Stanley announced the final concession, the grant

⁴⁶ Fitzpatrick, *O'Connell Corr.*, ii, 14.

of the franchise to £10 leaseholders for a term of twenty-one years (reduced during the debate to twenty years for technical reasons). He admitted that as originally conceived the plan of reform for the Irish constituencies was not perhaps sufficiently extensive.[47] As it passed into law, therefore, the Irish bill made important changes in the county franchise. Even though the 40s. freeholder was not restored, the extension of the vote to the leaseholders down to the £10 level effectively opened up the narrow electorate created by the 1829 act. Of the thirty-two county constituencies after the Reform Act only two (Louth and Sligo) were less than 1,000; another seventeen were less than two thousand; and the remaining thirteen ranged from 2,000 to nearly 4,000.[48] All these were of course two-member constituencies, so that the average number of Irish county electors per member was in fact only 947, smaller than the equivalent figure for either England or Scotland. That average figure, however, concealed no great range of variation and the Irish county system resembled, on a smaller scale, the English rather than the Scottish counties in providing almost without exception constituencies large enough to discourage bribery and offering at least the prospect of a popular election.

Once the question of the franchise was settled the remainder of the bill created little controversy. The chief problem was the question of additional seats. Since no disfranchisement was contemplated, this necessarily meant an increase in the hundred seats provided for Ireland in the Act of Union. For that reason alone it was impossible for the ministry to propose many additions. In the first draft of the bill it was arranged for four large towns— Belfast, Limerick, Waterford, and Galway—with populations according to the 1821 census between 28,000 and 37,000, to receive one extra member each. No changes were subsequently made in this initial decision. An addition was also proposed for Dublin University. In the place of the one existing member for the university constituency, there were to be two; and at the same time the constituency, which consisted of the provost, fellows, and junior scholars (i.e. members of Trinity College *in statu pupillari*), was to be enlarged by the admission of all former scholars whose names should within six months be placed on the books of the university.

This proposal received a good deal of attention because of the

[47] *Hansard*, XIII, 813, 1010.   [48] Mosse, *Parl. Guide* (1835).

religious issue involved. The position was that Roman Catholics could attend the university and take the degree of Master of Arts, but they were debarred from becoming either fellows or scholars of Trinity College which was a specifically Protestant foundation. The right of voting for the university member was vested in the provost and scholars of the college, and this had come to be defined as giving the vote to the existing provost, fellows, and scholars only. As the latter were limited to seventy, the constituency was extremely narrow even for a single member; and the suggested addition of the former scholars of the college would not lift it beyond a few hundreds. Yet in view of the undoubted increase in Roman Catholic influence made by the reform bill, the ministry was anxious to offset it by at least a symbolic strengthening of the Protestant interest in the shape of a second university member. By committing themselves to such a measure, however, they at once involved themselves in difficulty. Except on the naked ground of religious prejudice it was difficult to justify giving a second member to Trinity College. On the other hand, to throw open the university constituency to all M.A.s of Dublin, on the analogy of Oxford and Cambridge, as O'Connell proposed, would certainly produce a substantial electorate, but it would be a preponderantly Roman Catholic electorate. The compromise was therefore chosen of a moderate enlargement, and at the same time the preservation of the religious purity of the constituency, by bringing in the former scholars of Trinity College. This in fact was no great addition as the seventy scholars of the college normally held their places for five years. The Irish nationalists declared that the new university constituency would only amount to 200, though Crampton, M.P. for Saltash and Solicitor-General for Ireland, said the constituency would reach 600. Lefroy, the sitting member for Dublin University, mentioned a figure of 700.[49]

Even so it was not an easily defensible case, the less so since the proposed arrangements debarred from the franchise the fellow-commoners of the college who were disqualified from becoming scholars by reason of their property. In the end the government gave way and in the closing committee stage of the bill in July 1832, a week before it received its third reading, a private member's motion to extend the vote for Dublin University to all holders of M.A. and higher degrees was passed. It was a sudden and in

[49] *Hansard*, III, 870; XIII, 597–606.

many ways an unexpected surrender of what had appeared to be an essential point of principle. The secret of it was the profound uneasiness under which the whigs laboured in proposing an additional member for a constituency that barely deserved to have one. It is plain that the notion of a second university member had been taken up before its full implications had been realized. Once publicly committed to the project the ministers had only three courses open to them: to maintain the narrow Protestant basis despite the enlarged representation; to increase the constituency by admitting Roman Catholics; or to transfer the second seat to one of the large Irish cities. The first instinct of the cabinet had been to maintain its ground, however inadvisably that had been taken up.

> With respect to the member for the University [Grey wrote to Taylor in May 1832] though perhaps that addition was not sufficiently considered with a view to the nature of the constituency, very different from that of the English Universities, by which he is to be returned, having been once proposed, I think it cannot be altered; and this matter having been brought under the consideration of the Cabinet yesterday, it was determined to adhere to the bill in this respect, as it now stands.

Nevertheless Grey was not happy at the arrangement and admitted to Taylor the day after that he thought it would have been better to have proposed originally to give another member to Kilkenny rather than to the university, and that many supporters of the government were not satisfied with this clause of the bill.[50] The second university seat had in fact been a tactical error; but when the whigs decided to concede the point, they did so with good grace. To have attempted, at that late stage, to transfer the seat to Kilkenny or some other Irish town, and leave the Roman Catholic graduates of the university still unenfranchised, would have smacked of spite. As it was the concession was symbolic rather than real. Certainly no startling changes in university representatives resulted from the capitulation. Lefroy, the sitting member, comfortably retained his place at the head of the poll in the first election under the act, and was given as his colleague Frederick Shaw, the conservative Recorder of Dublin. Both men were returned unopposed in 1835. But the constituency for which they sat was now almost as large as that of Oxford University. The

[50] *Corr. Wm. IV and Grey*, II, 451, 456.

university electorate of over 2,000 that was registered in 1832 formed the fifth largest constituency in the list of Irish cities and boroughs. On the score of numbers alone it fully deserved its second member.

Nevertheless, even with the second university member and the additional seats for the large towns, the total Irish representation was only increased by five. To the Irish nationalists this seemed inadequate. As early as March 1831 in the initial debate on the reform proposals, O'Connell criticized the Irish provisions as being inferior to those for England and Scotland. He pressed for more representation for Dublin, on the analogy of the increase in the members for London, and more members for the Irish counties. He cited the position of county Cork, with a population larger than that of any English county except Yorkshire or Lancashire, and put forward a comprehensive request for additional representation for the counties of Antrim, Down, Galway, Kerry, Mayo, and Tyrone, all of which had populations of over 200,000.[51] The plea for more county members became the main theme of the Irish party. They pointed to the discrepancy between Ireland and Scotland. Scotland with a population of just over two millions was to have five members added to its forty-five; Ireland with over seven millions was to have five added to its hundred. They pointed to the discrepancy between Ireland and England. Seven English counties with populations of less than 200,000 were to receive a total of fourteen additional members; but a whole group of Irish counties with populations between 200,000 and 400,000 were to receive no additions at all. Even inside the country there were profound inequalities. Leader, member for Kilkenny, stated in debate in January 1832 that ten Irish counties contained half the acreage and half the population of Ireland and yet returned only twenty-nine members out of the hundred. He too asked for additional members for all counties with a population of over 200,000.[52] If that request had been granted, it would on the basis of the 1831 census have affected no less than fifteen counties—Antrim, Armagh, Cavan, Clare, Cork, Donegal, Down, Galway, Kerry, Limerick, Londonderry, Mayo, Roscommon, Tipperary, and Tyrone; and would have added from fifteen to thirty members to the Irish contingent.

This was not a proposition which the government was prepared

[51] *Hansard*, III, 196–7, 869–71. [52] *Ibid.*, IX, 611.

to put forward. In the first place they had never accepted the principle of population as the sole criterion in the redistribution of seats; and to apply it in Ireland would be to invite demands for similar application elsewhere. But more important than that, the redistribution or increase of Irish seats raised an issue that was not one of classes but of parties. Already the opposition had declared that the changes envisaged by the bill would lead to the displacement of Protestant by Catholic influence. In the majority of Irish cities and boroughs the corporations and freemen were mainly Protestant while the mass of freeholders and householders were Catholic. The opening up of the close boroughs meant, therefore, a Catholic ascendancy. Similarly the surrender of the narrow £10 freehold franchise in the counties and the creation of large popular constituencies would again weaken the party of Protestant ascendancy which depended on property and privilege for its survival. These fears may have been over-drawn; but they were not to be ignored. The ministry had gone further than they had originally intended in meeting the wishes of the Irish nationalists. It scarcely seemed advisable or even practical to exaggerate the inevitable change in the internal balance of power in Ireland by a substantial increase in Irish representation. The crux of the matter was stated very clearly by Sir Henry Hardinge when he told the House of Commons that five-sixths of the property of Ireland was in Protestant hands; five-sixths of the population was Roman Catholic; and that consequently any attempt to reconcile the principle of property and the principle of population in the Irish electoral system was doomed to failure.[53] The restricted constituency in the counties set up by the 1829 act, and the numerous borough oligarchies, could not be defended by reformers except with gross inconsistency. Yet any attempt to expand the electorate inevitably had a tendency to increase Roman Catholic and Irish nationalist influence. The whigs were clearly conscious of this dilemma and their original plan was a compromise between the interests of the English Protestant ascendancy, and the claims of rational reform: precisely the kind of compromise which Hardinge had denied could be achieved. Yet it is significant that where the ministers made the most important concessions to the Irish nationalists, on the question of the £10 leasehold in the counties, and the admittance of ordinary M.A.s to the university constituency of Dublin,

[53] *Ibid.*, III, 891.

they did so at those points where their initial scheme could not be reconciled to the general principles of reform they themselves had set up.

But if there was an unanswerable case for the reform of the franchise, the matter of increasing Irish representation was on a very different footing. Here there was a large amount of common feeling between whigs and tories; and no minister could afford to ignore the widespread reluctance of parliament to make any substantial addition to the number of Irish members. General Gascoyne's motion against a reduction in the existing representation of England and Wales which brought about the defeat of the first reform bill was in part at least designed to exclude Irish claims to a larger share in the membership of the House of Commons. Exactly the same point was made in Lord Wharncliffe's plan for an amended reform bill submitted to Grey in November 1831. 'If the whole number of the House is not diminished', wrote Wharncliffe, 'the door may perhaps be shut against any further or future demands upon the part of Ireland, by there being in fact no vacant representations to dispose of.' Grey himself was inclined to share this sentiment. The two essential features of the Irish bill, in the prime minister's view, were the continued disfranchisement of the 40s. freeholder and the absence of any additions to the county representation. Some additions to the Irish boroughs he thought were unavoidable, though unpopular.

> It appeared to me [he wrote in his account of the conversation with Lord Wharncliffe on 16 November 1831] absolutely necessary to make an addition to Scotland, and that doing so, a corresponding addition to Ireland could not be avoided. It was to the latter that I apprehended the chief objection was felt, and I was far from urging that it was unfounded, but that the necessity of it arose from the addition to Scotland, which was required by the altered circumstances of the country, the growth of large towns, etc.[54]

A spirit of reluctant justice rather than one of reforming zeal characterized the whig approach to the Irish problem.

It was not surprising, therefore, that the attitude of the Irish nationalists was one of bitterness and dissatisfaction. The reason was not merely in the relatively more favourable treatment dealt out to Scotland. It lay in the whole attitude of the government

[54] *Corr. Wm. IV and Grey*, I, 454, Appendices B and C, 467, 478.

towards the two subordinate kingdoms. The contrast in the atmosphere surrounding the two reform bills was profound. Over the Scottish bill the ministry had shown a friendliness and marked absence of jealousy or distrust, allowing the Scots to evolve almost unhampered their own scheme of reform and to carry it through the House. Towards Ireland their attitude had been one of guarded concession and extreme reserve, with the detail of the bill kept closely under cabinet control. The situation was made worse by the constant irritation engendered between the ministry and the Irish party. Grey himself, though he had no serious objections to the Irish bill as it entered its final stages in the summer of 1832, was sufficiently provoked by the conduct of some of the Irish members to tell the king on one occasion that the bill might well be defeated in the House of Commons and if so he personally would not regret it.[55] It is true that the whig ministry of 1830 merely inherited the incubus of past centuries of Anglo-Irish conflict. But the striking difference of approach to Scottish and Irish reform was characteristic of the fundamental dissimilarity between the Scottish and Irish Unions. The whigs perhaps dealt as justly towards Ireland in 1831–2 as the political circumstances of the time would permit and vindicated Stanley's claim that the government would not allow the issue of religion to act as a barrier to the progress of reform. But justice to Ireland was measured by different standards on the other side of St. George's Channel.

O'Connell himself, despite his earlier commendatory words in the House of Commons, was deeply disappointed by the Irish reform bill. His disillusionment was all the greater because he had entertained high, and perhaps extravagant hopes of the consequences to Ireland of a reforming ministry. At the outset it did not seem too much to expect actual legislative independence. In November 1830 he confided to Edward O'Dwyer his feeling that 'we may have an Irish Parliament soon' and expressed the view that never was there a time when 'an extensive demand for the Repeal of the Union would have a better effect'. And when his old friend Duncannon was taken into Grey's ministry he hailed it as 'the harbinger of peace to Ireland'. But this halcyon mood did not last long. His quarrel with Lord Anglesey and the refusal of the government to let the control of the Irish bill pass out of their hands soon caused the waning of the early enthusiasm. It is true

[55] *Ibid.*, II, 28, 451.

that the views of the Irish nationalists were not entirely ignored. In the summer of 1831 O'Connell was invited to a private conference with Althorp on what he described unhopefully as 'Stanley's humbug "improvements" in the Irish bill'; and in the autumn O'Connell and Sir John Newport[56] went as a delegation from the Irish members to discuss the bill at a joint meeting with Althorp, Russell, and Stanley. But the Irish efforts to amend Stanley's scheme of reform in accordance with their own ideas were not very successful. In October 1831 O'Connell was complaining to Duncannon that the whigs had been in office twelve months and had done nothing for Ireland; and in November he declared more roundly that 'Lord Anglesey and Mr Stanley have made the people of Ireland Repealers'. It is clear that the Irish party felt angry and frustrated. Their one ally in the ministry, Duncannon, was not in a position to intervene effectively in the conduct of the Irish reform measure nor was Stanley likely to tolerate such intervention. 'Has he consulted one single Irish member on the Irish reform bill', demanded O'Connell of his friend in December, 'I have an idea that you, my Lord, are as rigidly excluded as I am.' The deterioration in the relations between the government and the Irish nationalists was reflected in O'Connell's progressively pessimistic utterances over the bill. In July 1831 he was saying that the bill must be improved. Ten weeks later he thought the bill 'is very very bad as it stands but we hope we will ameliorate it'. But by December he was telling Duncannon that Stanley would have to resign from the government; and in May 1832 he was gloomily asserting that 'the Irish Bill is as bad as bad can be'. These impulsive phrases need not be taken at their face value. Even O'Connell would probably have preferred the bill as it passed to no bill at all. But nationalist Ireland did not enter on the reformed era with any marked sense of gratitude to the whig government.[57]

[56] The Rt. Hon. Sir John Newport, Bart., of New Park, co. Kilkenny, b. 1756, M.P. for Waterford 1803–32, Privy Councillor, Chancellor of the Exchequer for Ireland in the whig administration of 1806. 'Distinguished', said *Burke's Peerage* for 1830, 'for his activity as a senator, and his inflexibility as a patriot.'
[57] Fitzpatrick, *O'Connell Corr.*, I, 229–31, 253, 267–8, 271–9.

Chapter Three

THE CONSTITUENCIES

THE unreformed House of Commons had consisted of 658 seats. This total was made up of 188 county and 465 borough seats, representing 114 county and 262 borough constituencies, together with the five university seats for Oxford, Cambridge, and Dublin.[1] The makers of the reformed parliament adhered to the old total but altered its constituent parts. In England fifty-six smaller boroughs were totally disfranchised; Weymouth was reduced from four members to two; and thirty other boroughs were left with only one member each. Twenty-two new boroughs were created with two members each, and twenty with one member. A third member was given to seven counties; and twenty-six counties previously returning two members each were divided into two divisions, each with two members. The Isle of Wight received a separate member and Yorkshire was to send six in place of its previous four representatives to Westminster. In Wales the county representation was increased by three; the borough districts widened; one new district (Swansea) created; and separate representation given to another Glamorganshire town, Merthyr Tydfil. In Scotland eight new seats were given to the burghs and in Ireland four large towns and Dublin University received an additional member.

In this reshuffle of seats and constituencies three points are outstanding. Many old constituencies, it was true, had been abolished or reduced; and many new ones formed. This aspect was most visible in England where 126 new seats alone had been created. But not all the seats left vacant by the abolition of the boroughs of Schedule A or surrendered by the boroughs of Schedule B were given to new constituencies. Many went to increase the representation of existing constituencies. If the Reform Act introduced novelties in the representative system, it also strengthened some of the older parts. Secondly the county constituencies had gained in representation whereas the boroughs had lost. Instead of a mere 188 county members in the House of Commons, there were now 253. Instead of 262 boroughs and 465 borough members,

[1] In 1821 Grampound had been disfranchised and its two seats given to Yorkshire.

there were now only 257 boroughs and 399 borough members. The direct territorial interest had thus been fortified at the expense of the oligarchical system of corruption and influence. Lastly, the outlying parts of the United Kingdom, Wales, Scotland, and Ireland, had increased their representation at the expense of England. Before 1832 Wales had 24 members, Scotland 45 members, Ireland 100 members as compared with the 489 members for England. After 1832 Wales had 29, Scotland 53, and Ireland 105 members, while the number for England was reduced to 471. The difference was not great but it served as a reminder that a party which secured an outright majority in England would not necessarily be in a majority in a full parliament; and that the smaller countries of the United Kingdom could, with the assistance of an English minority, dominate parliament.

Even if modified by other factors, however, the group of new English boroughs were of obvious importance in the development of the representative system. For the most part they reflected the industrial growth in the north and midlands, and brought such household names as Manchester, Birmingham, Leeds, and Sheffield into the parliamentary roll. Of the twenty-two new boroughs returning two members, fourteen were industrial towns of the north and midlands.[2] Eight was, nevertheless, a substantial portion to leave for the south when it is considered that these were an addition to the already generous number of southern boroughs. London, of course (though the claims of London before 1832 to an enlarged representation tend to be unduly obscured by the more obvious deficiencies of the industrial north), took most of the southern share. It was already represented by the City, Westminster, and Southwark. Four new boroughs were now added to the 'great wen'—Tower Hamlets, Finsbury, Marylebone, and Lambeth—while a fifth, Greenwich, was near enough to be counted within the metropolitan orbit. The remaining new boroughs with two members are not without interest. They were Devonport, where naval and government interests might be expected to be strong; Brighton, growing rapidly under the encouragement of the frequent royal presence at the pavilion and the new fashion of holidays at the seaside; and Stroud, a pocket of industrialism in rural Gloucestershire, destined to provide a safe seat for Lord

---

[2] They were: Manchester, Birmingham, Leeds, Sheffield, Sunderland, Wolverhampton, Bolton, Bradford, Blackburn, Halifax, Macclesfield, Oldham, Stockport, Stoke-on-Trent.

John Russell in 1835 after his defeat in Devon. In addition to these, there were twenty new boroughs sending one member each. The composition of this group was more varied. There were the usual industrial towns of the north and midlands, such as Huddersfield, Rochdale, and Walsall; a few shipping and fishing towns: White-haven, South Shields, Tynemouth, and Whitby; towns that lacked a specifically industrial character, like Cheltenham, Frome, and Kendal; and another naval town in Chatham.[3]

The disfranchisement of rotten boroughs and the enfranchise-ment of new ones was the most obvious and striking change made in borough representation. But considerable significance also attaches to the less publicized changes made by the three Boundary Acts for England and Wales, Scotland, and Ireland respectively. The Reform Acts left four points, necessary for completion of the whole plan of reform, to be dealt with by subsequent legislation. These were, the division of the larger counties; the partition of counties into polling districts; the establishment of polling places; and the fixing of borough boundaries. Under the last heading was comprised not merely the legal and geographical definition of the new boroughs created by the acts of reform, but also the general enlargement of a number of old boroughs that had been undertaken as an integral part of the reform of constituencies. The extent of this boundary reform may be judged by the circumstance that in England less than twenty boroughs retained the old borough boundaries.[4] Not all, probably not the majority, of these changes made any great difference to the size or character of the electorates concerned. In many instances the redrawing of the borough limits was primarily for administrative convenience: to make parlia-mentary and parochial areas coincide, or to extend the legal borough to take in the physical growth of preceding generations. But not a few of these changes were deliberately intended to raise the size of the constituency to the minimum standards required by the ministry for continued parliamentary existence. The distinc-tion made by Lord Durham between curable and incurable parts

---

[3] The remaining towns in this group were: Ashton-under-Lyne, Bury, Dudley, Gateshead, Kidderminster, Salford, Wakefield, Warrington, Merthyr Tydfil.

[4] Only the following are delimited in the English Boundary Act simply as having the boundaries of 'the old borough'; Bedford, Abingdon, Reading, Cambridge, Derby, Colchester, Harwich, Maidstone, King's Lynn, Thetford, Northampton, Newark, Wenlock, Ipswich, Bury St Edmunds, Warwick, Evesham. But probably a few places such as Southampton that were 'counties of themselves' should be added to the list as having suffered no enlargement.

of the diseased body politic applied not only to those boroughs which would under the £10 household franchise receive an adequate electorate, but also to those which by a natural and judicious extension of their parliamentary boundaries could raise themselves above the level of the doomed boroughs of Schedule A.[5] Only those boroughs which no reasonable spatial enlargement could provide with a respectable constituency were handed over to the legislator's knife. The principle on which the boundary commissioners had worked was described by Lord John Russell when the House of Commons went into committee on the English boundary bill in June 1832. In the first place large overgrown towns had those parts added to them which were integral features of their social community although hitherto outside the old parliamentary boundaries. Secondly, towns large enough in themselves to justify their existing representation and with no integral features outside the old borough limits were left untouched. Thirdly, towns with an inadequate population had one or two parishes added to them to make up the required electorate, provided this could be done without extending the legal limits beyond a specified distance from the town itself.[6] It is the last of these provisions which is of special political interest.

The practice of curing corruption by throwing a borough into the 'country' was not of course new. In 1782, for example, Cricklade had been enlarged to include five adjoining hundreds which thus became a separate electoral district within the county of Wiltshire. In this case the franchise was also extended to the 40s. freeholder. In 1771 New Shoreham had been thrown into the Rape of Bramber with the right of voting similarly extended to the county freeholders in that area. The constituency retained the name of Shoreham although it was in fact a large rural area about ten miles wide stretching inland from the coast for some thirty miles. Only perhaps in Cornwall, where the county was small and the rotten boroughs numerous, was this method inapplicable. Grampound for instance was disfranchised in 1821 and not enlarged, because the hundred in which it was situated already contained four other boroughs. Hence the seats were given to Yorkshire. Other examples of this practice were Aylesbury, whose three hundreds combined in 1804 to form the electoral district; and East Retford, which, on the eve of the reform bill, was thrown

⁵ *Hansard*, III, 1025.   ⁶ *Ibid.*, XIII, 528.

into the hundred of Bassetlaw. The special status of all four of these hybrid 'boroughs' was preserved by a special clause in the Reform Act of 1832. The problem in 1831 was not to find a suitable device for the work of electoral salvation; it was to decide which boroughs on the brink of destruction were to be allowed to number themselves with the elect. In general terms Schedule A represented the incurable, Schedule B the curable section of the rotten boroughs. Provided that the necessary enlargement would not entirely alter the character of the borough and that the absorption of the surrounding population would not materially diminish the size of the county constituency, it was permitted to the boundary commissioners to essay the task of purification. Small boroughs with less than 300 £10 houses could be enlarged by taking in the whole parish; or if this was not enough, adjacent parishes up to a limit of four miles from the centre of the borough, if this could be done without the inclusion of a separate and distinct township with urban boundaries of its own. In the case of slightly larger boroughs with a basic complement of from 300 to 500 £10 houses, more licence was allowed in applying these rules. Parishes or parts of parishes could still be added but where a large geographical extension would only bring in a relatively small number of £10 houses it was thought better to leave the old boundaries and the old character of the constituency intact. In any event, all boroughs were taken as individual cases and judged on local circumstances.[7]

To judge accurately how strictly the commissioners followed these principles would involve retracing their itinerary over England and separately examining each borough whose boundaries they altered. Nevertheless it is clear their work formed an important, though neglected, aspect of the changes made by the Reform Act in the representative system. The main interest is in the changes made in the English boroughs. The boundary acts for Scotland and Ireland were primarily concerned with a more rational delimitation of the borough areas. The question of artificially enlarging the borough boundaries did not arise because in Scotland the small burghs were grouped in districts and in Ireland they had been swept away by the Act of Union. Even in Wales the method of associating small boroughs in electoral groups had been preserved. But in England the practice was different. About half the English boroughs were enlarged, about a third very extensively.

[7] *Ibid.*, x, 417–20.

Considerable changes were made in this way to many parliamentary boroughs that still kept their old name and old seats in
the House of Commons. In their desire to produce adequate
constituencies for the numerous small boroughs that had escaped
Schedule A, the commissioners were obliged to make wide use of
their power to include rural parishes within the parliamentary
boundaries. Constituencies were extended to take in not only
outlying parishes and suburbs but also whole tracts of surrounding
countryside, far larger than the original urban nucleus that still
lent its name to the nominal 'borough' seat. It was not unusual for
entire villages, sometimes even another former borough that had
been extinguished by Schedule A, to be included in these reformed
and reconstructed constituencies. Some notable changes were
thereby effected in the character as well as the size of some of the
sixty-five boroughs that underwent this drastic enlargement.
Croker argued, not without reason, that as a result of these
geographical extensions certain boroughs had in fact become small
counties rather than larger towns. Alternatively, he pointed out,
if this method of purification by absorption was legitimate, it
would have been possible to have saved all the Schedule A boroughs
by the same process.[8] It was certainly true that some extraordinary
constituencies now appeared, masquerading as boroughs. Wilton,
one of the examples Croker used to support his thesis, included no
less than twelve whole parishes and parts of five others. This was
an extreme case but there were others almost as striking. Buckingham comprised eight complete parishes after 1832; Shaftesbury
fourteen; Woodstock ten and part of another; Eye eleven parishes;
Rye eight and part of another; Midhurst seven complete parishes
and parts of eleven others; Malmesbury eleven parishes; and
Droitwich eleven and parts of four others.[9]

The effect on the parliamentary map of England was often
surprising. Woodstock, for example, sprawled across Oxfordshire
from Tackley to Church Handborough and from Kidlington to
Wootton. And not infrequently these geographical changes had
odd political effects. In general the enlargement of a constituency
worked in favour of greater independence. But it was not always

[8] *Hansard*, XIII, 514–17.

[9] For details of these boundary changes, see the statute itself (*English Boundary Act,
2 & 3 William IV, cap. 64*). See also the excellent series of maps in Lewis's *Parliamentary
History*, 1835 (vol. v of the *Topographical Dictionary of England*, by S. Lewis). Further
examples of the changes made in the physical size of many boroughs made by the
Boundary Act will be found in Appendix B of the present work.

so. At Stamford the addition of the parish of St Martin, on the farther side of River Welland from Old Stamford, tended to reinforce rather than weaken the influence of the Marquess of Exeter because it brought so much of his property into the constituency. This point was brought up at the committee stage of the bill but Althorp refused on principle to veto the logical extension of the boundaries of the borough to take in the whole township of Stamford, including the contentious parish of St Martin, simply because the change would increase the influence of one individual. A similar extension of aristocratic influence nearly happened at Arundel where it was at first proposed by the commissioners to include the township of Littlehampton in which there was a sufficient electorate to make up at one stroke the required constituency. As this, however, would almost rivet the power of the Duke of Norfolk on the whole constituency, and Littlehampton itself could in no sense be regarded as an organic part of Arundel, Lord John Russell agreed to remit the case to a select committee; and in the end the borough of Arundel was confined to the parish of the same name.[10]

Of more consequence perhaps were the changes made to small boroughs by the addition of adjacent rural parishes. Such alterations showed a tendency to alter the local political balance of power by transferring preponderant influence from the borough proprietor to the neighbouring gentry. More than one landowning family in the vicinity of an old pocket borough found that the effect of reform was to present them with a seat in parliament. At Rye, for example, where the Lamb family had formerly held influence, the extension of the borough boundaries transferred power to the Curteis family, a member of which sat for the borough from 1832 to 1852 with the exception of the years 1837–41. A similar case occurred at Wareham in Dorset. Before the Reform Act the electorate consisted of forty-one scot and lot voters and the borough was in the hands of John Calcraft, the son of the famous and wealthy army agent whose connexion with the place went back nearly half a century. Originally Wareham was placed in Schedule A for total disfranchisement; but it was finally reprieved with the loss of one member and put into Schedule B. In spite of its small electorate the boundary commissioners did not recommend any substantial enlargement of the constituency.

[10] *Hansard*, XIII, 555, 968 sqq.

A proposal in the House of Commons to join it to Purbeck was opposed by the government on the grounds that the latter would swamp the Wareham electorate; and an alternative motion to add Corfe Castle was eventually defeated after a discussion in which it was clear that local and party politics were inextricably mixed. It was alleged for example that the addition of Corfe would enable the former tory proprietors of that extinguished borough to reincarnate themselves in the Wareham constituency. Nevertheless, by the time the bill reached the House of Lords, the government had reconsidered their attitude and on the motion of the Duke of Richmond, who was in charge of the bill, both Corfe and Bere Regis were included in the new boundaries of Wareham.[11] As finally reconstituted, therefore, the borough included the old borough of Wareham, the parishes of Corfe Castle and Bere Regis, and parts of East Morden and East Stoke, being an area of some 14,000 acres. The electorate was thereby increased to 387 and by 1852 it had reached 418. Mr Drax of Charlborough, as a result of the extension of the boundaries and the increase of £10 householders on his own estate, was now able to dispute the hitherto dominant power of the Calcrafts. The following election results tell their own story.

> 1832   Calcraft 175 (returned)
>   Erle Drax 140
> 1835   Calcraft (returned unopposed)
> 1837   Calcraft 170 (returned)
>   Erle Drax 155
> 1841   Erle Drax 211 (returned)
>   Calcraft 187
> 1847   Erle Drax (returned unopposed)

This was by no means a unique instance. It is clear that in this as in many other ways, the Reform Act considerably strengthened the territorial power of the landed gentry, and that many constituencies classed as boroughs were in reality scarcely more than veiled rural districts. In these instances at least the old idea of the borough as a corporate body or a social unit had disappeared and the only touchstone remaining was merely the electoral qualification. In comparing the representation of town and country districts, the existence of this large class of bastard constituency must be borne in mind.

[11] *Hansard*, XIII, 965; XIV, 73, 200.

The study of these small 'ruralized' boroughs illustrates how far the £10 household franchise was from being the universal remedy for the inequalities of the English borough system. If this, the only reform common to all the boroughs, failed to guarantee an adequate electorate, it was obvious that the system would continue to exhibit wide variations of type. For, barring the boundary extensions, all that happened was that certain large towns had been enfranchised; certain small boroughs had been disfranchised. But the substantial basis of the reformed system was the unreformed system. Changes had been made but they were modifications not revolutions in the previous order. The most obviously rotten parts of the constitution had been cut away; the most obvious claims for increased representation had obtained varying degrees of recognition. But between the vanished Sarums and Gattons, and the new Manchesters and Marylebones, lay a wide and almost untouched field where the eccentricities and contrasts of the old system still found room to flourish. The counties, with their large electorates and few members, had always been the most orthodox and uniform part of the representative system. It was the boroughs that had provided the whole gamut of differences from the silent pastures of Old Sarum to the throng of Preston electors; and it was the boroughs, though shorn of their more scandalous elements, that continued to exhibit the greatest immediate anomalies in the reformed system. Even the coming of the £10 householder could not reduce the variety of English boroughs to a common standard.

There were, for example, after the passing of the Reform Act at least eight English boroughs where the actual number of voters in 1832 was less than 200. Their representation, nominal electorate and actual voters were as follows:

	No. of members	*Electorate*	*Voters in 1832*
Totnes	2	217	179
Tavistock	2	247	193
Lyme Regis	1	212	183
Harwich	2	214	186
Reigate	1	152	101
Horsham	1	257	188
Chippenham	2	304	183
Marlborough	2	240	198 [12]

[12] P.P. 1834, IX, 590–3.

That this, if anything, is a flattering picture of the actual voting strength of these boroughs is shown by the returns for the next election in 1835.

	Electorate	Voters
Totnes	217	no contest
Tavistock	289	177
Lyme Regis	250	no contest
Harwich	156	123
Reigate	165	99
Horsham	280	251
Chippenham	217	no contest
Marlborough	280 nominal 254 actual	no contest [13]

When in one constituency only ninety-nine electors voted in a contested election, making fifty electors capable of returning a member of the House of Commons; and when an absolute majority in seven other boroughs was obtainable at a figure that only varied between sixty-two and one hundred and twenty-six in two general elections, it could hardly be argued that the days of rotten and pocket boroughs had completely passed. It is true that this group of boroughs had been on the borderline between extinction and preservation at the time of the Reform Act. All of them were old boroughs; Reigate, Lyme Regis, and Horsham had only survived by each surrendering one of their members; and, significantly, all of them were in southern counties. Two were in Devon, two in Wiltshire, and one each in Dorset, Essex, Sussex, and Surrey. But their existence in the years after 1832, even at one end of the scale of boroughs, indicated at least the elasticity of the reformed system.

The inequality in the size of borough constituencies can be illustrated in another way by the figures of the largest electorates at the same date. In the election of 1832 eight boroughs had polled less than 200 voters. In the same election there were four boroughs that polled more than 7,000 voters.

[13] P.P. 1836, XLIII, 373 sqq.

	Number of Members	Electorate	Voters in 1832
Tower Hamlets	2	9,900	7,300
London	4	18,600	11,500
Finsbury	2	10,300	7,300
Liverpool	2	11,300	8,600

It should be remembered that these are only the largest borough electorates which went to the poll in 1832. Where there were no contests there were necessarily no accurate figures for the actual number of voters. But the polling figures, though not immune from error, provide a more certain index to the size of a constituency than the usually inaccurate or misleading register of voters.

Thus Totnes with 179 voters, Liverpool with over 8,000 voters each returned two members to parliament. In contrast to the eight boroughs where an absolute majority might have been secured in 1832 with a hundred votes or less, there were four others where a majority had only been assured at a figure between 3,600 and 5,700 voters. It is unnecessary to labour the inequality between the large and small boroughs or to emphasize the difference in political value (and monetary value too) between the vote possessed by the elector in Reigate or Harwich and that possessed by the elector of Tower Hamlets. Indeed, looking at the whole mass of English boroughs, the upper and lower limits are so far apart that it is difficult on casual observation to form any general picture. It is clear, however, that the great majority of borough constituencies possessed over 300 registered electors. Only thirty-one English boroughs fell below this standard and of these all but five were between 200 and 300.

The five small boroughs were:

Ashburton	Calne
Thetford	Westbury
Reigate	

The others were:

Abingdon	Lymington
Buckingham	Christchurch
Wycombe	Eye
Launceston	Horsham

Liskeard	Midhurst
Bodmin	Marlborough
Dartmouth	Wilton
Totnes	Malmesbury
Tavistock	Droitwich
Lyme Regis	Northallerton
Harwich	Richmond
Andover	Thirsk
Petersfield	Knaresborough

On the other hand, over twice that number of boroughs had over three times as many electors. There were sixty-four English boroughs that possessed over 1,000 registered electors in 1832. Of these, twenty-nine had electorates of more than 2,000. They were as follows:

Chester	Tower Hamlets	Lambeth
Exeter	Westminster	Southwark
Greenwich	Norwich	Birmingham
Preston	Northampton	Coventry
Manchester	Newcastle-on-Tyne	Worcester
Liverpool	Retford	York
Leicester	Nottingham	Hull
Finsbury	Oxford	Leeds
London	Bath	Sheffield
Marylebone	Bristol	

The thirty-five boroughs with electorates between 1,000 and 2,000 were as follows:

Bedford	Colchester	Salford	Wolverhampton
Reading	Stroud	Bolton	Ipswich
Aylesbury	Gloucester	Oldham	Shoreham
Cambridge	Portsmouth	Lincoln	Brighton
Stockport	Southampton	Yarmouth	Warwick
Derby	Canterbury	Newark	Cricklade
Plymouth	Dover	Shrewsbury	Beverley
Devonport	Maidstone	Stoke-on-Trent	Bradford
Sunderland	Lancaster	Stafford	[14]

[14] It will be noted that all four of the corrupt boroughs enlarged before 1832 are to be found in these lists of large borough constituencies. East Retford had over 2,000, while Aylesbury, Shoreham, and Cricklade had over 1,000 registered electors after

From these figures a picture with a little more substance emerges. The number of English boroughs represented in parliament was 187. Of these, thirty-one possessed 300 or less electors, five having under 200; and twenty-nine possessed electorates of over 2,000. Reducing the upper limit to 1,000 only included another thirty-five boroughs. By this method ninety-five boroughs have been accounted for; sixty-four being over the 1,000 line and thirty-one below the 300 line. There remained, therefore, ninety-two boroughs with electorates ranging between 301 and 999. In other words, half the English boroughs fell into this category.[15]

It should be remembered that the figures for the electorates are those on the official register. They do not represent the actual numbers that would vote in an election or even the actual number of possible voters. Some allowance has to be made for duplicate registration under the different franchise qualifications. The practical size of the English boroughs in 1832 must therefore be reached by scaling down to a slight extent these figures. The proportions, however, would probably remain roughly constant. Moreover, these figures only relate to the first year of the Reform Act. Their general validity, of course, extends to a rather longer period than that and can serve a useful purpose for the next ten or dozen years that saw the end of William IV's reign and the accession of Victoria. But in an age rapidly growing in wealth and population, the natural increase of the electorate must be taken into account. Indeed, the electorate, in England at least, tended to increase faster than the population. By 1852, when the population had increased by about one-third since 1831, it was reckoned that the county electorate had increased by about one-third and the borough electorate by about one-half in the same period. But to discover where and with what effects the greatest increases in the electorate had taken place, would need a separate investigation. Certainly the increase was too uneven to eliminate by natural means alone the small and potentially corrupt or pocket borough.

In the parliaments of 1830 and 1831 there was general agreement that the counties formed the best constituencies and that

the Reform Act. The new £10 householder franchise applied, of course, to these as to all boroughs, but the act also preserved the right of voting of those in possession of the old franchise at the time of the passing of the act subject to the usual condition of residence. It was this latter provision which accounts for the large electorates of these four 'boroughs'.

[15] P.P. 1834, IX, 590 sqq.

there was need for a larger number of county members. There was much to be said for this point of view. The devaluation over four centuries of the old Lancastrian 40*s.* freehold qualification had produced, long before the nineteenth century, a popular franchise which enabled the English counties in 1831 to act as the real spokesmen of public opinion. The general restriction of county representation to two members for each county had on the other hand created a gross anomaly which became apparent as soon as the notion of equating representation and electorate had entered the sphere of practical reform. The ministerial solution was to increase county representation by dividing twenty-five of the larger counties and giving two members to each division. In addition the three ridings of Yorkshire received two members each; Lincolnshire received two members for the part of Lindsey and two for Kesteven and Holland; and the Isle of Wight was made a county in itself separate from Hampshire. This method of fortifying the county representation did not pass uncriticized even from the tory benches. It was argued that the disruption of the large counties would diminish the prestige of the county member. No longer would the members for Yorkshire, as in the days of Wilberforce, rank as the uncrowned kings of the English commoners. More practically it was urged that county divisions by reason of their smaller size would be liable to fall under the influence of one great landowner or under the domination of any towns or industrial areas that they happened to contain. Finally it was said that the principle was bad in so far as it tended to destroy the organic basis of the constituency and turn it into a mere electoral district, devoid of local significance, for which any stranger might be returned. The government speakers, as was their duty, denied all these allegations. Althorp asserted that the division of the counties would check the prevailing tendency to arrange a compromise between the power of the biggest landowner and the 'independent' interest by which each returned a member. Smaller districts, he argued, would result in a truer local representation. Another and more cogent line of reasoning was that the division of the unwieldy county constituencies would materially decrease the cost of county elections and so make it possible for independent landowners of limited means to represent their own locality. Here, as at other points, the whigs claimed merit for increasing rather than diminishing the influence of the country gentry in the House of Commons. Peel's attitude to the question was one of conditional approval. He censured the splitting up of the historic county entities 'as a precedent for a departmental division of the country', but thought that the principle of strengthening the power of landowners in the House one of overriding importance 'as the means of maintaining the wrecks of aristocratical influence'. A final vote on the division of counties showed some interesting cross-voting. Some ministerialists voted against the clause and some of the opposition supported it.[16]

The view of the ministry that the landed interest needed protection was even more clearly expressed over the question of the three-member counties. An increase in county representation other than that produced by dividing the larger counties had not originally been contemplated by the ministerial plan of reform. But when it was found expedient to give more members to the boroughs, especially to certain manufacturing towns, it was decided to balance this additional urban representation by selecting certain two-member agricultural counties and increasing their representation by one more member. The essence of the arrangement, as Althorp made quite clear in the House of Commons, was that the seven new three-member counties[17] were chosen not so much because of their large electorates, as for the fact that they would be certain to return members representing the agricultural interest. It was thus a deliberate weighting of the county system in favour of the land. To some at least it seemed that the weight was too emphatic and Praed moved a resolution that in the seven 'triangular' counties each elector should only possess two votes. His object was to secure some more reliable means than the delicate operations of compromise for the representation of a minority opinion. But Althorp, appealing in his inimitable way to the practical experience of the county politicians around him, argued that there were always private and personal considerations in county elections that made the casting of the elector's second vote dependent on something other than mere party allegiance. He denied consequently that there was any danger of a majority tyranny. Whether this was true or not, there was no doubt that solid support existed on both sides of the House for any

---

[16] *Hansard*, v, 1221–48 (Committee stage of bill, 11 August 1831).

[17] I.e. Berkshire, Buckinghamshire, Cambridgeshire, Dorset, Hereford, Hertfordshire, Oxfordshire.

reinforcement of the landed representation and Praed's rather academic thesis made little impression.[18]

For an increase in county representation there was of course justification on numerical grounds alone. Even after the division of the larger counties, the English county constituencies were uniformly large. The only exception, and that a minor one, was Rutland which had a total population of just over 19,000 in 1831. But only four other counties, Bedford, Hunts, Monmouth, and Westmorland, had total populations of less than 100,000. The registered electorates in these counties were all large by the general standards of the day. Westmorland had an electorate of over 4,000; Bedford and Monmouth, of nearly 4,000; Huntingdon had an electorate of over 2,500 and even Rutland, the smallest county constituency in England, had an electorate of 1,300, which, if surpassed by many English boroughs, was still a large constituency by borough standards. Some of the Welsh counties were decidedly smaller; but only one, Merioneth, had an electorate of less than 1,000. At the other end of the scale the large county constituencies could stand comparison with any of the great industrial and metropolitan centres of population. In the election of 1832, for example, there were eight constituencies that polled more than 7,000 voters. Four of these were county constituencies.

	Number of Members	Registered Electors	Voters in 1832
Lincolnshire (Part of Lindsey)	2	9,100	8,300
Lancashire (Southern Division)	2	10,600	8,400
Staffordshire (Northern Division)	2	8,800	7,800
Yorkshire (North Riding)	2	9,500	8,600

The smallest poll of the four was thus larger than that at either Tower Hamlets or Finsbury in the same election. This moreover is only a comparison of constituencies where contests took place. The West Riding of Yorkshire does not appear for that reason although with an enrolled electorate of 18,000 it was obviously one of the largest constituencies in the kingdom. On the other hand, of the four county constituencies cited only two, Lincolnshire (Lindsey) and Yorkshire (North Riding) can be broadly classed as agricultural. A fairer test is perhaps provided by the seven

[18] *Hansard.* v, 1323–4, 1359–71.

agricultural counties specially selected for the grant of a third member. All these had electorates of considerable size, ranging from Hertfordshire with just over 4,000 in 1834 to Cambridgeshire with over 6,000. Even allowing for their third member, they formed more than adequate constituencies by contemporary standards.

In general, therefore, the county constituencies were uniformly large and displayed no extremes of size such as marked the borough system. The average number of electors in the English county constituencies was reckoned in 1834 to be over 2,000 while the corresponding figure for the English boroughs was just over 800.[19] This discrepancy appears in a wider comparison of county and borough electorates. In 1884 Gladstone argued that rural constituencies ought to have a disproportionately large share of the representation because they lacked the political effectiveness that accrued to the urban communities as a result of their concentrated population. Whether valid or not, the argument was not endorsed by the Reform Act of 1832. After the passing of that statute it was the boroughs that possessed not merely an equal but a disproportionately large share of the representation. In the whole kingdom the county electors numbered 464,000; the borough electors 349,000. The seats in the House of Commons were, however, distributed as follows:

Counties	253 seats
Boroughs (incl. universities)	405 seats

Thus the counties had 57 per cent of the electorate and only 38 per cent of the seats; while the boroughs had 43 per cent of the electorate and 62 per cent of the seats. These were the aggregate proportions; but they held good for most of the different parts of the kingdom. The 345,000 county electors of England controlled 144 seats; the 275,000 borough electors 327 seats. In Ireland there were 60,000 electors and 64 seats for the counties; 32,000 electors and 41 seats for the boroughs. In Wales there were 26,000 electors and 15 seats for the counties; 11,000 electors and 14 seats for the boroughs. The one exception was Scotland where the counties had 33,000 electors and 30 seats; the boroughs almost as many electors, 31,000, but only 23 seats. By far the greatest discrepancy was, of course, in England. The English counties provided 56 per

[19] P.P. 1834, IX, 269–70.

cent of the English electorate and had been given 31 per cent of the English seats; the boroughs had 44 per cent of the electorate and 69 per cent of the seats. The Reform Act had thus done little to counteract that gross disproportion between counties and boroughs that had so long been a striking feature of the English representative system. Of all the electoral classes, the English county voter had the most right to grumble. Not only did England possess fewer seats in proportion to the electorate than Wales, Scotland, or Ireland, but the English counties, which provided well over half the English electorate, had to be satisfied with under a third of its representation. Wales, Scotland, and Ireland, with a combined electorate, county and borough, of 193,000 returned 187 members; while the English counties, with an electorate of not far short of double that figure (345,000), returned only 144 members.[20] If the reformed parliament continued to be very largely a parliament of English landlords, the representative system did less than justice to the English county electors. In practice, of course, the balance was redressed by the large number of small boroughs, either rural by interest and connexion or actually including a large rural area, that returned representatives of the landlord class and were entirely agricultural in feeling and outlook. The continued enfranchisement of these boroughs in their existing shape, though condemned by radicals at the time, can in fact be defended as necessary to preserve the balance of representation. Without them, the country districts would have been grossly under-represented.

There were other unbalanced aspects in the representation which may be briefly observed. One such anomaly, which the Reform Act limited but did not entirely remove, was the over-representation of southern England as compared with the metropolitan and northern industrial, urban areas. The greatest disparities had, it is true, been abolished; the rotten boroughs of the south, particularly of Cornwall, had been the chief object of destruction. The majority of the new boroughs had been given to London, the midlands, and the north; and Yorkshire, after 1832, possessed six county members instead of the customary two or four. But a marked inequality still remained. The population of the ten southern counties of England was 3,296,000;[21] the total

---

[20] P.P. 1834, IX, 267.
[21] I.e. Berks, Cornwall, Devon, Dorset, Kent, Somerset, Hants (incl. Isle of Wight), Surrey, Sussex, Wilts. (P.P. 1831–2, XXXVI, *Population of Counties*.)

number of parliamentary seats in this area was 156. The urban and industrial districts composed by Middlesex, Lancashire, and the West Riding of Yorkshire here had a slightly larger population, 3,672,000, but only 58 members of parliament. In other words, the ten southern counties, with a quarter the population of England, had a third of the representation. Middlesex, Lancashire, and the West Riding, with over a quarter of the population of England, possessed an eighth of the representation. If the two adjacent counties of Oxfordshire (omitting the university constituency) and Buckinghamshire are added to the southern group, the discrepancy becomes even more striking. The two groups are now almost identical in population (3,672,000 and 3,595,000) but whereas the urban and industrial area has 58 members, the southern rural area has 174 members, or exactly three times as many.

It is worth noticing, moreover, in this comparison that the greatest inequality was suffered not by Lancashire or Yorkshire but by London. The general emphasis on the industrial and economic background to the movement for parliamentary reform has tended to concentrate interest on the increased representation demanded and granted to the north and midlands. In fact, the inadequate representation of London, though not the most publicized, was one of the most real deficiencies of the old system; and even after the Reform Act the former inequality still continued. A comparison of Yorkshire, Lancashire, and Middlesex at once reveals this aspect. The population of the three counties was roughly the same; Yorkshire 1,371,000; Lancashire 1,337,000; Middlesex 1,359,000. But Yorkshire had 37 members, Lancashire 26, and Middlesex only 14. The West Riding of Yorkshire alone, with a population of 976,000, had more seats in the Commons than Middlesex. The conclusions therefore are clear. The old domination of south England over north, although it had been diminished, still continued after the Reform Act. On the other hand, of the great urban, densely populated areas, it was not the new industrial towns of the north but the capital city itself that suffered most from lack of representation and had reason to complain of the partiality shown not merely to the agricultural counties of the south but to the industrial districts of the north.

A further set of anomalies existed as between the constituent parts of the United Kingdom. In spite of the increase in Scottish, Irish, and Welsh seats, and the decrease in the number of English seats, some obvious discrepancies remained. Scotland, which had nearly three times the population of Wales, had less than double the number of Welsh seats in parliament. Ireland, with over three times the population of Scotland, had less than double the number of Scottish seats. England, with a population of 13 millions as compared with the 11 millions of the rest of the Kingdom, had 471 seats as compared with the remaining 187. With just over half the total population, England possessed nearer three-quarters than two-thirds of the total number of seats. This, however, was merely the relationship between population and representation. A different set of anomalies emerges if an examination is made of the relationship between electors and representation. The proportion of seats to electors was roughly the same for Scotland and Wales. But Scotland, with more than two-thirds of the number of electors possessed by Ireland, had only half the number of seats in the House of Commons. Ireland had 92,000 electors and returned 105 members. Scotland and Wales together had 101,000 electors but returned only 82 members. England, on the other hand, with over three-quarters of the electorate, had under three-quarters of the total number of seats. In relation to population, therefore, England was over- and Ireland under-represented; in relation to electorate England was under-represented and Ireland over-represented. In theory, though perhaps in little else, the two sets of disproportions tended to cancel each other. Wales, with a population that was over-represented and an electorate that was fairly represented, secured perhaps the most favourable treatment; while Scotland had a fair representation of its electorate even if the population was under-represented. In general, therefore, the representation of the electorate in the United Kingdom was as equitable as could probably be obtained at the time. The chief sufferer, England, enjoyed in any case such a preponderance of voting strength that no real grievance could have been felt. On the other hand, the chief gainer by the distribution of seats, Ireland, was the country which had the largest proportion of unenfranchised population.[22] That in the end was perhaps the most important distinction.

In the creation of new boroughs and in the redistribution of county seats, statistics of population had been taken into account. The changes in the representative system made by the Reform Acts

[22] P.P. 1834, ix, 267.

reflected therefore to a limited extent the tendencies in the growth and distribution of population. The system itself, however, even after 1832 was far from giving an adequate picture of the comparative population of the constituent parts of the United Kingdom. To have attempted an accurate balancing of population and representation would have been a revolutionary project outside the powers and certainly outside the intentions of the makers of the Reform Act. Politically they achieved probably the most that was feasible at that time even if statistically their work was already many years out of date before it received the royal signature.

Chapter Four

THE ELECTORS

THE electoral qualifications sanctioned by the English Reform Act of 1832 were even more diverse and complicated than under the unreformed system. By the act the existing county franchise of 40*s*. freehold by inheritance was not disturbed but limitations were imposed on freehold tenure for life. Unless seized at the time of the passing of the act, none were entitled to vote in respect of such tenements unless they were in *bona fide* occupation of them or unless they were possessed of them by marriage, devise, or promotion to office or benefice, or unless the property was of the annual value of £10. The county franchise was further extended to the possessor of the £10 copyhold, the £10 leasehold of not less than sixty years, and the £50 leasehold of not less than twenty years, and to the tenant of lands or tenements paying not less than £50 per annum in rent. It is worth noticing that a freehold was not necessarily land. It could be anything in the nature of property or interest arising out of the land, such as rent, tithe, shares in rivers or canals, or market tolls.[1]

In the boroughs the central qualification for the franchise was occupation, as owner or tenant of one landlord, of buildings of the annual value of £10. But the famous £10 householder clause was hedged around by a mass of conditions and subsidiary franchises. Occupation, to be a qualification, entailed residence for the preceding twelve months at least. All rates and taxes had to be paid and the property rated to the poor rate before a legal claim to vote could be entertained. Tenants who compounded for rates with their landlords were thus placed in a peculiar and difficult position. In addition the old pre-reform franchises were allowed to continue in force during the lifetime of their owners. Freeholders and burgage tenants with the right of voting previous to the passing of the act were to retain the vote if they registered themselves and

---

[1] Besides the actual texts of the three Reform Acts, there are a large number of contemporary publications giving a summary of the acts together with explanations and other useful material. One of these (*Maxima Charta of 1832*) may be mentioned as a particularly useful compilation since it reproduces not only the main text of the three Reform Acts but also the three Boundary Acts, together with explanatory notes. Seymour, *Electoral Reform in England and Wales*, is the standard modern work.

continued in actual possession of their freehold and burgage tenements. Burgesses or freemen with a previous right of voting were to retain their vote on condition of continued residence in the city or borough, or within seven statute miles thereof, but no freemen created after 1831 could vote unless they were qualified by birth or servitude. All other persons with a right of voting previous to 1832 were to retain the vote as long as they remained duly qualified, except in the boroughs of Schedule A which were totally disfranchised. It was obviously the poorer classes that benefited in the main from these concessions as the rich were enfranchised in any case. The result was that the electorate was still wide and heterogeneous for many years after 1832 and only became narrower and socially more unified as the old franchise died out. But this was a process that required some twenty or thirty years for its substantial completion.

Many persons were of course qualified both for the old and the new franchises. Many persons too had qualifications for more than one constituency. On the other hand persons otherwise qualified were in some cases legally debarred from exercising the franchise. Receipt of parochial relief or alms was a disqualification in cities and boroughs though not in counties; no peers (except Irish peers), revenue officers, excise, customs, or post office officials, police magistrates or officers, were allowed to vote; aliens, women, minors, lunatics (except during lucid intervals), were also disqualified. Above all, for votes to be valid, all holders of the franchise had to be properly registered. As Maitland pointed out, since 1832 electoral qualifications are really qualifications for being put on the electoral roll; the qualification for voting is, strictly speaking, having one's name on the roll. Failure to be registered entails disfranchisement. The only modification of this principle which the Reform Act of 1832 provided was a clause permitting parliamentary election committees to consider the correctness of electoral registers in disputed election cases and to amend the register as they thought fit. But it was required that defects in the register must be shown to have arisen from the actions of the revising barristers; and votes amended must have been either cast or proffered at the actual election. Elaborate provisions were made, therefore, to ensure a frequent and impartial revision of the electoral rolls. The preliminary list of voters was drawn up in the counties and boroughs by the parish overseers, or in the case of freemen by the town clerk. Every year barristers appointed by the judges of assize held revising courts in boroughs and counties for the purpose of hearing and deciding applications for the erasement of existing or the addition of further names on the lists. The official register of voters was then entrusted to the clerk of the peace in the counties and in the boroughs to the returning officers appointed by the county sheriff.[2] A fee had to be paid for registration. In the counties every elector had to pay 1s. at the time of claiming his vote; in the boroughs the elector paid 1s. at the time of registration and 1s. a year thereafter. There was some discontent at this tax on voting and the authorities experienced considerable difficulty in collecting it, especially in the counties.[3]

Such, divested of its deeper intricacies, was the outline of the system under which the first generation of Victorians found themselves divided into the minority which voted and the majority which did not. One can sympathize with Baring's protest during the Reform Act debates that the ministry were 'weaving such a complicated web of franchise as would defy the ingenuity of man to unravel'.[4] The real question is what did this intricate electoral system (the word perhaps is a misnomer) represent in terms of voting strength and type of voter. It was inevitable in the first place that a property franchise would give an economic rather than a social representation. Not the numbers but the wealth of the country was enfranchised. It was reckoned by the authors of the act that half a million voters would be added to the electorate as a result of the new franchise and the creation of new boroughs. This estimate was excessive. The unreformed franchise had been less than 500,000. The electorate that registered in 1832 for the first time under the reformed system totalled 813,000. This was probably not a grossly inaccurate figure for the number of legally qualified voters at that date. Some no doubt omitted to register but on the other hand many were registered twice, under the old

[2] The registration procedure here described applied to England and Wales. In Scotland the initial list of voters was compiled in the burghs by the town clerk, and in the counties by the schoolmaster for each parish. Claims and objections were heard annually in the sheriffs' courts and the official register then made up by the sheriff clerk for the county and the town clerk for the burgh. In Ireland a special session for registering voters was ordered by the act to be held in each county, city, and borough, at which claims were examined and adjudged by the chairman of the sessions or assistant barrister. Thereafter voters were entitled to apply for registration at any sessions of the peace before the chairman or assistant barrister for the district in which the vote lay. Official lists of voters were issued annually by the clerk of the peace for each county, city, or borough.

[3] P.P. 1834, IX, 278–9.   [4] *Hansard*, VI, 309.

and the new franchise, and there were many plural voters.[5] The total was made up as follows: England, 619,000; Wales, 37,000; Scotland, 65,000; and Ireland, 92,000. The population of the United Kingdom by the 1831 census was slightly over twenty-four millions. The electorate was thus almost exactly one-thirtieth of the population. But to put the electorate against the gross population, especially in an age which did not count voting among the female functions, is not the most illuminating method of finding a significant proportion. Among adult males, a much fairer standard of comparison, the electors were in the ratio of one in seven. This was a composite figure for the United Kingdom. In England and Wales, however, the proportion was one in five; in Scotland, one in eight; and in Ireland, one in twenty. When these proportions are placed against the respective populations the picture begins to take some shape. In England, whose thirteen millions outnumbered the whole of the rest of the United Kingdom, every fifth man had the vote. By the standards of the time, it was not an inadequate representation. Little Wales, with her 800,000 maintained the English proportions. In Scotland one man in eight out of a population of less than two and a half millions had the vote. But Ireland, whose 7,800,000 was more than double the population of Wales and Scotland together, had a quarter the proportion of votes enjoyed by Wales and less than half the proportion in Scotland. The figures are an eloquent comment on the economic condition of 'John Bull's other island'. Among one-third of the population of the United Kingdom only one man in twenty possessed the franchise which in the richer half of the kingdom was possessed by one man in five. It is true, of course, that the Irish 40s. freeholder had been abolished and the English remained. But this in itself did not account for the difference. The electoral qualifications in Ireland were similar to those obtaining in Scotland where one man in eight had the vote.

A further contrast in the distribution of the franchise may be noticed. In the United Kingdom the county electors formed over half the total number, the actual figures being 464,000 in the counties and 349,000 in the boroughs. In England the proportions were almost the same; county electors numbered 345,000 and borough electors 275,000. Scotland had almost an exact balance between the two categories; county electors were 33,000 and

[5] P.P. 1836, XLIII, 405.

borough electors 31,000. Wales, however, with respective totals of 26,000 and 11,000 had well over twice as many electors in the counties as in the boroughs. While Ireland was almost in the same condition with 61,000 county and 32,000 borough electors. Translated into proportionate fractions, in the United Kingdom there was one elector in every thirty-seven of the county population; one in every eighteen of the borough population. In the different countries of the kingdom the proportions were as follows:

	County Electors	Borough Electors
England	1 in 24	1 in 17
Wales	1 in 23	1 in 17
Scotland	1 in 45	1 in 27
Ireland	1 in 115	1 in 22

Broadly speaking, therefore, in Scotland half the electorate was in the counties; in England three-fifths; in Wales over two-thirds; and in Ireland just under two-thirds. But the proportion of the electorate to the gross population in the Scottish counties was three-fifths of that in the boroughs; in the English and Welsh counties about two-thirds of that in the boroughs; and in Ireland only one-fifth of that in the Irish boroughs. The contrast between the two islands is again enormous. In England the chances that a borough inhabitant would have the vote were only half again as great as those of the county inhabitant. In Ireland, the borough inhabitant's chances were five times as great as those of the county inhabitant.[6]

The effect of the Reform Act on the character as distinct from the distribution of the electorate is harder to determine. That is partly because under a system of assorted franchises a voter might be qualified in several different ways; and partly because a fixed property qualification had different social implications in different parts of the country. In the counties the picture is not quite so obscure as in the boroughs since here the ordinary agricultural labourer, with his tied cottage and 10s. or 12s. a week wages when in work, fell far below the minimum property or rent qualification. The county electorate, if not a narrower constituency than in the towns, was probably a more homogeneous one. Nevertheless the precise political effect of the enfranchising clauses of the Reform

[6] P.P. 1834, ix, 267.

Acts had been the subject of acrimonious debate in 1831. The two chief controversial issues had been the 40s. freeholder in the towns and the provision which acquired fame as the Chandos clause. The 40s. freehold was, of course, by contemporary standards an absurdly low property qualification[7] and there can be little doubt that its disadvantages were keenly felt by most members of the House of Commons. To have attempted to extinguish such an ancient franchise would have been contrary to the spirit of the reformers and the conservative instincts of the opposition. But in the debate on the question whether the 40s. freehold situated in an urban constituency should carry a vote for the county, some of the deeper feelings of both sides emerged. The crucial issue was the position of the man who owned a 40s. freehold in a borough but was not qualified to vote in that borough either because he was not resident or because his property was less than the standard £10 annual value which would give him a vote as householder. Until the Reform Act an elector claiming a vote for the county under the property qualification had to be assessed to the land tax. This necessity was abolished by the act and the way was thus thrown open for a flood of 40s. freeholders from the urban and industrial areas to join the county electorates. The ministerial view was that such persons should vote with the county to prevent the smaller borough constituencies from being swamped by the facile multiplication of small non-resident proprietors. The opposition equally feared the swamping of the agricultural constituencies by a mass of miscellaneous urban freeholders, especially in the industrial areas. Reading the account of the debate it is hard to avoid the impression that neither side really cared for the 40s. freeholder, at any rate in the urban industrial districts. The tories did not want him in the counties because he did not belong to the purely agricultural interest; the government did not want him in the boroughs because of the corruption that would inevitably ensue. A further ministerial argument was put forward by Russell who advocated the inclusion of the urban freeholders in the county constituencies on the grounds that it would allay the conflict between industry and agriculture, and prevent the return of members pledged to the

[7] Blackstone estimated that by the middle of the eighteenth century the Lancastrian 40s. freehold qualification had diminished to about a tenth of its original value. Some indication of the relative standard of the 40s. freehold in the early Victorian period may be gained from contemporary wage-rates; about 10s. a week for an agricultural labourer, a guinea for Peel's new metropolitan police, about 33s. for the skilled artisan, 6s. or 7s. a day for a first-grade engine-driver.

sole support of one or the other interest.[8] In the end it was probably the passing of the Chandos clause in the face of ministerial disapproval that decided the government to maintain their ground over the 40s. freeholder. Althorp certainly gave that impression when he told the House of Commons that the ministers had originally intended to give the 40s. freeholder the right of voting in the boroughs but, in consequence of the Chandos amendment, had decided that this class of voter must be included in the county constituencies to balance their composition and prevent the agricultural electors from having the whole power of returning the county members.[9]

The famous Chandos clause might well have been known to history as the Sibthorp clause; since it was Colonel Charles Sibthorp, M.P. for Lincolnshire, who first moved an amendment to enfranchise the £50 tenant farmer. He mistimed his effort, however, and his motion was premature. In the end Chandos, who had a similar motion ready, was first called upon to make his amendment since technically he proposed it for insertion in the bill a few lines before the point selected by Sibthorp. One fancies that Sibthorp never forgave that episode. Certainly he protested indignantly in the House of Commons at what he styled Chandos's lack of courtesy and said he hoped the public at least would realize that he had been the first to demand enfranchisement for farm tenants. But full justice is rarely granted in this world, even to politicians, and it was as the Chandos clause that the amendment became known.[10] The fact that the motion was carried against the government by 148 votes to 232 is sufficient indication of the strength of feeling in its favour. Various factors contributed to this. Many no doubt welcomed any reinforcement of the landed and landlord interest. Many felt that the ministerial objections were not so much objections to the character of the farmer and his fitness to vote as reflections on the decency and integrity of the landowners. When 'influence' was a natural concomitant of politics, the farmer (who required at least six months notice to quit) was regarded as at least as independent as the small rural shopkeeper. Ultimately it seemed illogical to leave the vote to the 40s. freeholder and give it to the £10 householder, but deny it to the substantial farmer of £1,000 per annum or more. Radicals, too, of various shades of opinion, were attracted by the prospect of

---

[8] *Hansard*, IX, 983–4.   [9] *Ibid.*, VI, 689.   [10] *Ibid.*, VI, 270–83, 299.

enlarging the electorate. Mr Alderman Venables, M.P. for the City of London, supported the amendment on the grounds that it was a sensible and desirable extension of the franchise. Orator Hunt favoured it on the simple grounds that everyone should have the vote, though he accompanied his approval with the warning that it would soon lead to the ballot. Against this combination of agriculturalists and democrats the government was obliged to admit defeat. But their attitude was made clear enough. Althorp said plainly that the tenant-at-will in an agricultural area was more dependent on his landlord than the £10 householder in the town since the former not only resided on his farm but put his skill and capital into it for which he would get no compensation if ejected. The seven year lease, he argued, was the minimum guarantee of independence against the landlord. Lord Milton put the case even more strongly. He charged that the amendment was deliberately intended to make the influence of the landed aristocracy paramount at the expense of the independent freeholder; and at a later stage said bluntly that the clause would 'place the election of at least half the members of the counties, indeed, of all the counties exclusively agricultural, not in the hands of individuals but of an oligarchy chiefly composed of the members of the Bench of Quarter Sessions'.[11]

The 40s. freeholder and the tenant-at-will were thus envisaged as opposed elements on which the balance of power in the county constituencies would depend. What in fact were the relative proportions of these two classes of voters? Lord Milton had expressed the fear that in the agricultural counties the effect of the Chandos clause would be overwhelming. Yet it is clear that statistically, the freeholder element even in the non-industrial counties was the major and sometimes dominant factor. Among the published parliamentary papers for 1837–8 are to be found a list of English counties distinguishing between the various categories of electors registered in 1837. The categories adopted by the returning officers are not always uniform but a picture of some substance can be drawn from the statistics thus provided. In Cumberland, out of a total of 9,075 electors, the freeholders numbered 5,566, leaseholders and farmers 2,520. The remainder were composed of miscellaneous groups, mixed leasehold and freehold, copyhold, annuities, rent-charges, etc. In Derbyshire the

11 *Ibid.*, IX, 1116.

figures were freehold 8,520; leasehold and tenants 3,063, out of a total of 12,102. In Dorset, freehold 3,882, out of a total of 6,366. In Gloucestershire, freehold 11,487, out of a total of 14,687. In Hampshire, 6,597 out of a total of 9,214. In Huntingdonshire, 1,747 out of 2,805. In Sussex, 5,128 out of 7,951. In the North Riding of Yorkshire, 7,448 out of 11,716. In these eight districts, drawn from widely differing parts of the country, the freeholders formed anything from a half to three-quarters of the county electorate.[12] In spite of the 'Chandos clause' the effect of the Reform Act was not to deliver over the counties to the direct control of the tenant farmer. Even if encroachments had been made on the old freeholder system, the county electorate preserved outwardly at least much of its former independent character.[13]

One may indeed doubt whether the Chandos clause was as important politically as was hoped or feared at the time of the Reform Act. It would be interesting to know, for example, how many of the nominal 40s. freeholders in the unreformed days were also tenants with respect to other property. It would be difficult to maintain in any case that the counties were subjected after 1832 to a landed and aristocratic influence from which they had been free before. Probably the careful balancing of the urban freeholder and the tenant farmer ensured for the most part that there would be no striking change in the forces controlling county elections. On this, as on many other matters, the Duke of Wellington delivered an essentially sound and moderate verdict some time after the Reform Act. Discussing the effect of the act on county representation he observed that 'the gentry have as many followers and influence as many voters at the elections as ever they did' but that a new element had been introduced in the shape of 'the copyholders and freeholders and leaseholders residing in towns which do not themselves return members to Parliament. These . . . are everywhere a formidably active party against the aristocratic influence of the Landed Gentry.' This anti-aristocratic element he held to be fundamentally a dissenting party which joined up with the dissenters in the villages, 'the blacksmith, the carpenter

---

[12] P.P. 1837–8, XLIV, 553 sqq.

[13] In 1854 it was estimated that the total county constituency in England was composed as follows:

freeholders	321,559
other franchises	149,728
Total county electorate	471,287

(Banfield, *Statistical Companion for 1854*, 96).

the mason, etc.'.[14] Here the duke was specifically referring to the freeholders in the towns. But not all freeholders were of this description and while the statistics of 1837 are useful in proving the continued preponderance of the freeholder vote even in the agricultural counties, they throw no light on the different types of freeholder which made up the grand total. The factory owner in the industrial district not yet given borough representation; the dissenting blacksmith; the schoolmaster in perpetual office drawing his salary from a charge on the land; the retired professional man with shares in a canal or turnpike company; the shopkeeper who owned his house and garden; the small owner-farmer; the farmer who owned some land and rented more; all these were lumped together under the general heading of freeholder. The only common factor was property of their own. Apart from this there is nothing to fix their social status; still less their political convictions.

It is reasonable to assume on the basis of the parliamentary returns quoted that the voters subject to direct influence through the landlord-tenant relationship were in a minority in every county constituency. But mere aggregate totals of freeholders in separate counties can tell us nothing of the social and economic environment which affected their political behaviour. To regard the counties as areas in which the crude economic pressure of the landlord class was the only factor of weight would be a gross over-simplification of the situation. But it would be equally absurd to imagine that in the rural districts the mass of freeholders could be treated as a separate element divorced from, or at least opposed to, their rural context. Only in the industrialized or urbanized counties could the freehold vote upset the traditional political pattern of the countryside. In the ordinary surroundings of the market town and village, large farms and gentlemen's estates, the farmers and leaseholders enfranchised by the act were complementary rather than antithetical to the rural freeholder.

In the borough the electorate had been at different points both limited and enlarged. New boroughs had been created with a corresponding wide measure of enfranchisement; and a uniform qualification had been imposed on the old boroughs which broke down old franchise monopolies. On the other hand many boroughs

[14] *Croker Papers,* II, 206.

had been abolished and their electors disfranchised unless they happened to be qualified for other constituencies. It was true that in the boroughs that survived the Reform Act the old franchises were continued during the lifetime of their possessors; but the exercise of this right was made contingent on residence. This condition went some way towards confining the effects of the general concession. In several boroughs the electorate was actually reduced by the Reform Act because of the immediate disfranchisement of the non-resident voters. Only in the few cities or towns that were counties of themselves did the freeholders and burgage tenants have their franchise continued in perpetuity, along with the burgesses, freemen, and liverymen of the City of London. The old franchise was thus not transposed in its entirety to the new system.

On the matter of the proportions of the voters claiming under the old and the new franchise, a sample of actual conditions immediately after the Reform Act may be given as an illustration. At Andover there were 229 £10 householders and only seventeen freemen. At Ashburton there were 146 householders and fifty-two freeholders. Banbury had 326 householders and thirteen freemen or aldermen, but as ten of the latter were also qualified under the new franchise the total electorate was only 329. At Lyme Regis the total number of householders was given as 208, the number of freemen as fourteen; but the total electorate was returned as 212 which suggests that some of the freemen were also £10 householders. At Maidstone there were 456 freemen out of 1,108 registered electors. At Maldon there were 558 freemen among the 671 electors who polled at the 1832 election. The total registered electorate here was 716 so that it is probable that there were even more freemen on the lists than the number given. In the absence of more specific information, however, it would be unsafe to conclude that none of the freemen who voted were otherwise unqualified. Where there was a choice of qualifications under which an elector could be registered, it was possible that the older and more select franchise would be chosen. At Malmesbury there were 278 householders and thirteen freemen. At Marlow the holders of the old franchise (scot and lot) numbered 362, voters under the new franchise ninety-five. Here again it is likely that many of the 362 were also qualified as householders under the new act. At Wilton there were seventeen freemen of whom ten were also included among the 214 householders. At Woodstock the number of registered freemen was seventy-six, voters under the new franchise 241. Before the Reform Act the electorate at Woodstock had been exclusively composed of freemen who were entitled to vote wherever they were resident; they had numbered about 165. At Wycombe the total of registered electors was 298 of whom twenty-eight were burgesses; but as the greater part of these were also qualified as householders, only five were considered to draw their qualification merely from their burgess title. At Yarmouth the number of freemen was 1,040; that of the £10 householders 643; in all a total of 1,683. Whether any of the freemen were also householders is not clear.

These twelve boroughs have been taken at random from the alphabetical list. They form a sample, that is perhaps roughly accurate, of existing conditions; though the actual figures must be treated with some care as it is clear that the clerks responsible for making the returns did not always distinguish between voters with qualifications under the old and the new franchise. In many cases it appears that they were content to give, under the heading of new franchise, merely the number of electors added by the Reform Act, and leave the rest, whether qualified as householders or not under the heading of old franchise.[15] Nevertheless the broad picture these figures draw is not without meaning.

Among the conflicting tendencies in the general situation, certain tentative conclusions may be suggested. If, in the former open boroughs, many possessed the old franchise who were not qualified for the new, in the former close boroughs the electorate had already been to a certain extent of the £10 householder class. And in the forty-two new boroughs, of course, the £10 householder was in sole possession of the vote. In the thirties, therefore, while certain anomalies existed in the form of ancient franchises which required a generation for their extinction, most boroughs were probably dominated at once by voters who fell within the new £10 householder class created by the act. Nevertheless the perpetuation of the old class of voter is not without interest. Twenty years after the Reform Act the anomaly of the old franchise was still of tangible importance. In 1854 it was reckoned that they amounted to some 60,000 in a total borough electorate of 400,000; that is to say, more than one-seventh of the whole. Of these about

[15] P.P. 1833, xxvii, 111 sqq.

two-thirds were freemen.[16] Here again the nominal body of freemen almost certainly included many who would otherwise be
qualified as householders. In Derby, for instance, it was stated in
1848 that there were some 2,200 electors of which 450 were freemen; but of these latter 200 would have the franchise also as householders.[17]

Even among the orthodox £10 householders it is useless to look
for any real social homogeneity. There is in the first instance the
obvious point that the man who was literally a £10 householder
was at the bottom of the social scale in the borough electorate.
The average must therefore have been higher. But in that case the
fallacy of assuming that the £10, the £20, and the £50 householder
formed a single social or political class only needs enunciation to
be perceived. The phrase, 'Ten Pound Householder' is a convenient one but it involves taking the lowest class of urban voter as
a description of the whole. Lord Durham produced figures to
elaborate this point in March 1831. According to the tax-office
returns there were then only 379,000 persons in England and Wales
rated at £10 and over. Of these 116,000 were rated between £10
and £15. Only a third of the householders fell below the £15
standard. In Scotland there were 37,000 houses of £10 and over
of which 18,000 were rated at under £15.[18] In London, or at least
in certain London boroughs, the majority of the houses above the
£10 mark were also above the £20 mark. Althorp quoted figures
which were accepted by the opposition showing that in Tower
Hamlets, of the 26,000 houses of the value of £10 and above, only
13,000 were under £20. In Marylebone only 3,000 out of 23,000
were under £20. In Lambeth only 8,000 out of 17,000.[19] On the
basis of these three London boroughs, therefore, it was the £20
rather than the £10 householder that would dominate the electorate.

Yet to confine one's attention to the nominal value of the houses
occupied by the urban electors is scarcely the most illuminating
method of discovering what kind of electorate the new borough
franchise produced. Certainly if the same social class of elector
invariably inhabited houses of the same nominal value, some
roughly adequate conclusion concerning their status in society
could be drawn from the figures given in the preceding paragraph.
But it is precisely here that the superficial uniformity of the £10

---

[16] Banfield, *loc. cit.*; Bagehot, *Essays on Parliamentary Reform*, 69.
[17] Add. MS. 40600, fo. 202.   [18] *Hansard*, III, 1028.   [19] *Ibid.*, VI, 602.

householder suffrage disappears under analysis to reveal a wide range of different social and economic classes. The variation is not merely one between the £10, £20, and £50 householder. It is also the variation of social and economic status indicated in the different parts of the country by those house values. A property qualification is only uniform in its effects if the value attached to property is identical over the whole area under consideration. But such values are rarely constant; in early Victorian England they were subject to wide local variations. Indeed, the 'Ten Pound Householder' viewed as a type of elector was as much a legal abstraction, a constitutional myth, as the freeholder in the counties. As soon as one endeavours to translate the abstraction into flesh and blood, a host of different figures is revealed. It was asserted without contradiction by such opposed politicians as Croker and Hunt that in London the £10 qualification would in fact produce virtual manhood suffrage because the number of London houses of less than the annual value of £10 was negligible. On the other side of the kingdom, however, a £10 house in Cornwall indicated a person of some substance. The contrast was particularly striking in the industrial towns. Hunt told the House of Commons that in most English industrial constituencies the working classes lived in houses of £5 to £7 value and so would not be enfranchised although at least the upper level of that class was superior to the class that in London would be living in a £10 house. The general accuracy of this statement was admitted by the government. Russell said that the proportion of £10 houses varied in the towns from one-half to one-sixth, though the average was one-third or one-quarter, of the total number of houses. At Leeds, for example, the working classes would be largely debarred from the franchise because they lived in houses of £5 to £8 value. In Manchester on the other hand where rents were higher, a proportion of the working classes would be admitted. As an instance of the unequal incidence of the franchise qualification he quoted the case of Reading and Wigan. There was very nearly the same number of houses in both towns but the number of £10 houses in the first was double that in the second.[20] Again, a witness before a parliamentary committee of 1834 said that in the two Welsh boroughs of Newtown and Welshpool in Montgomeryshire, the occupiers of £10 houses were not tradesmen but 'principally workmen and men of that description'.[21]

[20] *Ibid.*, ix, 495–500; v, 1060; vi, 553.   [21] P.P. 1834, ix, 378.

The chief conclusion which emerges from this kind of evidence is that any generalization is apt to be misleading. At one end of the scale are the London boroughs where rents were so high that the £10 clause enfranchised most genuine householders. At the other were the raw industrial towns of the north and midlands which catered primarily for the new proletariat of the industrial revolution, and remote towns in rural areas where rents were low and £10 relatively a high rental. Between the two extremes were the ordinary, prosperous, middling boroughs of the English countryside. Brougham once described for the benefit of the House of Lords in 1831 the kind of person that occupied a £10 house in such places. 'Occupiers of such houses, in some country towns', he said, 'fill the station of inferior shopkeepers; in some, of the better kind of tradesmen [22]—here they are foremen of workshops—there, artisans earning good wages—sometimes, but seldom, labourers in full work; generally speaking, they are a class above want, having comfortable houses over their heads, and families and homes to which they are attached'.[23] The £10 household franchise was in fact an index neither of a class nor of a standard of living. In a few boroughs it included the majority of householders; in some it excluded entirely the manual worker; in many it took in the skilled while rejecting the unskilled labourer. The £10 qualification was a middle-class franchise in so far as it gave the vote to the majority of the middle classes living in the boroughs; but at many points it dipped below that class to take in a substantial element of the working class.

This regional variation in the significance of the urban franchise was of course commented on at length in the reform bill debates and more than one suggestion was put forward to level out its more obvious inconsistencies. Hunt, the only real democrat of the 1831 parliament, offered the simple solution of extending the franchise to all householders. This was rejected by the government on the equally simple grounds that it made the franchise depend on personal and not property qualifications and thus violated a fundamental principle of the bill. More complicated solutions were proffered by Polhill, M.P. for Bedford, and Mackinnon, M.P. for Lymington. The principle of both was the same: namely that boroughs should be graded in three different divisons according to

---

[22] It will be remembered that in early nineteenth-century phraseology a 'tradesman' meant a mechanic or artisan, i.e. a skilled workman who had learned a trade.

[23] *Hansard*, VIII, 239.

size and wealth and that the franchise qualification should be set at £5, £10, and £20 (by Polhill's plan) or at £10, £15, and £20 (by Mackinnon's plan), to correspond with the three groups, the larger and wealthier constituencies having the higher qualification. But the ministry was not prepared to be drawn from the safe refuge of the universal £10 qualification to pursue the elusive decoy of equity. Althorp, against whose cheerful and solid common-sense so many ingenious bubbles burst during the reform bill debates, freely admitted the inconsistencies which the uniform £10 franchise would produce in different parts of the kingdom, but neatly turned his critics' weapon in their hands by claiming it as an advantage of the ministerial scheme that such a diversity of electors would be admitted to the constitution. For the tories, who had claimed that diversity as a signal merit of the unreformed system, this was not easy to answer.[24]

The government indeed were well aware of the theoretical objections which could be brought against the bill and of the many anomalies created by it; they were also largely indifferent to them. If they had endeavoured to produce a logical and equitable franchise they would never have passed the reform bill at all. For nothing short of manhood suffrage would have been logical and equitable; and manhood suffrage would never have been accepted by parliament. Inconsistency and illogicality were bound to be present. It was enough if rough justice was done and the substantial ends of reform were met. The main object of the act, apart from the actual creation of new constituencies, was to consolidate rather than to extend. It was a rational rather than a democratic measure. Excrescences of all kinds, from the absentee freemen to the sheep-walks of Old Sarum, were lopped off and the whole brought within the framework of a neat and simple pattern. But the simplicity of the pattern was legalistic and not political. Within its confines there was a mass of vastly different franchises, including the characteristic perpetuation of the old franchises; and the edges of the pattern had a way of expanding and contracting in different parts of the country. But somewhere within those fluctuating borders lay the bulk of the property, education, and intelligence of the nation. For that reason it satisfied the country in 1832 and survived the epochal year 1848 when most of the other great European States saw their constitutions crumble in revolution.

[24] *Ibid.*, v, 1060; vi, 552–4, 576, 599–602.

Part II

THE WORKING OF THE SYSTEM

Chapter Five

THE PRICE OF POLITICS

ALTHOUGH payment of members of parliament had been proposed by various reformers before 1830, no alteration was made by the Reform Act to the principle that members should be men of independent means. The property qualification for members of the House of Commons was still continued; a landed estate of £600 per annum for the county member, £300 per annum for the borough member.[1] A slight change was made in 1838 when the qualifications were extended to include personal as well as real property.

By a curious anomaly no property qualification was required in Scotland. Before 1832 there had been one for the Scots county members but not for the borough members. The first draft of the Scottish reform bill continued this dualism although at one point a proposal was made to enforce a qualification on all Scots members as in England. This was dropped, however, partly because of the common evasion of the qualification and partly because of the general opposition in Scotland to any extension of the practice. Finally when the Scottish bill came up for debate most of the Scottish members expressed the view that there should be no qualification at all either for borough or county and Jeffrey accordingly withdrew the qualification clause.[2] In 1834 a parliamentary committee inquiring into election expenses recommended that the laws imposing qualifications on candidates in England and Ireland should be reconsidered.[3] But it was not until 1858 that the property qualification disappeared entirely.

In practice, however, the qualifications were not rigidly enforced and there were various familiar ways of evading the spirit of the rule. It was common, for example, for members to make friendly agreements with relatives and acquaintances, conferring artificial qualifications upon themselves during the election. Roebuck went so far as to declare that not one member in ten possessed the requisite qualifications until he came to make his candidature.[4] The

---

[1] The property qualification dated from 1710 (9 Anne, c. 5).
[2] *Hansard*, XIII, 1057 sqq.   [3] P.P. 1834, IX, 290.   [4] Leader, *Life of Roebuck*, 49–50.

limitations imposed by the property qualifications, if they were effective at all, could only have been slight. If, on the other hand, it had been the intention of the qualifying clause to restrict membership of the Commons to the upper classes, it was probably unnecessary. The social traditions of the British public ensured for the most part that their representatives were drawn from the upper classes of society. It has been abundantly demonstrated that the first reformed House of Commons was, like its predecessors, composed mainly of country gentlemen and members of the aristocracy. The middle-class banking, mercantile, and industrial elements were no stronger after 1832 than before.[5] To some extent the absence of remuneration assisted this conservative aspect of things. Where, as in the case of the early radicals, there was little prospect of securing a salaried office in the government, membership of parliament was a costly profession. Even if the election expenses were small or defrayed by supporters, residence in London and enforced absence from office or factory for half the year was a considerable tax on any professional or business man in the provinces. During the parliamentary session at least no conscientious member could combine his parliamentary duties with any full-time employment. Take, for example, the description given by Baines, the Leeds dissenter and back-bench liberal, of his typical day when the House of Commons was sitting.

> Monday—Rose at six, much refreshed by two successive good night's rest. Read Parliamentary papers and reports till eight; from the hour of post till half past eleven, corresponded with constituents; at twelve attended the House to present petitions, but standing low on the ballot list, had not been called when the House adjourned at three. Attended Committees till four; House resumed at five; debate continued till nearly midnight; real business then began; continued till three in the morning when the House adjourned. Walked home by morning twilight; pined a little after domestic comfort; soon forgot all cares, public and private, in sleep.

Baines was human enough to record rising at the late hour of seven the following morning. But it is little wonder that he added that 'a Bill should be introduced to enable Members to read and think by steampower'.[6] Baines was perhaps more assiduous in his duties than most; and as befitted a self-made Lancashire nonconformist, had a stamina even at the age of sixty that not

---

[5] See e.g. Halévy, *Hist. Eng. People*, iii, 63.   [6] Baines, *Life of Edward Baines*, 194–5.

all members possessed. Moreover even the reformed House of Commons did not invariably sit till three in the morning. Nevertheless only a minority of politicians could have defied the twin pressures of party whips and importunate constituents sufficiently to escape from the burden of parliamentary attendance.

When a member of parliament was appointed to a post in the ministry the immediate financial problem was alleviated. A fresh set of problems then presented themselves. Executive duties in addition to parliamentary attendance put any other kind of remunerative employment almost out of the question. Yet ministries were mortal; indeed, in the thirties their decease was often unexpectedly rapid; and no ministerial salary could be regarded as permanent. On the other hand, an M.P. without means of his own who had become a member of the administration always had a sense of economic dependence to curb his activities and to fret his conscience, if he possessed one. In an age which was still sensitive to the cry of 'placeman' and 'pensioner', the politician who had only his official salary to live on was in an uncomfortable position. In fact there was widespread agreement that no man could pursue a political career with integrity unless he had a competence of his own. It was this dilemma which deprived the whigs of Macaulay's services in the House of Commons for five important years. Poverty alone drove him to accept a lucrative post in India and abandon the political career which had opened so brilliantly in 1830.

> Every day [he wrote to his sister in August 1833] shows me more and more strongly, how necessary a competence is to a man who desires to be either great or useful. At present the plain fact is that I can continue to be a public man only while I can continue in office. If I left my place in the Government, I must leave my seat in Parliament too. For I must live; I can only live by my pen; and it is absolutely impossible for any man to write enough to procure him a decent subsistence, and at the same time to take an active part in politics.

To Lord Lansdowne, his patron, he wrote in a similar strain four months later.

> Every day makes me more sensible of the importance of a competence. Without a competence it is not very easy for a public man to be honest: it is almost impossible for him to be thought so. . . . You,

whom malevolence itself could never accuse of coveting office for the sake of pecuniary gain, and whom your salary very poorly compensates for the sacrifice of ease and of your tastes to the public service, cannot estimate rightly the feelings of a man who knows that his circumstances lay him open to the suspicion of being actuated in his conduct by the lowest motives.[7]

Politics therefore needed an independent income and before any man could embark on a parliamentary career he had to be assured not merely of the nominal property qualification that would satisfy the law, but of the financial qualification that alone would make possible his chosen profession. Macaulay solved the problem by turning himself into an Indian nabob; Peel was the son of a cotton millionaire; Gladstone was the fortunate offspring of a Liverpool East India merchant; Disraeli, with money-lenders and duns on his heels, married a wealthy widow; Baines was the proprietor of the successful *Leeds Mercury*; Cobden, the calico printer who nearly ruined his business by his devotion to the Corn Law agitation, would have been obliged to retire from political life in 1846 had he not been presented with a public subscription of over £75,000. It is not surprising that the independent landowners were by far the largest single group in the House of Commons, followed at a long interval by lawyers, merchants, manufacturers, and holders of military and naval commissions. It is true that payment of members had long been one of the stock radical reform proposals. It had appeared in the Westminster programme of 1780 and was one of the points of the People's Charter in 1838. Horne Tooke had proposed to give members £400 per annum, and that eccentric tory reformer, the Marquess of Blandford, had suggested £2 *per diem* for borough and £4 *per diem* for county members.[8] But as long as parliament and the country remained opposed to such a fundamental revaluation of the rôle of M.P.s as was implied in the payment of salaries, and as long as neither parties nor political and trade unions could afford to finance their parliamentary

[7] Trevelyan, *Life of Macaulay*, 1, 323, 343. For an almost identical attitude compare T. P. O'Connor's description of his state of mind when he was invited to stand for parliament in 1880. 'There was no Parliamentary salary in those days; nor, curiously enough, was there, as there was later, any public fund from which to draw support for the penniless members of the [sc. Irish] party. . . . Now, I had made up my mind that, so far as I could, I would never be dependent on politics for a living, I had a horror of the subserviency it might create, and I knew that it would always be an uncertain source of income.' (O'Connor, *Memoirs of an old Parliamentarian*, 1, 36.)
[8] Paul, *History of Reform*, 86, 103.

representatives, for so long would the legislature be in the hands of the wealthy and leisured classes.

The whole temper of opinion in early Victorian society insisted that this should be so. Despite the development of party and party organization, the highest respect, as Macaulay correctly stated, was reserved for the independent politician, in the sense not of one who was outside party but of one who was in party solely because of his conscientious opinion and perhaps traditional association. Integrity was held to be inseparable from intellectual independence; and intellectual independence inseparable in the long run from financial independence. All members and all candidates claimed to be independent in their opinions and votes because it was the contemporary ideal of what a politician should be, however far removed from reality that ideal was. A typical illustration of this feeling is the obvious homage paid by James Grant, the author of the well-known *Random Recollections of the House of Commons*, to the person of Thomas Wentworth Beaumont, M.P. for Northumberland in the 1833 and 1835 parliaments, whom he described as thoroughly independent, with no party allegiance, great integrity of character, and an income of nearly £100,000 a year.[9] A lower house composed entirely of Wentworth Beaumonts would have made government impossible. Nevertheless no constituency liked to feel that its representative was the hired hack of either party or executive. In such an atmosphere proposals for the payment of members were not likely to thrive and in fact the notion, along with annual parliaments, receded into the background of radical thought as the least practicable of future reforms. A sound, if illogical, instinct insisted that a member of parliament should be demonstrably capable of standing on his own feet. Despite all the services of Cobden in a cause which had become identified as a national cause, the fact that he accepted a public subscription made it impossible for the whigs after 1846 to take him into the government.

But quite apart from these material considerations, the English constituencies, except perhaps in the large industrial and metropolitan boroughs, preferred to elect as their representatives in the national assembly men whom they could regard as gentlemen by birth, education, and social standing. Even in the industrial towns it was not uncommon to find the seats split between a radical and a member of the more traditional governing class. Buckingham, for

[9] *Random Recollections of the Lords and Commons* (2nd ser.), ii, 66 sqq.

example, the radical M.P. for Sheffield, had as his colleague a more moderate reformer named Parker, who came of an old Sheffield family, and was well connected with the official classes of the town. His father had been chief magistrate there and Parker himself was a lawyer, an Oxonian, and an Anglican. His support, as might be expected, came mainly from the old, wealthy families.[10] In the election of 1835 at Leeds, Baines the dissenter was returned together with Sir J. Beckett, who was a member of a big Leeds banking family and connected with the Earl of Lonsdale.[11] And elsewhere, in the counties or in the ordinary boroughs, the electors usually chose as their members not their equals but their social superiors. Partly that was due to compulsion, partly to tradition, but partly also to a real preference. An illuminating remark of Lord Ellenborough may be quoted with respect to this: Writing in 1836 to Bonham, the party manager, on the possibility of returning a conservative member for Cheltenham, with the politics of which Ellenborough was intimately acquainted, he added, 'but then, he must be a man who can speak decently, who has some money, and who would fortify the ludicrous vanity and self-importance of the shopkeepers and idle inhabitants of Cheltenham by representing them'.[12] As long as the aristocracy could exercise material influence on one side and appeal to the social instincts of the electorate on the other, there was little need of artificial regulation to maintain the wealth and standing of the House of Commons.

Even the dissenters, as Halévy has pointed out, in spite of their numbers and importance in the constituencies, made no particular effort to return members of their own creed but were content to accept representatives from above. The House of Commons remained on the whole theologically as well as socially homogeneous. Moreover, the leading dissenter of the small group that did enter the House in 1833, Edward Baines, was steadfast in his loyalty to the whigs; and in that respect he was typical of many dissenters in the electorate. Baines had stood for Leeds as a liberal and not as a radical candidate, and he took his seat as a backbencher on the ministerial side. His parliamentary experience, which included dinners with Althorp, Brougham, and Durham, did not shake his adherence to the whigs and when in 1835 a prominent radical attempted to convince him that the whigs were a spent force and

---

[10] Turner, *J. S. Buckingham*, 251.   [11] *Life of Baines*, 186.
[12] Add. MS. 40617, fo. 27.

that the true struggle lay between tories and radicals, Baines retorted that he was sorry to hear it 'as I always had considered the Whigs the mainstay of the country', and added that it was impossible for him to join the radicals.[13] The old view of the dissenters as a solid and united sect supporting radicalism has undergone considerable revision. There is no doubt that dissenters often voted for a radical candidate; but on the other hand they voted perhaps equally often for a whig. And the Wesleyans, indeed, could be counted to a large extent among the supporters of conservatism. Even though the Tory-Wesleyan connexion tended, perhaps, to decrease after 1832, it was still an important point of contact for the conservative party.[14] Politically, the bulk of the dissenters may have supported the left wing in politics; socially they were probably as much a moderating as an innovating element. A long tradition connected the whig aristocracy with the dissenting communities in England and its strength was still unexhausted after 1832.

An example of this kind of attachment among the dissenters of one important town is provided by the evidence taken before a committee that inquired into the 1835 election at York. At that election Lowther, a tory, and Dundas, a whig, had been returned. A third candidate, Barkly, had stood as a liberal, in co-operation with Dundas, although there was a strong element of radicalism in his candidature. He was, however, left at the foot of the poll; 'being a stranger', one witness said, 'and not stating what family he was, it had an influence against him'. He had, it was true, come down armed with a letter from Joseph Hume but 'Mr Hume would not be much liked by the freemen of York'. Nevertheless, Barkly had received some support from the dissenters, including the Quakers. The chairman of his committee was an Independent, and the vice-chairman a member of the Society of Friends. The attitude of the Quakers was particularly interesting. There had been considerable bribery at York in the election of 1832 and their support of Barkly was an attempt to check corruption. On the other hand, their traditional support had always gone to the whigs. The vice-chairman of Barkly's committee stated that he had voted for both Dundas and Barkly, 'for the one on the ground of purity of election, and the other because he was a whig'. Another York Quaker, Joseph Rowntree, stated that he voted for Dundas alone.

[13] *Life of Baines*, 185, 191–5, 207–8.   [14] Cf. Hill, *Toryism and the People*, 20–1.

He did not vote for Barkly because 'my acquaintance with his qualifications was not such as in my opinion justified me in giving a vote, inasmuch as he was comparatively a stranger in York'. It was true, he acknowledged, that Barkly came down with a letter from that distinguished member of the Society of Friends, William Allen; yet 'we are accustomed to think for ourselves'.[15] While such elements of independent outlook, local feeling, aristocratic preference, and whig tradition, still remained to divide the ranks of the dissenters, no serious invasion could be expected of the prescriptive right of the old Anglican ruling classes of squires, merchants, and lawyers to govern the country.

For the ordinary member of the House of Commons, political life not only meant the prerequisite of a private income; it also entailed specific and sometimes heavy outlay. He had to keep himself respectably alive during session, certainly; but he had to win an election first. If he was fortunate he might find a constituency or a patron prepared to take that expense off his shoulders. Macaulay himself had been returned first for Lord Lansdowne's borough of Calne in 1830 and after the Reform Act for Leeds, where, if we are to believe his farewell address in 1834, he was elected 'without canvassing and without expence'. Another great city, Edinburgh, in the first flush of reform, returned two whigs, Jeffrey and Abercromby, free of expense in the first election after the passing of the bill.[16] When Gladstone was returned for the Duke of Newcastle's borough of Newark at the same election, the duke offered 'a handsome contribution towards expenses'.[17] But such cheap passages into the House of Commons were rare, and became rarer as reforming enthusiasm died down with the lapse of years. For most candidates the business of getting into parliament was a costly one.[18]

There was no novelty, of course, in this circumstance. Indeed one of the professed objects of the Reform Act was to reduce the cost of elections so that the respectable candidate of moderate means could put up for parliament without impoverishing himself and his family. But the act neither imposed a maximum for official expenses nor laid down any effective measures against

---

[15] P.P. 1835, x, 283 sqq., 423, 504, 518.
[16] Cockburn, *Life of Jeffrey*, 1, 339.   [17] Morley, *Gladstone*, 1, 66.
[18] For a discussion of the extent to which the two great organized parties could give financial assistance to their candidates in this period, see Appendix C, Party Election Funds.

bribery and corruption. Consequently it did less than was expected
to make elections cheaper than before. A fortune could be almost
as easily spent on a parliamentary election at the beginning of
Victoria's reign as in the age of George III; and for all the declama-
tion of the radicals against the wealth of the fundholder, the sine-
curist, the pensioner, the West Indian nabob, and the government
office holder, a considerable amount of the wealth acquired in
these and other ways flowed back to the lower and middle classes
of the population at each general election. The franchise was still
a financial asset; and even for the non-voter elections meant more
trade, free drinks, and easy money. For most candidates, therefore,
it was imperative to have a good supply of what was very literally
'the necessary'.

There were, in the first place, the legal and open expenses
incidental to candidature and election. The authorized charges
on the candidate were the expenses for erecting booths or hiring
rooms in which to take the poll; the official expenses of the returning officer and poll clerks; and the expenses for the administration
of oaths. In the counties the cost of polling places was not to
exceed £40 each; in the boroughs, not to exceed £25 each. Every
returning officer was to be paid two guineas a day, and every poll
clerk one guinea. In practice, however, election expenses were
settled between the local authorities and the candidate or the
candidate's agent, with little or no reference to the act of parliament regulating such matters. Not only were the statutory expenses
put at an exorbitant amount but all kinds of customary and incidental charges were made; and although the candidates were not
legally liable, they did as a rule accept a kind of prescriptive
liability and paid what was asked or at least roughly what they
thought was proper. In either case they would pay probably far
more than the actual services rendered could justify. The difference
they could put down to personal election expenses. It was difficult
not to be aware that a munificent and gentlemanly refusal to
quibble over financial items was a substantial recommendation for
any candidate. The most important of the standard charges not
authorized by law but commonly paid by the candidates were made
by local officials. Firstly there were the fees of the under-sheriff. A
high but not unusual figure, for example in Devon and Sussex,
was a hundred guineas. In the Cinque Ports, which retained their
separate organization for parliamentary purposes, the deputy

lord-warden made a fixed charge of £17 per candidate. In the
boroughs there was also a fee to the town clerk. This was usually
smaller although it could be as high as £85, as in Montgomery, and
even £105, as at Plymouth. Often there were fees and gratuities for
special services by the sheriff, the under-sheriff, and sheriff's
messengers, which might reach a total of £142 as at Bristol.
Preservation of the peace was another expensive item often borne
by the candidates. In many constituencies the sheriffs employed
special constables or posse men. The charge for such men, often
too peaceful themselves to be effective in inducing others to keep
the peace, was as high as £130 at Bedford, £144 in Berks, £127 at
Yarmouth, and £300 at Norwich. In the eastern division of Norfolk in 1832, 520 posse men were engaged at a total cost of £350.
The engagement of these officers was a matter in which the candidates had an interest other than financial. Often they were the
nominees of electors, who were thus indirectly bribed. In such
circumstances it was comprehensible that their numbers and
wages tended to be higher than seemed positively necessary. A
final item, which must have brought in a considerable sum to the
local authorities, was the charge for certified copies of the electoral
register. In Herefordshire the price was £25 a copy; in Berks the
total charge was £70, and in west Kent £133.[19]

All these were common and regular charges. There were
besides other subsidiary and miscellaneous categories such as
messengers and bannermen whose fees and expenses varied
according to place and circumstance. In Herts the cost of adver-
tising the election in local and London newspapers was £10, borne
by the candidate. At Brentford accommodation at the cost of £2 10s.
was erected for press reporters. At Andover there were more
picturesque items; 'ringers, band, bellman, gaoler, beadle, and
sergeants-at-mace: £35 1s. 6d. Gratuity to band and to men for
drawing in and chairing the members: £29 8s. 6d.' At Beaumaris
the court crier and the sergeants-at-mace received three guineas.
At Hastings the managers of a theatre, in front of which a polling
booth had been erected, were compensated with £30, although the
theatre had only lost two nights and it was alleged that its average
weekly takings were only £5. It appeared that the managers of
the theatre were the town clerk and his partner, which might
explain the circumstances. Frequently an unnecessarily large

[19] P.P. 1834, ix, 281–5, 328, 368–71, 409–10. The figures relate to the election of 1832.

number of poll clerks were engaged. In Middlesex, for the election of 1832, there were eight polling places with sixty-nine polling clerks. In the eastern division of Norfolk there were 114 polling clerks at a total cost of £336. Another item which could prove expensive was the charge for administering oaths. There were five or six oaths chargeable to voters—oaths of allegiance, supremacy, and abjuration, oaths as to identity and voting qualifications, and an oath against bribery—although in practice they were usually omitted. But it was obligatory to put them to any voter if a demand was made, and this was done on occasions to delay the poll or deter the supporters of an opponent. In any case it involved additional expense. In Carmarthenshire 10s. was charged for drawing up the oaths of allegiance, supremacy, and abjuration, and a further 10s. for translating them into Welsh. A similar but more costly item was the practice of objecting to particular voters. This was done to embarrass opponents; and even if the objections were proved to be invalid, there was considerable trouble and expense in getting the objected voter to appear personally to justify his right to vote. In the election of 1832 there was a notorious instance of wholesale objections for party purposes. A freeholder in west Somerset was employed by the solicitor of one of the candidates to sign forms of objection. He actually signed in all about 2,000 forms but nearly all in blank. At the election itself, however, there were no less then 1,700 objections made. Another man in Somerset was also in the habit of signing blank objections—'they were sent down to him in packets for his signature'.[20]

It is not surprising, therefore, that the official expenses of elections sometimes reached an extremely high level. In the election of 1832 the charge of the returning officer in the Lindsey division of Lincolnshire was £1,065. The electorate in that constituency was over 9,000 but in Berkshire with only 6,000 electors the charge was £752. In north Lancashire, another large constituency, the charge was £543. At an uncontested election in Herefordshire the charge was £235. Cambridgeshire cost £892; south Devon £703; east Gloucestershire £751; west Kent £734; and the North Riding of Yorkshire £781. The boroughs could be almost as expensive. Of the metropolitan boroughs Westminster cost £362; Finsbury £463; and the City £522. Charges were made of £426

---

[20] P.P. 1834, ix, 375–6. In 1835 electors were relieved of the obligation of taking the oaths of allegiance, supremacy, and abjuration (5 & 6 Wm. IV, c. 36).

at Brighton, £874 at Bristol, £729 at Manchester, and £444 at Preston. Newcastle-on-Tyne cost £422 and an uncontested election at Plymouth £130. These were the more expensive constituencies. The average charge made by returning officers in England and Wales was only £134. But this figure does not represent all the official expenses as often the candidates themselves made their own arrangements for erecting polling booths and paying the special constables. Moreover the large number of small boroughs, and the many constituencies in which there was no contest, bring down the average cost to a deceptive figure. A select average expense for contested boroughs, especially those above a certain size, would be at a considerably higher level. It cannot, on the other hand, be maintained that the election of 1832 to which these figures relate was abnormally expensive. As it was the first election under the reformed system, it is possible that the local authorities, out of ignorance or calculation, put more expenses on the candidate than was ultimately acceptable. But the figures for the general election of 1841, when authorities and candidates had experienced three general elections under the new conditions, show a barely perceptible decline from the highest charges of 1832. In the individual constituencies variations occur but there is no substantial change in the general scale of expenses. Among the county constituencies, the election in south Durham cost £718, in Herts £653, in the Lindsey division of Lincoln £681, and in the West Riding of Yorkshire £1,421. Of the boroughs, Bristol cost £452, Manchester £480, Birmingham £356, and Leeds £415. The metropolitan boroughs again ranked high. The cost at Tower Hamlets was £538, at Westminster £523, at Marylebone £442, in the City £404. But at Finsbury, where Wakley and Duncombe were returned unopposed, the charge was only £15 4s.[21]

These figures represent the total expenses charged by local authorities. The candidates divided the cost between themselves, usually in equal proportions but sometimes unequally, the greater share being paid by the successful candidates. It will be seen, moreover, that the greatest expenses usually occurred in the larger constituencies. In the boroughs of less importance the charges would be correspondingly less. On the other hand, it must be remembered that these were merely the formal and official charges

[21] P.P. 1834, IX, 281–2, 602–7; 1842, XXXIII, 623 sqq.; 1843, XLIV, 117 sqq.

which, although in many instances not actually authorized by act of parliament, were acknowledged and paid for by the candidates without any danger of incurring accusations of bribery and corruption. They formed the open and quasi-legal division of a candidate's election expenses. There were other, more individual, items of expense which the candidates were usually prepared to incur; some that were sanctioned by law or electoral conventions; and others that could less easily bear the light of public knowledge or parliamentary inquiry.

In the first instance, there were various forms of expense which occupied a middle ground between official charges and illegal practices. These were mainly concerned with inducing an elector to come to the poll and entertaining him when he was there. Canvassing was an unexceptional activity which yet could involve a good deal of expense, particularly in the county constituencies. Most of the work was no doubt done voluntarily by the candidate and his friends but often agents were employed and in any case the innkeepers probably profited. But for the candidate, perhaps the chief trials of canvassing were other than financial. Lord Seymour, canvassing Totnes in 1835, went round with his brother who 'shook hands and drank currant wine with the constituents'. Attwood, perhaps wisely in view of the size of his constituency, relied on kissing rather than currant wine. He wrote in 1837 that he had received about 10,000 kisses, chiefly from old women although some had come from the most beautiful women in the world. 'My lips', he added, 'are quite sore with the kisses of yesterday.'[22] More expensive, but involving less personal sacrifice, was the task often assumed by candidates of placing voters' names on the official list. This was done either by paying the ordinary cost of registration, or in the case of freemen, paying the dues for their admittance. At Maldon, for example, it was an established practice to pay the fee of £1 or £2 for the cost of admission to the freedom of the borough in order to secure the voter's interest at election time. Similar practices obtained at Coventry, Ipswich, and other towns.[23] Registration was an even more expensive and important factor.

The Reform Bill [wrote Peel in 1839] has made a change in the position of parties and in the practical working of public affairs,

[22] Mallock, *Letters of the Duke of Somerset*, 58; Wakefield, *Life of Attwood*, 320.
[23] P.P. 1835, VIII, 35–6, 65, 81.

which the authors of it did not anticipate. There is a perfectly new element of political power—namely, the registration of voters, a more powerful one than either the Sovereign or the House of Commons. That party is strongest in point of fact which has the existing registration in its favour. . . . We shall soon have, I have no doubt, a regular systematic organisation of it. Where this is to end, I know not, but substantial power will be in the Registry Courts and there the contest will be determined.[24]

Organization of a sort was in fact already in existence before that date.

It was soon realized after 1832 that where parties were evenly balanced, the decision of the revising barristers might decide the issue of an election, and that even under more unfavourable circumstances, the size of a hostile majority might be diminished before an election took place. Prospective candidates and local politicians began to make arrangements for the periodical registration courts. Lists of new supporters were added to the electoral rolls; rates and taxes were sometimes paid to qualify existing voters; lawyers were engaged to defend the qualifications of friends and disprove those of enemies; and occasionally, where the opposition was inactive, or taken unawares, lists of favourable but otherwise unqualified names were placed upon the roll for the sanction of the revising barrister. 'As a class', Joseph Parkes told a parliamentary committee in 1835, 'attorneys obtain more fraudulent votes than any other men in the country.'[25] The extent of this kind of party work, and the amount of money spent on it, depended of course on the initiative and the resources of the local politicians and their agents; but only rarely could it have been safe to neglect it entirely. For the sitting member it was a necessary item in the general nursing of his constituency; for the candidate it was the first skirmishing of the election campaign. Figures of the expenses in connexion with registration are difficult to obtain but the work of preparing the lists, bringing up witnesses, and feeing lawyers must have been extremely expensive. At Cheltenham it was estimated in 1840 that the conservatives had spent over £200 in getting between 600 and 700 adverse voters struck off the lists.[26] And in many cases the money for this kind of work came from the

---

[24] Parker, *Peel*, II, 368, where it is wrongly dated. See Aspinall, *Arbuthnot Corr.*, 210, n. 5.
[25] P.P. 1835, VIII, 113.   [26] Add. MS. 40617, fo. 94.

candidate's pocket, either directly or in the shape of subscriptions to the local party managers or associations.

Even when the preliminary work was over and the election actually arrived, most voters hoped to profit in some way from the generosity of their future representatives. It was to a certain extent more a question of hospitality than of bribery. The electorate as a whole expected entertainment at election time and the candidates who played no part in providing it suffered in the general estimation and on the hustings. Often there was no discernible trace in it of any kind of persuasion or bribery. This was most marked at the county elections where, owing to the nature of the constituencies, bribery was rare and the chief form of direct expenditure on the electors was the provision of vehicles to bring them in from the outlying districts. Entertainment, or in the phrase of the day, 'treating' of country voters was usually confined to actual polling days, and was rarely more than bread and cheese and a jug of ale for one's supporters before they set off home again. It was the habit in some counties for electors, after they had voted, to be given 5s. or 10s. refreshment tickets which could be spent in neighbouring taverns. But often the opposing candidate agreed to divide the cost of treating. In such cases the provision of entertainment tickets was merely a customary benevolence which could not be regarded in any sense as bribery. Without it, indeed, the poorer class of voters would often not inconvenience themselves by going to the poll. Free rides and free drinks were the necessary inducements for many country voters to exercise a franchise of which they were the custodians rather than the controllers.[27] In the boroughs, however, treating was carried on much more extravagantly and resembled more nearly a form of corruption. But even here there were often particular kinds of entertainment sanctioned by long custom and regarded by the electors less as a bribe than as a perquisite. At Coventry there was an institution known as 'hot suppers and hot breakfasts' for the electorate, and in addition, a 'peculiar election beverage without which numbers of freemen hang back and are unwilling to vote; it is called "buttered ale"'.[28] At Ipswich was a similar practice of giving election breakfasts. At Newcastle-under-Lyme there was a custom of distributing money among the poorer electors after the election under the name of 'market money' or 'dinner money'. Each person

[27] P.P. 1835, VIII, 34, 98.   [28] P.P. 1835, VIII, 95.

received about half a sovereign and it was apparently given by both parties.[29] Entertainment of a similar kind, even if lacking these picturesque names, was common in most borough constituencies. A popular and convenient method, which furnished some control over expenditure, was to issue tickets which enabled the holders to procure food and drink at various inns and beershops. In the elections at Leicester in 1832 and 1835 these entertainment tickets were issued by the agents at the beginning of the election campaign and the holders were entitled to go to public houses and eat and drink free of charge every day until the polling was concluded. The daily value of these tickets was estimated at 3s. 6d. or 5s.[30] At Bristol there was a similar system of giving away entertainment tickets valued at about 3s. Elsewhere it was usual for candidates or their agents to come to an agreement with the innkeepers and publicans of their party to furnish free drinks to their voters within moderation.

The state of the smaller and more corrupt boroughs, where this kind of free drink distribution might continue for several weeks previous to an election, can be left for a while to the imagination. What must first be stressed is the profitable trade which electioneering brought to innkeepers. The hosts of the White Lion and the Blue Boar, who hung out their party flags and competed for the custom of the drunken but ticketed electors, expected to be reimbursed somewhere; and at elections there was only one ultimate source of wealth—the candidate's pocket. An enormous quantity of liquor, even if only small beer and country-brewed ale, must have been consumed at the candidates' expense; and where no check on accounts could exist, it would have been unnatural had the landlords underestimated the total sums in the bills they presented for payment. Landlords, like lawyers, grew wealthy on elections, and it is clear that the whole system of treating was as much due to pressure from the electorate as to design on the part of the candidates and their agents. It was in the interest of the publicans for as much money to be spent in entertainment as possible, and irrespective of any party attachments they united to force a system of treating on the candidates.[31] From the candidate's point of view, the publicans formed an important element in the electorate which it was important to conciliate. Not only were they numerous in themselves (in Hereford there were forty publicans

[29] P.P. 1842, viii, 6, 84.   [30] P.P. 1835, viii, 125–6.   [31] P.P. 1835, viii, 34.

in a constituency of 900) but they had influence over others. Each inn or beershop had its regular customers who out of sociability or maudlin generosity might be induced to promise a vote to the candidate whose colours adorned their familiar taproom. Inns and taverns were, moreover, the social and organizing centres of election campaigns. It was there that committees sat, meetings were held, speeches were delivered, songs sung, drinks served, and sovereigns changed hands. In the election of 1841 in Southampton, where there was an electorate of 1,500, it was reckoned that the majority of the 48 inns and 102 beershops in the town were open for election time under the pretext of housing committees or furnishing committee rooms. The majority of these publicans were of course electors.[32] It was essential to have the public houses on one's side and their support was best secured by lavishly treating the electorate to the landlord's beer at the candidate's expense. A single item will indicate the amount of money which could be expended in this way. At the Hertford election of 1832 the election entertainment bill (beer, wines, cigars, meals, rooms) of one innkeeper in the tory interest came to £440.[33] Even in the rarer instances where the candidate did not foot the bill, the effect was much the same. Dawson, Peel's brother-in-law, reported during a by-election at Devonport in 1839 that he was having constant meetings at public houses where every man paid for himself.[34] As long as liquor was consumed and the reckoning paid, landlords had cause to welcome election contests. Indeed publicans themselves often became vote-mongers in a small way. At Southampton each little beershop keeper was said to have influence over four or five voters and could hope to gain more. 'When a lot of men get together and have plenty to drink,' observed one witness, 'they pledge themselves; they say, "These are nice fellows, I will vote for your party"; it influences many.'[35]

With such heavy sums involved and with doubtless some occasionally obvious profiteering on the part of the publicans, it sometimes happened that candidates refused or omitted to pay their bills. Even so the publicans rarely suffered. The unpaid accounts were held over to the next election and presented as a matter of course to the candidate of the party in whose interest they had been incurred. Often, therefore, candidates new to a borough

---

[32] P.P. 1842, VIII, 471.
[34] Add. MS. 40617, fo. 79.
[33] P.P. 1833, IX, 296.
[35] P.P. 1842, VIII, 507, 599.

were obliged, in order to have a chance of success, to pay the
debts of their predecessors. At Harwich, for example, Le Marchant found in 1841 an outstanding bill of £500, owed by a
candidate at the previous election, which he duly paid.[36] At
Sudbury, a corrupt and expensive borough that rarely had the
same members in successive parliaments, the practice had hardened into an institution. New candidates were obliged to pay the
unpaid bills of publicans and other election profiteers, and they
in their turn left a trail of debts to be settled by the next-comers.
These transferred debts were known as 'fixtures' and were usually
kept at a high level. One publican admitted that he sent in a bill
for £60 before the election of 1841 because he had been behind at
previous elections and wanted to make up his alleged deficiencies.[37]
But whatever arrangements were made, the publicans could
rarely have been out of pocket. Defaulting on election debts was
the one unpardonable sin for candidates or parties; and a strong
vested interest was in existence to chastise it with the punishment
of non-election.

This special attitude among the publicans was to a certain
extent reflected in the electorate at large. It is, in fact, easy to
overlook, in constructing a charge of bribery and corruption
against the candidate, the extent to which the electors expected
and insisted on bribery. At the time of the passing of the Reform
Act it was remarked by more than one member of the House of
Commons that though bribery was one of the chief evils of the
existing system, the bill would do nothing to check that evil.
Viscount Newark, for example, observed that 'as long as two
parties were found ready and willing to play at the game of
corruption, so long would it be continued'.[38] Russell himself
admitted that special legislation would be needed to deal with the
problem of bribery, and in introducing the second version of the
reform bill in the parliament of 1831 he held out hopes of such a
measure.[39] But the real stumbling-block was that the exchange
of money or other favours was firmly rooted in the electoral
system; and electors even more perhaps than the elected were
prepared to connive at any evasion of the anti-bribery laws.
Frankland Lewis, the member for Radnorshire, put this point
very clearly in August 1831. 'The alarming feature of the Bill', he

---

[36] P.P. 1842, v, 100.   [37] P.P. 1844, xviii, 260–75.
[38] *Hansard*, ii, 1128–9, 1174.   [39] *Ibid.*, iv, 339.

said, 'was that it confined its operations to prevent the rich practising bribery, without taking into consideration the readiness of the other classes to receive bribes.' He alluded specifically to 'a system which prevailed in great towns of keeping people in clubs, congregated to drink and to smoke, and by these means a constant system of bribery in the shape of feasting was continued from one election to another'.[40] The evidence supporting his view is considerable. There is the well-known passage in Greville's diary on the state of Maidstone: 'the one prevailing object among the whole community is to make money of their votes, and though . . . there are some exceptions, they are very few indeed'.[41] A less quoted but more sympathetic and revealing comment was made by T. P. O'Connor when discussing the state of political morality in his own town of Athlone at the period (1847–56) when William Keogh, later solicitor-general, attorney-general, and puisne judge in Ireland, was its representative in parliament.

> My native town [he wrote] was neither better nor worse than most of the Irish and English constituencies of the time. Its distinction was that the number of voters was small and that, therefore, the amount of the bribe was high. The bribe averaged £30 or £40 the vote; and there were tales of a vote having run up to £100 in one of Keogh's elections. With many of the people the periodic bribe entered into the whole economy of their squalid and weary lives. Men continued to live in houses who had better have lived in lodgings because the house gave them the vote. The very whisper of a dissolution sent a visible thrill through the town.[42]

Roebuck indeed went so far as to assert that this attitude was at the back of much opposition to the ballot. 'What they desire is to be well paid by the candidates and for this reason they dislike the ballot.'[43]

This last passage was written in May 1832 before the Reform Act had taken effect, but even the new constituencies and the new class of voter were not exempt from charges of venality. In the great majority of boroughs the old voters still exercised the franchise and the practices of the old régime which they naturally continued easily spread to the newly enfranchised electors. A good example of this kind of contagious process was afforded at Penryn

---

[40] *Ibid.*, VI, 606. [41] *Greville Memoirs*, III, 133. [42] O'Connor, *Memoirs*, I, 380.
[43] Leader, *Roebuck*, 34. The reference was to the electors of Christchurch.

and Falmouth. The old and notoriously corrupt borough of Penryn had been enlarged by the addition of Falmouth. But the only effect was to enlarge the area and extent of corruption. The systematized bribery at Penryn survived the Reform Act (the price of a single vote in 1841 was £4), and rapidly gained a hold among the more well-to-do electors of Falmouth. The only difference seemed to be that whereas among the poorer classes of Penryn, the price of a vote was stabilized at a fixed and moderate sum, some of the wealthier inhabitants in Falmouth made demands for larger sums more in keeping with their standards of living.[44] Those candidates and agents who hoped that the Reform Act would put an end to electoral corruption were soon disillusioned. The electors in general still attached a financial value to their vote and exerted an irresistible influence on the candidates to continue the old methods. An illustration may be given from Yarmouth. There it had been the custom to pay two guineas to each voter. At the first election under the Reform Act it was decided to discontinue this payment and the agents experienced in consequence considerable difficulty in making their canvass. The electors displayed an obvious reluctance to promise their votes and complained that the two guineas was their birthright and that the Reform Act had taken away their privileges and ruined them. In spite of their protests no money was paid out at the 1832 election and the result was a feeling of profound dissatisfaction among the electors, especially the freemen. At the next election, in 1835, little money was paid out before the polling but a strong rumour was current in the town at election time that the red or tory party would give two guineas each to their supporters. Not surprisingly the two sitting members, both whigs, were defeated and the tories, Praed and Baring, were elected in their place. About 550 electors who had voted tory were paid two guineas each after the election and there was a strong suspicion that bribery had actually been carried on by the tories even during the election. The number of registered electors was 1,600 and the successful candidates secured about 770 votes each.[45]

When reversion to the old technique of electioneering brought such immediate success, few candidates or agents could long withstand the temptation to concede to the prejudices of the electorate in favour of material inducements. When W. M. Praed was down

44 P.P. 1842, v, 236.   45 P.P. 1835, x, 12–77.

at Warwick assisting the tory candidate, Canning, at a by-election in 1836, he sent in a report to Bonham which illustrates the perpetual dilemma of electioneering in this period. 'There has been so much *trouble* in Warwick', he wrote, 'that a man cannot give away a glass of ale without tremblings and the canvass has been very dry. Many voters consequently hold back and bide their time. I hope the Blue faction will be as scrupulous as the Orange. But, alas! a Whig may steal a horse while a Tory, etc., etc.' Canning's principal agent told Praed that 'neither party could say whose election it is to be' and added significantly that '*management* might win it for either'.[46] According to Greville's informant on Maidstone, even the new electors were marked by the same general characteristics. 'I asked him what were the new constituency. "If possible worse than the old". The people are generally alive to public affairs—look into the votes and speeches of members, give their opinions—but are universally corrupt.'[47] This was not simply the after-dinner conversation of two cynical men of the world with a prejudice against the Reform Act and all it stood for. A great body of evidence confirms their generalizations. Not all boroughs were touched with corruption but the exceptions were rare. Not even the size of a constituency was a safeguard. Bribery and intimidation were features of at least two large constituencies, Westminster and Liverpool. At Liverpool it was said that the old voters demanded money, drink, and ribands, and would not promise their vote without them.[48] It was the opinion of Joseph Parkes, the whig parliamentary agent, that scarcely a single borough was free from venality; and few men in this period could speak from such a wide knowledge of electioneering as he possessed. 'I consider', he told a parliamentary committee in 1835, 'that almost every place has a system of corruption peculiar to itself where the same end is obtained and the same system of corrupt practices prevails but in different modes.'[49]

This being so, the path of the politician who wished both to preserve his independence and to be returned by the unpurchased votes of his fellow-countrymen, was beset with difficulties. If he sat for a large constituency he might find himself hedged round by the convictions or passions of his constituents, even by his own pledges to them. If he was returned through the influence of some

[46] Add. MS. 40617, fo. 21. [47] *Greville Memoirs*, III, 133.
[48] P.P. 1833, X, 18–19. [49] P.P. 1835, VIII, 92.

electoral magnate, there was inevitably the sense of dependence. If he put up for an ordinary constituency, he was forced into illegal expenditure. The career of John Cam Hobhouse, later Lord Broughton, is a case in point. In 1832, as candidate for Westminster, he had pledged himself to support the abolition of the house and window tax. After the election he became a member of the whig ministry which collectively insisted on the maintenance of the measure. Hobhouse, perhaps unduly squeamish, resigned both from the government and from the House of Commons, stood for Westminster, and was defeated. That was in 1833. The following year he was elected for Nottingham and retained his seat until 1847. His first election for that notorious borough cost him under £2,000; that of 1837 £4,000.[50] But clearly his position there was irksome. In May 1841 when the whig ministry was about to fall, he confided to his diary that

> I shall not go back to Nottingham, and have a great repugnance to looking elsewhere for a seat. After representing Westminster for so long, and maintaining, I trust, there and even at Nottingham, a character somewhat above the ordinary level of politicians, I think I should lower myself by dropping down to some insignificant and notoriously venal constituency or even by standing a contest for some large place upon the only terms on which such battles are now fought; for as a Minister I should have no chance at any town where ultra-Radical or anti-Poor Law pledges are required.

However, he did put up for Nottingham again in the general election of 1841 and was once more returned. The explanation appeared six years later in his diary after he had been defeated at the next general election.

> The truth was [he wrote in 1847] I did not feel angry; knowing that the election had been won because I had refused to do what I had before done, viz. *bribe the electors*. Wakefield told me that Gisborne's election in 1843 had been won by bribing one hundred and fifty voters, which was not found out. He mentioned this to Gisborne in my presence. Wakefield told me that, on this occasion, very small sums, even a shilling, had been given for a vote, and that six or seven hundred fellows waited until nine o'clock, not believing that I would not bribe them, and then took anything they could get; some, out of spite, voted for nothing.[51]

[50] P.P. 1842, v, 149.   [51] Broughton, *Recollections*, VI, 21, 198.

In such circumstances it was inevitable that most candidates were prepared to embark on expenditure other than the legal charges or the conventional treating of electors, and that most parliamentary agents found it necessary to resort to illegal forms of bribery and corruption which, if proved before a parliamentary committee, would render the election of their candidate invalid. Few borough members in the period after the Reform Act were returned by methods that were strictly in accordance with the law; and only tacit agreement between opponents, lack of proof, or lack of money to finance a parliamentary inquiry, prevented an avalanche of disputed elections after each general election. The most convenient and most effective of the illegal proceedings at election time was straightforward bribery. The price of a vote was often as well known after 1832 as in the halcyon days of the eighteenth century. At Leicester it was £1 or £2; at York £2 for a plumper[52] and £1 for a single vote. At Stafford in 1832 the prices began at £2 10s. for a single and £5 for a plumper but rose during the election to £7 and £10; it was said that the new voters were as corrupt as the old and that 852 voters out of a total poll of 1,049 were bribed. Sometimes, in exceptional cases, the price of a vote reached extraordinarily high levels. At Sudbury in 1841 £30 was paid for two votes and £20 for another: the average price at that election was £6 or £7. At Ipswich, in the same general election, £15 and £20 were being given for a vote and it was rumoured that as much as £30 had been offered.[53] At Ludlow, which the Clive family endeavoured to maintain as a pocket borough, at considerable expense to themselves, as much as £30 was actually spent on a single vote and on the polling days, especially towards the close, the price was said to jump to fantastic heights. It was alleged that 75 guineas was then regarded as a moderate figure and that one voter was offered as much as £250.[54] These last figures are probably exaggerated and in any case are exceptional. But there can be no doubt that in most borough elections bribery was practised even if it was not always the deciding factor. The better class voters often needed no inducement to vote for the candidate of

[52] In a two-member constituency each elector could, of course, vote for two candidates. If he 'plumped' for one candidate, leaving his second vote unused, he was said to have given a 'plumper'. The enhanced value to the recipient is obvious.

[53] P.P. 1835, VIII, 93; 1833, XI, 4–7; 1842, VII, 118–20, 211.

[54] P.P. 1840, IX, 86, 157, 161, 228. The evidence of some of these witnesses must be treated with caution, but there can be little doubt that very large sums of money changed hands at the Ludlow elections.

their principles; and in large constituencies it was financially impossible to pay more than two or three guineas to each voter. In the smaller boroughs, however, where every single vote was known and its importance at once discernible, the price of corruption rose proportionately, and it is comprehensible that towards the end of a closely contested poll higher sums would be offered for the few remaining unattached votes that might finally turn the scale. Often, indeed, many voters (those that Disraeli called the thoughtful voters), deliberately kept back their vote until late in the polling in order to command a higher price. At Bristol, for example, in the 1835 election, the parochial chairmen of Hobhouse's committee reported on the evening of the first day's poll that voters were hanging back in great numbers with the obvious calculation that there would be heavy bribery on the second day. In this instance they paid the penalty that was always risked by such enterprise; the reform candidate was withdrawn.[55]

Besides actual money payments, there were a variety of other rewards for the complaisant voter which could be exploited by the experienced party agent. Sometimes loans were made to needy tradesmen; sometimes the rent of a house was paid, or houses and land let on favourable terms. At Cacrnarvon borough before the election of 1835 the committee of one party secured the control of the contracts for a new harbour pier and advertised that contracts would be let out by the chairman of the committee. It was expected that the votes of about a dozen masons would be secured.[56] Sometimes politico-benevolent societies existed which were confined to the electors of one side and supported by the subscriptions of wealthy men of the party. At Lewes there were two of that nature; the *Bundle of Sticks Society* (liberal) and the *Constitutional Pruning Society* (conservative). At Bristol a conservative benevolent society was founded in 1832 for the freemen of the city, which distributed bread and beef among its members, the refreshment being known as 'blue beef'. Very few of the members contributed anything to the funds of the society and it was obvious that it was merely a cloak for wholesale treating of supporters. The number of members was over 1,000 and an average of 7 lbs. of beef was distributed among them in 1832, and 14 lbs. in 1835.[57]

---

[55] P.P. 1835, VIII, 400–1. It should be noted that following the 1835 election, polling days in borough constituencies were reduced from two to one (5 & 6 Wm. IV, c. 36).

[56] P.P. 1835, VIII, 115.   [57] P.P. 1835, VIII, 400–19; 1842, V, 202–3.

At Chatham after the election of 1835 the commander of the marines' barracks admitted four shopmen (of whom one had voted for the tory candidate, another had an uncle who had similarly voted, and the other two were neutral), to trade with the men in the barracks, while excluding four others, of whom one was a minor and the rest had voted for the whig.[58] Elsewhere tickets exchangeable for goods at local shops were issued, or labourers given appropriate presents of new shoes, clothes, and gardening tools. The better class of elector could be given posts in the customs, in government offices, on the new railroads that were beginning to thrust their lines into the countryside; or they could be bribed with contracts and the exclusive custom of wealthy families. 'I have', wrote Lord Seymour of his constituency at Totnes, 'in no way that I can understand neglected the wishes or the interests of the constituency but have obtained for many places under Government and applied for all who have asked me.'[59]

If the number of favourable voters was not adequate, there were often methods of increasing them. 'Frauds of the grossest description', reported a committee in 1834, were committed during elections by interested agents, especially the parish overseers responsible for sending in lists of electors. In one case 130 voters out of a total of 500 were either paupers or freemen outside the legal distance. At Westminster cases occurred of voters who impersonated dead men and others who discovered the numbers of certain electors from the register and voted with that number in place of the rightful owner. In another constituency 'all the paupers polled from the poorhouse at a guinea a head'. There was something almost importunate in this ingenious and civic desire to exercise the franchise. When even these enthusiasts failed to bring victory, the day was lost indeed. 'I do not see how we can win', whispered Mr. Rigby's agent towards the end of the second day's poll at Darlford, 'we have polled all our dead men and Millbank is seven ahead.'[60]

The central circumstance was that elections, particularly contested elections, brought money into the constituency. From the lawyers down through the publicans to the electors themselves, and even below to the unenfranchised mob who chaired the man of their own colour and groaned at the man who opposed him,

[58] P.P. 1835, IX, 3–12.   [59] Mallock, *Letters of the Duke of Somerset*, 86.
[60] Disraeli, *Coningsby*, Bk. V, Ch. 4. See also P.P. 1834, IX, 279, 309, 385.

the periodic parliamentary elections were like the regular playing
of the fountains of benevolence. It followed that the real as distinct from the official expenses of elections were usually high and
often outrageous. Greville reported that the election of Lord
Douro and Scarlett at Norwich in 1837 was said to have cost them
£50,000.[61] More authoritatively the Duke of Bedford told Lord
John Russell in 1834 that £28,000 had been spent by one side at
Bedford, and added not without reason, 'it makes my hair stand
on end'.[62] These reports, however, were probably both based on
hearsay and may be discounted accordingly; though they at least
indicate what contemporary opinion thought not incredible.
More sober calculations were provided by a parliamentary committee in 1842 which inquired into allegations of corrupt practices in certain boroughs in the 1841 election. The cost of the
elections to the successful candidates were stated as follows:

Harwich (2 members)	£6,300
Nottingham (2 members)	£12,000
Lewes (2 members)	£5,000
Reading (2 members)	£3,500
Penryn & Falmouth (2 members)	£4,000
Bridport (2 members)	£5,400

It will be borne in mind that this represented only the expenditure by the victorious candidates. At Nottingham, for example,
where Hobhouse and Larpent had defeated Walter and Charlton,
the two unsuccessful candidates had expended between £4,000
and £5,000, making a total of nearly £17,000 for the 5,000 electors
of Nottingham. In any case, however, these sums were merely the
estimates or statements of the election agents; and in view of the
circumstances under which the information was elicited, they were
probably underestimates.[63] At Southampton, at the same general
election, another parliamentary committee found that one side
alone had spent £5,000 and that both together had spent at least
£7,000 on a constituency of less than 1,500. It appeared that in
this borough expenditure at elections had been on the increase
since the Reform Act.[64] But perhaps the most expensive borough
of all that came under the scrutiny of a parliamentary committee

[61] *Greville Memoirs*, III, 387.   [62] Russell, *Early Corr.*, II, 66.
[63] P.P. 1842, V, 77–84, 88.   [64] P.P. 1842, VIII, 265, 470.

in this period was Yarmouth, a two-member constituency, where it was reckoned that the average expense on each side was as much as £10,000.[65] Judging by the evidence that came before these committees in the thirties and forties, a borough election costing each side from £2,000 to £5,000 could not be regarded as abnormal.

A rough check can be applied to these figures from sources not subject to the exaggerations of rumour or the caution inspired by official inquiries. The cheapest of all elections presumably were uncontested returns for pocket boroughs. Sir George Clerk's bills for his elections at Stamford show that in the by-election of 1838 he paid £258. This may not have been the final figure and in any case it represented a scaling-down of original charges totalling £270. For another by-election in 1845[66] a bill of £348 is preserved, composed of such items as lawyers' fees, printing and advertisements, hustings, bell-ringers, and band. All these, it will be observed, were legal items of expense. In enclosing the account his agent expressed the hope that Clerk would not find them excessive—'my instructions were to satisfy every person yet due regard being had to proper Economy'.[67] Even the most sheltered seats therefore had their price. In more normal constituencies of course expenses ran much higher than this. Bonham in 1836 was budgeting for an expenditure of £1,000 for a seat at Lincoln which for cheapness and certainty he thought would be hard to beat.[68] Lord Melville, when considering the prospects for starting his son as candidate for Leith in 1835, estimated that his expenses would be just over £1,000.[69] Praed, in a letter to Herries, said that his contest at Yarmouth in 1835 cost him £1,500 which he regarded as 'a very serious encumbrance to start with'.[70] Even so it was a more modest sum than would have been anticipated from the committee's report on Yarmouth referred to above which followed soon after the election. One does not know, however, how much of the joint expenses was contributed by the other successful tory candidate Thomas Baring,[71] who as a member of the great and wealthy banking family of that name would probably be in a better position to meet an untoward strain on his purse than his

[65] P.P. 1835, x, 19. [66] Consequent on his appointment as Master of the Mint.
[67] Welford to Clerk, 7 March and 20 March 1845 (Clerk Papers, T/188/81).
[68] Add. MS. 40422, fo. 289. [69] Add. MS. 40405, fo. 28.
[70] Add. MS. 40409, fo. 299.
[71] Second son of Sir Thomas Baring, Bart., and nephew of Lord Ashburton.

poetic and more talented barrister colleague. George Dawson told Peel that he estimated the costs of his election contest at Devonport in 1835 as £1,344. Sir Frederick Trench, who sat for Scarborough with the support of the Rutland interest from 1835 to 1847, told Peel once that his average expense at an election was from £1,500 to £1,600. This was clearly regarded as a moderate sum.[72] The local conservatives at Penryn and Falmouth considered £3,000 to be the minimum necessary to fight a by-election in 1839.[73] The same sum was required by the conservative party managers for fighting the Westminster constituency in 1841.[74]

In special circumstances the costs were naturally higher. Lord Hertford in 1841 was prepared to go up to £4,000 to get a seat in the House of Commons for Spencer de Horsey.[75] Sir James Graham, as a result of his secession from the whigs in 1834, was defeated in Cumberland, after having been five times returned as county member, in a bitter contest which cost him £4,000. He was prepared to spend that as a debt of honour to the party he had joined, but a repetition of such an outlay was more than he could afford, and he began to look about for a borough constituency where aristocratic and party connexion might stand in lieu of sovereigns.[76] At a by-election at Dublin in January 1842 the estimated expenses of a single candidate were even higher.

> Mr. Vance [wrote Eliot the Irish Secretary to Goulburn] has been pronounced to be an unfit man and has been thrown overboard somewhat unceremoniously. He was ready to put down £4,000 but was told that £8,000 at least was necessary. Gregory (a grandson of the old under Secy.) would stand if £3,000 or £4,000 were sufficient but cannot afford more. . . . Will our friends open their purse-strings? £2 or 3,000 would put success beyond a doubt.[77]

From the evidence of these sources where there is no reason to suppose either ignorance or a desire to falsify, it is clear that the figures produced by the various parliamentary committees of inquiry were not exaggerated or applicable only to unusual cases. In general there could have been few boroughs open to genuine

[72] Add. MS. 40411, fo. 160; 40598, fo. 190.   [73] Add. MS. 40427, fo. 278.
[74] Add. MS. 40496, fo. 86.   [75] Add. MS. 40485, fo. 325.
[76] Add. MS. 40616, fo. 84.
[77] Add. MS. 40476, fos. 92–3. Gregory was successful in the election. According to his later account, the contest on the conservative side cost £9,000 of which he paid £4,000, the rest being defrayed by supporters. One major item of expenditure recorded in the vouchers was, 'For 1500 freemen, gratification, at £3 per head, £4,500.' (Gregory, *Autobiography*, 58.)

contests which offered much hope to a candidate who could not back his candidature to the extent of at least a thousand pounds. Most successful candidates probably spent much more. When the parties on both sides were equally matched, equally wealthy, and equally determined, and where the constituency was large and corrupt, the expenses for a single candidate might easily rise from something under £2,000 to something over £5,000.

Even then one final, if contingent, item of expense had sometimes to be encountered: the cost of defending (or presenting) an election petition. Every general election of the period was followed by a large number of petitions controverting the validity of various election returns on grounds of bribery or other illegal practices. The 1832 election, for instance, produced some forty-nine disputed election cases though less than half were actually considered by an election committee, the majority being withdrawn or allowed to lapse. This was not exceptional. The elections of 1837 and 1852 were far more prolific in the number of inquiries to which they gave rise. The first twenty years after the Reform Act, covering six general elections, saw no less than 185 inquiries into disputed elections; and there were more than twice that number of petitions.[78] The expense to both sides in disputed election cases was often considerable. Indeed it was the main reason why the number of petitions that reached the inquiry stage was far less than the number of petitions originally presented; and why the number of petitions was far less than the number of elections in which grounds for an appeal existed. Even a candidate validly elected might well shrink from meeting the costs of a determined election appeal. One notorious example of this occurred actually during the reform bill debates. On 17 January 1832 Lord Ashley (later 7th Earl of Shaftesbury) announced in the House of Commons that in view of a petition that had been brought against his return for Dorset, he had decided not to resist it from sheer inability to meet the expense involved, although he solemnly declared on his honour that he believed his return to be a good one and he could prove it to be so.[79] Hume took the opportunity to say that this was one of the clearest arguments for reform that he had ever heard. But the Reform Act did nothing to make such occurrences impossible or even unlikely in the future. How expensive these election cases could be may be seen from the fact

[78] See Appendix A, Election Petitions 1832–52.   [79] *Hansard*, IX, 561.

that O'Connell estimated his cost in defending the Dublin election petition of 1835 as between £1,000 and £1,500. Yet he
thought that the petitioners had spent five times as much as the
defence.[80] Even if there was exaggeration in his conception of the
cost to his opponents, it was money well spent from the conservative point of view since the result of the petition was to unseat
O'Connell and his colleague and return two tories. Disputed
election cases of course affected only a small proportion of the total
number of successful candidates in any given election. Nevertheless, coming after the main verdict of the polls, they possessed a
kind of marginal importance which added to the keenness and
therefore to the cost of the parliamentary litigation they involved.
If, as often happened, the case was settled privately between the
two parties concerned after proceedings had begun before the
election committee, it was usually arranged on a basis of compromise in which the sitting member was obliged to give a *quid
pro quo* even if he retained his seat in the House. In any case, therefore, election petitions formed yet another financial risk in the
expensive game of politics.

The risk was all the more serious since the initial expenses of an
election might all be wasted as the result of the chance composition
of the election committee chosen to try the case. When few elections were free from illegal practices of some kind, the permanence
of the initial victory on the hustings depended on three factors: the
ability of the opposition to finance proceedings before a committee,
their skill in producing evidence that would prove their case, and
the composition of the committee itself. Until after the accession
of Victoria the machinery for trying disputed elections was still the
old Grenville committees. Only in 1839 were they abandoned for
committees chosen by a general election committee nominated by
the speaker.[81] Before that date, at least, party feeling played a
considerable part in guiding the committees towards a decision.
O'Connell on one occasion asserted that the decisions of parliamentary election committees were always partisan and challenged
the House of Commons to deny that the issue of every case depended always on the constitution of the committee and never
on the merits of the petition.[82] This was perhaps only an over-
statement of a good case. The conservative vote of censure on

[80] Fitzpatrick, *O'Connell Corr.*, I, 525; II, 13.   [81] See below, Ch. 10, p. 257.
[82] *Hansard*, XLI, 105–17, 265–70.

O'Connell for this reflection on the integrity of the committees of the House was merely a conventional party gesture. Most of them must have agreed in private on the substance of his charge. Goulburn, chatting with holiday friendliness to Macaulay a few months later, admitted as much.[83] 'Without adopting the libellous imputations of O'Connell', wrote Aberdeen to Princess Lieven in a more guarded strain, 'there is no doubt that the decisions of these committees have ceased to give satisfaction; and that in truth they are so often pronounced under a strong political bias, as to render some change absolutely necessary.'[84] It is fairly clear that when the evidence of petition and counter-petition was equally convincing or equally dubious, party loyalty contributed a decisive element to the final verdict of the committees. Where on the other hand there was a conclusive case, the composition of the committee might not be so important. Election petitions could be placed in two categories: strong cases that could stand on their merits before all but the most biased tribunal, and weak cases that needed luck in the ballot if they were to achieve success. 'We shall have six very good cases for petitions', wrote Hardinge to Peel after the general election of 1837, 'which no committee can prevent our getting, and about as many more of the usual class, exclusive of what may arise from Ireland.'[85]

Quite apart from the partiality of committees, however, the task of proving bribery before a parliamentary tribunal was a long and costly process. Until the act of 1841,[86] it was necessary to establish the connexion between the candidate and those responsible for the actual bribery before proceeding with the evidence for the bribery itself. Without proof of agency, the candidate could not be unseated. Elaborate precautions were therefore adopted to obscure the connexion between the candidate and the corruption practised on his behalf. The business of the election was commonly in the hands of the candidate's agent who took care to reveal to his principal as little as possible of the technique of management which secured his return. Money was made to pass from the candidate's bank to the pockets of the electors by circuitous and often untraceable routes; and strangers, arriving, acting and departing in a general atmosphere of finance and furtiveness, were often employed in the last stages of direct contact with the

---

[83] Trevelyan, *Macaulay*, II, 46.
[85] Add. MS. 40314, fo. 182.
[84] *Corr. Lord Aberdeen and Princess Lieven*, I, 103–4.
[86] See below, Ch. 10, p. 257.

electors. Even the relationship between the principal agent and the system of bribery was sometimes covered to prevent any proof of his knowledge or connivance. And as a last resource witnesses who were essential links in tracing the chain of complicity were sent abroad or otherwise concealed until the inquiry was over. After the 1841 act circumstances were eased for petitioners. It was now possible to begin the inquiry with proof of bribery and thus throw a great weight of suspicion on the challenged candidate before any attempt was made to prove agency. The moral presumption of responsibility thus created made proof of agency more convincing and in some cases unnecessary. The Sudbury case, in which bribery was proved without agency, was of considerable importance in establishing a precedent in this connexion.[87] After the Sudbury verdict, it appeared likely that other committees would accept its authority and base decisions on accumulative and circumstantial evidence.

After 1841 successful candidates seemed in consequence more vulnerable to attack than before. But even before that date there was one particular aspect of election law that worked inequitably against them. When a defeated candidate petitioned against the return of his successful opponent on grounds of illegal practices but did not claim the return for himself, it was sometimes ruled that no counter-evidence of illegality could be brought against the petitioner by the defendant. In an election, therefore, where (as usual) both sides had indulged in bribery and corruption, the election might be declared void on petition and the sitting member unseated and rendered incapable of again being returned, leaving the petitioner free to stand once more for election. This was not perhaps a common practice but it formed yet another hazard in the hard and costly road to Westminster.[88]

[87] P.P. 1842, vii, 853. For further details of the case see below, Ch. 7, p. 160.
[88] The committee that inquired into corrupt compromises at Harwich, Nottingham, etc., in 1842, drew attention to this point in their report (P.P. 1842, v, 77 sqq.).

Chapter Six

ELECTORAL VIOLENCE

WITH so much, financially as well as politically, at stake in elections, parties and politicians in many constituencies were apt to use forcible means to help ensure success. Indeed it is not easy to judge among the illicit influences brought to bear upon the electorate whether bribery or coercion was the major factor in impelling it towards a decision. The gentler technique was perhaps more widespread and probably more effective but it is hard to examine the available evidence without the feeling that force in various ways played an important part. In its more refined shape, intimidation could be exercised by the mere threat of dismissal from employment, termination of a tenancy, or refusal to continue patronage. As a rule, only an occasional deterrent example would be necessary to make the system work successfully, although instances of wholesale eviction were not unknown, especially in pocket boroughs. When his influence over Hertford was being threatened by the radical dandy, T. S. Duncombe, between 1830 and 1832, Lord Salisbury ruthlessly ejected tenants in order to secure political obedience; and Duncombe spent much money in finding homes for these domestic political refugees.[1] The system of 'exclusive dealing' or dealing solely with those shops and firms of approved political views, was another common practice. In fashionable towns or where large domestic establishments were maintained, it was an effective control over a certain class of voter. At Westminster, for example, it was said that the shopkeepers were considerably influenced by their wealthy customers. At Leicester the textile manufacturers were reputed to exercise political pressure on their workers by threatening to take away their frames. They only ventured to do this, however, when trade was slack. In better and busier times they were more dependent on their men and anxious to please them.[2] At Nottingham the practice of manufacturers obliging their workmen to vote as they directed was known as 'thumbing'. On the other hand

---

[1] Duncombe, *Life of T. S. Duncombe*, I, 129; P.P. 1833, IX, 200–1.
[2] P.P. 1835, VIII, 42, 131.

two could play at that game and the radicals were not so high-minded as to refuse to take a hand occasionally. At Stockport they revenged themselves on the publicans and shopkeepers who opposed Cobden at the 1837 election by boycotting all who had voted tory, with the agreeable consequence that the market-place soon began to resound with the cry of 'Cobden beef', 'Cobden potatoes', etc., from stall-owners anxious to assure their customers that they belonged to the popular side.[3] At Merthyr Tydfil in 1837 a large anti-Poor Law body of workmen held a meeting in opposition to the candidature of the whig member, John Guest the great ironmaster of Dowlais, and passed a resolution not to deal with any shop people who should vote for him. 'But this', wrote Lady Charlotte Guest, a devoted supporter of her husband though no great lover of the new Poor Law, 'will have but little effect as they were not persons whose custom was worth having. Had they been the respectable class of workmen it would have been otherwise.' On the other hand the moral influence of Guest's own workmen was not without some effect. When Lord Adare, the conservative candidate for the county in the same election, attempted to canvass Dowlais, Lady Guest related that 'a large body, they say 700, of our workmen collected around them and came up with them the whole way crying out "Guest for ever". They made use of no uncivility, but the Little Lord was so frightened that he did not canvass a single vote, and got the Constables to escort him safely back again.'[4]

All this, however, comprised familiar and relatively genteel tactics. Neither side would have had much to complain about had they no more to encounter in their election campaigns than a strict application of the accepted conventions of influence. But there were other, more direct and forcible methods. Among these was the practice of 'cooping', or taking electors into a kind of protective custody a short time before the election. In its milder form cooping was no more than the prudent habit of collecting the already bribed and attached, but unsteady voters a few days before the poll, and conveying them to some safe and comfortable retreat where they were lavishly regaled with food, drink, and tobacco as compensation for their temporary loss of liberty, until the time came for them to be escorted to the polling-booth on

[3] Morley, *Cobden*, 116.
[4] *Diaries of Lady Charlotte Guest*, ed. Earl of Bessborough, 49, 51.

election day to register a tipsy but valid vote for their careful host. Cooping of this nature was common at Nottingham and on one occasion at least gardens belonging to Lord Melbourne were used for this purpose. This was at the election of 1841 when a number of voters were cooped at various places some ten or eleven miles from the borough until polling day. About twenty were put in the grounds of Melbourne Hall, Derbyshire, and there were four other places similarly used. The voters were taken there three or four days before the election and made 'pretty drunk'. Both sides at Nottingham indulged in this practice and probably regarded it as a necessary measure of self-defence. At Leicester the out-voters (i.e. the holders of the old franchise who resided outside the borough but within the statutory limit of seven miles), especially the stocking-makers in the nearby villages, were usually collected into houses and locked up by one or other of the contending parties. They were given food and drink, especially the latter, and on election day taken into Leicester by carriage, 'the greater part of them brought as drunk as they can be to the poll'.[5] In 1847 Edward Seymour, whose son-in-law lost at Horsham by only nine votes, complained bitterly of the methods used by his opponent. 'It is said he gave a thousand pounds for five votes!!!', he wrote with more irascibility than credibility, and continued in a more moderate strain, 'certain it is that voters were made tipsy and locked up, besides all sorts of violence quite in the spirit of fifty years ago'.[6] At Cambridge in the 1835 election it was reported that 'the worst features of the old system were maintained of cooping and taking away voters and keeping them drunk'.[7] Cooping of the more unpleasant kind consisted in abducting the supporters of an opponent and keeping them out of the way until the election was over. Someone who had contested the borough of Lewes at more than one election remarked that one very expensive part of the Lewes election is putting the town in a state of siege, which we are forced to do to prevent carrying off voters'.[8] The first variety of cooping was of course often a safeguard against the second. 'Today', wrote Sir James Graham to Bonham during his election at Dorchester in 1841, 'two of our voters have been spirited away [sc. from Bridport] and brought over here in disguise, and I am now having an hunt made after them. I hope we

---

[5] P.P. 1835, VIII, 126–7; 1842, V, 127–8.
[6] Add. MS. 40599, fo. 131.
[7] P.P. 1835, VIII, 8.
[8] P.P. 1842, V, 186.

shall find them; if we do, we shall coop them up till Tuesday and send them to the poll.'[9]

In Ireland, as might be expected, cooping was carried on with a zest and colourfulness that sometimes reached spectacular proportions. In county Carlow, for example, it was the practice for the landlords to 'sweep the countryside' of voters several days before the election and keep them comfortably under watch and ward to prevent them being got at by the opposition. Refusal to submit to this kind of ceremonious abduction was considered a grave act of disobedience as it implied a refusal to vote in accordance with the landlord's wishes. In 1841 the nationalist party determined to retort in kind to these tactics and some 120 Carlow freeholders were rounded up and dispatched to safe-keeping with John O'Connell then busy on his own election at Kilkenny in the neighbouring county. For three whole weeks he kept them snugly quartered in an old brewery in the borough, fed most abundantly, and entertained during the day with the music of temperance bands and in the evening by political speeches. Kilkenny patriots guarded them all the while to see that none got away or were abducted by the other side. On nomination day in the Carlow election they all set off from Kilkenny. First came a stage-coach loaded with trusty nationalists; then a stage-car containing a temperance band to enliven them on the march; next twenty jaunting cars carrying the precious cargo of freeholders; and finally a 'guard' car brought up the rear. On either side of the column rode an escort of Kilkenny farmers on hacks to protect the convoy from guerrilla attacks. So they wended their way over the twenty-two miles that lay between Kilkenny and Carlow.[10] But it needed the special climate of Ireland for cooping to be developed on this superb scale. In England, though the practice was common, it was of a more limited nature.

The last extremity of intimidation was the threat of immediate and personal violence before the election and during the polling. Sometimes this might be no more than the drunken excesses of mobs or parties primed with beer and silver by an interested agent and secure in the protection of influential persons against the penalties of the law. Violence of this kind was common and few elections passed off without the breaking of a few heads and windows, or what the newspaper jargon of the time would call

[9] Add. MS. 40616, fo. 206.   [10] O'Connell, *Recollections*, II, 31 sqq.

'painful excitement'. Such a scene as the following deserves perhaps no more than the humorous pen of the young Charles Dickens. 'The other night there was a disturbance in Frome— mobs, broken windows, and fractured limbs; old Dr. Bush had his hands full, setting legs and selling plasters. —— who is, you know, lately in the yeomanry, was obliged to go and parade about all night. I lent him some pistols but I have not heard whether his military valour was called into action.'[11] One of the most potent stimulants to disorder was the traditional pageantry of processions and banners since it provided both the assemblages and provocations for a rough and tumble battle. Lady Charlotte Guest, who though a keen electioneer only rarely had personal experience of an actual contest, twice recorded election riots occasioned by such circumstances. At the Merthyr election of 1837 the tory supporters took along some weathercocks to the field where the hustings were erected as a symbol of derision against a Mr Crawshay, a prominent local supporter of John Guest, the whig candidate, in that election although he had opposed him in 1835.

> Our people took umbrage at it and a fight ensued, in which the said weathercocks were destroyed and sundry flags damaged. . . . The mob soon transferred their wrath from the flags to each other, and began a regular battle with stones.

John Guest came up on horseback, went into the middle of the crowd and called on them in Welsh and English to be peaceable. Eventually he induced the fiercest of the combatants to shake hands and the affair ended somewhat inconsistently with a cheer for peace and good fellowship.

In 1850 Lady Charlotte, by that date resident at Canford, went to see an election at Poole, being curious to see how it would compare with those she had witnessed in Wales. There proved to be little difference between the ironworkers of Merthyr and the countrymen of the young Thomas Hardy. The hustings were erected in the centre of the town near the town hall. The Guest influence was given to the liberal candidate, Seymour, whose procession was the first to arrive 'with a vast array of banners, musick, flags, ribbons, &c.' Soon the tory party made their appearance 'with a fine compact body of sailors, very few respectable looking voters and only a few flags'. The tory candidate, Savage, was

---

[11] Mallock, *Letters of the Duke of Somerset*, 40. The reference is to the election of 1832.

proposed and seconded but when the proposer for the liberal came forward the excitement began. One of the liberal free-trade banners showed a savage (a play on the tory candidate's name) bestriding a loaf and wielding a club to drive away starving labourers. The tory supporters made an attack on this ingenuous emblem and destroyed it. This in turn provoked a general outburst of disorder in which each side concentrated on pulling down their opponents' flags. The conservatives had the better of these exchanges partly because some of the 'so-called gentlemen of their party', as Lady Charlotte tartly observed, 'with very bad taste' took up the more obnoxious of their emblems to the shelter of the hustings. There was some hard fighting, or what seemed to be so to Lady Charlotte looking down on the scene from the security of the front-room windows of a neighbouring house, and she thought it all 'very disgusting and degrading'. But there was more to come. When Seymour's proposer again made an attempt to speak he was assailed by volleys of rotten eggs mingled with apples, turnips, and stones. The uproar was tremendous but fortunately the predominantly tory mob with a nice sense of humour suddenly changed their ammunition to balls of flour which even the partisan Lady Charlotte was obliged to record had a very ludicrous result, 'the flour sticking where the eggs had already taken effect and giving all the party on the hustings the appearance of being so many millers'. On this happy note the proceedings ended. The two candidates 'having both vainly tried to assure us what excellent members they would make', a poll was demanded and the two parties then left the hustings in safety if not with dignity.[12]

Sometimes, however, there was violence of a more serious nature than this. In the big industrial towns the poorer classes formed the raw material for mob-riots; and elsewhere, even in the smaller boroughs, the England of the luddites and chartists, and the investigations of Ashley and Chadwick, could usually provide the dissolute, the lawless, the unemployed, the professional bully, to carry out the will of any one with money and influence in the licensed saturnalia of the parliamentary elections. In the 1837 election Graham reported 'disgusting and brutal' scenes of violence in Cumberland and Roxburghshire. His son was knocked down by the mob and Graham himself assaulted. In Roxburghshire a

[12] *Lady Charlotte Guest*, 52–3, 246–8.

mob seized some of the electors, 'stripped them of their clothes threw them into the river and compelled three to run for shelter through the town in open day without a rag to cover them, in the presence of women and an assembled multitude'.[13] At Birmingham in the same election the tory candidate Stapleton, who put up against Attwood and Scholefield, was made the object of a fierce onslaught. His supporters were attacked and a mob, armed with stones from the churchyard, endeavoured to storm the hotel where Stapleton was staying. The military were called in to protect him and eventually he was 'got away in disguise smoking a cigar'.[14]. Electioneering indeed had its hazards for candidates as well as for voters. At the Nottingham election of 1841 there was considerable bitterness against the whig candidates occasioned partly by the anti-Poor Law agitation. As a gibe against Hobhouse, who had been Secretary at War in the whig administration, his opponents paraded round the town a cart containing a man stripped to the waist and another man flogging him. Hobhouse got his own supporters to break up the cart but naturally this led to an increase in rioting and violence. In the end the troops were brought in to protect the liberal side. 'I was informed by my friends', Hobhouse later told a parliamentary committee, 'that it was not safe for me to walk about, except well guarded, and indeed I was not permitted to do so; and when I did go out by myself, or rather with one or two friends, I was obliged to go by back streets, circuitously, in order to save my life.'[15] Hobhouse had ample experience of electoral mobs in this period. Not many years before at the by-election occasioned by his resignation over the window-tax issue, he had faced the fury of the crowd at Westminster. The description of the scene at Covent Garden on 7 May 1833, when Hobhouse went down with other M.P.s and a large body of friendly electors, is contained in his diary.

The moment I got into the Market the disturbance began: and it was not without difficulty not to say danger that I got within the rails of the church portico. The people were ferocious and if they had got me down, I should never have arisen again. . . . I was proposed in the usual way, but when I stepped forward to speak, I was instantly assailed with the most unsavoury missiles, and a storm of hisses and yells.

[13] Parker, *Peel*, II, 349.   [14] Add. MS. 40423, fos. 371–3.   [15] P.P. 1842, V, 149–53.

Returning to his house the day of the declaration of the poll, Hobhouse found his shutters up and heard that the police had sent a message to the effect that the chairing procession of Colonel Evans (his successful opponent) was going to pay him a visit and that a dozen constables were being sent to protect him. Hobhouse thought it advisable to send his wife and children to a friend's house till the danger was past although in the upshot the procession did not appear and contented themselves with pelting the house of Hobhouse's chairman.[16]

Perhaps the most vicious feature that marked these electoral disorders was the recruitment of gangs of paid bullies to break up musterings of opponents during the election campaigns and terrorize voters during the polling. The 1832 election at Hertford provided a picturesque illustration of this element in contemporary electioneering. Ingestre, the tory candidate, hired a gang of gipsies under the leadership of Nipper Price, a pugilist, to serve him during the election. The reforming candidate, Duncombe, not to be outdone, brought in a band of bargemen from Ware. On nomination day there was a fight between the rival gangs, and Duncombe's bargees beat Ingestre's gipsies. The next day, however, there was another clash between them; the bargees were beaten and left the borough that evening.[17] Other boroughs besides Hertford knew the excitement of gang warfare at election time. At Lewes such men were known as 'bullies'; at Nottingham they were called 'lambs', and were employed to abduct voters as well as break windows and assault opponents. Thomas Wakefield, an influential manufacturer in the constituency, said in 1842 that corruption and the employment of the 'lambs' first began in the election of 1837 and that the purity of the borough had declined since the Reform Act. He ascribed this to the growing poverty of the electors and the general decrease in political feeling.[18] At Warwick gangs of agricultural labourers from the Earl of Warwick's estates, stiffened by professional bullies, were brought in to assist at the election of 1832.[19] The Clive family at Ludlow fetched a body of fifty or sixty fighting men from Shrewsbury and quartered them on the borough during a by-election in 1839.[20] It would be foolish to suggest that most boroughs suffered from invasions of this sort but the practice was well established and

---

[16] Broughton, *Recollections*, IV, 310–12.   [17] P.P. 1833, IX, 50–1, 87, 99–101.
[18] P.P. 1842, V, 164–5.   [19] P.P. 1833, XI, 324.
[20] P.P. 1840, IX, 166.

illustrates with some sharpness the lengths to which candidates, parties, and borough magnates would go to establish their ascendancy.

It should be noted moreover that intimidation was not confined to the traditional whig and tory parties nor was it directed solely by the wealthy and privileged against the poor and defenceless. The radicals were no more innocent of violence than the more aristocratic politicians. The methods perhaps were different. On one side was the force of property and wealth; on the other the force of numbers. But the objectives remained the same. The constituencies where radical intimidation could be effective were probably fewer in number than the aristocratically controlled constituencies. Its influence, because the strength of mob-violence was inevitably temporary, was probably less powerful. Even so, the lot of a tory voter in a predominantly radical constituency must often have been as uncomfortable as that of a dissenting radical in a small village. In Birmingham, one of the safest radical seats of the period, there was an extensive system of intimidation by the lower classes of the town. Neighbours of a butcher, for instance, threatened not to buy any more meat from him unless he voted radical. In 1835, when it was reported that the innkeepers and public-house keepers were 'much incensed' against the two radical candidates, Attwood and Scholefield, their customers used their influence, often in a most forcible way, to deter them from opposing the radical cause. Men would go into public houses, ask the landlord how he voted, and if he was a tory, they would pour out his ale in the gutter, saying that it was tory ale, and that they wanted a reform drink. Sometimes the houses of tory publicans would be picketed by radicals to prevent customers going in. The following election, in 1837, witnessed the same kind of intimidation from below and the conservatives attributed their defeat, after a prosperous start at the polls, to the violent proceedings of a large mob which attacked the tory voters. In this election a police officer himself became a casualty and was taken off to hospital with his ear nearly torn off.[21] The radical candidates were possibly free from association or agency in this electoral intimidation and the people who practised it were for the most part non-electors. They were, however, connected with the political unions and formed part of the general radical strength of the town.

[21] P.P. 1835, viii, 246; Add. MS. 40423, fo. 371.

It was a striking example of the way in which the unenfranchised classes could influence parliamentary elections.[22]

This kind of radical intimidation was by no means confined to Birmingham. In all probability it existed in varying degrees in all the urban industrial areas. There were similar practices at Huddersfield and Walsall. It existed at Halifax together with the mobbing of tory voters by crowds of non-electors. The whole purpose of the rioting at Wolverhampton in 1835 which will be described later was to deter tory electors from polling. The influence of a radical population might even spread to other constituencies. At Warwick in 1832 the gangs drawn chiefly from the Earl of Warwick's estates which dominated the town for some days preceding the election, were attacked by men of the political unions who came over to Warwick from the radical strongholds of Birmingham and Coventry on polling-day. Serious rioting broke out; a great amount of destruction and damage was committed; and the Scots Greys were called in to put down the disturbance.[23] As between the introduction of the hired bully and the excesses of the local mob, perhaps there is something to be said for the latter. But a smashed window and a broken head would be felt in much the same way whatever the cause or motive. In any case the presence of intimidation and violence on behalf of the radicals and reformers was an element in the constituencies which should not be forgotten or underestimated.

On occasions even the radical leaders were not guiltless of encouraging such forcible demonstrations by their followers. Hunt was certainly charged with doing so by Lord Stanley in 1831. According to the latter's account, Hunt told people in Manchester on the first day of the Wigan election that every man in Manchester from the age of fifteen to that of forty-five should march over to Wigan and exercise 'constitutional influence' over the polling there. 'If you meet a voter . . . take care of him and see if you can't persuade him. . . . Use kind entreaties; and if these fail, I would advise you to take him by the arm, and give him a gentle squeeze. . . . I know you Lancashire men give something like a feeling squeeze when you like.' Stanley's tale was corroborated by Littleton, then member for Staffordshire, and indeed the charge was virtually admitted by Hunt.[24] In this belligerent electioneering

[22] P.P. 1835, VIII, 249.   [23] P.P. 1833, XI, 323–4, 404, 485.
[24] *Hansard*, III, 1502–9. At this election one conservative voter, Roger Holt Leigh (the brother of Sir Robert Holt Leigh of Hindley Hall), was so severely injured by

the radicals might fairly claim that they were merely imitating methods that the aristocracy had long employed. It would be idle to expect one side to be quiescent in the face of tactics pursued against them by their opponents or to assume that the radicals were more decent and law-abiding than the rest of their generation. But it also followed that violence was common to all parties.

The traditional Eatanswill picture of early Victorian elections is in fact not so much an exaggerated as a pale and euphemistic version of the contemporary scene. No doubt it was jocularly characteristic of some smaller rural boroughs but in comparison with what actually happened in many constituencies Dickens's account is under-drawn, conventional, and staid. This of course lay largely in the nature of the book. Dickens was too good a reporter not to know the material that was present even if he never had occasion to exploit it in a more serious vein. Take for example the short satiric sketch of 'Our Honorable Friend'[25] who was triumphantly returned for the constituency of Verbosity.

> It may be mentioned as a proof of the great general interest attaching to the contest, that a Lunatic whom nobody employed or knew, went down to Verbosity with several thousand pounds in gold, determined to give the whole away—which he actually did; and that all the publicans opened their houses for nothing. Likewise, several fighting men, and a patriotic group of burglars sportively armed with life-preservers, proceeded (in barouches and very drunk) to the scene of action at their own expense; these children of nature having conceived a warm attachment to our honorable friend, and intending, in their artless manner, to testify to it by knocking the voters in the opposite interest on the head.

Disraeli, had he been endowed with a taste for low life, might have redressed the literary balance. But even the account of the Darlford election in *Coningsby*, though one of the best of its kind, suffers from being burlesqued. Not all elections, it is true, were marked by street-rioting or the presence of the hired bully. Some were quiet enough (though quiet is a relative term and should not be given its modern value in Victorian accounts of elections); but it is perhaps worth while, in order to stress the other side of the

what his memorial tablet in Leeds Parish Church describes as 'an excited populace' when 'engaged in the exercise of his franchise as Burgess of Wigan', that he subsequently died. (I owe this interesting item of information to Mr Kitson Clark.)
[25] *Reprinted Pieces.*

picture, to give an account of a couple of elections as samples of what England of the young Victoria could occasionally produce in the way of election excitement.

The first, at Coventry in 1832, was marked by the employment of a gang of ruffians in the whig interest. The successful candidates were Edward Ellice, the well-known whig party manager, and Henry Lytton Bulwer; they secured an overwhelming majority of the 2,000 voters who polled in a constituency of over 3,000. Before the election came on, Randall, a pugilist who kept a public house at Coventry, collected a band of 'bullies', about fifty in number, to act during the election in Ellice's interest. The men were mainly drawn from the districts round Coventry, especially from Nuneaton, and included bricklayers, navvies, country labourers, and at least one other professional pugilist in the person of Hamilton, the 'Chicken Butcher'. A payment was made to them of 5s. a day (about three times the usual wage of the rural labourer at the time), and they were given gin to drink during the whole period of their employment. A dark blue handkerchief (dark blue was Ellice's colour) was given to each man to wear, and when they entered Coventry they were joined by other countrymen who swelled the mob to several hundreds, and they all 'marched round the town like soldiers'. They were given clear instructions to stop the tories from mustering and to keep the tory voters away from the hustings on the day of the poll. In this task they seemed to have been most successful. The worst intimidation took place on the polling days. Electors who cast a vote against Ellice, on coming out of the booths were 'most ferociously attacked and dragged backwards by the hair of their heads . . . when they fell to the ground they were kicked and beat; also their clothes were torn off their persons and thrown in the booth'. This description, given by a naval lieutenant who was a non-voter with no interest in the town, was genially confirmed by one of Randall's own bullies. 'We cut them down', he said, 'and kicked them about like a football.' Other voters known to be in the tory interest were forcibly prevented from voting by being pulled back from the polling booth as they were about to enter. One voter was dragged out of the booth and beaten; and had all his clothes torn off except his waistcoat and the top of his shirt. He did not vote. Another, who managed to force his way through, arrived on the hustings nearly naked with his clothes torn to pieces. Before the end of the polling one part of the polling booth was completely covered with torn shirts and parts of other garments. It is not surprising that several voters changed their intentions at the sight of the mob around the polling station. One elector was attacked and kicked unconscious at his first attempt to poll and though he went out again in the afternoon to see the polling from a distance, he was afraid to go up since he could see other voters being attacked. In general there was undoubted proof that many voters had been intimidated from polling. The election was challenged but a parliamentary committee confirmed the return of Ellice and Bulwer. They censured the sheriff, however, for providing only one polling booth in the city and for failing to keep order.[26]

A second example of extreme election disorder occurred at Wolverhampton at a county by-election in 1835. The chief feature here was the violence against tory voters exercised by a mob which seemed in this case to have been drawn from the inhabitants of the town although many no doubt were non-voters. The election took place on Tuesday and Wednesday, 26–7 May 1835. Dense crowds gathered in the streets on the morning of the poll and began yelling, jostling, spitting, hooting, and making 'gross and indecent observations' as voters started to make their way up to the polling booth. Everyone who did not wear a laurel leaf or some other whig emblem was jostled and threatened. If electors voted for Anson, the whig candidate, they were greeted with cheers; if they voted for the tory, Sir F. Goodricke, there were hisses and groans, and as soon as they left the booths they were knocked about and insulted. One elector who voted had 'an immense quantity of horse soil thrown all over me which got into my shirt and was very obnoxious'. Stones were thrown at his carriage and several windows broken. Numerous voters were knocked down, had their clothes torn, and were soiled with mud and spittle. A carpenter who tried to vote on the Tuesday found great difficulty in getting to the poll; and after he had voted, he was jostled, spit upon, knocked down in the gutter and had two or three persons pushed down on top of him. Dead rooks, stones, and other popular missiles were thrown into the polling booth and the deputy-sheriff threatened to stop the poll because of the interruption from the crowd. On Wednesday feeling increased.

[26] P.P. 1833, VIII, 143–287; *H. of C. Journals*, 1833, LXXXVIII, 72, 265–6.

Everybody that did not wear a laurel leaf or some badge of party, was most grossly used, and told that if he did not vote for Colonel Anson, he should have it; if they voted for Colonel Anson they were greeted with loud cheers, if they voted for Sir F. Goodricke, they were, so long as they continued in the booth, greeted with hisses and groans of the most horrible kind, and upon their leaving the square they were jostled about so long as I could keep my eye on them; in fact they could not quietly leave the square.

In the afternoon, when it became clear that the tory candidate would get in, it began to be dangerous for any of Goodricke's supporters to be seen in the streets. A crowd assembled outside the Swan Inn, where his committee had its headquarters, and started to assault all who attempted to pass in or out. A Shropshire farmer who had put up at the Swan was greeted with a yell of 'Tory' and a shower of stones. A shopkeeper, who had already suffered when he had voted for Goodricke the previous day, was again assaulted on leaving the inn. 'They spit upon me', he related, 'some made water in their hands and threw it at me.' In the end he was obliged to take shelter in a shop which he left by the back way twenty minutes afterwards. By the close of poll at four o'clock on Wednesday evening the crowd in the market-place outside the Swan Inn was estimated at over 3,000, 'yelling, groaning, and insulting everybody, throwing stones and all that sort of thing'. The Rev. John Clare, a magistrate, came to the balcony of the Swan and entreated the mob to disperse but his efforts only elicited a shower of stones which struck him and broke the window panes behind.

The civil force at the disposition of the magistrates to quell this disorder was originally a body composed of two constables, who were appointed by court leet and were notoriously inefficient, three or four deputies, who were unpaid except for fees for serving warrants and similar services, and a couple of tradesmen 'who never are expected to act, at least, not in the daily business of that office'. No deputy constables were appointed until the morning of the election, when fifteen or sixteen were enrolled. In consequence of the disorder on that day, about ten more men were sworn in as special constables. As the crowd seemed to be dispersing that evening, the special constables were not called out for fear of provoking fresh disturbances. On Wednesday the disorder was worse than on the previous day and the high constable of the town enrolled about forty more special constables. When he endeavoured to collect his men in the afternoon, however, he could only find about fifteen, 'not one of which durst show their faces'. Fortunately he had already advised the magistrates to call in military assistance, and in response to their summons a party of dragoons reached the town early in the evening. After the crowd outside the Swan refused to disperse at Clare's request, the magistrates waited for some twenty minutes longer. As the tumult still continued, Clare then read the Riot Act and ordered the troops to clear the streets. After some confusion the dragoons managed to clear the market-place. The rioters then retreated to a churchyard and locked the gates behind them. A party of them, estimated at over a hundred, climbed up to the church battlements and when the military arrived, they were met with a volley of stones from this impromptu fortress. For a while the dragoons remained passive under this attack while an attempt was made to undo the gates; but at last one of the horses was struck and killed by a stone thrown from the church and the captain in command then gave orders to fire. Thirty-five rounds of ammunition were subsequently returned as having been used though some of these may have had the ball bitten from the cartridge before being fired. The gates of the churchyard were finally forced and the mob cleared out by nine o'clock in the evening. The remaining streets (one of which was found barricaded with carts and chains) were cleared by ten o'clock, public houses and beershops between ten and eleven o'clock. On the following day, Thursday, and again on Friday, there were minor demonstrations. Crowds collected, groaning, hissing, and throwing stones; and the military had to be called out to disperse them. The official casualties were: one dead horse, a boy of seventeen shot through a leg which was afterwards amputated, a boy of eleven shot through an ankle, and a boy of fifteen shot through the heel.[27]

This affair at Wolverhampton was no doubt exceptional. But it is easy to exaggerate the extent to which it was exceptional. One elector, a resident in the town, who had himself been attacked by the mob and was only rescued by some special constables, said that 'he did not think that there was more danger on this occasion than on former occasions'; and several other witnesses seemed undecided whether there had not been a greater crowd and more violence used in the election of 1832 when the Riot Act had also been read and the troops called in. It is clear that in Wolverhampton, and probably in many other towns, violence was endemic among the lower classes, and election time provided merely the provocation and the opportunity. Much was due, perhaps, to economic distress; even so it must be admitted that there was more brutality and coarseness among the urban lower classes than has usually been recognized. The electoral mob at the time of Victoria's accession to the throne was in many ways more akin to the London of Barnaby Rudge than the Eatanswill of Mr Pickwick. Moreover, as the Hertford and Coventry elections showed, there was a considerable element of lawlessness and violence, formed by the manual labourer, the gipsy, the professional pugilist, and the vagabond underworld of the tavern, racecourse, highway, and slum, for which the eccentric George Borrow, philologist and social observer, is perhaps a better witness than the humorous, sentimental, humanitarian Charles Dickens. Where organized intimidation was added to popular riotousness, it is difficult to see in the results of elections the free and unbiased verdict of a chosen electorate. On the other hand it was useless to expect political elections carried out on the open hustings to be markedly superior to the social manners and administrative efficiency of the age. Politics after all was only one aspect of society itself. The educative and refining influence of the Victorian era is in fact best appreciated when it is realized how rough and indecent public manners were when Victoria came to the throne. In the light of the scenes at Coventry and Wolverhampton, Victorian propriety, Victorian prudery, and Victorian genteelism, are seen to better advantage. Their real justification, which was too often overlooked at the end of the century when the lessons had been learnt and the teachers outmoded, was to be found fifty or sixty years earlier. It was not uncommon then for the decent and the timid to look forward with dread rather than interest to a parliamentary election. 'He said there was likely to be an election, and I said yes, and I was very sorry for it, for it caused a deal of dissension and unpleasantness in the town; that I was very sorry that there was anything of the sort about to take place. O, he said, so was he, but it was very immaterial to a poor man which way he voted, for Whigs and Tories were both a bad lot.'[28] That was

[28] P.P. 1840, IX, 407.

said at Cambridge. Another witness before a parliamentary committee, from Southampton, echoed much the same sentiment when he spoke of 'the inconvenience to the innocent electors of an election . . . the electors would be glad if the town was disfranchised'.[29]

[29] P.P. 1842, VIII, 607.

Chapter Seven

CORRUPT BOROUGHS

FOR the would-be member of parliament who could not hope to be the popular candidate of a large city or the approved choice of his county, and who shrank from the riotous and expensive uncertainty of a closely contested borough, there still remained one familiar road of entry. He could buy a seat. The Reform Act had done much to eliminate the rotten parts of the constitution but it was still possible after 1832 to buy a seat in the House of Commons. The number of venal constituencies was certainly small; and in few of them was the financial aspect unmixed with other minor considerations. But they existed and a steady traffic in them went on behind the scenes in the informed and cynical offstage world of the professional politician, the party manager, and the country solicitor. The difficulty in compiling a list of the post-1832 corrupt boroughs derives chiefly from the circumstance that bribery was rarely the only factor deciding the issue. Most boroughs were corrupt in the sense that illegal inducements were habitually offered to voters and accepted by them. Few were corrupt in the sense that the collective decision of the electorate was based on a simple cash transaction. The task is one of discovering when bribery was the dominant, major, or subordinate element in the grand compound of motives that produced a verdict at the polls. At Warwick money had to compete with the direct territorial influence of the Earl of Warwick; at Penryn and Falmouth with the influence of government; at Leicester and Southampton with the restraining influence of a relatively free and incorrupt section of the electorate. Yet all these places, along with Hull, Ipswich, Lewes, Liverpool, Nottingham, Norwich, St Albans, Stafford, Sudbury, Totnes, and York, enjoyed varying reputations in this period as boroughs which were either rotten to the core or in which bribery had taken such a hold that it was doubtful whether it had not become the deciding factor. Any of the party managers and parliamentary agents of the day, Parkes, Coppock, Holmes, or Bonham, could have named offhand three or four constituencies where a passable candidate with a few thousand pounds would have a fairly certain prospect of success; and many more where members with no more qualifications than those had entrenched themselves so firmly in repeated elections that they could with some justice be considered to have bought the constituency.

It was of course by no means necessary for all or even the majority of electors to be venal for venality to assume a preponderant authority. It was enough if bribery could sway the balance between the conscientious voters on each side. An example of this marginal but decisive influence of bribery was to be seen at Liverpool. As a large constituency (it had over 11,000 on the electoral roll of whom over 8,000 voted in the 1832 election), Liverpool might have been expected to be pure from the sheer impossibility of corrupting such a huge electorate. But Liverpool had been a borough before 1832 and at any rate from 1827 onward had such a reputation for venality that Brougham was moved in the course of the reform debates to refer to it as 'the overgrown foul and corrupt borough of Liverpool'.[1] A large number of voters whose habits had called forth this unkind description survived the Reform Act to exercise their franchise under the new system. Of the 11,000 on the register for the first election after the Reform Act, 3,600 claimed under the old franchise. From the evidence of witnesses before a parliamentary committee in 1833 it is clear that at the election there was a peremptory demand from the old voters for money, and they refused to promise their vote without this and other customary perquisites. The result of the 1832 election was that the liberal candidate, William Ewart, a barrister and son of a Liverpool merchant,[2] was comfortably at the head of the poll with nearly 5,000 votes; Lord Sandon, a conservative, was next with 4,260 votes. Of the defeated candidates a liberal, Thorneley, only failed by less than 200 to beat Sandon out of the second place. The interest and the significance of the election rested in the composition of the votes cast for Sandon and Thorneley. Of the old franchise holders 2,107 had voted for Sandon, 857 for Thorneley. Of the new, 2,153 for Sandon, and 3,240 for Thorneley. At the close of the first day's poll the figures stood

> Sandon   2,521
> Thorneley   3,103

Sandon's majority was made up of old franchise holders who were

[1] *Hansard*, III, 1060.   [2] After whom Gladstone was named.

brought up in large numbers on the second day. On that day 1,109 old electors voted for Sandon and only 338 for his opponent. The select committee that inquired into the election found proof of bribery but no proof of agency. Nevertheless to anyone familiar with the processes of contemporary electioneering it was obvious what had happened. Moreover Sandon was returned for Liverpool at the next three general elections.[3]

An example of the power of the purse in a smaller constituency is to be found in Ipswich. This was a borough with some 1,200 registered electors. At the 1832 general election not much corruption was reported but it began to get a hold on the borough in the 1835 election in the shape of direct bribery, treating, payment of fees on becoming freemen, and the use of charitable funds belonging to the corporation. The common council at Ipswich was 'Blue' or tory as opposed to the 'Yellows' or reformers. In 1832 two liberal members were returned (Morrison, a wealthy wholesale haberdasher in the City, and Rigby Wason, a barrister), with easy majorities over their tory opponents, Goulburn[4] and Kelly. At the next election the tory candidates, Dundas and Kelly, beat the two sitting members by narrow majorities. A petition was laid against the return and a committee that heard the case declared the election void on grounds of bribery. One witness, a tailor, was offered £20 for his vote. He took the money but on arriving at the polling booth produced the notes, declared that they had been given him to vote for the Blues, and then proceeded to vote for the Yellows, saying he would give the money to the Suffolk Hospital. One is not surprised to learn that this stalwart vindicator of electoral integrity was a Unitarian and a 'decided reformer'. At the by-election consequent on the committee's decision, Messrs Morrison and Wason again secured handsome majorities over a different pair of tory candidates. At the 1837 election, although two liberal and two conservative candidates contested the borough, a closely fought contest ended with a conservative (Gibson) at the top of the poll, six votes ahead of a liberal (Tufnell), with their respective colleagues (Kelly and Wason) only two votes behind. But this time it was the turn of the conservatives and Kelly gained the second seat on petition against Tufnell. At the 1841 election the conservatives, on this occasion represented by Kelly and

[3] P.P. 1833, x, *Report of the Select Committee on the Liverpool Election Petition.*
[4] Edward, brother of the better known Henry Goulburn, M.P. for Cambridge University.

J. C. Herries, went to the borough with high hopes. Indeed they were assured by the local Blue managers that victory was certain. In the event they suffered an unexpected reverse at the hands of the liberal candidates, Wason and Rennie, who finished some fifty votes above them.

> It would seem [wrote Herries to Peel at the close of the poll on 2 July 1841] that money in large quantities has been sent down to the Borough (from what quarter I know not) and it has in the course of this day been applied in such profusion as to bring a considerable number of the voters who were bound by promises to us, to poll against us. I have much reason to believe that the proceedings of Attwood[5] at Harwich where extravagant sums are said to have been paid to individual voters, has increased the appetite for such feeding here which neither Kelly nor myself were willing, even if able, to supply. Even without that, the expense has been considerable and the labour of the canvass overwhelming; which is all we have got for our pains.

A few days later he wrote on the same melancholy theme:

> I really believe that the principal parties who persuaded us at the Carlton that on this particular occasion the seats were safe did not deal dishonestly with us. But they ought not to have been taken, as we were, by surprize. We now learn that the whigs have spent £6,000 at Ipswich to beat us; chiefly, perhaps, with a view to oust me.[6]

These were not just the idle accusations of a disappointed politician. From the evidence before the committee at the subsequent inquiry it is clear that heavy bribery had taken place both in 1841 and at earlier elections. In 1841 as much as £15 and £20 had been given for a single vote and it was rumoured that up to £30 had been offered. The subsequent history of the borough tells its own tale. The successful candidates of 1841, Wason and Rennie, were unseated on proof of extensive bribery. At the resultant by-election Lord Desart and Thomas Gladstone were returned only to have their own election declared void. They in turn were succeeded at a second by-election by John Gladstone[7] and Lane Fox in 1842. It is difficult to resist the conclusions that the borough had been

---

[5] John Attwood, elected M.P. for Harwich 1841.
[6] Add. MS. 40485, fos. 26, 139.
[7] Both John and Thomas were brothers of W. E. Gladstone.

growing steadily more corrupt since 1832 and that there was little
to choose between Yellows and Blues except in skill of tactics and
length of purse.[8]

Perhaps one of the purest examples, technically speaking, of a
rotten borough in the generation after the Reform Act is provided
by Stafford. Like many corrupt constituencies it had an electorate
larger than the average and was one of the old pre-1832 boroughs.
It had long been notorious for its bribery. Greville, with his
habitual exaggeration, spoke of it in 1837 as 'from time immemorial
a corrupt borough'. No improvement had been made by the
coming of reform. At the first election after the Reform Act the
initiative in demanding bribes, as in so many constituencies, came
from the electors themselves and corruption among the new £10
householders was reported to be as bad as among the old franchise
holders. Even before the election started 5s. and 10s. tickets had
been distributed to about 800 electors. There was evidence that
one side alone had paid out about £150 in 5s. tickets a week before
polling day. But this was chicken feed compared with what was to
come. When the election actually started the price of votes began
at £2 10s. for a single and £5 for a plumper, and gradually rose
to £4, £7, and even £10 for a vote. One agent alone paid out over
£1,000 in bribes to between 400 and 500 voters. Of the 1,000 odd
voters at the 1832 election it was calculated that 850 were bribed.
A parliamentary committee of inquiry that sat in 1833 found ample
proof of open and extensive bribery by both sides in the borough
('though probably not more so than many others', observed the
editor of *Mosse's Parliamentary Guide for 1835* with no trace of cyni-
cism), and although the election was not declared void, the borough
was recommended for disfranchisement.

The politics of the successive candidates for Stafford in this
period matter less than usual. In 1832 two army officers, Chetwynd
and Gronow, were returned; in 1835, when the constituency was
probably still in a subdued state from the threat of disfranchisement two years earlier, no less than five candidates put up, Sir
Francis Goodricke (a conservative) and Chetwynd (a nominal
liberal) being returned. At this election there was no allegation of
bribery and indeed some attempt was made to rehabilitate the
somewhat blown reputation of the borough. A witness before a
parliamentary committee in 1836 declared that the burgesses of

---

[8] P.P. 1835, VIII, 76–90; 1835, IX, 87–202; 1842, VII, 9–211.

Stafford did not 'concern themselves much about political opinions' and that their choice depended not so much on party or on bribery as on popularity. He instanced, to support this dubious thesis, the fact that both Chetwynd and Goodricke were members of Staffordshire families.[9] The House of Commons was not so easily convinced that Stafford had changed its character even if it had received a fright. When Goodricke took the Chiltern Hundreds in May 1835 in order to contest the county, the issue of a new writ for the borough was suspended and in the meantime a bill for the disfranchisement of the borough, in accordance with the recommendation of 1833, was brought forward. In the end nothing came of this penal measure although further evidence of the corruption of the borough was taken in 1836 and the disfranchisement bill even received a second reading. Finally in February 1837 the vacancy in the borough representation was allowed to be filled and Farrand, a tory, was returned. At the general election a few months later the sitting members, Chetwynd and Farrand, were re-elected though not without some opposition. Bingham Baring went down to Stafford, and if Greville is to be believed, spent £2,500 without success on his candidature.[10] Ten years later the old habits were still clinging. In June 1847 a correspondent of Graham, discussing the chances at Stafford, observed that 'the man who first appears on that field is almost always beaten. My impression is, that it may be carried by a *Coup*, after a little previous secret organization. On this point I should be glad to confer with Mr Bonham.' He added that 'I am told Wilkins is going there with £1,200 in his pocket.'[11]

Stafford escaped the danger that had threatened it in the thirties. But between the first and second Reform Acts two boroughs actually were disfranchised for gross bribery and corruption. They were Sudbury in 1844 and St Albans in 1852. The latter, since the Reform Act, had been in the hands of local managers whose task it was to bribe the electors on the one hand and recompense themselves at the expense of the candidates on the other. The electorate was small, just over 600 in the thirties, and was composed of freemen, old scot and lot voters, and the £10 householders. The case of Sudbury will be described in detail, partly because of the

---

[9] P.P. 1836, XIX, 77. See also P.P. 1833, XI, 4–73. Captain William Fawkener Chetwynd was the second son of Sir George Chetwynd of Brocton Hall, co. Stafford. For Goodricke, see below, Ch. 10, p. 250.
[10] *Greville Memoirs*, III, 390.   [11] Add. MS. 40616, fos. 328–9.

unusually full evidence that was brought to light by the parliamentary committee of inquiry concerning the actual machinery of bribery, and partly because Sudbury became a classic precedent in the history of election petitions.[12]

Sudbury was notorious long before 1841 for the way in which its electoral favours depended on money. It had become an established custom, for example, for supporters of the winning side to receive four guineas as a kind of victory medal. The centre of corruption was among the poorer handloom weavers of the town who as freemen retained their vote after 1832 and were reckoned to be about one hundred and fifty strong. But it is clear that the greater part of the constituency of nearly 600 voters took bribes at elections. The composition of the electorate is worth examination. Officially the registered electorate at Sudbury at the time of the election of 1841 was as follows:

$$
\left.\begin{array}{ll}
\pounds 10 \text{ householders} & 123 \\
\text{freemen} & 471 \\
\text{registered under both} & \\
\quad \text{headings} & \text{nil}
\end{array}\right\} \quad \text{Total } 594
$$

But of the 471 freemen, 149 were entitled to vote merely as householders so that the real division of the electorate was

$$
\begin{array}{ll}
\text{voters qualified as } \pounds 10 \text{ householders} & 272 \\
\text{voters qualified only as freemen} & 322 \\
\hline
\text{Total} & 594
\end{array}
$$

[13]

A party spirit of a kind prevailed in the borough but 'it is not a party spirit in reference to the general politics of the country; it is a contest of parties amongst themselves as to which shall make most money at elections. As to party, in reference to the country at large, the voters know very little and care even less. Amongst the educated classes party spirit, founded more or less on knowledge, prevails to a great degree.'[14] At the election of 1835 bribery took place on a great and unprecedented scale. It was estimated that the total sums spent on bribery averaged over £30 per voter. A

[12] See Ch. 5, p. 135. Cf. the evidence of James Coppock on this point (P.P. 1842, v, 237).

[13] P.P. 1842, xxxiii, 643.   [14] P.P. 1842, vii, 944.

similar expenditure was expected by the fortunate inhabitants of
the borough at the general election of 1837 occasioned by the
death of William IV; and many of the electors, from the commencement of the king's illness, began to neglect their work in pleasant
anticipation of heavy bribery ahead. In fact, it proved, by the
Sudbury criterion, to be a poor and disappointing election. Not
much money was spent on either side and as a result some of the
poorer and more optimistic electors found themselves in considerable distress. At the following election, however, by what was
perhaps a natural reaction, bribery on a large scale again took
place, and prosperity was presumably restored to the inhabitants
of the borough. It was the corruption on this occasion which
formed the subject of the subsequent parliamentary inquiry and led
to the disfranchisement of the borough in 1844.

The candidates at this election, as indeed was usually the case at
Sudbury, were strangers to the town, had no local connexions,
and in fact were unknown to the electors until a few days before the
election. Residents in the town had taken the lead in securing
candidates on both sides. Dyce Sombre and Frederick Villiers, the
liberal candidates, had been obtained by a Mr Peacock, a silk
manufacturer of Sudbury, through the medium of Coppock, the
whig parliamentary agent, and the Reform Club. An election
agent named Massey came down on their behalf a few days before
the election, introduced himself to various prominent inhabitants,
and opened public houses for treating. Three days before the
election Massey held a meeting of supporters at the Swan Inn,
which became the liberal headquarters. A list was read over and
a guinea paid out to each man that evening as a kind of 'refresher'
or token money. Villiers arrived at Sudbury two days, Sombre
one day before the election commenced. On the day of polling,
tickets were issued to supporters inscribed with each man's name
and number. Lists of electors were brought in from the hustings
as they voted and read out in the committee room. Those who had
voted in the liberal interest had second tickets made out for them
and were then chalked off the main list which hung up in the room.
This double ticket system enabled the organization of bribery to
function rapidly and efficiently. The hustings had been erected in
the market-place. On one side of the square was the Swan Inn;
on the other a public house called the Black Boy. An unknown
and anonymous agent, 'distinguished in the borough as the

Redhaired Man', was installed in a bedroom of the Swan furnished with a window or aperture giving out on to the landing of the stairs. Voters on the liberal side first went to the Black Boy and received two sovereigns in exchange for their first ticket. They voted and then went across to the Swan Inn where they received their second ticket. This they took up to the bedroom, and gave in at the window on the landing, receiving four sovereigns in exchange. Men with staves were posted at the bottom of the staircase in each house to keep order among the voters as they came and went. The liberal voters thus were paid in all seven sovereigns in cash apart from any miscellaneous treating. It was reckoned that fully two hundred electors received these tickets; and it is reasonably certain that towards the end of the polling, when the issue was still in doubt, Massey purchased at a much higher price the votes of six or eight electors who had hung back with just such an expectation. The total sum estimated to have been spent in the liberal interest was £3,000. This was not an exceptional sum to be paid for the privilege of representing Sudbury in the House of Commons. A former member for the borough, John Bagshaw, who headed the poll at Sudbury in 1835, said he should consider an election expenditure at Sudbury of £3,000 or £4,000 for one side 'rather perhaps in the extreme, not much'. It was enough to win the confidence of the Sudbury electors on this occasion. Villiers and Sombre were returned at the head of the poll with 284 and 281 votes, their nearest opponent polling 274.

The history of the other side is only slightly different. A resident of the borough, an attorney and a leading conservative, became acquainted with the two prospective tory candidates, Jones and Taylor, at the Carlton Club through the offices of F. R. Bonham. This attorney, Andrews by name, became their agent and the two candidates arrived in Sudbury a week before the election. Public houses were opened for treating and a few days before the election the first distribution of money took place. A sum of up to £200 was paid out to a number of electors called 'party makers'. These party makers, or in plain English, procurers of votes, formed a numerous and powerful profession at Sudbury. It was estimated that they formed some two-thirds of the whole body of voters. Apparently there were more officers than men in the rival electoral armies that were marched to the poll; and no doubt, as elsewhere, the leaders expected more pay than the rank and file. On the day of polling a sum of £1,500 in sovereigns was brought to an inn called the Rose and Crown, and at the close of the poll only £100 remained. In addition several claims for reimbursement of money expended in bribery came in after the election. The total expenditure in the conservative interest probably reached £2,000. Individual cases of bribery reached high standards. £10 was paid to one man under colour of a purchase; £20 to another for one vote; and £30 to a third for two votes. On both sides the most elaborate precautions were taken to cover the transference of the considerable amounts of money that were involved. On the liberal side Sombre had £3,000 placed in a separate account which he had opened with his bankers, and the money was immediately drawn out, by a clerk in Coppock's office, on the order of a bearer cheque. From there it probably went by hand to Massey, the election agent. In the case of the conservatives, a certain amount in cash was probably brought down with them and further sums, amounting to over £100, were borrowed locally by a supporter. The principal sum of £1,500 was supplied by a cheque signed by a brother of one of the candidates and cashed by a local bank. The money was deposited under lock and key by the bank, and the key given to a third person who allowed a fourth person and perhaps others, to have access to the money and distribute it among a body of men known as 'Raps' who finally passed it on to the electors.

The parliamentary committee that examined this election came to the conclusion that the whole system of illegal expenditure had originated with the inhabitants of the borough, was promoted by the leading men among them, and was forced on the candidates. This was borne out by the subsequent behaviour of the Sudbury electors. Some time after the election, when the case was already appearing before committee, the leading men on both sides in Sudbury held a joint meeting and agreed to put forward two candidates only at the next election, one liberal and one conservative, who should divide between them the representation of the borough. It was further resolved that if any other candidates appeared to contest the return of the two approved candidates, both parties would unite to oppose them. It was clear that this compromise was undertaken from two motives. There was undoubtedly a wholesome fear that any further scandal might result in the disfranchisement of the borough or at least some other form of penalization, and it was hoped that by dividing the borough seats amicably between the two parties, no challenge would be made to their return. Secondly, there was a considerable sum, between £300 and £400, outstanding from the last election and both sides were anxious to have their debts paid. But this gesture, like most death-bed repentances, came too late. The candidates invited by the meeting to stand for the borough at the next election both refused to pay the debts of their predecessors. A year later Sudbury terminated its parliamentary career.[15]

Sudbury, however, though it suffered an untimely fate and received some notoriety in consequence, was not the only place of its kind. Other venal boroughs existed even if they went about their business more discreetly. One significant aspect of the Sudbury case was the existence of a strong vested interest in the promotion of election contests, and the part played by certain leading inhabitants of the borough who acted as borough-mongers for that purpose. The same kind of activity by the same kind of persons was noted at St Albans, and they existed in other boroughs. Of Totnes, commonly regarded in this period as a semi-rotten borough, Lord Seymour (who sat for the borough from 1834 until he succeeded as Duke of Somerset in 1855) wrote as follows in 1839. 'I am . . . much obliged to the Duchess [of Somerset] for the zeal which she has displayed in defeating the intrigues of obsolete aldermen and unemployed attorneys; there is no doubt they wish to bring back the borough under the control of the small party who formerly governed it, and who obtained thereby patronage for themselves or their relations.'[16] Not merely the tradition but the actual profession of the borough-monger was still alive in early Victorian England. Without the costly and often notorious methods employed at Stafford, Nottingham, Ipswich, or Sudbury, there were yet ways of entering parliament by judicious negotiations and adequate payment. Two examples of these quieter but no less corrupt aspects of the representative system are recorded, even if incompletely, in the extant correspondence of the conservative party election manager, F. R. Bonham. The first was an interesting though ultimately abortive negotiation that took place in 1839 with the object of finding, or rather of purchasing, a safe seat for a nephew of Sir James Graham. This was Captain Blackwood and though the names of the boroughs concerned were

15 P.P. 1844, XVIII, 247 sqq.   16 Mallock, *Letters of the Duke of Somerset*, 86.

concealed, one of them was possibly Poole.[17] The initiative in the matter came from a local borough-monger, a certain James Bullock, who in July 1839 wrote to a friend called Jackson, stating that he would be able to return a member each for two boroughs in the county at the next election. 'One', he stipulated, 'must be a Whig (tho' moderate would do) and the other a Tory; the Whig seat would cost from £6[00] to 700 only; the Tory's from £2,000 to £2,500.' He added that as far as the first seat was concerned, more than half the voters were already pledged. In any case there would be no risk in the matter on the score of expense. If Jackson had any friends who might wish to take advantage of the offer, they could begin discussion of the details at once. In fact, if Jackson himself had a fancy for a seat in parliament and was qualified, Bullock could return him. Jackson, who was apparently well connected with political and parliamentary circles, communicated with the tory party manager, Bonham; and it was probably the latter who was responsible for the useful suggestion that a Stanleyite tory might do for the whig seat, so that both might be secured for the conservatives. At all events Jackson replied early in August that he had two persons in mind for the seats, although matters were not settled enough for negotiations to begin, and further inquired whether the constituency wanting a whig would be satisfied with a 'Whig of the Stanley school'. A few other business-like questions were also put. If the next elections in these boroughs proved to be by-elections, would the candidates be guaranteed a second return at low cost at the general election when the existing parliament came (as it seemed it soon would) to an end? And would an absolute guarantee of success be given in return for the sums named?

Bullock replied that the tory seat might be vacant before the end of the existing parliament but the whig seat not until then. 'One of the Stanley school will do admirably for the latter. If he has any general knowledge of the trade and commerce of the kingdom, the better . . . but before he appears personally, he shall receive a letter to the constituency for his consideration and in which the principles to which he must subscribe will be explicitly stated.' On the matter of guaranteeing the election, Bullock was more cautious. The course he suggested was for each candidate to

---

[17] Cf. Add. MS. 40616, fo. 100. Graham to Bonham, 6 October 1839, states that on former's return in about a month's time he will sound Blackwood on the subject of Poole and adds that Bonham must tell Graham the maximum of the necessary expense.

pay to him £100 for immediate purposes. If then, after the canvass and preliminary arrangements, both Bullock and the candidate should be satisfied with the prospect of success, half the remaining sum was to be paid over at once, and the other half when the candidate had been returned, after the lapse of the statutory period of fourteen days from the opening of parliament during which petitions could be laid against the return of members. Finally it was to be understood that the sums mentioned were exclusive of solicitors' fees. Jackson, acting no doubt with the advice of Bonham and the knowledge of Sir James Graham, then named Captain Blackwood as one of the prospective candidates. In return he asked for the name of the borough and the sitting members since 'as a man of honour, Captain Blackwood would not oppose a person of the same school of politics as himself'. He added that the tory seat was too dear as a chance, but that if it was a certainty, he had a party ready for it. In being so definite about Blackwood's candidature, Jackson was perhaps exceeding his instructions. Graham, who was acting on behalf of his nephew during the latter's absence abroad, refused to do anything for the time being except allow his name to be put forward. He told Bonham that though he knew his nephew would gladly pay £700 for a seat, he thought it was too great a risk to put down £100 on a chance. There the matter rested.[18]

Previous to the general election of 1841 Bonham was also active in searching for a seat for the relative of another grandee of the conservative party. For some years Lord Aberdeen had been anxious for his eldest son, Lord Haddo, to enter parliament and Bonham was looking round for a likely constituency as early as 1838. In the November of that year a vacancy at Penryn seemed likely to occur as a result of the prospective appointment of one of the sitting members, Sir Robert Rolfe, as Baron of the Exchequer. After consultation with Lord Aberdeen and Freshfield, the conservative second member for Penryn, Lord Haddo was established as the candidate for the borough. However, it appeared at one stage as though the expectation of a vacancy had been premature and that no contest would take place after all. Haddo, who had no personal desire to enter parliament and had only consented to stand in deference to his father's wishes, gratefully took the opportunity to depart abroad. The consequence was that when the seat

18 Add. MS. 40616, fos. 61–6.

did fall vacant, he was not available.[19] By the autumn of the following year Bonham was able to put forward further proposals, including a safe but expensive seat at Honiton. Aberdeen replied that he had not yet made any arrangements for his son and that 'in the event of a dissolution, I should much prefer the *certain seat*, at an expense not exceeding two thousand five hundred pounds, to the chances of a contest on more reasonable terms'. Though he would have preferred his son to enter parliament before the next general election, he confessed that he saw no prospect of that and therefore accepted Bonham's offer. Bonham then opened negotiations with a man whose name seems to have been Neale and who was apparently a local solicitor. He acted at least in the same capacity for Honiton as Bullock had done for his unspecified boroughs. It was agreed between them that the proposed candidate for the borough should be accepted on condition that, if he should be successful, a total sum of £2,500 should be paid on his behalf. Neale, however, was anxious to secure a preliminary payment of £1,000 to be spent before the election was decided and this Aberdeen was reluctant to promise.

> I approve of the terms of £2,500 for the seat [he wrote to Bonham] but I do not approve of the payment of £1,000 in the event of failure. This in fact renders nothing certain but a payment. Now it is clear that even for £1,000, I might have a *chance of success* in twenty places; and it is only in consequence of what may be considered a certainty that I readily acquiesce in paying the larger sum. I think such a stipulation as that proposed is calculated to invite defeat. . . . At all events it is quite different from that which I had contemplated; in which payment was to be contingent on success.

He admitted that, as a professional man, Neale must in any case be compensated for his labour but reiterated that he could not subscribe to any conditions which might seem to deprive the whole transaction of what, as far as Aberdeen was concerned, was its indispensable quality, viz. certainty. An agreement between the two parties was probably reached, as in the February of 1841 Aberdeen's son was ready to put up for Honiton at a moment's notice, although by that time his reluctance to enter parliament had so far taken effect as to render Lord Aberdeen less concerned

[19] Add. MS. 43061, fos. 220, 234; 40617, fo. 54.

to press his candidature and willing to withdraw from their engagement at Honiton if another suitable candidate could be found.[20]

It is clear, therefore, that the sale of seats and the pecuniary entry into the House of Commons persisted after the Reform Act. Moreover, as the two instances given above will demonstrate, the prices asked were by no means exorbitant, if in fact there was a practical certainty of return. The ordinary contested election often reached a higher level of expense than the sums quoted by Messrs Bullock and Neale and even then might bring no reward in the end. The only question was how far the seats bartered in this manner could be regarded as literal certainties once the cash was put down. Candidates and their friends were naturally cautious; borough-mongers were naturally optimistic. No doubt many a 'safe' constituency began to display curious obliquities once the candidate had been effectively detached from his money. On the other hand party managers and professional politicians were not the kind of sheep that are easily fleeced and if they seriously engaged in negotiations of these descriptions, it was presumably because there was a real prospect of a satisfactory bargain being made. Indeed with bribery so deeply rooted in the electoral habits of the age, it was inevitable that in some constituencies it should be systematized into what was virtually a commercial transaction. The isolated examples of disfranchisement presented by Sudbury and St Albans were insufficient to deter others from similar practices. It was the whole system that needed reforming because bribery was almost universal. All politicians were aware of its existence; most came to terms with it; a few exploited it. But it was not within the power of individual politicians any more than it was within the compass of the legislature to eradicate corruption in one grand reform of the political constitution. The statute books of the nineteenth century are littered with ineffective attempts to suppress bribery and other undue practices at elections. Where the law failed, a private individual could scarcely hope to succeed. Attempts to that end were made; but their record did not encourage other candidates to the pursuit of electoral virtue. Almost invariably, where a parliamentary candidate refused to become connected with illegal expenses, he automatically excluded himself from the House of Commons. Of this, the obverse of the medal,

[20] Add. MS. 40617, fos. 70–2, 91; 40427, fo. 157.

one illustration may be given to round off this sketch of the rotten part of the electoral constitution.

Norwich was an old corporate town (a county of itself) in which the 40s. freeholders as well as the freemen were entitled to vote. Both sets of voters retained their franchise under the Reform Act and as a result the constituency was unusually large. The total population of Norwich was just over 50,000; the electorate over 4,000. Included in the latter, however, were about 1,000 out-voters. Even before 1831 there had been no controlling influence in the borough, either personal or corporate, with the almost inevitable consequence that money came to fill the void. It was reckoned before the Reform Act that a contested election in the constituency cost about £4,000 and even an uncontested return from £1,000 to £1,500, since the out-voters always expected to be paid for their visit and unless they were duly recompensed were apt to look about for a third candidate.[21] By 1832, therefore, Norwich already had the reputation of a borough in which it was easy to spend a good deal of money. Much money had in fact been spent in Norwich by the well-known local banker, Richard Hanbury Gurney, who had been returned for the city in 1818, 1820, and again in 1830 and 1831 in the whig-liberal interest. In 1832 Gurney once more put up for Norwich but was defeated along with his liberal colleague by Lord Stormont and Sir James Scarlett in a contest notorious for its corruption. It was at this election, the first under the reformed system, that the traditional systematic corruption of the Norwich ward elections was transferred in its entirety to the parliamentary elections. J. J. Gurney, the Quaker philanthropist, and a near kinsman of the defeated member, was so far moved from his customary abstention from politics as to send a letter of protest to the *Norfolk Chronicle*.

> Our Ward elections [he wrote] and other contests of a merely local nature, have long been a scene of shameless bribery, licentious-ness and corruption. Thousands of pounds have been spent on both sides in the horrid work of depriving the poor voters of their best treasures: integrity and temperance. . . . In the meantime, the General Elections have been subject to some considerable degree of decency and restraint. Pure, indeed, they have never been in the view of the Christian moralist, nor by any means inoffensive in the

[21] *Key to Both Houses of Parliament 1832*, 371, quoting from an account of the con-stituency given by the *Spectator*, 2 January 1831.

eye of the law. . . . It is very probable that corruption may have
gone somewhat further on these occasions than I am aware of;
but the full introduction of Ward Election iniquity into the election
of members has unquestionably been reserved for our last contest.[22]

At the second election after the Reform Act Gurney transferred
his attention, with no better success, to the county and contested
the eastern division of Norfolk, finishing at the bottom of the poll.
In these circumstances the reforming party at Norwich approached
R. M. Bacon, the editor and proprietor of the *Norwich Mercury*, and
a friend of Lord Suffield, the reformer and philanthropist. Their
object was to secure the latter's son and heir, the Hon. Edward
Harbord, as liberal candidate for the borough. Suffield, who had
estates and property in sixteen Norfolk parishes and was one of the
most influential of the liberal peers in the county, replied as
follows:

> My dear Sir, . . . I have slept upon the proposition. Norwich to be
> had by such means as are commonly applied, I would *scorn*. Norwich
> to be represented by little or no accompanying expense, ranks in
> my estimation second only to East Norfolk. . . . I do not ask con-
> tribution towards the strictly legal expenses, but I do ask and insist
> upon an indemnification by competent persons, against all other
> expenses. . . .

On the same day, 29 November 1834, the council of the Norwich
Political Union passed a resolution to invite Harbord to become
their candidate. To this invitation the latter replied in suitable
terms but stating that 'I beg to be most explicitly understood, that
should the body of Reformers think fit to desire my services, I come
forward to vindicate purity of election in the strictest sense of the
words.' A meeting of Norwich electors, including bankers, traders,
and merchants, and a separate gathering of dissenters, were held
in favour of Harbord's candidacy; and a formal requisition,
signed by over a thousand electors, was put out for him to stand.
In Harbord's address to the electors of Norwich at the beginning
of December he again dwelt on the subject of purity of elections,
and added that 'under such a condition, I feel that the honour of
victory or the disgrace of success must rest upon yourselves . . . I
can be no more than the *image of your power*.'
To this was added a statement of his political principles, which

[22] *Memoirs of J. J. Gurney*, 1, 466.

were of the conventional liberal and humanitarian pattern. But the prime and almost the only point at issue was the stand against corruption. This was recognized by friends and foes alike. Lord Tavistock, for example, wrote to Suffield to congratulate him on his son's resolute attitude and followed this up a few days later with a second letter in which he hoped that 'you will carry out your principle to its full extent at Norwich, and that if your son's opponents take all the advantages they can derive from money, he will have recourse to the law for his shield, and avail himself of whatever protection it will afford him; otherwise you are engaging in a pure but hopeless contest with corruption. In case of defeat, I should petition against the other candidates merely for treating (or for bribery if it can be detected) without going into further expense.' J. J. Gurney, another friend of Suffield, added his meed of praise. 'One word more on purity of election . . . I rejoice that thy son purposes to take that ground. It is truly wise and right, and will in my opinion go far to secure his election.'

Here then was the issue of pure election *versus* corruption more clearly laid down perhaps than in any other contemporary election; and though the challenge had been put out in a constituency long famous for its venality, the combination of liberalism, dissent, and aristocratic connexion that Harbord brought to the hustings was not to be lightly estimated. Yet in the event, as Tavistock had correctly foreseen, it was a pure but hopeless contest. Lord Stormont and R. C. Scarlett were returned at the head of the poll, defeating Harbord and his colleague Martin by 300 votes. This was a larger margin than that which had separated Scarlett from Gurney in 1832. It was obvious that the issue of purity had not induced any noticeable number of voters to vote for Harbord in 1835 that had not done so for Gurney in 1832. The liberals of Norwich celebrated their gallant defeat by a dinner for the sixteen hundred unbought electors who had voted for Harbord and Martin. But little or nothing had in fact been done to eradicate corruption at Norwich. At the next election two conservative members, Lord Douro and Scarlett, were returned at a cost which if Greville was right could scarcely be repeated. This time, however, the defeated side did petition and Scarlett was unseated in favour of one of the liberal candidates, Smith. In 1841 Douro and Smith again shared the representation but this time without a contest. This truce was probably due, as one radical pamphlet suggested, to financial exhaustion on both sides and the deterrent effect of past expenditure on prospective candidates.[23] That indeed was one remedy which the corrupt borough periodically produced of itself; but its efficacy was apt to be brief and it could never in any case reach to the seat of the malady. Certainly the heroic prescription of Lord Suffield had been entirely without effect. The melancholy but indisputable fact remained that Harbord and Martin who alone fought their election campaign on the issue of electoral purity, were defeated by larger majorities and secured less votes than any other liberal candidates at Norwich in the first decade after the Reform Act.[24] It was a natural and instructive circumstance.

[23] *England and Ireland, A Political Cartoon* (1844), 23.
[24] For the history of Harbord's candidature, see Bacon, *Memoir of Lord Suffield*, 480 sqq.

Chapter Eight

INFLUENCE AND CONTROL

IN many constituencies of the kingdom the methods of bribery and intimidation gave way to or were accompanied by methods of control and influence. It is true that both sets of methods often overlapped; bribery might gild an inexorable pressure and violence might underline authority. But the distinction is clear enough. The first were temporary and specific devices; the second were based on a permanent disposition of circumstances.

In the towns the corporations were often identified with one or other of the political parties and exercised some effect on parliamentary elections. At York, for instance, the corporation was whig and the borough in consequence was usually considered a whig seat although in practice the seats were divided. At Ipswich the common council was 'blue' or tory; at Nottingham the corporation was whig—a circumstance which probably enabled Hobhouse to be returned for the borough in 1834 although he was not the popular candidate. At Leominster the corporation was said to control nearly 150 votes and the influence of the corporation at Harwich was said to be prevalent and irresistible.[1] Where, in addition to the usual petty patronage of a borough, the corporations controlled large charitable endowments and revenues, the power exerted must have been considerable. Charities, in many cases, were little more than permanent electioneering and bribery funds. At Bristol, where the town charities were made a source of parliamentary influence in this way, actual charitable disbursements amounted to over £16,000 per annum and loans to nearly another £6,000.[2] The corporation at Leicester was specially notorious for the political use it made of its public funds. It controlled various charitable and trust moneys, as for example, the Sir Thomas White fund of some £18,000 which was lent out in sums of £100 for nine years without interest to deserving tradesmen, together with other and similar patronage: a boys' school, for instance, the Green Coat school, where there were free places with clothing in

[1] P.P. 1835, VIII, 43, 57; 1835, IX, 202; 1835, X, 667.
[2] P.P. 1835, VIII, 385-7.

the gift of the corporation; or nomination to the Trinity Hospital which had over a hundred rooms. All these were used as political instruments to secure votes and it was reckoned that at Leicester, where a fifth of the electorate was in any case regarded as venal, the corporation controlled another six or seven hundred votes besides. The same misuse of charitable endowments went on at Ipswich, Coventry, and Hereford.[3]

The universities provided another type of borough influence which was parallel in many ways to that of the corporations. At Cambridge the university exercised a powerful influence over the town through the shopkeepers, the college servants, the lodging-house keepers and other classes dependent on colleges or university authorities. On one occasion the vice-chancellor sent round the marshal of the university before an election to recommend a particular candidate to the licensed lodging-house keepers. The number of these was between 200 and 300, and the majority, by reason of their profession, would no doubt come within the £10 householder class of voter. At the time of the by-election at Cambridge in 1834 the day for granting licences to the lodging-house keepers was significantly deferred until after the parliamentary election. Public-house keepers, who also needed a licence from the vice-chancellor, were equally dependent and controlled. In their case the butler of the vice-chancellor himself went round to recommend candidates whom his master signified for approval. Heads and tutors of colleges also possessed means of controlling the town electorate either through the college servants (over 100 of whom possessed the franchise at this time), or through trades-men by giving and withholding the custom of the college, or through the husbands of the college bedmakers. The practice was so notorious that in March 1835 several members of the university senate issued a circular protesting against interference by the university in the town elections 'in consequence of a very general impression that intimidation and persecution were employed by some members of the university'. A Cambridge solicitor believed that nearly 200 electors in the borough gave their votes under improper influence and there was an established case in which the private gardener of the president of Queens' College was dismissed for voting on the liberal side in 1834.[4]

It may indeed be stated as a generalization that wherever in

[3] P.P. 1835, VIII, 83, 113, 128–31.   [4] P.P. 1835, VIII, 8–27.

ordinary social and economic relationships there existed authority on the one side and dependence on the other, political influence was always liable to be exercised. One of the commonest methods was that of 'exclusive dealing'; that is to say, dealing exclusively with shopkeepers of one's own political persuasion or withdrawing custom from shopkeepers who had followed an opposed line at elections. This practice was to be found in most constituencies whether urban or rural and must have been one of the ordinary concomitants of business life in this period. But the habit of using this kind of pressure for political purposes was universal. Employers influenced contractors, manufacturers their work-people, masters their servants, customers their shopmen, landlords their tenants, clients their solicitors, breweries their tied houses, and clergy their congregations. Everything depended on the degree of pressure that could be brought to bear. The power of the landlord might be exercised in a small personal way like the spirited landlady at Hertford in 1832 who had the election colours of her late husband torn down by a gang of election bullies and retaliated by giving her tenant notice to quit unless he voted against the offending party.[5] Or on a grander scale like Planta's friend, the speculative builder of Rye, who purchased the whole sea-front between Hastings and St Leonards and built houses on it, 'every one of which will have a vote and will be under his Controul. This is doing things by wholesale. He told me yesterday (and he is quite a quiet man and no Boaster) that at an Election two or three years hence, if there be one, he shall have at least 100 fresh votes, and all for me.'[6] The power of the brewer may be exemplified by the firm of Mead & Co. at Rochester which was said in 1839 to make some thirty votes difference in the county election and probably as many in the borough.[7] Many of the clergy, both established and nonconformist, joined in the political controversies of their neighbourhood. Indeed to a large extent religion was itself a species of politics. In Essex, where it was stated that 'the dissenters . . . almost to a man adopt one line of politics; they are all of the Yellow party; they are Reformers as opposed to the Tories and Anti-Reformers', the clergy of both kinds vigorously joined in the 1835 election. No doubt the influence of clergy was often confined to admonition from the pulpit. But they were not entirely

[5] P.P. 1833, IX, 238.
[6] Planta to Wellington, 7 December 1834 (Add. MS. 40309, fo. 372).
[7] Add. MS. 40617, fo. 75.

free from more militant methods of propagating their political gospels. 'I find clergymen', one witness told a parliamentary committee, 'not only the most persevering and unscrupulous canvassers but also the best keepers of their promises in not continuing their custom or otherwise.'[8] One of the most active of canvassers on Palmerston's behalf in his Hampshire elections was Dr Thomas Garnier, Dean of Winchester and a zealous whig.[9] And Sir George Clerk, defeated in the county of Edinburgh in 1832, ascribed the result chiefly to the defection of voters from his side under clerical pressure. 'The principal reason of the defalcation of my supporters', he wrote to Peel, 'has arisen from the active interference of the Dissenting Ministers who have been the keenest partizans of Dalrymple.'[10] Since in the thirties and forties ecclesiastical legislation was one of the major issues dividing parties, it is not surprising that the churches took a keen interest in political affairs. Lord Lincoln who narrowly escaped defeat in the Falkirk district of burghs in the general election of 1847, reported that 'the Free Kirk, and all the Dissenting ministers, have been most active against me, and denounced the pains of Hell on Sunday last in their chapels against those who voted for a friend of the Papists'.[11] Lincoln's sin, of course, was not participation in the repeal of the Corn Laws, but his support for the Maynooth grant.

The poorer classes, too, even though unenfranchised, used their influence when and where they could. Leveson-Gower's election for Stoke in 1852 was an illustration of what could be done in this way. He put up for the constituency in the liberal interest together with J. L. Ricardo, a nephew of the great economist. Against them was the other sitting member, Alderman Copeland, who had considerable influence in the potteries and was backed by most of the great manufacturers except the Mintons. 'The working men then had no votes', wrote Leveson-Gower afterwards, describing the contest. 'In many streets the publicans were the only electors, but the working men were enthusiastic for Free Trade, and won the election for us by threatening the publicans and shopkeepers to withdraw their custom unless they promised to vote for us.'[12] There were occasions obviously when the absence of the

---

[8] P.P. 1835, VIII, 45, 55.   [9] Earl of Albemarle, *Fifty Years of My Life*, 75.
[10] Add. MS. 40403, fo. 150. Clerk's successful opponent was Lt.-Gen. Sir John Hamilton Dalrymple.
[11] Parker, *Peel*, III, 489.   [12] Leveson-Gower, *Bygone Years*, 239.

ballot was not without its advantages for the advanced liberals. In the closely-knit communities of the towns there must have been a multiplicity of influences converging on the individual elector which could not always have been very easy to bear. Joseph Parkes once spoke of 'very public spirited men in a remarkable manner . . . tortured as to their vote' and sometimes deciding that the exercise of the franchise was not worth the trouble it involved.[13] Yet if the franchise was to be regarded in any sense as a trusteeship, it was inevitable that pressure from many sources would be brought against the holder of the franchise and that this would be one of the penalties of the privilege. No doubt the position of an elector was not always a comfortable one. Yet it is possible that the decision of an electorate actuated in this manner corresponded more truly to the general interests of the constituency, interpreted as a combination of power, property, and numbers, than one produced by a secret ballot and representing merely the views and interests of the electoral minority. Because the result was secured by rough and frequently forcible methods, it was not necessarily a travesty of the political opinions of the community concerned.

One of the most interesting and widely spread forms of influence was that exercised by the landowner over his tenants. That influence was all the more effective because it was not based on a crude relationship of tyranny and subservience but on a more complex tie of mutual interest and obligation. In the towns the power of the landlord to evict his tenants played a prominent part; but in the country districts, where the landlords as a class were far more important, the situation was semi-feudal and the tenant followed the political tenets of his landlord as a kind of political service due to the owner of the land from the occupier. It would be a mistake to attribute this entirely or even mainly to coercion. 'I have now had a good deal of experience in county canvassing', wrote a local conservative politician to Lord Aberdeen in 1841, 'and I have been led to the conclusion that the tenantry of Scotland are on the whole very indifferent to points of mere civil politics—they feel no great interest in either party and therefore they will not quarrel with their landlords on such subjects.'[14] Joseph Parkes uttered a similar sentiment about the English rural voter. 'A great many county voters', he said, 'are persons without any decided opinion.'[15] And a witness before a

[13] P.P. 1835, VIII, 106. [14] Balfour, *Life of Aberdeen*, II, 92. [15] P.P. 1835, VIII, 107.

parliamentary commission stated that in Suffolk 'the individual feeling among the farmers is that their vote is their landlords'.[16] No doubt this attitude of indifference or passive obedience was assisted by the feeling that the tenant was in any case helpless against pressure from his landlord. But it is unlikely under any circumstance that the ordinary farmer of the thirties and forties took a great interest in or had much knowledge of home and foreign policy. When the agricultural community was stirred, as it was over the reform issue in 1831, or over the malt tax in the thirties, or over the corn laws in the forties, the county electorate could convey its opinions with considerable emphasis whether they were in agreement or not with the views of the landlords. Indeed, if any class was coerced in 1831, it was the landlords; and some of them equally certainly in 1846. But where the direct interests of the farming population were not affected, rural electors saw no particular loss of principle in voting in accordance with the known wishes of their landlords.

On ordinary political issues, therefore, the vote of the tenantry followed the views of the landlord. Joseph Parkes on one occasion committed himself to the statement that political influence in the county constituencies 'applies so much to the tenantry that the poll-book is almost a topography of the estates'.[17] Some examples of this characteristic were produced before a parliamentary committee in 1835. In Rattery, a parish of south Devon, twenty out of twenty-one electors were tenants of Sir Walter Carew. In 1832 Carew voted for Bulteel, the whig candidate, and all his tenants followed suit. In 1835 Carew voted for the tory, Parker, and all but one of the tenants did the same. In another parish, owned by Sir Thomas Acland, who made a similar change of side in the two elections, the great majority of electors voted whig in 1832 and tory in 1835.[18] So much was this kind of loyalty expected, that it was a matter of conventional courtesy at this time to seek the permission of the landlord before canvassing his tenants, even though he was of the same political party. Even that very radical whig, Joseph Parkes, did not consider it 'always an act of propriety to canvass among the tenants of a landlord on either side and particularly my own side without having the landowner's leave'.[19] It is true, of course, that even if leave were refused, many agents

---

[16] P.P. 1835, VIII, 89.
[18] P.P. 1835, VIII, 160–3.

[17] P.P. 1835, VIII, 105.
[19] P.P. 1835, VIII, 105.

would canvass without it; but this was not altogether a gentle-manly proceeding. It was not a general habit and when it oc-curred, it often evoked an indignant protest. In a county such as Herefordshire, for example, it was not the custom to canvass tenants on behalf of a political party or candidate to which the landlord was known to be opposed; and attempts to do so in other parts of the country were productive of bad feeling. The protest of one of the Grosvenor family against Gladstone's canvassing in the election of 1841 is well known, though the language will bear repetition: 'I did think that interference between a landlord, with whose opinions you were acquainted, and his tenants, was not justifiable according to those laws of delicacy and propriety which I considered binding in such cases.'[20] This may be capped with another and less known instance. Peel's old friend, the Rt. Hon. Dennis Daly, former M.P. for Galway, complained to him after the general election of 1837 that his son, James Daly,[21] had been defeated in Galway 'principally by a most extraordinary trans-action. Lord Mulgrave sent down one of his aide-de-camps to canvass Lord Clanricarde's tenantry to vote against my son in opposition to the written wishes of their landlord. I think I never heard of anything so monstrously unconstitutional.'[22] Obviously the custom of observing what might be called landlord right existed. But equally clearly there were occasions on which it was disregarded. Public opinion on the whole was still slightly shocked at any attempt to seduce a tenant from his political allegiance: but in the excitement of an election campaign both candidates and agents might refuse to accept the principle that the vote of the tenant was the property of the landlord.

Whether canvassed or not, however, landlords could usually control their tenants. Sometimes the mere knowledge of the land-lord's sentiments was enough. Lord Seymour wrote to his father in 1839, for example, requesting him to instruct his steward 'that the tenantry in Lincolnshire should be allowed to vote as they please, but certainly are not in any manner precluded from voting for Mr Handley.[23] They are, I hear, all really friendly to him but

[20] Morley, *Gladstone*, I, 178.

[21] M.P. for co. Galway 1832–4; defeated in the same constituency 1837; created Baron Dunsandle and Clan Conal (Ireland) in 1845.

[22] Add. MS. 40424, fo. 5.

[23] Henry Handley of Culverthorpe Hall, Sleaford, M.P. Lincolnshire (Part of Kesteven) 1832–41. He was a liberal, but also a strong agriculturalist who seconded the Chandos Malt Tax motion in 1835.

do not wish to vote in any way that might be unpleasant to you.'[24]
Sometimes a more formal hint was necessary. Old Lord Eldon
made the long journey to his northern estates in 1837 and had all
his tenants there to dine with him. He then delivered an election
address, the purpose of which was clear even if the language was
veiled. He said that it was of the greatest importance that a conservative member should be returned for the county; that his own
sentiments were well known, but that 'I should leave it to my
tenants to exercise the franchise which parliament had given them
in such a manner as should appear to them to be right and according to good conscience, and as most likely to uphold that Church
in which the purest doctrines of our religion are taught in the best
manner.'[25] Harsher terms were occasionally used. It was said
that in 1834 orders had been issued to the tenants of Lord Derby
as to the candidates for whom they were to vote; and Egerton
spoke of the last turn of the screw being given to a reluctant
tenantry by the great whig magnates of Lancashire, Lord Derby,
Lord Lilford, and Hesketh Fleetwood.[26] These were tories talking
of whigs and liable therefore to fall into a certain exaggeration.
Nevertheless there can be little doubt that on occasions peremptory instructions were issued. One instance of this was made
public during the reform crisis. In 1831 the Duke of Northumberland's tenants received a circular requesting their support for a
petition against the reform bill which was couched in these terms:

> The Duke's Commissioners send to Mr.———, for his own and the
> signatures of the tenants of his bailiwick, counterparts of Addresses
> to the King and the two Houses of Parliament, in respect to the
> present Reform Bill, the original of which his Grace has signed and
> in the promotion of which, his Lordship desires activity may be used
> as a return is expected in a few days; trusting that all persons con-
> nected with him will join in the prayer of the petitions, which their
> neighbours should have an opportunity of signing if they think fit.
> The Duke requires the names of tenants who do not sign and hopes
> that they will not embark rashly in politics, if they wish to place
> confidence in his opinions, which can only be truly learnt through
> his Commissioners.
>
> Commissioners Office, Alnwick Castle,
> April 5th.

[24] Mallock, *Letters of the Duke of Somerset*, 92.   [25] Twiss, *Life of Eldon*, III, 284–5.
[26] Add. MS. 40424, fo. 17; Parker, *Peel*, II, 266.

It is true that this missive appeared before the Reform Act. It may also be true that it was the action not of the duke but of his over-zealous agents. Sir Henry Hardinge, speaking in the House of Commons, put the blame for the document entirely on the commissioners and said that the duke had never seen it until a copy was reproduced in the local paper at Alnwick and printed in *The Times*.[27]

Nevertheless there is no reason to suppose that written instructions to tenants regarding their political behaviour were unknown in the period after 1832. Indeed, in the case of large estates with many tenants, it is difficult to see how otherwise a clear expression of the landlord's views could be made known to his tenants. How common was the practice is more difficult to ascertain since such documents would not usually be made public. But another example has been preserved relating to the north Staffordshire election of 1847. The candidates on this occasion were C. B. Adderley and Viscount Brackley, standing as conservatives, and Buller as the sole representative of the whigs. The position was complicated, however, by the relationship between Brackley and the great whig landowner, the Duke of Sutherland. The 2nd Marquess of Stafford, who from his seat at Trentham exercised a powerful influence over Staffordshire county politics, had married in 1785 the Countess of Sutherland and long afterwards, in 1833 was created 1st Duke of Sutherland. In 1803 his uncle, the 3rd and last Duke of Bridgwater, had left him the bulk of his fortune with the reversion to his second son, Francis Leveson-Gower. The latter assumed the family name of his benefactor, Egerton, and obtained in 1846 the titles of Earl of Ellesmere and Viscount Brackley (both subordinate honours of the former Bridgwater earldom). It was his son and heir, George Granville Francis Egerton, styled Viscount Brackley, who was now standing as conservative candidate along with the sitting member Adderley. He was thus in a somewhat equivocal position. On the one side, since he was a close relative of the Duke of Sutherland, there was in the early stages of the election campaign a general impression that the Trentham influence would be divided between Buller (on party grounds) and Brackley (on family grounds). On the other hand, many conservatives were annoyed at a relative of the whig Duke of Sutherland standing as a conservative in the duke's own

[27] *Hansard*, III, 1721-3.

county; and in fact there was in consequence of this connexion some doubts of the solidity of Brackley's conservatism even though he was at some pains to demonstrate his complete independence of the Sutherland family influence. Peel, for instance, though urged by Adderley to support both the conservative candidates, only recorded his vote for the latter. The whig-liberal interest was of course stoutly opposed to both Adderley and Brackley. A great deal therefore seemed to hang on the attitude of the Duke of Sutherland. Originally his interest was believed to have been given to Lord Brackley, but on the eve of the poll a general intimation was issued to his tenants that he desired them to cast a single vote only for Buller. This request was duly observed; the Sutherland tenants went to the hustings and gave plumpers for the whig candidate. The agent's circular which conveyed the duke's final decision ran as follows:

Trentham Aug. 7.

Dear Sir,

I have to inform you that the Duke's influence must be given to that Member who gives his confidence to the Government. Mr. Buller therefore has the Duke's good wishes.

(Signed) W. Steward.[28]

Undoubtedly, therefore, this type of formal direction of tenants continued after the Reform Act. Nevertheless it would be fallacous to assume that a great landowner could oppress and tyrannize over his tenants at every election. No proprietor who was dependent on his rents could afford to encounter the volume of discontent which such a course of action would encounter or risk the wholesale eviction of tenants which was his ultimate weapon. A more moderate and sensible comment was that of Palmerston when he was defeated in Hampshire in 1835. 'The event', he wrote to Russell, 'was the result of an immense combination of Tory influence assisted by the distressed state of the farmers, who being in arrear and looking for abatements, were more than usually dependent on the landlords.'[29] A tactful appeal was probably as often used by the landlord as the explicit threat. When Sir James Graham was faced with the task of leading his

[28] Add. MS. 40599, fos. 134, 183, 187. The result of the contest was: Adderley 4083; Brackley 4071; Buller 3350.
[29] Russell, *Early Corr.*, II, 72.

tenants from the whig to the tory fold after his own change of allegiance, he preferred to exercise persuasion and personal contact rather than give orders at second hand. He would, he wrote to Bonham, have 'some difficulty in persuading some of my tenants and odd adherents to vote for a Lowther; yet I will do all in my power to support him'. When the general election arrived, he went in person to Cumberland and reported to Bonham on arrival that 'for the next few days I shall occupy myself in a canvass of my tenants. It is fortunate I came down; they would have gone astray or remained neutral; now I think I shall succeed in bringing them to the post.'[30] It was important for a politically-minded landlord to control the votes of his tenants; it was hardly less important for him to retain their goodwill and respect. The better and wiser landowners managed to do both.

It must not be forgotten either that a few high-minded landowners were prepared to allow their tenants freedom of political conscience. The liberal and reforming Edward Harbord ranked in this period second only to Lord Ashley as an example of that unusual phenomenon, a humanitarian and religious peer. When he succeeded to his tory brother in 1831 as 3rd Baron Suffield, he publicly announced his desire to leave every individual on his large Norfolk estates free to follow his own inclination in politics. There is no reason to doubt that this liberty was genuinely and consistently maintained. It cannot be doubted either that such freedom was a rare and possibly embarrassing possession. After the county election of 1835 one of Suffield's tenants punctiliously wrote to him to explain 'my reasons for giving my vote yesterday in opposition to your Lordship's principles' and added that 'during a period in which two contested elections have taken place for this division of the county, never at any time in the slightest degree either directly or indirectly, has the influence which your Lordship (as my landlord) possesses over me, been exercised to induce me to give my vote contrary to my known principles'. The very effusiveness of the compliment betrays the singularity of the privilege.[31] Lord Ashley himself, though equally prepared to let his tenants vote as they thought best, unconsciously regarded any marked deviation from their landlord's views as insubordination. Writing to Bonham at the time of the general election of 1852, six years after Peel had outraged the agricultural constituencies by repealing the

[30] Add. MS. 40616, fos. 139, 209.   [31] Bacon, *Memoir of Lord Suffield*, 490.

Corn Laws, he informed him that there had been a revolt of tenants in Dorset and that some one had stirred them up to expect a return of protection in some form or other. All but three of his own tenants had not only refused to vote for Sturt but also refused to stay neutral. It may be observed, to underline the unusual nature of this defection, that Henry Charles Sturt was not only a local resident (his seat was at Crichel) and a member for the county from 1835 to 1846, but in addition he was first cousin to Ashley (who had succeeded as Earl of Shaftesbury in 1851), his mother having been Lady Mary Ann Ashley, daughter of the 4th earl. However, Shaftesbury had strong views on the freedom of election and so contented himself by informing his tenants that 'I should consider their support of Sturt "a personal kindness" to myself but that I must regard them as electors absolutely and entirely independent.'[32]

There were of course other elements in the county electorate besides the tenant farmer which were not always so amenable. The freeholder, the inhabitant of the small town, the artisan, the dissenter, were as familiar a part of the rural electorate as the tenant or leaseholder though their political opinions might often differ. Yet though a small opposition existed even in the most rural counties it was rarely enough by itself to outweigh landlord influence. Moreover as often as not it was denied the opportunity of a contested election to record its vote. In any case the network of patronage and influence was spread far wider than the tenant class. Freeholders and copy holders were dependent on men of authority; shopkeepers on men of wealth; the village artisans on farmers. There were discordant voices but the rural community was as much an integrated family as it was a battle-ground for jarring class struggles. The influence of the landlord was probably reinforced rather than diminished by the other elements in the rural electorate. There was at least no simple division of the electorate in political terms between the freeholder and the tenant. The apparent economic independence of the former made little difference to his exercise of the franchise. Freeholders were divided into parties and guided by local influences in the same way as the tenants. An analysis of the 1835 by-election in south Devon, made by one of the principal parliamentary agents in the county, revealed a curious identity of party grouping among

[32] Add. MS. 40617, fo. 282.

freeholders and tenants. The constituency was composed of seven
districts. In five of these a majority of leaseholders for either candidate was accompanied by a roughly proportionate majority for
the same candidate among the freeholders. The total figures of
the polling for the election were: whig, 1,894 freeholders and 1,234
leaseholders; tory, 1,897 freeholders and 1,840 leaseholders.[33] It is
clear that if influence was exerted, it applied as much to the freeholders as to the tenants and must therefore have been something
more pervasive and indirect than the mere threat to evict
tenantry. And, in fact, the influence of the landed classes can only
be appreciated when they are considered not only as owners of
land and landlords of tenants, but as magistrates, patrons, clients,
customers, holders of advowsons, controllers of appointments,
chairmen of committees, members of parliament, officials of the
government, subscribers to charity, local sportsmen, officers in the
militia, and finally as leaders of county society and the great agricultural interest.

It was these circumstances that enabled the great territorial
magnates, both whig and tory, to maintain their influence, and in
favourable conditions to exercise a preponderant power. If their
direct control had been limited through the abolition of pocket
boroughs and the widening of the corporation boroughs, the
Reform Act had done nothing to curb their authority when it
sprang directly from property and position. Indeed the purpose
of the act had been to destroy the illegitimate not the legitimate
influence of property; and the early Victorian conception of
legitimacy in this context was not fundamentally different from
that of the eighteenth century. Thus only the positions of the
Duke of Buckingham and the Duke of Bedford explain why
Buckinghamshire was mainly a tory and Bedfordshire mainly a
whig county. Similar territorial and family influences help to
explain the politics of other districts: the Marquess of Salisbury
in Hertfordshire, the Earl of Derby in north Lancashire, the Earl
of Orford in Norfolk, the Duke of Manchester in Huntingdonshire,
the Duke of Rutland in Leicestershire, the Duke of Devonshire in
Derbyshire, the Duke of Newcastle in Nottinghamshire, the Earl
of Shaftesbury in Dorset, Earl Spencer in Northamptonshire, and
Lord Segrave in Gloucestershire. Cumberland returned whigs in
the eastern division of the county and tories in the western division

[33] P.P. 1835, VIII, 159.

because the Earl of Carlisle was paramount in the former and the Earl of Lonsdale in the latter. In the smaller counties north of the border the power of the great aristocratic families was perhaps even more pronounced. The Duke of Gordon, the Duke of Sutherland, and the Duke of Buccleuch were dominating figures in Scottish politics from their territorial position alone. The Earl of Aberdeen had control of his native county as had the Duke of Argyll in his. Within a narrower range there were many others with great influence in their own localities: the Duke of Montrose in Dumbartonshire, Lord Galloway and Lord Selkirk in the Stewartry of Kirkcudbright, the Earl of Lauderdale in Berwickshire, Lord Douglas in Lanarkshire, and the Earl of Wemyss in Haddington burghs. Sutherland, like Rutland in England, was virtually a close borough.

In Wales the feudal tradition was carried on by the power of such magnates as Lord Cawdor in Pembrokeshire; or by families of lesser title but of as great an antiquity like the Wynns in Denbighshire and Montgomeryshire, the Mostyns of Flint, or the Bulkeleys of Anglesey. In Montgomeryshire the Hon. Charles W. W. Wynn had sat as county member for half a century and on his death in 1850 he was succeeded in his seat by Herbert W. W. Wynn. From 1832 to 1852 there was never a contested election in the county. In Flintshire, which his family had represented for a century and a half, the Hon. Edward M. L. Mostyn had an almost comparable record. He was elected in 1831, 1832, and 1835 without opposition; in 1837 he was narrowly defeated by a local rival, Sir Stephen Glynne (soon to be Gladstone's brother-in-law); in 1841 the struggle was resumed but this time Mostyn headed the poll after a fierce struggle in which every ounce of influence, legitimate or otherwise, was put into the scales.[34] A petition was brought against his return, however, and he was unseated in favour of his opponent. At the next election Mostyn was again returned, and once more in 1852. Two years later he succeeded his father as Lord Mostyn and was replaced in the House of Commons by Edward Thomas Mostyn who inflicted another defeat on the pertinacious Sir Stephen in 1857. In the small insular constituency of Anglesey Sir Richard Bulkeley was returned for every parliament except two between the first and second Reform Acts

---

[34] It was at this election that Gladstone, who assisted Glynne in his campaign, earned the reproof from the Grosvenor family repeated above.

(1832–1865). The exceptions were the elections of 1837 and 1841 when W. O. Stanley of Penthos, the second son of Sir John Stanley of Alderley, Cheshire, and through the collateral line of the Stanleys of Hooton a distant kinsman of Bulkeley, was returned unopposed. Anglesey indeed must have been almost impervious to party intervention. In 1836 there had been no contest in the constituency for half a century.[35]

Both for their own sake and for the sake of the power they still wielded in many different counties, the great landed families formed an important item in party and electoral calculations. The control of the House of Commons by the House of Lords may have been diminished in 1832 but through relatives, younger sons, supporters, and direct electoral influence, the peerage maintained after the Reform Act a direct and active interest in the members of the lower house. Their approval was sought for candidates in the constituencies where they held power; their relatives, friends or acquaintances were given preference in the complicated personal negotiations which often preceded the publication of a candidate's name; feuds between neighbouring magnates were assiduously smoothed down so that both could be brought into the field on behalf of the same candidate; the problems of bringing the right influence to bear in the right quarters through the right agents was carefully studied; attention was paid to the heirs of great estates or to the purchasers of such whenever they came on the market; and all the personal contacts which meant as much or more than abstract party loyalty or academic political principle were brought into play. Personal friends or official supporters could be approached directly and their assistance claimed as a matter of course. But outside that relatively small circle, more tactful and circuitous methods had to be employed. In 1832 when it became a matter of importance to the tories to secure the good will of Lord Abergavenny, it was arranged by Arbuthnot for the Earl of Rosslyn, one of the most influential of the party managers, to write to the Earl of Lauderdale as being 'the person most capable of influencing Lord Abergavenny'.[36] In 1837 when W. M. Praed was fighting a difficult contest at Aylesbury against Lord Nugent, he found the support he might have expected from Lord Carrington's tenants endangered by the presence of the latter's son, who was the sitting whig member for High Wycombe.

[35] P.P. 1836, XLIII, 406.   [36] Add. MS. 40617, fo. 2.

He therefore put in an appeal to Bonham. 'Ld. Carrington has many tenants here: mostly well disposed towards us but likely to be driven the wrong way by Robert Smith. Can anything be done with Lord Carrington through Ld. Granville Somerset or Lord Mahon to neutralise his son's mischief?'[37] In 1839 Sir James Graham endeavoured to persuade Frank Charteris to stand for Haddington burghs, a candidacy which could not fail to be successful if supported by the influence of his father, Lord Elcho, and his grandfather, the Earl of Wemyss. But Charteris, who had just attained his majority, was like many other young sprigs of nobility reluctant to embark so soon on the parliamentary career planned for him by his seniors and refused to stand for at least two or three years. Accordingly Graham hit on the project of persuading Lord Elcho to keep the seat warm, as the saying then went, until that period had elapsed by occupying it himself. He suggested to the party headquarters that an effort should be made to induce Elcho to consent to this proposition through the agency of the Duke of Buccleuch who until his retirement from politics owing to ill health in 1838 had been the leader of the Scots conservatives.[38]

The language in which these magnates were addressed on matters touching their political influence fully corresponded to their importance. An illustration of this may be given from Graham's own chequered career. Graham, together with the rest of the 'Derby Dilly', broke with Grey's ministry in 1834 although he did not for a time throw in his lot with the conservative opposition and floated uneasily between the two parties until the end of the 1835 session. His position at the general election of 1835 was therefore, from a party viewpoint at least, equivocal. Consider, however, the delicacy with which he, M.P. for the county since 1829, ex-cabinet minister, part-author of the Reform Act, and owner of 26,000 acres of land, approached the leading whig magnate of his constituency. Soon after Graham and Stanley had declined Peel's invitation to join the conservative ministry of 1834–5, the former wrote to the Earl of Carlisle about his political position. He said that he had not asked for Carlisle's support until the latter had the opportunity of seeing Graham's conduct with respect to the formation of the new government. But Graham's refusal to join the ministry, his public address to his constituents,

[37] Add. MS. 40617, fo. 32.   [38] Add. MS. 40616, fos. 47, 78.

and Carlisle's own knowledge of Graham personally 'will enable you now to judge whether you still think me worthy of representing in Parliament the division of the county in which you have so preponderating an influence'.[39] With such a formal etiquette of approach, even when party ties, personal acquaintanceship, and past connexion existed to sanction it, there can be little surprise that party managers frequently found it impossible to intervene in constituencies where the known presence of a specific electoral influence might make such activity seem gross interference. As a general rule both candidates and party men relied not on any identity of political attitude but on personal relationships to secure the influence they required. The principles governing such approaches were that they were only undertaken through personal friends, or where the potentate concerned was or had been a member of a ministry formed by the party on whose behalf his influence was being sought. Acceptance of office stamped a man as belonging to the inner ring of a political party and justified subsequent calls on his services. But mere general adherence to whig or tory principles did not of itself warrant a claim to the exercise of political influence in favour of any stranger professing the same brand of opinion. The leaders of the parties themselves, whether from fear of a rebuff or unwillingness to lay themselves open to future counter-claims, refused to make overtures that were not based either on private relationships or official connexions.

If, therefore, by carefully selected channels, local interests and family connexions could often be diverted to the advantage of the parliamentary parties, there also existed fields of influence in which party intervention was not practicable. Sometimes indeed even more complex situations arose to baffle the party loyalists. In a number of counties or constituencies there were no great landowners with commanding influence and ambitious views who might be susceptible to party and government blandishments, and could provide a point of leverage to influence a whole district. Power might reside in the hands of some ten, twenty, or thirty country gentlemen of comfortable wealth and independent outlook who decided among themselves the representation of the county in parliament and were not easily amenable to any form of central influence. Such men might occasionally prefer the claims

[39] Parker, *Life of Graham*, I, 221.

of family connexion, personal popularity, and good neighbour-
liness, to those of party loyalty and political principle. The relics
of a genuine county sentiment still remained to cut across and
occasionally stultify the conventional lines of party. An example
of this strong local feeling is provided by the gentry of Cornwall in
this period. The situation there is worth recalling for the light it
throws on the close personal relationships often present among the
country gentry and their relative indifference to the feuds of
reformers and anti-reformers that agitated the distant metropolis.

As far as the county representation was concerned Cornwall was
almost a whig preserve. In the western division of the county two
whigs, Edward W. W. Pendarves and Sir Charles Lemon, were
returned without a contest in the elections of 1832, 1835, and 1837.
The eastern division was almost as consistent. Sir William Molesworth and William L. S. Trelawney, one radical and the other
whig, were returned in 1832 and 1835; Lord Eliot, a conservative
and Sir Richard Hussey Vivian, a whig, in 1837. The difficulty
of upsetting these local arrangements was exemplified by the situation that arose in the western division in 1835. Of the two sitting
members for the constituency Sir Charles Lemon probably enjoyed the regard of both parties. He was the son of Sir William
Lemon, 1st baronet, who had represented the county from 1774
until his death in 1824. By his marriage in 1810 with Lady
Charlotte Anne Strangways he was brother-in-law to the Earl of
Ilchester and the Marchioness of Lansdowne, and thus connected
with one of the purest whig strains. On the other hand he was also
related by marriage to several of the tory families among the
Cornish gentry and was himself more representative of old whiggery than of new liberalism. He voted against his party on the
matter of the surplus Irish Church revenues which decided
the fate of Peel's ministry in 1835 and was absent from the
crucial division on the municipal corporations bill the same year.
Pendarves, his colleague, was a more liberal whig (certainly a
better party man), came of good Cornish stock, and was the senior
member, having first been elected county representative in 1826.
If then it came to an outright party contest in the division, the
probability was that Lemon as the more equivocal of the two
whig members, would be the chief sufferer.

Such a contest now threatened. Lord Boscawen,[40] the son of the

---

[40] Commonly so called; but more properly, Lord Boscawen Rose.

Earl of Falmouth, wished to contest the western division in the hope of unseating Pendarves, the more liberal of the two sitting members. To Falmouth's disgust, however, two of the most influential conservatives of the district, Mr Tremayne and Sir Thomas Acland, refused to support Boscawen's candidature on the grounds that it would endanger Lemon's seat. Lemon was a brother-in-law of Tremayne and it was clear that the latter, though a professed conservative, was primarily a supporter of his relative. The only other important tory magnate who might afford Boscawen sufficient hope was Lord de Dunstanville of Tehidy Park. To add the final irony, however, de Dunstanville was seriously ill just before the election and his affairs were being managed by his wife, who was Sir Charles Lemon's sister.[41] Lord Falmouth tried to obtain the intervention of the leader of the conservative party himself to end the deadlock. But Peel refused to interfere. Neither Acland nor Tremayne, he replied, had had any connexion with him in public life and his private interest with them was limited in the extreme. In those circumstances for Peel to write to them would do no good. In the end Boscawen was obliged to withdraw from the contest from the sheer unwillingness of the Cornish conservatives to oppose the existing whig members. Nobody, wrote Falmouth indignantly to Peel, could start for either division of the county while such conduct was met with from professed·conservatives. This 'league of Tremayne's', as Falmouth styled it, was sufficient to prevent a contest and return Lemon and Pendarves both in 1835 and again in 1837. In the 1841 election Sir Charles Lemon did not stand and Boscawen was at last admitted to share the representation with Pendarves. It would be interesting to know what negotiations preceded this arrangement. Boscawen, however, after his patient waiting was only a member for a year. In 1842 his father's death removed him to the upper house and Sir Charles Lemon came back to fill his vacant seat in the House of Commons. Pendarves and Lemon were re-elected at the general elections of 1847 and 1852. The

---

[41] Lord de Dunstanville had married Miss Harriet Lemon *en secondes noces* in 1824, his first marriage with Miss Hippisley Coxe having produced one daughter. According to Creevey's rather malicious account the second marriage with Miss Lemon, undertaken at the age of sixty-seven, was an 'old passion on his part'. However, the marriage remained childless and on his death in February 1835, the barony of Dunstanville became extinct. The subordinate barony of Basset passed to his daughter Frances (Gore, *Creevey's Life and Times*, 194–5).

former died in 1853 but Sir Charles Lemon sat till 1857, by which
time he was seventy-three.[42]

A similar demonstràtion of local and family feeling was afforded
by the 1835 election in Denbighshire. In that county the chief
electoral influence was held by Sir Watkin Williams Wynn who
had himself sat for the county in the tory interest since 1796 in
twelve successive parliaments. His own territorial influence was
mainly in Denbighshire and Merioneth for both of which he was
Lord-Lieutenant and Custos Rotulorum, as well as being head of
the Denbigh militia. But Charles Wynn of Montgomeryshire was
his brother and through his wife he was connected with the Earl
of Powis and the Duchess of Northumberland. Among his relatives he numbered no less than five M.P.s. After the Reform Act,
which gave Denbighshire a second county member, he shared the
county representation with a whig, Robert Biddulph of Chirk
Castle, a landowner and banker, whose family had a long-standing
connexion with Denbigh. In 1835 William Bagot, the youthful
son and heir of Lord Bagot, put up for Denbighshire as a second
conservative candidate. Peel, prompted no doubt by the party
managers, wrote before the election to Charles Watkin Williams
Wynn, whom he had just appointed Chancellor of the Duchy of
Lancaster, asking him to use his influence with Sir Watkin on
Bagot's behalf. Charles Wynn, however, returned a courteous
refusal to the request of his chief. A great number of friends and
neighbours, he explained, had supported his brother when he
stood for the county, although disagreeing with him personally on
politics; and he now felt that they possessed a claim on his services
and that the least he could do in return was to allow his tenants
complete liberty in voting at the forthcoming election. He promised to write to his brother but confessed that he could hardly see
what the latter could do. Possibly he was better than his word;
or perhaps Sir Watkin saw the desirability of strengthening a
ministry in which his brother held high office. At any rate Bagot
duly went to the poll, beat Biddulph in a close contest for the
second seat, and in 1837 and 1841 was returned with Sir Watkin
unopposed. But whatever the inner history of these events, the
language held by Charles Wynn to Peel is indicative of the disadvantages under which the official parties laboured when entering

[42] Add. MS. 40408, fos. 88–90; 40409, fos. 17, 19, 23; 40410, fo. 32. For a brief
sketch of the political attitude of the Cornish gentry a little later in the century, see
Leveson-Gower, *Bygone Years*, 243–8.

the complex field of local county politics, even when there was an official connexion to warrant the attempt.[43]

A kind of analogy to this local sentiment in the counties was to be found in what, for lack of a recognized description, may be called the family boroughs of the time. This type of constituency had been diminished by the Reform Act; but those that remained showed a considerable tenacity of life. They flourished on the strength of local influence and neighbourly attachment, on the inequalities of the borough system, and on the survival of the old franchises; and needed the enlargement of the franchise and the final abolition of the small boroughs for their extinction. But until 1867 at least they provided another item in the static forces of the representative structure. The category, it is true, is difficult to delimit and the family boroughs occupied a dubious position midway between the proprietary borough on the one hand and the independent borough on the other. But a general distinction may be made: a family borough was one which almost invariably returned a member of a particular family in the neighbourhood not merely because of the direct influence of their property but also from motives of local feeling, personal popularity, and respect for the family connexion. A proprietary borough was one that was so much under the control of one proprietor that the electors would return not only him or a member of his family but if necessary any one whom he chose to put forward in his interest. In the one it was the candidate, in the other it was the influence behind the candidate, that was the dominant aspect.

In practice, of course, the distinction was not always easy to maintain. Ludlow, for example, was a borough which in this period was almost impossible to define either as a rotten, pocket, or family borough, though it had elements of all three. The Clive family put forward candidates, frequently members of the family, at each election and were often successful in securing the return of their men. On the other hand there was a considerable amount of bribery and intimidation. Perhaps the most succinct account of the situation in the borough was that given by the landlord of the Golden Lion at Ludlow in 1840. On being asked whether there were no parties in the borough, he replied, 'we have no Tories and Radicals; the politics of Ludlow are whether we are to choose a member for ourselves, or have one family dictate to us,

[43] Add. MS. 40409, fos. 59, 61–2.

and we are called Cliveites and Reformers'.[44] The most famous of all the small boroughs of this period, Tamworth itself, though usually classed in contemporary literature as a pocket borough, is more accurately regarded as a family borough. The electorate invariably returned Peel and whatever second candidate he was thought to favour; but they did so from ties of property and residence and not because they were influenced or coerced. If there was embarrassment, it was because Peel would not sufficiently clearly indicate to the loyal Tamworth electors whom he wished them to send back with him to Westminster.

On more than one occasion Peel asserted that he used no pressure on the Tamworth electorate and once when doubts were cast upon that statement he was prepared to risk his life in vindication against the aspersion. In 1835, after the election in which he and his brother William Yates Peel had been returned unopposed, he stated in the course of a public speech that he had exercised no influence in the borough and that rather than subject the constituency to the feuds of a contested election he would prefer to abandon his own seat. At the following general election, in 1837, Peel and another conservative candidate, Captain A'Court, were returned against the unsuccessful opposition of Captain Townshend.[45] The latter was a member of the family of the Marquess Townshend, High Steward of Tamworth and owner of Tamworth Castle. The polling on this occasion was Peel 389; A'Court 249; and Townshend 185. In the customary speech from the hustings after the declaration of the poll, Townshend claimed that his defeat was really a triumph in view of Peel's failure to abide by the declarations he had made not to interfere with the second seat; and he went on to charge Peel's steward with exercising an undue influence upon the election. Peel contented himself on this occasion with a denial that he had either directly or indirectly interfered. About a month afterwards, however, at a reform dinner given at Tamworth on 20 August 1837, Townshend renewed and indeed redoubled his attack. 'Sir Robert Peel', he declared, 'under the mask of secrecy had exerted his utmost influence to return Captain A'Court and prevent his [Townshend's] election; and he had done it in utter contempt of reiterated declarations and promises solemnly and publicly made.' On 22 August Peel

---

[44] P.P. 1840, IX, 44.
[45] John Townshend, Capt. R.N., b. 1798, cousin of 3rd Marquess Townshend, whom he succeeded in 1855.

wrote to Townshend, through Hardinge, a letter which could only have had one outcome had not the latter substituted for it a note of his own. In the end, after considerable negotiation and delay, Townshend made an apology and retraction, and a retraction also appeared in the press. It is in fact incredible that a man of Peel's integrity would have staked his honour and life on a statement which was not true.[46]

Subsequent evidence, however, relating to the 1847 election confirms that if Peel was popularly considered to have the 'proprietary influence' at Tamworth, he made no attempt to exercise those rights. A'Court had again been returned as Peel's colleague in 1841 and from all appearances would stand once more in the general election of 1847. Some weeks before the election the calm of the borough was shattered by an early and unexpected announcement from William Yates Peel that he would come forward as candidate. It is unlikely that Sir Robert or any other members of his family were pleased by this unceremonious irruption. He had known nothing beforehand of his brother's intention and it could only lead, if persisted in, to the retirement of A'Court or a contest. A'Court had done nothing to deserve the one; and the other would entail an unedifying struggle between Peel's brother and Peel's colleague. Nevertheless Sir Robert remained faithful in this dilemma to the principles of non-intervention which he had proclaimed in past years. He announced his entire neutrality with regard to the second seat at Tamworth; he would not intervene or express an opinion; the constituents must decide for themselves. There is little doubt on the other hand that a clear direction from Peel would have been welcome to many of the Tamworth electors. Some of the usual conservative supporters were annoyed at William Peel's discourtesy and wished to run A'Court against him. The Tamworth protectionists for their part found it prudent to issue a poster denying that they were responsible for bringing William Peel forward to embarrass Sir Robert and unseat A'Court. Finally a body of conservative free-traders formally requested William Peel to retire and not disturb the peace of the borough by opposing the two sitting members. But the recalcitrant William persisted in his campaign, denying that he was in opposition to Sir Robert or acting unfairly to A'Court. In the end the unfortunate

---

[46] Add. MS. 40314, fos. 183–227; Cardwell Papers, P.R.O./G.D./48/53, fos. 103–10; Parker, *Peel*, ii, 350–1.

A'Court, unable to meet the expense of a contest, and fearing perhaps the effect of the family name of William on the Tamworth electors, withdrew from the contest and allowed the other two candidates, in the vernacular of the time, to walk over the course.

This, however, was not the end of the story. Shortly after the election William Peel's wife, Lady Jane Peel, died and even before parliament met the disconsolate widower, left with sixteen mother-less children, contemplated retiring from his newly won honours. As soon as parliament met (18 November 1847) the choice of his successor was actively canvassed. In the Peel family the keenest politician was Sir Robert's second brother, Edmund, who from his neighbouring seat at Bonehill House, Tamworth, kept his eldest brother informed of all the tortuous negotiations that occupied the local dignitaries at the beginning of December. The root of the difficulty was that A'Court showed no disposition to renew the connexion with Tamworth that had ended so unkindly in the summer. No obviously appropriate conservative candidate was available and Peel would have nothing to do with the matter. 'I really imagine', wrote Edmund on 29 November, 'we may return who we like but it will be by appearing to be quite indifferent on the subject. I think a contested election would be a horrid nuisance. As soon as William's intentions are made public, I think there will be a meeting of the Heads of Parties, and that there will be such an indifference evinced about Individuals that all will unite in electing the best Man.' In a later letter to his brother he wistfully asked, 'Can you think of anyone? I am sure there is a very strong feeling to elect anyone who it was thought would be acceptable to you.' But Peel would not stir and while Edmund was reviewing which local conservatives might be induced to come forward in the absence of an A'Court, the old enemy of 1837, Captain John Townshend, came forward as a declared candidate. Edmund was disgusted: 'what can he ever do for the Borough—a less influential Man could not have been found'. Nevertheless in the peculiar circumstances of the constituency nobody else could be found to contest the seat. With Peel indifferent, and certainly neutral, the whig candidate was duly returned for the second seat at Tam-worth.[47] This was not the hall-mark of a pocket borough, even though it was probably only Peel's disinclination to use his control that prevented it from becoming one. Perhaps the most significant

[47] Add. MS. 40598, fos. 303–7, 330–49; 40599, fos. 411–35, 454, 473.

aspect of all, however, is that into the vacuum created by Peel's deliberate withdrawal of his own influence rushed, not the independent verdict of a high-minded electorate, but the secondary influence of the next greatest local magnate.

Tamworth, perhaps, was a hybrid, an essentially pocket borough elevated into a family borough by an unusually scrupulous patron. But elsewhere it is possible to discern a small number of boroughs, about a dozen in all, characterized by small electorates, uncontested elections, and tenure of seat by the members of one particular family. They formed a permanent thread in the pattern of parliamentary membership: the Tyntes at Bridgwater, the Whitmores at Bridgnorth, the Pryses at Cardigan, the Neelds at Chippenham, the Cripps at Cirencester, the Kerrisons at Eye, the Arkwrights at Leominster, the Owens at Pembroke, the Jolliffes at Petersfield, the Prices at Radnor, the Heathcoats at Tiverton, the Blackstones at Wallingford, and the Lopes at Westbury. In some instances the influence seemed to be more that of an individual than of a family. W. S. Blackstone, a descendant of the great lawyer, sat for Wallingford from 1832 to 1852 as a respected and important local resident.[48] Joseph Neeld was one of the most influential conservative landowners of Wiltshire. He had inherited a fortune from his relative, Mr Rundell, a jeweller of Ludgate Hill, and through his marriage in 1831 with Lady Caroline Emily Cooper he was connected with both the Earl of Shaftesbury and the Duke of Marlborough. He sat for the borough of Chippenham from 1832 until his death in 1856. John Heathcoat, returned for Tiverton at every election between 1832 and 1852, was the proprietor of a large lace-manufactory there. The monopoly of representation was not always obtained without a struggle and the family dynasties sometimes experienced defeats and usurpations in the prosecution of their electoral policies. At Westbury, where Sir Manasseh Lopes was returned from 1820 to 1829 and was enabled on one famous occasion to give shelter to Peel himself, the Lopes' influence seemed slightly to decline after the Reform Act, probably as a result of the extension of the borough boundaries. Sir Ralph Lopes was elected in 1832 and 1835 but suffered a defeat in 1837 before his third success in 1841. At Petersfield, on the other hand, where the Jolliffe family had appeared to be losing the predominant power they once possessed, a revival of the family's influence

[48] See below, Ch. 11, pp. 279–81.

took place after 1832. Hylton Jolliffe contested the seat in that year and though placed in a minority at the polls he gained the seat on petition. Sir William Jolliffe was defeated in 1835 but thereafter was returned at each general election up to 1852, being unopposed in the last three.[49] The constituency here was only 234 in 1832 and 253 in 1852.

Leominster in the forties represented what might be described as an incipient family borough. George Arkwright of Sutton Hall, Derbyshire, the great-grandson of the famous inventor Richard Arkwright, was elected M.P. for Leominster at a by-election in 1842 and again at the general elections of 1847 and 1852, chiefly through the influence of another branch of the family, the Arkwrights of Hampton Court, Herefordshire. The by-election of 1842 was consequent on the promotion to the vice-chancellorship of the Court of Chancery of James Wigram, Q.C., of Lincoln's Inn, who had married Anne Arkwright, a grand-daughter of Richard. The family interest in the borough may be said, therefore, to have begun at least by 1841. In 1848 when the other sitting member, Barkly, was appointed governor of British Guiana, the conservatives wished to put up Frederick Peel, the second son of Sir Robert, for the vacancy. Goulburn and Bonham approached Wigram for assistance; the latter readily consented to write to the Leominster Arkwright and was confident that his support would be forthcoming. He added, however, a warning that the best service his relative could do Frederick Peel would be by not appearing openly on his side. The most embarrassing cry raised against himself personally at the 1841 election, Wigram continued, was that Hampton Court was trying to make Leominster a close borough; and as there was already one member for the constituency by the name of Arkwright the revival of such a cry might prove disastrous. But his relative could be trusted to do what was best. With this reply the conservative managers were more than satisfied. Barkly himself was equally encouraging concerning Frederick Peel's chances, 'I see no reason', he wrote to Sir Robert on 1 December 1848, 'why he should fail to secure the vacant seat at Leominster where political feeling has never run very high, provided he can secure a Whig agent whom I retained, & thereby prevent any united opposition being offered by that Party. My colleague's

---

[19] Sir William Jolliffe was unseated on petition in 1838, but was re-elected in 1841 and continued to sit for Petersfield until his elevation to the peerage as Lord Hylton in 1866.

friends I feel pretty sure will wisely rest content with the seat they have got.' Bonham, too, was reassuring. Of Leominster, he told Peel, 'tho' an habitual Croaker, I am disposed to hope & think well'. The protectionists in the constituency, according to his information, were few in number and though they might be disposed to raise an opposition to the son of Sir Robert Peel, such a step might react badly on the position of their own man Arkwright. Provided a quick start was made in the canvassing there was every reason to be hopeful. In this curious medley of forces in the constituency it may reasonably be surmised that the Arkwright family influence was one of the principal factors. The outcome justified the general optimism of Frederick Peel's supporters. He was duly elected M.P. for Leominster in February 1849. It was not perhaps merely coincidental that George Arkwright's next colleague in the representation of the borough was J. G. Phillimore, the elder brother of Gladstone's close friend, and like Wigram a Q.C. and a member of Lincoln's Inn.[50] This apparent consolidation of the Arkwright family interest is particularly interesting since at the time of the Reform Act there had been no special electoral influence in Leominster and it ranked technically as an 'open' borough.[51]

Another example of an incipient family borough, and that too in a constituency created by the Reform Act, was Merthyr Tydfil where Josiah John Guest was returned without a break from 1832 to 1852. As manager and principal proprietor in succession to his father and grandfather of the great Dowlais ironworks, Sir John Guest (he was created a baronet in 1838 by Melbourne) was not only the greatest employer in the town but also one of the greatest ironmasters in the kingdom. In the forties his employees at Merthyr numbered 7,000 with a pay-roll of a quarter of a million pounds per annum and it was computed that some 15,000 of the population were directly dependent on the ironworks in Dowlais alone. Like many other industrialists and commercial men in politics in this era, Guest's parliamentary activities did not begin with the Reform Act. In 1826 he had been elected for Honiton and retained this seat in 1830, losing it in the general election the following year. When Merthyr was enfranchised he put up for his native town and was returned unopposed. The next year he crowned his political

---

[50] Add. MS. 40600, fos. 531, 538, 540; 40617, fos. 255, 257.

[51] *Hansard*, III, 819 sqq. (list of patrons of boroughs in Schedule B of the original reform bill); *Key to Both Houses of Parliament 1832*, 347.

success by a social achievement through his marriage with Lady Charlotte Elizabeth Bertie, the daughter of the 9th Earl of Lindsey. In 1835 he received invitations to stand from both Honiton and Breconshire. But he remained faithful to Merthyr and was once more returned unopposed despite the threat of what Lady Charlotte described as the factious opposition of a local lawyer. In 1837 he stood both for the borough of Merthyr and for the county of Glamorgan; and perhaps in consequence of his temerity received opposition in both constituencies. He was successful in his own borough but was soundly beaten in the county where his whig colleague Talbot displayed a certain coolness to this third candidate who came to disturb an amical division of the representation between the parties. In 1841 there were alarms of a chartist opposition but Guest was again returned unopposed; and in spite of the removal of his family seat to Canford in Dorset in 1846, he was re-elected in 1847 with both whig and tory support. In 1852, with Sir John absent and in poor health, and the renewal of the Dowlais ironworks lease in doubt, his situation seemed weaker than at any time since 1832. But his friends in the borough of all shades of opinion assured him that so long as he chose to represent them he would not be disturbed. Some seven hundred electors, in a constituency that could scarcely have mustered more than that for a poll, subsequently sent him an address begging him not to expose himself to the fatigues of a canvass or even of an appearance on the hustings, and guaranteeing him a safe and untroubled return. The Merthyr electors were as good as their word. At the election, which came on in July, for the sixth and last time Sir John Guest was elected for Merthyr, in his absence and unopposed. He died five months later, the first and only representative his native town had sent to parliament up to that date. The insinuations which the tories sometimes cast against the independence of the borough of Merthyr are understandable. It was a striking example of what might not unfairly be described as a kind of industrial feudalism.[52]

Most of the other family boroughs were equally conspicuous for the solidity of the personal connexion. At Bridgwater, Colonel C. Kemeys Tynte sat for the borough from 1826 to 1837. He was the son of a former officer in the Guards who had married the heiress to the Tynte and Kemeys families and, as frequently

[52] See *Diaries of Lady Charlotte Guest*, Introduction and text, under election dates.

happened, assumed their surnames on succeeding to their extensive estates in Somerset and other counties. The son of the Bridgwater member, Charles J. K. Tynte, was elected member for the western division of Somerset in 1832 and 1835. But both of these were contested elections and finally he was beaten into third place by a margin of a hundred votes in 1837. In 1847 he put up for his father's old seat at Bridgwater and was returned at the elections of 1847, 1852, 1857, and 1859.[53] At Cirencester Joseph Cripps, a local banker and East India proprietor, sat for the borough from 1818 to 1841 and was succeeded by William Cripps who sat until his death in 1848. A Whitmore at Bridgnorth and a Pryse at Cardigan was elected at every general election from 1832 to 1852. At Eye, a small constituency of some 300 electors, a member of the Kerrison family was returned without a contest during the same period of twenty years and six general elections. Lt.-Gen. Sir Edward Kerrison, Lord of the Manor and Recorder of Eye, sat for the borough from 1824 to 1852 and on retiring from parliament was succeeded by his eldest son Edward Clarence, 2nd baronet, who was member for Eye from 1852 to 1868. In Pembrokeshire, where the Owens of Orielton had enjoyed almost hereditary power since the seventeenth century, Sir John Owen sat for the county from 1809 until 1841, and his son Hugh Owen[54] for Pembroke borough from 1826 to 1838 when he retired so that Sir James Graham, defeated in Cumberland the previous year, could be found a seat in the Commons. The Owen interest suffered a setback in 1839 when owing to the financial difficulties into which Sir John Owen had fallen, he was obliged for a time to shut his house and avoid his creditors. At the next general election it was deemed prudent to start another conservative candidate Lord Emlyn, son and heir to the other great Pembrokeshire magnate Lord Cawdor, for the county while Sir John took shelter in Pembroke, which he represented until his death in 1861. He never again ventured out of his borough stronghold to contest the county but in Pembroke his influence was virtually unassailable and in the fullness of time his son, the self-effacing Hugh Owen, succeeded to the electoral patrimony.[55]

[53] In the official *Return of Members of Parliament*, Pt. II, 404, the names of Frome and Bridgwater have been accidentally transposed in the column opposite the members' names relating to the parliament of 1847.
[54] Sir Hugh Owen Owen, 2nd baronet.
[55] Add. MS. 40616, fos. 78, 84, 87, 109, 119, 123, 127, 130, 135, 144, 146, 156, 187.

All these elements, landlords, corporations, universities, peers, parsons, and dissenters, political unions, and family boroughs, were at the roots of the representative system.[56] Reformer and conservative did not appeal to the impartial vote of an unattached electorate but to a mass of opinions and interests that were largely decided in advance. It is true that there did exist a field where rival programmes and past actions, the attractions and repulsions of Peel and Russell, Melbourne and Wellington, might exercise an important influence on the decision of the electorate even though the direct appeal of parties and leaders is difficult to trace through the obscurity of bribery, coercion, intimidation, and patronage. Genuine changes of opinion among the electorate did take place and might have decided the issue between the national parties, although the party managers did wisely to put their trust in wealth, organization, and influence. But these fluctuations of opinion and feeling were checked and their force diminished by the solid, immovable strength of these fixed interests in the electoral system. The 'floating vote', to use the modern phrase, was confined to narrower channels. Yet it was not so much that these interests were dependent on party as that the party was to a large extent dependent on them. The political and personal feelings of churches, corporations, the squirearchy, and the unions, naturally moved along the well-worn paths of whig and tory, reformer and anti-reformer, liberal and conservative, down which alone power, office, promotion, or patronage could flow. But if the party was the vehicle for opinions and interests, it did not always control those opinions and those interests. The university member, the leader of county society, the favourite of the unions or the dissenters, the member for the rotten borough or the family seat, all owed their position to strength and assistance from below and not to the decision or encouragement of party or government. Such men, though nominally members of a party, could bear lightly the claims of leadership and discipline. They contributed rather than received party opinion and although their power lay at the core of party strength, they often exhibited an independence at Westminster which sprang directly from their local security.

[56] Dod's *Electoral Facts 1832–52* contains besides details of elections, a mass of information relating to the various influences in the different constituencies during this period. As with most compilations of this sort, the editor tends to let his information get out of date; it should therefore always be checked against other evidence. Used with discrimination, however, it is an invaluable guide.

Chapter Nine

THE SURVIVAL OF THE PROPRIETARY BOROUGH

IT has frequently been observed that if at their worst pocket boroughs enabled a small clique of proprietors to obstruct beneficial legislation or wreck a ministry for a personal grudge, at their best they provided an early entry into politics for young men of talent, a means of security for indispensable ministers, a measure of justice to politicians of ability who lacked wealth and popularity, and a method of representing imperial and colonial interests not directly embraced by the elective system. Arguments and counter-arguments on this point were developed at length in the reform bill debates. All the well-known precedents were quoted: Chatham at Old Sarum, Pitt at Appleby, Burke and Canning at Wendover. Peel himself cited a list of twenty-two distinguished politicians who over a period of half a century had either entered parliament through a borough since doomed by Schedule A or at some time or other had been obliged to seek refuge in one.[1] The whigs in reply asserted that men of talent would always find a way into the House of Commons; and O'Connell asked pertinently: 'Are there no dull, drowsy members ever returned for [pocket] boroughs? Members without talent to join in a debate but with sufficient perseverance to be able to attend at the division?'[2] By both sides it was largely taken for granted that the Reform Act would end the nomination system, whatever its merits or demerits. This was a reasonable assumption; the whigs themselves had proclaimed it as one of the chief objects of their bill. 'The principle of the ministers', said Sir James Graham, 'was to go as near as possible to cut off all the proprietary boroughs.'[3] Even when the first shock of hearing the list of boroughs in Schedule A had passed away, and the proposals of the ministry came to be examined in greater detail, only a rare voice was raised to point out the inadequacy of the operation which the whig surgeons were performing on the rotten part of the body politic. Yet as early as the seventh day of debate Daniel Whittle Harvey, the radical M.P. for Colchester, observed that the forty odd boroughs of Schedule B left with one member

[1] *Hansard*, II, 1349.   [2] *Ibid.*, III, 206.   [3] *Ibid.*, III, 228.

each would come very close to providing the rotten borough element in the constitution which the opposition speakers appeared to desire.[4]

In point of fact, with all their evils and advantages (and they possessed both), pocket boroughs were still to be found in the representative structure between the first and second Reform Acts. Many of the most notorious had made in Schedule A their last bow to the world of politics which they had served so long; some that survived lost their proprietary character by the opening of the vote to the £10 householder. But there were others, saved from destruction by a few additional electors, by the timely erection perhaps of a row of £10 houses, or by a statutory enlargement of their parliamentary boundaries, that survived to carry on their task. Even if Tamworth is excluded, Gladstone at Newark, Clerk at Stamford, Fremantle at Buckingham, and Graham at Dorchester, demonstrated in one party alone the value of the pocket boroughs that had survived the massacre of 1832. Exactly how many pocket boroughs existed after the Reform Act is a different and more difficult question. The reform agitation had raised a storm which left gusts and eddies still blowing across the political scene when Victoria came to the throne. Public opinion was still sensitive to all implications of corruption, jobbery, and aristocratic influence; and many borough-owners found it prudent to mask their influence or their actual control by a tactful selection of candidates and a discreet intimation of their wishes. Even when the existence of a strong personal influence was obvious, it is not always easy to ascertain whether it exercised a dominant or merely partial and contributory control over the electorate. Lastly, bribery and intimidation were often introduced to strengthen the borough-owners in their possession and to complicate the task of disentangling the different motives that lay behind the verdict of the hustings.

In some boroughs undoubtedly the changes consequent on the Reform Act brought with them the end of a proprietor's dominating influence. At Droitwich, where the Foleys had reigned with almost undisputed power for over a century, the conservatives in 1835 put up John Barneby, a country gentleman of Hereford, and carried the seat by three votes. This was not an isolated victory; the conservatives were again successful in 1837 and 1841. At Lyme

4 *Hansard*, III, 272.

Regis in Dorset the electoral influence up to 1832 had for several generations been in the hands of the Earl of Westmorland who usually returned junior members of his family. The franchise here was confined to the corporation and freemen of whom in 1830 there were less than forty. The Reform Act reduced the representation to one member and enlarged the electorate to over 200. At the first election under the new system there was a triangular contest in which Mr W. Pinney of Somerton Erleigh, Somerset, son of J. F. Pinney, high sheriff and J.P., beat Lord Burghersh, the son and heir of the Earl of Westmorland, by nineteen votes. He retained the seat in the liberal interest at the next three general elections. Much the same happened at Grimsby, where the influence of the patron, Lord Yarborough, was diminished by the Reform Act and after 1834 successfully challenged by an ancient Lincolnshire family, the Heneages of Hainton. Edward Heneage was returned from 1835 to 1847, the last three times unopposed. At Malmesbury on the other hand the extension of the borough boundaries by the Reform Act resulted in a decline of the Pitt influence and its replacement by that of the Earl of Suffolk and Berkshire whose county seat was at Charlton Park, Malmesbury. Viscount Andover, the heir to the earldom, was returned from 1832 to 1837 and the Hon. J. Kenneth Howard, his younger brother, in 1841 and 1847.

An example of a close borough to all appearances completely unaffected by the Reform Act was Reigate. Up to 1832 the franchise in the constituency had resided in certain freeholds through the possession of which the patronage of the borough had long been in the hands of Earl Somers and the Earl of Hardwicke. In 1830 the sitting members were Admiral Joseph Yorke, half-brother to the Earl of Hardwicke, and James Cocks, cousin to the Earl Somers. It was the admiral who in March 1831 brought a somewhat quarter-deck atmosphere to the reform bill debates by observing that had honourable members sitting for small boroughs been given nine months' notice of the intention to base disfranchisement on population statistics, they could have taken care, as far as lay in their power, to ensure that their own respective constituencies should not be deficient in that respect.[5] Reigate, however, notwithstanding this rather literal argument *ad hominem*, duly passed into Schedule B and was deprived of one of its members.

[5] *Ibid.*, III, 235.

Indeed it was fortunate to survive at all since it had originally
been proposed for complete disfranchisement. Its survival
brought a tart comment from Hunt that it would be as much the
nomination borough of Earl Somers after the bill had passed as it
had been before. This home truth was denied by Viscount
Eastnor, who as eldest son of Earl Somers, and son-in-law of the
Earl of Hardwicke, was the family representative of the two
borough-owners in the House of Commons although at that date
member for Hereford.[6] The results of the elections after 1832,
however, could not but detract from the force of that denial. At the
first four elections Lord Eastnor himself was returned, unopposed
in 1832 and 1837, and beating two different opponents in 1835
and 1841 by overwhelming majorities. Another member of the
family, Thomas Somers Cocks (the younger), was elected in 1847
and 1852.

Nevertheless, for the pocket, or as they were usually called in this
period, the proprietary boroughs, that survived the act, the first
few elections after 1832 were not infrequently a testing time. Not
only was there a strong public opinion, stimulated by the triumph
of reform, that could be turned against the relics of exclusive
influence, but the new electoral conditions even in the small
boroughs invited challenges to old established connexions. It was
probably not a coincidence that in two of the most notorious
pocket boroughs in the country, where power seemed most
perverted and arbitrary, the control of the proprietors declined in
the decade after the Reform Act. The first of these was Hertford,
where Lord Salisbury's influence was the object of a hot attack by
T. S. Duncombe during the difficult period for borough magnates
between 1830 and 1832. Duncombe, a formidable antagonist by
reason of his property in the borough, his aristocratic connexions,
and his radical views, had sat for Hertford since the 1826 election.
On the other hand a large part of the borough was actually owned
by Lord Salisbury and tenants were evicted in 1831 for voting
against his wishes. At the 1832 election, when Ingestre and Mahon,
the tory candidates, were opposed by two radical whigs, Duncombe
and Spalding, Lord Salisbury took unusual pains to underline his
influence and his desires by heading an election procession through
the streets of Hertford displaying the tory colours. It was an
exceptionally hard fought contest. The Salisbury interest was

6 *Hansard*, v, 572.

determined to get rid of Duncombe once and for all; bribery ran high and a good deal of intimidation was exercised. In consequence of the dilemma in which many electors found themselves, between Salisbury's power and Duncombe's popularity, a good number of votes were split between the latter and Ingestre. But the influence of Lord Salisbury's property carried the day. He owned about 225 houses within the borough and all except about fifty were over the £10 rating. It is probable, too, that some of the occupiers of the smaller houses possessed the franchise under the old qualification, which had been owned by all resident householders not receiving alms. In a constituency of under 700, Lord Salisbury controlled, therefore, at least a quarter by direct means and perhaps as many by indirect methods, especially among the trading and professional classes in the town. One of the forms of bribery in the Salisbury interest was the issue of tickets exchangeable for goods at local shops. In this way both customer and shopkeeper benefited. At the election, Duncombe, the leading reformer, was fifty votes below Mahon and over 100 votes below Ingestre.[7]

After that decisive defeat, Duncombe, who had, it was estimated, already spent £40,000 in attempting to shake Salisbury's control of the borough, retired to the more welcome prospect of a candidacy for Finsbury. When he, radical by opinion, aristocratic by social connexions, popular with the crowd and backed by the whig party managers, had failed to make an impression, it seemed unlikely that another would succeed. The first election under the Reform Act thus reaffirmed rather than weakened the character of one of the best-known pocket boroughs in the kingdom. But the return of two Salisbury candidates in 1832, if not a Pyrrhic victory, was an achievement which did not bring much advantage. The immediate success was nullified by a parliamentary committee, which declared the election void, and by the House of Commons, which refused to grant a fresh writ for Hertford either in the 1833 or the 1834 sessions. And at the general election of 1835 Lord Salisbury was faced with a more formidable rival than Duncombe in the person of Lord Cowper, whose seat, Panshanger, was in the vicinity of Hertford, and who could appeal to the whiggish and radical elements in the borough. The result was the return of Mahon and the Hon. William Cowper, and the defeat of Ingestre.

[7] P.P. 1833, IX, 77–9, 200–1, 209, 452–3, 458–9, 463–7; *H. of C. Journals*, 1833, LXXXVIII, 23–4; *Life of Duncombe*, I, 124–9.

In the 1837 election Mahon successfully defended the Salisbury influence against the attacks of two liberals but this time Cowper was at the head of the poll. A position of equilibrium now seemed to have been reached between the forces of the two great magnates; and in 1841 and 1847 Cowper and Mahon were quietly returned without a contest. In spite of his efforts between 1830 and 1832, and his commanding position in the borough, Lord Salisbury had been compelled to surrender a seat to the opposing party.

Another example of an aristocratic pocket borough that in fact was weaker than its reputation, was Warwick. The Earl of Warwick had extensive property in and around the borough; he was Lord-Lieutenant of the county and Recorder of Warwick, and in the latter capacity he appointed the town clerk. The majority of aldermen and burgesses of Warwick were attached to the 'orange' or Warwick interest, and many were personally connected with the earl as solicitors, bankers, and tradesmen. The treasurer of the corporation, for example, was employed by the Earl of Warwick as his solicitor. The town clerk acted not merely as solicitor but as election agent for the 'orange' side. After the election of 1831, a large number of persons, chiefly dependent on the earl, were fictitiously rated to the poor of the parishes of Warwick and thus given a qualification for the franchise. Some of these were struck off by the revising barristers but a considerable number still remained on the register as electors. At the 1832 election the Earl of Warwick's brother, Sir Charles Greville, put up for election. The money for the contest seems to have come entirely from the earl who through his steward put £3,000 into the hands of the town clerk for election purposes. Both the town clerk and other aldermen were engaged in distributing money and hiring bullies on Greville's behalf. It is not surprising, therefore, that Greville was returned at the head of the poll. However, on a petition alleging bribery and illegal interference, he was unseated by a parliamentary committee; and, as in the case of Hertford, the issue of a new writ was suspended. The first election under the Reform Act had thus brought little profit. In 1835 Greville was again elected together with a liberal; and there was another tory success in 1836 when Greville made room for the Hon. C. J. Canning. But the halcyon days of Lord Warwick's influence were over. Though his power had not been destroyed, the notoriety of the attempts he had made to preserve it were beginning to impose some constraint. When Canning succeeded to the viscountcy early in 1837, his tory replacement was defeated in the by-election and for a few months Warwick was held by two liberals. But as at Hertford a balance of forces was reached. In the general elections of 1837, 1841, and 1847, the borough was divided between a liberal and a conservative member. It is worth noting, however, that in the two of these three elections that were contested the opposition came from a second liberal candidate and that on both occasions a liberal was at the head of the poll. The Earl of Warwick's influence, though returning a candidate at each election, was clearly on the defensive.[8]

A similar though less publicized attack on a prevailing interest after the Reform Act took place at Scarborough. The old franchise here was vested in the corporation or common council, a self-electing body which numbered under fifty at the time of the reform bill. The introduction of the £10 householder raised the electorate to over 500. Electoral patronage was exercised by the Duke of Rutland and Lord Mulgrave. The two sitting members in 1830 were Manners-Sutton, the Speaker, a cousin of the former, and Edmund Phipps, an uncle of the latter. At the 1832 election a hot contest took place. Sir Frederick Trench, who was the Duke of Rutland's candidate, was left at the foot of the polls. The two successful candidates were Sir John Vanden Bempde Johnstone, 2nd baronet, of Hackness Hall near Scarborough; and Sir George Cayley of Brompton, Yorkshire. After this there followed a kaleidoscopic series of election results as the borough magnates and local country gentry fought for the representation of the borough. In 1835 Trench and Johnstone defeated Cayley; in 1837 Trench and Sir Thomas Style, who was Cayley's son-in-law, defeated Johnstone; and in 1841 Johnstone and Trench defeated Colonel Phipps, a member of the Mulgrave family.[9] In 1847, however, Sir Frederick Trench decided to retire. His motives for this step are not clear since he had sat for the borough since 1835 and his position was to all appearances secure. But he was a Peelite and more than one follower of Peel had been driven by the events of 1846–7 into an unresolvable conflict between past associations and present opinions. Whatever the underlying circumstances, there was no doubt that he had built up a liberal-conservative party in the

[8] P.P. 1833, xi, 199 sqq.; *H. of C. Journals*, 1833, LXXXVIII, 96–8, 396.
[9] Lt.-Col. Charles Beaumont Phipps, an officer in the 3rd Foot Guards, younger son of the 1st Earl of Mulgrave.

constituency which was loath to see victory go by default. After Trench's decision not to contest the 1847 election became known, he was approached by Woodall, the head of the Old Bank at Scarborough, and one of his most influential backers, to get Peel to recommend a candidate. Trench forwarded the application to Peel, adding that he was aware of the volume of feeling in the constituency but that his own decision had been made on other grounds. 'I have little doubt', he continued, 'that the candidate who shall *succeed* in occupying my place may (by proper management) command the seat for life; as I feel I might have done.'[10] Nevertheless the attempt to import national politics into Scarborough was a failure. At the ensuing general election the Earl of Mulgrave[11] put up as candidate in place of his uncle, Colonel Phipps, who had vainly contested the borough in 1841. He was returned unopposed together with the other sitting member, Johnstone.

With that a position of equilibrium seemed to have been reached. The two men continued to share the representation of Scarborough at the elections of 1852 and 1857. Sir John V. B. Johnstone, indeed, was member for the borough until his death in 1869, two years after the second Reform Act; and was succeeded in his parliamentary seat by his son, Harcourt Johnstone,[12] who represented Scarborough from 1869 to 1880. Of all the families that contended for the constituency immediately after the first Reform Act, the Johnstones established the most effective and lasting influence. For almost half a century the electors of Scarborough only once failed to return a Johnstone to the House of Commons. It was a notable achievement, as significant in its way as the monopoly of the borough by the upper layer of the aristocracy which had existed before 1832. For it is clear that at any rate in the thirties the party issue though not absent from Scarborough was not the predominant factor in deciding the vote of the electorate. Johnstone was a conservative, as was Trench; the Cayley-Style interest was liberal. If the voting had gone on party lines it would be difficult to explain either the return of Johnstone and Cayley and the defeat of Trench in 1832, or the return of Trench and Style and the defeat of Johnstone in 1837. The key to the enigma may be found in the details of the voting. In 1832 the total number of

---

[10] Add. MS. 40598, fo. 189.   [11] Heir to the Marquess of Normanby, cr. 1838.
[12] 3rd baronet, cr. 1st Baron Derwent, 1881.

voters was 386, of whom eighty-two cast plumpers. Johnstone received eleven of these, Cayley ten, and Trench sixty-one. There were thus just over 300 electors who divided their votes between two candidates. Of these, Johnstone received 275, Cayley 245, and Trench 85.[13] It is therefore clear that the great majority divided between Johnstone the conservative and Cayley the whig, against Trench, the nominee of the patron. This isolated position of the Duke of Rutland's candidate was even more prominent in 1835. On that occasion Trench received no less than 128 plumpers; Johnstone 2; and Cayley 5. The split votes went as follows: 48 to Trench; 159 to Johnston; and 117 to Cayley. Again, therefore, the majority of electors who used both their votes divided between the two country gentlemen and refrained from supporting the ducal candidate. It is difficult to resist the impression from these votes that the real question at issue for many of the Scarborough electors was not the rivalry of tory and whig but the success or defeat of the Rutland interest.

In spite of these examples, however, it can scarcely be maintained that aristocratic influence exercised through the proprietary boroughs was a negligible factor after 1832. Nearly fifty boroughs and well over sixty members depended on the influence of great peers and landowners in England and Wales alone. Naturally the great era of the borough-proprietor had passed away for ever. Nobody now could return six, five, or even four members to the House of Commons. Peers who retained a half-share in some constituency could count themselves fortunate; and magnates like the Earl Fitzwilliam, the Duke of Rutland, or the Duke of Newcastle, with an interest in more than one constituency, could be numbered on the fingers.

One of the more notorious of these was Lord Segrave, formerly Colonel Berkeley, illegitimate son of the 5th Earl of Berkeley and unsuccessful claimant to the title after his father's death in 1810. Greville asserted, on the authority of Stanley and Spring Rice, that Segrave was given the Lord-Lieutenancy of Gloucestershire because he was able to return three members to parliament, more than any other man in England was able to do after the

---

[13] ? 88. There are three votes unaccounted for in the gross poll. Trench's total is given as 146. If the last digit was really a 9 accidentally inverted by the printer it would account for the deficiency. The details of the poll both in 1832 and 1835 are taken from Mosse, *Parl. Guide* (1835). The figure for the total poll in 1835 (267) must also be a printer's error for 297.

Reform Act. By the date of the 1841 election this figure had been raised to four, all brothers of the magnate in question, sitting respectively for Bristol, Gloucester, Cheltenham, and the western division of Gloucestershire. According to Grantley Berkeley's later and possibly prejudiced account, the barony of Segrave and the earldom of Fitzhardinge that Colonel Berkeley received at due intervals from a grateful whig ministry were the stipulated rewards for this increasing quota of liberal supporters. This perhaps even more than Greville's story needs corroboration before it can be accepted. The barony was in fact bestowed on the ambitious colonel in September 1831 at a time when only one Berkeley figured in the list of Gloucestershire members. The earldom was created in August 1841, after the results of the general election were known and shortly before the resignation of the Melbourne ministry. The coincidence may be significant but in view of the past political services of Lord Segrave, and the circumstance that only a disputed marriage date lay between him and his father's title, the reward he received was not more improper than many other peerages and does not necessarily bear the harsh interpretation put on it by his younger brother. In any case the material issue is whether in fact the four constituencies represented by the Berkeley clan in 1841, or even the three in 1832, were in any real sense pocket constituencies. Grantley Berkeley, who sat for the county, quarrelled with his elder brother over matters connected with the latter's mistress and a promised but unpaid allowance while on parliamentary duty; but though given notice by Earl Fitzhardinge to quit the county at the close of the 1841-7 parliament, he put up again in 1847 and beat his brother's nominee, their mutual cousin Grenville Berkeley, in an unpleasant election characterized by the employment on the earl's side of a gang of 'bludgeon men' from Ross armed with weighted cudgels. When Grantley Berkeley was finally defeated in the county at the 1852 election, the fact that counted against him more than the wrath of his fraternal patron was his effort in the 1847 parliament to induce the government either to repeal the malt tax or else restore a protective duty on corn, a policy not calculated to attract much liberal or popular support in a mixed county such as Gloucestershire.[14] Of the other constituencies, Bristol with over 10,000 registered voters, was clearly not susceptible to control of this

[14] Grantley F. Berkeley, *My Life and Recollections*, I, 341–71; II, 141–213.

nature. Gloucester, too, was scarcely a proprietary borough in any strict sense. Captain M. F. Fitzhardinge Berkeley, who won the 1832 election, was defeated in the borough at a by-election consequent on his appointment as a junior lord of the Admiralty. He was returned again for Gloucester at the general election of 1835 but was beaten once more in 1837. This is hardly an impressive record of control. Moreover all these Gloucester elections were closely contested affairs in a large constituency of some 1,400 electors which the local conservative party managers were far from regarding as an invulnerable whig seat. Cheltenham alone perhaps, where Lord Segrave owned considerable property and the registered electorate barely reached a thousand, could rank as a proprietary borough of the Berkeley family. Thus the legend of the Segrave influence shrinks on examination to very modest proportions. What is true in Greville's anecdote is that any man who could even claim to be in the position of returning three members to the House of Commons was a rarity at that date. After the Reform Act borough magnates counted their seats in the singular rather than in the plural.

Even so, over forty peers remained who could virtually nominate a representative to the lower house and there was often a marked social as well as political characteristic in the type of candidate they returned. Helston, for example, whose patron was the Duke of Leeds, elected successively S. L. Fox, husband of a younger daughter of the duke, in 1832; Lord Townshend, an uncle of the Marquess Townshend, in 1835; and Lord Cantelupe, eldest son of Lord Delawarr and a lieutenant in the Grenadier Guards, in 1837. Many owners of pocket boroughs seemed to regard them indeed as being primarily a means of entry to parliament for those members of the family that cared to interest themselves in politics. Richmond, the borough of Lord Dundas, enjoyed the following representation for the first three parliaments after the Reform Act.

1832 Sir R. L. Dundas, brother of Lord Dundas.
   Hon. J. C. Dundas, second son of Lord Dundas.
1835 Hon. Thomas Dundas, eldest son of Lord Dundas.
   A. Speirs, nephew of Lord Dundas.
1837 Hon. Thomas Dundas.
   A. Speirs.

When in 1839 Thomas Dundas succeeded his father as Earl of Zetland, he was replaced in the representation of Richmond by Sir Robert Lawrence Dundas, uncle of the new earl. In 1841 J. C. Dundas returned as member for the borough and only then did the exclusive family use of the constituency relax sufficiently for two ordinary whig party men, Colborne and Rich, to be accommodated in turn during the 1841 parliament.

At Calne, the borough of Lord Lansdowne, there was this record of unquestioned family supremacy.

1832   Earl of Kerry, eldest son of the Marquess of Lansdowne.[15]

1835   Earl of Kerry.

1836   (by-election consequent on the death of the Earl of Kerry) John Charles Fox Strangways, brother-in-law of the Marquess of Lansdowne.

1837   Earl of Shelburne, eldest surviving son of the Marquess of Lansdowne.[16]

1841   Earl of Shelburne.

1847   Earl of Shelburne.

1852   Earl of Shelburne.

All these elections were uneventful; indeed there were no contested elections at Calne from 1832 to 1852.

At Chester, a large constituency of over 2,000 registered electors where the influence of Earl Grosvenor (cr. Marquess of Westminster in 1831) was paramount, Lord Robert Grosvenor, the third son of the earl, was returned at the four general elections from 1832 to 1841; and the third Marquess sat (as Earl Grosvenor) from 1847 until he succeeded to the marquessate in 1869. At Chichester, where the Duke of Richmond controlled the borough from his neighbouring seat at Goodwood, a Lennox was returned from 1832 to 1852. At Marlborough, where the Marquess of Ailesbury was patron, the supremacy of the Bruces was challenged at the first election after the Reform Act by Sir Alexander Malet of Wilbury House, Wiltshire. But the second son of the Marquess, Lord Ernest Bruce[17] then a stripling of twenty-one, was comfortably

---

[15] William Thomas Petty Fitzmaurice, commonly styled Earl of Kerry.

[16] Henry Petty Fitzmaurice, commonly styled Earl of Shelburne. Both the Kerry and the Shelburne earldoms were subordinate honours held by the Marquess of Lansdowne in the Irish peerage.

[17] Ernest Augustus Charles Brudenell Bruce, styled Lord Ernest Bruce.

returned together with the other conservative candidate, Henry Baring. Thereafter the challenge lapsed and the same two members were returned unopposed in 1835, 1837, and 1841. In all, Lord Ernest Bruce and Baring sat continuously from the first to the second Reform Act; and when as a result of the latter the borough lost one member, Lord Ernest Bruce continued to occupy the remaining seat. He was still member for Marlborough when Disraeli formed his last ministry in 1874. At Morpeth, a pocket borough of the Earl of Carlisle, sons of the earl were returned at every election from 1832 to 1852 except between 1836 and 1840 when Granville George Leveson-Gower, commonly styled Lord Leveson, the eldest son of Lord Granville and nephew of the Earl of Carlisle, was allowed to occupy the seat during the absence on naval duty of the Hon. Edward Howard.[18] None of these elections were contested; as at Calne, the possession of the franchise by the 300 voters of Morpeth was a largely nominal privilege. At Lichfield, where the influence of the Earl of Lichfield[19] was enough to control the return of one of the two representatives, a member of his family was returned with one exception (1857) at every election from 1832 to 1865. At Wenlock, a former close corporation with voting confined to about 200 burgesses, the enlargement of the electorate to about 700 did little to loosen the tight control of the Foresters. George Cecil Weld Forester of Willey Park, Salop, a younger brother of Lord Forester,[20] was returned at every election from 1832 to 1865, bringing in with him on each occasion another conservative, James Milnes Gaskell of Wakefield, Yorks.

The predominant impression to be gained from an examination of the proprietary boroughs in this period is that they were used mainly to secure the return to parliament of members of the proprietors' families. Younger sons or retired uncles were provided with an interesting and not unimportant career in which their status as M.P. could not fail to lend distinction and influence to their relatives. Heirs to a peerage were enabled to acquire in the family seat an experience in the lower house not without its value against the day when they should succeed to the place and title in

[18] Fitzmaurice, *Life of Lord Granville*, 1, 26, 34. Both the Earl of Carlisle and Lord Granville had married daughters of the 5th Duke of Devonshire.

[19] The 2nd Viscount Anson, descendant of a nephew of the eighteenth-century navigator, Admiral George Anson, was raised to the earldom in 1831.

[20] 2nd Baron, succ. to the title in 1828.

the House of Lords. The use of the pocket borough as an avenue for talent is less apparent. A Macaulay at Calne, a Gladstone at Newark, are exceptions to the general practice. It was natural that this should be so. Maintenance of a controlling influence meant as a rule time, management, expense, and inconvenience to the proprietor. It might have been political wisdom, but it was scarcely in human nature, that the fruit of his labours should be willingly presented to a stranger. Had there been more pocket boroughs, or had more of them been two member constituencies, the generosity of the proprietors might have been more marked. But the Reform Act had taken away many and reduced others to a single seat; those that survived were consequently rare and treasured possessions. In an age which still regarded politics as the natural career of a gentleman, it was unreasonable to expect a borough-owner to send away his own relatives to seek the hard way into parliament while he ensured an easy return for some brilliant young man from Oxford or some loyal party official. Moreover there was the point of view of the electorate to consider. In the election of a son or relative of the proprietor a certain feudal and social aspect reinforced and therefore disguised the hard fact of control. A succession of strangers, however adorned with university prizes and double firsts, could only underline and render unnecessarily distasteful the real influence deciding the election result. It was even perhaps the sense of family obligation alone that in some cases prompted the borough patrons to perpetuate their influence in circumstances where they would otherwise have allowed it to lapse. There is at least a glimpse of this in the Duke of Devonshire's correspondence. At Derby a member or relative of the Cavendish family had, up to 1847, usually held one seat. The duke offered Frederick Leveson-Gower, his nephew, a seat there in 1847 in the vacancy created by Duncannon's succession to the Bessborough earldom. Leveson-Gower was duly returned at the by-election and again at the general election later in the year, though on the latter occasion he was unseated on petition together with the other sitting member, E. Strutt. But *à propos* of his offer, the duke wrote to his nephew that, 'It is quite true that you are the only person to whom I should consent to prolong that sort of interest with Derby.'[21]

There is of course a reverse side to this picture. Younger

[21] Leveson-Gower, *Bygone Years*, 237–8.

members of noble families destined for politics at an early age did not always relish the career which parental ambition had selected for them. It is of this period that Lady Dorothy Nevill, the daughter of the 3rd Earl of Orford, wrote 'great families used formerly to regard certain seats in parliament almost as their own property and peers often forced their eldest sons into politics against their will. At that time the sons of peers were often practically forced to stand by their fathers for constituencies which they had never visited, for which reason the Tories were often twitted by the Whigs for electing, what they called, "invisible members".'[22]

This family ambition, stronger perhaps than party feeling, made it possible for two magnates to share a constituency on the veiled understanding that each should return one member and that interlopers should be kept out. Where there existed ties of friendship and political unanimity there was of course everything to be gained by such a policy. But even when the two proprietors held opposed political views it was not uncommon for the dignity and power of both sides to be jointly upheld, and the divided state of the electoral influence exactly reflected, in the return of members to rival parties. Thus at Bury St Edmunds, which was controlled by the Duke of Grafton and the Marquess of Bristol, Lord Charles Fitzroy and Earl Jermyn were returned at the first four elections after the Reform Act against warm opposition. The former was the second son of the Duke of Grafton; the latter the eldest son of the Marquess of Bristol. The first was a liberal; the second a conservative. At Thetford there was another nice division of proprietary influence, in which the Duke of Grafton was again concerned. Control of the borough was divided between the whig duke and Alexander Baring (cr. Lord Ashburton in 1835) a conservative. On the Grafton side Lord J. H. Fitzroy, a younger son of the duke, was elected in 1832 and on his death the vacancy was filled in 1834 by his eldest brother, the Earl of Euston. With one exception a Fitzroy was returned at every election up to 1859. The exception was in 1841, the first contested election since the Reform Act, when a close struggle, in which an outsider took part, was finally determined by a decision of a parliamentary committee in favour of the Baring candidate and Sir James Flower of Woodford, Essex. On the Baring side Francis Baring, the second son of Lord Ashburton, was returned in the first three general elections

[22] Nevill, *Under Five Reigns*, 15.

after the Reform Act. In 1841 the Hon. William Bingham Baring, elder brother of Francis, continued to keep the seat warm until he succeeded his father.as Lord Ashburton. In his place, in 1848, came Francis Baring once more who in turn was succeeded by his own son Alexander Baring in 1857. There can be little doubt that in such constituencies there was a strong inducement for proprietors to preserve their interest even if that entailed a virtual agreement with a rival of another party not to encroach at each other's expense. Where two prevailing interests combined in this manner it was useless for a third candidate to intervene.

Not all the patrons of proprietary boroughs were peers. A few commoners remained to break with their more plebeian names the select list of those magnates who could return members to parliament by what was often little more than a process of nomination. At Rye, where the close corporation, in which the Lamb family had long been influential, controlled the borough in the Treasury interest, the extension of the boundaries in 1832[23] resulted in power passing to the Curteis family of Windmill Hill, Hurstmonceux. Edward Jeremiah Curteis (b. 1762) had been member for Sussex 1820–30; his heir, Herbert Barrett Curteis, succeeded him in the county representation from 1830 to 1837. Meanwhile a younger son, Edward Barrett Curteis, an officer in the 7th Dragoon Guards, successfully contested Rye in 1832 and 1835. In the general election of 1837 Herbert Curteis was defeated in the eastern division of Sussex and at the next election he withdrew to Rye which he represented until 1847. On his death, soon after the general election of that year, he was succeeded in the seat by his son and heir, Herbert Mascale Curteis.[24] This is perhaps an example of borough control where it is difficult to discern whether proprietary or family influence was the decisive feature; and the situation is further complicated by the rural nature of the 'borough' of Rye. At Marlow there was a rather clearer instance of a commoner securing proprietary influence. The influence here was possessed by the Williams family. Its history had started some forty years

[23] By the English Boundary Act 1832, the new constituency comprised the towns of Rye and Winchelsea, the parishes of Rye, Peasemarsh, Iden, Playden, Winchelsea, East Guildford, Icklesham, Udimer, and part of Brede. The Curteis family had, in addition to Windmill Hill, a second country seat at Peasemarsh Place.

[24] In the *Return of Members of Parliament* there is a printer's error in the details of the members for the Cinque Ports in the 1847 parliament (Pt. II, 407). Hythe should appear opposite Brockman and the remaining items in the constituency column from Rye to Sandwich moved down one interval.

before the Reform Act. In 1788 Thomas Williams of Llanidan, Anglesey, purchased the famous Temple Mills, near Marlow, that specialized in brass and copper manufacture. Within two years he was M.P. for Marlow and he represented the borough until his death in 1802. He was succeeded by his eldest son, Owen Williams of Temple House, Marlow (1764–1832), who also sat as member for the borough. He in turn was succeeded by his eldest son Thomas Peers Williams who was returned for Marlow at every election from 1832 to 1865. Some encroachment on the Williams' influence took place about 1830, when Colonel William Robert Clayton (succ. as 5th baronet, 1834), of the neighbouring seat of Harleyford Manor, built some houses in the borough and gained popularity by protecting voters who had been ejected by Owen Williams.[25] From 1832 to 1841 the borough representation was shared between T. P. Williams and Clayton; from 1847 to 1865 Williams' colleague was Lt.-Col. Brownlow Knox.[26] It is clear that the Williams' monopoly of at least one of the borough seats was continued until the second Reform Act.

Among the commoners who were proprietors two are distinctive in this period by virtue of their sex: Miss Peirse at Northallerton and Miss Lawrence at Ripon, the only two petticoated electoral magnates of their day. Henry Peirse of Bedale, Yorks (1754–1824), one of the largest proprietors in the North Riding and a former M.P. for Northallerton, left his estates to his three daughters and co-heiresses. Of these Charlotte, the eldest, married Inigo Thomas of Ratton, Sussex, by whom she had two daughters: Charlotte (d.s.p.) and Georgiana, sole heiress to her mother, who married in 1821 William Battie Wrightson of Cusworth, near Doncaster. Marianne, the second daughter of Henry Peirse, died unmarried. The third, Henrietta Elizabeth, who married in 1815 Admiral Sir John Poo Beresford, died in 1825. At the time of the Reform Act the borough of Northallerton, where the franchise was vested in certain burgage tenements, was generally regarded as divided between the Peirse family and the Earl of Harewood. This situation was reflected in the return at the general election of 1830 and 1831 of Sir John Poo Beresford and two successive members of the Lascelles family. The Reform Act by depriving Northallerton of one of its members prevented the continuation of this division of

---

[25] *Both Houses of Parliament* (1832), 358, quoting the *Spectator* of 2 January 1831.

[26] Possibly a relative of the Williams family. An aunt of T. P. Williams had as her first husband a Lt.-Col. Thomas Knox of the 1st Foot Guards.

the constituency. At the first election under the new system W. B. Wrightson, the son-in-law of Charlotte Peirse, was narrowly defeated by an outside opponent. Unlike the family into which he had married, Wrightson was a whig but this does not seem to have been a very material factor in the situation. It certainly did not prevent the Peirse interest from being deployed in his support. In 1835 and 1837 he was returned unopposed and in 1841 successfully beat off an attack by the Harewood influence. With that his position appeared to have been consolidated; he remained member for Northallerton for the next quarter of a century, being elected for the last time in 1859. Not until 1866 did the Lascelles family finally obtain the seat.

At Ripon the family history was similar although the influence of the patroness was put to less exclusively family use. Here the founder of the large Lawrence estates in Yorkshire and Leicestershire was George Aislabie who married Mary Mallory of Studley Royal in the reign of Charles II. John Aislabie, chancellor of the exchequer 1718–21 and of South Sea Bubble reputation, was his son. This Aislabie was a patron of Ripon, where he was mayor in 1702 and to the corporation of which he gave in 1720 the sum of £2,000. He died in 1742 leaving an only son, William, who was M.P. for Ripon from the time he attained his majority in 1721 to his death in 1781 and who made a substantial addition to the family estate by the purchase in 1768 of Fountains Abbey and Park. He was succeeded by his two daughters and co-heiresses, Elizabeth, wife of Charles Allanson (d.s.p.), and Anna Sophia, mother of Elizabeth Sophia Lawrence. It was this lady who was the celebrated Miss Lawrence of Ripon in the age of Peel.

She was born in 1761, the daughter of William Lawrence of Kirkby Fleetham, who was M.P. for Ripon in six parliaments. He died in 1798; her mother, Anna Sophia, in 1802. Her only brother (William) had died in 1785. She was thus left heiress to a large patrimony and in 1808 succeeded to the main Studley Royal estate on the death of her aunt, Mrs Allanson. Although probably the wealthiest woman of her time, Miss Lawrence never married and died at her seat at Studley Park in July 1845 in her eighty-fifth year. On the news of the death of the aged patroness of Ripon all shops and public places in the borough were closed and at the funeral a week later an impressive cortège assembled to pay a final tribute to the property and the influence of which she had so long been the representative. Besides her numerous relatives and friends, the Bishop of Ripon with the dean, chapter, and clergy, the mayor of Ripon with the corporation and constables, the tenantry on horseback, tradesmen and other inhabitants of the borough, all took part in a solemn mourning procession. It was a striking illustration, even if perhaps one of the last of its kind, of how much of the spacious eighteenth-century respect for the potency of landed property survived into early Victorian days.[27]

While she lived her electoral influence at Ripon was paramount. Only in 1832, under the immediate excitement of the passing of the Reform Act, was there any significant revolt against her control. Before the act the franchise had been held by less than 150 burgage tenants. The coming of the new franchise increased the borough electorate by another two hundred. The first election after the act witnessed a close struggle in which Miss Lawrence's two nominees were beaten by less than ten votes by two liberal candidates, Staveley and Crompton. This reverse brought about prompt measures to restore discipline. All the Lawrence tenants among the electors, to the number of nearly one hundred, were given notice to quit after the election. In the event only those, about nine in all, who had actually voted against their patroness's interest were actually obliged to move out. But the demonstration was enough. At the 1835 election all voted agreeably to her wishes. To render the borough proof against attack, however, a number of buildings qualifying for the vote were added to the existing estate property within the constituency by the usual process known as 'faggot-vote making'.[28] In April 1834 a petition was presented to the House of Commons from some of the inhabitants of Ripon, complaining of the manufacture of votes by means of 'cow-houses and other mean buildings' whereby the borough was being virtually swamped by the discreetly unnamed proprietress of much property in the neighbourhood. Baines, the member for Leeds, and Joshua Crompton of Sion Hill, Yorks, one of the sitting members for Ripon, supported the petition. The latter told the House that if the lady in question continued with her plans, it would soon be a mockery to call Ripon an open borough—'it would soon be emphatically her borough'.[29] But

[27] See the obituary notice for Miss Lawrence in the *Gentleman's Magazine*, October 1845.
[28] I.e. the manufacture for political purposes of tenements affording the bare minimum property qualification for voting.
[29] P.P. 1835, VIII, 194–5; *Hansard*, XXIII, 1 sqq. For a radical view of Ripon ten years later, see *England and Ireland* (1844), 26.

there was little that the House of Commons could do even if it felt the desire; and the petition was ordered to lie on the table. Every one knew that the Reform Act with its standard property qualification had made the manufacture of votes extremely easy. There was nothing in law to prevent landlords from erecting as many £10 houses as could be physically contained within the borough boundaries and passed by the revising barristers as legally qualifying tenements. Certainly after 1832 the constituency again relapsed completely into Miss Lawrence's hands. At the 1835 election Crompton did not offer himself for re-election. T. K. Staveley, of Old Henningford, Yorks, stood once more but was left at the foot of the polls, a hundred votes below the two conservative candidates. It was significant that of his 125 votes, no less than 112 were plumpers. With that the battle for the control of the borough was won and the next two elections at least were uncontested. Miss Lawrence was left the mistress of the smitten field.

Unlike Miss Peirse at Northallerton she used her borough for party rather than for family purposes. Indeed it was alleged by a radical pamphlet in 1844 that she had placed the two Ripon seats entirely at the disposal of the conservative party managers, allowing them to nominate and change members at pleasure. This was probably true enough, at any rate for the period after 1837. The successful candidates in 1835 were General d'Albiac, who had unsuccessfully contested the borough in 1832, and T. Pemberton, a barrister of Lincoln's Inn who had sat for Rye in 1831. In 1837 the general was replaced by Sir Edward Sugden, who had been Solicitor-General in 1829 and Lord Chancellor for Ireland in Peel's 1834–5 ministry. Sugden had last sat for St Mawes, Cornwall, in the 1831 parliament. Since the Reform Act he had been out of parliament although twice contesting the borough of Cambridge. He was now provided with a safe seat, and he and Pemberton were again returned in 1841. In the course of Peel's ministry of 1841–6 there were several official changes. On Sugden's re-appointment as Lord Chancellor for Ireland in 1841 he was replaced at Ripon by Admiral Sir George Cockburn, a Lord of the Admiralty. In 1843 Pemberton took the Chiltern Hundreds to make room for Thomas B. C. Smith, the Attorney-General for Ireland. Finally in 1846, following Smith's appointment as Master of the Rolls in Ireland, he was succeeded by Edwin Lascelles, a younger son of the 2nd Earl of Harewood. By that date, of course, the borough had passed into other though no less staunchly conservative hands. At her death in 1845 Miss Lawrence had bequeathed the greater part of her estates in Yorkshire to Earl de Grey and the Earl of Ripon. Both these peers were distantly related to her, being the great-grandchildren of Sir William Robinson by Mary, daughter of George Aislabie, the founder of the family fortunes. To each legatee his share of the property was limited to life; the whole was then to descend to Lord Goderich, the son and heir of the Earl of Ripon. The Studley Royal, Fountains Abbey, and Ripon estates passed in the meantime to the Earl de Grey who thus became the new patron of the borough.[30] But from 1837 to 1845 it was clear that Ripon was not only under the control of its proprietress but also at the disposal of the conservative party. Moreover, if the election of Staveley and Crompton can be taken as an index to the true state of feeling in the constituency, Ripon presented the spectacle of a borough largely liberal in sympathy, regularly returning members who were not only conservative but also strangers to the inhabitants, owing their nomination to decisions taken at Studley, the Carlton, and Westminster.

With boroughs as dependent on a proprietor as this, the special position of the patron was a well recognized feature of electoral politics. Even when he might seem to have abandoned interest in a seat, a punctilious inquiry as to his wishes was normally made by all those on his own side who chose to intervene in the constituency. At the time of the 1835 general election, for example, the liberals at Bury St Edmunds took a dislike to Lord Charles Fitzroy. An offer made by them to elect his elder brother, Lord Euston, was refused. They then sent an invitation to Lord Suffield's son, Edward Harbord, to stand as candidate. On receipt of this offer Lord Suffield wrote as a matter of course to the Duke of Grafton, stating to him all the circumstances, and adding that he would naturally entertain no such proposition on Harbord's behalf until he had received an assurance from Grafton that he had abandoned all thought of Bury St Edmunds for his son.[31] When the aspirations of a candidate in search of a seat turned

---

[30] The story went that the bequest to Earl de Grey was due to an early attachment between him and Miss Lawrence to which the lady had remained loyal all her life, and that accompanying the bequest was a tin box containing all the offers of marriage she had rejected for his sake (Wolf, *Life of Marquess of Ripon*, I, 13).

[31] Bacon, *Memoir of Lord Suffield*, 481.

towards a proprietary borough, the crucial question was his relations with the magnate and the probable view that the latter would take of his candidature. The correspondence of Sir James Graham throws some light on this aspect of political life.

After his defeat in Cumberland in 1837 Graham looked about for a safe and (in view of his expenses at the last election) cheap seat. The suggestion was made that he should have one of the seats at Stamford, the pocket borough of Lord Exeter. The latter himself told Peel that he would be quite prepared to support Graham and entertained no doubt that he would be returned by a large majority even if a contest took place. Graham, however, though anxious to return to the House of Commons as soon as possible, had some scruples about Stamford. Up to that time, he wrote to Granville Somerset, one of the Stamford members had always been a popular local man and that had served to mask the influence of Lord Exeter. If the latter succeeded in forcing Graham, a stranger, on the constituency, together with the other sitting member, Lord Granby (son and heir of the Duke of Rutland), the cry of 'nomination borough' would be raised which would only cause injury.[32] Eventually a seat was found for him at Pembroke but when after less than two years Graham was again on the hunt for a safe seat his thoughts were first turned to two other pocket boroughs, namely, Ripon and Thirsk. If, on the formation of a conservative ministry, he confided to Bonham, Sugden was comfortably disposed elsewhere, Ripon would suit him (Graham) very well. His father had represented the borough in several parliaments[33]—'I should not be unacceptable to Mrs. Lawrence. I am intimate with Ld. de Grey and Ld. Ripon, and the Inhabitants would hardly consider me a Stranger.' In default of Ripon there was another possible refuge at Thirsk. Before taking any steps, however, he sounded Bonham for his views.[34]

Thirsk was a small borough with an electorate of less than 300. At the time of the Reform Act the franchise belonged to a few score burgage tenements in the old borough. The majority of these were owned by Sir Robert Frankland of Thirkelby, Yorks, who later assumed the additional surname of Russell. He himself had sat for Thirsk during his father's lifetime for many years. The enlargement of the borough and the new franchise in 1832 made

[32] Add. MS. 40424, fos. 294, 299.
[33] Sir James Graham, 1st baronet, was M.P. for Ripon 1798–1807.
[34] Add. MS. 40616, fo. 78.

little immediate difference to the character of the constituency. At the first election after the Reform Act Frankland was returned unopposed. In 1834 he retired and was succeeded by a local man, Samuel Crompton of Wood End, Thirsk, who was also returned unopposed at the general elections of 1835 and 1837. In the House of Commons, it may be noticed, he sat as a liberal. He was replaced at the general election of 1841, again without a contest, by another local landowner, John Bell of Thirsk Hall. Sir Robert Frankland-Russell died in 1849 and was succeeded by his five daughters and co-heiresses. One of these married Sir William Payne Gallwey (2nd baronet) who became member for Thirsk on Bell's death in 1851. It would be interesting to know the detailed arrangements that lay behind these changes in the representation of the borough. From the strong local flavour to the successive members and the absence of any indications of a battle for possession, it would be reasonable to presume that the control of the constituency was vested in the hands of only one or two persons and that it fell into some intermediate category between a family and a proprietary borough.[35] To Graham in 1839, at any rate, there seemed a promising opening there. He was on friendly terms with Frankland and felt fairly confident of success if his support was forthcoming. A few months later he was asking Bonham whether, without committing Graham, he could ascertain the feelings of Sir Robert about Thirsk and the chances of success if Graham put up for the constituency.[36] A few days afterwards, when his own position at Pembroke seemed irretrievably lost, he wrote that he was disposed to think well of the Thirsk possibility provided that Frankland approved and was willing to support him to the utmost. In the end, of course, nothing came of the project. 'As to Thirsk', Graham wrote at the end of the year, 'the difficulty is to find a Yorkshire candidate: I am sure Sir R. Russell would support any good Conservative connected with the County who was agreeable to his neighbours.'[37]

By this time his attention was turned elsewhere: to Woodstock, commonly regarded as a close borough of the Duke of Marlborough. This reputation was certainly borne out at first by the members it returned to parliament after 1832. Deprived of one of its representatives by the Reform Act, it sent in succession the

[35] Cf. Dod, *Electoral Facts*, 302.   [36] Add. MS. 40616, fo. 119, 2 December 1839.
[37] Add. MS. 40616, fo. 142.

Marquess of Blandford, heir to the dukedom, and Lord Charles Spencer Churchill, the duke's second son, unopposed to the House of Commons. In 1837, however, a rift appeared in the patronage of the borough. Another conservative candidate contested the election of that year and Charles Churchill was defeated by less than ten votes. In less than twelve months the victor of 1837, Henry Peyton, withdrew from the scene he so oddly adorned. When he took the Chiltern Hundreds in 1838 his place was filled by the Marquess of Blandford after a contest with his own brother, Lord John Spencer Churchill. It must have been patent even to an outside observer that a family quarrel was going on inside the borough. If further proof of this was needed it was to be found in the fact that Lord Charles Spencer Churchill petitioned against Peyton's return in 1837 and that Lord John Churchill petitioned against the Marquess of Blandford's return in 1838.[38] It was at this delicate stage in the borough's history that Graham turned his thoughts to Woodstock. On the face of it he had much to recommend him in Oxfordshire. He was a near relative of the Churchill family, being a nephew of the Duchess of Marlborough, and was moreover one of the family trustees. As for the constituency itself, he told Bonham, if Blandford and the duke could agree to support the same candidate, the seat was a close one. He knew his relatives too well, however, to feel optimistic. They would both, he observed, try to screw money out of the transaction and at the critical moment one of them would fall away. But any port had its value for Graham in the storm that had blown up in Pembroke. He felt that he was the candidate on whom his combative kinsmen were most likely to agree, and so made up his mind to broach the matter verbally to the Marquess of Blandford when next they met.[39]

This speculative tour of English pocket boroughs, or some at least that were under tory control, eventually ended at Dorchester where Graham and Lord Ashley were returned without a contest in 1841. An easier return to parliament could scarcely have been procured anywhere. Nevertheless he left nothing to chance and preserved the decencies of electoral life by going down to Dorset to canvass the constituency. On 22 June he wrote back to Bonham that he had canvassed for six hours and obtained 105 promises out of 180 voters; and that he was alone in his glory, no other

[38] *H. of C. Journals*, 1837–8, xciii, 131, 513.   [39] Add. MS. 40616, fos. 127, 142.

candidate having appeared on the field. The next day he was able to report that he had called on every voter in the constituency and seen personally the great majority of them, securing promises from some two-thirds of the whole electorate. The feeling in his favour was more decided and he was hopeful that a contest would be avoided. Less than a week later he was a member for Dorchester.[40] Graham perhaps, as a leading parliamentary figure, a liberal-minded reformer, and a prospective member of the next conservative cabinet, was unusually scrupulous about his position. Even so his scruples were more concerned with securing the full and unreserved support of all the persons who influenced the particular constituencies under consideration than with appearing before the electorate as an independent and popular candidate. He had no objection to a seat for a pocket borough; he did object to being forced on a constituency against the wishes and opinions of the neighbourhood. In this his concern may have been chiefly for his public career. To the ordinary member of parliament these considerations would not apply with the same force.

Nevertheless, the relationship between the member returned for a pocket borough and the patron who had secured his return was inevitably marked by some delicacy. Naturally a Churchill at Woodstock or a Peel at Tamworth, even perhaps a Graham at Pembroke or Dorchester, was not hampered by any restrictions on his conduct. But Graham, well known and influential as he was, showed a punctilious deference to the views and advice of his backers. Lesser men, with no personal standing in the borough for which they sat and with insufficient parliamentary prestige to deal on equal terms with their patrons, were involved in a vague relationship of obligation and indebtedness which might seriously circumscribe their activities. It was not that they were servants sent to vote in the lower House according to the desire of the proprietor and bound by a gentlemanly convention to resign their seats if they were not prepared to pay him that service. But between the member and the patron there was an inevitable sense of duty on the one side and ownership on the other which could sometimes prove highly embarrassing. The pocket borough member might, for instance, be called upon to resign so that room could be found for a more indispensable politician. Lord Exeter was quite prepared to ask one of the sitting members for Stamford

[40] Add MS. 40616, fos. 198–208.

to give up his seat in order to assist the work of getting all the necessary ministers and officials into parliament on the formation of Peel's ministry in 1834. 'I shall have no scruple', he wrote to the Duke of Wellington on 20 November 1834, 'in requesting Col. Chaplin to relinquish his seat for Stamford in favour of any person of importance whom your grace and Sir Robert Peel may think essential to be in the House.' The only condition he attached was that the new candidate, whoever he might be, should pay the expenses of his election. As soon as Peel had arrived back from Italy he repeated his offer and added that he was keeping Chaplin back until the ministry's wishes were known. To have a safe seat put at his disposal was not unwelcome to Peel. Differences of opinion at that juncture with the Duke of Buckingham and his son and heir the Marquess of Chandos made it not unlikely that Fremantle, Peel's Treasury secretary and former member for Buckingham, would be unable to stand again for the duke's borough. Almost immediately, however, that danger passed and Peel was able to decline with grace to disturb so good a friend as Colonel Chaplin. Equally gracefully Lord Exeter replied that Fremantle would have been very acceptable and that the seat, the safety of which he could guarantee, was still at Peel's disposal even if it was not required for Fremantle.[41] In the event, therefore, Chaplin, who together with George Finch, son of the 8th Earl of Winchilsea, had been elected for Stamford in 1832, was again returned in 1835. The next election, which brought a crop of conservative casualties, necessitated a call for his services. Sir George Clerk, the conservative chief whip, had been defeated in his own constituency. In May 1838 Chaplin took the Chiltern Hundreds and Clerk replaced him as colleague of the Marquess of Granby, heir to the Duke of Rutland, who had been elected with Chaplin in 1837. Clerk and Granby were again returned in 1841.

This was one liability of the member for a pocket borough. Another was illustrated by the position of Sir Thomas Fremantle at Buckingham. Here was a case of an official party man sitting

---

[41] Add. MS. 40309, fo. 292; 40405, fos. 287, 289, 291, 293. The Marquess of Exeter owned many of the qualifying tenements in the borough and in 1835 there was reckoned to be a clear conservative majority of 170 in an electorate of between 700 and 800. An annotated roll of the Stamford electorate is preserved in the Clerk Papers which indicates that of the 580 valid voters on the register at the time of the 1841 election, 458 promised to support the 'official' candidates (the Marquess of Granby and Sir George Clerk). There is a note to the effect that of the remaining 122 electors many would probably vote Red (the Burghley colours) as only 79 were regarded as decidedly Blue (Clerk Papers, T/188/83).

for a proprietary borough whose proprietor did not always agree with the official party line. Fremantle was the type of hard-working and indispensable politician who more than most perhaps deserved the quiet and security of a close seat. With Sir George Clerk he had been secretary to the Treasury in Peel's first ministry and succeeded him as chief whip in 1837. His place in the hierarchy of party managers and his local connexion (he himself was a Buckinghamshire squire and related by marriage to Sir William Clayton of Marlow) made him a particularly suitable member for the seat at Buckingham controlled by the Duke of Buckingham which he had occupied since 1830. The difficulty that arose about his position in 1835 was due to the divergence of policy between Peel and the duke over agricultural relief. 'I ought to add', explained Peel in sounding Lord Exeter on the possibility of finding a refuge for Fremantle at Stamford, 'that his difference with Lord Chandos and the Duke of Buckingham arises solely from this, that he is ready to join me at this arduous crisis, without exacting from me a promise which they require from me (at least Lord Chandos who is deeply pledged upon it) that I will repeal wholly or in part the Malt Tax.'[42] The danger was averted in 1835 and Fremantle was re-elected in that year and again in 1837 and 1841. In 1845, however, the divergence of view between the agriculturalist patron and the Peelite minister became too wide for any compromise to be possible.

By that date Fremantle was chief secretary for Ireland. It was his second move in Peel's 1841–6 ministry. In 1844 he had been taken from the Treasury to be Secretary at War and early in 1845 he was transferred to Ireland. Each change of appointment had of course necessitated re-election. Already in January 1845 Fremantle had shown a strong sense of deference towards the patron to whom he owed his return to parliament on no less than seven occasions. On his appointment to the Irish secretaryship he wrote to Peel, asking permission to speak to the duke on the government's Irish policy before the by-election consequent on that promotion. 'If I obtain the Duke's promise of the return for Buckingham without opening the question', he pointed out to his chief, 'he may, when Parliament meets and the writ is moved, consider that I have not acted ingenuously towards him.'[43] All went smoothly, however, and Fremantle was duly re-elected for

[42] Add. MS. 40405, fos. 289–90.   [43] Add. MS. 40476, fo. 414.

Buckingham in February 1845. There followed the fateful summer and autumn that rotted the potatoes and wrecked the conservative party. By the end of the year the battle was joined between the free-traders and protectionists and the whole principle of protection for agriculture was at stake. Fremantle was now confronted with a much graver personal problem than the difference of opinion over the Malt Tax in 1835. As long ago as 1842 the Duke of Buckingham[44] had resigned from the ministry because of Peel's first adjustment of the duties on corn; now (20 December 1845) Peel had resumed office with the clear intent of a much more drastic change of policy than was ever envisaged in 1842. On 22 December Fremantle unburdened himself to his leader. He prefaced his letter with the statement that he had no wish to embarrass Peel and no wish to resign his office. He approved Peel's policy over the Corn Laws and would support him as far as he was able. But the circumstances under which he had twice in the last two years been elected for Buckingham made his position different from that of the others. In May 1844 in a public address to his constituents he had pledged himself to maintain the Corn Law of 1842; in February 1845—under pressure and after careful choice of his phrases—he had repeated that undertaking. Hence he was in all honour bound either to redeem his pledge or resign. He would cheerfully do the latter except that he did not know where he could find another seat and in that case his absence from the House of Commons might injure the government. Moreover the mere fact of vacating his seat would create a sensation and perhaps bring on other resignations. On that issue, therefore, he placed himself unreservedly in Peel's hands. There was, however, an additional consideration. In any case Fremantle was likely to lose his seat at the next general election. 'I can only obtain one thro' the influence of the Government at considerable expense to myself.'[45] The dilemma was ended in what was probably the only possible way. Fremantle resigned from the House of Commons and in February 1846 the Marquess of Chandos was returned in his place in time to be present for the crucial voting on the Corn Laws and the even more crucial division on the Irish coercion bill.

This was not the final repercussion. In default of another seat,

---

[44] The Marquess of Chandos (of Reform Act and Malt Tax reputation) had succeeded as Duke of Buckingham in 1839.

[45] Add. MS. 40476, fos. 577–9.

and these were hard to come by for Peelite politicians in the early weeks of 1846, it was necessary for Fremantle to relinquish the Irish secretaryship. A session in which Irish famine and Irish outrages formed the staple topic of parliamentary debate could not be entered on with no ministerial representative for Irish affairs in the House of Commons. Accordingly Lord Lincoln left the cabinet to take up the appointment only to be defeated himself in Nottinghamshire before finding a seat in Scotland. The politician thus entrapped between the exigencies of governmental policy and the obduracy of his patron's dissent was not forgotten. Fremantle was found a safe harbour as vice-chairman and later chairman of the Board of Customs, a post which he retained until 1873. He was not a wealthy man and he had a wife and family to consider. On both personal and public grounds his abandonment of the hazards of politics for the security of the civil service had much to recommend it.[46] Nevertheless it terminated the parliamentary career of a man who was one of the abler, certainly one of the most popular, of the second-line Peelites at a time when he was just attaining the lower slopes of ministerial eminence.

Whatever on balance were the advantages or disadvantages of the proprietary boroughs in the period after the Reform Act, there was at least one argument in their favour that could not easily be turned aside. As long as there remained on the statute-book the early eighteenth-century legislation enforcing the re-election of ministers on appointment, it was of great practical benefit, almost indeed a necessity, for the efficient government of the country that those ministers should have a secure entry into the House of Commons should their original constituency fail them. To expose ministers to the anxiety and expense of a double election, or to deprive the country of the services of men simply because their re-election could not be guaranteed, was an anachronism which neither tories, nor whigs, nor radicals were seriously disposed to defend. The defects of the law on this point were widely realized. An alteration might with propriety have been introduced into the Reform Act which took away so many of the close boroughs that had previously robbed the place acts of their stringency. The question was in fact seriously considered by the whigs; and Lord John Russell told the House of Commons at one point that if the

---

[46] Cf. Graham's remarks to Bonham, Add. MS. 40616, fo. 307, 22 January 1845, at the time of Fremantle's appointment to Ireland.

reform bill passed, it might be advisable to alter the act of Queen Anne requiring vacation of seats on appointment as minister. Hunt rejoined that there would be enough boroughs in Schedule B, some with no more than three hundred voters, where the application of five or six thousand pounds would do the business without the need for statutory changes.[47] This was an over-simplification. Proprietary boroughs were approachable through the patron not through the purse; on the other hand contests in venal boroughs were always risky matters. In any case to affix a contingent fine of £5,000 to every ministerial nomination was scarcely a defensible aspect of the constitution.

But the opportunity passed and, as it happened, nothing was done in the matter until 1867. But though custom to some extent obscured the disadvantages of the system, its penal aspect was extremely real after 1832 when nomination boroughs became precious commodities. The crux of the matter was the continuation of the old constitutional practice within the new electoral structure. As early as May 1834 Peel wrote to Sir George Clerk of the 'extraordinary state' which had been reached in the conduct of public affairs. 'The King's prerogative as to the appointment to the most subordinate office connected with a seat in Parliament paralyzed by the Reform vote. The sole question is not who is fit for the office, not who will accept it, but who dare vacate.'[48] In little over six months he was to have personal experience of the importance of the question. For it was precisely this problem of finding seats for ministers that was a material factor in Peel's decision in 1834 to dissolve parliament without waiting to meet it with the new ministry. His failure to secure a majority in the general election of 1835 exposed him to the censure of those who held up the example of Pitt's conduct in 1784 as the model to be followed in such circumstances. The critics argued that Peel should have met the old parliament, developed his policy and made his case; and only then, if he still met with an adverse hearing, appeal from a partisan House of Commons to an informed and sympathetic country. But such criticism ignored the changes that had taken place since Pitt's day. If Parliament had not been

---

[47] *Hansard*, v, 714. The Marquess of Northampton subsequently introduced a bill into the House of Lords to repeal for certain offices (cabinet posts and the principal law appointments) the clauses in the act of Anne requiring re-election on appointment. The Duke of Wellington, while expressing his sympathy with the object of the bill, deprecated a measure which he thought should be introduced by the ministry in the House of Commons.   [48] Clerk Papers, 8 May 1834 (T/188/81).

dissolved there was a real danger that Peel would have been obliged to meet a hostile House of Commons with half his ministry absent in the country endeavouring to obtain re-election. The losses among ministerial candidates at the general election, when the opposing forces were dissipated over the whole kingdom, demonstrated what might have happened if they had been able to concentrate their strength on a few selected ministerial by-elections. 'If anything were wanted', wrote Peel to his brother-in-law towards the close of the elections, 'to justify the dissolution, it would be the proof that those places wherein it might be supposed the influence of Government would prevail, have been most unfavourable.' There would have been little chance, he added, that a strong government could have been formed which had to vacate its seats in the first session.[49] The difficulties were of course greatest, and the inconveniences of defeat most vexatious, at times of crisis. In 1846 when Peel reshuffled his ministry preparatory to repealing the Corn Laws, he saw Rous (appointed to the Admiralty) and Lord Lincoln lose their seats on seeking re-election and Gladstone unable to find a seat at all.[50] The first defeat, though it concerned only a junior minister, was particularly galling since it is unlikely that Rous would have been appointed a lord of the Admiralty if his success at Westminster had not been considered certain.[51] Lincoln's position on the other hand was clearly more doubtful; but a victory for him would have been worth double that of Rous.

> The great difficulty [Peel wrote to the queen] is his return for the county of Nottingham. If that return could be carried in defiance of the Duke of Newcastle, and of that sort of dictation to members of the House of Commons which is proceeding to very dangerous lengths, it would be a great triumph not only to your Majesty's servants, but to the constitutional freedom of election. The risk is great . . . but the advantage of success would greatly overbalance the risk of failure.[52]

[49] Add. MS. 40410, fo. 18.
[50] The extent of the losses among ministers seeking re-election at this time has been perhaps exaggerated by Halévy, *Hist. Eng. People*, IV, 108. Not all were unsuccessful. Carnegie (lord of the Treasury) was re-elected at Stafford; Neville (lord of the Treasury) at Windsor; Wortley (Judge-Advocate-General) at Bute. The casualty list would have been much higher, of course, had Peel's 1841–6 ministry actually resigned office at the end of 1845. As it was, the greater part of the losses at this juncture were due to voluntary resignations on the part of free-trade conservatives who felt themselves bound to defer to their protectionist constituents or patrons.
[51] Parker, *Peel*, III, 334.   [52] *Ibid.*, III, 338.

But even in less abnormal times than the crisis of 1845–6 the problem of places for ministers was always present in the calculations of whips and prime ministers. In April 1845, before the Corn Laws began to totter, Peel recommended Forbes Mackenzie for a lordship of the Treasury on the double grounds of having supported the Maynooth grant and being able to carry his county election without difficulty.[53] In Bonham's list of ministerial appointments (drawn up for Peel's guidance in September 1841), a list of ten names was included from whom the lords of the Treasury and the civil lords of the Admiralty were to be selected. Of these, four were asterisked with the explanatory note: 'Those marked (*) could not probably vacate safely and I would apprize every man that if he lost his Seat, he must resign his Office.'[54] Certainty of tenure was, therefore, especially for the young politician on the fringe of office, a marked asset to a parliamentary career. The real criticism of the close boroughs from the executive standpoint was that too many of them were reserved for dependent friends and relatives, too few for official men. Patrons like Miss Lawrence at Ripon, Lord Exeter at Stamford, or Lord Sandwich at Huntingdon (who returned Jonathan Peel[55] and Sir Frederick Pollock, the conservative Attorney-General, from 1832 to 1841) were extremely rare; and though there were many proprietary boroughs there were not many which the government or party could command. Yet there were some and though perhaps the pocket boroughs after as well as before the Reform Act sent more 'dull, drowsy members' than men of talent to sit on the House of Commons benches, yet to some extent they lightened the burden of government that the Duke of Wellington had thought would be impossible in a reformed, that is to say, an independent parliament.

But there was a price to pay. Official men in close seats were hostages to the proprietors, as the fate of Fremantle amply demonstrated. There was in fact no easy solution to the difficulty. Expense in a venal constituency; obligation in a close constituency; the restraint of pledges and pressures in a popular constituency: these were the trinity of evils from which it was not easy to escape. To fly, like Hobhouse, from promises at Westminster might be to

---

[53] Parker, *Peel*, III, 176.   [54] Add. MS. 40489, fo. 393.
[55] Jonathan Peel once told his daughter-in-law, Lady Georgiana Peel, that in all the years he represented Huntingdon, the only question he was ever asked by his constituents was 'How are you?' (*Recollections of Lady Georgiana Peel*, 209).

fall into bribery at Nottingham. The most fortunate politician perhaps was a man like Peel who had himself returned for his own family seat. Whatever the theoretical advantages of standing for a wider constituency which have sometimes been urged against Peel's refusal to move from Tamworth, the practical conveniences of staying there were immense. Under this heading there came not only the certainty of election but the absence of any trammels on his political conduct. After the passing of the repeal of the Corn Laws in 1846 Peel could have had his pick of half a dozen great urban constituencies; but he refused them all. There was of course some sentiment in his reluctance to abandon Tamworth. But this was not the sole reason. To Brougham, who wrote more than once to induce him to stand for the City of London, he confessed that

> so much of feeling enters into my decision in respect to the ad-
> herence to Tamworth, that I am scarcely accessible to reason. But
> [he continued significantly] even if I were, I should long hesitate
> before I relinquished the advantage of that independence which
> the representation of a small place enables a man to enjoy. I
> greatly doubt whether I cannot render greater public service by
> means of that independence than by being the organ of even such
> a constituency as that of London.[56]

But even when the member for a close borough was not his own patron, it would be wrong to assume that his obligations would be more irksome than if he sat as representative of a wider body of voters. The hydra-headed electorate of a large constituency could be as rapacious and ungrateful as a ducal proprietor. Gladstone, a politician of conscience and integrity, sat for the Duke of New-castle's borough of Newark from 1832 to 1845 without any special qualms. It was only when he accepted office in Peel's last cabinet that he refused to invite a rebuff by standing again for his protec-tionist patron's constituency and in consequence was out of parliament till the general election of 1847. He had therefore no special cause to love the nomination system. Yet his reactions to the various attempts made by Bonham to find him a seat in the interval indicate no insuperable objection to sitting for some other close seat; and certainly he showed no desire to put up for a popular constituency. No less than eight constituencies were

[56] Parker, *Peel*, III, 486.

jointly reviewed by Bonh'am and Gladstone in as many months. But every opening seemed attended by objections or afflicted by fatalities. At St Ives an alleged interest possessed by Lord Mornington and offered through his uncle, the Duke of Wellington, to Gladstone, turned out on closer inspection by Bonham to be quite hollow. A speculative vacancy at Whitby under the auspices of Hudson, the railway promoter[57] but on terms of 'perfect independence' was regarded rather coolly by Gladstone who drew attention to Hudson's ties with the protectionists and doubted 'whether any verbal stipulation as to independence would entirely get over this difficulty'. An invitation then came from the city of Aberdeen for Gladstone to stand as candidate for that constituency. But he was unwilling to start except with a reasonable guarantee of success and Bonham was unable to hold out much hope of that in view of the dissensions among the conservatives in Scotland over the Free Church question. To atone for that discouragement, however, the party manager then raised two further possibilities. At Newcastle-under-Lyme one of the sitting members, Colquhoun, was dangerously ill and though a successor for him had been designated in the person of Lord Brackley, it was conceivable that the latter's father, Lord Ellesmere,[58] would be prepared to give Gladstone the seat for the brief remainder of the existing parliament. Alternatively C. P. Villiers, M.P. for Wolverhampton, was shortly to be nominated as governor of Bombay and if Gladstone put up, 'your name might tell with the predominating Liberals' of that borough. However, Colquhoun was disobliging enough not to die; the Court of Directors of the East India Company refused to accept Villiers' nomination; and so the hunt was resumed. A couple of months later, in November 1846, Bonham sent off a hasty note to Gladstone informing him that Sir George Cockburn, M.P. for Ripon, had just had an apoplectic fit of the most severe kind—'at 75 this is serious. . . . If he dies, Ld. de Grey will have the return for Rippon. Could *you* not manage this?' But Gladstone replied as cautiously as ever. He did not know Lord de Grey very well and did not think that Lord Ripon had any reason for obliging Gladstone. In

---

[57] Hudson, then almost at the peak of his reputation and influence, was a leading Yorkshire conservative and had property interests at Whitby.

[58] Lord Francis Egerton (formerly Leveson-Gower), second son of the 1st Duke of Sutherland, became Earl of Ellesmere in July 1846 on the retirement of Peel's ministry. He had sat as liberal-conservative for south Lancashire from 1833 to 1846. His son and heir, George Granville Francis Egerton, styled Viscount Brackley (1846–57), was liberal-conservative member for north Staffs, 1847–51.

the end there was no need for these scruples. Cockburn despite age and apoplexy rallied sufficiently to live on until 1853, and, what was more to the purpose, retained his seat for Ripon for the remainder of the 1841–7 parliament. In December a third political invalid came under Bonham's professional scrutiny. 'Jemmy' Bradshaw, the strong tory and protectionist member for Canterbury, was rumoured to be in a hopeless state and fit to die at any time.[59] Of late years, Bonham reported guardedly to Gladstone, that constituency had been very conservative. Did Gladstone know any of the cathedral clergy there? But Gladstone commented truly though unhelpfully that it had the reputation of being a very corrupt borough and showed an inclination to hark back to an earlier project. 'Ripon wd. be delightful,' he wrote nostalgically, 'but is too good to hope.' Finally, in February 1847 an opening seemed to present itself at Wigan which both Young, the Peelite chief whip, and Bonham, hastened to bring to his notice. He had already been a prospective candidate for that borough in the previous session but a by-election had been averted at the last minute by the protectionists.[60] He was now prepared to make a second attempt, he wrote to Bonham, provided it was on the same footing as in the preceding year, namely the consent of both parties, since he felt indebted to both. Whether or not this last condition was too stringent, nothing came of the Wigan project and no more seems to have been attempted until the general election of 1847 when a haven was found in the university seat for Oxford.

In all these negotiations Gladstone showed a degree of caution that almost amounted to positive disinclination. At the outset he explained to Bonham that though he would prefer a seat in the next session, he would not refuse one immediately; and then added, 'if you think I ought to be more keen and will be so charitable as to give me your advice I shall, as I know from all previous experience of it, be much obliged to you'. A few weeks later when deprecating an approach to Hudson in connexion with Whitby, he told Bonham that he was not anxious to incur any great expense for a seat in the existing parliament 'and with illegal expense of course I could not have anything to do'. A sudden rumour which reached Bonham in August 1846 chiefly through

---

[59] The rumour in this case did not prove false. Bradshaw did die, but not until the following March. He was succeeded at Canterbury by Lord Albert Conyngham.
[60] Morley, *Gladstone*, I, 213.

the Duke of Buckingham to the effect that the whig ministry intended an early dissolution made him more than ever concerned for Gladstone's political future. But on investigation Bonham was able to reassure his correspondent and devoted himself once more, therefore, to the task of finding Gladstone a seat for the final session of parliament. Indeed Gladstone himself wrote to express a hope that he would have 'a hole to creep in at before February'. Yet when each project foundered on real or imagined difficulties, he began to feel some embarrassment. After Bonham's suggestion about Canterbury he replied that he feared his chilly answers would entirely stop Bonham's indefatigable labours 'in a field so unprofitable as that of my parliamentary interests'. At last something of the real truth showed itself.

> I suppose the real trouble is [Gladstone continued] though I have scarcely yet spoken it out to myself, that I feel a great repugnance to introducing myself to the leaders of any constituency in the way of solicitation. I cannot get over the belief that such a step requires as a condition previous, my being prepared to take up bodily their presumed views and opinions upon all leading questions.[61]

It was perhaps with some personal relief that Bonham saw Gladstone safely lodged at Oxford. To a politician with the electoral sensitivity which Gladstone was exhibiting at this period, a university was possibly the only appropriate constituency. Yet it is worth remarking that he was considerably more sensitive to the drawbacks of a popular constituency than he was to those of a pocket borough. It was not until eighteen years later that he finally left the cloisters of the university for the broad electorate of Lancashire. By then the political world with which Peel and Palmerston had been familiar was about to break up for ever.[62]

[61] Add. MS. 44110, fos. 175, 183, 185, 194–218.
[62] For a general list of proprietary boroughs and their patrons in the period immediately after the Reform Act, see Appendix D.

Chapter Ten

COMPROMISE ELECTIONS

IT may be observed as a generalization that the composition of the House of Commons in the age of Peel was decided almost as much by the elections that were not contested as by those that were. After the Reform Act there were 401 constituencies that returned members to parliament. In the five general elections that took place between 1832 and 1847 the average number of those that were contested was only just over half. The figure of course fluctuated considerably. The 1832 election, with the electorate still under the influence of reforming idealism, was by contemporary standards hotly contested. The 1835 election was quieter. The 1837 election, which was the crucial contest between conservatives and whigs in the period between the Reform Act and Peel's death, almost reached the abnormal figures of 1832. The 1841 election, which merely ratified a Peelite victory long made inevitable, was less warmly disputed even than 1835; and the 1847 election, coming at a time when the old party ties were loosened and sometimes shattered, was the quietest of all. In round proportions, just over two-thirds of the constituencies were contested in 1832; just over half in 1835; just under two-thirds in 1837; less than a half in 1841; and just over two-fifths in 1847.[1]

These proportions are of course large by comparison with elections before 1830. Nevertheless it is a singular reflection that at the general election of 1841, which installed in office one of the most memorable ministries of the century, the electors were only called upon to record a vote in about 190 constituencies. The circumstance, moreover, that on an average only about half the electoral area was the scene of party contests, emphasizes the contemporary difficulty of producing a rapid alteration in the balance of party strength in the House of Commons. The recovery of the conservative party in less than a decade from the disastrous position in which it had been left by the reform crisis of 1831–2 owed much, certainly, to its own energy and skill; but it was aided perhaps equally by the unprecedented and largely fortuitous

[1] See Appendix E for a further discussion of this subject.

occurrence of four general elections in the space of nine years. It took three appeals to the country to whittle away the commanding majority enjoyed by the whigs in the first session of the reformed parliament. The swing of the pendulum characteristic of the late Victorian electoral system with its mass electorate and tightly organized party warfare could scarcely operate with the restricted franchise and equally restricted area of electoral competition that marked the period between the first and second Reform Acts. Too many dams and obstructions existed for the tides of public opinion to flow with either freedom or power along the electoral channels. Personal and family influence withdrew some constituencies entirely from the currents of national feeling; others, where bribery and intimidation were the dominant factors, were also in a degree exempt from the pressure of public opinion even if not from party conflict. Yet it would be an error to assume that in those constituencies where there were no contests, there were in no sense electoral verdicts. The choice was not expressed by the electorate in the full meaning; but it was not infrequently the result of an agreement by the influential leaders of the constituency, of personal bargains between rival candidates, or of compromises between the organized parties themselves. To that extent the uncontested elections of this period were often in fact elections contested and decided by means other than the hustings. As such they cannot be ignored in any analysis of the political conditions of the time.

Two factors made this kind of electoral compromise possible. One was the strength of local feeling and local personalities as against the more partisan and uncompromising views of party managers and the central organizations. The other was the existence of the two-member constituency as the characteristic unit of the British representative system. Wherever two members had to be chosen to represent one constituency, the door to a compromise was permanently unlatched. This circumstance had been recognized by both supporters and critics at the time of the reform bill. Peel had argued against the single member constituencies of Schedule B on the grounds that double membership allowed minority representation and diminished the undue preponderance of one class of interests or opinions.

> There is an immense advantage [he told the House of Commons] when contending parties are nearly balanced, in having the means of effecting an amicable compromise, and of warding off the necessity

of absolute triumph and unqualified defeat. What is it that gives keenness to election contests? Not merely general politics but local and hereditary attachments, the preference of this family to that, the influence of property newly acquired contending against that of ancient family and long established connexion.[2]

Other speakers even maintained that the two-member constituency was a principle of the constitution; and there was considerable support for the view that double seats by avoiding contests and leading to compromises gave a better because more accurate representation of the electorate. This was not simply a tory opinion. Lord Milton, a supporter of the bill, actually moved an amendment in committee to give two members to the Schedule B boroughs on the grounds that 'the minority out of doors should have a minority in the House' and that an accumulation of narrow majorities in contested elections would mean a large national minority completely unrepresented in parliament.[3] During the discussion in committee on the principle of dividing the larger counties the same idea recurred; although Althorp argued that the division of the counties would weaken the compromise tendencies inherent in the larger and more unwieldy county constituencies and create a better and more direct representation by members resident in the districts.[4] There is little evidence, however, that the county divisions, themselves double member constituencies, were any less immune from the spirit of compromise than the old county units.

The theoretical case for the two-member constituency was therefore precisely that it led to balance and compromise in the choice of members and produced a truer because more composite national representation. The circumstances that made such compromises desirable, as distinct from those that made them practicable, were naturally more varied. Sometimes, when contending parties were evenly matched, a compromise was resorted to as much on grounds of justice as of convenience. It may be observed moreover that compromising tendencies might be operating even in a contested election. At York, where the parties were evenly divided though the corporation was predominantly whiggish, it was customary to return one whig and one tory. Petre (whig) and Baynton (tory) were returned in 1832; Dundas (whig) and Lowther (tory) in

---

[2] *Hansard*, v, 408–9. [3] *Ibid.*, v, 775–6.
[4] *Ibid.*, v, 1226–32, 1359–70. See above, Ch. 3, p. 78.

1835 and 1837. All these elections were contested but there were special reasons for this. The Reform Act had caused a dissension among the tories of York between reformers and anti-reformers, since Baynton had in fact voted for the bill. Each faction therefore put forward in 1832 its own candidate, whereupon the whigs also brought forward a second candidate to balance the two tories. The contests in 1835 and 1837 bear a simpler explanation, being caused by the intervention of a radical candidate.[5] Elsewhere a compromise might be the result of a strong family desire to ensure the safe return of one of their members irrespective of the politics of his colleague. Where the family concerned enjoyed considerable electoral influence, it was often extremely difficult for party managers and more partisan politicians to overcome this type of passive obstruction. In Huntingdonshire, for example, Viscount Mandeville, the son and heir of the Duke of Manchester, was returned unopposed in the tory interest at the general election of 1832 together with a local whig landowner, J. B. Rooper. At the next election, in 1835 when Peel's first ministry was in office and in desperate need of every vote they could secure in the Commons, not only did the same two candidates again put up for the constituency but the Duke of Manchester, whose influence in the county was immense, refused to lend his support to a second conservative candidate. Lord Sandwich, a lesser tory magnate in the same county, complained of his conduct and endeavoured to move his party chiefs to write to the duke on the matter. But Wellington refused to intervene on the grounds that the Duke of Manchester was not a member of the government. Sandwich then approached Peel who in turn declined on exactly the same grounds. Mandeville and Rooper were once more returned unopposed; and in April the government retired.[6]

The primary reason perhaps for entering into a compromise was fear of expense. There were few elections that did not cost the candidates a considerable amount of money; and beyond the inevitable expenditure in the constituency there was the contingent risk of a petition. For many politicians this personal argument outweighed all other considerations. Simple compromises based on these motives were a common feature of contemporary elections both in boroughs and counties. In south Devon Russell and another whig, Bulteel, were elected in 1832 against the opposition

[5] P.P. 1835, x, 291, 667.   [6] Add. MS. 40409, fo. 314.

of the tory Buller. At the next election some of the leading tories in the county suggested that there should be an uncontested election, each side returning a member. One of Russell's chief supporters strongly recommended him to accept this offer, in view of the cost and danger of a contest. Accordingly Bulteel, despite his personal claims (as Lord Grey's son-in-law), retired from the arena and Buller was returned with Russell to the next parliament.[7] At Norwich the conservatives held out against strong opposition in 1832 and 1835 but after the 1837 election, almost certainly by collusion between the two sides, yielded one seat on petition, Mr B. Smith being declared elected *vice* Scarlett. At the next election the sitting members, Lord Douro (conservative) and Smith (liberal) were returned unopposed by agreement between the contending but probably exhausted parties.[8] At Newark the same kind of equilibrium was reached in the 1835 election with Gladstone as the more fortunate tory candidate. In 1832 there had been a smart contest which ended in the second tory candidate, Handley, being run to a margin of some seventy votes by the whig candidate, Wilde. In 1835 the 'Blues' and 'Reds' at Newark came to an agreement and Gladstone, who by his exertions had unexpectedly placed himself at the top of the poll in 1832, was returned without a contest but with a whig colleague.[9]

How far this unwillingness either to meet unlimited expense or to disturb existing political patterns affected both sides, especially in the county constituencies, may be illustrated from the history of the Northamptonshire election of 1832. From 1806 to 1830 the representation of the county had been shared by Viscount Althorp and W. R. Cartwright, the popular tory squire of Aynhoe Hall. Althorp's election in the first instance probably owed much to the extensive property in the county owned by his father, Earl Spencer, and to the direct influence emanating from the latter's Northamptonshire seat at Althorp. But his continuance as the county representative soon became an established feature which was not disturbed even by his marriage to Miss Acklom and consequent migration to Wiseton Hall in Nottinghamshire in 1814. As county member, master of the Pytchley Hunt in succession to his father and grandfather, chairman after 1830 of the Northamptonshire Quarter Sessions, and a noted agriculturalist, Althorp had

---

[7] Walpole, *Russell*, I, 222–3.   [8] *England and Ireland* (1844), 23.
[9] Morley, *Gladstone*, I, 69, 89.

a position in the county that transcended the ordinary divisions of party and he numbered many tory landowners among his political adherents. Before the Reform Act he was almost invariably returned without opposition together with his tory colleague and even in 1831, at the height of the reform agitation, there would have been no move to oppose him had not a second whig candidate been put up to break the peace of the county. Althorp himself was far from welcoming such embarrassing aid; for in such a rural constituency, with a large tory electorate certain to vote against all reformers if it came to a contest, he knew how precarious his seat was. But at the last minute, on the actual day of the nomination, Lord Milton was put up as candidate by a Northampton radical. As son of the Earl Fitzwilliam, who was the proprietor of considerable estates in the county with a seat at Milton Hall, Peterborough, his intervention even in the eleventh hour was not to be ignored. The indignant tories consequently put up Sir Charles Knightley, a local landowner, as colleague to Cartwright, and Althorp found himself bereft of many of his usual supporters and with an unexpected contest on his hands. The combination of reform zeal and his own popularity proved too formidable for his opponents and in the end not only Althorp but also Lord Milton were returned for the county, the latter just beating the sitting member Cartwright by a margin of little over a hundred votes.[10]

By the Reform Act Northamptonshire was split into two divisions. Althorp stood for the southern and his recent colleague, Lord Milton, entered on a contest for the northern division. A contested election also seemed to await Althorp. Lord Euston, who had his seat, Salwey Forest, in the county, evinced a desire to stand as the second whig candidate for the southern division. But a repetition of the 1831 contest was more than Althorp was disposed to bear.

> I think that my seat may be secured [he wrote to his father in September 1832] whether Euston perseveres or not, but it will cost more than it is worth, and I have decided that if it is probable that the expense will exceed £1,000 I will take to the Tower Hamlets.[11] That is to say, if it appears that it will be necessary to pay for bringing up the voters to the poll, I will not undertake it. I consider that if I do resign, I can never show my face here again, but that is an

---

[10] Le Marchant, *Memoir of Viscount Althorp*, 314–18.
[11] For which constituency he had been invited to stand free of all expense.

evil which must be submitted to—one is not compelled to go to an absurd expense, because some wrong-headed people choose it and insist upon dragging me into it against all reason and common sense.[12]

Simultaneously, however, there were divided counsels of prudence and daring on the other side. Arbuthnot, who at his Woodford estate maintained a listening-post in Northamptonshire politics, told Bonham on 4 October that Cartwright would be head of the poll if a contest took place and perhaps even two tories might be returned for the southern division. But that experiment would not be made 'as Cartwright dreads expense'. A few days later he renewed his complaints. In Northamptonshire, he wrote, the tories would divide the county with the enemy but not more. 'Lord Althorp must have been driven out had not Ld. Euston upon his earnest solicitation withdrawn. Lady Euston cut Ld. Althorp for his treatment of her husband. Cartwright has prevented a Contest from fear of expense. Ld. Brudenell is as opposed to a Colleague on the Northern side.'[13]

In the other division, however, though Arbuthnot considered that the tories would win both seats if the whigs put up another candidate besides Milton, his judgement was not so good as on the southern half of the county. The northern division was contested and produced, characteristically, a compromise result. Milton, the whig, and Brudenell, the tory, were returned with almost identical polls. In the south, Althorp and Cartwright were returned without a contest. In both divisions of the county, therefore, as the result of private negotiation in the one and open contest in the other, the result was the same: the division of the constituency between a whig and a tory. The candidates themselves in the southern division, and a decisive proportion of the electors in the northern division, were agreed in subordinating the rigours of party politics to other more local and personal considerations. Althorp's own county had thus provided one of the earliest and most striking exemplifications of all that he had said in the reform bill debates of the peculiar characteristics of rural politics.

In the case of southern Northamptonshire in 1832 both sides had been reluctant to engage on a contest. Frequently, however, the initiative in proposing a compromise came from the weaker party. It was natural that those were foremost in advocating a

---

[12] Le Marchant, *Althorp*, 442.   [13] Add. MS. 40617, fos. 2, 4.

compromise who had most to gain and least to lose from an amical share in the representation. Judicious politicians, by playing on the timidity or parsimony of their opponents, might often extract an advantage unlikely to fall to them by way of a direct trial of strength. Much therefore depended on the accuracy with which rival party polls could be estimated in advance of the elections. In large constituencies this was not always easy to do. In the eastern division of Norfolk two whigs, Windham[14] and Keppel,[15] were returned in 1832 with clear if not excessive margins over their opponents. Major Keppel, however, put himself in disgrace with his agricultural constituents by voting with the government against a revision of the Pension List and against a resolution for the repeal of the Malt Tax. He had in any case somewhat sinned against the proprieties of county politics by coming forward independently as candidate for the division in 1832 while the leading whig landowners were still arguing over the choice of a second string to Windham. It was commonly accepted, therefore, that he would not be elected again and by December 1834 Keppel had arrived at that conclusion himself. Richard Hanbury Gurney, the Norwich banker, then joined Windham as second whig candidate while the tories brought forward Edmund Wodehouse and Lord Walpole. Yet it is probable that the tories were by no means confident of success, especially perhaps with their second string, Walpole, who had only reluctantly allowed himself to be tied as a sacrifice to the political altar. Wodehouse too had earlier offended the Norfolk electors by his support for Catholic Emancipation and his inclination to ascribe the difficulties of the agriculturalist to currency policy rather than to the pressure of taxation.[16] At all events the conservatives made a proposition to a select meeting of the leading members of the liberal party in the constituency, offering a compromise on the basis of a withdrawal by Lord Walpole and a guarantee of a quiet return for Windham and Wodehouse. Most of the liberals at the meeting were disposed to accept the offer and the veteran Coke[17] was the only person of consequence

[14] William Howe Windham, eldest son of Admiral Windham, of Felbrigg Hall, Norfolk.

[15] Hon. George Thomas Keppel, second son of the 4th Earl of Albemarle, one of the leading whig magnates in the county. For Keppel's own account of this election, see *Fifty Years of My Life*, by George Thomas, Earl of Albemarle, 365–7.

[16] Wodehouse had sat for the county of Norfolk from 1817 to 1830 in four successive parliaments.

[17] Thomas William Coke of Holkham, cr. Earl of Leicester 1837, formerly member for the county for many years.

among them not prepared to entertain the notion of a compromise. Subsequently Lord Suffield used his influence against the truce and in the end a contest took place. Only then was it seen that the conservatives had underestimated the reaction in their favour and that the liberals had erred in rejecting the bargain offered to them. The two tories, Wodehouse and Walpole, were elected, the latter beating Windham for the second seat by a hundred votes despite being an absentee candidate who did not appear before his constituents until the election was over.[18]

At other times the threat of a contested election was hung over the opposing and superior party with virtually the sole object of frightening them into a compromise. This species of bluff needed careful organization and much work if the show of resistance was to appear real; and for that reason might be undertaken long in advance of the actual election period. Even when it did not produce the effects wanted, its employment sheds further light on contemporary election tactics. Graham's activities in Cumberland from 1839 onwards, for example, were chiefly directed to this end. In 1837 he was beaten in the eastern division and two liberals returned. That this would probably happen had been indicated by the events of the previous year when on the retirement of Graham's colleague, W. Blamire,[19] a radical was selected to replace him in the person of W. James, backed by the influential Howard family and unopposed by the conservatives. Graham's candidature and defeat at the following election was a debt of honour to the past rather than a premium for the future and it was not long before he was turning his thoughts to more practical measures. For himself, he considered the game was finished in Cumberland. A political turncoat would always be the candidate most hotly opposed by his former friends and most coldly supported by his former enemies. But he had hopes of securing at least one seat for his newly adopted party. There was a probability, he wrote to Bonham in October 1838, that Lord Morpeth[20] would put up for east Cumberland at the next election and that in such a

---

[18] Bacon, *Memoir of Lord Suffield*, 402–5, 480 sqq.; Nevill, *Reminiscences of Lady Dorothy Nevill*, Ch. 2. Lord Walpole is described by his sister as having possessed 'a truly indomitable indolence' and the brunt of the electioneering in 1835 was borne by his cousin, Spencer Walpole.

[19] William Blamire of Thackwood, Carlisle, a landed proprietor and a well-known northern stockbreeder.

[20] Viscount Morpeth, eldest son of the Earl of Carlisle, the head of the northern Howard clan.

case it might be worth while for himself to stand down, as the enmity towards him was so great that the whigs would tolerate a conservative colleague rather than himself. A year later he wrote in more decided terms that the hostility of the Howards towards him was too implacable to leave him any hope of returning to east Cumberland and that any compromise, to be successful, must exclude him. Nevertheless, if Morpeth stood for the whigs, Graham had every hope that the second seat might be gained for the conservatives by private management. The man best able to effect that, he considered, was Lord Lowther[21] who could probably arrange a compromise for any conservative barring Graham himself. In that case he expressly authorized Bonham to sanction negotiations on such a basis.

The way was now clear for battle or at least going through various warlike gestures designed to intimidate the enemy. A meeting of the conservative association for east Cumberland was held in December 1839 and matters put in train for a contest or a compromise of one seat. Sir George Musgrave,[22] the high sheriff and Graham's brother-in-law, was ready with funds but the search for a suitable country gentleman as candidate proved more difficult than had been expected; and eventually Graham appealed to Bonham for his assistance in persuading Colonel Sowerby and the eldest son of Colonel Lowther[23] to come forward. Given these two as candidates, Graham felt that the party could then arrange a compromise which would put Lowther in for east Cumberland and Sowerby in at Carlisle. To do that, it was essential to contest both seats at both places. As it happened the whig ministry clung resolutely to office for another eighteen months after these plans were being hatched. But even at the beginning of 1841 Graham was still hoping for a double compromise in east Cumberland and Carlisle. Lord Morpeth was still the probable whig candidate for the county and another member of the family, Philip Henry Howard, was certain to contest Carlisle where he was one of the sitting members. Provided the conservatives could put

[21] Viscount Lowther, eldest son of the Earl of Lonsdale, at that date M.P. for Westmorland. Succ. as 2nd earl 1844.

[22] Sir George Musgrave of Edenhall, Cumberland, b. 1799, succ. as 10th baronet 1834, m. Graham's sister Charlotte in 1828.

[23] Henry Cecil Lowther, younger brother of Lord Lowther, colonel of the Cumberland militia, M.P. for Westmorland. His eldest son, Henry Lowther, b. 1818, sometime officer in the 1st Life Guards, was M.P. for west Cumberland from 1847 until his accession to the upper House as Earl of Lonsdale in 1872.

up serious candidates in opposition, Graham's hopes were strong that Lord Lowther could effect, possibly through Edward Ellice the whig party manager, a compromise which would give them a share of both constituencies. The Howard clan, he assured Bonham, would be strongly desirous of a quiet return for Morpeth and 'Philip the Papist'.[24] In the circumstances the game was a sound one to play but Graham perhaps was over-sanguine. The Howards were not so easily to be intimidated or defeated; nor were the candidates put forward by the conservative party of the type necessary for Graham's scheme. No Lowther came forward in east Cumberland at the general election of 1841. A conservative candidate by the name of Stephenson contested the constituency with the support of the Lowther and Graham interest and was narrowly defeated, with a margin of only eighty votes, by the Hon. G. Howard[25] and W. James. Nevertheless Graham professed himself satisfied with a hard fought contest which made future victory certain. At Carlisle also the Howard interest stood firm. The conservatives ultimately put up Serjeant Goulburn but he lost by a margin of fifty votes in a small constituency to the Papist Philip and William Marshall of Patterdale Hall, Westmorland, the eldest son of John Marshall, the great Leeds textile manufacturer.[26]

In all these Cumberland negotiations the official conservative party managers were privy to the arrangements and no doubt approved them as offering an opportunity, perhaps the only one, of establishing a foothold in two predominantly liberal constituencies. But there were other compromises where the advantages were less discernible from the strict party viewpoint and over which the party officials were neither consulted nor considered. An example of this kind of compromise, carried out entirely by the county magnates of the constituency and admitting no interference by the central authorities, occurred in Staffordshire at the general election of 1841. In the southern division of the county the position of the rival parties had reached a kind of balance by the middle thirties. In 1832 two whigs, Littleton[27] and Wrottesley,[28] had been

[24] P. H. Howard, eldest son of Henry Howard of Corby Castle, and related both to the Earl of Carlisle and to the Duke of Norfolk, was one of the few English Roman Catholics in the House of Commons at this time.
[25] Charles Wentworth George Howard, b. 1814, younger son of the 6th Earl of Carlisle.
[26] For the correspondence between Graham and Bonham on Cumberland politics, 1839–41, see Add. MS. 40616, fos. 21, 84, 105, 109, 133, 135, 139, 187, 212.
[27] E. J. Littleton, 1st Lord Hatherton, 1791–1863.
[28] Sir John Wrottesley, b. 1771, of Wrottesley Hall, Staffs.

returned without a contest. Littleton, at least, hardly expected a repetition of these favourable circumstances at the next election. 'I expect', he wrote to Wellesley in December 1834, 'a bitter contest in Staffordshire. The Tories will all desert me and the Radicals will support me. I had rather it were the other way. But *Defensoribus istis tempus eget.*'[29] Nevertheless the tories held their hand and he and Wrottesley were once more given a quiet return in 1835. Shortly after that election, however, Littleton was elevated to the peerage and at the resultant by-election in May 1835 the conservative candidate Goodricke[30] defeated his whig rival, Colonel Anson. Goodricke, a wealthy and popular Warwickshire landowner, was the sitting member for Stafford borough and had recently been created a baronet by Peel's short ministry of 1834–5. He deliberately resigned his seat in parliament in order to contest the county and his victory was hailed by his party as a signal reward for an act of uncommon coolness and courage. With the peace of the county thus disturbed, the election of 1837 saw four candidates in the field. Colonel George Anson, the brother of the Earl of Lichfield, stood with Wrottesley in the whig interest; Viscount Ingestre[31] and Dick Dyott[32] for the conservative. The result proved once more the difficulty of making county politics conform to party requirements. Anson the liberal and Ingestre the tory were head of the poll, each leaving a defeated colleague below him.

The explanation of the result lay in the personal circumstances attending the election. Anson and Ingestre were well-known Staffordshire men, both belonging to powerful aristocratic families. Both were first in the field on their sides. Dick Dyott, the son of old General Dyott, though backed by prominent tory landowners, was a young army officer still in his late twenties who had not previously taken part in county politics and was only just being introduced by his father into the inner circles of county society.

---

[29] Add. MS. 37311, fo. 190 (Wellesley Papers).

[30] Sir Francis Lyttleton Holyoake Goodricke, Bart., of Studley Castle, Warwickshire, b. 1797. He came of the old Warwickshire family of Holyoake, but had adopted the surname of Goodricke on succeeding in 1833 to the large estates in Warwickshire, Yorkshire, and Ireland, of his friend Sir H. Goodricke.

[31] Henry John Chetwynd Talbot, styled Viscount Ingestre, the eldest surviving son of the 2nd Earl Talbot, who was Lord-Lieutenant of Staffordshire. He succeeded his father as 3rd earl in 1849.

[32] Richard Dyott of Freeford, Staffs, b. 1808, subsequently J.P., lt.-col. Staffs militia, high sheriff 1857. His father General Dyott (1761–1847) was a magistrate and deputy-lieutenant for the county.

Indeed, one of the motives that prompted General Dyott to incur the expense of the election was the thought that, whatever the result, 'the application of so influential a list of electors would naturally introduce him to the county, and place him in a situation of high respectability in future life'.[33] Wrottesley, the other defeated candidate, as an active county politician and a farming landowner, was a more formidable competitor than Dyott. But he only came forward to offer himself as candidate on the actual day of nomination, much to everybody's astonishment and to the particular indignation of General Dyott who took it as a sign of weakness on Anson's part. If so the manœuvre was successful. Anson finished at the top of the poll though Wrottesley, who had helped him to that eminence by drawing votes from the other two candidates, was at the foot. Nevertheless the voting was extraordinarily close. Only some hundred and eighty votes separated the top and bottom of the poll. In the northern division where W. B. Baring, a conservative, and Edward Buller, a whig, had been elected in 1837, much the same kind of equilibrium had also been reached. Baring, though not a Staffordshire man, had unsuccessfully put up for Stafford borough and was on that score considered a fit man to be put in nomination for the northern division by the local conservatives. With the parties so closely balanced in both divisions of the county, it was obvious that the next general election would produce nothing certain except hard knocks and much expense. It was of this situation that was born the compromise of 1841.

The election of 1837 in the southern division cost the two conservative candidates £7,000. Of this amount some £6,400 had already been subscribed, including a sum of £500 from Dyott himself and presumably as much or more from Ingestre. There remained after the election therefore a debt of six hundred pounds to be paid off by the two candidates. Old General Dyott privately considered that 'the noble lord as the winning candidate should have settled the debt without calling upon the unsuccessful candidate'.[34] But Ingestre was not the kind of man to exercise charity at his own cost even towards a neighbour and a colleague. Indeed it was almost certainly Ingestre's determination not to be led into similar expense that led to the events of 1841. As early as 1839 there were significant straws in the wind. In May of that

[33] *Dyott's Diary*, II, 258.   [34] *Ibid.*, II, 276.

year Dick Dyott was sounded on his parliamentary ambitions for
south Staffordshire by a Mr Benbow, a trustee for Lord Ward, one
of the most influential tory landowners in the southern division of
the county. The Dyotts naturally took this as encouragement and
Dick prepared to abandon a prospective candidature at Lichfield
to enable him to stand once more for the county. But it soon
became apparent that the intention was otherwise and that
local conservatives were being advised from the same source to
put aside thoughts of another contest. 'We have pretty good
reason', wrote General Dyott indignantly, 'to believe that Mr
Benbow is a snake in the grass, and using underhand means to
secure Lord Ingestre's seat.'[35] The Dyotts turned for advice to
Peel, their friend and neighbour. But he told them that he had
not been consulted in the matter and could proffer them no
hopes. Dick Dyott accordingly fixed his thoughts once more
on Lichfield.

Matters rested in this state until the eve of the dissolution of
parliament in 1841. The conservatives in the northern division
had made their dispositions for the expected contest the previous
December. But it was not until the beginning of March that
Ingestre summoned a meeting of the principal party members at
Wolverhampton to consider what was to be done in the south. At
that meeting the first proposal, put forward by a friend of Ingestre,
Edward Monckton of Somerford Hall, but believed to have
originated with the former, was that unless the whigs put up two
candidates, the conservatives should refrain from forcing a contest.
This was rejected almost unanimously. A resolution was then
passed that a second conservative should be adopted. Bowing
temporarily to the force of opinion Ingestre pointed out that if the
election was to be supported by a subscription, it would be only
proper, in view of his services in 1837, to invite Richard Dyott to
stand as Ingestre's colleague. It was decided, therefore, that the
terms of the offer should be that the candidate should be required
to put up £1,000, the remainder of his expenses to be defrayed by
subscription; and that a short list of candidates, headed by Dyott,
should be asked in turn to stand for election with Ingestre. The
Dyotts, however, preferred to take their chance at Lichfield
and were confirmed in this opinion by Peel. In consequence a
Mr Forster of Walsall agreed to come forward as the second

[35] *Dyott's Diary*, i, 296.

conservative candidate for the southern division on the terms prescribed by the Wolverhampton meeting.

The party of compromise having thus failed to achieve their object in the county, the next step was to remove the proceedings to the more pliable environment of the London clubs. Shortly before the dissolution of parliament and some time before the general election started, a conference of Staffordshire gentry from both divisions of the county was held to discuss what could be done with regard to the southern division. The company included Earl Talbot, the Earl of Dartmouth,[36] Viscount Sandon,[37] Viscount Ingestre, William and Charles Bagot, C. B. Adderley,[38] Hay of Hollybush, and Webb, the conservative agent for north Staffordshire. At this meeting Webb stated that some time previously the agent of Lord Lichfield, a Mr Henry Wyatt, had thrown out a hint that if the conservatives left south Staffordshire undisturbed, the whigs would not interfere in the north. It was therefore agreed that one of the conservatives at the meeting, Mr Monckton, who had been the advocate of compromise at Wolverhampton, should endeavour to ascertain whether the whigs were still of that mind. He succeeded in broaching the matter to Lord Hatherton, one of the leading Staffordshire whigs, and as a result was able to confirm the readiness of the other side for a compromise. At the same time he acted upon a suggestion made at the tory meeting, and tried the effect of raising the price of the bargain. The conservative seat in the northern division, he told Hatherton, was unassailable in any case and that if the party were to agree to divide the southern division, they would probably expect their second string, Dyott, to be given a quiet return for Lichfield. This last proposition had a certain audacity. The borough of Lichfield, which was under the influence of the Earl of Lichfield, had split between a tory and whig in 1832 and 1835 but at the last election in 1837 had returned two whigs (Lt.-General Anson and Lord Alfred Paget). In effect, therefore, the conservatives were asking for an additional borough seat as a consideration for not provoking a contest in either of the two county constituencies. Lord Hatherton duly conveyed this

[36] William Legge, 4th Earl of Dartmouth, b. 1784. His first wife, Frances Charlotte, was the daughter of Earl Talbot.

[37] Dudley Ryder, b. 1798, eldest son of the 1st Earl of Harrowby, whom he succeeded in 1847.

[38] Charles Bowyer Adderley, b. 1814, the conservative candidate for the northern division.

suggestion to his party and it was considered at a meeting at Stafford House in London at which the Duke of Sutherland,[39] Lord Anglesey, Lord Wrottesley,[40] the Earl of Lichfield, and Hatherton himself were present. This whig conclave rejected the Lichfield demand with indignation, real or feigned, but consented not to interfere with the *status quo* in south Staffordshire.

The conservative bluff having been called, it now rested with them whether to accept the simple compromise for the two county divisions or to take up the challenge in south Staffordshire. There were not lacking potential conservative candidates even though the expense of a hotly contested election was a material deterrent. Sir Edmund Hartopp, of Sutton Coldfield in neighbouring Warwickshire, and a relative by marriage of C. B. Adderley, only needed encouragement (according to Charles Bagot) to come forward and would have furnished £2,500 towards the cost of election. Simultaneously Captain A'Court,[41] Peel's colleague in the representation of Tamworth, approached both Peel and Bonham on behalf of a Mr Pye[42] who in his zeal for the party professed himself, in default of any other candidate, ready to stand 'provided the Gentlemen of the County (as he has a large family) would *guarantee him beyond a certain sum*. He did not say what that certain sum was, but I should *suppose somewhere about £800. It might be £500 or it might be £1,000.*'[43] Surely, wrote A'Court, some of the wealthy gentlemen of the county, Lord Ward,[44] Colonel Greville Howard and others, could furnish such a guarantee?

Even had this offer arrived in time, however, it is extremely unlikely that the Staffordshire gentry, wealthy as some of them were, would have committed themselves to such an unlimited expense on behalf of the domesticated Mr Pye. Even Hartopp received little encouragement to draw on his much more substantial financial resources. But by the time that A'Court was writing

[39] George Granville Leveson-Gower, 3rd Marquess of Stafford.

[40] Son of Sir John Wrottesley, the unsuccessful whig candidate for south Staffs in 1837. He succeeded his father as 2nd Baron Wrottesley in March 1841.

[41] Edward Henry A'Court, Capt. R.N., b. 1783, brother of Lord Heytesbury.

[42] Henry John Pye, of Clifton Hall, Staffs, b. 1802, high sheriff of Staffs 1840.

[43] Add. MS. 40429, fos. 357–8. A'Court to Bonham, 22 June 1841 (copy sent to Peel). Pye was a Staffordshire magistrate and a friend of General Dyott. According to the latter, Pye was actually proposed and accepted as candidate for the southern division on condition he was indemnified beyond a certain sum (*Dyott's Diary*, II, 345).

[44] William Ward of Himley Hall, Staffs, b. 1817, succeeded his father as 11th baron in 1835.

his letter to Bonham, it was already too late. The wealthy proprietors of Staffordshire had displayed a marked reluctance to
engage on a contest and counsels of prudence had finally prevailed.
A second meeting was held at the Carlton by the men of south
Staffordshire, as a result of which a general assent was given to the
original whig proposals to share the two county constituencies
without a contest. In order, moreover, to provide a guarantee of
good will, and perhaps to deter any independent conservative from
breaking the county compact, it was also agreed that should any
candidate, professing to know nothing of the arrangement, put
up for the county, the party on whose side in politics he should be
deemed generally to act, should refrain from giving him support,
while the opposing party should be released from their undertaking
not to run a second candidate. Care was taken nevertheless to
ensure that all the influential conservatives in the county were
made cognizant of the bargain. Lord Ward, who was not at the
meeting, was told of what had been transacted by his agent,
Mr Gifford, and it was confidently expected that Lord Bradford[45]
would also consent to the arrangement. The articles of the
compact, duly set out in writing, were formally exchanged
between Monckton, the conservative negotiator, and Walter
Wrottesley,[46] on behalf of the whigs. Nothing could be more
formal, and for practical purposes, more binding.

There were of course some voices raised in criticism and
opposition. General Dyott, on being informed by a letter from
Monckton of what had passed in London, issued a resounding
protest at any meeting of individuals presuming to settle the representation of the county without ever consulting the district
conservative association which had been working vigorously since
1837 for just such a contest as was now declined.[47] A'Court wrote
belatedly to tell Peel that the sum he had mentioned as being
presumably what Mr Pye would be prepared to pay was in fact
much less than the actual figure to which he was ready to go. But
all this was now immaterial. A'Court added, however, that he
could not understand the reasons for the compromise. The seat
for north Staffordshire was safe and Lords Lichfield and Anglesey

[45] 2nd Earl of Bradford, b. 1789, succeeded to the title in 1825. His seat was
Weston Park, Shifnal, Staffs.
[46] Younger brother of Lord Wrottesley, b. 1810, sometime Fellow of All Souls
College, Oxford.
[47] *Dyott's Diary*, II, 343.

were moving heaven and earth to defeat Dick Dyott at Lichfield.[48] Charles Bagot, who had been at both the Staffordshire conservative meetings, also deplored the outcome privately to Peel. The effort should have been made, he told his leader; financial difficulties did not form a very good excuse and Ingestre who, as sitting member, had most to lose from a contest, would have been prepared to fight had the meeting thought the contest less hazardous. Ingestre himself expressed dissatisfaction at the compromise. Nevertheless he could scarcely withdraw from a bargain once it was made and indeed shortly after the decision was taken he went down to Wolverhampton to explain to a meeting of his supporters the exact nature of the arrangement. It was in the highest degree unlikely that another conservative would come forward to an inevitable and costly struggle since all the parties to the compact on the tory side made it clear that they would be unable to give any assistance, financial or otherwise, to a second candidate. Yet there is a certain disingenuous air about the excuses of Ingestre and Bagot, and the attempt to pass on responsibility to the meeting of county magnates at which both were leading participants could not have been very convincing. General Dyott had personal reasons for distrusting Ingestre but he was probably right in his conclusion that 'there was no difficulty in discovering the cause of this *daring* attempt at compromise, which was done at the instigation of Lord Ingestre's friends, headed by (I believe) Monckton to prevent a contest, which must occasion a considerable material which his lordship lacked, *Money*'.[49] It was Ingestre in fact who finally made a contest impossible. He told Peel, and no doubt others, that should he see a decided disposition in the constituency to put forward two conservative candidates, he would probably feel himself obliged to retire altogether.

In the face of this solidarity on the part of the Staffordshire magnates it was clear that nothing could be done either in the way of an individual venture or by pressure from party headquarters. In the event Russell and Adderley were returned for the northern division, Anson and Ingestre for the southern. No contest marred the peaceful partition of the county although Lord Leveson

---

[48] Their efforts were successful. Sir George Anson and Lord Alfred Paget were again returned although Dyott ran the latter to a bare margin of eight votes. A petition subsequently brought against Paget's return was abandoned after a few days' proceedings in committee.

[49] *Dyott's Diary*, ii, 343.

who went down to Lichfield to assist in the electioneering reported to his father that none of them knew whether there would be a contest for south Staffordshire until they were actually on the hustings. A 'Mr Smith of London' had apparently put out an address but failed to materialize on the platform. All passed off quietly, therefore, except for an attack on Leveson himself by Ingestre's seconder for the double crime of being both a whig and a stranger to the county.[50] What is striking about the whole story, however, is the almost complete political autonomy of the county gentry. Peel himself, who if not as party leader then at least as a Staffordshire landowner might have been considered a fit person to consult, does not appear to have been informed of what was happening until he made personal inquiries. As for the views of the party managers, it was obvious that they were ignored throughout, even though the meeting that decided the fate of the constituency was held under the same roof at the Carlton Club. Writing shortly afterwards to Peel about the Staffordshire meetings, Bonham told him that 'no one connected with the general management of the Elections was present or consulted'.[51]

In a class by themselves, though illustrating under special conditions the same tendency for candidates to avoid trouble and expense by private negotiation, were the 'corrupt compromises' which became notorious in consequence of a parliamentary inquiry in 1842. The characteristics of these agreements were that they followed and did not precede election contests, and were designed to evade parliamentary scrutiny.

In 1841 two acts of parliament made much more precarious the position of a candidate defending his return against charges of bribery and corruption. The first, introduced by Sir Robert Peel (4 & 5 Vic., c. 58), effected improvements in the existing methods of choosing the committees that considered controverted election cases[52] and had some influence in producing more impartial and therefore more stringent tribunals. The second, introduced by Lord John Russell (4 & 5 Vic., c. 57), enabled election committees to inquire into general evidence of bribery before specific proof of agency.[53] Of these two acts it is clear that the second was the

[50] Fitzmaurice, *Life of Lord Granville*, I, 34–6.
[51] Add. MS. 40435, fo. 2. For the general history of this episode, see Add. MS. 40429, fos. 357, 359, 372, 441; and *Dyott's Diary*, II, 329–45.
[52] Peel's act simply effected certain improvements on his earlier act of 1839 (2 & 3 Vic., c. 38).
[53] See above, Ch. 5, p. 135.

more instrumental in driving contending parties into a compromise. Being passed shortly before the 1841 election, however, the
significance of the act was not generally realized until election
cases arising out of the general election came up for consideration.
A succession of void election decisions (notably Sudbury, Ipswich,
and Southampton) showed that a keener wind was now blowing at
Westminster and even before the final results of these cases were
officially announced, the panic started. At the beginning of May
1842 rumours were rife of hasty arrangements being patched up
to stave off the inexorable inquisitions of parliamentary committees. A number of withdrawn petitions and resignations from
the House of Commons proved that the rumours had some basis
of fact. A petition alleging bribery had been brought against the
return of the two members for Reading. The committee appointed
to try the case held two sittings on 29 and 30 April before adjourn-
ing over the week-end. On Monday, 2 May, the petition was
abandoned. On 4 May Sir George Larpent, recently returned for
Nottingham, accepted the Chiltern Hundreds and a new writ
for the borough was due to be moved the next day. On 5 May,
however, Roebuck gave notice that he intended to put the
following questions to the successful candidates for the boroughs
of Reading, Penryn and Falmouth, Nottingham, Lewes, and
Harwich:

> Whether either of them is cognizant of, or party to, any arrange-
> ment by which it has been agreed that one or other of these honour-
> able members is to accept the Chiltern Hundreds, in order to vacate
> his seat, notwithstanding they have been declared duly elected by the
> Select Committee appointed to try the merits of the petitions presen-
> ted to this House against their return.

In the debate which ensued (6 and 9 May), Roebuck made out a
clear *prima facie* case for the charges which he was levelling at the
members for those named constituencies. He was supported by
Peel, the prime minister, and on 9 May 1842 the House of
Commons set up a select committee to inquire into charges of
corrupt compromises made in order to avoid investigation into
allegations of bribery at Reading, Harwich, Nottingham, Lewes,
and Penryn and Falmouth. On 1 June Bridport was added to the
list. The report of the committee was ordered by the House to be
printed in July 1842. It completely vindicated the unusual and

outspoken course followed by Roebuck in a matter which had become one of common notoriety.

At Harwich two conservative members, Attwood and Beresford, had been returned by a narrow majority over their whig opponents, Bagshaw and Sir D. le Marchant. Three petitions had been presented against the return on grounds of bribery, treating, and corruption. A compromise was therefore entered into by the agents of Attwood and Beresford on the one side, and Le Marchant's agent on the other. The terms of the agreement were: that Beresford was to retire within one month of the date of the agreement; that at the ensuing by-election Le Marchant was to be allowed to stand without opposition; and that Attwood was to deposit £2,500 as a guarantee that the engagement entered upon by himself and Beresford would be kept. In consequence the petition against the sitting members was withdrawn and the proceedings arrested. At Nottingham Hobhouse and Larpent had been returned against John Walter and Charlton. Two petitions were presented against the return by the party attached to Walter, while a third petition was got up in the interests of the sitting members, designed to give them an opportunity of making a counter-case against the petitioners. The first two petitions merely prayed that the election should be declared void and did not ask for Walter to be declared duly elected.[54] On 4 May, after the appointment of a committee to inquire into the election but before it had actually commenced proceedings, a compromise was reached between the agents of the sitting members and Walter's party. The terms of the agreement were: that all petitions arising out of the election should be abandoned; that one seat at Nottingham should be vacated within four days; that £1,000 should be paid to the petitioning party to reimburse them for their expenses; that the leading members of the whig party at Nottingham should engage not to oppose Walter at the ensuing by-election; and that lastly a promissory note for £4,000 should be deposited with a named firm of bankers, under the direction of two referees, on behalf of Hobhouse or Larpent, to be forfeited if the conditions of the contract were not fulfilled.[55] At Lewes, Harford and

[54] For the point of these tactics see above, Ch. 5, p. 136.
[55] Larpent duly resigned; Walter put up again at the by-election and was returned, though only by a close margin in a hotly contested election, as the chartists and lower middle-class radicals combined to put forward a Complete Suffrage Union candidate against him. On taking his seat Walter in turn was petitioned against and unseated

Elphinstone were the successful candidates and a petition alleging bribery and corruption was presented against their return by their defeated opponents, Fitzroy and Lord Cantelupe. A committee was appointed to try the case but its proceedings were arrested by a compromise entered into by the two parties. The only novelty in the Lewes arrangement was that Fitzroy and Elphinstone, by a pre-arranged scrutiny before the election committee, were to be placed at the head of the poll, and Harford in consequence to be unseated.[56] A safeguard was inserted in the agreement, however, that should it not be possible to place Fitzroy in a majority by means of a scrutiny, one of the sitting members was to resign in the orthodox manner.

Of the three remaining cases, two conformed to this general pattern. The case of Reading will be considered elsewhere.[57] At Penryn and Falmouth a petition was brought by the supporters of one of the defeated candidates praying for a void election to be declared in the case of one only of the sitting members; and the committee appointed to try the case had almost completed its hearing of the petitioners' evidence when the proceedings were stayed by the compromise. The agreement in this instance was merely verbal and apparently without the knowledge of Captain Plumridge, the candidate against whom the petition had been directed. But it was not explained how his agent, who had made the compromise, proposed to persuade Plumridge, according to the terms of the agreement, to apply for the Chiltern Hundreds.

At Bridport the simple inquiry into the existence of a corrupt compromise which the committee had in mind was so entangled with various cross-issues of a private and personal nature that the committee of inquiry refrained from presenting the evidence and

by the parliamentary committee that considered the case. Rather unreasonably, Walter then claimed the surety of £4,000 (under the 4 May agreement) on the grounds that he had not secured the seat, and was unwise enough to sue Hobhouse for the money in a court of law (*History of 'The Times'*, II, 6, and Appendix II, 540–1).

[56] By the Reform Act of 1832 it was open to the petitioners to impeach the correctness of the electoral register before a parliamentary committee and such committees had the power to alter the poll by adding or striking out individual voters. As only two votes separated Elphinstone from Fitzroy at the original poll, it would be a simple matter to invalidate three of the former's votes to put the latter in second place. In fact, on the hearing of the petition for the Lewes election, the attention of the committee had merely been drawn to a scrutiny of the votes and after several days investigation, Harford's majority was reduced to a minority and he withdrew from the inquiry. The poll at the election had been Harford 411, Elphinstone 409, Fitzroy 407, Cantelupe 388.

[57] See below, Ch. 11, p. 296.

confined themselves to a report on the public issues involved. In this case there were three candidates involved. At the general election Warburton and Mitchell were declared duly returned, Cochrane being the defeated candidate. Soon after the election Warburton heard that a petition was to be presented against his return as well as that of Mitchell. He therefore made an offer to Cochrane which was finally reduced to writing on 27 August 1841. By the terms of this document Warburton wrote a conditional application for the Chiltern Hundreds which was then deposited with a third party on condition that it was not to be used within the period of fourteen days allowed for the presentation of petitions after the first meeting of parliament and was to be returned to Warburton in the event of Mitchell accepting the Chiltern Hundreds within that period. In accordance with this agreement Warburton finally vacated his seat and Cochrane was elected without opposition. The story then becomes complicated. After Warburton had undertaken to resign, a petition was brought by Cochrane's party against Mitchell. The latter then cross-petitioned against Cochrane alleging bribery and corruption at both the general election in June and the by-election in September. Legal actions for penalties in respect of bribery were also brought by both sides against each other. Meanwhile Cochrane had become involved in a separate bargain at Bridport. Before the by-election he came to an agreement with certain electors there to withdraw all actions for bribery provided no opposition was raised to his election. Furthermore he promised to prosecute the petition against Mitchell's return on documentary evidence only, since oral evidence might implicate the parties in the borough with whom he was negotiating. This was less of a concession than it appeared, however, since Cochrane possessed documentary evidence of bribery on the part of Mitchell's friends which had been given to him by Mitchell's own agent at Bridport who had since quarrelled with his former employer. Finally in March 1842 an agreement was reached between Cochrane and Mitchell before the time appointed for hearing the petition against the latter's return. The substance of this last compromise was that Mitchell agreed to withdraw both his petition against Cochrane's return and all legal actions commenced by him against Cochrane's supporters. Cochrane on the other hand agreed to withdraw his petition against Mitchell. There were thus, in this tangled and unelevating situation, no less than three separate compromises: between Cochrane and Warburton; between Cochrane and certain Bridport electors; and between Cochrane and Mitchell.

What was of special interest in these cases were the motives inducing the parties concerned to come to a compromise. At Harwich both the sitting members and their agents concurred in the belief that the seat could not be held in view of the clear evidence of bribery by persons who could be proved to be agents. Since Beresford had not contributed to the expenses of the winning side, he was selected for sacrifice; and Le Marchant, who had spent three times as much as his colleague, was for equally sound reasons chosen as beneficiary. At Nottingham the motives for compromise were the certainty of enormous expense if the case was defended before committee and the probability that both the sitting members would be unseated for bribery and treating on the part of their agents. In the Lewes case the compromise was apparently precipitated by the agent of the sitting members. He told them flatly that it was lunacy to continue to defend the petition and that they only had about fifteen hours in which to decide whether to strike a bargain or not. In the Penryn and Falmouth case the agent responsible for the defence stated that he had, indeed, exhausted all the funds available to him but that even if he had been able to prolong the battle he would have declined to do so. In his considered opinion such a circumstantial case had been built up that the committee would undoubtedly accept as proved the existence of extensive and systematic bribery in the borough. In the Bridport case Warburton stated that his initial reason for opening negotiations with Cochrane was to save his supporters and friends from the exposures with which they were threatened; and that subsequently he was anxious for an inquiry to clear his own name from the imputation of illegal practices but was too deeply committed by his bargain with Cochrane to retire from it with honour. Mitchell, reasonably enough in view of his turncoat agent's disclosures, was simply anxious to avoid being unseated on a charge of bribery. Cochrane, who appears to have stirred singularly deep and muddy waters in his efforts to represent the borough of Bridport, was apprehensive of the consequences of various investigations to both himself and his friends. This he might well be since at the time of his third and final compromise several actions were due to be tried at the Somerset Assizes against certain of his supporters.[58]

The Roebuck committee of 1842 necessarily confined its attentions to the boroughs named in its terms of reference. It is clear, however, that these only represented some of the corrupt compromises known, or at any rate believed, to have been entered into after the general election of 1841. Indeed exception was taken in the House of Commons to the original motion for a committee of inquiry on the grounds that it was unfair to single those boroughs out for special indictment. Palmerston, for instance, professed himself 'opposed to any partial investigation of the cases of half a dozen individuals to be selected from the herd in order to be held up to undeserved obloquy. . . . These individuals are only a few out of many, and they cannot without gross injustice be singled out.'[59] There was general agreement in the House of Commons that compromises of this description affected many other constituencies besides those named by Roebuck. Wakley argued for a more extended inquiry on the grounds that 'it was perfectly well known that there were upwards of fifty more members as deeply committed'.[60] Nor was the practice merely born of the special legislation of 1841 though that undoubtedly had been an aggravating feature. 'It would be the greatest hypocrisy', said Palmerston, 'to say that they have now for the first time been made and that the practice has not been generally and notoriously prevalent.'[61] Lord John Russell concurred in this observation and instanced the case of Norwich in the 1837 parliament; but he added that 'in the present Parliament it is notorious that a much greater number of those cases have been compromised'.[62] Moreover the system of compromise embraced not only agreements between parties with respect to a particular borough but also, through the medium of the party managers, a method of 'swopping' (in the race-course slang of the day) or exchanging one constituency for another. That is to say, one party would withdraw its petition against a seat held by an opponent in consideration for the withdrawal by its opponents of a petition against one

[58] For the details of all these corrupt compromise proceedings, see *Report from the Committee on Election Proceedings*, P.P. 1842, v, 76–88, and minutes of evidence, 97 sqq.; *H. of C. Journals*, 1842, xcvii, esp. 263, 268, 330, 498; *Hansard*, LXIII, May–June 1842, 209–34, 271–309. The *Westminster Review*, xxxix, 113 sqq., published an interesting and informative article on the subject in 1843 which contains a reprint of the committee's report.

[59] *Hansard*, LXIII, 284. [60] *Ibid.*, LXIII, 234. [61] *Ibid.*, LXIII, 282. [62] *Ibid.*, LXIII, 289.

of its own seats. In the nature of things evidence of this kind of political barter is not easy to obtain but there can be no doubt that such exchanges took place. Disraeli possibly owed his seat in the 1841 parliament to a 'swop' of this kind. A petition had been brought against his return for Shrewsbury; at the same time there was a tory petition pending against the return for Gloucester. By mutual arrangement both petitions were dropped. 'This great *coup*, almost, in the present state of affairs, as great as my return', wrote Disraeli to his sister, 'was effected in the most accidental and happy manner by my agent, Bailey of Gloucester, without any interference and barely knowledge of the great parties. On his own responsibility he paired off Shrewsbury against Gloucester.'[63]

As an instance of a compromise not covered by the inquiry of 1842 may be given the case of St Ives. The constituency was a small one with some six hundred voters, and the preponderant interest was held by James Halse, the proprietor of mining works adjoining the town, and in politics a tory. He was first returned for the borough in 1826 and though opposed by two other candidates in 1832 was elected at the first three general elections after the Reform Act. Halse died in 1838 and a struggle then took place between his earlier rivals, Praed[64] and Stephens. The former, who had also contested the constituency in 1837, was successful in the by-election consequent upon the death of Halse, and was again returned in 1841. On the latter occasion he was opposed by Mr Edwin Ley of Penzance, the nephew and heir of Mr Halse. A hard contest resulted in a narrow win for Praed by only four votes. In September 1841 Ley petitioned against his opponent's return on grounds of bribery, corruption, and invalid votes and prayed for Praed's return to be declared void and for himself to be declared duly elected in his place. Initially the matter was referred to the general committee of elections. Then, in the following April, before the case had come before a select committee, the petition was withdrawn. What had induced Ley to abandon his case? The answer was supplied several years later

---

[63] Monypenny, *Disraeli*, II, 134.

[64] William Tyringham Praed, to be distinguished from the better known Winthrop Mackworth Praed who d. 1839. The two men were cousins and at his kinsman's invitation W. M. Praed had contested the borough in 1832. The family estate at Trevethow gave W. T. Praed some influence in the constituency but not enough to prevail against Halse, many of whose tin-miners were resident in the borough, and who was reckoned to control by direct means more than half the electorate.

by Bonham who perhaps had been cognizant of it at the time. Praed induced his rival to withdraw his petition on the understanding that at the expiration of the parliament elected in 1841 Praed should retire from the representation of St Ives and transfer his interest in the borough to Ley. The presumption was therefore that Ley would be returned at the next general election without opposition.

The uncertainties of long-term contracts were now to be vividly illustrated. Praed, having successfully negotiated the undisturbed possession of his seat during the lifetime of the 1841 parliament, evaded all further responsibilities in the most absolute manner possible by dying in 1846. The situation in the borough was now extremely fluid and as usually happened in those circumstances various claimants appeared on the scene. Lord Mornington,[65] who had been member for St Ives before the Reform Act and indeed had been credited in 1830 with the patronage of both the seats which the borough then possessed, appeared to be imbued with a desire to revive his vanished influence and even offered to put his interest in the borough at the disposal of his illustrious relative, the Duke of Wellington. But an even older aristocratic connexion began to reassert itself. The borough of St Ives had once been in the hands of the Powlett family, of which Lord Bolton was the head, and though their interest had apparently been alienated long before 1832, sufficient was left of the old relationship for the family interest to be revived. Lord William Powlett,[66] the second cousin of Lord Bolton, was elected to the vacancy caused by Praed's death and was again returned by a large majority in a contest at the general election of 1847. 'As to St. Ives', wrote Bonham to Gladstone between the two elections, 'I ascertained that Ld. Mornington on the score of a former *idle* expenditure had offered the seat to his Uncle without the possibility of *obtaining a single Vote* against the *united* determination to

[65] William Pole Tylney-Long Wellesley, b. 1788, nephew of the Duke of Wellington and of the Marquess Wellesley, and son of the 3rd Earl of Mornington whom he succeeded in 1845.

[66] William John Frederick Powlett (formerly Vane), styled Lord William Powlett. He was the second son of the 1st Duke of Cleveland who married Katharine, daughter of the 6th Duke of Bolton. On the death of the latter the title lapsed, but the Bolton estates passed by special entail to Jean-Mary Powlett, the illegitimate daughter of the 5th duke. She married in 1778 Thomas Orde, a secretary to the Treasury in 1782, who took the additional surname of Powlett and in 1797 was created Baron Bolton. He was succeeded in 1807 by his eldest son, William Orde-Powlett, 2nd baron, who d. 1850.

support the old *Bolton interest* in the person of Ld. Wm. Powlett.'
It may be concluded that on balance Praed had derived the
greater advantage from his compact with Ley in 1841.[67] But the
episode at least illustrates yet another mode in which a compromise could operate without attracting the inquisitive eye of
radical purists.

It would in any case be unwise to assume that the inquiry of
1842 put an end to the practice. A quarter of a century later, in
the general election of 1868 (the first after the second Reform Act),
Leveson-Gower fought a contest at Bodmin against his former
colleague there, Mr Wyld. After his defeat Wyld brought a
petition against the return but on the eve of the trial offered to
withdraw the petition on payment of a sum of £2,000. Leveson-
Gower refused and won his case. By virtue of the recent statute
(31 & 32 Vic., c. 125) the petition was tried in the Court of
Common Pleas. But if justice was thereby more secure, the
expense was almost as great as in the days of Peel. In spite of being
awarded costs, Leveson-Gower estimated that the case cost him
£1,000.[68]

A few concluding observations may be made. Compromise
elections were essentially agreements to share political spoils on
the rough principle of equality of reward for equality of sacrifice.
The dominating, though not the only, consideration was desire to
avoid expense or at least to secure value for what had already been
spent. Even corrupt compromises, in the technical sense of a
mutual agreement to withdraw cases from the scrutiny of election
committees, were merely ordinary compromises arranged at a
higher level and at a later stage. The motives, however, were the
same. More often, of course, for obvious reasons, the compromise
was effected at the earlier stage and so avoided a contest altogether.
The large proportion, by modern standards, of uncontested
returns was thus an index to the expensiveness of contemporary
electioneering rather than a mark of apathy among electors
or elected. In some cases it was thought useless to throw away
good money in challenging an impregnable seat; in others the
two sides came together in an agreement to divide the seats
and refrain from a contest of which the only sure outcome was

---

[67] For the whole affair see Add. MS. 44110, fos. 175, 177, 183; *H. of C Journals*,
1841, xcvi, 557; 1842, xcvii, 189; Hudson, *Poet in Parliament*, 190–4.
[68] Leveson-Gower, *Bygone Years*, 251.

expense. From a logical point of view this expedient might seem to have something of the absurd. A constituency that returned one tory and one whig to vote against each other in the House of Commons could be regarded as stultifying itself in the national assembly. But from the party, and indeed from the national, point of view this was unimportant. A whig from the same borough as a tory was as valuable as one from a single-member constituency a hundred miles away. What mattered was the aggregate of party numbers, not the indivisible expression of the will of one constituency. Indeed, if facts were to be opposed to logic, it might well be inquired how many constituencies were there in which the opinion of the electors was so unanimous that it was an absurdity for them to be represented by two members of different views. It could even be argued, as it was during the reform bill debates, that split elections were substantially just in that they secured representation for both parties in a constituency instead of registering a deceptive victory for the slightly stronger side. Compromise elections therefore provided a kind of proportional representation. If the object of the electoral system was to furnish an accurate reflection of the divisions of sentiment in the country, compromise elections were more likely to effect that end than brute contests in which all the seats went to the party with a bare numerical advantage. To criticize the compromising tendencies endemic in early Victorian politics on the ground that they prevented a clear expression of the views of the electorate would be manifestly wrong.

It is true that perhaps the most significant aspect of these uncontested and, as Russell styled them, compromised elections, was the ease with which the governing classes in general, and especially those in the counties, could dispense with any formal consideration of the views of the electorate and virtually themselves decide on the proper representation of the constituency. Yet a close examination of county elections, for example, whether contested or uncontested, suggests that too many other factors were operating to make a clear party victory certain even if the decision was carried to the polls. The country gentlemen were certainly the political and social leaders in the rural constituencies but it would be misleading to suppose that they either wished or could afford to disregard the feelings of their humbler constituents. Compromises were offered and accepted on the basis of an existing division of power. They reflected, therefore, influences at work among the electors as well as among the leaders.

If criticism of the compromise elections was to be made, it would have come more appropriately from the side of the ministers and the party leaders. From the point of view of the executive, the objectionable feature was that in every compromise the stronger party inevitably conceded something to the weaker. What was bad in compromise was not that it falsified electoral sentiment but that it did not do so enough; that is to say, that it frustrated the innate tendency of an electoral system based on simple majority decision to exaggerate movements of opinion and thus produce a marked, because exaggerated, inequality of parties. What governments and party whips wanted was not an accurate transcription in terms of M.P.s of the national outlook, but powerful parties and strong majorities. The party system was best suited by an electoral structure which turned shifts of opinion into parliamentary landslides. But that could only happen if every possible seat was contested and no quarter given.

'I do hope', wrote Graham at the height of the 1841 election, 'that Middlesex, West Surrey, North Northumberland and E. Somerset will be fought to the last extremity; individual feelings and interests must be disregarded in an emergency of such danger and importance.'[69] These were the authentic accents of party; but they were not always echoed in the counties and small boroughs, nor always by party leaders themselves in their own constituencies. Yet in proportion as local interests and individual feelings were consulted, the prospect of decisive victory or defeat tended to recede. Compromise elections, and the spirit of compromise in the electors, like all systems of proportional representation, possessed an equalizing tendency. In so far as they stabilized and balanced the composition of the House of Commons, they worked against the efficiency of party as the basis of government and, therefore, after 1832, against the efficiency of government itself. But these considerations were scarcely such as could be used with effect at this time. If compromise favoured local and personal interests rather than party discipline or strong government, it was after all an age which on the whole preferred the former to the latter. Indeed it was fortunate for the cause of parliamentary government that there were other factors in politics and that the

[69] Add. MS. 40616, fo. 209.

aristocratic order itself was divided on the means of government. An aristocracy that controlled parliament and was homogeneous politically as well as socially would have provided the country with a problem of some gravity. As it was, the rough sporting contests between the two historic parties, so derided and detested by the radicals, were not without their profounder advantages. If elections brought with them not only wooing with promises and bribery with gold but also intimidation with menaces and repression by violence, they did at least keep the parliamentary system alive. Even a compromise at least presupposed the existence of two different sides.

Chapter Eleven

POLITICS IN THE PROVINCES: BERKSHIRE

In this study of political life in the age of Peel an account of the politics in one particular county may not be without value. An analysis of certain selected features drawn from a wide field of human action has certain self-evident dangers. A more comprehensive and consecutive narrative of events in a smaller area may to some extent serve as a corrective to any arbitrariness and distortion in the larger picture. There is another justification. In one sense all politics are provincial politics. What Peel, Melbourne, or Russell could do in the Houses of Parliament depended primarily on what happened in the constituencies. It is true that provincial politics were not immune from central influence; it is equally true that national politics were given their peculiar colour and flavour largely by provincial representatives and provincial interests and opinions.

At the time of the Reform Act Berkshire was an ordinary prosperous English county with little to distinguish it from its neighbours. The one unusual feature was the royal seat at Windsor. But for the most part it was neither industrialized nor rurally remote; it had no urban agglomerations to form strongholds of radicalism; no small boroughs that were centres of corruption; no titled magnate to dominate the countryside. Indeed it was a peculiarity of the social and economic structure of the county, remarked by many observers, that it lacked any great aristocratic leaders. Mavor, in his *General View of Agriculture in Berkshire*, published in 1809, had commented on the rarity of large landowners, the respectable body of yeomanry, the numerous and increasing freeholders, and the comparative absence of any influence of power and property.[1] Twenty years later it was the same story—'in Berkshire a great many small proprietors or yeomen who cultivate their own farms consisting of 40, 50 or 80 acres'.[2] Some years later Sanford and Townsend in their *Great Governing Families of England* considered only three family seats in

[1] Pages 49–52.   [2] Add. MS. 28660, fo. 59 (Richards MSS.).

the county worthy of inclusion in their map of great landowners, namely, the Earl of Abingdon at Wytham Abbey, the Earl of Radnor at Coleshill Park, and Earl Craven at Ashdown Park. Old Fuller in the seventeenth century had observed that the lands in Berkshire were very skittish and apt to cast their riders; and it remained true in the early nineteenth century that there were few outstanding families of any very ancient lineage. The Fettiplaces, Purefoys, Hobys, Vachells, Riches, and Blagraves were names that had ceased to count in Berkshire politics. Of the few old families that still maintained a place in the constantly shifting county society, the only two of note and influence were the Cravens of Ashdown in the south-west corner of the county, who came into Berkshire in the early seventeenth century and were perhaps the largest landowners in the county; and the Eystons, the oldest of all the Berkshire landed gentry, who had owned the manor of East Hendred since the fifteenth century. Among the others the Puseys of Pusey were, as often happened, a new family that had taken on the old name when they inherited the estates towards the end of the eighteenth century; and the Berties (Earl of Abingdon) had inherited by marriage the estates of the Norreys family in north Berkshire. The county presented, therefore, a singularly pure sample of contemporary rural society with its opinions and representation undistorted by propertied or traditional influence.

Agriculture was of course the basis of the county and agriculture had been complaining ever since Waterloo. Berkshire had felt the financial crisis of 1813 and the weight of post-war poor relief. Like most other counties that had drifted into Speenhamland methods (though by 1830 the Speenhamland system was not more noticeable in the county of its origin than elsewhere), it had economized in wages and labour and the result had been the memorable winter of 1830–1 when the Berkshire labourers, imitating their fellows in Kent, Sussex, and Hampshire, had revolted against the conditions imposed on them. For the farmer, the squire, and the justice of the peace, the pleasant pastoral landscape of the Thames and Kennet valleys, the forest-land of the eastern division of the county, and the open sheep-walks of the Berkshire Downs, were riddled with economic depression, unemployment, and crime. Yet there were other things in the county besides agriculture and Captain Swing. Several towns, some small and some of moderate size, some with a strong tradition of dissent and most with special economic interests, broke the rural uniformity of the countryside. If the older textile manufactory had decayed by the beginning of the nineteenth century, other industries were filling the gap. Reading, the county capital, was something more than a mere market town. It was prosperous, middle class, and expanding. The Thames and the great Bath Road linked it to the rich market of the metropolis; it boasted native industries in addition to its vital position as *entrepôt* for the trade between London and the adjoining counties; and besides opulence and activity, it had some pretence to culture and social life. Windsor, with the castle, the chapel royal, and Eton College, was a centre for retired gentry and aspiring tradesmen. Newbury, at the other end of the county, was now long past the heyday of its fame as a clothing town but it still retained importance as a market. It was on the high road from London to Bath and Bristol and in the thirties some three dozen coaches passed daily through its streets. Through it also ran the Kennet and Avon canal which connected the Severn to the Thames. The chief local industries were malting and milling but it was in addition a big corn and provision market, and a distributing centre for coal, manufactured articles, groceries, and building material from London and Bristol.[3] Its population of 7,000 (including Speen) was larger than that of any other town in Berkshire except Reading and Windsor. The citizens of Newbury were not unmindful of their urban importance and at the time of the reform bill they petitioned parliament for a restoration of the representation of the borough in the House of Commons which it had enjoyed in medieval times.[4] Elsewhere the towns were smaller and more embedded in the life of the countryside. Some had industries of a kind—ironworks or textiles—while two, Abingdon and Wallingford, were parliamentary boroughs.

Berkshire was thus a county characteristic of that part of England as yet untouched by the direct results of the industrial revolution. The plough and the threshing machine were still the masters and all the other industries in the area were to a greater or less extent ancillary to them. It was for this reason that it was selected together with other agricultural counties for additional

---

[3] P.P. 1835, XXIII (*Corporations of England and Wales, 1st Report*), Appendix, Pt. I, 228–9.

[4] *Hansard*, III, 1745, 21 April 1831. The petition was presented by the Earl of Carnarvon, whose seat at Highclere was only five miles south of Newbury, across the Hampshire border.

representation in the shape of a third county member by the Reform Act. Not surprisingly therefore Berkshire, county and boroughs, was almost solidly protectionist in 1846. The only exception was formed by the members for Windsor; but it is an exception that merely emphasizes the cohesion of the rest of the county. Windsor politics will be described in some detail at a later stage and the borough will not in consequence be considered further in this chapter. But its omission will in no way impair the unity of a section devoted to Berkshire politics since the royal borough for political purposes was outside the county orbit. Like the court itself, it was a foreign body, in but not of the county; and its primary issue, that of town against castle, was one from which the Berkshire gentry for obvious reasons held aloof. The county family with most interest in Windsor were the Vansittarts of Shottesbrooke. In the election of 1806 Arthur Vansittart had been defeated for the second place by Richard Ramsbottom. But no attempt was made by that family to recover their influence in the borough in this period and the inhabitants of the borough were left to accept or reject the royal influence as best they might without help or hindrance from the county. So strong indeed was this sense of the political isolation of the borough that the *Windsor Express* once described it as being in 'a state of political quarantine'.[5] Its exclusion from this chapter therefore creates no anomaly.

Before 1832 the county had been represented in the House of Commons by nine members. Two stood for the county constituency; two each for Reading, Windsor, and Wallingford, and one for Abingdon. The Reform Act retained the aggregate but changed slightly the composition. Wallingford lost one member and the county gained one. It is worth comment that in 1831 Berkshire was almost as solidly in favour of the reform bill as it was against the repeal of the Corn Laws in 1846. The two political manifestations of the same area at an interval of only fifteen years epitomizes much of English political history in this period. In 1831, besides the two county members, both of whom were whigs, most of the borough members were also reformers. There can be little doubt that this was mainly due to a genuine feeling in the electorate which was particularly evident in the election of Throckmorton and Dundas as the county members. Robert Throckmorton of

[5] 15 December 1832.

P.A.P.— U

Buckland House, near Faringdon, was a whig squire who owed his position as county member almost entirely to the fact that by 1831 the Berkshire freeholders were stirred to independent action on behalf of the reform bill. He had not previously represented the county and his success was an illustration of the power of the county electorate even in the unreformed system. The other county member, Dundas owed his place to something more than a transitory enthusiasm. He had sat as member for the county for over thirty years and occupied a unique place in county politics. Yet this had depended on his personal popularity and influence rather than on the tangible weight of his property. He was indeed an important landowner but there were others in the county with equal or greater property. For Dundas, however, the parliament of 1831 was his last. He died in 1832 at the age of eighty-one shortly after his elevation to the peerage as Baron Amesbury. His death left a gap in the county representation which was difficult to fill. Both personally and politically, therefore, the passage of the Reform Act marked the end of a well defined era in the county representative history.

I. THE BOROUGHS

Abingdon   To the electors of the small, comfortably thriving town of Abingdon, the Reform Act brought little that was new. Possibly because it had always returned only one member, it had largely escaped the attentions of the borough-mongers and could most fittingly perhaps be placed in the class of family boroughs. Like most of the Berkshire boroughs it had possessed a scot and lot franchise[6] before 1832 and the new franchise made no striking alteration either in the size or composition of the electorate. In 1830, 253 voters (the highest total for thirty years) had polled out of a population that remained slightly above 5,000 in this decade. At the first election under the reformed system only 201 voters polled and the total of electors on the register was only 300. In 1836, when the electorate had risen to 306, an analysis showed that 217 of these were old scot and lot voters of whom all but ten were also qualified as £10 householders. Thus the Abingdon constituency was composed of eighty-nine electors who owed their franchise to the Reform Act; ten who were electors because of the provision for the retention of the old franchise during the lifetime

---

[6] I.e. inhabitants rated and paying parochial taxes.

of the holders; and 207 who would have been electors whether under the old system or the new. Substantially the Abingdon electorate after 1832 was little different from that before. A more significant change would have come with an alteration in the borough boundaries. This was originally contemplated but the Earl of Abingdon secured an amendment in the House of Lords confining the boundaries to the old borough. This, like all the other amendments in the upper house to the boundaries bill, was accepted by the House of Commons because of the need for haste and so Abingdon was spared the process of ruralization that overtook its neighbour Wallingford.[7]

The member who had previously represented Abingdon was J. Maberley who sat for the borough from 1818 to 1831 as a liberal whig. No doubt he had looked to the management of his limited constituency since one of his customs was to distribute every Christmas £100 worth of coal among the poor of the town. But Maberley's own finances were in disorder and he finally went bankrupt, paying a modest dividend of 2s. in the pound. In spite of the declarations of his friends that this was merely a temporary embarrassment, it clearly ended his parliamentary career. At the general election of 1832 a local squire, Thomas Duffield of Marcham, came forward to succeed to the broken Maberley influence. He was elected without serious opposition. Another local man, T. Bowles, put up as candidate but withdrew on the eve of the election. A Colonel Maberley, son of the late member, then entered the lists to defend the family seat before it finally slipped from their grasp but he only polled 43 votes against Duffield's 157. The first trial of strength was decisive; and uncontested returns in 1835, 1837, and 1841 demonstrated that Duffield had taken Maberley's place as the acknowledged patron of the borough. Even the annual distribution of coal was continued and perhaps this weighed as much with the electors as the political views of the new member. In fact Duffield was a tory, though with fairly independent views which he could well afford in the comfortable circumstances of his seat. Like most of the Berkshire gentry he had opposed the reform bill and put his name to the *Berkshire Declaration* of 1831 protesting against that measure. In 1835 he told the electors of his determination only to support the conservatives on the professed grounds they had put forward (an allusion to the

[7] *Hansard*, xiv, 171; P.P. 1833, xxvii, 111; 1837-8, xliv, 580 sq.

Tamworth Manifesto) and that if they failed to uphold the principles there stated, he would cease to assist them.[8] In 1837 he made a reference to the valuable work in saving the government from defeat done by 'the party with whom he generally acted'.[9] No doubt a flavour both of reform and independence went down well with the little crowd of Abingdon citizens who were responsible for returning one member to the House of Commons. But Duffield was a member of the Carlton and probably in most respects an ordinary tory country member, more stirred by agricultural topics than anything else. He voted for the Chandos Malt Tax motion in April 1835 and his election speech in 1841, at a time when corn laws and cheap bread almost monopolized the utterances from the hustings, followed the party line in supporting the principle of a sliding scale as against the whig proposal for a fixed duty. In the great crisis of 1846 he played an even more outstanding rôle. At the indignation meeting of Berkshire agriculturalists at Reading on 31 January Duffield was one of the most outspoken of the gentry in condemning Peel's policy and himself moved a resolution to that effect. His constituency may have been urban but his point of view was indistinguishable from that of a county member.

It was an ironic circumstance, therefore, that by that date Duffield was no longer member for Abingdon and the vote he might have cast against repeal in fact went to the staunch minority of 112 conservatives who followed their leader into free trade in corn. It was (barring Windsor) the only Berkshire vote in the House of Commons that was to be found among them. What had happened was that in 1844, when the great conservative party was still united, Duffield had taken the Chiltern Hundreds in order to provide a seat for the conservative Solicitor-General, F. Thesiger. Duffield's paramount position in the borough, unchallenged since 1832, had given Abingdon almost the appearance of a nomination borough. No one came forward to challenge Thesiger in 1844 nor again in 1845 when he had to apply for re-election as a result of his appointment as Attorney-General. Thesiger, therefore, now Sir Frederick, seemed to present the spectacle of a ministerial nominee, ensconced in a safe pocket borough, duly supporting the ministry in their Corn Law policy. But Abingdon was not so complaisant as this picture would suggest. At the general election of 1847 there

[8] *Berkshire Chronicle*, 10 January 1835.   [9] Add. MS 28673, fo. 15 (Richards MSS.).

was a bitter contest, the first for fifteen years, and Thesiger only scraped through by two votes against General James Caulfeild.[10] There were 315 electors on the register, and all but eleven voted. A petition was entered against his return but without success. Nevertheless the escape had been too narrow for comfort. In 1852 Thesiger removed to the safer precincts of Stamford and Caulfeild enjoyed a quiet return for Abingdon; though, as he died on the first day of the assembly of the new parliament, it could hardly be counted a fruitful one.

Politically, therefore, Abingdon does not fall into a ready-made category. It was not entirely a pocket borough nor was it quite of the same texture as the surrounding countryside, however much it depended on the latter economically. The ease with which the electors transferred their favours from a whig to a tory in 1832 and from a resident country gentleman to a member of the 'red tape squadron' sent down from London in 1844, suggests that the dominating factors were personal rather than national. Yet even the easy-going Abingdon electorate, as the election of 1847 showed, had a sting within it that vindicated its old reputation as a borough in which aristocratic corruption and influence had never obtained the mastery. If Abingdon in this period attests to anything, it is to the danger of generalization.

Wallingford. Unlike Abingdon, Wallingford even in the economic sense was merely an agricultural market town with no industries of its own. There was a certain amount of distress in the town arising out of the inadequate employment offered in the surrounding agricultural district; and the poor rate was rising. The Reform Act enhanced the rural character of the constituency. The old borough boundaries had barely extended beyond the built-up area of the town. The Boundary Act extended these limits to take in, besides the old borough, the parishes of Brightwell, Sotwell, north and south Moreton, Bensington, Crowmarsh and Newnham Murren, and large parts of the parishes of Cholsey, Aston Tirrold, and Aston Upthorpe, including the three villages of those names. The constituency which went by the name of Wallingford after 1832 was thus a large stretch of essentially agricultural countryside, some five miles from north to south and

[10] James Caulfeild, major-general in the East Indian Army, director of the East India Company, d. 4 November 1852 at the age of 67 at Copswood, co. Limerick (*Annual Register*, 1852, 325). In politics he was a whig.

about six from east to west, comprising numerous villages, besides
the town of Wallingford itself, some of which were on the Oxfordshire side of the Thames. The Reform Act both widened the
electorate and altered its character. Before 1832 Wallingford had
been the smallest constituency in the county. In the thirty years
preceding the act the highest poll at an election had been 212.[11]
The reconstruction of the constituency at first doubled that figure.
For the general election of 1832 there were 453 nominal electors on
the register and 367 actually voted   There were, however, some
obvious errors and duplications in this first estimate of the new
electorate. By the time the 1835 election took place, the registered
list had been reduced to 366 and even then there were many
duplicate entries on account of plural qualifications which made
the aggregate of voters appear larger than it really was.[12] There
was no contest in that year but at the next election there was a poll
of 277 electors out of a register of 360. The latter figure was composed of 297 householders and 63 scot and lot voters. But it is not
clear how many of the £10 householders were also old scot and
lot voters. Probably the enlargement of the constituency had made
a greater addition to the electorate than was experienced at
Abingdon. Moreover the population of the Wallingford constituency was now larger than that of Abingdon and increasing at a
faster rate. By 1841 it contained nearly 8,000 inhabitants. Windsor
itself with its two members could only muster some 9,000.

Besides these changes in the nature of the constituency one of the
two seats which Wallingford had previously held was taken from
it. From being a small borough with two members it had changed
to a moderately sized, semi-rural constituency with only one seat.
The effect on the character of the Wallingford constituency was
clearly marked. Before 1832 the borough had enjoyed some
reputation for venality. Oldfield had described the corruption in
the borough in 1816 as having gained 'a systematic establishment'.[13] And in the course of the reform bill debates Wynn had
used Wallingford to illustrate his argument that small boroughs
would be rotten still despite the changes in the franchise. Wallingford, he said, had 287 resident householders of whom 218 were
above the £10 standard. Was it likely, therefore, that the alteration
in the franchise would make any difference to the notorious

[11] P.P. 1830–1, x, 24 sqq.   [12] P.P. 1833, xxvii, 231; 1836, xliii, 403.
[13] *Representative History*, iii, 41.

corruption of the borough? Was it not indeed more probable that the attractions of the franchise would turn all the Wallingford houses into Ten Pounders, since men would as an investment willingly pay more than an economic rent for the sake of what they would recover at election time?[14] Nevertheless the Reform Act brought a change for the better; partly because the constituency was enlarged; and partly because as a single-member constituency it was less attractive to the borough-mongers. These two factors enabled a gentleman of the neighbourhood, W. S. Blackstone of Castle Priory, a grandson of the famous eighteenth-century lawyer, to secure a position in the borough as powerful as that of Duffield at Abingdon.

The Blackstones were a local family. He himself was a native of the town, had property in the district, and was patron of the living of Wallingford. He had contested the borough without success in 1831 but like many other country gentlemen he found his political influence strengthened by the effects of the Reform Act and was able to secure the seat in 1832 with little opposition. Blackstone, for what it matters in this context, was a tory and his name appears in the membership of the Carlton in 1836. But like Duffield he owed his election not to his politics but to his local position. Another squire of the neighbourhood, Charles Eyston, contested the borough in the whig interest. The Eystons were perhaps the oldest of the county families, having been settled in Berkshire since the marriage of John Eyston to Isabel Stowe, heiress of East Hendred, in the fifteenth century. At the time of the Reformation the Eystons had remained true to the old religion and despite the difficulties and persecutions of the sixteenth and seventeenth centuries, had probably succeeded in maintaining the continuous observance of their traditional worship either in the old medieval chapel of the manor-house or at their secluded house at Catmore on the Berkshire Downs. Soon after the passing of Catholic Emancipation in 1829 Charles Eyston[15] was appointed J.P. and served as high sheriff for the county in 1831, in which capacity he openly expressed his sympathy with the reform candidates in the elections of that year. The previous year he had been the author of a *Letter to Viscount Althorp, Reasons in Favour of a moderate Constitutional Reform*

---

[14] *Hansard*, VI, 694–5.
[15] B. 1790, eldest son of Basil Eyston; J.P., D.L., high sheriff 1831; m. Maria Theresa Metcalfe of Barnborough Hall, Yorks; d. 24 February 1857. See also, Humphreys, *East Hendred, a Berkshire Parish*, 96.

of the Commons House of Parliament. He was thus the outstanding liberal among the county gentry of the period. Nevertheless from his seat at East Hendred in the Vale of the White Horse, some miles from Wallingford, he could scarcely exert the same influence enjoyed by Blackstone from his residence within the constituency; and a religious prejudice probably further lessened his chances. He withdrew from the contest during the poll and Blackstone was elected by 202 votes to 165.

As at Abingdon the first round was decisive. After 1832 Blackstone's position was never seriously challenged. At the next election he met with no opposition whatever and was returned with scarcely a word of comment in the local newspapers. In 1837 a little more activity was shown in testing his hold on the constituency. Eyston had apparently not entirely abandoned all hope and as the general election of 1837 drew near he began to sound the ground once more. In July, however, he announced that, following a canvass of the Wallingford electors, he had concluded that he stood no chance of defeating the sitting member. It was not, he explained, merely a question of political principles. Blackstone's residence in the borough, his property in the district, his connexions with many of the tradesmen in the constituency, were factors of such advantage in the limited electorate that the best efforts of Eyston and his friends were unlikely to make any impression.[16] Another candidate, more optimistic, then came forward. This was Thomas Teed, a magistrate for Middlesex, and a retired solicitor of the East India Company. He defined himself as a liberal but not a radical, an Anglican but favourable to relief for dissenters. But the result of the polling was as might be expected. Blackstone secured 159 votes; Teed 118. The next general election (1841) saw Blackstone once more in undisturbed possession of the seat.

Even more than at Abingdon the representation of Wallingford seemed to have become the acknowledged perquisite of a family or, at least, of an individual. There may have been bribery but there was no public allegation of such methods. There was of course a certain amount of money spent on official fees and expenses which could not have been unacceptable to the recipients. All that the borough paid was the cost of registration. The rest fell on the candidates, especially the successful candidate; and no doubt the items were not examined too closely. The under sheriff received

[16] *Reading Mercury,* 1 July 1837.

five guineas; the hall-keeper four guineas and the sergeants-at-mace four guineas; the town clerk was paid twenty guineas for his general services and expenses.[17] But in 1832 all that the two candidates had to pay as official expenses was £43 beside the fees for indentures and returns.[18] It would be difficult to attribute to such small sums any particular political importance. The decisive factor was the social and personal position of Blackstone in the borough. He entered the House of Commons without responsibility to any except himself and his neighbours. And they no doubt were not greatly concerned with his political opinions as long as they were of the kind that could be held without discredit by any country gentleman of the time, and without infringing the agricultural interests and prejudices of the constituency. Of this there was little likelihood, for Blackstone was a typical example of the ultra-tory country member. Ballot, Dissenters, and Poor Law, all came under his condemnation; he supported the Corn Laws and voted for the repeal of the Malt Tax. Not only was he an 'agricultural radical' but he was one of the knot of independent and intransigent members who formed an insubordinate and potentially dangerous element in the conservative party long before the rise of Disraeli and the Young England party. Along with Vyvyan of Cornwall and Tyrell of Essex he was at the heart of the threatened revolt of the country back-benchers over the speakership in 1841. Inevitably, therefore, he was with the majority that broke with Peel in 1846 on the issue of the Corn Laws. Yet his independent and sometimes truculent attitude towards the party leaders was a reflection of the invulnerable and almost autonomous position he enjoyed in his constituency. A man so circumstanced was almost beyond the threats and cajoling of the whips.

Reading. The county town, steadily rising towards the 18,000 of the 1841 census, had a population almost equal to that of the other three parliamentary boroughs of Berkshire put together. Politically and socially it was the one great urban centre of the county. Its connexions with the countryside were of course important. The flourishing trade with London in flour, timber, malt, and other agricultural products depended on its position as the collecting and distributing point for the sales and purchases of the rural area around it. But economic dependence did not mean

[17] P.P. 1834, IX, 434, 518.   [18] P.P. 1833, XXVII, 231.

political dependence; and Reading possessed in addition industries of its own. Though the clothing trade had almost disappeared, the great beer, seed, and biscuit companies of the nineteenth century were already emerging. The dozen or so breweries in the town at this time included that of Messrs Simonds; and the commissioners that inquired into the state of the corporation in 1835 commented on the influence of brewers on the town council.[19] By the forties Sutton and Sons were established as seedsmen and florists in the market-place. In 1841 the young Quaker, George Palmer, came to join Mr Huntley in his bakery and biscuit business and so began the expansion of the Reading biscuit industry. While these were yet in their infancy the gap was filled by a variety of small but flourishing trades—breweries, banks, ironworks, water-works, brickyards, timber-yards, and gunsmiths—that helped to give rise to a specifically townsmen's attitude, more pronounced in Reading than anywhere else in the county. Socially, moreover, the borough had a long tradition of civic independence and religious dissent. At the beginning of the nineteenth century Reading was well known for the number and variety of its sects. Independents, Baptists, Quakers, Congregationalists, Methodists of both kinds, Unitarians, and Presbyterians, all assisted to give the town a marked puritanic and radical temper.[20] Reading had protested against the repressive legislation of the government at the time of the Revolutionary and Napoleonic Wars. It had passed resolutions in public meeting for the abolition of slavery, for greater missionary effort in India, and for Catholic emancipation. In 1809 a town meeting of over a thousand resident inhabitants had declared almost unanimously in favour of parliamentary reform; and the following year the town petitioned the House of Commons against the commitment of Sir Francis Burdett. A generation later it returned two members to parliament in 1830 and 1831 to vote for the whig reform bill.

Even before 1832 it had been a large constituency and the Reform Act did little at first to extend the franchise. In the Reading election of 1826 over 1,000 electors had voted. This admittedly was a record poll; but even the total of registered electors after the Act scarcely exceeded this figure. In 1832 there were 1,001 voters on the register; in 1835, 1,002; in 1837, 1,032; and in 1841, 1,194. In such a thriving town as Reading the old scot and lot

[19] P.P. 1835, xxiii, Appendix, Pt. I, 251.
[20] Man, *History of Reading*, 129–30; Childs, *Reading during the Early Nineteenth Century* 53–6, 63–5.

franchise had in effect been as wide as the new £10 householder franchise. Indeed the *Berkshire Chronicle* suggested in 1837 that the electorate of the borough had, if anything, been diminished by the Reform Act.[21] It quoted the polls at three elections, one before and two after the act, to prove its case. On each occasion there had been three candidates and the voting figures had been as follows.

1830	*1835*	*1837*
497	643	468
459	441	457
430	384	448

Allowance, moreover, must be made in the post-1832 registers for duplicate entries. But it is clear that after 1832 the constituency numbered about 1,000; this, by contemporary standards, was a borough larger than the average.

At the time of the passing of the Reform Act the members for Reading had been C. Fysshe Palmer and C. Russell. Both were reformers although Russell was neither whig nor radical in any precise sense. Palmer came of an old Berkshire family connected since the seventeenth century with the parishes of Sonning and Hurst in the vicinity of the town. A Roger Palmer had sat for Windsor in 1660 and a Richard Palmer was high sheriff in 1680. C. F. Palmer, six foot three inches tall, 'upright as a pike', and commonly called 'long Fysshe', was an outstanding and respected whig not only in his own county but in the unreformed House of Commons. His whiggery was of the Fox and Grey school, moulded in the internal strife of the Revolutionary Wars. He told the House on one occasion of his vivid recollection of the Muir and Palmer trials in Scotland in 1793 and his visit to Palmer[22] as he lay in the hulks, 'loaded with irons and placed amidst housebreakers, footpads, and highwaymen'.[23] Through his wife he was connected with the Scottish aristocracy, having married in 1805 Lady Madelina, widow of Sir Robert Sinclair of Stevenson, Haddingtonshire, daughter of the 4th Duke of Gordon, and sister to three duchesses and one marchioness. His colleague, Russell, was of rather a different type. His father, Sir Henry Russell, had been chief

---

[21] *Berkshire Chronicle*, 29 July 1837.
[22] Thomas Fysshe Palmer, his uncle,
[23] *Hansard*, XII, 1180. Cooper, *Worthies of Reading*.

justice in Bengal. His brother, also Henry Russell, had been chief resident at Hyderabad, and after many years service with the East India Company he survived, as his obituary stated with equal tact and realism, to enjoy for over twenty years the honours and emoluments he had earned in India. He succeeded his father, the 1st baronet, in 1836 and from his seat at Swallowfield, a few miles south of Reading, was able to assist his younger brother's electoral fortunes. In 1840, for instance, he sent a copy of one of Charles Russell's speeches in the House of Commons to the editor of the *Berkshire Chronicle* with directions how to introduce it and explain the context.[24] Charles Russell himself was in close touch with the world of commerce and finance. He was a West India proprietor and a few years after the Reform Act he became the chairman of the Board of Directors of the Great Western Railway. In many ways he was far less liberal in his outlook than his elderly colleague. He had the reputation, justified by his subsequent political career, of being opposed to the abolition of slavery and to municipal reform. There was thus a decided and curious contrast between the two Reading members. Palmer, the old-fashioned aristocratic whig, brother-in-law to the Duke of Gordon, and connected by marriage to the great houses of Richmond, Bedford, Manchester, and Cornwallis, was a strongly liberal whig. Russell, son of a West Indian nabob who had secured a baronetcy for himself as late as 1812, and with extensive city interests of his own, leaned towards a form of conservatism that rapidly became indistinguishable from toryism. A simple theory of politics that would seek in this period to identify whig-liberalism with capital and toryism with the land would find these circumstances awkward; yet it is improbable that either Palmer or Russell saw anything anomalous in their respective positions.

Palmer had sat in the House of Commons as a member of the whig opposition since 1818. Russell was first elected for the borough in 1830 when he and Palmer defeated Dr Stephen Lushington. At the general elections of 1831 and 1833 they were returned unopposed as liberal reformers. In the excitement and passions of 1831 this was a natural event. It seems clear that even in 1832 the conservatives despaired of capturing a single seat. But Russell received considerable support from the conservative elements in the borough and indeed he had in the first instance been proposed

[24] Add. MS. 28671, fo. 180 (Richards MSS.).

by the anti-reform party. His speeches, however, showed a proper appreciation of the general trend of feeling in the town. He declared himself in favour of church reform, revision of the Corn Laws, and free trade. On the delicate subject of slavery, where he was most suspect, he finally announced himself as an abolitionist, provided due consideration was paid to the interests of the planters. Hence, although he was welcomed by the tory *Berkshire Chronicle* as a conservative, he so far conciliated liberal opinion in Reading as to be accepted as a suitable representative. The town, though reforming, was not radical. A leading article in the *Reading Mercury* deprecated the violence to be expected from the radical party in the new House of Commons. 'The sound, the influential part of the community', it added, 'are not desirous of violent changes—they only wish for effectual Reforms in the abuses which have crept into the institutions of our Country.'[25] No doubt this was a fair reflection of the views of most Reading liberals. The town was too solidly middle class and prosperous to welcome extreme measures either for their own sake or as party tactics against the tories. Neither in the House of Commons nor in the constituency did there seem much danger from the shattered and discredited opposition.

Two years later the circumstances were materially different. The whigs were out; the tories in. Peel was coming home from Italy but in the meantime the head of the new government was the Duke of Wellington who was regarded by a large section of the public as the arch-representative of tory reaction. John Walter, the proprietor of *The Times*, sounded Berkshire opinion at the beginning of December 1834 in preparation for his own candidature for the county and was deeply impressed by the strong feeling among the liberal party in the towns and their 'unreasonably angry hostility' to the duke.[26] The Reading electors had in addition their own reasons for discontent. Palmer had shown himself too orthodox a supporter of the ministry to please the extremer elements among his supporters and there were taunts that he had too close an acquaintance with the treasury officials and the pension list. This was an unjust accusation but it had enough basis of fact to make it a recurrent and troublesome feature of Palmer's political career. The truth was that not he but his wife, Lady Madelina Palmer, was in receipt of a government pension. The

[25] 31 December 1832. [26] Add. MS. 40405, fos. 24–5; *History of 'The Times'*, I, 340–1.

matter had come up before but the House of Commons had decided in 1818 that it did not debar Palmer from sitting in the House since Lady Madelina was already in possession of the pension at the time of her marriage to Palmer and it had been granted to her in recognition of the public services of her first husband, Sir Robert Sinclair. Nevertheless the slur stuck and Palmer's enemies in the liberal-radical camp made the most of it. Russell on the other hand had shown beyond doubt in the first reformed parliament that his political affinities lay with the moderate Peelite conservatives; and Reading had thus been confronted with the sight of their two 'reforming' members voting on opposite sides in the House. The combination of these public and private motives produced some important changes.

On the eve of the election the more radical party in the borough brought forward a new candidate, a Mr Oliveira who was, incidentally, a nephew of Sir John de Beauvoir, the parliamentary candidate for Windsor, and as much a stranger to Reading in 1835 as his uncle was to Windsor in 1832. He was a radical with a pure enough programme to satisfy Bentham himself—the ballot, triennial parliaments, governmental economy, municipal reform, and church reform. His election agent was a local solicitor called Weedon, who had formerly been agent to Palmer and according to most accounts had led the radical malcontents against him. Whether that was true or not, the presence of a second liberal candidate weakened rather than strengthened the liberal cause. Oliveira's supporters claimed that their intention was to defeat Russell; in fact the result was to make Palmer withdraw. What his precise motives were in taking this step are not quite clear. Publicly he said that he did not feel justified in incurring the expense of a contested election. His friends suggested that the real reason was his abandonment by his agent and the feeling that there had been a conspiracy to get rid of him. He was an old man and such a human emotion may well have guided his conduct. In any case his resignation was accepted by the Reading liberals and in his place they put forward Serjeant Talfourd. This was undoubtedly a politic choice. To the outer world Thomas Noon Talfourd already had some reputation as a barrister, journalist (he was an important contributor to *The Times* and at one time on their staff), and author. In Reading, besides all these things, he was the son of a Reading tradesman and the grandson of a Reading dissenting minister. His mother Miss Noon, the daughter of a well-known independent minister of Broad Street Chapel, had married Talfourd, a brewer and a deacon of that chapel. He himself was a native of the town and was educated at Reading School under the famous Dr Valpy, that 'venerable and excellent master' who had been the leader of Reading liberalism during the Revolutionary Wars. After qualifying as a barrister T. N. Talfourd had joined the Oxford circuit, thus retaining this connexion with Reading, and continued to take a part in local politics. In 1819 for instance he had denounced the Peterloo Massacre at a meeting in Reading Town Hall. It was on these latter connexions that he prudently laid most stress in his electioneering. In a brilliant final speech to the electors that gleams even through the cramped and faded newspaper print of a century ago, he appealed to them as old school-fellows and Reading citizens 'to show to their sons that by keeping the straight path of integrity and honour, they might receive what he now asked at their hands, the highest reward which they could bestow'.[27] On personal grounds alone his success was probably assured; but in addition he put forward those moderate liberal views that were entertained by most of the electors he addressed.

The chief electoral interest lay with the other two candidates. Russell carefully defined his position as an independent reforming conservative of the Peel school. He stressed the progressive weakness of the whig ministries, lamented the failure of the king to secure a coalition of moderates, and proclaimed his belief that the new conservative government, in spite of the absence of one or two names (clearly a reference to Stanley and Graham), would win the confidence of the people. He enunciated the principles of the ministry in a list apparently drawn straight from the *Tamworth Manifesto*—the preservation of the fundamental balance of the constitution and the moral government of the church, a cautious but searching revision of institutions to eradicate abuses. He admitted the need, while stressing the difficulty, of church reform in England and Ireland; and lastly, with an obvious concession to his constituency, he advocated the promotion of dissenters to a position of perfect civil equality with the established church. Oliveira, on the other hand, presented himself as an independent man of property, a stranger certainly to the town but also (a hit at

[27] *Berkshire Chronicle*, 10 January 1835.

Palmer) to the pension list. He pointed out that Reading in returning members of opposite parties had in effect not been represented
at all; it was his wish to assist in ending that position and carrying
on the great work of reform.[28] The end of the first day's polling
showed Talfourd well ahead of the field with Oliveira leading
Russell by thirty votes. But less than half the constituency had
voted; perhaps the bribeable section of the electorate was hanging
back for a harvest of bribes on the second day. At any rate Russell
came along with a rush on the following day and finished sixty
votes in front of Oliveira. In one day he polled ninety votes more
than his rival and Reading once again had two members of
opposite political views.

In a subsequent analysis of the election the *Reading Mercury*
pointed out that over a thousand votes had been cast for the purple
or reform party and only 441 for the blues. But this was to burke
the issue. Personal as well as party motives decided the election.
Quite apart from his politics Oliveira as a complete stranger could
not have attracted the more prosperous and old-fashioned classes
in the town. It was too often the weakness of the radicals that
local men of standing would rarely join them so that they were
obliged in consequence to bring in candidates who were foreign
to the constituency. De Beauvoir at Windsor and Oliveira at
Reading both smacked of the outlandish and the parvenu. Even
the *Reading Mercury* admitted that Russell's local connexion had
much to do with his victory. There were other recriminations.
The *Berkshire Chronicle* attacked Weedon for deserting Palmer and
engineering the latter's exclusion. It was denied by the other party
that there had been any motive in bringing Oliveira forward other
than to secure the return of two reformers. Whether true or not,
the fact remained that Weedon had ensured that there would be a
contested election and that he belonged to a class that profited
most from such contests. The main lesson of 1835, however, was
that there was not enough support in the borough to return an
outside radical purely on the merits of his abstract programme.

At the next election no more was heard of Oliveira. In his place
Palmer again stood as liberal candidate. The prospects of the
reforming party were now good. Talfourd, 'the Pride of Reading',
was certain to be re-elected; and Palmer's temporary retirement
had perhaps enhanced, rather than otherwise, his value to the

[28] *Berkshire Chronicle*, 10 January 1835.

electorate. Accordingly the Reading liberals went cheerfully into the contest under the cry of the 'Queen and Liberty', and 'Down with the Tories, the King of Hanover, and the Orange Lodges'. Talfourd had an enthusiastic reception from the constituency and in an able speech to the electors he vindicated both his liberality and his independence. He had voted, he said, for all the great measures of the government—including municipal reform and Irish Church reform—but he had opposed them in his advocacy of three particular measures: factory legislation, abolition of military flogging, and triennial parliaments.[29] This humanitarian liberalism could only have strengthened his position with the Reading electors. A touch of independence in their man made him preferable to a mere party hack and Talfourd erred, if he erred at all, on the side of generous feeling. As for the other two candidates the crucial issue for them as for their constituents was the question of the church. Russell acknowledged (and it was an important confession) that the body of Reading dissenters had been against him and he endeavoured to make capital out of his attachment to the Anglican Church. He admitted that he had opposed municipal reform for Ireland because it would be prejudicial to the Protestant interest in Ireland. He was a reformer, he said, but not when reform would harm the established church and religion. Palmer took him precisely and almost exclusively on these points and expressed his own determination to do justice to Ireland by reforming both the Irish corporations and the Irish Church. In the course of the election campaign the *Reading Mercury* made great play with the association of the queen and reform; but the real issue was clearly religious. The polling was close and in the end twenty votes covered all three candidates. Russell, however, was at the foot of the list, nine votes behind Palmer. An analysis of the voting published later[30] showed that 880 electors had polled; of these 377 had given plumpers for Russell and 71 had divided between Russell and one of the other candidates. It is clear that the body of Russell's supporters, most of them presumably conservatives, had voted solid and unbroken for their man. The liberals on the other hand had divided evenly between their two candidates. Talfourd received only seven plumpers; Palmer only three; but 422 had divided between Talfourd and Palmer. The cross-voting, as usually happened in

[29] *Reading Mercury*, 1 July 1837.   [30] *Berkshire Chronicle*, 29 July 1837.

tripartite contests, had decided the issue between two compact and powerful parties. Up in London the indefatigable Bonham added another name to the list of conservative losses.[31]

In these three elections the pattern of events is unusually clear and public issues alone explain the verdict of the polls. The liberal party in Reading had undoubtedly the majority of the electorate on their side and with one exception they returned what they believed to be liberal representatives in three successive elections. The exception, Russell's return in 1835, can easily be explained by the substitution of a radical stranger for the familiar and respected figure of Palmer. Yet it is difficult to believe that, in the course of a contest between two strong parties in a constituency of over 1,000, no venality existed among any of the electors and that no recourse to illegal methods was ever had by the contending sides. Untampered opinion and conscientious principle perhaps played the main part in deciding votes; but where opinion and voting was so evenly divided even a small minority of corrupt voters could, in fact, settle the issue. The question which must be faced, therefore, is whether illegal practices took place in the Reading elections and whether they had any marginal significance. The first three elections after the Reform Act brought occasional denunciations from one side or another of the undue methods of their opponents. After the 1837 contest the *Berkshire Chronicle*, the organ of the defeated party, published an interesting list of accusations against the liberals. The mayor had shown partiality; some electors were impersonated at the hustings; others had been 'cooped'; and others still had been 'hocussed' by drinks mixed with laudanum.[32] These were of course partisan charges, not necessarily false, indeed probably true, but not necessarily the attributes of one side only. No doubt such things went on even in respectable middle-class Reading, but they were the small change of electioneering and not greatly resented by either side. Moreover it was difficult to prove agency in such matters and in themselves they were insufficient to secure a reversal or quashing of the election by a parliamentary committee. But a few years later more detailed and trustworthy evidence on the political morality of the borough was forthcoming as a result of an inquiry into the election of 1841. The information procured by the parliamentary committee then was of interest not only for the preceding but for earlier elections.

[31] Add. MS. 40424, fo. 44.   [32] *Berkshire Chronicle*, 29 July 1837.

After the liberal success in 1837 the conservatives made great efforts to strengthen their position. A Reading Conservative Association was set up with a member of the important local family of Simonds as chairman and it was clear from the support which Russell had received at the last contest that the movement would not lack numbers. Efforts were then made to get a second conservative candidate for the constituency. The details of these negotiations are obscure but at one point at any rate Bonham was drawn into it. 'What', asked one of his correspondents in 1839, 'are the state of Politics at Reading? I have been asked whether there would be a good opening for a Conservative there—against Serjeant Talfourd as I suppose. F. Palmer is safe—my man of course would like to be No. 1 in the field and has some tolerable local interest though not known personally there.'[33] Whatever came of that particular inquiry another conservative candidate besides Russell was found to contest the borough in 1841. This was Viscount Chelsea who on general grounds seems to fit the description given by Bonham's friend. He was a descendant of the famous William Cadogan, Marlborough's Quartermaster-General, who had been raised to the peerage as Baron Cadogan of Reading in 1716 and created Viscount Caversham in 1718, the latter title being taken from the village in Oxfordshire across the Thames from Reading and now a suburb of the town. These titles, however, had become extinct and the only formal relic of the original connexion still surviving in the dignities of the Cadogan family was the subordinate title of Baron Oakley of Caversham created for the 2nd Earl Cadogan in 1831. Henry Charles, Viscount Chelsea, in 1841 a young man of twenty-nine, was the eldest son of the 3rd earl. Wisely enough, in view of this tenuous association, he based his claims on party rather than local recommendations. In his printed address to the Reading electors he made a passing reference to the slight 'ancient connexion' of his family with the borough but stated that he preferred to take his stand as a conservative on conservative principles. Charles Russell, while making no mention of conservatism or any party connexion, indicated his support for 'an ample protection for those great interests, both Agricultural and Colonial, which is essential not only to the well-being of your own town' but also to the prosperity of the whole country.[34] By 12 June 1841 both conservative candidates were already in the field.

---

[33] Add. MS. 40617, fo. 77.   [34] *Reading Mercury*, 12 June 1841.

The liberal force they had to encounter was not the vigorous party of 1837. Indeed for a whole week there was no opposition at all and no indication of where it could come. from. Of the two sitting members Talfourd was the first to state that he would not stand for re-election. He had not been the success in the House of Commons that his reputation outside had promised. Able as he undoubtedly was, the House had found him too erudite, refined, and poetical for their taste.[35] Moreover it could not have been easy for him to combine an active participation in the business of parliament with his legal practice. But these were not the reasons he gave for his retirement. In a letter to the Reading electors published on 12 June he told them that though willing to stand again, he could not feel assured of the clear and undivided support of the Reading liberals. Even before the 1837 elections, he observed, news of another liberal candidate canvassing the borough had obliged him to leave the House of Commons and come down hastily to Reading. Now, in 1841, he had just received information that some of his supporters intended to introduce a fresh candidate with whom they had already been in communication without previous notice to Talfourd or his friends. Talfourd indeed had good reason to feel aggrieved; for efforts had been made only the preceding week to secure another liberal candidate. Certain persons in the borough had turned their attention to an even greater literary figure than their sitting member—his own friend, Charles Dickens. With *Pickwick, Oliver Twist,* and *Nicholas Nickleby* already to his credit and his readers still damp-eyed from the death of Little Nell the preceding January, Dickens had already reached the pinnacle of fame as a popular novelist and a humanitarian radical. Shortly before the opening of the election campaign of 1841 he was approached by a Mr Lovejoy on behalf of some Reading liberals with an invitation to stand for the borough. His reply expressed his gratification at the offer and his readiness to accept 'if there were any reasonable chance of success'; but he said plainly that he could not afford the expense of a contested election. Nevertheless he went down to Reading for an interview in which it was made equally plain to him that though the liberals would like him as candidate they would not be able to contribute to the cost of returning him. On 9 June, when the two conservatives were about to begin their

[35] Grant, *Random Recollections of the House of Commons,* 360 sqq.

electioneering in the borough, Lovejoy made a final effort to get Dickens to come forward. He mentioned a reasonable sum as the likely cost of his candidature and suggested that the liberal party headquarters in London might be induced to contribute. But Dickens was not to be tempted. He pointed out that he could not afford any expenditure on an election since the mere fact of being a member of parliament would entail a financial sacrifice on his part; and he did not feel that an application to the government for assistance would be compatible with the independence which he himself as well as his constituents must wish him to preserve. Reading therefore lost the distinction of electing as its member the immortal creator of Eatanswill.[36]

In view of the friendship between Talfourd and Dickens, the former may have had direct information of these negotiations. In any case it may reasonably be presumed that he intended a reference to them in his letter of 12 June. With pardonable indignation Talfourd now felt it no longer incumbent on him to contest the constituency once more. It was in fact almost a precise repetition of the incident in 1835 which had provoked Palmer's withdrawal. It is difficult to escape the impression that the radical element in Reading was constantly subject to schismatic impulses, preferring to put up a candidate of extreme views rather than accept two moderate liberals. Undeterred by the failure to secure the candidature of Charles Dickens, and virtually ignoring the position of Palmer, who was still nominally in the field, the liberals at once placarded the town with handbills announcing that two ministerialist candidates were ready to take the field. No names were given, probably for the good reason that the candidates in question had not yet been obtained. In all this work Weedon the solicitor, whose breach with Palmer had led to the introduction of Oliveira in 1835, probably took a leading part. Certainly he became the agent of the first of the new liberal candidates to appear. This indiscipline as a party played straight into the hands of their opponents. For Palmer, now seventy-two years old, took this opportunity also to resign from the representation of the borough. It is possible that he would have continued had he been sure of a peaceful return. But any hope of this was dashed by the appearance on 17 June of a new liberal candidate,

[36] *Letters of Charles Dickens*, I, 44–5; Pope-Hennessy, *Charles Dickens*, 123. Talfourd's conduct in the 1841 election does not support the surmise in the latter work that Talfourd was responsible for the overture by the Reading liberals to Dickens.

Thomas Mills. Two days later Palmer announced his retirement 'in consequence of advanced age and increasing infirmities'.

On that same day a second liberal candidate, Tooke, presented himself to the Reading electors. The two new liberals who now came forward in place of Talfourd and Palmer were far less distinguished than their predecessors. Mills was a Hertfordshire resident described by his party press as a 'gentleman of liberal politics, and a large landed proprietor in that county'.[37] In his electioneering he made what capital he could out of his agricultural connexion and pledged himself never to do anything that would harm the agricultural interest. Nevertheless his platform was the stock party programme of 'The Queen, good government, and cheap provisions.' In his printed address to the electors he came out on the side of free trade and the 'removal of all restrictions' (though with no specific mention of the Corn Laws), civil and religious liberty, and progressive reform. Tooke, a London lawyer who had been member for Truro from 1832 to 1837, was even more decidedly radical. He stood, he announced, for civil and religious liberty in the fullest sense; Religion and Moral Education; Free Trade and the revision of the Corn Laws; Cheap Bread with the maintenance of Liberal Wages. Though he himself was a member of the established Church he made a marked bid for the dissenting interest and drew attention to the part he played in supporting the foundation of University College, London.

If the 1837 election had been fought primarily on the religious issue, that of 1841 revolved, overtly at least, round the question of the Corn Laws, presented to the electorate in the simplified form of cheap bread *versus* protection for agriculture. On that issue the Reading electorate was deeply divided. Though it was an urban commercial community with a strong dissenting leaven, it was also a market town, the centre of a predominantly farming country, and bound by close links to the soil. The battle for the county town was one that roused the whole county. At the height of the election a *Petition and Address to the electors of Reading* was published by the agriculturalists of the neighbourhood, urging them to give their votes to the conservative candidates. It was answered on the liberal side by an *Address from the Poor and Working Classes, inhabitants of the borough*. This purported to be the

[37] *Reading Mercury*, 19 June 1841.

expression of the views of a meeting of some 4,000 non-electors of the borough held on 25 June, pointing out to the 1,000 odd electors their duties and responsibilities to the 18,000 non-electors of the town who depended on them for the protection of their interests in parliament.[38] Polling day was 29 June and the two conservative candidates went into the lead from the start, being about a hundred in front after the first hour. The close of the poll saw Russell on top with 576 votes closely followed by Chelsea with 564, while Mills and Tooke were left to fill third and fourth places with 409 and 396 votes respectively.[39] The result was scarcely surprising in view of the character of the candidates. Russell was probably certain of re-election and was the only one of the four with a genuine local association. It was significant that on nomination day he had been proposed by Henry Simonds, a member of the brewing and banking family, and seconded by W. Blandy, the representative of another old and respected Reading family. Chelsea, it is true, was a stranger to the borough; but at least he came as a true-blue conservative with the additional lustre of an heir to an earldom. Mills and Tooke, on the other hand, must have presented to many Reading electors the appearance of carpet-bag politicians, coming down by train from London less than a fortnight before polling-day with only the asseverations of their backers to give them any kind of status. In part this was a circumstance made inevitable by the last-minute retirement of Talfourd and Palmer. Yet it was indisputable that Mills and Tooke had been sent down to the borough by a London solicitor (probably Coppock) in response to a requisition from certain interested parties in Reading for a couple of liberal candidates to oppose the two conservatives already in the field.

There were other factors. In the first case there can be little doubt that following the formation of the conservative association in 1837 the organization of the party had immensely improved. The *Reading Mercury* alleged that the conservative party in the borough had been for several years in 'a perfect state of organization and preparation' whereas the liberals had neglected the registration and allowed many objectionable conservative votes to remain on the list. After the election the same paper published an analysis of the poll which, though its data cannot now be

[38] *Reading Mercury*, 26 June 1841.
[39] The final state of the poll as given subsequently to a parliamentary committee was respectively, 570, 564, 410, 397.

checked, made two interesting and reasonable suggestions. The first was that the conservatives polled 96 per cent of their supporters and the liberals only 80 per cent; the second was that nearly eighty electors previously reckoned as reformers on this occasion voted conservative. The explanation proffered for this was the unprecedented intimidation exercised to prevent liberals from casting their vote and the reluctance of many liberals during the election to vote for what from the outset seemed to be the losing side.[40] In any case the two conservatives had enjoyed the advantage of a clear week's start in their election campaign during which they were in 'exclusive, uninterrupted and tranquil possession of the borough'. This in itself was due of course not only to the slackness of the liberals but also to the preparedness of the conservative candidates. But beyond all these open features of the election there were other and less reputable circumstances. Mills and Tooke had lost the election but there was still the possibility of an appeal. Mills at any rate proved a tenacious opponent and at the opening of the new parliament he brought a petition against the return of Russell and Chelsea on grounds of bribery and corruption. The resulting inquiry not only made the Reading election case one of the corrupt compromises given notoriety by Roebuck in 1842 but also threw some light on the electoral methods pursued in the borough.

The general charge against the sitting members was that of 'gross and systematic bribery and corruption', but before the election committee had finished its investigations the petition was abandoned as a result of private agreement between the two parties concerned. This agreement was an important item in the general disclosure of corrupt compromises in 1842. In the case of the Reading petition the compromise was of a particularly business-like character. As soon as the committee had commenced its work, the liberal side was approached by an agent of the two conservative members and an agreement was eventually reached in time to stop the proceedings of the committee on the third day. The compromise was embodied in a document in two copies, signed by the three principals: Russell and Chelsea on one side, Mills as petitioner, on the other. It was laid down in the first place that the petition should be withdrawn with such reasons to be assigned to the committee as should be jointly agreed on; secondly, that

[40] *Reading Mercury,* 3 July, 10 July 1841.

one of the sitting members should vacate his seat in time to allow a new election to take place in the current session and that both the sitting members should use their utmost endeavour to assist the return of the petitioner at the next Reading election without opposition, whatever the occasion of the vacancy, and to induce the conservative electors of the constituency to do likewise; thirdly, that in the event of the petitioner not being elected in the manner proposed, the sitting members should pay him forthwith the sum of £2,000. It is to be presumed that the financial clause of this contract eventually came into operation. Viscount Chelsea duly applied for the Chiltern Hundreds but by that time the whole business of corrupt compromises had come out and Goulburn, the chancellor of the exchequer, refused the application. He would not, he said, 'make myself a party to transactions which I do not approve and of which the House of Commons has implied its condemnation'.[41] The compromise was thus defeated and before the election committee was stopped short in its work, enough had been elicited to prove the existence of bribery at Reading. It was obvious that the whole motive of the conservatives in entering upon an arrangement whereby they sacrificed one seat was the fear that if the committee pursued its inquiries, both seats would be lost in spite of any expense to which they might go in defending the petition.

'Reading is, I suppose', remarked a solicitor in the course of the proceedings before committee, 'no purer than other constituencies in the kingdom.'[42] This was the aspect which emerged most clearly from the mass of evidence brought forward. A considerable sum of money had been spent, and perhaps was habitually spent, on the contest; and there was no doubt as to the destination of one part of it. Russell spent about £1,500 on the 1841 election. In two previous contests (1835 and 1837) he had spent on each occasion between £1,600 and £1,800. Viscount Chelsea admitted that his election expenses had been about £2,000. On one side alone, therefore, an amount probably exceeding £3,500 was spent on a single election. It cost the liberals just as much. Mills stated that he imagined the contest in 1841 would cost him about £1,000. In fact it had cost him £1,600. Thus it would not be far wrong to assume that a fully contested parliamentary election

[41] P.P. 1842, xxxiii, 641. In consequence of this refusal, Russell and Chelsea remained members for Reading during the 1841–7 parliament.
[42] P.P. 1842, v, 212.

with four candidates brought the town something between £6,000 and £7,000. Exactly how these sums were expended it was of course impossible to prove. But it was generally admitted that a section of the electorate was corrupt and that bribery was a well established feature of Reading elections. Russell, the candidate in 1841 with the greatest experience of the town, modestly confessed that he could not refrain from thinking that 'in the town of Reading money is illegally given, as I believe it is in every town in this kingdom'; though he said he was not personally cognizant of it. But it was the function of agents and committees to see that candidates never were cognizant of such things.

The most compact statement came from Weedon, the solicitor previously mentioned. He described the contested elections of 1835 and 1837, and said that by 1841 the two incorrupt, *bona fide*, political parties in the borough were evenly matched, 'as near equal as possible'. The balance therefore was held by that section of the electorate which was notoriously influenced by bribes. He estimated that at least a hundred voters took money at elections. In the 1841 election there were further developments. By that date the Great Western Railway was pushing its iron fingers across the county and it was alleged that Russell, who was chairman of the board of directors, had made promises of positions on the railway to various electors.[43] These accusations were naturally denied by Russell's party. What was not to be denied was that the secretary of the G.W.R. Company, a Mr Saunders, had taken a leading part in securing the compromise with the liberals when the petition was brought after the election. Weedon also said that some sixty or seventy electors in the constituency had been intimidated into neutrality by the threats of the farmers and landlords in the neighbourhood 'in consequence of the stir relative to the Corn Bill'.[44] All these specific allegations came from hostile sources; they would hardly have come from friendly ones. But they need not be too heavily discounted on that score. The cost of bringing the petition against Russell and Chelsea was between £1,200 and £1,500. It is unlikely that either Mills or his party would have undertaken that expense without strong proof of corrupt practices on the part of the successful candidates; nor would the successful candidates have committed themselves to the

[43] The Great Western line reached Maidenhead in 1838, Reading in 1840, and Bristol in 1841.
[44] For details of the whole inquiry, see P.P. 1842, v, esp. 25–6, 82–3, 207–35.

contingency of paying Mills £2,000 unless they had good cause to fear investigation. They were certainly unable to present a very solid front to the charges brought against them. On the opening day of the inquiry it transpired that the town clerk of Reading, Mr J. J. Blandy, was on holiday in Italy. There was every reason to suspect that he had been sent abroad out of reach of the speaker's warrant in order to wreck or delay further proceedings on the petition. As a result there was some difficulty in getting hold of the poll-books of the election and two whole days, Friday and Saturday, were spent in formalities and legal arguments (when the books were finally produced) whether they came out of proper custody. Only at the very end of the Saturday's hearing did the committee decide to go on with the examination of witnesses brought by the petitioners. As soon as it was clear that evidence on bribery was going to be taken by the committee, the defendants hastened to come to a compromise agreement. It cannot seriously be doubted that in spite of the placid and respectable appearance which Reading presented to the outside world, corruption had a hold on a small section of the electorate which in certain circumstances might be decisive.

Some other reflections suggest themselves. What were the motives and what was the rôle of John Weedon, the solicitor who was in turn election agent to Palmer, Oliveira, and Mills, and always seemed identified with measures calculated to ensure a contested election? A sum of £1,600 presumably passed through his hands on behalf of Mills in 1841; nearly as much perhaps on the earlier occasions. How far had he shared in the golden harvest of four contests in eleven years? How far, indeed, was it the interest of lawyers to promote contests from which as a class they invariably benefited? But above all personal factors such as these, the final consideration must be that Reading, a centre of whiggery and liberalism for many years, and solid for reform in 1831, had swelled with its two seats the national movement that put Sir Robert Peel into office in 1841. The motives that had led it into this essay in conservatism were many: superior organization, more money, more energy, and perhaps more unscrupulousness, on the part of the conservative party in the borough; the intensity of feeling in a rural area on the subject of the Corn Laws which was capable of affecting the county town: finally the divisions and weaknesses, almost the irresoluteness, of the liberals, and the defection of some

of their number to the other side. It should also be remembered
that Charles Russell, who represented the constituency at the
start and at the end of this period, was a reformer in 1831 and a
protectionist in 1841. The whirligig of time that put Grey into
power in 1830 and Peel in 1841 played tricks with representatives
as well as electors. Russell was probably not the only politician
who found it prudent to wear a reforming costume at the beginning of the thirties—and a perhaps equally theatrical protectionist garment ten and fifteen years later.

II. THE COUNTY OF BERKSHIRE

The county constituency, with a registered electorate in this
period of about 5,600, was five times as large as the biggest borough electorate and two and a half times as great as all four of the
county boroughs put together; though it returned only three
members to their aggregate of six. It was not of course purely
rural and agricultural in character. The small towns below the
dignity of the parliamentary boroughs—Maidenhead,Wokingham,
Newbury, Hungerford, Wantage, and Faringdon—constituted an
element in the county constituency that was socially if not always
politically different. Some of them, indeed, especially Maidenhead at the eastern end of the county, Newbury and Hungerford
in the west, had a reputation for political radicalism and religious
dissent. Yet for the most part it was the rural environment—the
flat water meadows, the rolling hill country and downland, the
spinneys, plantations and coverts of the game preserves, the
parsonage and hall, the corn-market and sheep fair—that dominated the outlook of the electorate. In the ordinary ephemeral
issues of politics the countryside as a whole was not greatly
interested. 'In the villages and in the agricultural districts', wrote
Walter in 1834, 'politics are less cared for and the party spirit
can hardly be said to exist.'[45]

Yet over the great issue of reform the Berkshire freeholders had
indeed been stirred. One of the county members, Robert Palmer,
though himself an opponent of the ministerial plan of reform, presented a petition in February 1831 from the gentry and freeholders of Berkshire praying for a 'national, fundamental, and
effectual reform', which had been approved by a county meeting
of the 'highest respectability'. He told the House, moreover, that

[45] Add. MS. 40405, fos. 24–5.

at the same meeting a resolution in favour of the ballot had been passed with only a few dissentient voices. Dundas, the other county member, concurred with Palmer's speech and said that the petition was supported by all parties and opinions. Of the general determination for reform there could be very little doubt; equally little of the motives which principally inspired it in this essentially rural constituency. The bulk of the electorate, in a county which Cobbett had frequently traversed and harangued, had come to agree with Cobbett's primary thesis that it was not the times, but the government, that was bad. Agricultural distress, the tithes, the return to cash payments in 1819, the fluctuations in the price of wheat, the misery of the unemployed labourers, and the slender working margin of the farmers, all in the end were attributable to the actual measures of the House of Commons. Thence came the disease; there must be applied the remedy. The population in the countryside, like that of the town, had been taught by a generation of radical criticism to believe that the troubles that beset society after the Napoleonic Wars were due to one thing only— misgovernment; and that only a reform of government could restore them their old prosperity. Old Charles Dundas, the whig, sitting in his eleventh parliament, now found himself, his constituents, and the government for once in accord. For his colleague, Robert Palmer, a tory who had sat for the county since 1825, the case was different. At the general election of 1831 he, like, Dundas, offered himself for re-election but in view of the opposition which he had presented to the reform bill, the county reformers brought forward a whig squire, Throckmorton, to contest the seat. This unusual and in normal circumstances unpopular .step was justified by the temper of the constituency. It was true that in reply to the county reform petition a *Berkshire Declaration* against the ministerial reform bill was issued by a number of leading landowners, including the Earl of Abingdon, Lord Barrington, Duffield, Philip Pusey, Blackstone of Wallingford, and William Mount of Wasing.[46] But whatever the sentiments among the upper crust of county society, the majority of farmers and freeholders were bent on reform. In their eyes the cause of parliamentary reform and the cause of agriculture were not only complementary but identical; and they could not be blind to the undoubted increase in agricultural representation which the

[46] *Reading Mercury*, 18 April 1831.

ministerial bill provided. In a public letter to the farmers of Berkshire, written over the telling pseudonym of *Speed the Plough*, this aspect of reform was firmly stressed.

> Some persons [the anonymous writer observed] are opposing Mr Throckmorton on the ground that as a Reformer, he is an enemy to the agricultural interest. Now let us see in what way the Reform Bill can be injurious to Agriculture. And, firstly, it gives an additional number of Members to the Counties—are County Members injurious to Agriculture? It gives Copy-Holders and Lease-holders of various descriptions the right of voting—are these descriptions of persons more hostile to agriculture than Freeholders?

And on polling day at Abingdon (where the county elections were held) Mr Blandy, in a speech supporting Dundas, spoke of the 'wise and salutary consideration for the agricultural interest' shown by the reform bill.[47]

But the decisive proof of the feeling in the county came at the election. On nomination day Robert Palmer announced his retirement from the contest. For this there was only one reason: the tide of public opinion which he found setting against him. In a subsequent letter to the county freeholders he frankly admitted the great volume of support for the reform bill. 'Many of those friends', he continued, 'who on all former occasions, had been my warmest supporters, distinctly stated that, owing to the opposition I gave to the Ministerial measure of reform, they could not conscientiously give me their support.'[48] The two reform candidates, now alone in their glory, went forward to a popular and undisputed election. It was a notable triumph for reform; it was not, however, a triumph for the whigs; and still less a triumph of one party over another. Indeed the whole subsequent development of politics, not only in Berkshire but in the country at large, is scarcely explicable if the Reform Act is regarded as a party victory. The Berkshire electorate, it could be said with little exaggeration, was ignorant of and indifferent to the claims of mere party allegiance. However mistaken in its motives and disappointed in its hopes, the reform movement was a genuine vindication of a principle. If the principle is to be associated with a party, it was in a truer sense the last successful demonstration of the old eighteenth-century 'country party' against the 'government' rather than a victory

---

[47] *Reading Mercury*, 2 May, 16 May 1831.   [48] *Ibid.*, 16 May.

of whig and radical over tory. The whigs certainly were in office; but they were there as the representatives of the mass of the British middle classes, rural as well as urban, pledged to amend the structure of government at a vital point. It was an index of this essentially 'country' feeling that the speeches of Dundas and Throckmorton at this election concentrated on a description of the miseries of the country under the rule of the old borough-mongering monopolists and by implication promised an end to these afflictions by a legal reform of parliament. There was little in their speeches of which Cobbett would not have approved, though Cobbett only a dozen years earlier had come under Dundas's censure as an incendiary. The temper that prevailed in Berkshire, as in most other agricultural counties at this time, was a simple non-party agricultural radicalism, directed not against nor on behalf of any one party, but against the whole system of government. But though the form which that protest took was radical and political, the impulse behind it was rural and economic. Reform of parliament and aid for agriculture did not seem incongruous things in 1831; and it was with perfect consistency that the county which voted for the reform bill under Grey opposed the abandonment of protection under Peel. Indeed the changes in the representation made in 1832 enabled the county to protest to greater effect against the repeal of the Corn Laws fourteen years later. Not without reason did the county reformers claim that in the agricultural areas the Reform Act would strengthen the agricultural cause. The real interest was how the politicians and the parties would adjust themselves to this basic and not very tractable political material.

Both the Berkshire members returned to the last parliament of the unreformed system were county landowners. Dundas had property in the south near Newbury; Throckmorton in the north at Buckland. Dundas, or Lord Amesbury as he had recently become, died in 1832. There was no direct heir; the title became extinct; and the property passed to Captain Dundas R.N. who had married Lord Amesbury's only child. Captain Dundas was little known in the county and had political ambitions elsewhere. In the first reformed parliament he was returned as whig member for Greenwich. The vacancy in the county representation left by Charles Dundas's elevation to the peerage was filled by the same Robert Palmer who had been virtually rejected by the electorate in 1831. This in itself was a less remarkable circumstance than might at first appear. By June 1832, the date of Palmer's return, the battle of the reform bill was over and the abnormal situation which had caused so many of Palmer's usual supporters to hang back no longer existed. In view of the inevitable dissolution of the 1831 parliament as soon as the details of the reformed constituencies were settled, there was little object in contesting Palmer's residuary right to so short a parliamentary term. It was only his views, not his person, that had incurred displeasure. Robert Palmer of Holme Park, Sonning, was connected with the same family of which Charles Fysshe Palmer was the nearest descendant. But he lacked the latter's traditional position in the county and the rise of his own branch of the family was a fairly recent achievement. His grandfather had made a considerable fortune as agent to the Duke of Bedford and towards the end of the eighteenth century had reverted to his ancestral origins by purchasing the manor of Sonning a few miles east of Reading. However, wealth, property, and a connexion with one of the older families in the county, formed a good foundation for a political career; and the grandson was elected member for the county constituency in 1825, 1826, 1830, and 1832.

In the first election under the reformed system Palmer and Throckmorton put up for re-election. Two other candidates appeared to contest the three seats that were now available. Both in their different ways were of more than local standing and importance; though that circumstance did not necessarily assist them in the county. The first was John Walter, the proprietor of *The Times* and owner of Bear Wood, a small estate in the eastern part of Berkshire. The second was Philip Pusey, a member of a branch of the Bouverie family that had assumed the surname of Pusey on inheriting the considerable estates of that family in north Berkshire.[49] It was Walter's first venture into politics, in a county in which he was as yet little known except through his connexion with the great newspaper he controlled. Pusey first entered parliament at a by-election for Rye in 1830, but was unseated on petition. He was elected for Chippenham at the general election of 1830 and for Cashel in 1831. From these boroughs of doubtful reputation he now turned at the age of

---

[49] He was the eldest son of the Hon. Philip Bouverie (half-brother to the 1st Earl of Radnor), and brother of Edward Pusey the Tractarian. In 1828 he succeeded to the family estates of some 5,000 acres.

thirty-three to the county in which he was so considerable a landowner. Pusey—politician, agriculturist, pamphleteer, the friend
of peers and statesmen—was better known and appreciated in
London than in the county of his residence. Moreover, his liberal,
individualistic views unsuited him for the harness of party, and
there was a strain of brilliance in him that was perhaps not much
to the liking of the ordinary Berkshire squires and fox-hunters.
At this time he was a Peelite; after 1846 he tended to follow Lord
John Russell. Though yielding to none in his devotion to agriculture, his reason and intelligence led him ultimately to believe
that free trade was inevitable and that its coming would not be
fatal and might even be salutary if farming was developed scienti-
fically and tenants given adequate protection for their improvements. But this was scarcely the kind of champion that was to
the taste of the more ignorant and prejudiced farmers and freeholders on whose votes the county member for Berkshire must
necessarily depend.

The rough party divisions were between Palmer and Pusey,
the conservatives, and Throckmorton and Walter, the reformers;
but party divisions were not particularly stressed and the main
argument centred round specific items of legislation. All four
men emphasized the importance of agriculture and all thought
it prudent to deny being in coalition with any of the others. It
was clear that the electorate at least liked to think that each
candidate came forward to be judged on his personal merits
without the cloak of party or alliance. In the speeches on nomination day, which were the final test of a candidate's position, the
important topics were tithes, Corn Laws, and slavery. On these
matters there was remarkably little difference of opinion between
the four candidates. All four wished to see an adjustment of tithe
that relieved the farmer without harming the Church. Three
were in favour of the immediate emancipation of the slaves;
Palmer alone expressed a sense of the difficulty involved. All were
in different ways protectionists. Throckmorton said he was not
opposed to the Corn Laws, though he would consider any reform
that would protect the farmer; Palmer promised to support the
existing law unless an equally efficient mode of protection were
devised; Pusey thought the scheme of a variable duty superior
to the fixed scale; Walter would support whatever the best judges
approved as the most effective protection for the agricultural

industry. With such a large unanimity among the opposing candidates, personal and territorial influences no doubt decided the election. The sitting members, Palmer and Throckmorton, were re-elected with a heavy majority, and Walter beat Pusey by forty votes for third place.[50]

The details of the poll were not without some interesting features. All the candidates obtained striking support in the districts where they resided. Palmer, in the Reading district; Throckmorton and Pusey, in the Faringdon district, were at the head of the poll. Walter shared the Wokingham district, in which his property lay, with Palmer, whose estate was just outside it. The ties of property and local connexion were clearly very strong. But there were indications of another kind of influence. The Newbury and Maidenhead districts, containing two of the largest non-parliamentary boroughs and noted for their radical dissenting strength, voted heavily in favour of the liberal candidates, Throckmorton and Walter, and were the only areas in which the two reformers were together at the top of the poll. Walter made no secret of the kind of support to which he believed he owed his return. 'With a few splendid individual exceptions', he stated in a public letter after the election, 'I owe little to that order which calls itself or is considered, the aristocracy of Berkshire. The middle and industrious classes . . . are they to whom I feel myself most sensibly indebted for the eminent though arduous station to which I have been raised.'[51] Walter's election, though not a social revolution, was certainly something of a social invasion. He was not a typical country squire; he was a relative newcomer to the county; he was, as the *Berkshire Chronicle* disparagingly observed, 'without an acre of cultivated land or a single tenant'. His two proposers on nomination day had been Sir Francis Burdett and Fysshe Palmer, the Reading member, neither of whom were the type of county landowner who usually performed these services for the county candidates. Against Throckmorton, the whig, there had been far less animosity displayed by the conservative opposition; only his association with Walter had been deplored. Walter, on the other hand, had resentments of his own. In his speech immediately after the declaration of the poll he hinted strongly at the influence and intimidation that had been

[50] *Berkshire Chronicle*, 22 December 1832.
[51] *Windsor Express*, 22 December 1832.

brought to bear against him. Narrow as the margin was, however, he had got in at his first attempt.

Thus the conservatives, as they had already begun to call themselves in Berkshire, obtained only one of the three county seats. At the next election the situation was more favourable. A committee under the chairmanship of an influential landowner, Benyon de Beauvoir, was early in the field on the side of Palmer and Pusey; and both those candidates issued public statements stressing the support they had given and would continue to give to the cause of agriculture. Palmer asserted that he had frequently assisted the efforts of Lord Chandos to force the subject on the attention of the government and had voted five times in the previous parliament for the reduction or repeal of the malt tax. Pusey's address was to much the same effect. He advocated the repeal of the malt tax and assessed taxes, and their substitution by some kind of property tax. Both stressed their attachment to the established Church and opposition to any encroachment on its essential rights. Walter, who again put up, was in a more equivocal position. By the end of 1834 *The Times* had completed its transition from the whigs to the conservatives. The political movement of its proprietor had followed in a similar orbit; and in 1835 Walter offered himself to the county of Berkshire as a Peelite reformer. In an open letter to his constituents he pointed out that he was not a party man but a reformer; that the new ministry was more capable than the whigs of carrying through reform measures because it would meet with less obstruction in parliament; but that he would only support the conservatives if they were also reformers. It was not, he concluded, he that had gone over to the conservatives, but they had come over to him. On the great question of agriculture that agitated his constituency more perhaps than abstract discussions of party connexions, he said he favoured the repeal of the malt tax and a fixed duty on corn. This change of allegiance was not unnatural; Walter was never a whig. But the county whigs equally naturally resented it and a fierce altercation broke out between themselves and their former ally which still further consolidated the position of the conservatives.

Throckmorton, the sitting whig, retired unexpectedly and abruptly on the eve of the election. In his place, and with his assistance, came forward Captain Dundas, the son-in-law of the old Berkshire member. At the previous election Dundas had given his influence in Berkshire, for what it was worth, to Throckmorton and Walter. He was therefore vexed, somewhat unreasonably, at finding the coalition dissolved in 1835. But Walter himself had reason for dissatisfaction. Throckmorton, though acting as his colleague in 1832, had concealed from him his intention to resign in 1835; and after his resignation, according to the reports of Walter's election agents, he instructed his tenants and followers to vote against Walter despite the fact that his share of the joint expenses of 1832 was still unpaid. Walter accepted the clear implication of this situation and in turn canvassed against the new whig candidate. This brought an irate protest from Dundas. An explanation from Walter failed to placate him; and finally, after an exchange of views, Walter made public the correspondence that had passed between them, including the final threat from Dundas that 'I was mainly instrumental with my brother reformers in seating you for Berks in 1832 and I shall now do my best to turn you out.'[52] Walter's position was obviously endangered. He had broken with the whigs; he was not yet identified with the conservatives; he could not be sure how far the liberal middle-class elements in the constituency would approve of the line he had taken. He thought it prudent at least to make use of the powerful channels of influence now open to him.

The correspondence between Dundas and Walter took place in the last week of December. At the very end of the month Barnes, the editor of *The Times*, wrote an anxious letter to Lyndhurst regarding Walter's prospects in Berkshire and enclosed a list (which could hardly have come from anyone but Walter himself) of influential persons in the county whose interest it was of importance to secure.[53] Lyndhurst communicated with Peel; and the prime minister, breaking his usual rule of never intervening in an individual election, wrote on 1 January 1835, both to Sir Herbert Taylor, the king's secretary, and to the Duke of Wellington, on Walter's behalf. The former he asked to use his influence with the Windsor clergy, 'to make them favourably disposed towards Palmer, Pusey, and then Walter, in preference to Dundas'. Taylor promised to write to the vicar of Windsor and two or three other active and influential persons; but he added that the chapter was generally absent and had little local

---

[52] *Berkshire Chronicle*, 10 January 1835.   [53] See Appendix F, The 'Berkshire List' 1835.

interest.[54] On the same day Peel wrote to the duke. 'Can you', he inquired, 'do anything from your neighbourhood to, and knowledge of, Berkshire with any of the persons in the enclosed list in favour of Palmer and Pusey and then Walter.' The relegation of the original subject of the letter to third place in the favours of the influential was a noticeable detail in both communications; and Wellington carried the process of elimination still further. 'I return your Berkshire list', he wrote a few days later. 'I can do something with Dr Winter of St John's College, Oxford, and with Lord Downshire, I think for all excepting Walter. Walter and his friends in Berks have been very troublesome in their opposition to Lord Downshire's views, and I am afraid that he would not listen to an application to support Walter. But I'll try.'[55] It was as well for Walter's peace of mind and the maintenance of cordial relations between *The Times* and the government that he was unaware of the use to which his list was ultimately put. But as it happened he suffered no disadvantage. Dundas, convinced by his preliminary canvass that he had no chance of success, retired from the contest and allowed his three rivals the luxury of an unchallenged return.

All that remained was the pageantry and the speech-making. On nomination day the candidates rode into Abingdon, the ancient county capital that still retained the right of staging the county elections, attended as the custom was by their followers. The cavalcade of yeomen and farmers who attended Palmer and Pusey contrasted conspicuously with the strings of coaches and other vehicles that clattered out from the towns to support Walter. The proposing and seconding of the candidates was a matter of routine, and if the speeches tended to revolve round the question of agriculture, that in itself was no new thing. Only one voice was raised to point out that without even a contest the county was drifting into the anti-reform camp. This belonged to Marsh, a well-known Berkshire freeholder, who in a racy and popular speech lamented the decline in the reforming spirit of the county and observed half-humorously that they were now returning two conservatives and a tory reformer. The three members, who had

---

[54] Add. MS. 40302, fos. 131–3; see the *History of 'The Times'*, 1, 345.

[55] Add. MS. 40310, fos. 3, 5. St John's College had taken a leading part in securing Wellington's election as chancellor of the university in 1834. Wellington's seat at Stratfield Saye was a bare dozen miles south of Reading on the Berkshire border and Lord Downshire, at Easthampstead Park, Wokingham, was thus a not too distant neighbour.

all given ample assurance of their fidelity to agriculture, were
chiefly concerned to place themselves in a liberal light. Palmer
defined himself as a Peelite reformer and quoted the recently
published *Tamworth Manifesto*. Walter referred to the constant
communication he had maintained with his constituents on all
public questions. Pusey stated that he was returned not as a mere
partisan, but as one simply anxious to give the government a fair
trial. Walter, changing with a changing world, had no doubt
mollified much of the original feeling against him. A significant
letter from him, published after the election, declared that while
as in 1832 he was chiefly obliged to the 'middle and industrious
classes' for his return, there had been witnessed on the present
occasion 'a new and increasing friendship on the part of the clergy
and of the county aristocracy' which he hailed as a sign of the
growing amity among the various classes of society.[56] Perhaps
Taylor's letter to the vicar of Windsor and the Duke of Wellington's influence with Lord Downshire had not been without
effect.

Indeed, it was not Walter but the whig gentry and the middle
classes that were stranded between the two parties. Faced with
the opposition of the tory rural party and unable to wrest from
Walter the towns and the dissenters, Dundas had done nothing
but harm by his abortive candidature. The *Reading Mercury*, the
leading liberal newspaper in the county, had warned him of the
folly of his quarrel with Walter. The people, wrote the paper,
knew Walter as a tried friend of reform; of Dundas they knew
little and that little, as a result of the Bucklebury enclosure bill,
was unfavourable.[57] This reference to Dundas's previous activities
is interesting. With so little ostensible difference between the
candidates who competed so amiably on the hustings for their
votes, and with party distinctions deliberately kept in the background, the Berkshire electors who took their politics seriously
could only judge their men by what they did in parliament. It
was their conduct there that revealed their true political character
and decided to some extent at least their relationship with the
county.

Pusey for instance was a representative who though passing as a
conservative could not be defined by any party formula and was
not elected on mere party grounds. In March 1835, despite his

[56] *Berkshire Chronicle*, 17 January 1835.   [57] *Reading Mercury*, 5 January 1835.

repeated professions of attachment to the agricultural interest, he had assisted Peel's ministry by voting against the repeal of the malt tax. There was some grumbling even then from the Berkshire agriculturalists—enough at least for the king himself to express a hope to Peel that Pusey would not be induced to resign merely because the vote he had given was at variance with the feelings of part of his constituency.[58] But his fault then was on the side of party discipline even if not very congenial to the supporters of that party. Some of his subsequent activities were neither partisan nor agricultural. Not only did he support the Poor Law Amendment Act but he voted with the whigs on the Irish Church bill of 1835. For this he had to face the indignation not only of the Carltonians but of his constituents. Indeed, in view of the opposition of many of his usual supporters in the county to his conduct, he wrote to the chairman of his election committee, Benyon de Beauvoir, offering his resignation. But Benyon replied in the true vein of the independent country gentleman, expressing the hope that he would remain in his seat as his friends would wish him to retain his opinions unfettered until he should have an opportunity of explaining them in the natural course of events at a general election.[59] This personal independence of Pusey cut across all party lines and secured him a similar general, non-party support in the county at the next election. In 1837 the conservatives made no opposition to his return—no doubt the influence of such men as Benyon de Beauvoir was enough to secure that—and the liberals not unjustifiably were able to claim him as a virtual representative of themselves. A meeting of the liberal county electors was held shortly before the election in July 1837 and it was decided to sound Pusey on three specific points: Irish tithes, Irish municipal reform, and the question of Church rates. Charles Eyston, the whig Catholic squire of East Hendred, announced that if Pusey failed to give satisfaction on these topics, he would come forward himself as liberal candidate for the county. Pusey, however, came in person to a subsequent liberal meeting, gave satisfactory answers on the first two points and approved the principle of the third. The assembly then declared itself perfectly satisfied with his attitude and resolved that there would be no need for Eyston to come forward.[60]

[58] Add. MS. 40303, fo. 67.   [59] *Windsor Express*, 1 August 1835.
[60] *Reading Mercury*, 22 July 1837.

Walter was another Berkshire member who pursued an individual line of policy in the House of Commons, the ultimate failure of which reacted keenly on his political career in the county. As befitted the proprietor of *The Times* he led that cross-party attack on the new Poor Law which was a curious blend of genuine humanitarianism, the prejudice of country gentry against the bureaucrat, and the party animus of the conservatives against the whigs. Walter had already given proof of his tory-democratic sympathies when in 1834 he had successfully opposed a bill introduced by Robert Palmer and supported by Throckmorton to enclose Bucklebury Common, a tract of gorse and bracken lying between Reading and Newbury. In the sessions of 1836 and 1837 came Walter's main effort, the attack on the Poor Law Amendment Act of 1834. That campaign ended in failure and at the following general election Walter surprised both his friends and his opponents in Berkshire by announcing his retirement from politics. In a public letter to his constituents he acknowledged that there were other reasons besides the pressure of business and the decline in his health. Experience had taught him, he wrote, that the Reform Act had done little that was advantageous either with respect to the composition of the House of Commons or of the ministry or to the despatch of important public business. His chief reason for withdrawing from his seat was his 'dissatisfaction with the present state of the House of Commons, as an assembly brought together for advancing the real interests of the people, or as a system of machinery through which any independent and disinterested man, unfettered and therefore unsupported by party, can hope for clear, fair, and impartial justice in his exertions for what he conceives to be the public good'.[61] The ground of his complaint and the tone of disillusionment in which it was couched are deeply revealing. It was the spirit of the pessimistic radicals of 1835 and 1837. Optimistically and unrealistically they had hoped for much from a new parliament based on a new electorate. By 1837, because it had done neither what they wished nor what they expected, the radicals were ready to condemn both.

Unperturbed by Walter's retirement Berkshire politics entered once more on the familiar but perennially exciting routine of a general election. In his place the conservatives put forward

[61] *Reading Murcery*, 8 July 1837.

Lord Barrington[62] of Becket House in north Berks, an influential landowner and chairman of the quarter sessions, who was supported by an impressive list of gentry, clergy, and other electors. The substitution of a tory of the first water for the humanitarian figure of John Walter was unpleasant for liberal circles in the county which had hitherto indulged in the pleasant luxury of allowing their opponents to return two candidates of whom they themselves approved. But the attempts made to secure a liberal candidate to contest the county showed how completely the initiative had been let pass into the hands of the conservatives. The *Reading Mercury* appealed in a leading article for some liberal gentleman of the county—Mr Goodlake of Letcombe Regis, Mr Clayton East of Hall Place, or Mr Dundas—to stand as candidate. There was clearly considerable sentiment in favour of a liberal move; the difficulty was to secure a candidate. Whether because the handful of liberal squires were unable to stand the cost of election; or whether, as is equally likely, they were unwilling to put themselves forward without substantial approval and support from the body of landowners in the county, the liberal electors found it impossible to find a candidate. A requisition was made to Clayton East to stand but he refused, as he afterwards said, on account of 'prudential motives connected with his own family'. Nomination day arrived with only three candidates in view and another uncontested election seemed inevitable. After their names had been formally proposed, however, Henry Marsh, the liberal freeholder who had spoken on nomination day in 1835, made another humorous, satirical speech, bantering Lord Barrington in particular, and ended by proposing Clayton East. A seconder was found and the election therefore went to the poll. Marsh's action was taken entirely on his own initiative. He had informed Clayton East of his intention shortly beforehand and the latter, unable to dissuade him, had left the hall before the business of nomination commenced. He explained afterwards that he could not by his presence seem to countenance the proposal but on the other hand he felt it his duty not to interfere with the right of the county liberals to express their political convictions. He himself had in fact merely gone over to Abingdon to support Pusey.

[62] William Keppel Barrington, Viscount Barrington in the Irish peerage, was a descendant of the ancient family of Shute which in the early eighteenth century had become possessed by inheritance of the extensive property near Shrivenham, Berks, of the Wildman family. He had succeeded to the title in 1829, and at the time of his election was forty-four years old.

The result of an election contested in such a manner was almost foregone. Palmer and Barrington, the orthodox conservatives, headed the poll. Pusey, who in a frank speech from the hustings had told the electors that he could not act with satisfaction to himself or to them unless his opinions were free, was beaten into third place by a margin of less than fifty votes. Clayton East, the candidate *malgré lui* was left behind at the foot of the poll. But his polling figures, though only half that of Palmer and a thousand votes behind Pusey, were not without significance. He had been brought into the contest unannounced, and as was known at the time, against his will. There was no canvassing on his behalf, no organization, no expenditure of money by his party. There were no conveyances to take his supporters to the polling stations; no shelter or refreshment for them when they arrived. At Wokingham there was not even a poll-clerk in the liberal interest. He had publicly disclaimed all responsibility for Marsh's action. Yet with all those adverse circumstances he polled 1,300 votes—most of which were plumpers—and in the Newbury area he had headed the poll. It was strikingly evident that there was a great reserve of liberal feeling in the county constituency largely unexploited and unexpressed.[63] A whig or liberal country gentleman, working on that feeling, backed by some territorial or family influence, and making some concessions to the special agricultural interest, might well have secured a place in the county representation. But no liberal candidate stepped forward from the solid social caste of the country gentry. There was only one John Walter; Charles Eyston, the best known of the whig landowners and in all other circumstances the ideal liberal candidate, was handicapped by the fact of being a Roman Catholic; and so the Berkshire liberals were stultified for want of a leader. It was not so much that the county constituency, including as it did tradesmen, craftsmen, dissenters, and small towns, was impenetrably conservative, as that the county was controlled for ordinary political purposes by a small unified class in which social and personal considerations were probably dominant. The formation of a conservative association for the county in the autumn of 1837 assisted perhaps not merely to increase the control of the country gentry over the county electorate but to harden that control into a party and parliamentary

[63] *Reading Mercury*, 5 August, 12 August 1837; *Berkshire Chronicle*, 8 July, 22 July, 5 August 1837.

mould. Yet at the time when Victoria came to the throne the primary consideration was still the social and personal position of the candidates; their political views, though important, were only secondary. On the one side this is shown by the diversity of views exhibited by such men as Palmer, Pusey, and Throckmorton; on the other by the independence which the first two at least, though in different ways, displayed towards their professed party and leader.

Nearly all these aspects were implicit in the election of 1841. Although devoid of incident, that in itself was highly significant. It was the first county election since the Reform Act in which three regular conservative candidates were given an undisputed return and it was the quietest of the four. Palmer, Pusey, and Barrington, the sitting members, stood once more for the county and in the absence of any opposition were duly elected. The election issue was clearly the Corn Laws and the whig policy of a fixed duty. All three candidates delivered speeches on nomination day stressing the importance of agricultural protection and, even more pointedly, acknowledging that as the representatives of an agricultural constituency they must consider the interests of their constituents and protect in parliament the cause of agriculture. In accordance with the custom which treated nomination day as a licensed occasion for the expression of all shades of county feeling, the high sheriff then asked whether any other elector wished to address the meeting. Charles Eyston, who had played an influential part on the liberal side at every election since 1830, then made what was the most illuminating and in many respects the most interesting speech of the day. He began by expressing his pleasure that no one had come forward to offer a vexatious opposition to the noble lord and his two colleagues which could have no reasonable chance of success. At the last election there had been an ill-advised attempt which could not have failed to end as it did; and though his political convictions obliged him to support the unsuccessful candidate, he had deprecated the contest and had had no hand in its promotion. Having thus paid a compliment to the essentially neighbourly feeling of his class, he then went on to utter some thoughts on the Corn Laws which perhaps struck a responsive note in some of his fellow gentry though they could scarcely have been to the taste of the farmers in his audience. On the matter of protection, the real topic of the day, he admitted that the whig fixed duty of 8*s.* a quarter was generally recognized as inadequate; yet, 'he thought the time had arrived when the Corn Laws should be fairly and dispassionately discussed; for looking at the two years passed, 1839, and 1840, prices had been undoubtedly too high for the consumer'. In general, he continued, as wide a freedom of intercourse as possible with other countries was desirable and the whole question of the Corn Laws needed examination. As for the Poor Law (on account of which Lord Barrington as chairman of the Board of Guardians had come in for a few hisses when he rose to speak), he considered that it had brought benefit especially where administered in the proper spirit.[64]

This was not the only indication during the 1841 election that some at least of the Berkshire gentry were not carried away by the unreflecting championship of the Corn Laws that characterized the bulk of the agricultural electors. Lord Radnor, whose seat at Coleshill made him one of the few resident peers of the county, sent a letter to the *Reading Mercury*, published on 21 June, raising two fundamental questions capable of destroying the whole case for protection. Were the Corn Laws, he asked in the first place, really efficacious in providing protection for agriculture? And secondly, was agriculture really in need of protection? One may wonder how far these pregnant heresies were echoed in the mind of his kinsman, Philip Pusey, one of the great exponents in the mid-nineteenth century of the scientific farming which was the answer to protectionism, and who shortly before his re-election for Berkshire in 1841 had become president of the Royal Agricultural Society.

But whatever the private thoughts of some of the landed gentry, there were no reservations in the minds of the rural electorate either in 1841 or, more ominously, in 1846. It was on 22 January 1846, the first day of the assembly of parliament, that Peel announced his intention to reduce the duty on corn to a few shillings and ultimately to abolish it entirely. On 29 January a meeting took place of the Hungerford and Newbury branch of the Berkshire association for the protection of agriculture. This meeting called for a general gathering, fixed for 5 February, of all those interested in the defence of agricultural protection. That was a Thursday. On the following Saturday, 31 January, being the day of the corn-market in Reading, a large number of farmers and some squires were present during the forenoon in the county town

[64] *Reading Mercury*, 10 July 1841.

and feeling ran so high over the Peel proposal that it was finally decided to hold a protest meeting the same afternoon. The mayor lent them the use of the council chamber and one of the county M.P.s was present. This was Palmer, who explained that he had come down to Reading that day in order to consult with his agricultural friends on the course to be adopted towards the government's declared policy. In a carefully phrased and non-committal speech he said that he was of course aware in general of the views of the constituency on the subject of protection but he now wished specifically to know whether the action of the prime minister and the arguments with which it had been accompanied had affected their earlier views. If, he concluded, they were still opposed to any tampering with the Corn Laws, they might perhaps express their opinion in a formal resolution. 'He had only one object in view, viz. to represent as far as he was able the feelings and opinions of those who sent him to Parliament.'

Of the reality of the last sentiment there can be little doubt. Not only was it a repetition of what the county members had said on the hustings five years before, but the whole tenor of Palmer's speech left it open to the meeting to accept Peel's change of policy or at any rate to modify the uncompromising protectionism which had seemed so safe in 1841. If that had been Palmer's private hope, it was decisively shattered. One or two squires and several farmers spoke in succession and at the end there was no room for mistaking the temper of the meeting. One farmer spoke of their assembly as 'the spontaneous effort of farmers who were aware of their dangerous position'; another of the 'atrocious' measure of Sir Robert Peel; and it was Duffield of Marcham Park, late member for Abingdon, who finally proposed a resolution, which was passed by acclamation, condemning the government's proposal as calculated to ruin the agricultural industry. If further evidence was needed it came at the meeting on 5 February of the Newbury and Hungerford branch of the agricultural protection society, presided over by William Mount of Wasing and attended by a large number of farmers and gentry. It was a renewal of the Reading meeting and the most cutting and characteristic speech came from a well-known Berkshire farmer by the name of Job Lousley who said of Peel in words that typified the attitude of most protectionists from Bentinck down to the humblest tenant, 'the farmers had brought him up, nourished him, and supported him all along, and now he

turns round and gives them such a bite as they never had before'.[65]
In a subsequent speech in the House of Commons Palmer stressed
the solidarity of protectionist feeling in the county as attested by
numerous public meetings. Tradesmen as well as agriculturalists,
tenants as well as proprietors, all believed that their prosperity
depended on the Corn Laws.[66]

It was in deference to this attitude that not one of the three
Berkshire county members were to be found among the 112
conservatives who voted with whigs and radicals to give Peel leave
to bring in the repeal bill. All three voted with the protectionist
minority. Yet it would be unsafe to assume that all three were
inveterate protectionists. Pusey certainly was not; his vote on
27 February was largely a token of his duty towards his constituents.
He abstained from voting in the other two critical divisions arising
from the second and third reading of the bill.[67] Even Palmer, if
one may speculate on the evidence of the Reading meeting, might
have been prepared to compromise had he seen signs of compromise
in his constituency. If one thing is clear in this analysis of Berkshire politics it is that though the country gentry ruled the county,
they were not its despots. As a class they showed an extraordinary
cohesion which made the party barriers that loomed so high at
Westminster or in the clubs shrink to relative insignificance in the
market town, the sessions-room, or the hunting-field. Where
rivalries and animosities occurred they were usually over personal
and ephemeral issues. But the country gentlemen were not living
in isolation and the impulses which came to them from below were
perhaps as important as the influence they could exert down-
wards. They, for the most part, selected the parliamentary
candidates from among their own number; but it was the constituency, even in an uncontested election, which shaped and coloured
much of the county member's views. It would be going to extremes
to say that if the squirearchy made the county members, the electors
made their opinions. But no view of county society is tenable that
does not recognize the great force of public opinion in a county like

---

[65] *Reading Mercury*, 31 January, 7 February 1846.   [66] *Hansard*, LXXXIII, 1100 sqq.

[67] Together with his other two colleagues Pusey was re-elected without opposition
in 1847. It is significant for the relative importance of corn and religion in the minds of
the electors that when, in 1852, Vansittart drove him out of the county representation,
it was primarily on the issue of Pusey's support for the Maynooth bill and his brother's
connexion with Tractarianism. Cf. Bonham's remark to Peel over the fortunes of the
Peelites in the general election of 1847. ' "Maynooth" has certainly destroyed several
of our friends. "Free Trade" hardly any.' (Add. MS. 40599, fo. 122.)

Berkshire where there were no great landed magnates to limit or distort the relatively free expression of the rural electorate. The tendency of the landed gentry was in fact to dampen controversy and avoid vexatious contests. But when the county electorate was moved, it could impose its will. That will, however, was not necessarily a reflection of conventional party politics. In 1831 the Berkshire electors returned two whigs to support Grey; in 1841 three conservatives to support Peel; and in 1846 used their strength to oppose Peel. On all three occasions it was not party feeling but a vigorous and unselfconscious country feeling that impelled them. To this feeling the country gentry bowed at the time of the reform bill; it is a matter of some interest how many of them were bowing to the storm in 1846. Clearly if the gentry had been their own masters in 1831 there would have been no Reform Act; it is at least possible that had they been similarly unencumbered in 1846 there might not have occurred the disruption of the conservative party.

It might not have been lost on the contemporary observer that the political vicissitudes in the county of Berkshire reflected the general trend of parliamentary history between 1832 and 1846. In 1832 the Berkshire M.P.s were mainly whig; in 1841 mainly conservative. A tory squire sat for Abingdon; another for Wallingford. The county town of Reading, that had sent two reformers to the House of Commons in 1831, 1832, and again in 1837, provided the conservatives with two seats in 1841. The county constituency, that elected two whigs in 1831, returned three conservatives only six years later. Equally significantly Berkshire followed the majority of the House of Commons in accepting Grey in 1831, and Peel in 1841; and in rejecting Peel in 1846. Indeed, excluding the members for Windsor, only one Berkshire M.P. supported Peel over the issue of the Corn Laws and he was a stranger to the county, sitting as a ministerial nominee in a quasi-pocket borough. The county was almost solidly reforming in 1831 and almost solidly protectionist in the forties. Part of the explanation consists in the differences between the two parties. The liberals by 1841 lacked unity, leadership and the sense of purpose that had characterized them in 1831. The conservatives on the other hand appeared to be superior in organization; they bore the imprint of coherent leadership; and they had a vigour and urgency that was absent among their opponents. Part of the explanation is the effect of the

Reform Act which in the agricultural districts strengthened the country gentry and the farming interest as a whole by providing a more direct and enlarged representation. Abingdon, Wallingford, and the third county seat, in their post-1832 form constituted a reinforcement of the rural political interest which the accidental presence of Thesiger in the 1844–6 period only temporarily weakened. But beyond all these considerations was the even more fundamental circumstance that the changes in the political constellation of the county occurred primarily because the issues placed before the electorate had themselves altered. It was not that substantial numbers of the electors had changed from whig to conservative, though perhaps some had; but that in judging successive issues by the touchstone of its own interests and prejudices the electorate gave verdicts that in the early years of the decade happened to favour the whigs and in the latter years the conservatives. But party was still only a vague and half-recognized element in Berkshire provincial politics. It existed as a division in the electorate but it was no more and possibly less important than the other divisions, that for example between Church and dissent, or between town and country, or between the personal attractions of individual candidates. Interest, class, religion, personalities— these rather than party loyalties were the ingredients of local politics.

Part III
DIRECTION FROM ABOVE

Chapter Twelve
'GOVERNMENT' BOROUGHS

FOR a system of influence to survive in politics, two constituent elements were necessary. In the first place the means of influencing persons had to be present; in the second place opinion at large had to sanction or at least tolerate the employment of those means. Patronage that created humiliation or disgust was neither efficient nor durable. These considerations were particularly relevant to the use of government patronage in specific constituencies. An arbitrary use of influence by an individual borough-owner only involved his own reputation and perhaps that of the member he returned. When exerted by the government it involved not only some of the leading politicians of the day but the whole credit of the executive. If public opinion was tender on the question of jobbery, coercion, and improper interference in the sphere of personal rights, the executive even less than the borough magnate could afford to bring down criticism on its use of power.

In the fifty years that had elapsed between Burke's Place Act of 1782 and the Reform Act of 1832 both the ability of the government to affect the course of elections and the assumption that it should endeavour to do so had suffered a steady erosion.[1] But the change in the 'climate of opinion' on such matters was at least as important as the actual reduction in the means of influence. Even after the reform bill there remained methods whereby the government of the day could take a hand in elections. But these methods were severely circumscribed by the alteration in the attitude towards them not only of the general public but also of many leading politicians on both sides. The campaign for greater efficiency, economy, and purity in the public service was waged by the leaders of all parties as well as by public opinion and the press. Even before the first reformed election Sir James Graham, whose administration at the Admiralty forms a landmark in the history of governmental development in the nineteenth century, was

[1] See Mr Foord's article on 'The Waning of "The Influence of the Crown"' (*E.H.R.*, LXII, 484 sqq.)

refusing to use his patronage to reward the supporters of the so-called 'dockyard M.P.s'.

> If [he wrote in September 1832] I had opposed an objection on the ground of political inexpediency, and of an election quarrel, in my opinion I should have betrayed my duty, and been false to those liberal principles which we profess. . . . If I am swayed by other motives, in the difficult and odious task of distributing patronage, I should be altogether unworthy of the office which I hold. . . . I cannot refuse rewards which past services render due to officers who may oppose you; nor can I give promotion solely on the score of relationship to an editor of a newspaper who supports you. [And the next day he wrote] all promotion in the Dockyards will henceforth be given as the reward of merit, on the recommendation of the Admiral Superintendent. As patronage I have ceased to exercise it.[2]

It is true that the battle was only joined, not won. Graham incurred the same reproaches from the whigs for alienating friends and conceding to enemies that Peel was later to hear from the tories. The patronage secretary wrote to acquaint him with the 'murmurs of your friends and the jeers of the enemy', and begged him pathetically to endeavour, when fresh vacancies should arise, 'to discover meritorious individuals of our own caste to fill them'. But the practice and example of such men could not be without their effect; and the area of influence and the choice of means continued to shrink after the Reform Act as they had been shrinking in the half-century before. Nevertheless, the government possessed and exercised certain methods of influencing parliamentary elections.

Actual Treasury funds, in spite of a popular belief to the contrary, were probably not used for this end. After 1832 various sources of money capable of being used for this purpose had been withdrawn from the control of the government and it is most unlikely that the party in office diverted the secret service funds to finance their own elections.[3] To the suspicious nose of a radical reformer or the prejudiced one of a partisan, the name secret service still breathed a tainted air; but in this matter popular belief had long been overtaken by events and no politician who knew anything of the inner workings of the executive paid any heed to such anachronistic charges. There was an interesting illustration of

---

[2] Parker, *Graham*, I, 162–4.
[3] See Aspinall, 'English Party Organisation' (*E.H.R.*, XLI, 401–2), for a discussion of this subject mainly in the period before 1832.

this in the House of Commons not long after the passage of the Reform Act. In the course of an inquiry into an otherwise unconnected matter a committee of the House elicited the fact that during the general election of 1831 Edward Ellice, being at that date secretary to the Treasury, had received an application for financial assistance on behalf of the liberal candidates at Colchester and that a sum of £500 had been sent down for their use. The circumstances being immediately reported to the House of Commons, an explanation was naturally demanded and obtained. From his seat in the House Ellice admitted that in the 1831 election the reform party, like its opponents, had received subscriptions for election purposes. He himself had been charged with the general arrangements for the election, not in his official capacity but 'simply as an humble individual most anxious for the success of that great constitutional principle for which they were contending', and in consequence was habitually consulted on the disposal of election funds. It was true that he had caused £500 to be advanced for the promotion of the liberal contest at Colchester and indeed he acknowledged that he had been the instrument for the apportioning of the liberal election funds throughout the country. In making that confession he was content to leave his conduct to the judgement of the House. 'After what he had stated', he said in conclusion, 'he thought it quite unnecessary to add, that not one single shilling of the fund had been contributed from the public money.' A short discussion followed. Hume, whose zeal for the purity of public finance would hardly have allowed him to be partial in such a matter, expressed himself satisfied that the £500 had not come from government money. Rigby Wason, a barrister and liberal member for Ipswich, introduced a sour note by observing parenthetically that it was perfectly clear that the government in recent elections had been in the habit of assisting candidates of their own side and that one advantage of their present discussion was that it would draw the attention of parliament to the need for discontinuing or reducing the secret service money. This innuendo from a ministerialist brought an immediate rejoinder from the opposition benches. Sir Henry Hardinge, the Peninsular War veteran, announced that having held office on several occasions[4] he felt he must say, upon his honour, 'that he

---

[4] Hardinge had been successively Clerk of the Ordnance, Secretary at War, and Chief Secretary for Ireland, between 1823 and 1830.

had never known a single instance of the public money having been applied in the way alluded to by the hon. gentleman who had just spoken', and asserted his complete satisfaction with Ellice's statement. This evidently was the general feeling of the House and there was no real support for a suggested committee of inquiry.[5]

Nevertheless, the 'Secret Service' tradition died hard. In a debate in 1842 on the secret service grant a Mr Williams moved a reduction of that part expended by the Home Department on the grounds that there was a general impression in the minds of the public that it was employed for electioneering purposes. Graham whose integrity can no more be doubted than that of Hume or Hardinge, rose to say that 'the hon. gentleman was labouring under a great error in supposing that the Secret Service money was expended for electioneering purposes. For the last three years no Secret Service money had been voted for the Home Department.' Palmerston confirmed the denial and assured the House that 'no part of the Secret Service money was applied to electioneering purposes'.[6] The statements of these eminent politicians, both whig and tory, cannot be dismissed without more evidence than has yet been produced. But even if the home secret service fund had been drawn upon, its effect would scarcely have been noticeable on the result of a general election. The total sums granted for the whole secret service in the period 1833–5, for example, were as follows:

$$
\begin{array}{ll}
1833 & £39,400 \\
1834 & £37,000 \\
1835 & £36,800
\end{array}
$$

Of this not very lavish sum the part set aside for domestic use was

Home Secret Service	*Irish Secret Service*
1833 £10,000	£21,000
1834 £10,000	£15,000
1835 £10,000	£9,000 [7]

In view of the immense expenditure on elections in this period, the annual home secret service fund, even if entirely devoted to electioneering, would have been almost negligible in its effects, and

[5] *Hansard*, xxv, 284, 298–302; *Annual Register*, 1834 (History), 315–18.
[6] *Hansard*, lxv, 182.   [7] P.P. 1835, xxxvii, 155; 1840, xxix, 693.

certainly not worth the risk of exposure in its use. But there is no reason to suppose that it was so used.

There were, however, other and more legitimate ways of exerting government influence besides a crude misappropriation of public funds. There existed certain government boroughs, that is to say, constituencies usually at seaports or garrison towns, where the presence of barracks, dockyards, depots, and packet-stations formed the permanent basis for an 'influence' of the usual kind with the one difference that it was under the control of a department of State. Despite the spread of reforming ideas and the example of such ministers as Graham, there can be no doubt that the power of the government was strong in these constituencies and was generally recognized by the public at large. The government department almost solely connected with this kind of electoral influence was the Admiralty. This was partly due to the size of the home dockyard establishments. In 1853, for example, the financial vote for wages for the home establishment was £683,600 and the total number of men employed 9,653. In the thirties and forties both sets of figures were probably higher since certain economies had been effected after 1846.[8] But it was also due to the concentration of the home establishment in a relatively small number of towns. The Admiralty dockyards in this period were only seven: Deptford, Woolwich, Sheerness, Chatham, Portsmouth, Devonport, and Pembroke. In these places it is apparent that the reforming policy initiated at the top took many years to spread effectively to all the lower levels of the home establishment. Even in the Admiralty reform came more as sporadic and fluctuating aspirations than as a settled and consistent policy. There was always the pressure of colleagues and party managers as well as sheer inertia to assist the relaxation of principles, especially at election time. Immediately below the ministerial regions, the commanding officers and dockyard superintendents might on their own initiative build up a network of patronage unknown to the Admiralty; and the lowest class of all, the men employed in the dock- and victualling-yards who were also voters for the constituency, would tend to advance their claims for promotion by voting for the candidate presumed to be favoured by their superiors. Even outside the ranks of the dockyard employees, many an elector in the dockyard towns would direct his electoral support to those

[8] P.P. 1852–3, xxv, 14.

quarters which could reward it by the appointment of his friends and relations to the government service. It can scarcely be a matter for surprise, therefore, that throughout this period the Admiralty was perpetually faced with the recurrence in their establishments of a political atmosphere which seemed to spring up whenever their vigilance was relaxed.

From 1833 onwards there were various attempts to control appointments and promotions by the institution of set regulations; but none of these were very satisfactory until after 1846. After the return of the whigs to office in 1835 an Admiralty order was issued, dated 18 July 1835, stating that representations had been made to their lordships of attempts by officers at dockyards to influence the voting of their workmen, and strictly enjoining each admiral superintendent that 'in any future election for the town or county in or near to which the yard under your superintendence is situated, the exercise direct or indirect, of any influence on the part of superior officers to induce workmen to vote in any way is to be carefully avoided'. To guard against even the appearance of political pressure, canvassing in the dockyards was forbidden except in the case of employees actually resident within them. There is no reason to suppose that this order was effective in suppressing local patronage and in all probability there continued to be considerable laxity in the matter of political appointments and promotions which the secretary to the board of the Admiralty (himself a professional politician) was either unable or unwilling to prevent. Critics of the system, both inside and outside the service, even declared that so much did political motives enter into promotion, that money and manpower were wasted on overloaded establishments, while the good workman in the royal dockyards was at a disadvantage with his fellow in the private yard where the pay was better and promotion went by merit. In 1847 the Admiralty issued another notable circular to all admirals and captains superintending H.M. Dockyards. After referring to the steadily increasing financial vote for wages, stores, buildings, and equipment, consequent on the development of steam machinery and growth of the admiralty establishments, the circular passed to the question of political partisanship in appointments and promotions. It was evident that in the view of the Admiralty there was no confidence among the dockyard workers that success in their careers would depend solely on merit; and it was urged that every effort should be made to instil that confidence. Certain rules for the admittance of apprentices to dockyards and the promotion of dockyard workers were then laid down whereby it was made clear that the Admiralty formally dissociated itself from all motives of political patronage in making promotions. The new system was to be as follows. On the occasion of a vacancy the principal officers concerned in the department were to draw up a list of three names to be presented to the superintendent of the yard. The latter was then to investigate the claims of all three candidates, strike out the name of the one least qualified, and submit the remaining two recommendations to the Admiralty together with all the documents. The Admiralty then made the appointment from one of the two names thus submitted to them.[9] At the same time as these new regulations were introduced, an appeal was made for the assistance of all officers engaged in the dockyards to co-operate in this plan for establishing a system of promotion based entirely on merit and known regulations.

This point was raised the following year by a committee on army, navy, and ordnance expenditure. H. G. Ward, the secretary to the Admiralty, stated emphatically that 'we have foregone all patronage whatever with regard to the promotion of the men' and assured the committee that the Admiralty only promoted men from the list submitted to them by the dockyards concerned. But it was precisely at this level that the system was most open to suspicion and Graham at once asked whether the superintendents of dockyards used their influence to interfere in elections. Ward replied that no suggestion of such practices had been made at the previous election (1847) which was the only one of which he could speak from personal knowledge. As an additional precaution, however, Sir Francis Baring, when first lord in 1849, introduced the rule of requiring all dockyard superintendents to give him a personal assurance that they would not interfere with the politics of the town in which they held their post.

There was general agreement subsequently that the circular of 1847 was effective in suppressing any widespread system of electoral influence in the promotion of dockyard employees. In 1849 its good intentions were reinforced by a change in the method of transmitting recommendations. Formerly, recommendations

---

[9] It should be noted that the circular of 27 February 1847 only relinquished patronage of promotion, not of first appointment.

from the dockyards passed through the hands of the secretary to the Admiralty for final decision by the board. In that year an order was issued that all such recommendations were to go in the first instance to the Surveyor of the Navy, a professional naval officer of high standing, to be forwarded in due course to the Admiralty with his own observations and recommendations attached to the original documents. This change, really a reversion to an old practice, was due to a suggestion from the then surveyor, Sir Baldwin Walker, who pointed out that vacancies were being filled locally which he, with his general knowledge of the whole range of naval establishments, could fill more economically by transfers from other yards. The proposal was discussed and approved by their lordships and though never the subject of a formal minute was put into force by a circular of September 1849 on the authority of the first lord. While the ostensible reason for the change was the administrative economy thereby effected, it is clear that the intervention of the surveyor would still further weaken the power of dockyard superintendents or their officers to make promotions on political grounds.

It was this latter reform that led to the well-known Admiralty scandal in the first Derby ministry of 1852. The importance of the affair is perhaps easy to exaggerate although if the practices adopted by the unfortunate O'Brien Stafford had been allowed to pass unchecked, they would have had a disastrous effect on the slow growth of political impartiality in Admiralty establishments. As it was, the chief interest of the incident was the light it shed on the general working of the system of promotion in dockyards rather than on the foolish behaviour of the Admiralty secretary. The conservative ministry entered office in February 1852 and the new board of the Admiralty took over control early the following month. The government did not possess a majority in parliament and its continued existence depended on the general election. It is reasonably clear that from the first the secretary of the Admiralty, O'Brien Stafford, came under heavy pressure from his colleagues, including the prime minister, Stanley, and the chancellor of the exchequer, Disraeli, to manipulate admiralty patronage in such a way as to benefit his party at the polls. With unimportant exceptions the first lord, the Duke of Northumberland, gave up all civil patronage to the secretary. Towards the end of March Stafford's own secretary, Grant, tried to induce Baldwin Walker to waive his right under the 1849 circular of scrutinizing recommendations and making his own submissions on them. The surveyor refused to be party to any jobbery. A few days later Stafford wrote a letter to him expressing the dissatisfaction of the party at the way in which promotion was being administered in the civil branches of the Admiralty and hinting at the withdrawal of the 1849 circular. He told the surveyor in revealing terms that 'there is a general impression that all these things are dispensed among political opponents, insomuch as there seems no alternative but to resume the system which existed previous to September 1849'. The surveyor's reply to this candid epistle pointed out that while it rested with the board of the Admiralty to rescind the 1849 circular as they thought fit, it was the circular of 1847 that regulated promotion. An interview between the two men followed in which, according to good testimony, Stafford told the surveyor quite frankly that he was being pushed hard by his political superiors and could not help himself. On 19 April Stafford signed an order revoking the circular of 1849 and restoring to the board direct control of promotions. Walker, not unnaturally taking this as a reflection on his own integrity, promptly sent in his own resignation and it needed all the tact of the Duke of Northumberland and the issue of another explanatory circular to induce him to stay on.

There was undoubtedly some substance in the argument that Stafford subsequently advanced in the House of Commons that the long rule of the whigs had resulted in 'every hole and corner in the yards' being stuffed with 'whig officials and underlings' and that the working of the 1849 circular was 'not to make appointments to the dockyards non-political, but to make them one-sided'. Yet Stafford himself ruined whatever case he had by making personal appearances in the dockyards at Chatham, Deptford, and Devonport, shortly before the election of 1852, and conspicuously displaying himself before the dockyard employees in the company of the local conservative candidates, their agents, and chairmen. Moreover, the rescinding of the 1849 order was widely taken as a sign that there was to be a return to the old system of promotion by patronage. Whatever the justice of the conservative complaints, the attempt to restore a political balance in the yards by direct action of this nature was a step that ran counter to the whole course of development during the previous twenty years. It was in itself a symptom of changed feeling on the subject that the matter was immediately brought up in the House of Commons and the decision taken to appoint a select committee of inquiry into the rescinding of the 1849 circular and the general question of promotion in the dockyards. In the evidence before the committee there was ample proof that the conservative ministry of 1852, contrary to the practice of recent years, had made a number of promotions only explicable on political grounds. 'Officers of high character in the Navy', said the unanimous report of the committee, 'distinguished alike for professional abilities and unblemished honour, observed the course of promotion in the dockyards during the last summer with apprehension, with feelings of humiliation, with dismay, and even with disgust.' Following on the committee's report a private member of the Commons, Mr H. Keating, M.P. for Reading, moved a vote of censure on the conduct of the recent ministry for having used Admiralty patronage for political purposes. A long inconclusive discussion took place in the small hours of the morning of 6 July 1853 and the matter was eventually suspended by the adjournment of the House. It was clear that the coalition government, which had by that time succeeded the unsuccessful conservative ministry, was content to let the matter rest under the publicity given to it by the committee of inquiry.[10] This was probably the wisest policy. The conservatives, without perhaps being guilty of a deliberate attempt to corrupt a newly purified department, had been inexperienced, desperate, and extremely foolish; and their folly had recoiled on their own heads. On the other hand, if the ministry of Derby and Disraeli had fallen into a crude temptation after a fashion that would have been unthinkable in the conservative party when led by Peel, it was easy for the whigs to be politically virtuous. Between 1830 and 1852 they had been in office for sixteen out of the twenty-two years. Throughout that period all original appointments had remained under direct Admiralty control and it was inevitable that the long continuance in office of one political party should result in a corresponding preponderance of their followers in the Admiralty establishments. This is not to say that the whig attempts at reform were not genuine or were not attended with any success. They were probably both; but the whigs could afford to be reforming and

---

[10] The main sources for the history of dockyard patronage after 1832 and the Stafford case of 1852 are: *Hansard*, cxxvi, 33–122 and cxxviii, 1290 sqq.; P.P. 1852–3, xxv, *Report of Select Committee on Dockyard Appointments*. The latter includes the full evidence of witnesses and a documentary appendix.

disinterested because the advantages in any case lay heavily on their side. They had so much that they could afford to give away a little.[11]

Even so the evidence suggests that until 1847 corrupt practices were not uncommon in the dockyard constituencies. If in the period 1830–50 they were under a reforming régime, it could not be assumed that they were themselves already reformed. Certainly the election results in four of the most important 'admiralty boroughs' in the thirties tend to support the view that they were the entrenched strongholds of whig and ministerialist power. Even the bare recital of places, dates, and names is in itself impressive.

Chatham (one member)
  1832 Lt.-Col. Maberley (whig)
      Clerk of the Ordnance.
      Appointed 1834 Commissioner of Customs.
  1834 G. S. Byng (whig)
      Son and heir of the Earl of Strafford; junior lord of the Treasury in Melbourne's first ministry, 1834.
  1835 Admiral Beresford (conservative)
      Lord of the Admiralty in Peel's 1834–5 ministry.
  1837 G. S. Byng (whig).

Devonport (two members)
  1832 Sir George Grey (whig)
      nephew of Earl Grey; under-secretary of State for the Colonies.
      Sir Edward Codrington (whig)
      vice-admiral of the White.
  1835 Sir George Grey
      Sir Edward Codrington
  1837 Sir George Grey
      Sir Edward Codrington

Falmouth and Penryn (two members, of which the government was reputed to return one)
  1832 R. M. Rolfe (whig)
      solicitor-general in Melbourne's first ministry 1834.
      Lord Tullamoore (conservative)

[11] It was acknowledged in the report of the select committee that patronage of first appointments would probably give preponderant power to the party which had been in office for a continuous term of years (*loc. cit.*, 13).

1835   J. W. Freshfield (conservative)
      solicitor, former M.P. for Penryn.
      R. M. Rolfe
      re-appointed solicitor-general in Melbourne's second
      ministry 1835.

1837   J. W. Freshfield
      Sir R. M. Rolfe.

Plymouth (two members)

1832   J. Collier (whig)
      merchant, ship-owner, agent for Lloyds.
      T. B. Bewes (whig)
      local landowner.

1835   Collier
      Bewes

1837   Collier
      Bewes

At first sight this seems a convincing record of governmental, official, and naval influence in these four boroughs. In fact the picture is hardly so impressive as it appears. In the first place it was a natural and politic custom, not unknown in other periods, to put up naval and official candidates in this type of constituency. For admirals, members of the government, and ship-owners to contest port and harbour constituencies did not necessarily imply any more concealed manipulation of the electorate than the selection of country gentlemen for county constituencies or middle-class merchants and bankers for the metropolitan and industrial boroughs. It was merely the elementary application of the rule of 'horses for courses' and on that basis alone the presence of so many official names is readily comprehensible. In the second place even the proof of a marked tendency among the electors to support governmental candidates irrespective of party does not by itself imply an illegal use of governmental influence. There is sufficient evidence in this period of laxness of political opinions and indifference to party among the electors to render a characteristic and almost innocent air to the desire among shopkeepers, contractors, and dockyard employees to be on good terms with the government of the day. There must have been a great deal of completely spontaneous support for the official candidates, based on the expectation of favours to come rather than on the fear of what might befall. In these seaport and dockyard towns government influence might be strong not because it coerced but because it attracted voters.

An illustration of this aspect of government influence was provided by the general election of 1835. Peel had come into power; the offices in the Treasury and the Admiralty, to name the two that had most consequence for domestic patronage, had been filled by conservatives; and all the official means of influencing electors in the 'government constituencies' formerly in the hands of the whigs were now possessed by their opponents. It was in fact the only occasion when the conservative party under Peel was able to appeal to the country as the duly appointed government of the kingdom. Yet at the general election the government, except in one constituency, entirely failed to break the whig control of the four boroughs cited above. At Chatham alone, where the tory lord of the Admiralty, Sir John Poo Beresford, defeated the former whig lord of the Treasury, Byng, did the official government candidate get in. Lord Tullamoore, with the good wishes of the executive behind him at Falmouth, and Dawson, the secretary to the Admiralty at Devonport, were both beaten by whig opponents. The outstanding reason for the failure of the conservative ministry of 1834-5 to carry these government seats is clear. That ministry had been formed not as the result of a vote in the House of Commons but in consequence of a decision of the monarch which depended for its success on forces outside his control. At the 1835 election, said a witness before a parliamentary committee on bribery a few months later, many people voted whig because 'a Tory administration had just got into office, and there was a strong belief current that they would not last long, and the fear of offending the succeeding administration operated very powerfully'.[12] The whigs, though temporarily on the opposition benches, possessed, in fact, all the attractions of the true possessors of power; while the conservatives, though temporarily in office, were rendered uninfluential by the prospect of an early resignation. But if this analysis is correct it carries with it an important corollary. The implication is that the power exercised by the government in these constituencies was the power of attraction rather than coercion. The actual control of government resources during the

[12] P.P. 1835, VIII, 43.

period of the elections was of less significance than the certainty
and security of a long possession of patronage and power. The
influence of government in the dockyard towns was based not on a
sudden mobilization of official forces for the purpose of winning an
election but on a permanent control of appointments and promotions. The conservatives failed to capture the government boroughs
in 1835, largely because the whigs were still vested in the public
eye with actual political power.

But though this was perhaps the determining factor in the
government constituencies, it would be wrong to assume that
government did not for its own part exert particular efforts to
influence the immediate results of elections. The conservatives, for
example, made full use of executive authority in their attempts to
win the dockyard towns in 1835; and Lord Rosslyn, the leading
member of the party election committee, included among his
other activities in London a visit to the Admiralty to obtain votes
for various conservative candidates.[13] Active government participation in elections was still a normal and admissible feature of
contemporary politics. The principle was not yet seriously
contested although its application received criticism from government opponents. 'The government influence', complained a
conservative in Hampshire after the 1837 election, 'was used beyond
all precedent, both in the town and dockyard at Portsmouth, and
in the New Forest, amongst the lower classes of labourers to the
number of 30 who were directed to vote for its candidates altho'
they had promised their votes to Fleming and Compton [the
conservative candidates], or lose their work at ten shillings a week
in the forest enclosures.'[14] Granville Somerset, the chief election
manager of the party at the same election, confessed to Peel that
'with such large constituencies and with such unsparing use of
government influence', it was hazardous to predict the outcome of
the general contest.[15]

The fact of government intervention in elections is indisputable.
What is more doubtful, and certainly more difficult to elicit, is
how far such intervention was decisive. Was popular opinion
correct in considering certain boroughs as government preserves?
Or was it that in certain constituencies the influence of government was simply one more factor in the sum of forces? The

---

13 Add. MS. 40409, fos. 146–7.   14 Add. MS. 40424, fo. 21.
15 Add. MS. 40423, fo. 346.

answer can only be discovered by an examination of the so-called government boroughs themselves. Generally speaking the boroughs in England and Wales commonly regarded as under government influence in the period after the Reform Act were Chatham, Dartmouth, Devonport, Falmouth and Penryn, Greenwich, Harwich, Plymouth, Portsmouth, Rochester, and the Cinque Ports with the omission of Rye (viz. Dover, Hastings, Hythe, and Sandwich). This list does not of course exhaust the number of constituencies where government influence was present. But there, if anywhere, government influence was to be found in its most powerful manifestation.

A detailed examination of six of these constituencies (Appendix G) shows, however, that other factors entered into the situation besides the direct influence of the government. Bribery, the individual reputation and connexions of well-established members, the calculations of the electors as to their ultimate as well as their immediate interests, the ordinary ebb and flow of party popularity, all assisted to clog and frustrate the automatic operation of a system of governmental nomination. At Chatham alone perhaps was the influence of the ministry of the day invariably decisive. Twenty years after the passing of the Reform Act the borough (itself a creation of the act) was formally recommended for disfranchisement by a parliamentary committee of inquiry which observed that on no single occasion had its electors failed to return a candidate recommended to them by the government. At Devonport, too, the dockyard vote was probably the final decisive element that tipped the balance in a constituency which otherwise reflected the general recovery of the conservatives during the thirties. At Falmouth and Penryn the marriage of a notoriously corrupt pre-1832 constituency with a new electoral area containing material for government influence, produced a highly complex situation. But after 1837 it was plain that the power of the purse was beginning to gain on the power of the government. This was the aspect which led to the corrupt compromise of 1841. By that date the constituency could no longer be classed as a government borough even if fragments of government influence still remained. The naval establishment at Falmouth was too small and the contagion of Penryn too infectious for either party in or out of office to be sure of a seat. At Harwich, for which J. C. Herries had sat since 1823, the personal connexion he had built up under tory rule in the twenties enabled him to maintain his position during the reform agitation of 1831–2 and the almost unbroken nine years of whig rule that followed the Reform Act. In the three general elections of 1831, 1832, and 1837, he provided the unusual but significant spectacle of an opposition member retaining his hold on a 'government seat' despite all the efforts of the aggrieved whigs to dislodge him. By the time he was finally driven from the place, bribery as much as government influence was becoming the important factor in the Harwich elections; and the corrupt compromise between the two parties after the 1841 contest indicated, as at Falmouth, that in proportion as government interest receded, its place was taken by the highest private bidder. The history of the other two constituencies examined, the Cinque Ports of Hastings and Sandwich, also testifies to the dangers of generalization on boroughs popularly accepted as under ministerial control. At Hastings where Planta, who had represented the borough in earlier years, continued to build up his personal influence after 1832, he failed to secure election in 1835 when he had government backing but wrested a seat from the whigs in 1837 when he lacked that support. At Sandwich, on the other hand, which had a long tradition of Admiralty control, it was evident that the government continued to exert a marked influence even after the Reform Act. As regards one at least of its seats that power was probably decisive in the sense that it was the deciding factor between the two parties.

In the whole field of government boroughs, therefore, a few outstanding features are discernible. It is clear, in the first instance, that public opinion accepted the fact of government influence in certain specific constituencies; that government influence was in fact exerted; and that there were not lacking the men to endeavour to perpetuate and even extend a system of government nomination boroughs. The outlook, the vocabulary, and the practices of the unreformed system are still to be found ten and twenty years after the passing of the Reform Act. Yet the politicians who worked to create a nomination borough at the disposal of the executive were not noticeably successful; government itself was growing increasingly cautious and self-conscious in its use of patronage for direct electoral purposes, and public opinion probably erred on the side of generosity in estimating the real power of the executive in such constituencies. For the last there was a natural excuse. To a radical reformer bred up in the traditions of the eighteenth-century reform movement, to a journalist looking for copy, to a compiler of parliamentary guides necessarily dependent for much of his information on common repute or handbooks printed several years earlier, the existence of government influence at Chatham, Plymouth, or Greenwich was so palpable that it was taken as the decisive factor in all such constituencies. It was not easy for an outside observer to acquire a knowledge of all the personal and purely local forces that modified and sometimes annulled the influence of the executive. To generalize on the topic of government influence was in fact both tempting and plausible. Yet even on a preliminary analysis that influence tends to shrink to much smaller proportions than was commonly allowed in this period, at least, among the uninformed. Of the dozen or so constituencies usually accepted as being specially susceptible to government influence, six have been singled out for examination. Of those six, only three (Chatham, Devonport, and Sandwich) show convincing marks of conformity to the government of the day; at Harwich, though executive influence was probably decisive in the mid-thirties, it was being rapidly replaced by direct corruption; and at Falmouth and Hastings, local and temporary influences seem to have counted for more than any pressure which the Admiralty could bring to bear. If this is a good sample of what the others were like, it means that the number of boroughs in England and Wales in which government influence was really important was probably nearer six than twelve. The numbers involved are of course too small for such a sample method to be reliable as a means of assessing the whole. But weight is given to this provisional conclusion by the contemporary and authoritative opinion of F. R. Bonham. Writing to Peel in 1840, when the party leader was weighing the relative advantages of coming into office before a dissolution of parliament or waiting for the whigs to dissolve with the prestige of government still with them, the party electioneering expert gave it as his considered opinion that 'in England & Scotland the result would be nearly the same tho' in Ireland *your* election might make a difference of five or six seats in our favour. There are about six seats *at most* in England which would depend on the Ministry of the day. *At this moment* I doubt whether there are so many.'[16]

16 Add. MS. 40428, fo. 14.

Ireland was of course in a class by itself and a study of executive influence there would need separate investigation. But in the remainder of the United Kingdom there is no reason to assume that the government in this period could decide the issue of an election in more than half a dozen constituencies. Moreover, since Bonham must certainly have been including Windsor in his reckoning, the number of true government boroughs was perhaps even less than six. These were not in all probability a fixed and known list remaining constant over the whole period but an average dependent on the conjuncture of time and place. Direct government control over the constituencies did not therefore survive the Reform Act in any degree of strength that would warrant regarding it as a tangible factor in general parliamentary tactics. With so many other independent and incalculable forces in the House of Commons, the possession of six or even twelve seats out of a total of over 600 was relatively insignificant. If indeed the government seats could have been treated by the party in office as literally nomination boroughs and used to return the indispensable ministerial men defeated elsewhere, their qualitative value would have been great despite their paucity of numbers. But in fact they were not used and could not be used for governmental convenience in this way. Obviously they formed useful and appropriate constituencies for certain types of governmental candidates. But the whigs could not use even Chatham as the conservatives used Ripon. The nature of the constituencies themselves imposed restrictions on the use of government power and the kind of representative on whose behalf it was exerted.

In spite of the complaints at every election by both sides in turn of the undue use of governmental influence, that influence was negligible in the sum of electoral forces. As an indication of the ethics still prevailing in parliamentary circles it has a special interest; as an element in the making and un-making of governments it no longer counted. The access of parliamentary strength to be derived from the mere fact of being in office, while still perceptible, was so slight that it could be ignored. To Bonham, surveying the mustering of forces, actual and prospective, of the rival parties in 1840, it was a matter of indifference whether whigs or conservatives presided over the dissolution of the existing parliament. 'Tho' on the first blush it may appear extravagant . . .', he assured Peel, 'I think myself prepared to prove, as far as such matters admit of actual demonstration, the soundness of my conviction that excluding Ireland, *their* Dissolution will be no injury to us.'[17] Much as the influence of government had declined in the half century previous to the Reform Act, he was probably the first manager of a party in opposition who could have made such a remark with such confidence.

[17] Add. MS. 40428, fo. 14.

Chapter Thirteen

POLITICAL PATRONAGE

GOVERNMENT patronage was not of course confined either to select constituencies such as the dockyard towns or to the kind of person most conspicuous in them. In its widest sense it covered all classes and all parts of the Empire. Political motives entered into the award of honours; the grant of titles; creations and promotions in the peerage; appointments to lord lieutenancies, magistracies, bishoprics, and canonries; and the disposal of regius professorships or pensions on the Civil List bounty. Even commissions and promotions in the army and navy were still on the fringe, at any rate, of the patronage system and became accordingly the object of eager and incessant solicitation at the Horse Guards or the Admiralty. The patronage chapters in the published correspondence of Melbourne and Peel[1] demonstrate that prime ministers were cautious and sparing in their exercise of general patronage powers; and a dozen were disappointed for every one sent joyful away. Nevertheless it is equally clear that though honours and appointments were made with careful attention to the merits of the candidates, yet the exclusion of extreme political opponents, the reward of faithful supporters, and the attachment of important classes and individuals, were the main principles which governed the distribution of governmental favours. In this the early Victorian era was not peculiar. To many contemporaries, however, the criticism was not that these principles were followed, but that they were not followed far enough.

"The Statesmen of the present day', observed the Marquess of Londonderry in 1837, 'seem not to know that a body acting together must have the rewards of ambition, patronage, and place always before their eyes and within their expectation and belief of grasping, as well as the fine expressions of love of their country, and the patriotism which is a virtue.'[2] This attitude was neither uncommon nor, within limits, unduly cynical. Goulburn, a politician of perhaps greater principle than Lord Londonderry, had

---

[1] *Melbourne Papers*, Ch. XIV; Parker, *Peel*, III, Ch. XV.
[2] Buckingham, *Memoirs of the Courts of William IV and Victoria*, II, 287.

argued the matter with Peel a couple of years earlier in language that was more restrained but led essentially to the same conclusion.

> Let me however observe [he wrote] that where there are no superior qualifications evidently marking out a man for an office, it is, I think, impolitic to select for an appointment those men who have been uniformly opposed to a Government or only recently converted. I may live in a peculiar society but I can assure you that I found nothing more prejudicial to our interests than the impression which prevails that such is our course. It deadens the exertions of zealous friends and it makes the large mass, namely those who act on interested motives, oppose us as a matter of profitable speculation.[3]

As both these quotations indicate, there was a divergence of view between political leaders and political partisans. The difference was not of course an absolute one. It was a difference of emphasis rather than of principle. The personal considerations of ambition, wealth, and power are inseparable from the pursuit of a political career and a 'spoils system' is in some shape or other the concomitant of any party organization. The effective distinction is between what is recognized as the legitimate and the illegitimate rewards for political services; and that is a question of contemporary opinion and practice. It is here that the differences assert themselves. In the two examples given Londonderry was grumbling because he thought Peel and Wellington were refusing to overthrow a whig government which lay open to their attack; and Goulburn, though agreeing in general, obviously regarded as unduly principled a remark of Peel's that 'judicial offices ought always to be filled up without reference to any personal considerations whatever'.[4] If the difference between leaders and followers on the proper use of patronage in this period is unusually prominent, it is because the men that composed the political world, and the public opinion that did much to shape it, were not entirely coincidental. In particular public opinion was extremely sensitive to charges of governmental corruption and political leaders were extremely sensitive to public opinion. One of the most powerful elements in the movement for parliamentary reform had been the exaggerated public notion of the corruption, jobbery, and extravagance of government, and one of the main objects of that reform

[3] Add. MS. 40333, fo. 247.   [4] Add. MS. 40333, fo. 245.

had been to secure cheap and honest (the two qualities were synonymous) administration. Party leaders were therefore peculiarly anxious to prevent such charges being levelled at their own ministries; and, to do them justice, honestly concerned to avoid not only the imputation but the fact of using patronage for improper purposes.

Both parties reflected this change in public opinion. Melbourne, who does not usually pass for a purist, set up new standards in the distribution of higher patronage, especially peerages. His familiar and deflating answers to seekers after honours ('Confound it, does he want a Garter for his other leg?') though inspired primarily perhaps by fastidiousness, were in accord with the temper of his time. If the bishops 'positively died to vex him', it was characteristic that he devoted much scholarly correspondence to the disposal of the vacant sees, even though his appointments did not always please those of his party with whom politics was a stronger point than theology.[5] Under Peel the conservative party showed equal scrupulousness. In 1843, for example, Peter Borthwick, the eccentric and unreliable member for Evesham, asked for a diplomatic appointment. But the party managers were agreed on his unsuitability. 'I own', wrote Fremantle regretfully, 'I should be glad to get rid of him and have Evesham at our disposal. If he is now disappointed, I suspect he will join the party of malcontents, G. Smythe, D'Israeli & Co., but anything is better than an improper appointment.'[6] The following year a particularly crude proposal was indignantly rejected by the prime minister as 'a regular Irish job'. Boyd, the conservative member for Coleraine, approached Fremantle with an offer to resign his seat in favour of Peel's nephew, Captain Dawson, on the understanding that Boyd's son (aged 22) should be appointed to the office of registrar-general in Dublin under the new Irish Marriage Registry Act at a salary of £800 per annum. "This is a gross job, according to the most approved old Irish practice', wrote Peel subsequently to Lord Heytesbury, the Lord-Lieutenant. 'As it is a job from which a relative of mine would derive advantage, I am doubly anxious that it should be discountenanced and defeated.'[7]

Such evidence as this, however, sheds light on only one side of the question. Government by patronage had disappeared but

[5] *Melbourne Papers*, 495–506.   [6] Add. MS. 40476, fos. 266–7.
[7] Parker, *Peel*, III, 425; Add. MS. 40476, fos. 375–9, 380–1.

patronage in government remained as an important element of political solidarity. For every party the authority, profit, and reputation of official position were the natural and legitimate objects of ambition; and every party leader when called upon to form a ministry was obliged to consider not merely the claims of merit but also the conciliation of the influential and the satisfaction of the party as a whole. The judicious allocation of office was in fact one of the bases of party unity and it would not be too fanciful to ascribe some of the disunity of the English radicals in this period to the absence of this disciplined incentive. The distribution of the upper political posts was of course a relatively straightforward task. Certainly it was the object of much previous intrigue and subsequent heartburning. But these are universal phenomena. Of more importance was the fact that by this time it was clearly and generally recognized that such posts could only be given to men of official experience or high standing in parliament, and that for the most part they would be held by the leading members of the party, or what an Edinburgh reviewer once styled the 'red-tape squadron'. This was merely the ordinary functioning of the party system. It was not so much the means of constructing a working majority as the political reward to which a working majority, formed and organized, could properly look. Patronage in the sense of making a friend, detaching an enemy, or conciliating a neutral, was of a different order. There was a clear distinction between the discriminating assignment of office to important members of a party and the indiscriminate grant of place and salary to enlarge the area of party support. Yet it would be a mistake to assume that patronage in this narrower sense had disappeared from politics after the Reform Act.

It is true that by 1832 there were few sinecures among government posts that could be used for this kind of beneficiary patronage. The ministers that succeeded Lord Grey found themselves not at the beginning but at the end of a long process of retrenchment, reform, and purification that had started half a century before. Indeed the ministries of Liverpool and Wellington were in the not unprecedented position of reforming governments which by their own reforms had weakened their ability to resist further changes. To some extent, therefore, the whig political reforms of 1832 were the consequence of antecedent tory administrative reforms. From 1782 onwards the physical means whereby the executive could control the conduct of members of parliament had been whittled away by successive reforming measures to which Burke, Rockingham, Shelburne, Pitt, and Liverpool had all contributed. Public funds were no longer used in any direct way for political purposes; public opinion no longer sanctioned the dismissal of army and navy officers who sat in parliament as members of the opposition; and the virtual disappearance of sinecure posts during the same period was confirmed by a Select Committee in 1834 which found that of about a hundred nominal sinecures still in existence at the time of the inquiry, only half could be regarded as such. Almost the only form of major patronage still left to the government was the Honours List. But though Pitt had made use of this substitute patronage, Melbourne, Russell, and Peel were singularly sparing in their grant of titles. The ministers of the young Queen Victoria did without almost all those means of influencing the legislature that had been possessed by Walpole, Newcastle, and North.[8] Even if the government after 1830 had wished to employ the eighteenth-century arts of appealing to the large mass of politicians 'who act on interested motives', they would have been unable to do so. The upper slopes of patronage had been washed away by the tide of economic reform, leaving the small ministerial group at the summit in a position of decided, and occasionally dangerous, isolation.

Their difficulties would have been greater had the lower slopes also disappeared. But they had not; and patronage in this period is primarily a question of the lower reaches of the government service. It existed, but it concerned smaller men and smaller posts. What characterized Victorian patronage, as compared with that of the eighteenth century, was mainly the scarcity of those desirable offices under the government which required no particular experience or understanding, which provided a salary on which a gentleman could make shift to live, and which involved no loss of social status to hold. The even more desirable offices that did not even require personal attendance were of course virtually extinct. But there did exist a large number of minor employments in the government which were habitually distributed for political purposes or among political partisans. Certainly there were fewer of these available at any one time than a hungry public or a heavily committed politician was apt to believe; and

[8] Foord, 'The Waning of "The Influence of the Crown"' (*E.H.R.*, LXII, 484 sqq.).

conventions and regulations within the civil service itself tended to restrict the range and quality of vacancies when they did arise. But the extent to which politics controlled appointments to the civil service is sufficiently indicated by the fact that the civil service reform controversy of 1853–5 turned almost exclusively on the elimination of government patronage. 'Patronage in all its varied forms is the great abuse and scandal of the present age', wrote Trevelyan in his *Thoughts on Patronage* (1854). Elsewhere he wrote that 'the Civil Establishments have hitherto been treated as a *corpus vile* for providing at the expense of the Public for the personal and political followers of the Party in power', and argued that reform would end, not government by party, but 'the old abusive practice of strengthening Parties by mere personal support obtained by interested motives'.[9] In their zeal for reform Trevelyan and Northcote overstated their case and came very near to parodying the actual state of the unreformed civil service. In fact the impact of political patronage was muffled by the control exercised by heads of departments in matters of promotion and dismissal, and by departmental regulations on age limits and entrance examinations. The real key to the efficiency of the service lay not so much in the choice of recruits as in the principle of promotion.[10] Yet when all allowance is made for the restrictions on political patronage, there is no doubt that the public was left with the impression of a vast amount of minor offices at the disposal of the government and enough actually existed to account for much of the time and correspondence of every politician from the prime minister to the youngest member of the House of Commons.

The central figure in the exercise of government patronage was the first lord of the Treasury. The offices which were at his disposal included a wide range of departments. The Customs had posts ranging from boatmen, messengers, and tide-waiters at an average of £60 per annum to searchers and coast-waiters at salaries up to £200. Most of these officers of course were eligible for promotion. In the Excise Department a private arrangement existed whereby half of what was known as 'House patronage' was exercised by the Treasury, each department nominating to alternate vacancies. The officers that came into this category were

[9] Printed by Professor Hughes in *E.H.R.*, LXIV, 69, 85, 86. For an authoritative account of the state of the civil service and the civil service reforms of 1853–5, see the articles by Professor Hughes, *E.H.R.*, LXIV, 53 sqq., 206 sqq.; *History*, XXVII, 51 sqq.
[10] Hughes, 'Civil Service Reform' (*History*, XXVII, 56).

of the nature of clerks, messengers, and permit-writers. Other agreements with the Excise gave the Treasury a substantial share in the rest of the Excise patronage. Of the appointments as excise officers, the Treasury took fifty-five out of every hundred; of the remainder, thirty-five were left to the excise commissioners and ten reserved for the sons of deserving officers of the service. Hop assistants, employed temporarily during the hop season, were nominated by the Treasury in the proportion of about one-third. In the department of Stamps and Taxes all posts were at the disposal of the Treasury; as were appointments to the Audit Office, the Stationery Office, and the Record Office.[11] In the majority of cases, age limits which appear to have been generally observed were imposed on original appointments to these offices. Moreover, there was a clear line drawn between appointments and promotions. Thus in the important Customs Service not only did the Treasury control all original appointments but also no promotion could take place without its approval. Technically, indeed, promotion in the Customs was made by the first lord of the Treasury on the recommendation of the Commissioners of Customs. Nevertheless this power was largely nominal. The Treasury seldom interfered with the recommendations of the Customs Board and the responsibility was held to rest with the latter.[12] Broadly speaking, therefore, the Treasury patronage was for practical purposes confined, as Peel once told a correspondent, to 'revenue situations of a subordinate character but with prospects of promotion on account of zeal and faithful service.'[13] The other main categories of governmental patronage were certain legal appointments in the hands of the Lord Chancellor; administrative posts at home under the Secretary of State for the Home Department; diplomatic appointments under the Foreign Secretary; colonial appointments under the Colonial Secretary; post office appointments under the Postmaster-General; appointments connected with military and naval establishments under the War Office and Admiralty; and the Irish appointments in the hands of the Lord-Lieutenant.

Superficially impressive as this list might seem, the actual freedom of choice of those nominally in control of departmental patronage was severely limited by departmental regulations, the necessity in

---

[11] See Appendix H, Memorandum relating to the Patronage of the First Lord of the Treasury.
[12] Add. MS. 40476, fo. 311. Cf. Hughes, *History*, xxvii, 56.
[13] Add. MS. 40570, fo. 240.

many cases for specific professional qualifications, and the devolu-
tion of power to permanent officials. In practice the real powers of
patronage exercised by ministers were surprisingly small. An
illustration of this may be taken from the Colonial Department.
In 1845 Sir George Clerk, a former conservative chief whip and at
that date Vice-President of the Board of Trade and Master of the
Mint, applied to Lord Stanley with a request for the nomination
of his son to some post in Australia. Stanley's reply was an interesting revelation of the practical limits to the Colonial Secretary's
powers of patronage.

> Virtually [he wrote back to Clerk] the patronage of all the
> Colonies is vested in the respective Governors; and . . . every vacancy
> which occurs must be provisionally filled up on the spot, and con-
> sequently in the case of the Australian colonies, held by the person
> so appointed for at least a year, before the supersession by the
> Secretary of State can take place. This becomes consequently a
> most invidious course of proceeding. It dissatisfies the Individual
> displaced, the Colonists generally, and especially the Governor, who
> feels his authority weakened by having his recommendation dis-
> regarded. Practically therefore I have little or nothing at my
> disposal. It sometimes happens that an office is vacant . . . for which
> no qualified person can be found in the Colony; but this can hardly
> be the case in Australia, where consequently, I feel myself bound
> to take the recommendations of the local authorities.

As a concession to his colleague, Stanley added that if Clerk would
tell him exactly where his son was, he would see what a note of
recommendation to a governor would do—

> but I have had from several of them urgent entreaties that in the
> present state of colonial affairs, I would abstain from even this
> amount of interference.[14]

The effective patronage at the disposal of the government for
political purposes was thus marked by two characteristics: it was
poor in quality and deficient in quantity. Once the higher political,
legal, diplomatic, and service appointments needing special qualifications were excluded, little remained except the beginners' posts
in the lowest grades of the public service. One part of every
minister's duties in this period was to disabuse all those ambitious

---

[14] Stanley to Clerk, 9 July 1845 (Clerk Papers, T/188/82).

fathers and fond mothers who sought through patronage to secure elegant and remunerative employment for their untried offspring. In 1835, for example, Peel had to tell Lady Isabella Blachford, a daughter of the 3rd Duke of Grafton, that employment except in a professional capacity was almost out of the question. At the Treasury there were no intermediate appointments between a lordship and a clerkship of £90 per annum. The same applied, he added, to nearly all the other State departments; and he civilly lamented the scarcity of avenues open to young men of birth and talent in the administrative service of the country. To the Duchess of Gordon, another fair applicant, he regretted that there were no longer appointments other than those which required personal attendance for the discharge of the duties attached to them. Offices tenable by gentlemen were chiefly those parliamentary appointments which became vacant with changes of ministry.[15] Not only were such posts scarce but, in the initial stages at least, they offered far less attractive conditions of work than private employment; and seekers after patronage were perpetually being astonished at the subordinate positions and meagre salaries which were all that harassed ministers and chief whips had to offer. Fremantle described once how, when to the advocate of some young man's claims, he 'hinted at a Clerkship worth £80 a year, he smiled and said that he paid some of his own Clerks from £150 to £300'.[16] Even if the salary was acceptable, the nature of the work was such as to offer little appeal to the sons of wealthy and aristocratic households. Thus, in discussing with Bonham the choice of office for a son of Lord Francis Egerton, Peel concluded that only the Foreign Office would be suitable. 'The Treasury offers nothing but the dullest routine—it would give a nausea for public life. But the daily routine of the F.O. is one of great interest.'[17] If this was the character of the central departments of the government, the great network of provincial appointments in the customs and excise, which formed the mainstay of political patronage, was attractive only to a much lower grade of recruit; and not always to them. One of these wrote to Clerk at the end of his first probationary month as a tide-waiter at Greenock, that his office was one 'the duties and disagreeableness of which I am unable to undergo, particularly the night watching and the

[15] Add. MS. 40411, fos. 209, 260.   [16] Add. MS. 40476, fo. 76.
[17] Add. MS. 40550, fo. 253.

knocking about wet and dry in oftimes confined and dirty ships
... moreover the class of men holding Commissions as Tidewaiters
are not by any means those from whom much profitable is to
be learned.'[18]

Yet despite low pay and dull or disagreeable duties, the other
characteristic of government patronage at this time was the
enormous pressure of applicants, far exceeding the number of
vacancies, for such appointments. If the civil service offered
nothing else, it did provide security and respectability. These
qualities alone would probably have attracted more than sufficient
recruits even if it had not also been an age of commercial uncertainty and periodic trade depression. Every vacancy in the civil
service, therefore, even those that barely offered a decent living
wage, was sought after with drab and pathetic tenacity by a host
of aspirants. The correspondence of ministers, of the patronage
secretary, and of every member of parliament belonging to the
party in office, was full of appeals from candidates, their parents,
relatives, or friends, of which the great majority were doomed to
disappointment. Even applicants who had perhaps flattered
themselves on the modesty of their requests and the consequent
certainty of speedy satisfaction were liable to receive curt and
discouraging answers. To a request from some one for a post as
landing-waiter or gauger in the Customs, John Young who replaced Fremantle as conservative patronage secretary in 1844,
replied succinctly that 'the situations which he seeks to obtain are
the best at the disposal of Sir Robert Peel and the pressure for
these places prevents me from holding out to him any expectations
of appointment'.[19] On another occasion, when refusing an importunate suitor from north of the border, Young replied that 'the
patronage of the Treasury does not afford the means of providing
for one in a hundred of the persons recommended for appointments in Scotland'.[20] The inexhaustible appetite of the Scots for
public patronage had long been proverbial in politics and Young
(who was an Irishman) no doubt was allowing himself a certain
luxury of exaggeration. But there could be no doubt that the
demand grossly exceeded the supply.

---

[18] MacFarlane to Clerk, 30 April 1844 (T/188/84). A tide-waiter or tides-man was
a customs officer who remained on board a merchant ship until its cargo was landed
in order to prevent evasion of duty.
[19] Young to Clerk, 6 August 1844 (T/188/83).
[20] Mure to Clerk, 28 November 1844 (T/188/83).

It was because of this pressure from without, burdensome and distasteful both to M.P.s and ministers, that most departments followed the practice of keeping official lists of candidates waiting for an appointment. During Peel's 1841–6 ministry, for example, Fremantle and Young in succession kept the Treasury list; Lord Lowther as Paymaster-General kept one; Stanley at the Colonial Office had a list kept by his private secretary; and Hardinge as Secretary at War had a list. There is every reason to assume that all the major departments of State were obliged to do the same. Moreover the volume of applications coming in to these departments is shown by the fact that nearly every future vacancy was booked up two, three, or even four deep by candidates on the waiting list. Hence even the happy few who succeeded in having their names put upon the list might wait months or years before an offer of a vacancy came their way. The pressure was greatest of course on the better paid offices. 'It is now eighteen months', wrote Peel to Bonham in November 1844, 'since I had an office to dispose of which in the language of this letter [an application by Sir David Scott on behalf of his son] "a Gentleman can hold". I speak not of purely professional or Parliamentary office, but of ordinary civil office. You can well conceive what must be the accumulation of applications and claims for employment.'[21] But conditions could have been little better for aspirants to lowlier situations. 'I wish', wrote William Bowles of the Admiralty to Sir George Clerk in February 1846, 'I could do what you wish with respect to Mr. Goodson but we have a sadly overloaded list of candidates for Clerks Assistants and there are already many young men now serving in inferior situations, hoping for this miserable advancement.'[22]

In these circumstances it is inconceivable that political considerations should not have entered into the distribution of patronage. The limited quantity of loaves and fishes at the disposal of the government could not possibly feed all the hungry multitude that thronged the entrances to the public service. In the face of so many candidates of apparently equal merit, political discrimination at least provided some means of selection as well as some contribution to the stability of the government. The influence of the patron was therefore of more consequence than the ability of the candidate in catching the attention of harassed

[21] Add. MS. 40554, fo. 231.   [22] Bowles to Clerk, 12 February 1846 (T/188/83).

ministers and whips. The rewarding of loyal party men, the conciliation of the territorial magnate, the tactful handling of the newspaper proprietor, were all powerful factors in the calculation of the patronage secretary. Thus in 1842 Delane, the editor of *The Times*, wrote to Peel requesting promotion for his brother who was in the Customs service. Peel passed the letter on to Fremantle with the suggestion that 'we say a good word for Mr. Delane' as it might prove of great service to them.[23] Lady Fremantle in 1843 wrote direct to Peel to ask for a Landing Waitership for a young man in whose fortunes she was interested and Peel promptly granted her request.[24] Early in 1835 the post of Distributor of Stamps at Cork fell vacant. Among others who applied for the appointment was a cousin of the Rt. Hon. Frederick Shaw, M.P. for Dublin University and leader of the Irish conservatives. The cousin was given the post and Peel went out of his way to express his pleasure in making the recommendation. 'I have many applications for it,' he wrote to Hardinge, the Chief Secretary, 'but I must say that a relation of our friend Shaw has I think a prior claim to anybody.'[25] Even when there was no such cordiality, it was sometimes judged prudent to keep influential personages in good humour by a regular if limited share in patronage. 'The Duke of Buckingham presses me for another Clerkship', wrote Fremantle at the end of 1841 when the conservatives had only been in power four months, 'and says he must have it in the *month of January*. I have no vacancy, but if I had, I could not in justice to others give it to him. He has had one, and many others must be served before his turn comes round again. Unless you say anything to the contrary, I shall write to him in this sense.' But his leader was less intransigent. Whatever his personal merits, which were few, the Duke of Buckingham was a figure of importance in the party. As an agriculturalist his inclusion in the cabinet of 1841 had been taken as a sign of the conciliation of interests in the new government just as his resignation from it a few weeks after this correspondence was regarded as the first open breach between Peel and the strong protectionists. For whatever reason, the prime minister urged soft speaking upon his impatient whip. 'I think', he wrote to Fremantle a couple of days later, 'you

[23] Add. MS. 40476, fo. 211.
[24] Add. MS. 40476, fo. 276–8. A landing-waiter was a customs officer who supervised the landing of goods to ensure payment of duty on them.
[25] Add. MS. 40314, fos. 23, 27.

P.A.P.— BB

had better tell the Duke of Buckingham that you will do what you can to comply with his wish for a Clerkship.'[26]

One remarkable aspect of the business of patronage, to which this last episode bears witness, was the intensive interest with which peers and party magnates, as well as the humbler members of the Commons dependent on their constituents, pursued even the meanest vacancy on behalf of their friends and clients. The Duke of Buckingham with his clerkship could be matched with many similar examples. In September 1842, for example, Fremantle had a place as landing-waiter vacant at Greenock. Two politicians claimed the nomination: Lord Bute and the prospective conservative candidate for Renfrewshire, Colonel Mure. The chief whip's predilection was for the peer. But Lord Bute had another aristocratic rival in the Duke of Argyll who had been pressing the Treasury for a Collectorship of Taxes for one of his friends and would no doubt be prepared to accept a Landing-waitership in place of the superior office. In the end probably both peers were satisfied, as Fremantle was eventually able to offer the Duke of Argyll a Surveyorship of Taxes.[27] An even better illustration is furnished by Lord Lonsdale's administration of the Post Office patronage. In May 1845 he wrote a personal letter to Sir George Clerk, informing him that the post of letter-carrier at the little town of Lasswade in Midlothian was vacant, carrying with it a salary of £25 per annum. Lasswade was some six miles from Clerk's seat at Penicuik and Clerk himself had been at one time member for the county. The offer was thus in accordance with the etiquette of patronage even though the post was scarcely one of the richer nominations. Lonsdale inquired therefore whether Clerk knew of any one who would be glad of the employment. A couple of days later, before Clerk had replied, another letter in Lonsdale's hand came through the post. It informed him apologetically that since the original offer of the vacancy Lonsdale had received so pressing a communication from Lord Melville for the situation that he had been induced to give him the nomination. Gratified by his success, but anxious to mollify any annoyance that Clerk might be feeling, Lord Melville then wrote himself to Clerk to explain the transaction, and again a little later to inform him of the name of the candidate appointed to the post. Here then were four letters, two from Lonsdale and two from

[26] Add. MS. 40476, fos. 83, 85.   [27] Add. MS. 40476, fos. 161, 166.

Melville, not to mention Clerk's replies and the correspondence that had passed between Melville and Lonsdale. Two peers of the realm and a baronet, two of them ministers of the Crown, exchanged therefore some eight or nine letters full of compliments, apologies, and requests; and the occasion of it all was a post that brought in ten shillings a week.[28]

From any survey of early Victorian patronage several general aspects clearly emerge. On the personal side there were first of all the actual controllers of patronage; that is to say, the prime minister, the patronage secretary, and the political heads of the government departments. At their disposal was a range of appointments, wide in extent but for the most part poor in quality, for which no outstanding abilities were required and for which, therefore, within the limits of age and promotion laid down by the departments themselves, the actual selection of candidates was abstractly a matter of little importance. Outside the service was a huge and importunate mass of applicants, hungry for the smallest place of profit and inscribing their names three and four deep on the departmental lists for anything that might turn up. Inside the government and the party in power there was a smaller but more formidable array of ambitious politicians and magnates, ranging from influential dukes to defeated parliamentary candidates, jostling for their share in the distribution of patronage and exercising a constant pressure on the ministers and patronage officials. In this welter of interests and ambitions all order and control would have disappeared had there not been evolved known and generally observed rules of procedure. Indeed no account of the patronage system in this period would be complete without some description of the ethics and conventions which governed the distribution of the limited supply of loaves and fishes to a waiting multitude that lived in apparent expectation of a miracle of plenitude for all. Method and order in themselves could not alter the inadequacy of the existing supply but they could ensure a tolerably even distribution of what was available and a certain degree of protection against indiscriminate demands for those charged with the invidious task of distribution.

The central figure in the management of patronage was of course the parliamentary or 'patronage' secretary to the Treasury.

[28] Lonsdale to Clerk, 27 May, 29 May; Melville to Clerk, 30 May, 31 May 1845 (T/188/84).

Trevelyan, in his *Thoughts on Patronage,* stressed at the outset the 'portentous significance of the fact that a Functionary of high standing is attached to the Central Department of the Government with the recognized official duty of *corrupting* Members of Parliament and the Constituencies'.[29] It should be observed, perhaps, as some counterbalance to this forthright utterance, that the patronage secretary was usually also the chief whip and during the session therefore had a great deal more to do than sit at his desk in the Treasury corrupting electors and elected. The conduct of patronage, even for the patronage secretary, was not a full-time occupation. Nevertheless he was charged with the general supervision of government patronage and commonly recognized as the chief accessible source of authority in that sphere. Theoretically indeed all requests for patronage passed through his hands. Some years later Earl Grey described for the benefit of the Victorian public the general functions of the official so sturdily denounced by Trevelyan. Members of parliament, he explained, who sought patronage for their relatives or friends first approached the parliamentary secretary to the Treasury who forwarded the request with his own endorsement thereon to the minister concerned. In turn the parliamentary secretary, in his capacity as chief whip, had a corresponding counter-claim on the votes of members so assisted.[30] This, as a generalization, was both neat and accurate. Even in the middle of the nineteenth century the original connexion between patronage and the maintenance of a governmental majority in the House of Commons was not lost from view. Indeed one of the arguments against the reform of the civil service in the fifties was precisely that it would weaken the power of the executive. Fremantle himself, by that date a civil servant, so far remembered his unregenerate past as to express the view that it would not do for the Whipper-in to have nothing but his whip.[31] Nevertheless it would be wrong to assume that patronage secretaries in this period invariably kept such a strict control as the description given by Earl Grey would suggest. Certainly under Peel the practice was much looser and more flexible. Applications were often made direct to ministers, and ministers in turn made appointments without reference to the patronage secretary. Bonham himself, whose position in the party but (for

[29] *E.H.R.*, LXIV, 69.   [30] Grey, *Parliamentary Government*, 42–3.
[31] *E.H.R.*, LXIV, 214.

the most part) out of parliament made him in some sort a complementary figure to the chief whip, was frequently the recipient of
requests for patronage, some of which he passed to Fremantle,
others he took up directly with Peel.

This relative laxity of control was of less consequence than it
might have been if patronage had been the only or even the main
basis of the executive majority in the Commons. In practice the
area of patronage was defined in advance by the existence of
organized party. Patronage was consequent on the success of the
party in securing power; it did not create that power. It was a
contingent reward, not a specific bribe. But once the party was in
office, all its members qualified for a share in patronage unless
there were particular reasons to the contrary. Like a limited
liability company, a party could go for many years without showing a profit; but once a profit was made, all the shareholders
received their dividend. And if the shareholder was the member
of parliament, the unit of dividend-bearing stock, so to speak, was
the parliamentary constituency. The first rule in the administration, of patronage was that local appointments should always be
made at the request or with the consent of the local M.P. if he
was a supporter of the government. Usually, of course, the M.P.s
themselves or their local agents would keep an attentive eye on the
vacancies that occurred in the constituencies and would be ready
with their recommendations. In some of the dockyard constituencies, where patronage might be expected to be usually brisk,
regular patronage committees sat to assist the member in his
duties.[32] But even when no recommendations were forthcoming
from the local member, and requests came in from other quarters,
it was the practice to consult him before making any appointment
in his constituency. Thus in October 1841, when the conservatives had only been in power a few months, Fremantle received a
recommendation from a Dr Cook for a vacancy as postmaster in
Carrickfergus. But both Peel and Fremantle were agreed that
Kirk,[33] the sitting member, must be consulted. Indeed Fremantle
expressed the view that it would be best to take no action for the
time being and wait for a letter from Kirk in the hope that he
would recommend the same person as Cook had done. But he

[32] There were patronage committees, for example, at Chatham and Rochester.
At Devonport, according to Tufnell, each ward had a committee and the ward committees sent a representative each to the central committee (P.P. 1852-3, xxv, 183,
344, 347). [33] Peter Kirk of Thornfield, M.P. Carrickfergus 1841-7.

thought that if the government took the first step and recommended the man to Kirk, the latter would not be likely to concur.[34]
This prescriptive right of the sitting member to control the
government patronage in his district proved a source of frequent embarrassment to those candidates for office who had the
misfortune to live outside the constituency in which the desired
position was located. In September 1843, for example, there was
a vacancy at Eyemouth for a tide-waiter for which a man named
Crerar came forward as apparently the sole candidate. Eyemouth is in Berwickshire and in normal circumstances, therefore,
the application for the post should have gone to the conservative
member for that county, Sir Hugh Campbell. But Crerar was
from Musselburgh in Midlothian and Campbell knew nothing of
him nor did the Musselburgh conservatives know much of Campbell. It was conceivable that Crerar could apply through his own
member; but unfortunately the M.P. for the Leith, Portobello,
and Musselburgh district of burghs was Andrew Rutherfurd, the
former whig Lord-Advocate for Scotland. In this dilemma an
approach was made to Sir George Clerk, the nearest influential
conservative. What his advice was is not recorded; but it is not
hard to guess.[35] Sometimes the embarrassment was caused to
the patronage secretary who had to reconcile the claims of competing patrons. In 1844, chiefly owing to the exertions of Mr
Chief Justice Doherty, a post office was opened at Killiney, near
Dublin. Young, the patronage secretary, duly wrote to Hamilton,
the conservative member for Dublin county, asking him to submit a name for appointment as postmaster. In the meantime
Doherty showed signs of interest in the vacancy and no doubt considered that he had good cause to be consulted. Hamilton was
informed of this but it was agreed in London that nothing could
be done until Hamilton's reply was received.[36]

This acknowledged claim of the local member to control the
patronage in his constituency was subject to limitations. The most
obvious of these was that a member of the opposition could no
more expect a share in government patronage in his own district
than anywhere else. Had it been otherwise of course, it would have
destroyed the whole value of patronage as a means of consolidating governmental support. It is true that the administration of

[34] Add. MS. 40476, fo. 53.   [35] Milne to Clerk, 20 September 1832 (T/188/86).
[36] Doherty to Clerk, 3 September 1844 (T/188/83).

patronage in certain constituencies gave an appearance to the contrary, and at all times there were complaints that the opponents of the ministry were being favoured at the expense of their supporters. Here for example is a typical complaint in 1844. It was sent to Burroughes,[37] the conservative member for east Norfolk, from a conservative supporter in Yarmouth, which at that time was represented by two liberals. The letter referred to 'our Political opponents almost monopolising the Patronage as it falls' and went on to say that 'we as a party do think it hard that our Friends should not at least have their share of it under a Conservative Government although I am ready to admit from the Representation of our Borough that we are not in a situation to ask for much but when parties are wanted to carry out particular measures to have them chosen from our most violent opponents is not quite the thing, and somewhat disheartening'.[38] Patronage secretaries of both parties were well hardened to this kind of accusation and despite the tendency of politicians to regard even impartial administration as deliberate favouring of the opposition, there was not infrequently apparent cause for dissatisfaction. But good reasons usually existed for such departures from convention. In the first place not all patronage of government was under political control. Fremantle drew Peel's attention to this anomaly in 1842 when pointing out that the Commissioners of the Board of Excise themselves appointed to nearly half of the vacancies occurring in the service.

> Allow me to call your attention [he wrote] to the question of patronage vested in the Comsrs. of that Board. Out of every 100 officers appointed the Comsrs. nominate 45. Much to their own inconvenience, for they have considerable correspondence connected with the appointments & much to the injury of the Gov. of the day, for the patronage is frequently given to persons in direct hostility to the Administration, on the recommendation of opposition members of Parliament. Ld. Granville Somerset had this question under consideration, when engaged in the Comsn. of Enquiry & was & is of the opinion that it is advisable that this patronage like all the patronage in the Customs (excepting of course promotion in the service) should be vested in the Treasury.[39]

[37] Henry Negus Burroughes, M.P. east Norfolk 1841–7.
[38] Add. MS. 40617, fos. 177, 179.
[39] Add. MS. 40476, fos. 191–2. Professor Hughes' comment on this letter in his article on 'Civil Service Reform' (*History*, xxvii, 58) is liable to misinterpretation.

There was, in the second place, notwithstanding the intense pressure on all places at the government's disposal, a certain amount of patronage exercised for the benefit of the existing officers of the department concerned rather than for any political motive. Thus as early in Peel's administration as November 1842, Fremantle was writing to him about 'the several appointments which you have made up to this time in favour of the relatives of public servants on public grounds. To this must be added a long list of supernumerary Surveyors of Taxes, sons of the existing Surveyors, selected chiefly on the grounds of the experience the young men have had of the duties of the office by working as clerks to their fathers.'[40] When the combined incidence of patronage outside political control and patronage set aside for service and professional reasons is taken into consideration, it is easy to see why the supporters of government, for whom all patronage had a political significance, should complain bitterly and frequently of the incomprehensibility of government action.

The basic principle still held good, however, that only supporters of the government could expect the patronage secretary to pay any attention to their requests. When opposition members had occasion to approach him, or any of the government whips, with a suggestion that might be thought to bear on that subject, it was made with circumspection or else was doomed to contemptuous rejection. Thus Tufnell, the whig member for Devonport, in forwarding to Clerk in October 1841 a memorial from the mayor of the borough to the Treasury for the establishment of a customs-house there, added that 'the question is taken up by all parties in Devonport and all shades of politicians are equally interested in its success—I have therefore no scruple in requesting the early attention of the Government to the Memorial'.[41] Tufnell, as the opposition chief whip, was himself an official man and knew the delicacy of such proceedings. Others were less discreet. On one occasion Fremantle received a recommendation from a radical member for Tavistock. It was not an application for a specific place but merely a general recommendation of a particular man's fitness for some kind of government post. Even so Fremantle thought it 'rather an impertinent proceeding' for an opposition member to approach him with such an object.[42] It is quite

---

[40] Add. MS. 40476, fo. 202.
[41] Tufnell to Clerk, 21 October 1841 (T/188/85).   [42] Add. MS. 40476, fo. 273.

obvious that an M.P.'s influence in the disposal of local patronage was entirely dependent on whether his party was in power, so far as those appointments were concerned which were controlled by the government. 'Happy the man', wrote John O'Connell after an entertaining description of Irish patronage-hunters, 'who is in Opposition, and who can meet all requisitions with the incontestable fact, that he is out of favour with the Minister.'[43]

There were in addition a number of other conventions which circumscribed the privileges of a member of parliament even when a supporter of the ministry. Promotions for example within the civil service were for the most part regulated by the appropriate department and were immune from political interference. As an extension of that principle, local vacancies caused by internal promotion were not usually held to be in the gift of the sitting member, even though a supporter, since the vacancy had been created by the department itself. Accordingly local vacancies created by promotion were regarded as being at the disposal of the central department with no obligation to consult the M.P. in whose constituency they occurred.[44] They formed, therefore, a useful addition to the patronage normally administered directly from the centre. Again all attempted encroachments by M.P.s on patronage outside their own constituency were carefully watched by the patronage secretary. The pretext for such enlargements of authority were most likely to arise when an adjacent constituency was represented by an opposition member. In such circumstances, especially when there was no acknowledged government candidate nursing the district, there was always the temptation for members to indulge in a kind of political pluralism. Up to a point there were some advantages in this from the party point of view. Occasional irrigation of an infertile district might bring a profitable harvest at election time. But such vicarious exercise of patronage was always granted as a privilege and not as a right. In general it was conceded that a county member had a kind of general responsibility for his whole area, including even the boroughs, if they were not already represented by a government supporter. But there was less readiness for allowing borough

[43] O'Connell, *Recollections*, 1, 204–5. This chapter contains perhaps the most engaging of all self-recommendations for patronage: 'I am past twenty-one years of age, six feet one in height, and can play at the cudgels with any man in the barony.' It came from an Irish applicant who wished to get into foreign military service.

[44] Add. MS. 40476, fo. 272.

members to claim a share in county patronage where the county members were of the opposing party. Borough members in such cases might be consulted from motives of prudence or courtesy; but there was no obligation on the patronage secretary to do so.[45] Similarly, small appointments some distance from a county member's own immediate locality were not invariably referred to him. In December 1841, for instance, the post office at Fazeley in Staffordshire fell vacant, carrying with it a salary of £30 per annum. Since as patronage it was relatively unimportant, and geographically was near Peel's house at Drayton, Fremantle asked his leader to dispose of it. 'As the county member', he wrote, 'would not wish to trouble himself with so small a piece of patronage at a distance from his residence, you will perhaps select some fit person to be appointed when you are at Drayton.' He added that he would not write to Lord Ingestre, the conservative member for south Staffordshire, except at Peel's direction. In fact Fremantle had erred in his topography. Fazeley was actually part of the borough of Tamworth and so properly within Peel's gift, as he apparently reminded Fremantle in his reply.[46]

In a category by themselves were the politicians who were not members of parliament but who had established some claim on the gratitude of the party in power and had some title to be considered in the patronage of a particular district. These were usually the defeated party candidates at previous elections or the prospective candidates at the next. Here the amount of patronage made available to them was a matter chiefly for the sense and good judgement of the patronage secretary. They could not be given as much as a sitting member or else an incentive to secure election would disappear. On the other hand a sample of the benefits likely to ensue should they be eventually elected would materially assist them in working up their chosen constituency to a proper frame of mind at the next election. 'It is not well', pronounced Fremantle on one occasion, 'to treat unsuccessful candidates with the same consideration that is paid to sitting members.'[47] Yet gratitude and calculation both ensured that consideration of a kind would be paid to this class of party supporter. The chief difficulty was to prevent them from claiming too much. How far the claims of energetic and ambitious candidates could reach may be seen in the following episode. In November 1844 Clerk

[45] Add. MS. 40476, fo. 264.   [46] Add. MS. 40476, fos. 86–7, 90–1.
[47] Add. MS. 40476, fo. 161.

received a long tirade from Colonel William Mure of Caldwell, the prospective conservative candidate for Renfrewshire mentioned earlier, about the administration of patronage in the constituency. Mure had been narrowly defeated in the general election of 1841 and was ultimately returned at a by-election in 1846. The intervening years he spent in an indefatigable nursing of the constituency and incessant applications to Fremantle and Young, the successive ministerial patronage secretaries. Both of them gave him things from time to time but not enough to satisfy him nor as much as he thought was due to his position.

> During the late Whig incumbency [he wrote heatedly to Clerk] the whole patronage of the district, shire and borough, was disposed of for the benefit of the party within its bounds. Wallace[48] was uncontrolled lord of Greenock, P. Stuart, as its prospective M.P. of the county, together with a share in the borough allotted him by Wallace & which, in itself, told sufficiently to make his majority against me.[49] On the accession of Sir Robert Peel his supporters naturally (I admit unreasonably) expected a *similar* harvest to fall to their lot. I am aware that circumstances unnecessary here to dwell on placed this out of the question nor am I any advocate for carrying one's measure by such means, but as long as human nature is constituted as it is, the supporters of a government, in a district, will expect, and are I think entitled to expect, that at least a moderate share of the government good things within its limits should come their way, and if sorely disappointed will become at least lukewarm in the cause. Within the first year or so after the change of ministry one or two appointments in the ports were placed at my disposal (it being agreed as you may remember that I was to be the medium of forwarding such applications) and as Sir T. Fremantle even in his refusals was always kind & conciliatory, I managed to keep people upon the whole in good humour. For the last two years, however, I am not aware at least that any appointment has been bestowed in consequence of any application from me; and as Mr Young seems still less favourably disposed than Sir Tho. judging by the very little intercourse I have presumed to hold with him, I much fear that the disappointment & soreness now prevalent both in county and borough may have the most prejudicial if not fatal effects, if some remedy be not interposed.

[48] Robert Wallace of Kelly, M.P. for Greenock 1832–45, and advocate of Post Office reform.
[49] He defeated Mure in the election for Renfrewshire in 1841 by fourteen votes. The *Return of Members of Parliament* gives his correct name as Patrick Maxwell Stewart. On his death in 1846 Mure succeeded to the seat.

Having thus established his general grounds for complaint, Mure
then brought forward two specific requests. The first was for some
appointment to gratify Sir John Maxwell of Pollok whose father
had been one of the pillars of whig strength in the county. Having
recently by his father's death succeeded to the considerable family
estate he might be brought over to the conservative side if the post
he had asked for could be given to him. Secondly Mure requested
that 'a portion, however limited, of the Renfrewshire borough
patronage (which formerly be it remembered in Whig times was
all kept within the county) should be understood to be allotted for
its individual behoof, and consequently, according to the present
arrangements should pass thro' my hands'. Under this broadside
Clerk succumbed and wrote to Young the following month recommending that Maxwell's *protégé* should be given the tide-waitership
he desired and that an answer be given to Mure on the remainder
of the letter.[50]

Niceties of patronage etiquette apart, however, the material
question was how far political patronage contributed to the
strength of the government in the House of Commons and in the
constituencies. In February 1854 Trevelyan suggested to Delane
that the counties and larger boroughs such as Leeds, Manchester,
and Liverpool, secured very little patronage because their constituencies were too large to be bought. Equally so at the other
end of the scale the small pocket boroughs, like Calne and Midhurst, also received very little because there was no need to buy
them. Thus the bulk of patronage was absorbed by the middling
boroughs small enough to be affected by patronage and independent enough to make some form of persuasion necessary.[51] It is
doubtful, however, whether such a neat analysis can be accepted
without more authority than is afforded by Trevelyan's bare assertion. Trevelyan was a man of greater clarity than insight. Moreover he was engaged in making a case against the unreformed civil
service and in providing a newspaper editor with materials for
such a case. The gravamen of his charge was that the civil
service was corrupt because it was used for corrupt purposes. But
it is precisely here that he is open to criticism. The service was not
so corrupt as he implied and patronage was not simply a system
exploited by politicians to seduce the electorate. It was also a

[50] Mure to Clerk, 28 November 1844; Clerk to Young, 27 December 1844 (T/188/
83).
[51] Trevelyan to Delane, 6 February 1854 (printed by Hughes, *E.H.R.*, LXIV, 84).

system riveted upon politicians by a public which could scarcely conceive any way of entering the public service except by grace and favour. No prolonged study of early Victorian patronage is necessary to demonstrate that an M.P.'s constituents expected, indeed positively required, him to distribute patronage among his supporters. It is even arguable whether there was not a greater pressure on the individual member to dispense patronage than there was to dispense bribes. Bribery, after all, was outside the law; patronage was the accepted convention of the day. There was no sinister implication attached to the word; it meant merely the power of appointment. As such it was an object of ambition to many electors who would have scorned a bribe. Most constituencies expected their member to represent their interests and views in parliament and with the government; but one of the chief interests in the eyes of the constituents was a proper share in government appointments. A member who failed to secure that would be fortunate indeed not to be regarded as failing in one of his primary duties to his constituency.

To equate patronage with bribery, as Trevelyan appeared at times to do, was to falsify the issue. No doubt in small boroughs a judicious administration of patronage could so consolidate a member's position as to render it almost impregnable. But it would be difficult to sustain the thesis that counties, large boroughs, and pocket boroughs, were content to go without their share of governmental appointments or that the members for those constituencies were prepared to see the inevitable local vacancies that must have arisen from time to time given over to the control of another member of the party. The fundamental rule that the local member if a government supporter must be consulted in local patronage in itself ensured a basic distribution of patronage over all constituencies. In a populous constituency the number of vacancies might well be relatively small; in a pocket borough it might be absolutely small. But in neither case would it be easy to show that the sitting member was thereby dispensed from his duty of watching over the interests of his constituents. This was true even of pocket boroughs where the actual choice of the representative was scarcely within the compass of the legal electors. When that austere administrator Sir James Graham was M.P. for Dorchester his deficiencies in this vital respect led to a natural grumbling among some of his constituents against him because they felt that he ought to 'look after his own borough'.[52] Or to cite an example from a large constituency, there was the case of Arber at Westminster. He was a master-builder of Hanover Square who was chairman of the Westminster conservative committee at the general election of 1841 and had undertaken to bear all the costs of the contest after the first £1,000. After the election, in which a conservative candidate had been returned, he asked for a situation in the government service for his son who was nearsighted and unfit for the building trade. 'If therefore Westminster was worth having', wrote Bonham to Fremantle after detailing Arber's services to the party, 'I know not the man living who has an equal claim to your patronage to that extent.' The appeal was irresistible and Peel replied in due course that he would have great pleasure in promoting young Arber's claims.[53]

Perhaps the truth of the matter was that so long as patronage was in the gift of the politicians the public at large would not only solicit it but would take steps to place the politicians in their debt by political services, or at least regard their political services as meriting reward. And politicians, necessarily thinking of the immediate need to bind political support to themselves and their parties, inevitably used patronage to satisfy their public. But the politicians themselves were as much the hunted as the hunters. 'Government offices', observed that genial but none the less acute observer of the Victorian scene Surtees, in *Soapey Sponge's Sporting Tour*, 'are supposed to be receptacles for all improvident and unfortunate men, and youths without a profession. "Oh, a man with his connection is sure to get something—his friends will get him a berth in a government office, or something of that sort"; and forthwith every member of parliament, and every person of note within range of the family acquaintance, is besieged and pestered with importunate applications.'[54] It was not simply, as Trevelyan wrote,[55] that the majority of those members of the House of Commons that voted for the government expected the accustomed dole; but also that the majority of those electors that voted for a member of the successful party expected it as well. The individual member of the Commons was between the nether stone of his constituents and the upper stone of ministers and patronage secretaries schooled in the routine of 'civil refusals'.

[52] Horsford to Hope, 8 January 1845 (T/188/84).   [53] Add. MS. 40496, fos. 84–6.
[54] Ch. 69.   [55] *Thoughts on Patronage*.

The ordinary daily correspondence of a politician such as Sir George Clerk shows him as the target of innumerable requests for patronage: requests from constituents, requests from friends and relatives, requests from neighbours and fellow Scots, requests from political colleagues and from peers of his party, requests from Edinburgh, from Midlothian, from Stamford, from Southampton, from London. Some were written in beautiful copperplate by the young and hopeful candidate himself, some were from fathers, mothers, family friends, clergymen, solicitors, or local M.P.s. Most of the petitions were for first appointments, either specific or general; but others were for promotion, for transfer, for grants of pensions, removal from the supernumerary to the permanent estab-lishment of the department, even for reinstatement after dismissal, or re-appointment after resignation. Some were illiterate, some pompous, some pathetic. Some pleaded mere charity and com-passion; some the ties of locality; the majority political services. They had voted for Clerk in the past, or their relatives had, or their friends might in future. Here are two examples that may stand for many.

Stamford, May 31 1846.

Hon^{d.} Sir,

Pardon the liberty I am taking in asking the favour of your Interest in obtaining a Situation for my Son in the Excise, or Customs, he has received a very liberal Education, and having been left a Widow with a large family, such a favour conferred would always be acknowledged and I should consider such an act of benevolence bestowed on that family whom the lamented Parent was a strenuous supporter of yours, could never be erased from memory by, Hon^{d.} Sir,

Your ob^{t.} & humble Servt.

Ann Boyden.

23 Landport Terrace,
Southsea, Portsmouth.   31 October 1843.

Sir George,

I am really ashamed of again encroaching on your Kindness, time & patience; in behalf of my youngest Son; a fine active & intelligent youth, going for 17 years of Age; & for whom I should feel extremely grateful, if through your kind assistance, he could procure the

Situation of a Clerkship in the Department of Customs; I have
given him a good Classical & Mathematical Education, with French
& Drawing.

Under any circumstances, I hope you will allow me to crave your
indulgence; for this Intrusion; the offspring of the feelings of an
anxious Father.

> I have,
>> the honor to be,
>>> Sir George,
>>>> Your most Obed.ᵗ Servant,
>>>>> Joseph Roche Com.ʳ R.N.[56]

It was inevitable that politicians, political agents, and party
managers, in the face of a mass of patronage solicitations such as
these, should regard direct and tangible political service as the
only workable criterion of reward.

At the Treasury [as Fremantle told Gladstone in 1843] we must
look first to the claims of our political supporters & our patronage is,
as you know, quite inadequate to meet the applications of members
of the H. of C in favor of their constituents, who naturally consider
all our patronage as theirs. The son of a good voter at Newark
would stand a better chance under your recommendation than the
son of a poor clergyman who probably made it a point of duty not to
interfere with politics. . . . Pray excuse my frankness in explaining
to you how these things are viewed within the corrupt walls of a
Sec[retary of the] Treasury's room.[57]

Clerk's correspondence is an ample sermon on this text. He
was of course more than ordinarily exposed to patronage hunters.
As a member until 1837 for Edinburgh county, and one of the
most prominent Lothian conservatives, he was inevitably expected
to consider the interests of his Scottish neighbours. As member for
Stamford from 1838 to 1847 he was also required, like Graham, to
'look after his own borough'. Having, in addition, between 1841
and 1846, as secretary to the Treasury and then vice-president of
the Board of Trade and Master of the Mint, some personal influence in the disposal of patronage, he was also liable to be approached by other M.P.s on behalf of their constituents. There
must, however, have been many politicians with similar wide

---

[56] Boyden to Clerk, 31 May 1846 (T/188/81); Roche to Clerk, 31 October 1843
(T/188/82).
[57] Quoted by Hughes, 'Civil Service Reform' (*E.H.R.*, LXIV, 67).

obligations. But among all the applications that came to him from these diverse sources, the refrain was usually political service. An application was made on behalf of a young man friendly to the writer by the secretary of the conservative association for the city of Perth. An application from Stamford referred to the fact that 'my strenuous efforts have been for this 40 years past of serving the Interest of the House of Burghley'. There was advocacy for the claims of a 'distinguished individual in the Conservative cause', Mr Neill, who had signalized himself at Clerk's election in 1834 by 'bringing to the Poll a Voter whom nobody else could get up, and took him out of the hands of two of the enemy's Committee, who were actually arm-in-arm leading him to vote for the whig candidate. . . . Mr Neill on occasion of our stirring up Voters to enroll this last autumn at once met us with open arms, split up his Property into *five* Votes, and gave Dispositions.' When the conservatives came into power this zealous creator of faggot votes asked for a situation for his son-in-law in the Excise; and in November 1842, eight years after his cutting-out operation at Clerk's Lothian election, he was rewarded with a tide-waiter's post at Leith.[58] Electors clearly had long memories. John Hope recommended a certain Bartholomew, 'who did you good service in the west of this county' and 'is sadly in need of some small office'. He was appointed messenger in the Stamps and Taxes office at Edinburgh.[59] Lord Melville pressed the claim of a Mr Brooks of Lasswade. 'You know as well as I do Brooks' great exertions in electioneering matters in this county and as there can be no question that under the administration of your predecessors his service would not have been overlooked, I think it important if possible that something should be done for him.'[60] But the list could be prolonged indefinitely. 'Hunt is a most worthy character and *staunch conservative*—he voted for *yourself and your worthy colleague* at the last election & he is likewise a member of the St. Mary's Conservative Association.' 'My Father who is a conservative elector of Lambeth and obtained by canvassing at the last election above thirty votes for Mr Thomas Cabbell & Mr Baldwin, the Conservative candidates'—'Son of Mr Thomas Scotland, Parish Schoolmaster of North Leith, who is, I may mention, a registered voter in the Conservative interest'—'a worthy man and

[58] Stewart to Miller, 19 January 1842 (T/188/84).
[59] Hope to Clerk, 13 December 1843 (T/188/86).
[60] Melville to Clerk, 2 October 1841 (T/188/86).

staunch Conservative'—'all my relatives reside in, or near, Edinburgh . . . and are, and ever have been staunch supporters of the present conservative Government'.[61]

Human nature being fallible, especially where its own interests are concerned, these claims were not always accepted at their face value and not infrequently old poll-books were hunted through to see whether an applicant was as 'entitled' to ask for patronage as he alleged himself to be. In the case of a busy politician this scrutiny was usually undertaken by his constituency agent who acted as a general consultant on all matters of patronage within the district and sometimes himself named suitable candidates. In 1844 for example Clerk had two vacancies for Stamford which he referred to his local man, Phillips, who supplied in due course a couple of names for the posts. Conversely Phillips kept a vigilant eye on any unauthorized approach to the sitting member. 'I have not', he wrote to Clerk in July 1845, 'been able to discover that Mr King has any particular claim to your consideration as I believe he has never given you a vote but has been generally considered *doubtful*.'[62] On the occasion of another suspect application he warned Clerk that the man concerned had no claim on them. He had at one time been a scot and lot voter but after giving one vote for the conservatives he had voluntarily and knowingly given up his franchise by moving to another house. He was therefore no longer in possession of a vote and Phillips advised that his letter should be ignored.[63]

Even where there was no regular agent to watch over the party interests, jealous pens were often ready to point out any case of a miscarriage of political justice. One such case is preserved among Clerk's Scottish correspondence. In July 1842 Clerk received a letter from a certain George Fenwick of Edinburgh, asking for his assistance in securing the transfer of the writer's son, Geo. F. Fenwick, from the Board of Excise to the Board of Customs. Clerk was unable to do anything for the moment but sent back an encouraging reply. In acknowledging this, Fenwick, with the obvious hope of spurring Clerk on to fulfil his wishes, referred to his own influence and exertions among 'my Catholic brethren and friends, in this City or County' and added that he would spare no

---

[61] All these extracts are taken from different applications for patronage preserved in the Clerk Papers.
[62] Phillips to Clerk, 11 July 1845 (T/188/84).
[63] Phillips to Clerk, 11 May 1843 (T/188/85).

effort 'to render them available to that side of politics of which you have the honor to be a distinguished Member'. At some subsequent date he visited Clerk at his house at Penicuik and was told that his son's name had been placed on Fremantle's list for a vacancy in the Customs. In August, however, a very different complexion was put on the affair by a letter from a Mr Stillie of Edinburgh who wrote 'as an old Tory and having served upon all our Conservative Election Committees'. He warned Clerk that Fenwick had been boasting of having had a promise from Clerk that his son would be transferred from the Excise to the first vacancy in the Customs department át Leith. Then came the exposure. At the time of the Reform Act, he asserted, Fenwick had '*joined the Whigs*, and has ever since continued a bitter and active Whig-Radical, voting with, and supporting them on every occasion'. When O'Connell visited Edinburgh he had acted in his support and was a member of his committee. In 1838 he had qualified for the county franchise as one of a batch of faggot voters created on the estate of Sir James Gibson-Craig but was eventually struck off the register by Clerk's own agent for want of value in the stamp. 'Knowing all this, and as there are too many good and trusty conservatives who are deserving of notice & patronage, I felt it my duty to put you in possession of the simple facts.' This intervention was decisive and a pencilled endorsement on Stillie's letter gave the conclusion of the affair. 'A note has been made that Mr. Fenwick's son is not to be transferred.' So the younger Fenwick was left to languish in the Excise and when after months of fruitless waiting Fenwick senior wrote in March 1843 to remind Clerk of his previous assurances, the letter was docketed with that routine direction that spelled disaster to innumerable hopes—'civil refusal'.[64] Of such stuff did one aspect of politics consist. It was not the most elevating and probably not the most important aspect of political life; but it was one that few working politicians could afford to neglect however much they wearied of the task.

What degree of positive power either politicians or parties derived from the exercise of patronage is a doubtful question. Patronage, for what it was worth, tended to strengthen party ties both at Westminster and in the country. It ranked with other forces in diminishing changes of opinion among voters and

[64] Fenwick to Clerk, 16 July, 20 July 1842, 11 March 1843; Stillie to Clerk, 2 August 1842 (T/188/85).

in producing the characteristically sluggish electorate of early Victorian politics. Administratively it fortified the executive; politically it favoured the party in possession. Nevertheless it was only one factor among many. Patronage did not prevent the whig electoral strength from crumbling after 1832; the absence of it did not keep the conservatives from the triumph of 1841. At most there is the presumption that patronage acted as a check on the decline of the one and the recovery of the other. If even in the highly concentrated areas of government patronage afforded by the dockyard boroughs the influence of government was less than commonly supposed, the electoral effects of the same kind of influence spread more thinly over the whole kingdom can scarcely be expected to be discernible. To the individual politician, or to the party managers engrossed in immediate concerns, patronage must have often seemed an inescapable but burdensome duty with little more than marginal value attaching to it.

Chapter Fourteen

THE INFLUENCE OF THE COURT IN PARLIAMENTARY ELECTIONS

AMONG the several methods of influencing the electoral system still open to the executive government after 1832, the personal power of the crown has a certain intrinsic interest; for though the constituencies affected by it were too few to form more than a minor item in the calculations of the party managers, the part played by the court in elections has obviously a wider political and constitutional significance than the equivalent activities of private politicians, or even ministers of State.

The most favourable field for court intervention was in the boroughs of Windsor and Brighton, the public and the private residences of the monarch, where the electorates were small enough, even in the latter town, to give the royal household a tangible and ascertainable influence. It is true that these two boroughs did not provide the only opportunity, nor did the household servants and royal tradesmen form the only vehicle for crown intervention. The territorial influence of the Duchies of Lancaster and Cornwall was both invoked by ministerial candidates and exercised on their behalf in this period. But working in the wider county constituencies, and faced with the rivalry and sometimes with the jealousy of private landowners, it was more difficult for the crown to exercise any commanding influence over elections. In Staffordshire, where the extensive possessions of the Duchy of Lancaster might be expected, if anywhere, to have political significance, the changes in the representation during this period are more indicative of the ordinary party fluctuations between liberal and conservative than of the control of the government. In the general elections of 1832 and 1835, Mosley and Buller (whigs) were elected for the northern division, Littleton and Wrottesley (whigs) for the southern. In 1837, although the whigs were still in office, two seats were won for the conservatives by Bingham Baring in the northern, and Viscount Ingestre in the southern division. In the western division of Norfolk, an isolated conservative candidate, William Bagge, applied for the support of the Duchy of Lancaster tenants in the constituency at the election of 1835 and finished at the foot of the poll. In 1837, when he could not have obtained that support since his party was out of office, he was one of the tory candidates who captured the division from the whigs.[1] It is improbable that the influence of the scattered Duchy possessions was more effective in county elections elsewhere. The Duchy of Cornwall was similarly ineffective. It possessed and used some influence but it was entirely unable to compete with the local gentry. Grey, Peel, and Melbourne in turn wielded government influence at a general election but in the two Cornish divisions, during the first three reformed parliaments, there was only one contest which produced a change in the representative personnel. In the western division Pendarves and Lemon (whigs) were returned without a contest in the general elections of 1832, 1835, and 1837. In the eastern division Molesworth and Trelawney (whigs) were returned in 1832 and 1835, Eliot (conservative) and Vivian (whig) in 1837. The subordination of Duchy influence to local interests was illustrated by the election of 1835 in the western division. Lord Boscawen wished to contest the constituency and his father, Lord Falmouth, wrote to Peel warning him that 'the vigilance of the Dutchy Council or of the Lord Warden will be necessary as to the Dutchy officers and their connections' and requesting that the influence of the Duchy should be exerted on behalf of Lord Boscawen. Peel accordingly communicated with Sir Herbert Taylor, the king's private secretary, who promised to write to the secretary of the Duchy in Boscawen's interest. He added, however, that they were on 'ticklish ground' there and that Lord Falmouth had previously shown himself a bitter opponent of Duchy rights.[2] But the leading Cornish conservatives were not prepared to support Boscawen and the whole scheme fell through. The influence of the Duchy, though an accessory, was clearly not a dominant factor in Cornish politics.

For what it was worth, however, crown influence both in county and borough was added to the power of the government at elections and helped to give some substance to the theoretical advantage possessed by the ministerial party in an appeal to the electorate.

[1] Add. MS. 40409, fos. 139–40. Bagge's application for government help in the 1835 election was made to Peel who forwarded the correspondence to Wynn, the Chancellor for the Duchy of Lancaster. Such a request from a government supporter would normally be granted and there is no reason to suppose in this case that it was refused.

[2] Add. MS. 40302, fos. 144, 156; 40408, fo. 88; 40409, fos. 17, 23.

But it is in the royal boroughs rather than in the royal counties that any decisive influence of the crown must be sought. In the borough of Windsor the castle had long been the central factor in local elections. A generation before the Reform Act Windsor politics had revolved not round the faction fight of tory and whig but round the contest between the 'loyal' voter who affected, and the 'independent' voter who opposed the 'countenance of the hill'. The first sustained encroachment on royal influence came at the beginning of the century. In 1802 Richard Ramsbottom, a local brewer and banker famous for his 'Windsor ale', contested the borough and was defeated by what appeared to be a coalition of two court candidates. A second attempt in 1806 was successful, however, and when he retired from parliament in 1810, his nephew John Ramsbottom succeeded to his seat.[3] From 1810 until his death in 1845 John Ramsbottom sat continuously as member for Windsor, sharing the borough with the court interest. By 1832 his position was unassailable. Like his uncle he was an important brewer and banker; he was connected with the London firm of Ramsbottom and Newman, and he was a deputy chairman of the Hope Life Assurance Company. Among more miscellaneous qualifications he was a provincial Grand Master of the Freemasons and a former officer of the 16th Dragoons. For over a third of a century, therefore, Windsor as regards one of its two members, was a family borough of the Ramsbottoms.[4] Electoral interest was thus confined to the other seat. This, until the Reform Act, had been consistently occupied by the candidate 'recommended', as Stanley had delicately phrased it in a speech to the Windsor electors in 1831, '. . . from a quarter to which you have invariably paid that deference which is due not less to the station itself, than to the personal character of the illustrious individual to whom I may not more particularly allude'.[5]

Stanley himself indeed was characteristic of the type of member to which the borough had long grown accustomed. He had been returned for Preston in the general election of 1830 but on seeking re-election after his appointment as Chief Secretary in Grey's ministry he had been defeated by Hunt. As soon as it appeared

[3] *Handbills Concerning the Windsor Election* (Windsor 1802); Knight, *Passages of a Working Life*, I, 47–8 (Charles Knight was editor of the *Windsor Express*); Oldfield, *Representative History*, III, 46–7.

[4] There is an obituary notice of John Ramsbottom in the *Gentleman's Magazine* for December 1845.

[5] *Election of Representatives for the Borough of New Windsor* (Windsor 1831).

that he was likely to lose his seat, William IV made an offer of Windsor to the prime minister. Lt.-Gen. Sir Richard Hussey Vivian, the sitting court candidate, duly retired, and Stanley took his place in February 1831 in time for the opening of the reform debates. Though quite safe, however, the seat was not without some incidental expenses to the favoured candidate. In conveying the royal offer Sir Herbert Taylor told Grey that 'having been member for Windsor, I may state that the expenses of the election will amount to about £1,000 and the annual subscriptions, charities, etc., to something less than £100'.[6] But with certainty almost guaranteed this was not an unreasonable sum to pay. The real question was how much longer was that certainty to last. By 1832 the prescriptive division of the borough between Ramsbottom and the court no longer went unquestioned. Windsor was beginning to expand from the lazy, narrow life which Charles Knight described for an earlier period[7] and the Reform Act had inspired some at least of the electors with the hope of radical change even in the shadow of the castle. Such feelings inevitably directed themselves against the existence of a recognized court candidate, for Ramsbottom had disarmed liberal criticism by supporting reform, and his material hold on the borough was too strong to be shaken after twenty years' possession.

On 8 December 1832 the *Windsor Express* came out with a leader headed 'Is Windsor to be a rotten borough?' The election was fought on that issue. The court candidate was one of the whig lords of the Admiralty, Sir Samuel John Brooke Pechell.[8] Against him the reformers in the borough brought forward, less than a week before the election, Sir John de Beauvoir of Connaught Place, Middlesex, a politician of radical principles who was accompanied by a London electioneering agent of the same persuasion. Ramsbottom's return was a matter of course and the contest lay between Pechell and de Beauvoir. The election took place in considerable excitement. Pechell was shouted down at public meetings and the royal servants were hissed when they came up to vote. But the close of the poll saw Pechell twenty-five votes ahead of de Beauvoir with Ramsbottom at the top of the poll by a great majority. A subsequent petition to the House of Commons, complaining of the intervention in the election of the Earl of Belfast,

[6] *Corr. Wm. IV and Grey*, 1, 20.   [7] *Passages of a Working Life*, 1, 47–9.
[8] He was a lord of the Admiralty 1830–4 and 1839–41.

Sir Frederick Watson, and other officers of the royal household, was allowed to lie on the table; and one brought by de Beauvoir against Pechell's return was abandoned before a decision was reached.[9]

At the next election in 1835, when the court candidate was also a tory, the system of court influence was subjected to a severer strain. Pechell had been a court nominee but he had also been a supporter of the whig government that had passed the Reform Act. Sir John Elley, a major-general in the army, who now came forward under the auspices of the castle, was faced with a coalition between Ramsbottom and de Beauvoir. By the time of the election the contest had narrowed to one between the court party aided by the genuine Windsor tories on the one side, and the liberals, radicals, and independents on the other, fought primarily on the issue of nomination or free election. In the end, though the court servants came up from Brighton to poll plumpers for Elley (a significant change from 1832 when they split between Pechell and Ramsbottom), de Beauvoir beat the court candidate by nine votes for second place. From the first it was certain that this defeat would not go unchallenged. Elley at once petitioned against the return on the ground that de Beauvoir had polled invalid votes; and according to the latter he was also threatened by an emissary of the Carlton Club. Undeterred he voted with the opposition on the address to the king's speech and on Russell's crucial Church of Ireland motion; but in April 1835 he was unseated by the committee that tried Elley's election petition. Not content with this vindication of royal power, two members of Elley's committee then prosecuted de Beauvoir for perjury in connexion with his property qualification oath. He was found not guilty but this final experience of the powerful system he had challenged might well have made him reluctant to enter on a third trial of strength in 1837. That he did so was a sign more of tenacity than judgement. The Ramsbottom interest was now arrayed once more on the side of the court candidate who on this occasion was Robert Gordon, secretary to the board of control in Melbourne's second ministry,[10] while the Windsor tories brought forward a candidate

[9] The account of the elections at both Windsor and Brighton in the period 1832–7 is only given here in summary form. For further details and sources, reference should be made to my article 'The Influence of the Crown at Windsor and Brighton in the Elections of 1832, 1835, and 1837' (*E.H.R.*, LIV, 653 sqq.).

[10] He was the son of a Bristol merchant and West India proprietor, and had sat for Cricklade in the parliaments of 1833 and 1835. In the first whig ministries after

of their own, Captain Thomas Bulkeley of the 1st Life Guards. With the opposition split in this fashion Ramsbottom and Gordon were returned with easy majorities over the radical and the tory. Even before the election the loss of the seat had been regarded as certain 'on local grounds' by the conservatives;[11] and de Beauvoir who at first sight thought it futile to stand was only reluctantly persuaded by his supporters to enter the contest.

The evidence on these three Windsor elections, though largely circumstantial, is irresistible. The old system, whereby the crown invariably returned one of the Windsor members on behalf of the ministers of the day, survived the 1832 reform intact even if not unchallenged. Under Grey's ministry, a whig; under Peel, if only as the result of a successful petition, a tory; and under Melbourne another whig had been returned by a faithful court interest. The reforming enthusiasm of 1832, the united prejudices against toryism and the court in 1835, and the combined opposition from tories and radicals in 1837 had all been successfully surmounted, and at the commencement of Victoria's reign the influence of the court at Windsor seemed more firmly entrenched than at any time since the Reform Act. A change, if a change there was to be, could only come from an altered attitude on the part of the crown. It was too much to expect that any government, however high-principled, would deliberately deprive itself of a safe government seat so long as the crown itself sanctioned the practice. It remained to be seen what the new monarch would do.

The results of the 1841 election at Windsor, with a whig queen at the castle and a whig ministry in office, showed one departure from tradition. A court candidate (Fergusson) came forward but he was unexpectedly defeated by a tory-radical coalition in favour of R. Neville, after de Beauvoir halfway through the polling abandoned hope of success and transferred his supporters to the conservatives. For most of Peel's ministry, therefore, the Windsor seats were divided. But in the autumn of 1845, at the very beginning of the Corn Law crisis, the unpredictable happened. Ramsbottom, who had represented the borough for thirty-five years in eleven parliaments, died on 8 October 1845. His passing seemed to herald a new era in Windsor politics. Immediately, the way was now clear for the return of yet another conservative; ultimately, it might even be

the Reform Act he was a commissioner of the board of control, and since 1835 its secretary.
[11] *Berkshire Chronicle*, 22 and 29 July 1837.

possible for both seats in the borough to be controlled on behalf of the government of the day. Even before his decease, the watchful Bonham drew Peel's attention to the impending vacancy.

My friend Col. Reid of the Life Guards and *therefore* connected with the Court as acting in his turn as Silver Stick is anxious to fulfill an intention announced more than two years ago of offering himself as a Candidate *provided* the Government *or* the Palace do not meditate bringing forward any friend of their own and would give him whatever indirect support they might fairly influence. I should state to you that the Colonel has considerable local connexion thro' the principal Brewery and Bank which are in the hands of his Family. He also informs me that unless there is an avowed Court Candidate, he can rely on the strenuous support of the Clergy of both Windsor and Eton.[12]

The need for expedition, or at least decision, on the part of the ministry was the more urgent since John Walter, the proprietor of *The Times*, was already in the field. Four years earlier Walter had secured an unenthusiastic endorsement from the conservative party managers in his contest at Nottingham. But since then the gap had widened and he could not by any stretch of party discipline be considered still as a follower of Peel. He was not for that reason any less formidable an opponent. His estate at Bearwood in east Berks gave him the status of a local landowner; his connexion with the great journalistic organ of the middle classes gave him a national position among liberals; and his constant attacks on the new Poor Law could scarcely have been without effect in the county which was the birthplace of the Speenhamland system. Nor was he lacking friends inside the borough of Windsor. Aided by an influential builder by the name of Bedborough he had started an active canvass of the constituency and even before the vacancy had actually occurred, he had gained the support of a strong party in the town. One of Bonham's local informants assured him that he had seen a strongly anti-ministerial address in the hands of Walter's agent, ready for publication the moment Ramsbottom's death was announced. All were agreed that Walter would be a powerful candidate almost certain to succeed unless active measures were taken and a good man found to put up against him. The position of the conservatives, however,

[12] Bonham to Peel, 29 September 1845 (Add. MS. 40574, fos. 376–8).

was complicated by the continued presence of Captain Bulkeley, who by reason of his earlier efforts had some kind of a claim on the borough and yet by reason of his personality would almost certainly be defeated. Nevertheless Bulkeley was reckoned to possess about a hundred solid votes and had begun privately to canvass the borough in the conservative interest.

In these circumstances it seemed to many conservatives at Windsor that outside intervention was necessary if their cause was not to founder through personal weaknesses and divisions. On 28 September Sir William Fremantle,[13] for many years a court official at Windsor and at one time himself prospective candidate for the town,[14] wrote to his nephew Sir Thomas Fremantle, lately conservative chief whip, to inquire whether the ministerial whips were aware of the impending vacancy at Windsor. 'The Borough', he assured his nephew, 'will be easily attained with a good Candidate supported by the Government.' But that was precisely the difficulty. From Reid's point of view the problem was twofold. He had to secure the backing of the court; and he had to induce Bulkeley to resign his pretensions as the recognized conservative candidate. Once these objectives were obtained, he would have little cause to fear even the proprietor of *The Times*, for Reid himself had a strong personal position in the borough, which, in combination with the favour of the castle and the support of the conservative organization, would prove irresistible. To a limited extent, indeed, he was heir to the old Ramsbottom influence, since some seven years before his death the latter had transferred his brewery to a member of the Reid family; and as a good tory he was generally credited with possessing the support of both the clergy and Eton College. His position at Windsor, therefore, was not that of a mere court candidate, coming to the town as a stranger and departing with the next change of ministry. In his own right he was a good local candidate, endeavouring to profit by his party's tenure of office to secure the additional asset of royal patronage.

The first task was to establish his candidature with the party headquarters. They alone would be able to influence the court and they might also be able to negotiate Bulkeley's withdrawal. An interview with Bonham in London on 29 September proved satisfactory to both sides. A few days later, when he had gathered

[13] The Rt. Hon. Sir William Henry Fremantle, K.G.H., P.C., Treasurer of the Household and Ranger of Windsor Great Park, d. 19 October 1850.
[14] *Corr. Wm. IV and Grey*, I, 20.

more information from independent sources on the state of politics in the borough, Bonham wrote again to his leader to express the opinion that in view of the unusual relation between Walter and the conservative party 'it therefore now becomes a most important consideration for the Govt. to consider whether they should give the most strenuous *or* no opposition to Mr Walter'. Peel, whom he had asked to make confidential inquiries at Windsor, replied that he did not know 'whom to consult at Windsor respecting the prospect of success on which must mainly depend the policy of interference. The competing Conservative candidates should meet. A promise of support given to one might offend the other and thereby diminish the chances of success.' By this time Bonham, who was still pursuing his researches into Windsor politics, had convinced himself that Reid, if strongly supported by the court, would easily beat Walter and that no other court candidate would have the same chance of winning. Indeed some of his informants thought that if Reid declared his candidacy at once, Walter would not even go to the polls. But Reid was unwilling to move until more sure of his ground; or, more precisely, until he received the necessary support from the party managers. This Bonham now proceeded to secure. On 4 October he again wrote to Peel, reminding him of the position at Windsor, and reiterating his view that 'if it is not considered expedient to support Col. Reid, it would be far better not to exasperate Walter by an unavailing opposition'. Meanwhile Reid had opened up negotiations with Bulkeley who promised to go up to town to consult his friends and was expected to call on Bonham in the course of his visit. '*If* this be so', Bonham reported a trifle cynically, 'he only means to make a merit of resigning what he well knows that he could not accomplish.'

Ramsbottom died in the middle of these proceedings, with Bulkeley still in the field and the court patronage unsecured by any one. Peel was engaged to dine at Windsor two days later; on the morning of that day, in his determination not to let slip the golden opportunity, Bonham sent round an urgent note to his chief.

10 October 1845

My dear Sir Robert,
    Ramsbottom died on Wednesday evening and Col. Reid is a Candidate for Windsor but if he does not get the Government

support, I do not believe that he will persevere. You will meet him at dinner today at the Castle, but I will call at Whitehall at four to take the chance of seeing you.

With this note he enclosed a letter from Sir William Fremantle who emphasized once more that 'the Conservatives *united* would I think be pretty certain of carrying the Seat, and they would be united if the government and the Palace avowed their support of *any one* respectable Individual'. Thus adjured Peel set off for Windsor on the evening of 10 October. It was not the kind of commission for which Peel usually had much liking. But he was not unreasonable and there can be little doubt that he had agreed with Bonham to raise the question of court support for Col. Reid. At Windsor he received a note from the prospective candidate indicating his requirements, and he had some conversation with Sir William Fremantle. He also had a conversation with the Queen and Prince Albert. In its way it was a crucial episode even though it merely concerned the fate of an obscure by-election in an unimportant little borough. For what passed between the prime minister and the royal couple was a turning-point in the whole history of the intervention of the crown in elections. When the subject of the Windsor candidate was broached Victoria and Albert made it clear that they were not prepared to continue the practice whereby the court had virtually secured the right of nomination to one of the Windsor seats. It was true that such interference had taken place at previous Windsor elections since Victoria's accession but that, they assured him, had not been with royal acquiescence. To Col. Reid there was no personal objection at court and indeed he was regarded there both from his character and local connexions as an admirable candidate. But, wrote Peel to Sir William Fremantle the following day,

the Queen does not wish to interfere in Elections and there is no separating in this matter the Court from the Sovereign.

The Prince tells me that the interference that did take place during the late administration was contrary to the express wishes of the Queen and himself. Non-Interference must therefore be the Rule— and I cannot authorise any acts or any declarations at variance with that principle. I cannot promise (to take the case specified by Col. Reid) 'that all the persons belonging to the Royal Establishments who have votes, shall be *required* to support Col. Reid'.

Neither can I sanction 'an authorized intimation to the Royal Tradesmen that Col. Reid has the best wishes of the Court'.

Such things would be wholly at variance with that principle to which Her Majesty wishes to adhere, not with reference merely to this Election but to all Elections at Windsor.

The principle of non-interference, Peel continued, was not intended as a prohibition on political activities by individual members of the court. Sir William Fremantle was at perfect liberty, along with any person connected with the castle, to play what part he pleased in favour of Col. Reid.

Individuals may exercise their franchise as they please, but it is not wished to bring the Influence of the Court, that is, of the Sovereign, to bear upon the election at Windsor.[15]

To this categoric refusal on the part of the crown to exercise the traditional royal influence at Windsor, Peel of all men would be the least likely to demur; and no one else was in a position to do so.

In the event the neutrality of the castle proved less disastrous than the conservatives at Windsor had feared. Prudent negotiations with Col. Reid were carried on by Sir William Fremantle, who told Peel on 14 October that there was so much support for a conservative candidate among the influential residents in the borough that he had every hope of success. He added handsomely that 'I think also these Gentlemen are pleased with the decision which Her Majesty has avowed of not allowing Her name and influence to be used on this occasion or in any future election at Windsor.' As Bonham had foretold, Bulkeley proved acquiescent and indeed did much to bring round the ultra-tory element in the constituency in the teeth of the influence of the protectionist party in London and the lukewarmness of the college towards a Peelite candidate. Even Walter in the end withdrew from the contest and in November Col. Reid was duly returned to parliament. At the general election of 1847 he was re-elected together with Capt. John Hay without opposition although by that date Peel had been out of power for many months. The question phrased, perhaps a trifle inaccurately, by the *Windsor Express* in December 1832 had at last been answered; but the change had come not as a result of the

[15] Add. MS. 40575, fos. 29–31.

Reform Act under William IV nor at the hands of a Reform Ministry but from the decision of the Victorian monarchy and under a conservative government. Not an organic change in the political structure of the constituency but a reforming spirit in the castle itself and perhaps a new Germanic notion of the constitutional proprieties had ended the history of crown nomination in the borough of Windsor.[16]

In Brighton, the other royal borough, circumstances were substantially different. Windsor was a small constituency with a population of about 7,000 and electorate of about 500. The system of crown control had been well established before 1832 and there were ample means to exert influence not only through tradesmen and the household but also through the military garrison and the Windsor clergy. At Brighton, on the other hand, the task was not merely to preserve but to create a system of influence. It was one of the new parliamentary boroughs made by the Reform Act and along with such great constituencies as Manchester, Birmingham, and Marylebone had been given two members. The population was over 40,000, the electorate over 1,600 in 1832 and both rapidly increased in the succeeding years. In addition to the unwieldiness of the constituency, there was a strong radical element in the town which would also obstruct any attempt to set up a court faction. Opinion at large, viewing only the outline of the situation, expected the mere presence of the court to be decisive, and the return of two radicals as the first members for Brighton was greeted as a proof of the strength of the new electoral force which was threatening to break up the older party divisions.[17] Nevertheless, the relative success of the court in the face of numerous difficulties may with some justification be regarded as of greater significance.

The first contest in a new and important borough attracted a number of candidates. The outstanding radical among them was Faithfull, a lawyer and a dissenting preacher, and the first choice of the political unions which played a prominent part in the election. In the absence of a second thorough radical, the unions' other candidate was a liberal, Wigney, a member of a wealthy local banking family and a magistrate for the county. The two traditional parties were represented by Crawford, a whig, and

[16] For the general account of this episode, see also Add. MS. 40575, fos. 7, 9, 12–14, 15, 17, 25, 27, 33; 40590, fos. 3–4; and Peel, *Private Letters*, 272.
[17] *Raikes' Journal*, I, 122; Dod, *Parl. Companion* (1833), 58. See also Maccoby, *English Radicalism 1832-52*, 76, for a similar impression.

Dalrymple, a tory. Finally there was the recognized court candidate, Captain George Richard Pechell, a naval officer who had retired from active service in 1830 and had been appointed the following year an equerry to Queen Adelaide.[18] By his opponents he was described as a royal nominee and 'the minion of the court'; by his supporters as 'a personal friend of our beloved sovereign' who would therefore have it in his power to be 'locally as well as nationally useful'. Because of his connexion with the court, Pechell was singled out for attack by the political unions, and it was almost impossible for him to get a public hearing. In spite of that and although he was largely a stranger to the electorate, he finished third at the poll. Wigney was at the head with 873 votes, Faithfull second with 722, Pechell third with 613, and the other two candidates brought up the field with 391 (for Crawford) and 32 (for Dalrymple).[19] The triumph of the radicals was outstanding but the other aspect remained for those who cared to examine it; that at the first attempt the acknowledged court candidate secured nearly a quarter of the total votes cast in the two-member constituency.

Pèchell at least thought that Brighton was worth cultivating, for in the interval before the next election he engaged in many local activities especially on behalf of the fishing population. Harbour improvements were made and a vessel of war sent to stop the depredations of French fishermen on the home fishing grounds. All this was put to Pechell's credit and helped to swell his influence.[20] Unfortunately, however, when the prospect of a general election came in 1834, it was with tory ministers in power who might reasonably expect the court candidate to be one of their own supporters. Pechell's whig opinions, which were one of his qualifications in 1832, complicated his position in 1835. The alternative seemed to be between standing as court candidate at the sacrifice of his political consistency and standing as the whig candidate at the sacrifice of his court influence. But the court was not at Brighton at the time, and with naval resource Pechell at once started his canvass of the borough without publishing any party connexion and still assuming the position of court nominee. His somewhat

[18] He was a younger brother of Sir Samuel John Brooke Pechell, the Windsor member.

[19] *Brighton Gazette*, 6 December; *Brighton Guardian*, 12 December, 19 December; *Brighton Herald*, 17 November 1832. The figures for the poll given in Dod, *Parl. Companion* (1833), 58, differ slightly but not importantly, from those quoted in the text taken from the local press.   [20] *Brighton Gazette*, 8 January 1835.

equivocal position was not unnaturally the subject of ribaldry in the election that followed. But in the course of the contest he broke his leg and by that timely accident was spared the necessity of appearing in public to answer awkward questions from his constituents on his future voting in the house. Horace Smith, the contemporary wit and punster, observed that Pechell's broken leg was in fact the only leg he had to stand on.[21] Sir Herbert Taylor arrived in Brighton towards the end of December and was pardonably aggrieved at Pechell's conduct. But the crown influence in the borough was still a young and precarious growth, and it seemed that Pechell by reason of his appointment would be amenable to ministerial control. After some hesitation between 'Sir A[dolphus] D[alrymple] who would be a staunch supporter or . . . Captain Pechell who *must* become so', Taylor finally ranged the court influence behind the intrinsically stronger candidate. At the same time he wrote to warn Pechell that if he did not on election support the government, he would lose his position in the queen's household.[22] At the election Pechell was duly returned at the head of the poll with Wigney as his colleague. Nevertheless the result put him in a serious quandary. In the first reformed parliament Pechell's political opinions had coincided with his political obligations. In the second he found it impossible to reconcile consistency in his parliamentary conduct with the loyalty to the government expected of him. During the election campaign he had been careful not to express himself against the new ministry. But the stricter warfare of the House of Commons demanded a more unequivocal attitude. He absented himself from the division on the speakership despite a strong hint from Taylor[23] and voted with the government on the address in answer to the king's speech. After that one concession he began to diverge and his insubordination culminated with a vote for the opposition on the Church of Ireland motion. Even before that act of defiance the ministerial whips had been pressing the court to use its influence and Taylor sent another warning to Pechell reminding him of his earlier letter and adding that in the past the king had in similar circumstances invariably demanded from members of the royal household that they should either support the government or resign their posts. Pechell came to see Taylor and pleaded that as an equerry of the

21 Earl of Albemarle, *Fifty Years of My Life*, 378.
22 Add. MS. 40302, fos. 97, 99, 106; 40303, fo. 153.
23 Clerk Papers, Taylor to Clerk, 3 February 1835 (T/188/81).

queen, he did not owe the same duty to the government expected from members of the king's household. Taylor refused to accept the argument and quoted precedents to show that no such distinction had been or could be made.[24] After this clear exposition of his duty, Pechell's action in voting against the government on 2 April seemed to demand immediate disciplinary measures.

On 4 April the king and Lord Denbigh, the queen's Master of Horse, drew up a letter to be sent to Pechell on the queen's behalf, asking for a personal confirmation of his vote on a specified occasion (probably the Irish Church motion), with a view to his dismissal if the vote was acknowledged to be hostile to the ministry. Taylor was consulted and he suggested a few emendations designed to make the authority of the king more patent and thus shield the queen from any suspicion of independent action. Lord Denbigh then proposed that the letter should be submitted to Peel before it was dispatched, but this was opposed by Sir Herbert Taylor and both their majesties on the ground that it would embarrass Peel and possibly prevent the queen from taking a step of which the sole object was to support him. The letter was therefore sent to Pechell the same day without any previous communication to Peel.

The fear that Peel would not entirely approve of the action was well founded. From the minister's point of view, it was ill-timed and clumsily performed. Two issues were involved; the inquiry by a peer as to the vote of a member of the lower House; and the separate intervention of the crown in what was clearly a political matter. On either count there would be enough material for his opponents to launch an attack which radical opinion in the country could not fail to approve. To Peel, struggling to keep a government together in the face of an adverse majority in the Commons, such an outcome to the incident would be far more damaging than the mere loss of a single vote. To crown all, the imprudence had been committed of sending out a letter which half the London press would pay considerably to print. Peel's first care was for the recovery of the correspondence. That done, he proceeded to deliver a gentle admonition to the court.

Secret 5 April 1835. My dear Taylor, . . . I am glad to hear that Lord Denbigh has recovered the letter which he wrote yesterday to

---

[24] Lord Howe had been dismissed for voting against the ministry on the second reading of the reform bill in 1831, while holding the post of Lord Chamberlain in the queen's household (*Corr. Wm. IV and Grey*, 1, 370–2).

Captain Pechell. I think any public use made of that letter would have greatly increased our present difficulties; and I earnestly hope that while the present state of things continues, no step will be taken, having a bearing upon political matters, and upon our position in the house of commons, without consultation with the responsible advisers of the crown. I am sure you will feel that an enquiry made from a member of the house of commons *by a peer*, as to how he voted on a particular question, with a view to his dismissal from office, is in the present state of public affairs, a *political act*, although the office may not be of a political character, and that the necessity of my having to avow that although the king's name was mentioned in the letter approving of the act of dismissal, yet that the resolution had been taken without any knowledge of it on my part, would have placed me in a painful situation. It would have been very difficult for me to state the fact without stating whether I approved of it or not and unless I distinctly declared my approbation of it, the inference would have been that I did not approve of it. Now any appearance of separate action on the part of the court would be (however intended, as I am sure this communication to Captain Pechell was, to strengthen the government) very unfortunate and embarrassing. The dismissal of Captain Pechell *on the grounds* stated by Lord Denbigh, would I assure you, have had in my opinion a very unfortunate effect, and I sincerely rejoice that the matter has been settled as it has been.[25]

Sir Herbert Taylor replied, acknowledging the force of the particular arguments which Peel had put forward, but still upholding his conviction of the general propriety of their action. 'I own I felt', ran his unregenerate opinion, 'that Captain Pechell had incurred the penalty of which he had been forewarned and that I had not the slightest desire to save him.' Nevertheless, he had shown Peel's letter to the king and could assure him that 'nothing will be done in this circle on any future occasion having a bearing on political matters'.[26] Pechell was thus allowed to continue in the anomalous position of a royal servant who opposed the royal ministers until the return of the whigs a few days later regularized his situation.

[25] Add. MS. 40303, fos. 149–50.
[26] Add MS. 40303, fo. 155. It may be noted that Sir John Elley, M.P. for Windsor in 1835–7, voted consistently with the conservatives although after April 1835 they were in opposition. But his position was not the same as Pechell's. He was not a personal servant of the crown, and the conservatives had actually been in office when he appeared as court candidate for Windsor. Pechell had accepted official support under a conservative ministry and subsequently opposed them.

At the next election the complications from which he had so narrowly escaped in 1835 no longer arose. On the other hand, the opposition to him locally as a nominee of the court had increased in temper and outspokenness as a result of his success. As before, the other candidates were Wigney, Dalrymple, and Faithfull; and as at Windsor, the identification of Victoria with the whigs played a material part in the election. Even Wigney, whose return in 1832 had shocked the London clubrooms, made use of the queen's name, while Pechell openly called on the electorate to 'rally round the queen and her government'. His own position must have been enormously strengthened at the beginning of the election campaign by his appointment as groom-in-waiting to the queen. Alarmed by this alliance of crown and whig influence, the radical and tory opposition directed their attack to Pechell's connexion with the court. Dalrymple, embittered perhaps by the way in which he had been deserted by the court in 1835, accused Pechell of being a royal nominee, devoid of political principles, whose whole intent was to convert Brighton into a ministerial borough; and a leading article in the tory *Brighton Gazette* referred to the shameless and unprecedented foothold which had been obtained in Brighton, a creation of the Reform Act, by court and governmental influence.[27] Faithfull, who at first had declined to contest the borough again, entered the campaign less with the hope of election than to prevent the return of both Pechell and Wigney. In this he was successful. Pechell was again returned at the head of an exceptionally large poll but Dalrymple beat Wigney for the second seat by eighteen votes. The tories and the whigs divided between their own men and Pechell; and some fifty electors who split between Dalrymple and Faithfull decided the fate of the other candidates. The radicals rejoiced that they had broken the 'base coalition' between Pechell and Wigney and claimed that the way was now open for a purer contest in future.[28]

The fact remained, however, which even Faithfull could hardly ignore that of the two ministerial candidates, it was the party man who had been rejected and the nominee of the court who had been successful. The fluctuations of electoral fortune that had put Wigney and Faithfull at the head of the poll in 1832 and in 1837 at the foot, served only to reveal the steadiness of the influence which

[27] *Brighton Gazette*, 3 August 1837.
[28] *Brighton Herald*, 29 July, 12 August; *Brighton Gazette*, 17 August; *Brighton Guardian*, 2 August 1837.

Pechell and the court had built up in less than half a dozen years after the Reform Act. It is true that the system was neither so efficient nor so impersonal as at Windsor. Much was clearly due to the combination of Pechell's individual standing at Brighton with his connexion with the crown. Unlike the brief figures that flitted across the hustings at Windsor, he had achieved a position of stability and repute. On the other hand, it is impossible to separate his private from his public character. It was as a member of the royal household that he had attained his power and it was because he was a member of the royal household that obedience to the ministry of the day was expected of him. A certain care and discretion in the use of crown influence, superfluous perhaps at Windsor, was probably necessary in Brighton. But that influence was undoubtedly used by the court and the royal name undoubtedly invoked by the candidate. The incident of Pechell's threatened dismissal in 1835 may be taken as a sign of weakness in the system of court candidatures. But even if it had inaugurated an era in which members of the household were no longer penalized for opposition to the ministry, it would have done nothing to check the system at its source; namely, the construction of a definite court interest in a constituency and its assignment to a specified candidate. In any case, Peel's attitude cannot be so taken. Expediency rather than principle dictated his intervention to save Pechell. A majority government would have dealt less tenderly with a rebel. Moreover, at the very date when the incident occurred, Peel was already convinced that it was useless to carry on the government; in such a case the support or opposition of Pechell was a matter of indifference.[29] As it was, the real importance of the affair for Peel lay in its potential effect on public opinion at a critical period in the evolution of the conservative party. A leader, working under difficulties that were already numerous enough to gain the confidence of the middle classes of the electorate, might well refrain from an action which though justified by the political ethics of the day was inadvisable owing to the exigencies of the moment.

A more normal statement of the conventions, by a prime minister in more normal circumstances, was provided within a few weeks of the Pechell incident. On his return to office in April 1835, Melbourne in a memorandum to the king laid down as a

29 Parker, *Peel*, II, 302–3.

principle that 'it is necessary for the conduct of public affairs under our constitution that the ministry should possess, and be known and felt to possess, the full confidence of the crown (and) the advantage of all the influence which it can command'. He referred to the position of the members of the royal household and stated that he had no wish to interfere 'provided those who compose it, and who have seats in either house of parliament, are prepared to give your majesty's servants a firm, unequivocal support'.[30] By the general standards of the time, therefore, two things were clear; that the crown was entitled to use its influence to return supporters of the government; and that members of the royal household engaged in active politics should reflect their loyalty to the monarch in their obedience to his ministers. As long as those elements remained in the constitution the theoretical conditions for a system of crown influence were assured. The important hindrances were material: the increase in the size of the electorates and popular prejudice against a royal nominee.

In Brighton neither of these at the accession of Victoria was as yet 'decisive; nor on the other hand was the court influence the preponderant factor that it clearly was at Windsor. It had, it is true, shown remarkable vigour and resilience in establishing itself in the new constituency. But Pechell himself would clearly be a difficult man to shift; and the size of the constituency enabled public opinion to have a much freer play than in the small borough of Windsor. Even if Victoria and Albert had not inaugurated a new era of crown politics, it was improbable that the influence of the court would ever have been more than one factor among many in the Brighton constituency. But the royal purchase of Osborne in the spring of 1845, the visits to Balmoral from 1848 onwards, and its ultimate purchase in 1855, made inevitable the decline of Brighton as a royal residence. In proportion as the splendours of the Pavilion paled before the domestic charms of the Isle of Wight and the romantic deer-forests of Deeside, the prospect of establishing an effective court party at Brighton became remote.[31] By 1850 there was little to distinguish the constituency from any other large prosperous seaside town with more than its share of wealthy and retired families. It was conservative though

---

[30] *Melbourne Papers*, 270–1. For a reference to the position of the queen's household, see *ibid.*, 275.

[31] According to Fulford (*The Prince Consort*, 77), Victoria and Albert paid their last visit to the Pavilion in 1845, and it was finally sold to Brighton Corporation in 1850.

not tory; liberal but not radical. In the 1841 election Pechell and Wigney were again returned, defeating the tenacious Dalrymple by a substantial margin. In May 1842 Wigney took the Chiltern Hundreds and was succeeded by Lord Alfred Hervey,[32] a Peelite conservative. Pechell and Hervey were returned at the general election of 1847 in a triangular contest, and again in 1852. Pechell indeed continued to sit for Brighton until his death, as Vice-Admiral Sir George Brooke Pechell, Bart., in 1860.

[32] Alfred Hervey, styled Lord Alfred Hervey, sixth son of the 5th Earl of Bristol, b. 1816. He was included by Bonham among the inner ring of Peelites in 1852, and was appointed a lord of the Treasury in the Aberdeen ministry.

Chapter Fifteen
CLUB GOVERNMENT

IT was not accidental that the decade that witnessed the Reform Act should also see the foundation of the two famous clubs, the Carlton and the Reform. Indeed it would be true to say that the period between the first and second Reform Acts was as much the golden age of the political club as of the private member. There was, moreover, a direct relationship between these two characteristic aspects of contemporary political life. The first was the necessary corrective, at once effective and flexible, to the independence of the last. In the history of party management it was an age of what Edward Ellice once called 'club government' to an extent never realized before or since. The political independence of the House of Commons had of course been growing for a generation or more before 1830 and the Reform Act was but one of several landmarks in the process. But the circumstances surrounding the passing of the act compelled politicians to consider more urgently this developing problem. Equally truly the club as a political centre was not a novelty. In the course of the eighteenth century it had become a feature of the political life of the capital. But what distinguished the Carlton and the Reform from their predecessors was that the earlier political clubs were social centres in which politics had gradually taken a hold, whereas the former were from the outset designed as party political organizations. Both Brooks's and White's, as their names indicated, had originally been proprietary clubs. The first was a gambling club established in 1764 by the famous Mr Almack and subsequently taken over by Brooks, a wine merchant, as a business venture. White's started in 1693 as a chocolate-house in St James's Street and early in the eighteenth century became a private gambling club kept by a Mr Arthur. The Carlton and the Reform, however, followed the new development, conspicuous after the Napoleonic War, of founding large public subscription clubs deliberately catering for a clientele with a special interest or profession. The Travellers' Club (1814), the United Service Club (1816), and the Athenæum (1824) were the first clubs of this new type.[1] The Carlton (1832)

[1] Timbs, *Club Life of London*, I, 241.

was the first of this new type to be based on common political associations and objects. 'It was no mere new club established for the social meeting of gentlemen generally professing the same opinions, as Whites' or Brookes',' said a hostile account in 1835, 'from the first it was a political association organized for party and parliamentary purposes.'[2] This was equally true of the Reform Club founded a few years later. The period also saw the beginning of modern party organization in the form of constituency associations; the appointment of central managers, concerned not only with elections and candidates but also with the recruitment of party electors; the formation of central registration committees; and the growth of election agents as almost a profession in itself. But all these unexpected developments of the registration clause of the Reform Act took time to build up and encountered distrust and opposition even within the party they were designed to serve. Not until after the second Reform Act were the local party organizations in the constituencies able through their central association meetings to make a direct and effective contribution to party solidarity at the centre and to the formation of party policy. In the gap thus intervening during this period between local and central party organization came the political club. It was less obnoxious to the old-fashioned whig or tory because of its long established rôle in politics, but refurbished and directed specifically to party purposes it was able to meet the immediate needs of the new situation. Within the limitations imposed by its constitution, it com bined the functions of central office and national party conference; and as such it was the characteristic feature of early Victorian politics.

In both the main parties of the period the provision of a club as a social bond of union was inextricably entwined with the organization of central machinery for the supervision of the register and the conduct of elections. Yet the manner in which the conservative and liberal parties conformed to a common political situation differed in almost every point of detail. With the conservatives the formation of a club preceded by several years the effective establishment of a central organization. With the liberals the foundation of the Reform Club was subsequent to, and grew out of, the early efforts at registration machinery. There can be no doubt that the sharper minds on both sides realized at once the implications

[2] *Edinburgh Review*, LXII, 171.

of the Reform Act for the management of parties and elections, and in particular, the immense importance of the registration clause.[3] But the marked difference in the way in which the two parties as organizations reacted to the new electoral structure throws a suggestive light on the character of the two bodies.

The first impulse towards the founding of the Carlton Club came not so much from the details of the Reform Act, however, as from the victory of the reforming party that made the act possible. It was the sting of defeat that drove the tories to undertake their first important measure of re-organization and the initial object was little more than to construct a permanent political centre for the forces of conservatism. The first move was made in 1831 immediately after the general election that gave the whigs their massive reform majority. Fifteen members of the tory party drawn from both houses met at an address in Charles Street, off St James's Square, formerly occupied by Planta. They agreed to rent the house as a party headquarters and to defray the cost by subscription. The intention was to use the place not merely as an office but also as a point of assembly for the party in general. A considerable amount of money for that purpose was in fact raised though also rapidly expended and by 1833 there was an unpleasant legacy of bad debts and threatened legal proceedings to be settled. Nearly a thousand pounds was owing on past and current expenses and it was necessary to raise a fresh subscription before the ill-starred 'Charles St. office' could finally be liquidated. One of the primary objects of the new headquarters was that it should serve as a centre for press management and indeed when it was first set up the independent press fund of the party under the control of Planta was merged in the general Charles St. fund under the control of Holmes, the chief whip, and Fitzgerald, the secretary of the office. But equally clearly it was a centre of general party organization. In August 1831 for example Peel told his wife that 'I went this morning to Charles St. and told the persons assembled there that I could not undertake to continue in town . . . I found several people, such as Lord Chandos, Sir C. Wetherell, and Lord Stormont, dissatisfied with this and prepared to go on interminably on the present system [i.e. parliamentary opposition

[3] For a general discussion of the connexion between registration and party organization in the nineteenth century, see J. Alun Thomas, 'Registration and the Development of Party Organization 1832–70' (*History*, xxxv, 81 sqq.).

to the reform bill]. Others were disposed to agree with me and seemed anxious to bring the business to a close. We parted not in very good humour.'[4]

It was the circumstance that the Charles Street house was a party rendezvous as well as an office that made it the indisputable progenitor of the Carlton. Within six months indeed Holmes had come to the conclusion that the premises were too small to serve as a party headquarters and favoured turning them into a club. At the same time he was inclined to deprecate the excessive concentration on press management which had been one of the original objects of the place and was already leading them into some difficulty and much work. It was from this situation that the Carlton Club took its rise. Throughout its brief career the Charles Street office bore the marks of hasty and amateurish improvisation. Its main defect was that it was involved too deeply in the treacherous coils of press management and that as a permanent establishment it called for recurrent subscriptions at a rate that could not be maintained in the absence of any personal advantage to the subscribers. In October 1831 a remarkable proposition was laid before the Duke of Wellington by Lord Mahon in the shape of a draft letter, to be issued by Holmes or Fitzgerald from Charles Street, requesting each member of the tory parliamentary party to contribute £50 towards the attainment of 'an object of great and pressing importance to the constitutional cause'. This sanguine and ingenuous circular, reminiscent of the best days of the South Sea Bubble, was calculated by the party managers to be likely to raise £10,000; and the money was to be used to finance the *Herald* or the *Ledger* newspaper for party purposes. 'Supposing', observed the duke dryly in return, 'that there are 200 gent^n able to part with such a sum without inconvenience, which I think doubtful, you would scarcely expect that they would not require an explanation of the objects of the subscription.'[5] An organization conducted in this optimistic spirit was not likely to endure. Nevertheless the men concerned in the Charles Street venture comprised, with the significant exception of Peel, all the leaders and organizers that the party could boast at that date. In the first category were Wellington, Buccleuch, and Aberdeen; in the second Arbuthnot, Holmes,

---

[4] Peel, *Private Letters*, 134.

[5] For the history of the Charles Street office, see Aspinall, *Politics and the Press*, 336–40, and the Apsley House MSS., printed in the Appendix, 467, 471–3. See also Ellice's reference to Charles Street in *Hansard*, xxv, 298.

Herries, Charles Ross, Granville Somerset, Rosslyn, Hardinge, and Goulburn. The notable absentee was Peel and that absence could hardly have been without effect. So strong indeed was the impression of his aloofness that Greville wrote that he never gave a farthing to the funds raised by the Charles Street organization and that from the time when it became a question of subscriptions he ceased to go there.[6] But, Peel apart, there was an obvious desire in the party for greater cohesion and direction in the party affairs. Out of the failure of Charles Street came the Carlton.

The second session of the 1831 parliament opened on 6 December 1831. In an atmosphere different from that of midsummer, with spirits renewed by the autumn recess and numbers strongly mustered for the last and critical battle of reform, the conservatives now took up seriously the project of founding a party club. 'We are going', wrote Arbuthnot to his wife on 21 December, 'to form a great club to be the best in London. The duke and Peel are to be of the Com[tee.] & I have promised to ask the D. of Portland etc. etc. to be of it also.' To many people the certain triumph of reform and the revolutionary excitement of that autumn were in themselves a stimulus to fresh efforts on the side of the party of conservation. 'The idea of the Club is admirable', commented the Marquess of Londonderry, '& should be anxiously & zealously work'd. Communication between those who were formerly *not allies* should be cherish'd & sought.' Some preliminary meetings were held in the Charles Street premises and by the spring of 1832 the scheme was ready for launching. At a meeting held at the Thatched House Tavern on 10 March, with the Marquess of Salisbury in the chair, a committee was appointed to arrange the housing and management of the new club and it was made known that Lord Kensington's house in Carlton Terrace would be available as a club building. At a later meeting on 17 March the title of the Carlton Club was formally adopted. A large number of persons had been circulated and before the end of the month some five hundred had agreed to become members. The membership of the club was tentatively fixed by the rules at 700 and raised to 800 the following year.[7] One material reason for the rapid success of the club was that it supplied a very real need for a social centre in the party.

[6] *Greville Memoirs*, II, 328.
[7] Information on this and several other points connected with the early history of the club I owe to the courtesy of the secretary of the Carlton Club.

In April that fashionable man about town Raikes noted in his journal that the new tory club had been formed. 'The object is to have a counterbalancing meeting to Brooke's, which is now purely a Whig reunion; White's, which was formerly devoted to the other side, being now of no colour, and frequented indiscriminately by all.' In November Raikes was present at 'a house dinner of tories at the Carlton Club' which was attended by the leaders and officials of the party, Peel, Scarlett, Grant, Herries, Bonham, Holmes, and others, all apparently in high spirits at the progress of the election. In January the amenities of the club were improved by the engagement of a French cook.[8] Perhaps in consequence Arbuthnot could report a couple of months later that the club was always full and flourished greatly with many dinners.[9] The club was first housed at Lord Kensington's residence at 2 Carlton Terrace but in 1835 it moved to the new club-house designed by Sir Robert Smirke in Pall Mall. The steady growth in membership enabled new premises to be taken in on the west side in 1846 and various other extensions and alterations to be made.

But the Carlton was not, and was never intended to be, a mere social centre for gentlemen of the same way of thinking. Politics and political management were dominating considerations from the start; and the Carlton was designed to be a point of union and the centre of organization for the whole party. Within a few years of its foundation the club contained the substantial strength of conservatism in England. There was a row of impressive names for the trustees of the club: the Duke of Buccleuch, the Marquess of Salisbury, the Earl of Verulam, the Earl of Lincoln, and Lord Redesdale. Men like the Earl of Rosslyn, Hardinge, Francis Baring, Sugden, and Sidney Herbert served on the committee of management. The full complement of members was maintained and there was a long waiting list of applicants. Its membership included not only the great bulk of the actual parliamentary party but all who counted for influence and activity among the recognized leaders of conservatism in the provinces, in the diplomatic service, and in the fighting forces.[10] Membership of the club thus became both a token of adherence in the party and to the outside

---

[8] *Raikes' Journal*, I, 21, 110, 141.

[9] For Arbuthnot's share in the founding of the club, see Aspinall, *Corr. of Charles Arbuthnot*, 149, 155, 157, 168.

[10] There is a list of the members of the club dated April 1836 in the British Museum (908. d. 18/14).

world a badge of allegiance. When in 1841 Sir James Graham, with an eye for the effect on the ensuing session of parliament, wished to make a public demonstration of his and Stanley's adhesion to the conservatives, he arranged that they should be elected to the Carlton and their nomination for membership should be known before the session started. It would be useful, he told Arbuthnot, as 'a proof of cordiality and perfect union'.[11] Stanley consented to the move and the formal history of the 'Derby Dilly' closed at the committee meeting at the Carlton in January 1841 that elected Stanley and Graham to the membership of the club.[12] An example of this attitude in reverse came in 1842 when Lord Ashley, as a result of the breach between himself and the party over the Ten Hours bill, thought it obligatory to offer his resignation to the club. He wrote to Bonham, explaining the line of action he proposed to take up over the bill, and inquired 'whether such a course would not leave me in a very curious position as a member of the Carlton Club, engaged, as I shall be, in decided and vigorous opposition to the ministers?' Bonham consulted Graham and in the end Ashley was persuaded not to persist with his resignation. He remained a member of the club from its foundation until 1868.[13]

It is significant nevertheless that lack of conformity with the official policy of the party leaders could be regarded as a disqualification for the club. Not all individual eccentrics were as sensitive as Ashley but it is clear that the main body of the club attempted on occasions to exert a social and moral pressure in order to secure conformity. Philip Pusey, the Berkshire member, came under this form of boycott in 1835 as a result of his vote for the whigs on the Irish Church bill. Even Croker felt impelled to write to Peel asking him to use his influence with the 'madmen' at the Carlton to stop their attacks on Pusey. '*A majority*', he pointed out, 'might brand *deserters*—but if there are to be no deserters, how are our Carltonians ever to be in a majority again? Moreover think of the indecency in times like these of claiming mere party votes.'[14]

[11] *Arbuthnot Corr.*, 225.
[12] Add. MS. 40616, fos. 180, 183, 185, 195. According to Graham, Stanley said that 'if his accession to the Carleton [*sic*] would reconcile or prevent differences, the Time is in his opinion come, when our juncture is a matter of course; for after some years of mutual probation it is more natural that we should be members than we should not'.
[13] See my article, 'Ashley and the Conservative Party' (*E.H.R.*, LIII, 679 sqq.).
[14] Add. MS. 40321, fo. 156.

Another victim was William Lascelles, son of the 2nd Earl of Harewood, who had been a member of the managing committee of the club in 1835. According to Monckton Milnes, himself a local resident, the defeat of Lascelles at Wakefield in 1841 was largely due to distrust emanating from London. 'My friend William Lascelles', he wrote to Peel, 'has lost his election & the party a vote in consequence of the gossip of that political scullery, the Carlton Club, & the stupid violence of party newspapers. The Tories at Wakefield had been made believe that he had deserted his profession and would take no pains about his return.'[15]

The club was also the hub of the party election machinery. In the Carlton was to be found the centre of electoral information; the home of the party election committees; the office of dispatch for the whips' correspondence; and the main collecting-point for the party subscriptions. By means of its central position constituencies that were vacant and politicians that were unattached could be put in touch with each other. The pleasant chapter in *Coningsby* which deals with the Darlford delegation in search of 'a very rich man, who would do exactly as they liked, with extremely low opinions and with very high connections' and their final introduction at the Reform Club to young Mr De Crecy who 'looked like the rosebud which dangled in the button-hole of his frock-coat' probably owed much to Disraeli's observations of similar scenes in the Carlton. Sometimes the more active members of the club intervened directly in the election contests of the constituency in which it was situated. Hardinge described to Peel how on the occasion of Burdett's election at Westminster in May 1837 the club decisively whipped up its supporters in the constituency on the day of the poll. The local conservative committee, he said, was not good but 'our young men of the Carlton, about 120, divided into districts, were at their posts before 7 o'clock, urging the voters who had promised to the Poll'.[16] Disraeli has a characteristic entry in his diary on this episode. 'Distinguished myself very much in the election of Burdett for Westminster; the success mainly attributable to myself; proposed and organized the youth of the Carlton including all the nobility, fashion, and influence of our party— Lord Forester, and his brother,[17] Codrington, H. Baring, Pigot, Sir H. Campbell, etc. etc.' From other documents written in a more

---

[15] Add. MS. 40485, fo. 108. Lascelles was subsequently seated on petition.
[16] Add. MS. 40314, fos. 175–6.   [17] Cecil Forester.

credible vein it appears that the Carlton Club mapped the constituency into districts and that Disraeli along with others was
allotted to the Mayfair area and so was 'obliged to canvass' in the
curious colony of servants, grooms, and cooks which he later
described in the first chapter of *Tancred*.[18]

The strong political complexion of the Carlton gave particular
significance to the formation of the second party club, the Conservative, in 1840. Ostensibly this was an ancillary society designed
for those who were unable to gain admission immediately to the
crowded membership of the Carlton. It is clear, however, that it
also possessed something of the nature of a dissident opposition
body and was regarded as such by the party managers. Writing
to Arbuthnot in June 1840 on the differences within the party over
the Canada bill, Graham added pessimistically 'there is also a new
Club about to be formed, an offshoot from the Carleton, from
which I anticipate great mischief and a serious schism in the conservative ranks. All this is most unfortunate, when we are on the
verge of success and when at any moment our victory may be
decisive.'[19] Bonham, though not so despondent as Graham,
certainly shared his view that the Conservative Club was what a
later Victorian generation would have called a 'cave' of malcontents. However, he set to work to gather information about the
new society and when the first list of members was drawn up,
succeeded in procuring a copy in spite of the efforts made to keep
it secret. On 17 September 1840 he wrote a cheerful letter from
Brighton to inform Peel that after all the excitement about the
new conservative club, the mountain had only brought forth the
proverbial mouse. The list of members included only ten members
of the House of Lords and twenty-seven of the House of Commons,
and with two ducal exceptions hardly a man among them of even
average influence. Some of the members had joined, he thought,
on a false apprehension of the real character of the club and its
relations to the leader of the party; but generally speaking the
names were what would be expected, as well as the motives.
Another letter, written some ten months later, in July 1841 showed
that his distrust was still active. In a discussion of the nomination
to the borough of Athlone, which he said would unquestionably
be in the hands of Lord Castlemaine at the next election, he added
that it was essential that it should not fall into the hands of the

---

[18] Monypenny, *Disraeli*, I, 367, 370.   [19] *Arbuthnot Corr.*, 218.

conservatives with whom that peer was closely connected 'in their new Club', and who he had every reason to know lost no opportunity of strengthening their own particular interests.[20] It is obvious therefore that the Conservative Club was regarded at the outset as a potentially disloyal organization. Writing a generation later John Timbs the antiquarian observed that though many of the conservative chiefs were honorary members of the club, they rarely visited it; and instanced the fact that Sir Robert Peel was said never to have set foot in the club except once to view the interior.[21] Certainly the existence of two conservative clubs in the forties was not a mark of strength; and though the Conservative was in no real sense a rival to the Carlton, it is not easy to say how far it constituted a disruptive element.[22]

Nevertheless the outstanding fact was that the conservative party was the first to establish a club of the new type and that in comparison with their political opponents they accomplished it with little difficulty or internal disagreement. For this there were perhaps several reasons. One was that the tories had not previously possessed a specifically party club of their own; another was that adversity had served as a stimulus to effort; and lastly there was the circumstance that as a party they were socially more homogeneous than the motley body of reformers. The whigs on the other hand already had in Brooks's a convenient party centre; their comfortable parliamentary majority between 1831 and 1837 made any further party reconstruction seem less urgent; and any development would probably confront them with the awkward dilemma of either admitting radicals to the sacred precincts of Brooks's (which the radicals themselves would conceivably neither wish nor be able to afford) or starting a new society which would be a rival to the old whig club. In view of the barely civil relationship between many of the whigs and their undesired but indispensable allies, there may well have been a private apprehension that to surrender Brooks's as the social centre of the party would be to surrender the party itself to radical penetration. The radicals themselves, as the acrimonious history of the founding of the

[20] Add. MS. 40428, fo. 303; 40485, fo. 357.

[21] Timbs, *Club Life of London*, I, 276.

[22] It is an extraordinary circumstance that Greville, who frequently refers to the Carlton as the 'Conservative Club' during the thirties (and so misleads his editors), apparently lived from 1840 to 1854 thinking that the Carlton and the Conservative were one and the same club until his error was exposed by a letter he wrote to *The Times* in the latter year (*Greville Memoirs*, VII, 7).

Reform Club makes plain, certainly attributed these motives to their colleagues. It is not surprising, therefore, that the Reform Club did not appear until several years after the Carlton and that but for radical pressure it would not have come even then.

The institutional origin of the Reform Club may be traced back to two separate sources. The first of these was the radical political association known first as the Westminister Club and then as the Westminster Reform Club, founded in 1834. The type of politician present at the preliminary meetings—John Wilks, Rigby Wason, Daniel O'Connell, and Whittle Harvey—showed its unmistakable radical texture; and it was housed at 24 Great George Street, the residence of Alderman Wood, a London hop-merchant and former Lord Mayor, who was a radical M.P. for the City. It was for this club that Disraeli, in the early and ambiguous manœuvres of his political youth, was proposed and elected as member though his actual association, such as it was, only lasted about six months. He withdrew in February 1835 and the club returned his subscription. The same month that Disraeli ended his connexion, Hume became a member; and it was Hume who suggested that the title of the society should be changed to the Westminster Reform Club. It is unlikely that it was then more than an extra-parliamentary gathering of radicals, formally constituted and financed by subscriptions. Ordinary club amenities could not have been present to any great extent and Hume at least felt the need to extend its compass.[23] It was from this desire among the radicals to form a central and national focus for the liberal element in politics, foreshadowed in the partial and limited experiment of the Westminster Club, that the Reform Club proper eventually emerged.

There was a second current setting in the same direction, also under radical inspiration. Joseph Parkes of Birmingham, who had been engaged in registration work in Warwickshire after the Reform Act, early perceived the need for money and organization in that crucial sphere of party activity. His friend and patron, Lord Durham, himself one of the authors of the Reform Act which had set the problem, was also keenly aware of the futility of individual sporadic efforts if radicalism was to be the potent force in politics which its supporters hoped and its opponents dreaded. Durham and Parkes had worked in close collaboration over the question of registration and in 1834 Durham founded the Reform Association

[23] Fagan, *The Reform Club*, 19–32.

primarily as an organization for registration purposes. In the
general election of 1835 he publicly advocated the necessity for a
general organization of liberal supporters throughout the country.
'The great nail to drive home is the formation and organization of
political associations in every town and village of the Empire', he
declared; and the result of the election seemed to justify his assertion
to Parkes that 'for four years the Whigs have never tried to rally
talent and zeal to themselves'.[24] In July 1835 Durham left for
Russia but Parkes, whose appointment in 1833 as secretary to the
Municipal Corporations Commission brought him into contact
with radicals all over the country, carried on with the work of
improving and extending the Reform Association. A registration
office was opened in London; branches were established in the
provinces; and an active correspondence set up.[25]

Thus by 1834 the Westminster Club and the Reform Association were in existence side by side; and by 1835 both were showing
signs of expansion. With prominent radicals sharing in the activities of both organizations (Parkes, the leading spirit behind the
registration office was also one of the founders of the Westminster
Club), it was an obvious step to attempt a fusion of the two concerns. What was clearly wanted was something that the conservatives already possessed in the Carlton Club: a place of social
amenities for liberal parliamentarians, rooms for party managers
and organizers, and a point of contact for liberal politicians both
metropolitan and provincial. Durham had already in 1835 urged
the necessity of such a club, in addition to a registration committee;
and the shock administered by the dismissal of the whigs and the
formation of Peel's ministry in 1834 seemed to provide the necessary
impetus for action. Following the formation of the grand parliamentary alliance of whigs, radicals, and Irish to defeat the conservative government in February 1835, a serious proposal was
made to form a liberal club of which both whigs and radicals
should be members. Besides Durham, other whigs such as Mulgrave appeared to favour the project and for a moment it seemed
on the verge of realization. 'It will be like the Athenaeum', wrote
Molesworth enthusiastically to his mother on 19 February, 'a good
dining club. The great object is to get the Reformers of the country
to join it, so that it may be a place of meeting for them when they
come to town. It is much wanted. Brooks' is not liberal enough,

[24] Reid, *Life of Durham*, II, 3–4.   [25] Buckley, *Parkes of Birmingham*, 136–8.

too expensive, and not a dining club.'[26] But there was no real response from the whigs and the idea was still-born. 'It failed', said Molesworth subsequently, 'in consequence of the Whigs being opposed to it secretly.' In view of their attitude twelve months later there can be little doubt that this was true; but true or not, the radicals believed it and their belief coloured their future actions. Obviously a club that set out to provide the facilities of the Carlton or the Athenæum would find it difficult to dispense with the subscriptions of the whig gentry. But though temporarily repulsed the more pertinacious of the radicals were still determined to have their club, with the whigs or without.

During the recess before the beginning of the 1836 session a dozen of the radical leaders, including Hume, Parkes, Molesworth, Grote, and Ward, took up the project. Hume, to whose veteran authority both whigs and radicals attached much weight, was pressed by Molesworth to exert himself in forming a club, independently if necessary of the whigs, leaving them to join later if they thought proper. Hume consented and the self-appointed group of radicals at once began to look about for a suitable building to house the new foundation. E. J. Stanley, Ellice, and one or two other liberal whigs were informed but their attitude was lukewarm and for a time the project hung fire once more. Ellice, who in some respects was one of the most important links between the parliamentary radicals and the main body of whigs, proved particularly disappointing. During the winter recess he was over in Paris but Parkes, Hume, and Stanley wrote to him repeatedly on the subject; and Parkes, with whom he was on good terms, strongly urged him to support the new club. But Ellice's instincts were not nearly so radical as his friendships. He replied cautiously, recommending moderation and telling Parkes to consult with other leading radicals before deciding finally on anything. The following letter, though undated, was probably written at this time and in any case uncovers some of the motives for Ellice's opposition to the proposed reform club. It was sent to Parkes.[27]

> I have written to Jo. Hume about his club, stating that my ultimate opinion will depend upon the grounds he could show for the success of the undertaking on a large scale, and if they were not clear, we should rather endeavour by degrees to enlarge the foundations of

---

[26] Fawcett, *Molesworth*, 74. See also, Chester New, *Lord Durham*, 275.
[27] Ellice Papers, Ellice to Parkes, undated, but endorsed 1836, in a different hand.

our Reform association, than risk the failure of a greater speculation under present circumstances. I *have serious doubts* whether any attempt to carry this club system further would be popular, and how far many of the Town Councils would be frightened by the cry that would immediately be set up of 'club government'. Suppose some of the liberals, for you know they are not all radicals,—Coventry[28] for instance,—think one way, some another. Would a division be a good thing or tend to give the ennemy [*sic*] a more wholesome opinion or apprehension of our strength?

In view of the generally quiet state of affairs, he continued, his preference would be to remain on the defensive.

However, I have written to leave the whole thing open till the week after the meeting,[29] when I propose to call a meeting of the General Committee of the other Club[30] and hear how opinions were on the larger concern. . . . I will march with the mass, if only to guide it, but do not let us lose our reputation for prudence and good management. . . . If it is only desired to change the *local* of the Club, to nearer Westminster, I have no objection to that, and I will endeavour to take the present House off their hands.

Faced with this kind of attitude from one whom they had reason to regard as among the most friendly of the official whigs, the radicals decided that the only hope of success lay in prompt and independent action. Parkes and Molesworth told Hume that 'now was the time or never' and he agreed to a meeting. On Tuesday 2 February, the day before Ellice returned from Paris and two days before the meeting of parliament, the mine was exploded. The three radical conspirators called together a select handful of supporters. Only seven came, of whom five were members of parliament. It was formally determined that there should be a Reform Club, and Molesworth, Parkes, Grote, Ward, and some others drew up a memorandum to that effect. To this document was attached a list of some fifty names, forming an alleged committee. Most of these were M.P.s known or believed to be favourable to the project, though according to Molesworth none of them would have consented individually to the particular transaction for which their names were used. The slender composition of the little junto that hatched out these proceedings was concealed by the simple

---

[28] For which Ellice was M.P.   [29] Presumably, of Parliament.
[30] From the succeeding reference this is presumably a reference to the Westminster Club.

expedient of omitting a list of those present at the meeting. The document was dated London, lithographed, and launched on an unsuspecting world. As Molesworth wrote:

> This was a most bold and impudent blow. And I don't believe, except the five who were present, any other persons of our party would have consented to such a proceeding. We took the best of the Radicals and no Whigs [sc. for the list of the committee members] On Thursday the House met. Many of the circulars had been presented; the Whigs consequently saw them and were thunderstruck. . . . A shell had been thrown into the midst of them and had exploded; who threw it they could not make out. They went about trying to trace who had been present at the meeting which issued this circular. They could only trace Parkes, Hume and myself.

Even the few whigs who had been apprized in general terms of the radical wish for a new club could scarcely have been other than surprised and a little indignant at this sudden and arbitrary move. Molesworth, who was in a provocative mood, threw oil on the flames by inquiring tauntingly of Ellice on meeting him the same day whether he had come over from Paris to assist them in making a club. The following day, Friday, 5 February, what Parkes described as 'a House of Commons row' took place. Ellice went to Molesworth as he was going out of the House and requested him to say exactly what the radicals were about. Molesworth told him that they were forming a club and when Ellice asked why they had not consulted him and the more liberal whigs, he replied flatly that they had twice frustrated the radical efforts to that end in 1835; that now the radicals were determined to have a club; that the whigs might join them, and if they did, the radicals would be delighted to welcome them. They desired all reformers to assist in the work and proposed to circularize the members of the Reform Association the next day. Ellice then asked if the radicals wished to lead the whigs, as if they acted in that manner they would break up the party. Molesworth retorted that if the whigs thought they could lead the radicals just as they thought fit, they were mistaken.

On Molesworth's own confession the conversation was not of the most courteous description. The upshot was that Molesworth and Ellice, joined by E. J. Stanley, the whig whip, went to Parkes' residence at Great George Street. There, still with some heat, the debate was continued. Parkes pointed out that Ellice had been told repeatedly of what was being planned while he was in Paris; that Ellice had urged Parkes to consult Grote, Blackburne, Warburton, and other radicals; that this had been done; and that those gentlemen fully approved. Ellice and Stanley then mentioned several reformers in parliament who were opposed to the project or had stated their ignorance of it. Parkes asserted that all the names mentioned were men who had either attended many meetings held in connexion with the formation of a new club, or had expressed their approval of it. The debate then moved to wider issues. Ellice and Stanley urged the objections to a club; Parkes and Molesworth stated decisively that a club was going to be founded and the only question was whether the whigs would co-operate. They made it clear, however, that they both thought it desirable that the club should embrace all classes of liberals. The two whigs then began to yield ground. Ellice complained of the exclusively radical character of the published list of the committee. Parkes countered by saying that it was merely a list of those known to be favourable and that the following day it was intended to secure the accession of all the members of the Reform Association and then proceed to the final organization of the club. At this the whigs threw in their hands. They agreed that they would have no objection to such a union of reformers if the committee could be made representative of all sections and included the names of the leading whigs. To this Parkes and Molesworth readily agreed and an amended committee list was drawn up on the spot in Ellice's handwriting. Most of the suggestions were made by Ellice and Stanley, though mutual concessions were made, and it was at Ellice's request that O'Connell was added to the list. It comprised in its amended form some thirty-five names of whom twenty were radicals and fifteen whigs. Ellice then said that if the radicals on their side agreed to this revised committee, he would lend his endeavours to form a club and had no doubt that the whigs as a party would cordially participate. Parkes and Molesworth for their part promised to do their utmost to get the radicals to concur in what had been done.

Left to themselves the two radicals were in high feather. They knew, and had known all along, that it would be virtually impossible to form a club without whig assistance. The whole of their tactics had been to create a situation in which the whigs would be obliged to follow a radical lead. They had succeeded almost beyond their hopes. 'We had them now,' wrote Molesworth jubilantly a few days later, 'they had come to us; they had assented to a list written out by themselves; it was impossible for them to retract.' Nevertheless there were still some pitfalls to be avoided on the radical side. The first step was to secure the consent of Hume, the third member of the radical triumvirate. This was accomplished without difficulty the following morning. The next task was to induce the body of radicals to accept the new development, including the necessary omission from the second committee list of the majority of those who had been on the first. Any difficulty here would provide the whigs with a pretext, if they wished, to withdraw from the transaction. But all passed off harmoniously, though Ellice complained of the publicity given to the bargain on the radical side before he had secured the consent of Lord John Russell to the party's commitment. However, that was the last shot, and having taken the decisive step, the whigs amply vindicated Ellice's pledge of wholehearted co-operation. Indeed, wrote Parkes a few weeks later, 'Ellice having taken it up, pets the child (the adopted) as if begat by himself'. Most of the cabinet became original members, along with two eminent whig peers, the Duke of Sussex and the Duke of Norfolk. And though Spring Rice, Lord Lansdowne, and Lord Howick, for a while hung back, the success of the club was assured from the start. By the end of February it had a membership of a thousand, including 250 members of parliament. The first formal committee meeting of the club was held in May, when a body of trustees and a managing committee were appointed. The five trustees were the Duke of Norfolk, Earl of Mulgrave, Lord Durham, Ellice, and General Ferguson; and the committee included Ellice, Grote, Hume, Shaw Lefevre, Le Marchant, Molesworth, O'Connell, Pendarves, Romilly, E. J. Stanley, Hussey Vivian, and Warburton. On 24 May 1836, the birthday of the Princess Victoria, the Reform Club formally opened its doors at 104 Pall Mall. The figure originally fixed for the membership was so rapidly exceeded that it soon was found necessary to enlarge the building. The famous *chef de cuisine*, Alexis Soyer, was engaged to superintend the catering and the club acquired a European reputation among gastronomes, thereby fulfilling one at least of Molesworth's ambitions. Meanwhile the old Westminster Club, the subscriptions and interest that had

nourished it being diverted elsewhere, began to wither away. Its
finances fell into disorder and it was quietly wound up in 1838.
Not long afterwards the Reform Association also closed down.
The Reform Club had made both unnecessary.

The radicals, particularly those whose forcing tactics had been
responsible for making the long-debated project a tangible fact,
were naturally gratified at the success of the venture. Yet its very
success was a powerful counterweight to the purely radical programme. They had dreamed of capturing the whigs; it is at least
arguable that they themselves were ensnared in the net they had
woven. For the numbers and material prosperity guaranteed to the
club by the whig membership could not fail to be without its
silent insidious effect on the political independence of the radicals.
Reluctant victims of Parkes' guile as they had seemed to be, it is
possible that the whigs in the end could count the foundation of
the Reform Club as one of the greatest single factors in prolonging
the life of the whig parliamentary party. In the early days some
radicals thought otherwise. Molesworth, writing to his mother,
thought the foundation of the club was in fact the radical victory
it seemed to be.

> Our success is certain. It will be the best club in town, and the
> effect will be to break up the whig party by joining the best of them
> to the Radicals, and the club will be the political centre of the
> Empire, and augment our power immensely. All we want is or-
> ganisation. This we shall now obtain. We had no place of meeting.
> Ten Radical M.P.s were never to be found together except in the
> House, consequently no one knew what his neighbour was about.
> This disorganisation the Whigs desired and on this account they have
> always in secret been opposed to a club. Now their only remaining
> hope is to join us in such numbers as to have the predominance;
> they will fail in this respect. They have never been in social contact
> with us yet; I don't fear their influence; some few they may seduce,
> but very few, whilst we shall gain many of them, for in all arguments
> we are their superiors. The most intelligent of them are aware of all
> this and have made up their minds to it.

These ingenuous lines were penned when Molesworth had not
yet reached his twenty-sixth birthday. An older man might have felt
less confidence in the readiness of politicians to change their sympathies when confuted by superior arguments. Whig contact, whig
habits, whig sociability were in the long run calculated to work

a profounder change in the outlook of the radicals than doctrinaire arguments were on the whigs. In politics, as in other human relationships, proximity can be a more seductive instrument than principle. The single-mindedness, the integrity, the characteristic acidity of the radicals that flourished in frigid isolation, could not easily survive transplantation to the convivial atmosphere of the Pall Mall clubrooms. A few years after the foundation of the club, the party which in 1835 Molesworth had prophesied would destroy both whig and tory had virtually disappeared as an independent element in parliamentary life. If Molesworth and Parkes had seriously envisaged the Reform Club as a kind of Trojan horse within the whig camp, the horse was soon docilely eating from the whig manger. 'The degeneracy of the Liberal party and their passive acquiescence in everything, good or bad, which emanates from the present Ministry', wrote Grote as early as 1838, 'puts the accomplishment of any political good out of the question.'[31] And a year later Graham and Bonham, going over the parliamentary list to assess the strength of the enemy, placed the number of independent radicals at a mere ten or eleven.[32]

A more realistic appreciation of the potentialities of the Reform Club came from Durham. At the beginning of March 1836 Parkes wrote to tell him about the formation of the club and the comments in Durham's reply were eminently practical.

> I am confident [he wrote from his distant watch-post at St Petersburg] that out of the club will arise, at least if it is well-managed, such organisation and concentration as will set all Tory measures at defiance. To be useful it should be in communication with every town in the kingdom, either through its members, or through correspondence. Some plan should be devised by which any of the chiefs of the Liberal Party coming to town should become acquainted with the Committee, and why should they not, being *bona-fide* temporary sojourners, be admitted into the club-rooms as foreigners are at the Travellers'?

It was in fact on these lines that the Reform Club developed, as the centre of liberal organization and the rival to the Carlton. 'Club government' had come to stay.[33]

---

[31] *Life of Grote*, 127.   [32] Add. MS. 40616, fo. 78.
[33] For the history of the foundation of the Reform Club, see Fagan, *The Reform Club*, 19–36; Reid, *Durham*, I, 325–8, II, 74–81; Fawcett, *Molesworth*, 72–81; Buckley, *Parkes*, 134–40.

With club government came, too, the new-style party manager. Ostrogorski, in his description of the central party machinery which appeared after the first Reform Act, has delineated the main characteristics of the species in a few bleak but incisive sentences.

> The Whip was assisted by a general agent of the party, whose special business it was to watch the electoral situation in the constituencies. This chief agent had correspondents throughout the Kingdom. In places where there were associations their secretaries communicated with him. The information being concentrated in his hands, he in his turn was in a position to assist the Whip and the leaders of the party in general with his suggestions. At a time when the provincial Press possessed but little importance, and when it was credited in London with much less than it really possessed, local life was imperfectly known. . . . Consequently the electoral situation in different parts of the country appeared somewhat hazy, even to politicians. The general agent of the party was supposed to see through it, and he enjoyed the same respect in party circles as country folk have for the local bone-setter. A Prime Minister, before risking a dissolution of Parliament, closeted himself with the agent of the party to consult him on the chance of a general election.[34]

As a generalized description this is extraordinarily accurate. The men who in actual fact carried out these functions in Peel's day departed, of course, to a greater or lesser degree from this abstraction. There was no identity between the two parties on this point even though in their own way both saw to it that the duties were carried out. Indeed it might even be said that the office filled by F. R. Bonham in the conservative party between 1832 and 1846, was on the whig side put into commission between the two radical attorneys, Joseph Parkes and James Coppock. Another distinction may be noted which is perhaps of greater importance since it reflects the difference between the tories and the whigs already exemplified in the history of the two party clubs. Bonham was a typical member of his party in the sense that his views approximated to the average opinion of its members and his social admissibility was unimpeachable. He was more of a tory in many respects than Peel, and though not himself a member of the aristocracy in the strict sense, he came of good family. On the

[34] *Democracy and the Organisation of Political Parties*, I, 146.

other side it was entirely characteristic that just as the whigs had left the initiative in founding the Reform Club to the radicals, so they left it to the radicals to provide the two men who played the leading rôles in the extra-parliamentary organization of the liberal party in this period. Bonham and the Carlton were evolved from the heart of the conservative party; Parkes, Coppock, and the Reform were alien appendages forced on the whig party by radical pressure and the lesson of events.

Francis Robert Bonham, the conservative party agent during the whole time of Peel's leadership, was M.P. for Rye 1830–1 and for Harwich 1835–7, Storekeeper to the Ordnance 1834–5 and 1841–5, and assistant whip 1835–7.[35] On his father's side he was descended from a substantial though not outstanding Irish Protestant family, a branch of which was until comparatively recently settled at the family seat of Ballintaggart, co. Kildare. On his mother's side he came of more distinguished stock. Her father, Edward Herbert, had sat for Innistioge in the Irish parliament, and her grandfather was member for Ludlow in the parliament of Great Britain from 1754 until his death in 1770. Through her Bonham was kinsman to the Peelite Sidney Herbert, son of the 11th Earl of Pembroke. He was thus a scion of the Anglo-Irish governing class of the eighteenth century with more than a tincture of aristocratic connexion and some family tradition of parliamentary membership. It was this background that nourished the sturdy, tory Anglican views which he retained to the end of his life. He wrote once of himself as 'entertaining from infancy a strong (possibly) prejudice in favour of the Church' and a 'dread of any proposed reforms'.[36] What is remarkable is not that he entered political life but that he reached the age of forty-five before he became an M.P. After taking his degree at Oxford he entered Lincoln's Inn and was called to the bar in 1814. It does not appear, however, that he ever practised as a lawyer. A parliamentary guide in 1830 gave his occupation as that of landowner. But all ordinary M.P.s at this time were theoretically landowners, and in view of the general evasion of the property qualification no particular importance can be attached to this description. In all probability he was living the life of an independent gentleman. His father, who died in

---

[35] The following sketch, while embodying some fresh material, is based on the more detailed account of Bonham's career and activities given in my article in *E.H.R.*, LXIII, 502 sqq. See also Appendix K for further biographical details.

[36] Add. MS. 44110, fo. 202.

1810, was a man of considerable means and a substantial legacy of money and property passed to his son.

In 1830 F. R. Bonham was living at the Old Steyne, Brighton, and already on friendly terms with Peel and Planta, the secretary to the Treasury and M.P. for the neighbouring borough of Hastings. It is not unreasonable to suppose that this acquaintanceship facilitated his entry into politics. At the general election of that year he successfully put up for Rye, a borough commonly regarded as one in which the Treasury nominee was invariably returned. From that point onwards Bonham's career takes on the clear outlines that marked it for the next quarter of a century. In the spring of 1831 he was assisting Holmes and Planta in the management of the tory party in the House of Commons. He was a foundation member of the Carlton and by the date of the general election of 1832 he had displaced Holmes, the chief whip, as the party's principal election manager.[37] There is no reason to suppose that he was deliberately installed by Peel after the Reform Act in order to carry through a reform of the conservative central organization. Such a reform did take place but not until after 1834 and even then mainly as a result of the growing experience of the party organizers both central and provincial rather than in response to any directive from the official party leaders.[38] But it is clear that from 1832 onward Bonham was the cardinal figure in the extra-parliamentary management of the party. His industry, his knowledge, and his enthusiasm, more than anything else were responsible for that technical superiority of the conservative organization which was a feature of the first two general elections of Victoria's reign.

Though he held junior office in both Peel's ministries and was assistant whip in the 1835 parliament, Bonham's essential work was done at the Carlton rather than on the floor of the House or in the voting lobbies. He again played a central part in the 1835 election though even at that date there existed no permanent organization (other than Bonham himself) to prepare for an election as distinct from an *ad hoc* committee set up to fight it. In May 1835, after the election was over, in a discussion with Peel on the

[37] William Holmes, treasurer of the Ordnance 1820–30, was the last tory chief whip in the unreformed House of Commons. He took some part in the general election of 1832, but his inability to secure election to the new parliament ended his long rule as whip.

[38] For further discussion of this point, see my paper, 'Peel and the Party System' (*Trans. R. Hist. Soc.*, 5th ser., I, 47–51).

possibility of a sudden whig dissolution, Bonham advised the formation of 'a very small and *quiet* but active committee to obtain information and prepare for such an event. . . . For myself I am ready *to devote my whole time* out of the H. of C. to this work.'[39] He clearly assumed that he would take a part, and in point of activity the leading part, in such preparations; and there can be little doubt that he was already in the position of a permanent election-eering expert within the party. 'One of the most important points for the attention of a committee', he wrote two days later, 'would be to ascertain precisely the comparative effect of the two registrations in each particular constituency.' Whether in this or some other way the work was undoubtedly accomplished. In 1836 he was so satisfied with the state of the conservative preparations that he was hoping, with a conservative ministry in office, for a gain of fifty seats in England alone. When the general elections came the following year the strength which the party put in the field reflected the work carried out since 1835. 'So far as I recollect', wrote Granville Somerset to Peel on the eve of the contest, 'we have 445 candidates in the 3 Kingdoms & I have no doubt that 10 or 12 more will appear in Ireland, and some few in this country. In 1835 my recollection is that we did not exceed 390, and as we had not above 180 in possession of seats, and we now have about 310, the fair inference is that we shall gain on the general results.'[40]

In the next few years the preparations of the party managers were even more intense. In the autumn of 1840 Bonham was engaged in a 'rather extensive correspondence as to the Registrations, and the ensuing Municipal elections' which gave him grounds for confidence. Unlike most tories he did not consider that the Municipal Reform Act had, in England at least, weakened conservative influence in the borough constituencies and he kept a careful scrutiny of the municipal elections as pointers to the growing national strength of the party.[41] Before the start of the new session he was able to give a comprehensive and definite answer to a request from Peel for a forecast of the result of a dissolution at the hands of a whig, or alternatively a conservative, ministry. The reply was clearly one which would have a direct bearing on Peel's parliamentary tactics and Bonham's reply, reached after four

[39] Add. MS. 40420, fo. 126. [40] Add. MS. 40423, fo. 346.
[41] Add. MS. 40428, fo. 342.

pages of evidence, was that from the party standpoint an early
dissolution would be welcome and that it would make no difference what ministry actually dissolved. 'So entirely too are we
prepared', he added, '(some elections will always *regulate themselves
at the last moment*) that I should *relatively to their preparation* be glad
Parlt. was dissolved next week.'[42] Graham, who had been kept
informed of this correspondence, arranged to come down to
London early in January 1841 to confer with the other party
managers so that Peel could be put in possession of the most full
and accurate information before parliament met. 'Thanks to you',
he wrote to Bonham, 'and your indefatigable industry, no Party
out of office ever before possessed such sources of intelligence and
such means for active war.'[43] When the general election came six
months later the conservative party machine functioned with the
ease and effectiveness born of long preparation. Nearly five hundred candidates took the field and the results spoke for themselves.
Less than a decade after the Reform Act that had seemed to put the
conservatives out of power for a generation, the party was returned
with a solid majority in both houses of parliament. Even Arbuthnot
who had no great love for Bonham, was moved to write that
'you have laboured well and satisfactorily; & you ought to be
proud'.[44]

In the triumph of 1841, as at other general elections, Bonham's
work did not merely consist in invigilating over registrations and
preparing his annual 'book of knowledge' as Graham termed it.
A major part of his duties was to find seats for aspiring candidates
and candidates for vacant seats. Moreover his desk at the Carlton
was not simply a clearing-house for candidates and constituencies;
it was also the means for a measure of control and his official
recommendation of a candidate became a badge of orthodoxy
recognized by politicians and local associations alike.[45] Even in
the peaceful years between general elections his interests were
spread wide and his activities unending. Though in appearance
older than his years, he endeared himself to a wide and varied range
of acquaintances by his good humour, zest, and sociability. To the
Wharncliffes, who gave nicknames to almost everybody within
range of their family circle, he was 'mon ami' Bonham; and it was
probably his qualities of warmth and friendliness that secured him

[42] Add. MS. 40428, fos. 13–16.   [43] Add. MS. 40616, fos. 191–4.
[44] Add. MS. 40617, fo. 101.
[45] See e.g. his letter introducing Disraeli to the Taunton conservatives in 1835,
printed in Appendix J.

the *entrée* to circles such as that of the Duke of Buckingham not conspicuous for loyalty to Peel. Not only was he deep in the inner conservative counsels and on a confidential footing with the grandees of the party but he was also a frequent visitor at the great tory country houses, one of the most familiar figures at the Carlton, and accessible to every member. Above all he was the devoted friend and confidential adviser of his leader, and acted as his chief intelligence agent on all matters affecting the political scene. There was hardly a ripple of opinion within the party that was not reported to Peel by his watchdog at the Carlton. Indeed it is clear that Bonham was under express orders from Peel to keep him permanently informed of what was passing in the political world. 'Tho' there is absolutely no news which would justify my troubling you,' he wrote to Peel in the summer recess of 1841, 'yet I think myself acting in the spirit of your instructions in doing so.'[46] On a variety of subjects he was called in for active consultation especially where his wide knowledge of local conditions and the subtle network of personal relationships within the party were directly relevant. His peculiar position, in the party but outside the House of Commons, gave him a detached viewpoint which was not without its advantages. He once told Peel that he was in the position of a looker-on who sees and knows more of the game than the players.

The disruption of 1846 put an inevitable termination to his political career. Loyal to Peel and an unforgiving opponent of the protectionist rebels, there was no place for him outside the diminishing and disorganized band of followers that still surrounded the fallen prime minister. Even in December 1846 he told Gladstone that he had almost abandoned his general interest in election matters and seven months later he found himself in almost solitary superintendence of the Peelite fortunes at the general election. Thereafter his activities slowly withered away. His knowledge and professional connexions were still at the disposal of his immediate circle of acquaintances and he was a constant visitor at Drayton. But Peel's death in 1850 was the irretrievable stroke. Occasionally in after years he still breathed the familiar air of politics. With Graham he maintained a desultory exchange of letters chiefly on parliamentary topics and between 1852 and 1857 his services were sought at times almost in the old

[46] Add. MS. 40486, fo. 101.

style by Gladstone. But by then Bonham had fallen on hard days. After 1850 the ill-health noticeable in earlier years began to gain on him and the decay of his political activities was accompanied by the sharper sting of poverty. It fell to Gladstone, as chancellor of the exchequer in the Aberdeen ministry, to be the medium whereby the Peelites paid their debt to Peel's old party manager. In August 1853 Bonham was appointed Commissioner of Income Tax. Ten years later he died at his house in Knightsbridge at the age of seventy-eight, a forgotten and unnoticed figure. In contrast to the full obituaries given to Parkes and Coppock, a single announcement of his death appeared in the private columns of *The Times*; there was no editorial comment.

Long after the events and personalities of the age of Peel had become a distant memory, Lord John Manners (then Duke of Rutland) set down in a few lines his sixty-year-old recollection of the obscure conservative agent of the forties.

> He was in 1841 an elderly man, dressed in a long brown coat and carrying a large strapped book, full of electioneering facts, figures and calculations. He was not in Parliament but was Sir Robert Peel's trusted agent in matters relating to elections and party management; whether he held some subordinate post in one of the departments I forget. . . . For the rest my recollection of Mr Bonham is distinctly favourable—rough, faithful, honest, indefatigable, the depositary of a thousand secrets and the betrayer of none.[47]

Of the two radical agents that served the liberal party in the generation after the Reform Act the better known, the more fortunate, though not necessarily the more acute, was Joseph Parkes of Birmingham.[48] A native of Warwickshire, after a characteristic radical education at a school near Worcester and at Glasgow University, he entered the legal profession and for eleven years practised as a solicitor in Birmingham, specializing to a considerable extent in election work. About 1822–3 he was active in Cornwall and served as clerk in the Camelford committee of inquiry. He was employed as election agent in a contest at Leicester in 1826 and in another at Stafford in 1827. By the time of the reform bill agitation, therefore, he had much practical

---

[47] See Appendix J, The Hayter Letters.   [48] See his *Life* by Jessie Buckley.

knowledge of the electoral system and took an important part in the campaign to secure representation for his native town of Birmingham. By 1835 his electoral experience had widened to cover the boroughs of Birmingham, Coventry, Warwick, and Stamford, and the counties of Warwickshire, Worcestershire, and Staffordshire.[49] This decade of apprenticeship could have left him with few illusions concerning the nature of popular elections and contributed perhaps to the strong vein of realism which distinguished him from most of the parliamentary radicals of the period after 1832. As befitted a friend and disciple of Bentham his radicalism was of an intellectual rather than an emotional nature and it was this reputation for sense and moderation which caused the whigs to single him out as a member of the extreme reforming party in the country with whom they could deal in a rational manner. At the height of the reform crisis Althorp employed him to moderate the excessive zeal of Attwood and the Birmingham Union; and his success in that mission was the foundation of his future career.[50] The whigs on the whole did well by the men that served them. Moreover the fundamental reform legislation they undertook after 1832 required the employment of a number of men trained in business and administrative habits which they were scarcely able to supply from their own ranks. Sydney Smith's joke about the whigs' 'favourite human animal, the barrister of six years' standing' was a very real comment on the extent to which the administration was forced to rely on a new type of bureaucrat, drawn predominantly from the legal profession, for the execution of its measures.[51] For men like Edwin Chadwick, Parkes, Bowring, and Southwood Smith, therefore, the passing of the Reform Act opened up a fair prospect. In 1833 Parkes was appointed secretary to the commission for inquiring into municipal corporations. He now moved permanently to London, leaving his practice at Birmingham in the hands of his partner, Solomon Bray, who later became the first town clerk to the Birmingham Corporation. Parkes established himself at 33 Great George Street, Westminster, where he presently built up a practice as a parliamentary solicitor. He had already been

---

[49] See his evidence in P.P. 1835, VIII, 92.
[50] Le Marchant, *Althorp*, 368; Butler, *Passing of the Great Reform Bill*, 316.
[51] Cf. Wm. Johnston, *England as It Is* (London, 1851), II, 150–1. Johnston, himself a barrister, considered that government patronage of this type had the effect of increasing the numbers and lowering the standard of entrants to the profession.

concerned in the management of the first general election after the Reform Act and soon became the trusted friend of men such as Ellice and Durham. At the same time, however, being brought by his work on the municipal corporations commission into contact with radical reformers all over the country, he began to form a wide national connexion which must have greatly enhanced his position in the background of the radical parliamentary party.

Parkes was thus a point of intersection for three different spheres of activity. He was one of the leading Benthamite administrative reformers; he had a foothold in the world of the whig party managers; and his house in London was a meeting-place for the metropolitan and parliamentary radicals. As his position became secure, his energy and activities seemed inexhaustible. Besides his official employment on the municipal corporations commission and his unofficial work in connexion with the Reform Association, the Westminster Club and the Reform Club, he also engaged in what he described to Durham once as 'bread-getting engagements', and at one point seems to have contemplated an attempt to enter parliament.[52] His contacts were wide and increasingly influential. From 1834 to 1840 he was in constant communication with Durham and when the latter went to Russia, he kept him amply informed of all the shifting sands of contemporary politics, especially on the liberal side. Over the Municipal Corporations Act he was in close touch with Ellice, who had only recently ceased to be the party whip and played a leading part in the party's management; he assisted E. J. Stanley, who became the liberal chief whip in 1834; and was on good terms with Melbourne, who was not above discussing political matters with him. He ventured into the treacherous realm of press management and tried to influence the *Morning Chronicle* against Palmerston's 'Tory system of diplomacy'.[53] Mackay, who became sub-editor of that newspaper in 1835, records that Parkes was a constant visitor to the *Chronicle* office about this time, bringing social news and sometimes getting political news in return.[54] Parkes also cultivated the friendship of the *Spectator*, whose proprietor, Rintoul, he found perhaps more amenable than Black, the editor of the *Chronicle*. In 1837, when Cobden made his acquaintance in London, he was at

[52] Reid, *Durham*, II, 82.   [53] Buckley, *Parkes*, 134.
[54] Mackay, *Forty Years Recollections*, I, 95.

the height of his reputation. Certainly he impressed the young and as yet scarcely known Manchester calico-printer far more than Grote, Molesworth, or Roebuck did.

> One of the cleverest men I have ever met with is Joseph Parkes, late of Birmingham, the eminent constitutional lawyer and writer. He was employed to prepare the Municipal bill and other measures. He is not only profound in his profession, but skilled in political economy, and quite up to the spirit of the age in practical and popular acquirements. He was very civil to me.[55]

Parkes told him, moreover, that Durham, from distant St Petersburg, had inquired after the authorship of Cobden's anonymous pamphlet on Russia, and had declared that its writer showed more sense than the whole British cabinet. It is possible that Cobden, like all authors, even calico-printers, was not immune to flattery, and that the compliment tinged his views of the person who so thoughtfully conveyed it.[56]

Other men who knew Parkes were not quite so enthusiastic. Le Marchant has left in print a condescending eulogy that hardly squares with Cobden's tribute. 'He became professionally concerned for the Whigs in election matters and was much trusted by them. I knew him well, and invariably found him zealous, honest, and able in his vocation.'[57] Perhaps the obituary notice printed by *The Times* was as reasonable and sound a judgement as any.

> Few men in a secondary position were more trusted than he, few had a larger circle of friends, few were more completely in the current and full tide of political life. . . . If anyone on his side of politics wanted information. . . . Mr. Parkes was the man to apply to. If he could not at once give it, he could get it. So people clung about him, and he was a most useful man in his party—useful not only because he was so well informed and had such a wide circle of friends but also because his judgement was of the soundest, and he was ever active and loyal in offices of friendship.[58]

[55] Morley, *Cobden*, 138.   [56] Reid, *Durham*, II, 92.
[57] Le Marchant, *Althorp*, 369n.
[58] Quoted by the *Gentleman's Magazine*, XIX, N.S. (1865), 646, in the notice of Parkes' death.

What seems beyond controversy is that he was a sharp, brisk, energetic man, competent in his work, active in his politics, and able to speak his mind firmly to whigs and radicals alike without incurring enmity. Like most radical and self-made men he was apt to be limited and dogmatic in his judgements and perhaps was not specially qualified to climb any higher than he did. But he was admirably adapted to serve as a link between the ordinary, moderate whigs and the quarrelsome, impetuous, and impatient radicals that found themselves thrown uncomfortably together after 1832. There were few politicians who could have played his rôle with greater success and when in 1847 he finally retired from active political work, the whigs fittingly rewarded his services with the post of taxing master in the Court of Chancery, an appointment which he held until his death in 1865.

Among all Parkes' various activities it is not easy to lay bare his precise part in the management, particularly the election management, of the party; nor was that work of a kind that courted publicity. Professionally he was one of the small number of lawyers who specialized in parliamentary work on the whig and liberal side. Theoretically all solicitors could undertake the management of parliamentary business; but inevitably some firms tended to make a feature of such work, particularly the conduct of disputed election cases, and in proportion as their reputation and experience grew, the monopoly of such business fell into their hands. Moreover, as the solicitors in such cases acquired a considerable amount of knowledge concerning the inner working of electoral management, there was a natural tendency for political parties to engage lawyers of known fidelity to the side that employed them. It was, as need scarcely be added, a very lucrative branch of the profession. In Parkes' case, not only was he a well-known figure in liberal circles but he already possessed a wealth of knowledge on election proceedings which made him an outstanding member of his class. But that part of his work was not of course the real basis of his position in the party. Besides such assets as his information, his influence, and his range of contacts, his main rôle seems to have been that of a third man, interposed between the real party managers on the one side and Coppock, the real party agent, on the other. One of the interesting minor items elicited by the parliamentary committee which inquired into the Sudbury election of 1841 was that Parkes, acting on behalf of Ellice, who was apparently still the chief liberal party election manager, was paying over sums of money to Coppock for election purposes.[59] Parkes' interests, and perhaps his ambitions, were too widely spread[60] for him to settle down to the narrow and highly specialized work of party agent. For this subordinate function he found a henchman in James Coppock, a study of whose activities would shed a great deal of light on the electoral organization of the liberal party between the Reform Act and the Crimean War. Parkes, though not born to the parliamentary purple and never actually a member of the House of Commons, at least made for himself a respectable place in the party. Coppock who in many respects was the indispensable party factotum, came from an even lower social grade, and won neither the prestige nor the status of his superior. It is characteristic, for example, that Greville, who has one or two familiar references in his diary to 'Joe Parkes', nowhere mentions Coppock. Yet if the impact of his personality was less than that of Parkes, his work in its technical aspect was at least as important.

James Coppock, two years junior to Parkes, was born in 1798 at Stockport, Cheshire, the eldest son of a respectable mercer to whose business he was bred up. In 1820 he was placed as a clerk at a wholesale haberdasher's in London but soon began operating in the silk trade on his own account. This business venture, however, did not turn out profitably. He then turned to the law and articled himself to a solicitor in Furnival's Inn. Here for five years he industriously pursued his new profession. The passing of the Reform Act brought him into politics and he took an active part in the first election contest in the new borough of Finsbury.[61] His voluntary efforts on behalf of the liberal organization in London brought him to the notice of the leading radicals and when after the 1835 election Parkes began to reorganize the Reform Association, he selected Coppock for the post of secretary and installed him in the central London office of the association in Cleveland Row, Westminster, with a salary reported to be £300

---

[59] P.P. 1844, xviii, 557–8.

[60] He was the author of several works, including a *History of the Court of Chancery* (1828), and in his retirement gathered materials for a life of Sir Philip Francis subsequently completed and edited by H. Merivale in 1867. Le Marchant said of him that 'he was no mean scholar and could write with clearness and spirit'.

[61] In 1835 he was honorary secretary to the Finsbury Reform Club, and published in that year his only recorded work, *The Elector's Manual*, a stereotyped digest of electoral law, which he dedicated to the club.

per annum. His work here brought him a wide circle of acquaintances among liberal agents and solicitors throughout England and
Wales and he was soon recognized as the party authority on
electoral information. By the following year his position was so
well established that when the Reform Club was founded, he was
appointed the first secretary. How far he could have combined
the very different functions of club secretary and election agent is
doubtful. It is possible, moreover, that the whig grandees did not
care for a man of Coppock's humble origin in such a post. Whatever the cause, in two weeks Coppock was succeeded as secretary
by Mr Walter Scott and given a life membership of the club as a
consolation for the abrupt termination of his appointment.[62]
Nevertheless his political career suffered no setback. In 1836 he
was admitted as an attorney and when a few years later the Reform
Association was wound up, Coppock took over the lease of the
house in Cleveland Row and set up in practice as parliamentary
agent. In this work his extensive connexions with liberal constituency associations, his industry, and one may perhaps guess
also a certain native sagacity, soon brought him a considerable
reputation. Serjeant Ballantine, who as a young barrister was
contemporary with this period of Coppock's activities, described
him in after life as 'one of the acutest of Parliamentary agents'.[63]
At the same time he did not abandon his functions as the party
electoral agent and his office in Cleveland Row, within a short
distance of the Reform Club, became a centre of party intelligence.
In the selection of candidates for constituencies and constituencies for candidates Coppock became the indispensable guide
and mediator; and much of the obscurer financial transactions
of the party election campaigns must have been trusted to his
execution.

In the notorious Sudbury election of 1841, for example, it was
Coppock who had been responsible for getting the two liberal
candidates for the borough in response to a requisition to the
Reform Club, just as it was Bonham at the Carlton, a little farther
down Pall Mall, who had introduced the two conservative candidates to the Sudbury conservative agent who came up to town for
the purpose of securing representatives for his party. The investigations of the parliamentary committee showed Coppock's office
to be deeply concerned in the financial operation of the election in

[62] Fagan, *The Reform Club*, 36.   [63] *Serjeant Ballantine's Experiences*, 284.

that financially-minded constituency. Three days before the election one of the liberal candidates placed £3,000 in a separate account which was immediately drawn out by a bearer cheque presented by a clerk in Coppock's office. At the same time this clerk changed two other notes, one for £1,000 and the other for £500. The latter had been paid out of the account of Edward Ellice and by his direction placed with other sums in the hands of Coppock for election proceedings not connected with Sudbury.[64] It was Coppock too who was instrumental with Parkes in launching Cobden on his parliamentary career. 'Cobden wants to stand against the Tories at Stockport', wrote Parkes to Durham in September 1836. 'Luckily Coppock came to me and asked me about him, and I said he would be an honour to them, not they to him.'[65] At the general election the following year Cobden duly stood as the liberal candidate although in the event he was left at the bottom of the poll.

At the fierce Ludlow by-election in 1839 Coppock acted as a direct agent on behalf of Alcock, the liberal candidate, with consequences that might easily have been more unfortunate than they were. At the subsequent inquiry it was proved that Coppock in person had paid a sum of £30 to the landlord of the Three Compasses at Ludlow as a bribe for a specific elector. A legal action (*Marsh* v. *Coppock*) was then brought against him for damages of £500 under the existing bribery law. In this awkward situation Coppock acted with energy and lawyer-like resource. He immediately brought a similar action against the actual voter he had bribed for having taken the bribe and won his case, the verdict going against the defendant by default and (one may suspect) by collusion. Coppock next petitioned under the old Bribery Act (2 Geo. II, c. 24) for permission to plead as a defence in his own case the fact that within twelve months of the alleged bribery, he had successfully prosecuted another person similarly offending. The petition was refused on technical grounds and the case went to trial at the Shrewsbury Assizes in August 1840; but after three hours' deliberation the jury finally returned a verdict in Coppock's favour.[66] Juries were noticeably reluctant to convict in bribery

[64] P.P. 1844, xviii, 247 sqq. [65] Reid, *Durham*, ii, 93.
[66] P.P. 1840, ix, Ludlow election petition; *Annual Register* 1840 (Chronicle), 65; *Standard*, 8 August 10 August 1840, where Coppock is described as the secretary of the Reform Club. For the point of law involved in Coppock's defence, which was again brought forward by his counsel when the case was heard at Shrewsbury, see Stephen's *Commentaries*, ii, 399–400.

cases and it was to this popular feeling that he owed his escape. But it was a lesson not to appear personally in these dubious transactions.

The nature of Coppock's work, which both in its legal and political aspects kept him in the background of events, inevitably cast its obscurity over his personality. But occasional evidence suggests a certain sharp and incisive turn of mind. In 1848, for instance, with reference to some alleged complaint by Sir Edward Bulwer-Lytton of the ingratitude of the party, Coppock told him to his face that any talk of ingratitude was nonsense. Bulwer-Lytton had been made a baronet; his brother enjoyed a place of £8,000 a year; he had been helped by the party purse at elections; and then had turned half-tory, half-protectionist.[67] Obituary notices are proverbially generous, but there is no reason to suppose any reservation in the stress that was laid after Coppock's death on the respect and trust paid to his character and invariable confidence placed in his word by opponents in all arrangements and compromises. Nor need one doubt the assertion that his moderate fortune had been earned by his profession as solicitor rather than in some corrupt and devious manner. There was little enough money in party organization on either side to encourage men to take up the career of party agent for the sake of personal profit. Neither Bonham nor Coppock died in affluence. Moreover, as not infrequently happens, Coppock was perhaps better as an agent than as principal. His last years were clouded by business anxieties owing to the failure of the Surrey Gardens, of which he was shareholder and director, leaving him as the chief creditor. In August 1857 his long service to the party was recognized by his appointment as county court treasurer. But he lived only a few months to enjoy it, dying at his house in Cleveland Row in December 1857. 'Probably our future electoral system', said *The Times* ambiguously, 'will never create, nor need, a second James Coppock.'[68] Parkes had by that date already retired to the peace of literary pursuits; and Bonham, whose main political work had ended in 1846, was eking out his last few years as a civil servant. When, after the Palmerstonian interlude, the next great movement of party organization began, the Brands, Gorsts, and Schnadhorsts of the new era were men of a different stamp and

---

[67] Broughton, *Recollections*, VI, 208.
[68] See his obituary notice printed in the *Gentleman's Magazine*, February 1858.

moving in a different political world. Yet they could not have accomplished half that they did, if they had not been able to build on the foundations laid by their half-forgotten predecessors in the first generation after the Reform Act of 1832.

APPENDICES

A. Election Petitions 1832–52.

B. The Enlargement of Boroughs in 1832.

C. Party Election Funds.

D. Proprietary Boroughs after 1832 (England and Wales).

E. Contested Elections 1832–47.

F. The 'Berkshire List' 1835.

G. Six 'Government' Boroughs.

H. The Patronage of the First Lord of the Treasury (1834).

J. The Hayter Letters.

K. Biographical Note on Francis Robert Bonham.

APPENDIX A

In the first twenty years after the Reform Act 443 election petitions
were presented to parliament. In some cases two, three, or more
petitions concerned the same election. When a decision was reached
on one of several petitions, the remainder were not pursued. But
the majority of cases were withdrawn and the number of actual
inquiries in this period was 185. The table below, taken from Banfield,
Statistical Companion for 1854, gives details of these inquiries. But the
incidence of controverted elections was narrower than these bare
statistics reveal. Of the void and undue elections, only two occurred
in Scotland or Wales; and of the remainder, seventy-five occurred in
England. Moreover, the greatest number of cases concerned boroughs.
The void and undue elections include no English county and only one
county each in Wales, Scotland, and Ireland. Few county elections
were controverted and those that were usually ended in the petition
being withdrawn (Banfield, *op. cit.* p. 98).

Parliaments	Void Elections	Undue Elections	Elections made good	Total Inquiries
1833	6	7	10	23
1835	1	5	10	16
1837	3	14	30	47
1841	6	11	9	26
1847	15	1	8	24
1852–3	27	0	22	49
	58	38	89	185

NOTE.—A 'void' election was one in which the whole proceedings
were quashed by decision of the committee of inquiry, whereupon a
new writ was usually though not invariably issued.

An 'undue' election was one in which the committee of inquiry
found the sitting member not duly returned and the return was
amended by the substitution of the name of another candidate.

An election 'made good' or confirmed was one in which the committee of inquiry upheld the original return.

APPENDIX B

A *Return of Boundaries of Boroughs* (P.P. 1859, XXIII, 121 sqq.), published some years after the Reform Act, shows the changes made to the actual physical size of boroughs by the boundary alterations of 1832. The main changes of importance were among the English boroughs and according to this list some 111 English boroughs were enlarged. Allowing for a number of defective returns the actual figure was probably nearer 120. Some of the more extraordinary cases of enlargement are given below. The arrangement is by counties.

Borough	Area in Square Miles		County
	before 1832	after 1832	
Wallingford	0·6	25·6	Berks.
Buckingham	8·0	28·9	Bucks.
Wycombe	0·2	9·8	Bucks.
Bodmin	4·5	26·2	Cornwall
Launceston	2·6	22·3	Cornwall
Liskeard	3·7	12·7	Cornwall
St. Ives	2·8	17·6	Cornwall
Cockermouth	3·9	13·3	Cumberland
Tavistock	0·5	17·4	Devon
Shaftesbury	0·3	35·0	Dorset
Wareham	0·7	47·7	Dorset
Christchurch	0·7	35·3	Hants.
Petersfield	0·4	35·5	Hants.
Huntingdon	1·9	10·5	Hunts.
Clitheroe	3·6	25·3	Lancs.
Grimsby	2·6	24·5	Lincs.
Morpeth	0·4	23·3	Northumberland
Woodstock	0·1	33·7	Oxon.
Bridgnorth	1·8	12·8	Salop.
Tamworth	0·3	17·9	Staffs.
Eye	6·4	30·8	Suffolk
Horsham	0·3	17·7	Sussex
Midhurst	0·9	39·5	Sussex
Rye	1·6	32·3	Sussex
Reigate	0·1	9·6	Surrey
Calne	1·6	14·2	Wilts.
Chippenham	0·1	16·1	Wilts.
Malmesbury	0·2	32·3	Wilts.

Borough	Area in Square Miles		County
	before 1832	*after 1832*	
Westbury	0·04	19·3	Wilts.
Wilton	0·2	49·4	Wilts.
Bewdley	3·2	11·2	Worcs.
Droitwich	2·7	35·3	Worcs.
Malton	0·1	10·7	Yorks.
Beverley	3·6	17·4	Yorks.
Pontefract	4·2	11·9	Yorks.

One of the obscurer aspects of electioneering in this period is the extent to which there existed permanent party funds for election and other expenses as distinct from special subscriptions raised locally or in London for particular candidates or elections. It is clear that important constituencies and important candidates were made the object of special exertions by the parties. In the 1837 election, for example, the conservatives in London raised £2,400 for Dublin City and £3,300 for Westminster. In 1842 Eliot, the chief secretary, appealed for a party subscription of two or three thousand pounds for the Dublin by-election. When a by-election was anticipated in Middlesex the following year another party subscription was opened for the conservative candidate, though Fremantle told Peel that 'it is doubtful in the present state of the party whether the Conservatives will come forward as readily as they have done on former occasions'.[1] Similar efforts were made for individuals. When Disraeli contested Taunton in 1835 a subscription was opened for him at the Carlton. In 1846, after Lord Ashley had resigned in deference to the feeling of his Dorset constituents over the repeal of the Corn Laws, a few members of the party including Peel and Graham subscribed £2,000 to enable him to stand again for the county, though in the event Ashley declined the offer. Party funds were also raised to fight election petitions.

But what is less certain is whether there existed any general permanent fund for party purposes. The correspondence of the conservative party managers throws some light on this question. It is obvious in the first place that not only was little known to the general public of such resources, but that even in the party at large there was no question of there being a party chest into which all could dip. 'I hear', said one of Herries' correspondents in 1832, 'that there is no idea of assisting any candidate with money, so Holmes tells us, and Bonham, and all who can be supposed to have means of knowledge.'[2] On the eve of the 1835 election Rosslyn told Lord Melville that there would be no fund for electioneering expenses. 'I am sorry to hear it', replied Melville,'—not with reference to Leith or even to Scotland generally— but to England, where I am quite sure it will be wanted. I am not aware that such a fund will be of any avail or will be required in

---

[1] Add. MS. 40476, fos. 298–301.　　[2] *Memoir of J. C. Herries*, ii, 162.

Scotland; I think we get on very well without it, or at any rate, with local subscriptions where necessary.'[3] In 1837 Lyndhurst wrote tentatively to Bonham to say that Smythe had been put to such continual expense in politics that he would be unable to stand without some pecuniary aid. 'Can it', asked Lyndhurst, 'be obtained?'[4] In connexion with a by-election in January 1840 the Newark conservative association sent in an application for financial assistance to the Carlton Club which was refused in such uncompromising terms that it evoked from the disappointed constituency the suggestion that a central fund for helping conservative candidates should be started.[5]

Such a central electioneering fund did however exist. It may not have been present in 1832 but there was certainly one in the general elections of 1835, 1837, and 1847; and there can be little doubt that one existed for the 1841 election. Rosslyn's statement to Lord Melville seems, to say the least, to have been misleading or misunderstood. There may not have been a fund to which all members could indiscriminately apply. But there was a sum of money administered by the party managers for election purposes and in 1835 Rosslyn himself was one of the principal executors of the fund. A good deal of secrecy necessarily surrounded this aspect of party organization. No party could undertake to assist candidates in every contested constituency and to advertise the existence of such a fund would merely provoke requests that could not be met. The fund was probably raised by subscription from the wealthier members of the party. A note in the Hardinge papers[6] relating to the 1837 fund gives a list of contributions mainly from peers totalling nearly £7,000. Much more than this, of course, would be necessary to make any appreciable impact on the general electoral fortunes of a party in an age when one hard-fought contest in a single large constituency could by itself swallow up the greater part of such a sum. In all probability the party fund represented only an insignificant fraction of the total outlay by one side in a general election and was used therefore merely to assist a limited number of candidates who from their personal circumstances seemed to deserve exceptional support.

Some evidence is available for the distribution of subsidies from the central fund of the party in the 1835 election. In Buckinghamshire Sir George Rose and other conservative supporters, who wished to bring forward a candidate named Watts, applied to Rosslyn for assistance on the grounds that success was certain if they could obtain £500.

---

[3] Add. MS. 40405, fos. 30–2.
[4] Add. MS. 40617, fo. 45. [5] Add. MS. 40427, fo. 259.
[6] I owe this reference to the kindness of Mr Michael Brock of Corpus Christi College, Oxford.

Rosslyn told them he could neither give nor promise anything; nevertheless he wrote privately to Peel, describing the situation and asking whether he wished to give any instructions on the matter. Simultaneously Rosslyn was approached by Lyndhurst, probably after an earlier and unsuccessful application, who informed him that nothing less than the £500 demanded would enable another Buckinghamshire candidate, none other than Disraeli, to start for Wycombe; and that if the money was not forthcoming he would resign the next day. This second application on behalf of another conservative in the same county clearly embarrassed Rosslyn. Disraeli was not a candidate who possessed the confidence of the leaders; on the other hand it would be a delicate task to assist Watts and refuse at the same time to assist Lyndhurst's *protégé*. 'There is rather more difficulty in giving money here', wrote Rosslyn in a second letter to Peel, 'than in any other place from D'Israeli's connection with this county.' The following day he reported that he had started Farrand for Peterborough upon letters from Lord Westmorland and the Duke of Wellington. Fortunately 'Mr Farrand pays for himself and saves £500 which the Duke would have given.' As for the earlier problem, 'the Duke has authorised me to give £500 to D'Israeli besides Sir Harry Smith.[7] I have seen the Chancellor and told him. I know not if it be in time.'[8]

The repetition of £500 in these three instances reads like a routine subsidy and it also is apparent that Peel and the duke were trustees for the sums which Rosslyn administered. Given discreet and parsimonious handling, a relatively small fund could be stretched to cover a number of contests and even leave something in the party chest between elections. It is possible that at most times between 1835 and 1847 there existed at the disposal of the leaders a small fund for extraordinary expenses or special grants. Thus, when Lord Lincoln was obliged to defend his seat for Falkirk burghs in the general election of 1847 after having fought two by-elections the previous year, Young the conservative chief whip put the case before Peel as justifying financial assistance. 'The subscribed fund', he added, 'has been very little trenched upon, and you will perhaps think L's. case one which deserves aid.'[9] Not all grants from the party funds concerned elections. Fremantle suggested in 1841 a grant of one or two hundred pounds to assist Painter, the editor of the *Church of England Review* to start a new weekly paper aimed at counteracting radical influence with the working classes. And in 1843 he passed to Peel a proposal to give financial

[7] Presumably Sir George Henry Smyth, of Beerchurch Hall, Essex, who was returned as conservative member for Colchester at this election.
[8] Add. MS. 40409, fos. 114–15, 146–7.
[9] Add. MS. 40599, fo. 217.

assistance to a Dr Hugh who was running a campaign against the Anti-Corn Law League in Lancashire and Yorkshire. Peel, though sceptical, told the whip that if he thought it might be of use, 'I make no objection to the employment of a specific sum entailing no further liaison with the Doctor'.[10]

[10] Add. MS. 40476, fos. 70–3, 290–5; Aspinall, *Politics and the Press*, Appendix, 409.

The work of classifying constituencies is full of pitfalls and only a local historian can hope to reach finality. The following is offered as a provisional working list of the proprietary boroughs still in existence after the Reform Act of 1832 in England and Wales.

No. of Members	Borough	No. of Members returned by patron	Patrons
1	Arundel	1	Duke of Norfolk
1	Ashburton	1 ?	Lord Clinton
2	Aylesbury	1 ?	Duke of Buckingham ?
2	Buckingham	1	Duke of Buckingham
2	Bury St Edmunds	2	Duke of Grafton: Marquess of Bristol
1	Calne	1	Marquess of Lansdowne
1	Cheltenham	1 ?	Lord Segrave
2	Chester	1	Marquess of Westminster
2	Chichester	1	Duke of Richmond
2	Chippenham	2	Joseph Neeld esq.
1	Christchurch	1 ?	Sir G. Rose
2	Cirencester	1	Earl Bathurst
2	Derby	1	Duke of Devonshire
2	Dorchester	2	Earl of Shaftesbury
1	Droitwich	1	Lord Foley
1	Dudley	1 ?	Lord Ward
2	Grantham	1	Earl of Dysart
1	Haverfordwest	1	Sir R. B. Philipps
2	Hertford	2	Marquess of Salisbury: after 1834 shared with Earl Cowper
2	Huntingdon	2	Earl of Sandwich
1	Kidderminster	1 ?	Lord Ward
1	Launceston	1	Duke of Northumberland
2	Lichfield	2	Earl of Lichfield
2	Ludlow	2 ?	Earl of Powis
2	Lymington	1	Sir H. Neale
2	Lynn	2	Duke of Portland: Earl of Orford
1	Malmesbury	1	Influence of the Pitt family decreased as a result of the extension of the borough boundaries and after 1832 successfully challenged by the Earl of Suffolk

No. of Members	Borough	No. of Members returned by patron	Patrons
2	Malton	2	Earl Fitzwilliam
2	Marlborough	2	Marquess of Ailesbury
2	Marlow	2 ?	Mr Williams: Sir W. Clayton
1	Midhurst	1	Earl of Egmont: Earl Digby
1	Morpeth	1	Earl of Carlisle
2	Newark	2	Duke of Newcastle
1	Northallerton	1	Miss Peirse
2	Peterborough	2	Earl Fitzwilliam
1	Reigate	1	Earl Somers: Earl of Hardwicke
2	Retford	2 ?	Earl Manvers
2	Richmond	2	Lord Dundas (cr. Earl of Zetland 1838)
2	Ripon	2	Miss Lawrence
2	Scarborough	1	Duke of Rutland
1	Shaftesbury	1	Marquess of Westminster
2	Stamford	2	Marquess of Exeter
2	Tamworth	2 ?	Sir R. Peel
2	Tavistock	2	Duke of Bedford
2	Thetford	2	Lord Ashburton: Duke of Grafton
1	Thirsk	1	Sir R. Frankland Russell
2	Warwick	1	Earl of Warwick
2	Wenlock	2	Lord Forester
1	Westbury	1	Sir R. Lopes
1	Whitehaven	1	Earl of Lonsdale
1	Wilton	1	Earl of Pembroke
1	Woodstock	1	Duke of Marlborough

SUMMARY

Boroughs

accepted	42
queried	10
Total	52

Members returned by patrons

accepted	59
queried	14
Total	73

NOTE.—For a list of 'family' boroughs, many of which can scarcely be distinguished from 'proprietary' boroughs, see Ch. 8, Influence and Control, pp. 193-201.

APPENDIX E

CONTESTED ELECTIONS 1832–47

It is surprisingly difficult to get agreed figures of contested elections in this period. The official *Return of Members of Parliament* does not indicate whether elections were contested. The voluminous parliamentary reports and papers dealing with the working of the electoral system after 1832 rarely include total figures for election contests. When they are given they are usually reliable for Wales, Scotland, and Ireland, but are apt to be inconclusive for England partly owing to the curious habit of still treating the counties as single electoral units and partly owing to defective returns. Nevertheless they form a useful check on figures obtained by other means. Unofficial compilations of election polls in the individual constituencies are numerous but suffer from varying degrees of inaccuracy; and the process of reaching the total by means of a numerical count introduces a fresh source of error. The main authorities on which the following table is based are:

Parliamentary Papers (esp. P.P. 1834, IX; P.P. 1836, XLIII; P.P. 1842, XXXIII; P.P. 1843, XLVI).
MacCalmont, *Parliamentary Poll Book.*
Dod, *Parliamentary Companion.*
Mosse, *Parliamentary Guide.*
The Annual Register.
The Westminster Review, XXXVI (Tabular View of the Elections of 1832, 1835, and 1837).

In addition the *Extraordinary Black Book* of 1835 quotes some figures of contested elections for the general election of 1832; and Jephson, *The Platform*, has figures of contested elections in England, Wales, and Scotland for the first four elections after the Reform Act. Mr Woolley, in his 'Personnel of the Parliament of 1833' (*E.H.R.*, LIII, 251), gives a modern estimate for English and Welsh contests in the 1832 election. All these authorities rarely agree exactly but there is in nearly all cases a sufficient general coincidence to justify the hope that the margin of error in the table given below is not a significant one.

GENERAL ELECTIONS 1832–47

Constituencies	1832		1835		1837		1841		1847	
	uncontested	contested	uncontested	contested	uncontested	contested	uncontested	contested	uncontested	contested
England and Wales (284)	92	192	120	164	94	190	138	146	159	124
Scotland (51)	15	36	23	28	22	29	29	22	37	14
Ireland (66)	17	49	31	35	34	32	46	20	40	26
U.K. (401)	124	277	174	227	150	251	213	188	236	164
Total	401		401		401		401		400*	

* Sudbury disfranchised 1844

CONTESTED ELECTIONS: ENGLAND AND WALES, AND SCOTLAND
1832–41

	1832	1835	1837	1841
Previous Table	228	192	219	168
Jephson	227	192	219	170

Jephson does not give the authority for his figures but they provide substantial confirmation for the figures produced by independent calculation in the first table. Mr Woolley's figure for contested elections in England and Wales in 1832 is slightly higher than either of the above estimates. He notes 150 borough and 48 county constituencies as having been contested, being a total of 198. If to this figure is added the generally undisputed figure of 36 contests in Scotland in that election, the result would be a total of 234 contests for England, Wales, and Scotland. But the figures given in P.P. 1834, IX, for the contested returns in the 1832 election, which are unusually complete, confirm Jephson's rather than Mr Woolley's calculations.

APPENDIX F

(Add MS. 40310, fos. 3–7)

Peel to Wellington, 1 *January 1835.* 'The enclosed list is sent by *Barnes* to the Chancellor with the expression of much anxiety on the subject.'

Wellington to Peel, 3 *January 1834.* 'I return your Berkshire list. I can do something with Dr. Winter of St. John's College, Oxford; and with Lord Downshire I think for all excepting Walter.'

Enclosure in the preceding letter:
List of people who have considerable influence in Berkshire.

1. The Windsor Clergy:
2. The Revd. J. Cleaver of Great Coxwell:
3. Dr. Vansittart of White Waltham:
4. Dr. Haskins of Appleton:
5. Lord Barrington:
6. The Bastards of Devonshire: near Faringdon
7. Revd. J. Bastard of West Lodge, Dorset:
8. Dr. Winter of St. John's College, Oxford:
9. ·Revd. Mr. Cotton of Denchworth:
10. Revd. Mr. Wapshare of West Hendred:
11. Lord Braybrook:
12. Lord Downshire
[13.] Lord Craven.'

NOTE. Last three names and 'near Faringdon' in different writing.

EXPLANATORY NOTES

(1) See Ch. 11, p. 308.
(2) The patron of the living of Great Coxwell was the Bishop of Salisbury.
(3) The Vansittarts were a family of German commercial origin who settled in Berkshire in the early eighteenth century. The head of the family in 1835 was Arthur Vansittart of Shottesbrook Park, near White Waltham, b. 1807, succ. his father 1829, d. 1859. The Dr Vansittart referred to in the list is probably Charles Vansittart, uncle of the preceding, who was in Holy orders.
(4) The Rev. J. Haskins, D.D., was the incumbent of this parish, of which the patron was Magdalen College, Oxford.

(5) Irish peer; the family had inherited the Berkshire estate of Shrivenham in the Vale of the White Horse. See above, Ch. 11, p. 313.

(6) John Pollexfen Bastard, a member of the well-known Devonshire
(7) family, d. 1816, had married Sarah Wymondesold of Lockinge, co. Berks. The family produced several Berkshire M.P.s and J.P.s; a John Pollexfen Bastard was a justice of the peace for the county in 1836.

(8) The president of the college. St John's College had considerable property in Berkshire, especially at Appleton, Fyfield, Longworth, Frilford, and Wittenham; and was the patron of several Berkshire livings.

(9) The patron of the living of Denchworth was Worcester College, Oxford.

(10) Charles Wapshare, rector of East (not West) Hendred, 1806-58. According to Foster's *Index Ecclesiasticus* he was rector of Sproatley, Yorks, 1806; vicar of Kilmersdon, Somerset, 1806; and rector of East Hendred, October 1806. Whether he held all three livings together is not clear but there is little doubt that he held the two rectories for the remainder of his life. (Humphreys, *East Hendred*, p. 207.)

(11) Lord of the manor of Warfield; high steward of Wokingham; patron of several livings. His Berkshire seat was at Billingbere, near Wokingham.

(12) Marquess of Downshire; possessed a considerable estate at Easthampstead, near Wokingham, and was the patron of several livings.

[13] Earl of Craven; possessed extensive property at Kintbury and Enbourne near Hungerford, and at Ashdown, near Lambourne, on the Berkshire Downs; patron of several livings. Was probably the most important landowner in the county.

APPENDIX G

SIX 'GOVERNMENT' BOROUGHS

The following brief sketch of six so-called government boroughs of the 1830–50 period may serve to amplify and illustrate the more general conclusions discussed in Chapter 12.

Chatham. It is an example of the difficulty of effecting a change of system by legislation that Chatham, the best known perhaps of all the government boroughs in this period, was itself a creation of the Reform Act of 1832. Even at the time of the reform debates it was suggested that the new constituency would become a government 'close borough' and Grey admitted in the House of Lords that at Chatham and Plymouth the ten-pound householders would probably tend to give their support to the government of the day.[11] From the start therefore it was generally accepted that Chatham was a borough in which government influence would be extremely strong. The electorate in the new constituency was less than 700 at the first registration and of these a considerable proportion were probably employees of the Admiralty. It was estimated twenty years later that of the 1,200 or so voters on the register some four or five hundred worked in the dockyards. In all it was reckoned that about one-third of the electorate was subject to government influence. At every election between 1832 and 1852 a 'government' candidate, so designating himself, put up for election; and at every election the government candidate was returned.

Significantly enough, the only conservative returned for Chatham in the thirties and forties was in 1835 when a conservative ministry was in power. His election was made the occasion for an election petition complaining not of him personally but of the conduct of the commandant of the Royal Marines barracks at Chatham, a Colonel Tremenheere. The complaint was that shortly before the election the commandant forbade the admittance to the barracks of all slopsellers and pawnbrokers; and that after the election a few were admitted by special permission. Of the favoured few, one had voted for the government candidate, Admiral Beresford; two were neutral; and a fourth had an uncle who had voted for Beresford. Of the four refused admission, three had voted for the whig candidate, Captain Byng,[12]

[11] *Hansard*, XII, 21.

[12] Hon. Capt. G. S. Byng, eldest son of Lord Strafford (cr. Earl of Strafford 1847) and son-in-law of the Marquess of Anglesey. He was elected for Chatham 1834 *vice* Lt.-Col. Maberley, and again in 1837, 1841, and 1847. After his defeat at Chatham in 1835 he sat for Poole, 1835–7, in the seat rendered vacant by his father's elevation to the House of Lords as Baron Strafford.

and the fourth was a minor. It was also asserted that Colonel Tremenheere had told one elector that he hoped, if Chatham did not return Admiral Beresford, that the government would take such measures as would cause half the shops in the town to be shut up. The bulk of the evidence against Tremenheere was given by small shopkeepers, but the witness to the remark about closing up the shops was the returning officer for the borough, a respectable man of evident sincerity. Tremenheere's explanation of his exclusion order was that he was expecting a large draft of men to be paid off whom he wished to protect from the Jews. In fact he greatly overstated the number of men paid off during the period of exclusion though this was subsequently attributed to a clerical error on the part of the paymaster who supplied him with the figures. In all his defence was not convincing and the general onus of the evidence was against him. It was significant that the exclusion order was withdrawn immediately it had been agreed to get up a petition against him. The select committee which inquired into the charges refrained, however, from drawing any direct conclusions as to Tremenheere's alleged attempt to interfere with the freedom of election. In the debate in the House of Commons on the petition two minor but interesting points emerged. One was the statement that the regimental colours of the Royal Marines were taken off their flag-staffs and borne in Admiral Beresford's election procession; the other was the fact that at the previous election, when the whigs were in office, Tremenheere had voted for the whig candidate, Captain Byng. As Warburton, the radical member for Bridport, unkindly observed, the latter circumstance merely proved that the colonel was a friend to the government whatever that government might be.[13]

The episode of Colonel Tremenheere, though illuminating, is not perhaps conclusive. In any case Admiral Beresford was left in undisturbed possession of the seat until 1837. At the general election of that year, Byng was returned unopposed. It is clear that at one point Beresford considered standing again but with a whig government now in power abandoned the constituency as hopeless. He was one of the three conservative candidates at that election who retired before a contest could come on, 'which', wrote Granville Somerset to Peel on 18 July 1837, 'the influence of Government fully accounts for'.[14] In 1841, with the whigs still in power, Byng again retained his seat although he had to meet a challenge from Lord Dufferin. He comfortably survived this, however, polling nearly double his opponent's total of votes; sat through Peel's ministry; and with his party once

[13] P.P. 1835, IX, 1–83, see esp. report of committee, pp. 3–12, and the evidence of witnesses pp. 39–42; *Hansard*, XXVI, 1194 sqq. and XXVII, 204–13. It may be noted that Admiral Beresford had formerly been commander-in-chief at Sheerness.

[14] Add. MS. 40423, fo. 346.

more in office was returned for the fourth time in 1847. The long run of whig elections ended in 1852 when the Derby ministry, with a minority in the Commons, appealed to the country in a general election. A fresh set of candidates now appeared. The government, that is to say, the conservative candidate, was Sir Frederic Smith on whose behalf the secretary to the Admiralty made a personal appearance in the dockyards shortly before the election. As was by now customary in Chatham, the government candidate won the election. But a petition was launched against his return, alleging the usual catalogue of electoral sins in such a constituency: bribery, corruption, offers of place, promotion and preferment, intimidation and undue influence. As isolated matters of fact it was subsequently shown that one of the dockyard employees, a prominent supporter of the government candidate, was afterwards promoted to a post at Portsmouth. Another elector was rewarded by the appointment of his son as letter-carrier in the post office through the influence of the successful candidate.

The report of the committee which considered this petition was perhaps the most important outcome of the 1852 election at Chatham. The committee found that Sir Frederic Smith was not duly elected and that the election was void. In addition, it passed the following resolution.

> That it was proved before the Committee, that a large number of the Electors are employed in Her Majesty's Dock Yard and other public departments at Chatham, and that they are under the influence of the Government for the time being; and that it appears that there is no instance of a Candidate being elected for this Borough who has not had the support of the Government. Under these circumstances it will be for the House to determine, whether the right of returning a Member should not for the future be withdrawn from the Borough of Chatham.[15]

Devonport. 'The Government influence', says Mosse's *Parliamentary Guide* for 1835, 'is considerable in this borough.' Like Chatham it was a new constituency created in 1832, but with a considerably larger electorate (over 1,700 at the first registration). It was estimated in 1852 that, taking dockyard and ordnance employees together, about one-third of the electorate was subject to government influence.[16] The borough had two seats and between 1832 and 1852 these were filled by an impressive row of whig politicians. Sir George Grey, who sat from 1832 to 1847, was successively under-secretary for the colonies, advocate-general, and chancellor of the Duchy of Lancaster under Melbourne, and became home secretary in Russell's first cabinet in 1846.

---

[15] P.P. 1852–3, IX, 207 sqq. (*Report Sel. Comm. Chatham Election*); *H. of C. Journals*, 1852–3, CVIII, 34, 315.
[16] P.P. 1852–3, XXV, 348.

Sir Edward Codrington, who was his colleague from 1832 to 1840, was vice-admiral of the White and generally considered to be a particular favourite of the Admiralty. Henry Tufnell who succeeded him in 1840 and was re-elected in the general election of 1841, was a junior lord of the Treasury in Melbourne's ministry and after 1841 was for many years the liberal chief whip. John Romilly who succeeded Grey in 1847 became first solicitor-general and then attorney-general in Russell's ministry and finally master of the rolls.

At the first election in 1832 the return of Grey and Codrington was unsuccessfully challenged by a local candidate, Leach, with no strong party affiliations. He was left at the foot of the poll some 300 votes below Codrington. There was not a great amount of government influence reported in this first election in the new borough, but it is significant that Leach was put forward by a townsmen party in order to prevent two government candidates from monopolizing the borough. In 1835 a more formidable competitor appeared in the person of George Dawson, brother-in-law to Peel, and recently appointed secretary to the Admiralty. He embarked on the contest with confidence and told Peel at the end of December 1834 that there was every prospect of a good fight with 'Conservatives, Churchmen, moderate Dissenters and Government on the one side—and the Ten Pounders, extreme Dissenters, Radicals & Whigs on the other'. All the influence that government could exert was brought into play, reinforced by the expenditure on Dawson's part of some £1,300.[17] All these resources failed, however, and though polling over 300 plumpers Dawson was defeated by a margin of some 200 votes. It was alleged many years later, by a solicitor employed on the conservative side, that Dawson did not receive the full support of the dockyard electors because they were pleased at the promotions that had taken place in the preceding years under a whig régime and did not expect Peel's government to last very long.[18]

At the following election Grey and Codrington were returned unopposed, but in 1840 there was a by-election in consequence of Codrington's promotion to commander-in-chief at Portsmouth. The new official candidate was Tufnell and against him the local conservatives invited George Dawson to stand once more for the borough. Bonham approved the project but enjoined secrecy as 'it is very desirable to keep the other parties in the dark and squabbling with each other until our canvass has commenced'.[19] The situation was in fact rendered more hopeful by the re-emergence of Leach who was expected by the conservatives to draw a number of votes from the whigs. Not

[17] Add. MS. 40408, fo. 32; 40411, fo. 160.
[18] P.P. 1852–3, xxv, 341.   [19] Add. MS. 40427, fo. 244, 20 November 1839.

unnaturally there was a good deal of feeling between the Tufnell and the Leach factions and Dawson could reasonably anticipate being left in the position of a *tertius gaudens*. The election campaign started in December 1839, and at the end of the month Dawson was able to send in a hopeful report to headquarters. After canvassing 2,000 houses he could record 802 positive pledges together with 57 who would probably be on his side though they would not pledge themselves. Some 460 were pledged to Tufnell and about 400 to Leach; though these figures would no doubt increase. He was therefore confident of success. Bitter warfare existed between the other two parties and it seemed certain that they would both go to the poll. If either retired it would only assist the conservatives. Tufnell's retirement would give the dockyard vote to Dawson; Leach's retirement meant that his followers would coalesce with the conservatives.[20] But, not for the first time, something went wrong with these neat electoral syllogisms and when it was all over Tufnell was found to have maintained the official tradition at Devonport by being returned at the head of the poll in January 1840. It was said afterwards, probably with truth, that though Dawson had strong support in the constituency, the decisive dockyard influence was used against him with all its power.

In the general election of 1841 Dawson again put up as the single conservative candidate and was once more defeated, though on this occasion by a margin of only 150 votes. Writing to Peel after the result, he said that 'the government influence, which is very great, was strained to the utmost against me, and you have no idea of the profligacy on their part to maintain the two seats. . . . A change of government would make a wonderful difference here.'[21] Complaints of the methods used by opponents were common form in all letters from defeated candidates; but the last sentence was probably just. Had Dawson fought the 1841 contest as secretary to the Admiralty the verdict might well have been reversed. Yet so many factors entered into an election that it is unsafe to dogmatize. By 1841, if not before, a perceptible transfer of moderate support to the conservatives had taken place in the country at large which probably swayed some votes at Devonport and helped to increase Dawson's poll. Moreover, 1841 was the third contest in the constituency in which Dawson had been engaged and the ability to take punishment and come back fighting was a quality appreciated in the political as well as the boxing ring. It is an interesting fact that Dawson, attacking a weak ministry in 1841, had done better than as secretary to the Admiralty in a minority ministry in 1835. But allowing for a strengthening on other grounds of his position at Devonport, the probability is at least that the dockyard vote

[20] Add. MS. 40617, fo. 79.   [21] Add. MS. 40485, fo. 34.

was the final decisive element that tipped the balance towards the whigs in 1841. It may tentatively be concluded, therefore, that the government influence at Devonport, though not the dominant factor that it was at Chatham, was a major force. As usual, exceptional personal popularity or doubts as to ministerial permanence might blunt its effectiveness; but in combination with other sources of strength it was irresistible. Without it, though otherwise in favourable circumstances, the whigs had triumphed in 1835. It is doubtful whether they would have retained the borough without it in the general whig debacle of 1841. Some weight is added to this conclusion by the events of 1852. At the previous general election Romilly and Tufnell had been returned once more for the whigs. But in 1852, with a conservative ministry in power and a secretary to the Admiralty taking an active part in the election on behalf of conservative candidates, Romilly was displaced by Lieutenant-General Berkeley. The two seats were thus shared between the two parties for the first time in the history of the borough. Where the conservatives had courted Devonport in vain under the leadership of Peel in 1841, it is hard to believe that the constituency had succumbed conscientiously to the attractions of Derby and Disraeli in 1852.[22]

Falmouth and Penryn. Falmouth, like Chatham and Devonport, was a new constituency. Unlike them it had received representation not in its own right but in conjunction with the old and notoriously rotten borough of Penryn. There was no dockyard at Falmouth, but it was commonly regarded as subject to government influence because of the naval packet-station there. Penryn on the other hand was technically an 'open borough', that is to say, one open to the highest bidder. The control over this dual constituency was therefore divided between the government and the purse, though in what proportions it was never easy to tell; nor whether they were in themselves decisive. It was not a large constituency, there being less than 900 registered voters for the first election after the Reform Act, and it was characteristic of the complex nature of its politics that it customarily returned members of both parties. For the whigs Sir Robert Monsey Rolfe, an able lawyer who was solicitor-general in Melbourne's government, held one seat from 1832 until his elevation to the bench in 1839. For the tories Lord Tullamoore,[23] the only son of the Earl of Charleville, was elected in 1832. His unsuccessful conservative colleague on this occasion was

---

[22] The polling in this 1852 election was extremely close: H. Tufnell 1,079; Lt.-Gen. Sir G. Berkeley 1,056; Sir J. Romilly 1,046; Sir J. H. Maxwell 1,032. In such an even contest, Stafford's intervention almost certainly gained a seat for his party.

[23] He succeeded his father as 2nd Earl of Charleville in October 1835. The courtesy title he held as eldest son is frequently, but wrongly, spelled Tullamore.

another lawyer J. W. Freshfield, who had sat for Penryn in 1830. At the next election Freshfield was returned and it was Tullamoore's turn to be left at the foot of the poll. Rolfe and Freshfield were again elected in 1837.

At the election of 1835, when the conservatives were in office, they made a particular effort to secure both seats. Their failure to do so, the result largely of a personal quarrel between their two candidates, throws an interesting light on the limitations of central control over such a constituency. The two conservative candidates were once again Tullamoore and Freshfield. Tullamoore, as the sitting member, was not overlooked by the watchful eye of Bonham. He reminded Peel towards the end of December 1834 not to forget Lord Tullamoore; 'as representing Falmouth, Ld. G[ranville] S[omerset] ought to have recommended him for the Board of Admiralty'.[24] He was not put there but Peel remembered him sufficiently to give him an appointment in the king's household. In the constituency itself, however, the election was marked on the conservative side by mismanagement and division from the very start. Rolfe was tacitly accepted by both parties as certain of re-election. There remained only one seat to be competed for by the two conservatives. Freshfield, who assumed as soon as possible the rôle of government candidate, showed an ominous tendency to ally with Rolfe against his nominal party colleague. Tullamoore, though he had been pressed from the party headquarters to continue his candidature, found himself the object of distrust by the local naval superintendent, and considered himself a much aggrieved man. The outcome of a confused and angry situation was that none of the regular government voters at Falmouth supported the unfortunate Tullamoore and what he indignantly described as 'the coalition between Messrs. Rolfe & Freshfield' went forward to an easy victory. Lack of control from London, Tullamoore's tactlessness, Freshfield's jealousy, all conspired to deny to the conservatives an outright victory in this, a reputedly government, borough.[25]

A letter written to Peel by one of Freshfield's committee shortly after the election helps to explain both Tullamoore's failure and the special nature of the Falmouth constituency. The letter was prompted by the rumour that Rolfe was about to resign. If so, thought Peel's correspondent, a little 'judicious management' would secure the second seat for the government. But certain conditions would have to be fulfilled.

[24] Add. MS. 40407, fo. 62.
[25] Add. MS. 40405, fo. 113; 40409, fos. 53, 93; Clerk Papers, Tullamoore (to ? Peel), dated Devonport, 25 January 1835, and a copy of a printed manifesto to the electors of Penryn and Falmouth following his defeat, by Lord Tullamoore, dated 16 January 1835 (T/188/81).

If Mr Rolfe's resignation should be brought about, a government man cannot be too early in the field; and to ensure success that man should by all means be a Lord of the Admiralty. I have no hostility to Lord Tullamoore, though by an unhappy concurrence of circumstances, I did, as a friend of Mr Freshfield's, stand in an antagonist position to that young nobleman at the last election; but I must be bold enough to say that no man but one who is immediately connected with that Department of the government upon which this town more particularly relies, will have a fair chance here. Any other person, and Lord Tullamoore particularly, would seem to come rather as a *Tory* than as a *Government* candidate; and his standing in that character might perhaps excite a feeling in the Reformers too likely to rally them round their old colours, and to make them, in the ardour of their political predilections, unmindful of those interests, to a just understanding of which they seem now to be returning.[26]

There was, however, another side to the Falmouth and Penryn constituency besides government influence and a just understanding of the true interests of the electorate. It had long been known that the old voters in Penryn were amenable to money and it was not long after the Reform Act when indications began to appear that their example was having an influence on the new voters in Falmouth farther down the estuary. Considerable bribery had taken place in 1835 and the appetite for it had probably increased as a result of a contested by-election in 1835 and a contest in 1837. When, towards the end of 1839, the promotion of Rolfe as baron of the exchequer made another by-election certain, there were probably many individuals in the constituency of no special political views, who were anxious that his successor should not be returned unopposed. In any case the conservatives in the district were looking out for a candidate, and Bonham assured them that he would produce one. But this was not easy. The original plan, to run Aberdeen's son, Lord Haddo, broke down on the latter's absence at the crucial time,[27] and other prospective newcomers were distinctly apprehensive of the expense likely to be encountered in such a venal constituency. Freshfield, the sitting member, was consulted along with others, and the general conclusion was that the seat was within reach of the opposition since the government was under a temporary cloud at Falmouth owing to the transfer of the packet-boats to another station.[28] But reach and attainment were not the same thing. 'The first *rich* man of either party that goes to Falmouth will certainly win', confessed Bonham to Peel at the end of November; the difficulty was to find the rich man. The Penryn conservatives urged the desirability of finding a candidate, but added 'that to save trouble it would be idle for any man to go down

---

[26] Clerk Papers, Wm. Kirkness to Peel, 25 January 1835 (T/188/81).
[27] See above, Ch. 7, p. 166.　　　[28] Add. MS. 43061, fo. 234.

who was not prepared to spend *Three Thousand Pounds*'. Bonham, who had already expressed his doubts of finding any one ready to spend such an amount in the uncertain state of parliament, felt justified in his pessimism as no less than nine persons to whom he broached the matter declined such a speculation. At the last minute, however, a candidate was found in Benjamin Bond Cabbell, a lawyer of the Middle Temple, who had unsuccessfully contested St Albans, another venal borough, in 1837.[29] Bonham duly packed him off to Falmouth early in December with a letter of introduction, but warned him that he must be guided in his course by the result of his talks with the local conservatives. The party manager's lack of enthusiasm for both candidate and constituency was probably shared by Cabbell himself when he discovered the true character of the electorate whose suffrages he was to invoke. 'Mr Cabbell', reported Bonham to Peel on 30 December, 'I fear will bolt as it appears *entre nous* that of the Penryn voters, 409, three only do not expect their payment and Falmouth is learning the good lesson.'[30]

Harwich. Before the Reform Act, Harwich had been a close corporation under the influence of the Treasury. After the Reform Act the corporation was still strong and the government still influential. Neither of these things was surprising in view of the size of the constituency which was one of the smallest in the country. The number of voters who registered in 1832 was only 214; and only 186 actually voted in the first election after the Act. A more favourable field for influence could scarcely be found. It was in the logic of the situation, therefore, that both parties, besides seeking their own immediate electoral advantage, worked to transform or rather maintain Harwich as a government borough; the whigs in order to consolidate their existing tenure of power; the conservatives against the day when Peel should enter upon his inevitable period of office. J. C. Herries, who was the tory member that maintained this unequal contest, was better qualified than any one else in the party for the task. He had first been elected for Harwich in 1823 when he became financial secretary to the Treasury under Liverpool. He kept his seat in the difficult period between 1830 and 1834, and was appointed secretary at war in Peel's first ministry. At the ensuing general election he celebrated his return to office by bringing in Bonham, the party manager, as his colleague at Harwich.

Before the election, and indeed even before Peel had returned from Italy, Herries sent to the new prime minister a memorandum on the

[29] He was defeated again at Marylebone in 1841, but secured election for St Albans in 1846 (a by-election) and for Boston in 1847 and 1852.
[30] Add. MS. 40427, fos. 238, 264, 278, 297, 363.

state of politics at Harwich in the expectation, as he explained to
Peel, that his leader would have 'more than one application for the
nomination to the borough'. The memorandum divided the constituency into three parties. Firstly there was the old 'Blue' or conservative party that had consistently supported Herries irrespective of
what government was in office. Secondly there were the whigs and
radicals who had returned the former liberal member, Tower, and
were still in touch with members of the late government. Lastly there
were the independents who kept themselves separate from the other
two groups and were conscious that they could decide the issue of an
election since the conservatives, though numerous, could not defeat the
whigs and independents combined. In 1832 the independents had
given the conservatives a measure of support and Herries had been
labouring to induce them to assist in returning a second conservative
candidate. This, he reported, they seemed inclined to do if that candidate were an official man 'and recommended to them by the government itself'. The memorandum continued, 'I feel confident indeed
that if the business be discreetly managed and through the influence
of those who have it now in hand, the joint support of those two parties
to two *government* candidates may be depended upon in the event of a
dissolution.' The advantage of such an arrangement extended not
only to the present occasion but also 'with a view . . . to making Harwich available as a government nomination borough permanently
hereafter'. The choice of a second candidate, Herries concluded, was
a matter of indifference as he had prepared his followers to receive
and support him, whoever he might be, as the nomination of the
government.[31]

In the light of this exposition of the inner mysteries at Harwich, the
external details of successive elections are more than usually intelli-
gible. In 1832, the first under the new system, there were four candidates who at the close of polling were only separated by eight votes.
Herries finished on top with ninety-seven votes; the other elected member was the whig, C. T. Tower, with ninety-three; while a radical,
Leader, and a fourth candidate (probably a second whig), Disney,
occupied the bottom places with ninety and eighty-nine apiece. The
key to this election was an agreement between Herries' 'Blue' party
and the independents who supported Leader, whereby the latter also
voted for Herries in return for the votes of most of the conservatives
for Leader. It was this neat balance between tory and independent
strength on the one side, whig and governmental strength on the other,
which produced such a close finish. In 1835 the conservatives were now
also the ministerial party and Herries was obviously confident of

[31] Add. MS. 40404, fos. 274, 276.

success not only for himself but for a second conservative. Bonham, now storekeeper to the Ordnance, was selected for the honour of being his colleague, and though rarely optimistic about his own political fortunes, he told Peel early in January that he felt safe about their election at Harwich—'Herries of course is safe.'[32] This confidence was justified. Herries again polled ninety-seven votes; Bonham received seventy-eight; and their solitary opponent Verner was left at the post with thirty-six. On this evidence the combination of conservative and government influence was clearly irresistible. If a hostile journal is to be believed, everything was done during Peel's short ministry of 1834-5 to make it permanently so. No fewer than seventeen places of profit, alleged the *Edinburgh Review*, were showered on the heads of the fortunate Harwich electors in the four months of conservative rule.[33] Nevertheless, when Herries and Bonham put up for the borough again in 1837 it was without the backing of the official situations they both held in 1835, and this time the whigs returned in full force. They put up two candidates, Tower and Alexander Ellice,[34] a naval captain, and in a close run contest Herries and Ellice tied with seventy-five votes, beating Tower by a single vote, while Bonham was nine votes behind with sixty-six.

Herries himself could scarcely have been satisfied with such a narrow victory and in the few years that elapsed before the next trial of strength his position steadily weakened in the face of the persistent attacks of the whig governmental forces. In 1841 his principal supporter at Harwich was driven from the borough by what was alleged to be governmental influence. When the general election came on the same year Herries gave up his long contest and retired to what he hoped would be more favourable ground at Ipswich, only to meet there the defeat which he regarded as inevitable at Harwich. According to his biographer, Herries never bribed nor consented to bribery on his behalf at his elections, and it was because under whig pressure his seat became too precarious to survive without bribery that he preferred to go elsewhere. The piety of a family historian is to be respected. 'I have maintained,' ran Herries's own more ambiguous account of his stewardship, 'out of office, at a considerable cost, during more than ten years and at four elections, against all the power of the Government, a seat theretofore invariably at the disposal of the Treasury for the time being', and he claimed that he was only driven at length from the struggle by the overwhelming weight of that power.[35]

[32] Add. MS. 40409, fo. 124.   [33] *Edinburgh Review*, LXII, 173.
[34] Not to be confused with Edward Ellice, the whig party manager, M.P. for Coventry.
[35] *Memoir of J. C. Herries*, I, 119; II, 124-7, 188-9, 191-204.

What is not open to doubt is that bribery was taking an increasing hold on the borough. In the 1841 election, when an entirely fresh set of candidates appeared in the constituency, there was some heavy expenditure. Le Marchant spent £1,000 and yet finished at the foot of the poll with seventy-four votes; and no fewer than three petitions were brought against the return of the two successful candidates, Attwood and Beresford, on the usual grounds of bribery, illegal practices, and intimidation. As described elsewhere[36] a compromise took place between the two parties in order to evade a parliamentary inquiry. In the resultant investigations Joseph Parkes, the whig election agent, testified to the borough's reputation for bribery and corruption.[37] It was not to be expected perhaps that a whig party man should advert to government influence in a period when the whigs had formed the government. Yet the significant aspect of the 1841 election at Harwich was that although the whigs were in office, it had been the two conservative candidates who had actually received the majority of votes polled. Herries' analysis of 1834 had suggested that the floating vote which decided the issue between the two regular parties was mainly influenced by the prospect of government patronage. By 1841 it was direct bribery that was becoming the deciding factor. All the evidence seemed to show that in proportion as government influence receded, its place was taken, at Harwich as at Falmouth and Penryn, by the power of the highest private bidder.

The Cinque Ports. (a) Hastings. Until 1832 Hastings, like Harwich, had been a close corporation under the influence of the Treasury. The franchise was vested in the mayor, jurats, and resident freemen, and the electoral influence had been managed by a local attorney named Milward in the governmental interest.[38] The Reform Act increased the electorate from about 200 under the old franchise to 500 in 1832 and 600 in 1835. In 1830, with a conservative ministry in power, the borough presented a familiar picture. Its two representatives were both tories and both official men: Joseph Planta, secretary to the Treasury, and Lieutenant-General Sir Henry Fane, surveyor general to the Ordnance. At the following election, fought under the auspices of a whig government, these two were displaced by two whigs, Frederick North and John Warre. Both of these were local gentry, the former (a direct descendant of the Roger North who wrote the famous *Lives*) being indeed a resident of Hastings. At the time of the reform bill he used his considerable personal influence in the borough to bring it over to the cause of reform although he was himself far from being an

[36] See above, Ch. 10, p. 259.
[37] P.P. 1842, v, 100–14; *H. of C. Journals*, 1841, XCVI, 487, 489, 556.
[38] *Key to Both Houses*, 334.

orthodox party man. It was his rather unexpected adoption of reform principles in 1831 that had really been responsible for keeping Planta out of the representation of the constituency. These two whigs were again returned at the first election after the Reform Act. In 1835, however, with a change of government, the conservatives launched a counter-offensive. On the liberal side North, who had inherited the old Milward interest and claimed in addition the reforming vote, was the most powerful competitor. He was now joined by a more radical colleague in H. Elphinstone, a nephew of the well-known radical member for Bridport, Warburton, and connected by marriage with the Curteis family who had considerable influence in the county of Sussex and the borough of Rye. Against these a challenge was put up by Planta who since his exclusion from the borough in 1831 had been steadily cultivating his interest in the constituency.

Early in December 1834 Planta wrote to the Duke of Wellington, who, as Lord Warden, was frequently the victim of the electoral confidences of tory candidates for the Cinque Ports in spite of his continued refusals to exercise any of his powers there for electoral purposes. On this occasion Planta announced that he had met with a good reception in Hastings and St Leonards and was hopeful of success in 'this one of your Grace's Cinque Ports'. He had, he related, been fortunate enough to secure as his agent a Mr Manser of Rye, who owned a good deal of property, was consequently influential in that locality, and was a stout conservative. This paragon had recently purchased the whole of the frontage on the sea between Hastings and St Leonards, nearly a mile in extent, and was running up £10 houses which would all be within the constituency and all for Planta.[39] That, however, was a development for the future and pleasing as the prospect was, Planta had to consider the immediate present.

> The very successful canvass [he continued] which I have made here has been chiefly owing (barring some respect for my private character of which I hear) to my connection with the King's Govt. The two things which the people in this town most care about are: foreign licenses for the fishermen, and a question of derelict crown lands, on which renewal of leases may or may not be granted. On these two subjects I have not committed myself in my canvass to any line of conduct. I have only said, what is obvious: that a man connected with the government must have more influence on such questions than any other person. This has got me the fishermen almost to a man, and a great many votes in a district called America which is Crown property. Now this influence I shall lose if I am not permanently connected with the government.

He therefore requested the duke to allow him to retain his former

[39] Cf. above, Ch. 8, p. 175.

connexion with the Treasury. If, he added persuasively, he stayed on in the borough, he was convinced that he would be able to make 'an Interest at Hastings which nothing would be likely in future to shake, and prepare the way for the Introduction at a future time of a second Tory Member'.[40] This was exactly the same language and the same inducements as were being put forward by Herries with reference to Harwich at almost the identical time. Official connexion greatly assisted a candidate at a 'government borough'; but conversely, success in such a constituency seemed to warrant a request for an official appointment to make it permanent. Peel, to whom this eloquent appeal was forwarded, thought it inadvisable to put Planta, who was already in receipt of a government pension, in the Treasury; and the latter's application for a government appointment was met with an offer of nomination to the privy council.[41]

In the event neither Planta's personal character nor his connexion with the government nor even his friendship with Mr Manser, was able to secure his return. North was at the top of the poll with 374 votes; Elphinstone, the suspect radical, was second with 291; while Planta and the other conservative candidate Brisco languished at the bottom with 159 and 157. It had generally been assumed beforehand that Brisco stood no chance; and it is possible that his candidature damaged the position of Planta. But this alone would scarcely have accounted for the wide margin between the successful and unsuccessful candidates. Either government influence had ceased to be the dominant factor in the constituency or the prudent electors of Hastings did not trust in a long continuation of Peel's ministry. Planta perhaps did well to put his hopes in the line of new houses going up along the sea-front. At the next election, two years later, by which time they should have been completed, he was carried into first place with 400 votes. The other elected candidate was a local liberal, R. Hollond of St Leonards, and the only other contestant was the unfortunate Brisco who polled 312. With this election a temporary equilibrium seems to have been reached, and at the 1841 general election Planta and Hollond were returned without a contest. In 1844, when Planta retired from parliament, Brisco at last secured a seat and he was re-elected together with Hollond at the general election of 1847.

The evidence here suggests, therefore, that neither government influence nor party organization was the decisive force at Hastings. The old personal connexion taken over from Milward had been engrafted by North on the new liberal interest; while Planta's own attempt in 1834–5 to restore governmental control on behalf of the conservative party completely failed. It is to other, more local, factors

[40] Add. MS. 40309, fo. 372.   [41] Add. MS. 40405, fo. 272.

that the success of the conservatives in capturing and retaining one of the seats from 1837 onwards is to be attributed.

(*b*) *Sandwich*. In this borough there was a long history of Admiralty influence even though from the end of the eighteenth century there had on occasion been symptoms of an independent interest. The latter was made possible by the size of the electorate formed by the freemen of the borough who in 1830 numbered about 700, the majority being non-resident. The borough was originally placed in Schedule B of the reform bill and ranked technically as an 'open' borough.[42] In the end it survived the Reform Act with its two members intact. Its boundaries were enlarged, however, to take in the parishes of Deal and Walmer so that, despite the loss of the non-resident freemen, its new electorate at the first registration was over 900. Nevertheless it was alleged more than once during the reform debates that the constituency would be under government control. Sir George Warrender, who had been member for Sandwich from 1818 to 1826, suggested that it would become 'a very snug nomination borough in the hands of the Admiralty'.[43] Nothing occurred at the first reformed election to disturb the established conventions of the borough. Joseph Marryat, a banker, merchant, and shipowner of London, and Sir Edward Troubridge, Captain R.N. (a son of the Admiral Troubridge of Battle of Nile fame), who had sat for the borough in 1831, were again elected in the whig interest in 1832, defeating two conservative opponents by substantial margins. In 1835, with a conservative ministry, Troubridge was left alone to uphold the whig colours and though beaten into second place, contrived to maintain himself in the representation of the borough against two opponents. His tory colleague, who polled nearly 150 more votes, was Samuel Grove Price, a barrister and eminent parliamentary counsel, who had been elected for the borough in 1830 and unsuccessfully contested it in 1832. About half of Troubridge's poll came from plumpers, but it is obvious that many electors split between him and Price. In 1837, with a whig ministry once more, the borough returned two whigs. Troubridge, who in 1835 had been appointed a junior lord of the Admiralty in Melbourne's second administration, was top of the poll and brought in with him a second liberal in the person of Sir James Carnac. The two conservative candidates, of whom Price was again one, were beaten by a clear if not overwhelming majority. Price, for example, polled only 13 more votes than he received in 1832 and nearly 180 less than he received in 1835. It is difficult not to associate these fluctuations with the changes of ministry in the three successive elections.

The whigs who represented the constituency after 1837 were both of

[42] See the list published in *Hansard*, ii, 819 24.   [43] *Hansard*, v, 494.

an 'official' character. Carnac was subsequently appointed Governor of Bombay and was succeeded in his seat for Sandwich by another whig in 1839. This was Sir Rufane Shaw Donkin, K.C.B., an army officer who had fought in the Peninsular War and by this date had reached the rank of lieutenant-general. Not until the death of the latter early in 1841, when the Melbourne ministry was patently at the end of its resources, did the conservatives manage to take a seat. The man who achieved this success, H. H. Lindsay, was returned again at the general election a few months later with Troubridge still in possession of the other seat. There was no opposition to this division of the borough between the two parties. Once restored to power, however, the conservatives were not disposed to remain content with a half share in an 'official borough'. Even while the whigs were enjoying their last few weeks of office in the summer of 1841, the conservative party managers were turning their thoughts to Sandwich. There was a rumour in August that Troubridge was to be appointed to the governorship of South Australia. Fremantle, the conservative chief whip, wrote off promptly to Peel to warn him of the impending vacancy and recommended that they should be prepared with a 'Government candidate'. His suggestion was that they should put up Sir George Cockburn (appointed a lord of the Admiralty a few weeks later) or some one of that calibre to fight the by-election.[44] But nothing came of this project because Troubridge did not go to Australia and indeed remained member for Sandwich until the general election of 1847. By that time the great Peelite ministry was a thing of the past.

Circumstantial as this evidence largely is, it seems reasonable to conclude that the government of the day continued to enjoy special influence in the constituency after 1832 and that, as regards one seat at least, that influence was perhaps decisive in the sense of being a deciding factor between the two parties. The only occasions when the conservatives gained a seat at Sandwich were firstly in 1835 when a conservative ministry was in power, and secondly in the two elections of 1841 when the whig government was weak, discredited, and approaching its end. The extraordinary difference, having regard to the smallness of the electorate, between the votes attracted by Price in 1835 and 1837 needs in particular some special explanation if it is not attributable to the change of government.

[44] Add. MS. 40476, fo. 38.

APPENDIX H

(Add. MS. 40408, fo. 249)

Customs

The offices which fall to the disposal of the Treasury in this Dept. are:

Age of admission above 21 and under 30

Searchers
Coastwaiters, etc.

Salaries ranging from £200 to £80 according to the magnitude of the post.

Above 16 and under 40

Clerkships

Salaries £80 or £70.

Above 21 and under 30
under-Messengers
above 18 and under 40

Tidewaiters
Weighers
Messengers
Boatmen

Emoluments consisting principally of day pay averaging £60 p.a.

Searchers are eligible for promotion to Landing Surveyorships, Comptrollerships & Collectorships.

The Collectors Clerks may also succeed to Comptrollerships and Collectorships. Tidewaiters may succeed to Tidesurveyorships, and Weighers to Lockerships. All appointments in the Customs emanate from the Treasury and no Promotion can take place without the approval of that Board.

Excise

The patronage of this Dept. is vested in the Commissrs. by their Patent and by Act of Parliament but by a private arrangement lately made with them one half is ceded to the Treasury and each Dept. nominates to alternate Vacancies.

Age of admission to Excise Offices varies in every appointment—Clerks from 18 to 30 Export Officers 21 to 35 Permit Writers 21 to 45

The Appointments which fall to the disposal of the Treasury under this arrangement are in the nature of Clerkships, Permit Writers, Messengers, etc.

The above arrangement refers only to what is termed the House Patronage.

Expectants in the Excise 19 to 30. Persons having more than 2 children are ineligible.

Other arrangements have been made at different times respecting the Appointment of the Officers who are called Excisemen. Of these the Treasury have now 55 out of every 100—35 fall to the disposal of the Commrs. and 10 are reserved for the sons of deserving Officers.

Hop Assts. no limitation as to age.

Another agreement again applies to the Appointment of Hop Assistants—temporary Officers employed during the Hop Season—of these about a third are nominated to the Treasury.

The promotion in the Excise Department is exclusively in the hands of the Commrs.

Stamps & Taxes

No limitation as to age
  Survrs. of Taxes 21 to 30
  Stampers 21 to 35
  Messrs. 21 to 40
  Clerks no limitation

All appointments in this Dept. are at the disposal of the Treasury. They consist of Distributors of Stamps, Surveyors of Taxes, Clerks, Stampers, Messengers, etc.

Audit Office

The Appointments in this Dept. consist of Clerkships and Messengers which are at the disposal of the Treasury.

The same applies to other Depts. subordinate to the Treasury such as the Stationery Office, etc.

(Unsigned and undated, but from its position in the Peel Papers may reasonably be assigned to December 1834.)

APPENDIX J

Transcripts of three letters in the possession of L. H. Hayter, esq., of Bridgwater, are reproduced here by his kind permission. The first two concern Bonham's activities in the Taunton by-election of 1835 when Disraeli unsuccessfully opposed Labouchere, and are a good example of the kind of control exercised by the central managers in many constituencies. The third, written by the Duke of Rutland in 1905, was in response to inquiries as to Bonham's identity prompted by Mr Hayter after the first two had passed into his hands.

(1) Letter to Mr Beadon, solicitor, Taunton.

25 Dorset St. Monday.

Dear Sir,

In the absence of Lord Granville Somerset who I believe mentioned to you the name of Mr D'Israeli as a Gentleman for whom all the Conservative Party are most anxious to obtain a seat in the H. of Commons, I take the liberty of introducing him to you as the Bearer of this Letter. He is the son of Mr D'Israeli well known in the literary world and is himself a very able man.

He contested Wycombe at the last Election, and Ld. Lyndhurst as well as Ld. Chandos and all the leading Conservatives in Buckinghamshire where he resides were I know most anxious for his success. With the extreme probability amounting almost to certainty that the present Parlt. must be of very short duration he would not of course be disposed to incur any very considerable expense but this is a point on which he will be able to converse with you more explicitly than I could.

I have only therefore to repeat my assurance that nothing would be more gratifying to all our friends in London than to learn that Taunton had returned so powerful an accession to their cause.

Believe me, my dear Sir, yours very truly,

F. R. Bonham.

On recollection I believe that I also mentioned the name of Mr D'Israeli when you did me the honor of calling on me. I hope we shall be able to send you a letter tomorrow which will secure the interest of Ld. Ashburton.

(2) Letter to Mr Beadon, solicitor, Taunton.

25 Dorset St.
April 24'th. 1835

My Dear Sir,

I have written to Mr D'Israeli urging him in the strongest manner to poll the Borough as far as his means will go to the last man.

I cannot promise him any money *this day* but I hope tomorrow to have made up the greater part if not the whole Three Hundred Pounds he wants—however I cannot *now* guarantee it.

I have seen letters to Mr Bainbridge from persons who mean to vote against us, but yet admitting that our man has made great way, and is very popular.

I shall be really disappointed if we do not make a good fight if not beat him.

At all events I am satisfied that we have sent you a good Candidate.

Very truly yours,
F. R. Bonham.

(3) Letter from the Duke of Rutland to Lady Henrietta Turnor.[45]

July 24 1905
Belvoir Castle,
Grantham.

Dear Lady Henrietta,

Victoria[46] has given me your letter anent Mr Bonham and I will endeavour to give you my recollection of him.

He was in 1841 an elderly man, dressed in a long brown coat and carrying a large strapped book, full of electioneering facts, figures and calculations. He was not in Parliament but was Sir Robert Peel's trusted agent in matters relating to elections and party management; whether he held some subordinate post in one of the departments I forget. A strange scene, which occurred in the House of Commons in 1845 or 1846, originated in Mr Bonham being confused with his brother Col. Bonham, a violent Radical, who, in Lord Liverpool's stormy days, was tried for sedition or something of the kind. Sir Robert was able to expose the whole mistake (which originated with Walter of '*The Times*'), and vindicate his Friend. The whole story no doubt is set out in *Hansard*.[47] For the rest my recollection of Mr Bonham is distinctly favourable—rough, faithful, honest, indefatigable, the depositary of a thousand secrets and the betrayer of none.

Yours sincerely,
Rutland.

[45] Lady Henrietta Turnor was the wife of Algernon Turnor, private secretary to Disraeli 1874–80.
[46] Presumably Lady Victoria Manners, daughter of the 7th Duke of Rutland.
[47] For an account of the 'Despard incident' (an allegation by Disraeli in 1845 that Bonham had been concerned in the Despard plot of 1802), see my article in *E.H.R.*, LXIII, 506–7. The duke seems to have conflated Colonel Despard with Bonham's half-brother John, and placed the affair under Liverpool instead of Pitt. It is not clear whether he meant that Walter originally supplied Disraeli with the misleading information or whether he thought that Walter himself had brought the charge against Bonham in the House of Commons.

APPENDIX K

Unlike Parkes and Coppock, F. R. Bonham has found no place in the *Dictionary of National Biography*. The following details may therefore be worth putting on record.

He was born 5 September 1785 in London and baptized at St. George's, Hanover Square. His father, Francis Warren Bonham, came of an Irish family, was educated at Trinity College, Dublin, and later called to the Irish Bar. Some time before the end of the eighteenth century he settled in England and died 8 September 1810 at Richmond Hill, London. By his first marriage, with Mary Ann Leslie, he had a son John, imprisoned for suspected complicity in Irish nationalist activities in 1798, and a daughter Mary Ann (Joyce) who died unmarried at Hammersmith in 1796. By his second marriage he had five children, of whom only two survived infancy: Francis Robert, and a daughter Susan born in 1780. Neither married and they lived together for at least the last thirty years of their life. After F. R. Bonham's death the two volumes of his correspondence now in the Peel Papers were purchased from Miss Susan Bonham by Peel's literary executors.

His mother, Dorothea Sophia, who died at Hertford Street, Mayfair, on 23 June 1820, was a member of the famous Herbert family and was in direct line of descent from Sir Richard Herbert of Coldbrook, the ancestor of the earls of Pembroke and Montgomery. On her mother's side she was the grand-daughter of Lord Desart of Kilkenny, who sat for Thomastown, co. Kilkenny, in the Irish parliament of 1715–27.

F. R. Bonham was probably privately educated until 1804 when he matriculated as a gentleman commoner at Corpus Christi College, Oxford, on 27 January. He took his B.A. degree in 1807 and his M.A. in 1810. In 1808 he entered Lincoln's Inn and was called to the Bar in 1814. His father, besides providing for his widow and elder son, left by his will in 1810 the sum of £5,000 each to Francis Robert and Susan. In addition, F. R. Bonham received a further sum of £5,000 from the estate of his half-sister Mary Ann, and was his father's residuary legatee. There is also a family record of certain property at Clongaffyn, co. Meath, which came to him on his father's death and which he sold. He died in his seventy-eighth year, on 26 April 1863, at his house in Knightsbridge. His sister, Miss Susan Bonham, died only six months later and their common gravestone may still be seen in Brompton Cemetery.

BIBLIOGRAPHY

(except for printed periodicals, place of publication is London unless
otherwise stated)

A. MANUSCRIPT SOURCES

1. BRITISH MUSEUM (ADDITIONAL MANUSCRIPTS)

Peel Papers (including the Bonham Papers, 40616–17): the main
manuscript source for this book. Reference has been made in the
text to some seventy-five volumes, numbered between 40302 and
40617. The period covered is 1829–50 though the Bonham Papers
contain some letters of later date.

Gladstone Papers: correspondence with Bonham, 1835–60 (44110).
Some use has also been made of:

Aberdeen Papers: correspondence with Bonham (in 43061).

Wellesley Papers: (37311–2, 37316).

For Berkshire politics use has been made of:

Baigent Collection: (39989–92).

Richards Collection: (28660–78).

Miscellaneous collections of letters, newspaper cuttings, etc., relating to the general social and political history of the county.

2. PUBLIC RECORD OFFICE

Cardwell Papers: (G.D. 48/49–50, G.D. 48/53).

Home Office Papers: Municipal and Provincial Correspondence
1834—Berks (H.O. 52/24).

3. REGISTER HOUSE (EDINBURGH)

Clerk of Penicuik Papers: (T 188/81–87), eight boxes of unsorted
papers relating to Sir George Clerk of Penicuik (1787–1867).

4. SCOTTISH NATIONAL LIBRARY

Ellice Papers (1st instalment): miscellaneous correspondence of
Edward Ellice senior (1781–1863).

B. PARLIAMENTARY PAPERS

1. HOUSE OF COMMONS (ACCOUNTS AND PAPERS): the reports of committees
of inquiry, and evidence before election committees, form the
largest single printed source for the working of the electoral
system after 1832.

Reference has been made in the text to the following:

1830–1, X (statistics).

1831–2, XXXVI (statistics).

1833, VIII, Coventry; IX, Hertford; X, Liverpool; XI, Stafford, Warwick; XXVII, election expenses.

1834, IX, election expenses.

1835, VIII, bribery at elections; IX, Chatham, Ipswich; X, Yarmouth, York; XXIII, corporations England and Wales, 1st Rep.; XXXVII, secret service; XLVI, Wolverhampton.

1836, XIX, Stafford; XLIII, electoral statistics.

1837-8, X, Evesham, Ipswich; XI, Kingston-on-Hull; XII, Shaftesbury; XLIV, county elections 1837.

1840, IX, Ludlow, Cambridge.

1841, IX, St Albans, Coventry, Walsall.

1842, V, corrupt compromises; VI, Lyme Regis; VII, Ipswich, Great Marlow, Sudbury; VIII, Newcastle-under-Lyme, Penryn, Southampton; XXXIII, election expenses 1841 (counties).

1843, VI, Cambridge, Nottingham, Durham; XLIV, election expenses 1841 (boroughs).

1844, XVIII, Sudbury.

1852-3, IX, Chatham; XXV, Dockyard Appointments.

1859, XXIII, Boundaries of boroughs.

2. OTHER PARLIAMENTARY PUBLICATIONS

Return of Members of Parliament, Part II (1878).
Interim Report of Committee on House of Commons Personnel and Politics, 1264-1832, Cmd. 4130 (1932).
Journal of the House of Commons.
Hansard's *Parliamentary Debates*, 3rd ser.

C. PERIODICALS, PAMPHLETS, WORKS OF REFERENCE

1. NEWSPAPERS

The Times   *Essex Herald*
Standard   *Brighton Gazette*
Berkshire Chronicle   *Brighton Guardian*
Reading Mercury   *Brighton Herald*
Windsor Express

2. OTHER PERIODICALS

Annual Register   *Edinburgh Review*
Gentleman's Magazine   *Westminster Review*
Quarterly Review

3. PAMPHLETS

Appendix to the Black Book, by the original editor, 3rd ed. (1835).
Carlton Club, list of members, etc., April 1836 (1836).
England and Ireland, a Political Cartoon (1844).
Letter from Sir H. Verney, Bt., to one of his Constituents (1848).

O'Connell, D., *Letters on the Reform Bill* (1832).
On Pledges (National Political Union Pamphlet no. 15).
Wakefield, D., *Pledges Defended, Letter to the Electors of Lambeth* (1832).
Handbills concerning the Windsor Election (Windsor, 1802).
Election of Representatives for the Borough of New Windsor (Windsor, 1831).

4. WORKS OF REFERENCE
British Almanac & Companion.
Banfield, T. C., *Statistical Companion.*
Crosby, G., *Parliamentary Record*, two vols. (Leeds, 1849).
  Political Reference Book (Leeds, 1838).
Dod, C. R., *Electoral Facts 1832–52*, 2nd ed. (1853).
  Parliamentary Companion.
Gooch, R., *Book of the Reformed Parliament* (1834).
Key to Both Houses of Parliament (1832).
Parliamentary Pocket Book for 1833 (supplement to the *Key to Both Houses*, etc.).
Lewis, S., *Parliamentary History* (vol. v of Lewis's *Topographical Dictionary of England*) (1835).
Maxima Charta of 1832 (1832).
MacCalmont, F. H., *Parliamentary Poll Book* (London and Nottingham, 1879).
Mosse, R. B., *Parliamentary Guide* (1835).
Oldfield, T. H. B., *Representative History of Great Britain and Ireland*, six vols. (1816).
O'Byrne, R. H., *Representative History of Great Britain and Ireland*, two vols. (1848).
Present and Last Parliaments (1833).
Burke's Peerage and Baronetage.
Burke's Landed Gentry of Great Britain & Ireland.
The Complete Peerage, by G. E. C., new ed., by the Hon. Vicary Gibbs, etc. (1910–).
The Annual Peerage of the British Empire, ed. A., E. and M. Innes.
Ridgway's Peerage of the United Kingdom.

D. OTHER PRINTED WORKS

1. ARTICLES IN LEARNED REVIEWS, ETC.
The English Historical Review.
  A. Aspinall, 'English Party Organization in the Early Nineteenth Century' (XLI, 389).
  A. S. Foord, 'The Waning of "The Influence of the Crown"' (LXII, 484).

N. Gash, 'Ashley and the Conservative Party in 1842' (LIII, 679).
'The Influence of the Crown at Windsor and Brighton in the Elections of 1832, 1835, and 1837' (LIV, 653).
'F. R. Bonham: Conservative "Political Secretary" 1832–47' (LXIII, 502).
E. Hughes, 'Sir Charles Trevelyan and Civil Service Reform, 1853–5' (LXIV, 53, 206).
S. F. Woolley, 'The Personnel of the Parliament of 1833' (LIII, 240).

History
E. Hughes, 'Civil Service Reform 1853–5' (XXVII, 51).
J. Alun Thomas, 'Registration and the Development of Party Organization 1832–70' (XXXV, 81).
C. K. Webster, 'The Accession of Queen Victoria' (XXII, 14).

Transactions of the Royal Historical Society
G. Kitson Clark, 'The Electorate and the Repeal of the Corn Laws' (5th ser., I, 109).
N. Gash, 'Peel and the Party System, 1830–50' (5th ser., I, 47).

The Economic History Review
G. Kitson Clark, 'The Repeal of the Corn Laws and the Politics of the Forties' (2nd ser., IV, 1).

2. SEPARATE WORKS
Aberdeen, Correspondence of Lord, and Princess Lieven, two vols., ed. E. Jones Parry, Camden, 3rd ser. (1938).
Albemarle, George Thomas, Earl of, *Fifty Years of My Life* (1877).
Arbuthnot, Correspondence of Charles, ed. A. Aspinall, Camden, 3rd ser. (1941).
Aspinall, A., *Politics and the Press, c. 1780–1850* (1949).
Bacon, R. M., *Memoir of the Life of Edward, third Baron Suffield* (Norwich, 1838, privately printed).
Bagehot, W., *Essays on Parliamentary Reform* (1883).
Bagenal, P. H., *Life of Ralph Bernal Osborne* (1884).
Baines, E., *Life of Edward Baines* (1851).
Balfour, Lady Frances, *Life of George, fourth Earl of Aberdeen*, two vols. (1922).
Ballantine, Mr Serjeant (Wm. B.), *Some Experiences of a Barrister's Life* (1883).
Berkeley, Hon. Grantley F., *My Life and Recollections*, two vols. (1865).
Broughton, Lord, *Recollections of a Long Life*, ed. Lady Dorchester, six vols. (1910–11).

Buckingham, Duke of, *Memoirs of the Courts of William IV and Victoria*, two vols. (1861).

Buckley, J. K., *Joseph Parkes of Birmingham* (1926).

Butler, J. R. M., *Passing of the Great Reform Bill* (1914).

Childs, W. M., *The Town of Reading during the early part of the Nineteenth Century* (Reading, 1910).

Cockburn, Henry, *Memorials of his Times* (Edinburgh, 1856).

Some Letters . . . with passages omitted from the Memorials, ed. H. A. Cockburn (Edinburgh, 1932).

Journal of (continuation of the *Memorials*), two vols. (Edinburgh, 1874).

Life of Lord Jeffrey, two vols. (Edinburgh, 1852).

Letters . . on Affairs of Scotland (1874).

Cooper, J. J., *Some Worthies of Reading* (1923).

Cory, W., *A Guide to Modern English History,* two vols. (1882).

Creevey Papers, ed. Sir Herbert Maxwell (1923).

Creevey's Life and Times, ed. J. Gore (1934).

Croker Papers, ed. L. J. Jennings, three vols. (1884).

Dickens, Charles, Letters of, ed. M. Dickens and G. Hogarth, three vols. (1880).

Disraeli, B., *Coningsby* (1868).

Lord George Bentinck (1872).

Driver, C., *Tory Radical, The Life of Richard Oastler* (New York, 1946).

Duncombe, T. H., *Life and Correspondence of T. S. Duncombe,* two vols. (1868).

Dyott's Diary (General Wm. Dyott), two vols., ed. R. W. Jeffery (1907).

Fagan, L., *The Reform Club* (1887).

Fawcett, Mrs, *Life of Sir William Molesworth* (1901).

Fitzmaurice, Lord Edmond, *Life of the second Earl Granville,* two vols. (1906).

Fitzpatrick, W. J., *Correspondence of D. O'Connell,* two vols. (1888).

Fulford, R., *The Prince Consort* (1949).

Gladstone to his Wife, ed. A. Tilney Basset (1936).

Grant, James, *Random Recollections of the House of Commons, 1830–35* (1836).

Random Recollections of the House of Lords (1836).

Random Recollections of the Lords and Commons, two vols. (1838).

Gregory, *Autobiography of Sir William,* ed. Lady Gregory (1894).

Greville Memoirs, ed. L. Strachey and R. Fulford, seven vols. (1938).

Greville, Charles, & Henry Reeve, Letters of, 1836–65, ed. A. H. Johnson (1924).

Grey, Earl, *Parliamentary Government* (1858).
Grote, H., *Life of George Grote* (1873).
Guest, The Diaries of Lady Charlotte, ed. Earl of Bessborough (1950).
Gurney, Joseph John, Memoirs of, ed. J. B. Braithwaite, two vols. (Norwich, 1855).
Halévy, E., *History of the English People*, III (1927), IV (1947).
Herries, E., *Memoir of J. C. Herries*, two vols. (1880).
Hill, R. L., *Toryism and the People, 1832–1846* (1929).
Hodder, E., *Life of the seventh Earl of Shaftesbury* (1890).
Holland, Lady Elizabeth, to her Son 1821–45, ed. Earl of Ilchester (1946).
Holloway, W., *History and Antiquities of the Town of Rye* (1847).
Hudson, D., *A Poet in Parliament, Life of W. M. Praed* (1939).
Humphreys, A. L., *East Hendred, A Berkshire Parish* (1923).
Jephson, H., *The Platform*, two vols. (1892).
Johnston, W., *England as it Is* (1851).
King, Cooper, *History of Berkshire* (1887).
Kitson Clark, G., *Peel and the Conservative Party, 1832–41* (1929).
Knight, C., *Passages of a Working Life*, three vols. (1873).
Leveson-Gower, F., *Bygone Years* (1905).
Maccoby, S., *English Radicalism 1832–52* (1935).
Mackay, C., *Forty Years Recollections*, two vols. (1877).
Man, J., *History and Antiquities of the Borough of Reading* (Reading, 1816).
Marchant, D. Le, *Memoir of Viscount Althorp* (1876).
Mavor, W., *General View of Agriculture in Berkshire* (1809)
Maxwell, H., *Life of Wellington*, two vols. (1899).
Melbourne, Papers of Lord, ed. L. C. Sanders (1889).
Monypenny, W. F., *Life of Disraeli*, two vols. (1910).
Morley, J., *Life of Gladstone*, three vols. (1912).
  Life of Richard Cobden (1920).
Nevill, Lady Dorothy, *Under Five Reigns* (1911).
  Reminiscences of, ed. R. Nevill (1906).
New, Chester W., *Lord Durham* (1929).
O'Brien, R. B., *Life and Letters of Thomas Drummond* (1889).
O'Connor, T. P., *Memoirs of an old Parliamentarian*, two vols. (1929).
Omond, G. W. T., *The Lord Advocates of Scotland*, two vols. (Edinburgh, 1883).
Ostrogorski, M., *Democracy and the Organisation of Political Parties*, two vols. (1902).
O'Connell, John, *Recollections and Experiences*, two vols. (1849).
Parker, C. S., *Life and Letters of Sir James Graham*, two vols. (1907).
Paul, A., *History of Reform* (1884).
Pease, Sir Alfred, *Elections and Recollections* (1932).

Peel, Private Letters of Sir Robert, ed. G. Peel (1920).

Peel, Sir Robert, from his private papers, ed. C. S. Parker, three vols. (1891).

Peel, Recollections of Lady Georgiana, ed. E. Peel (1920).

Pope-Hennessy, Una, *Charles Dickens* (1945).

Raikes' Journal, 1831–47, three vols. (1856).

Reid, S. J., *Life and Letters of the first Earl of Durham*, two vols. (1906).

Reid, T. Wemyss, *Life of W. E. Forster* (1889).

Life . . of Richard Monckton Milnes, first Lord Houghton, two vols. (1890).

Roebuck, J. A., Life and Letters of, ed. R. E. Leader (1897).

Russell, Early Correspondence of Lord John, ed. R. Russell, two vols. (1913).

Sanford, J. L., and Townsend, M., *The Great Governing Families of England*, two vols. (1865).

Seymour, C., *Electoral Reform in England and Wales* (Yale Historical Publications, New Haven, 1915).

Somerset, Letters . . of Edward Seymour, twelfth Duke of, ed. W. H. Mallock (1893).

Stephen, H. J., *Commentaries on the Laws of England*, four vols. (1841–5).

Timbs, J., *Club Life of London*, two vols. (1866).

'The Times', History of, three vols. (1935–47).

Torrens, W. M., *Memoirs of Viscount Melbourne* (1890).

Trevelyan, G. O., *Life and Letters of Lord Macaulay*, two vols. (1876).

Turner, R. E., *James Silk Buckingham* (1934).

Twiss, H., *Life of Lord Chancellor Eldon*, three vols. (1844).

Wakefield, C. M., *Life of Thomas Attwood* (1885).

Wallas, G., *Life of Francis Place* (1918).

Walpole, Spencer, *Life of Lord John Russell*, two vols. (1891).

Wharncliffe, The first Lady, and her Family, by her grandchildren, two vols. (1927).

William IV and Earl Grey, Correspondence of, ed. Earl Grey, two vols. (1867).

Wolf., L., *Life of the first Marquess of Ripon*, two vols. (1921).

INDEX

Biographical details given in the text are not repeated in the index

Principal Abbreviations

Adm.—*Admiral*
Bdy(s)—*Boundary(ies)*
Bn.—*Baron*
Bnss.—*Baroness*
Bt.—*Baronet*
co.('s)—*County(ies)*
Ctss.—*Countess*
D.—*Duke*
Div.—*Division*

Dss.—*Duchess*
E.—*Earl*
El.—*Election(s)*
Gen.—*General*
M.—*Marquess*
Mss.—*Marchioness*
n.—*footnote*
parlt.—*parliament(ary)*
Visct.—*Viscount*

Abercromby, James (cr. Bn. Dunfermline 1839), 112
Aberdeen, 44, 236
Aberdeen University, 47
Aberdeen, George Hamilton Gordon, 4th E. of, 135, 166–7, 177, 186, 392 n., 396, 451
Aberdeenshire, 186
Abergavenny, Henry Nevill, 2nd E. of, 187
Abingdon, 67 n., 75, 272–9, 309, 313, 317, 319–20
Abingdon, Montagu Bertie, 5th E. of, 271, 275, 301
Abinger, Lord, *see* Scarlett
Acklom, Miss Esther, 243
Acland, Sir Thos. Dyke, 10th Bt., 178, 191
A'Court, Capt. Edward Henry, 194–6, 254 and n., 255
Act of Union (Ireland), xiv, 50–2, 57, 69
Act of Union (Scotland), 36, 43–4, 51
Adare, Visct., Edwin Richard Wyndham-Quin (succ. as 3rd E. of Dunraven 1850), 138
Adderley, C. B., 181–2, 182 n., 253 and n., 254, 256
Adelaide, Queen, 385, 387
Admiralty, home establishment, 327; electoral influence, xii, xx, 323–4, 327–33, 336, 338, 444 ff.; 1847 circular, 328, 329 and n., 331; 1849 circular, 330–2; 1852 scandal, 330–3
Agricultural interest, and Reform Act, 6, 14, 300–3, 320

Agricultural Protection (*see also* Corn Laws), 230, 276, 281, 291, 294, 303, 305, 307, 315–18
Agricultural Protection Societies, xv, 316–17
Agricultural Society, Royal, 316
Agriculture, and politics, xiv–xv
Ailesbury, Chas. Bruce Brudenell Bruce, 1st M. of, 214, 439
Aislabie, George, 220
Aislabie, John, 220
Aislabie, Mary, 223
Aislabie, Wm., 220
Albert, Prince, xii, 382–4, 391
d'Albiac, Gen. Sir James Chas., 222
Alcock, Thos., 425
Allanson, Chas., 220
Allanson, Eliz., 220
Allen, Wm., 112
Almack, Wm., 393
Althorp, Visct., John Chas. Spencer (succ. as 3rd E. Spencer 1834), 17, 20, 34 n., 42, 48, 64, 71, 78–9, 92–3, 101, 110, 419; and division of co.'s, 78, 241; and Northants elections, 243–5
Amesbury, Lord, *see* Dundas, Chas.
Andover, 76, 114; old and new voters, 96
Andover, Visct., Chas. John Howard (succ. as 17th E. of Suffolk and 10th E. of Berkshire 1851), 205
Andrews, Mr, 162
Anglesey, 186–7
Anglesey, Henry Wm. Paget, 1st M. of, 63–4, 254–6, 444 n.

472